# THE HISTORY
# OF THE
# UNITED STATES
VOLUME II·1850 TO THE PRESENT

# THE HISTORY OF THE UNITED STATES

## VOLUME II: 1850 TO THE PRESENT
## SOURCE READINGS

*Edited by*

NEIL HARRIS · DAVID J. ROTHMAN · STEPHAN THERNSTROM

*Harvard University*     *Columbia University*          *Brandeis University*

Holt, Rinehart and Winston, Inc.

*New York   Chicago   San Francisco   Atlanta   Dallas   Montreal   Toronto   London   Sydney*

Design by Arthur D. Ritter

# Preface

This collection is an instrument that will aid the user in understanding the history of the United States. It is designed to bring to life the people and events of the past. History should not be a dry chronicle of names and dates; it deals with characters as real as those of whom we read in the daily newspaper. The documents here assembled will bring the reader close to the figures of earlier eras and thus help explain the evolution of the American nation.

It takes an effort of the imagination to understand that the strange costumes of seventeenth- and eighteenth-century portraits clothed living human beings. Through the curious antique lanes of old towns and through the forest clearings of the wilderness, moved men and women whose emotions, ambitions, and ideas were not exactly the same as our own but also not entirely discontinuous with ours. The student of history must try to comprehend these people, different though they were. Fortunately he can do so through the written material they left behind. The collection that follows has arranged such materials so as to illuminate the development of the Americans through their whole history.

The aim of making these records of the past interesting and understandable dictated the standards of selection as well as the organization of this volume. The editors wished each document to speak directly to the students who will read it. Each selection treats an important subject in a way that will attract and hold the attention of twentieth-century young people who are not themselves historians. Furthermore each item drawn into the collection is long enough so that the student, once immersed in it, can learn something not only of the subject concerned, but also of the language and style and therefore of the way of thinking of the era represented.

The collection is unique in the range of materials represented. The selections touch on all the important aspects of the history of the United States, economic, social and intellectual, as well as political. Each document is presented in a form full enough to convey its own flavor; yet each also fits into a coherent pattern which, taken as a whole, provides a vivid introduction to the American past.

Historians refer to sources such as are here assembled as primary. By this they mean that the books or manuscripts from which the selections are drawn are first-hand or eyewitness accounts, printed or written at about the same time as the events with which they deal. Such material is always valuable as evidence of something. But these written survivals from the past fall into several categories, which the reader must understand if he is to make effective use of them.

Some primary sources are produced in the course of contemporary transactions. The people who wrote them intended such documents to serve only specific purpose. A bill of sale or a contract, for instance, completed a business deal, and no one considered the possibility that it might some day prove useful to a historian. Such records consequently are reliable; they are just what they say they are, although what they mean must be explained by interpretation. Among other sources of this sort on which historians depend are acts of legislation and decisions of courts, the journals of legislatures and conventions, and petitions to such bodies about important issues of the times.

Even more useful are materials produced without conscious guile in the normal course of some transaction. Farmers and businessmen keep records for their own use and therefore try to be as accurate as possible. These records are evidence of how such enterprises really operated. By the same token, letters written for a specific purpose reveal the political concerns of the writers or describe military or domestic events.

Still another kind of primary material is that recorded by participants and observers with some conscious purpose. The reasons why each document was written must therefore be understood, for that may have influenced its contents. Yet the account may nonetheless be valuable. Among such records are journals and diaries, set down from direct observation, as well as the narratives of settlers and travelers. Contemporary histories are usually even more interpretive, for their authors generally wish to make some point that will persuade future readers. More often than not, too, there is some purpose behind the writing of an autobiography. As a man looks back over his life, he wishes to set down the facts, but also to justify his past actions or to draw a moral from them; and he may not be able to separate the two aspects of his writing. The same caution applies to newspaper accounts. Reporters have a professional purpose in chronicling the news, yet their views may well color their stories.

Some contemporary documents, of course, are clearly and explicitly cases of argument or pleading. The authors intend to make a case and select and organize the facts accordingly. The value of these materials lies less in the facts they detail than in the ideas they express. American history is rich in tracts of this sort, whether published originally as pamphlets or as articles in periodicals. Whether the argument is presented with restraint or with fanatical zeal, its importance for the student lies in the view it offers of the thinking of its author.

Other forms of persuasion are also common. Newspaper editorials directly express opinions and thus reflect the ideas of their writers and of their readers. Orations and sermons were long the most familiar means of persuasion; they remain important because they often held the close attention of Americans.

In a quite different category are the unconscious expressions of attitudes and ideas that appear in popular and formal literature. A story, a poem, or a play often reveals the underlying beliefs of people, particularly when written without artifice. Satires and campaign songs thus convey a good deal of information about current political practices, for they show what symbols and concepts aroused popular enthusiasm or mockery.

In arranging their selections from the great variety of primary sources in American history, the editors have held in view the needs of the students who will use this collection. They have held to the highest standards of accurate scholarship. But in the interest of clarity and readability they have modernized antique spellings and punctuation, and they have omitted ellipses from certain passages. Without in the least altering the meaning of the originals, they have sought to make these documents completely accessible to the modern student. The result will enrich the understanding of the American past.

*Cambridge, Massachusetts*                         Oscar Handlin
*February 1969*

# Contents

## PART SEVEN
## The Thrust of Progress, 1890–1912

Introduction

**PART EIGHT**
The Quest for an Old Order,
1912–1929

**PART NINE**
The End of the Old Order,
1929–1947

## PART TEN
## Peace in a World of Conflict, 1945–1968

# THE HISTORY OF THE UNITED STATES

## VOLUME II: 1850 TO THE PRESENT

## PART SIX

# Industrialization, 1850–1890

In the four decades between 1850 and 1890 the United States underwent a stunning economic and social transformation. Midcentury America was an agricultural and rural society. It had more slaves than factory workers and still more independent farmers. Only one-eighth of its population lived in cities of more than eight thousand. The United States ranked well behind England, France, and Germany in the value of its manufactured goods.

By 1890 nearly one-third of the American population lived in cities, and the remaining two-thirds were tied to the swelling urban industrial centers in a variety of ways. The United States was the leading industrial power of the world; its manufactures almost equalled those of England, France, and Germany combined! As late as 1880, American rural and urban real estate were of approximately equal value, $10 billion. Ten years later, farm property had risen to $13 billion, urban property to $26 billion! The gross national product more than doubled between the end of the Civil War and 1890.

An efficient national transportation and communications network was laid down in these years. Railroad mileage increased eighteen-fold, shipping costs fell dramatically. The telegraph, and later the telephone, allowed instant contact between cities on opposite sides of the continent. These and other developments called into being a national distribution system for goods and services. Woolworth's five-and-ten-cent stores, the A & P grocery chain, Montgomery Ward's mail-order catalog, Macy's, and nationally advertised brand names like Baker's chocolate, Singer sewing machines, Swift meats, and Kellogg's cornflakes all appeared during this era.

The availability of a national market spurred specialization, increased production, and created costly new labor-saving machines. The giant textile factories built in Lowell, Massachusetts, in the 1820s were rare exceptions to the general pattern. By 1890 firms employing several thousand operatives were commonplace. The prospect of sales to millions of customers across the country made it profitable to invest in elaborate machines and processes that could make a product more cheaply than the individual craftsman, utilizing relatively unskilled working men and women.

The new technology, however, required investment on a scale few individual entrepreneurs could provide. The dominant form of business organization quickly became the limited liability corporation, not the family firm, generating its capital by selling its stock to the public through investment bankers like J. P. Morgan. There were a variety of attempts by major corporations to obtain primacy and protection from competition by purchase of rivals, pools, mergers, and trust agreements.

The rising city was the point of concentration for much of the explosive economic energy unleashed during this period, and the spectacular growth of the cities was a dramatic symbol of the emergence of a new America. No less than one hundred and one American cities doubled their population in the 1880s. The new factories were in many cases outside the major urban centers—Homestead, Pennsylvania; Pullman, Illinois; and Winston, North Carolina; for instance—but the control of manufacturing gravitated toward the metropolis, for there the financing, distribution, and sales were accomplished. The growth of the cities and the consequent need to build housing, roads, warehouses, bridges, water and sewage systems was itself an increasingly important source of economic dynamism as the nineteenth century drew to a close.

Even the prairie farmer, hundreds of miles from a factory or large city, found his way of life transformed. The American farmer had never been a true peasant, securely rooted in a plot of land that had been his family's for generations. He had always been a restless soul, quick to scent new opportunity and to move on in search of it, and he was likely to concentrate his efforts on the production of a cash crop—cotton, tobacco, and rice in the South, corn, wheat, meat, and dairy products elsewhere—for sale at a market. Farming was usually a business for him, and speculative. Gains from selling his farm for more than he paid for it were often on his mind. But in this period, farming became more of a business, and a more dangerous business than ever before. Improved transportation and communications opened up vast new areas that had never been available for cultivation before, and drew farm products from these areas into a world-wide market. There were tempting new opportunities for profit, but a number of new risks as well. The market fluctuated more wildly than ever before, responding now to events far across the seas. The farmer was more likely to be living on borrowed money, due to both the competitive pressure to invest in new farm equipment and improvements and to the temptation to accumulate large land-holdings on the assumption that prosperity would continue forever. The city, and city institutions—the bank, the railroad, the grain exchange—seemed increasingly to control his life, and it was the city to which his children drifted when they came of age.

Most Americans in this era were becoming richer in material terms. Real wages in manufacturing edged slowly upward, though interrupted by depressions in the late 1850s and the 1870s. The owners and managers of the growing corporations as well as their lesser white collar employees received some fraction of the new wealth generated by improved productivity. Even the farmers, despite their bitter protests in the 1880s and 1890s, shared to some degree in these gains. There were large groups of desperately poor people in the new America—the tenement dwellers Jacob Riis describes in *How the Other Half Lives*, for instance; but few were deprived of all opportunities for increased economic security and social mobility. The poorest tended to be those most recently arrived in the urban, industrial world, from the farms of Europe or of rural America. In time they found their way out of the slums, for the most part, and into the American mainstream.

A booming economy and a fluid social order lent credence to the optimism of Horatio Alger, Russell Conwell, and other preachers of the gospel of success. Belief in the sacredness of hard work had deep roots in the American past; the values Lucy Larcom and E. W. Howe learned in early childhood could be traced back to Benjamin Franklin and even to Puritan divines of the seventeenth century. But in the latter half of the nineteenth century these ideas became a national obsession, and in the process were vulgarized to the point where many believed that worldly wealth was the ultimate measure of human worth. The gospel of wealth, fortified by Darwinian ideals about the survival of the fittest, was used to excuse ruthless business practices and cold disregard of the sufferings of the unfortunate. The social philosophy of Conwell met with criticism, especially toward the end of the period, but a sufficient number of Americans were surviving and prospering in the new order to give Social Darwinism and laissez-faire political economy considerable plausibility for a time.

Despite the optimism fostered by an expansive social and economic setting, many Americans felt significant reservations about the new order. There was some nostalgia for the old ways, and revulsion from the machine and the dollar. For all of his committment to progress, Mark Twain preferred the steamboat to the screeching locomotive, and he looked wistfully backward to Tom Sawyer and Huck Finn's life in sleepy Hannibal, Missouri. There was popular suspicion of the new class of fabulously wealthy "robber barons" who accumulated unprecedented fortunes in the Gilded Age, often by methods that seemed incomprehensible if not positively immoral. If the poor were not getting poorer, the rich were getting very much richer, and the contrast between the two became increasingly sharp. The cities were bursting at the seams with newcomers, many of them packed like sardines into dark, dirty tenements. The newcomers were often immigrants, speaking strange tongues, practicing alien ways. Every year more Americans were exposed to the harsh discipline of the factory, and to the disintegrating pressures of life in the urban jungle. Although industrial America produced more wealth, the national market was more sensitive to fluctuations; undreamed of prosperity in boom times was followed

3

by devastating setbacks at other times. The social order had changed more radically and more rapidly than the typical American's conception of it, and it is probable that the ordinary citizen felt more helpless, more driven, more at the mercy of implacable external forces at the end of the period than at the beginning.

The national political system in this era did not prove very responsive to these new difficulties and concerns. The major efforts of the national government to deal with the problems generated by rapid urbanization and industrialization came after 1890, though some states made significant attempts in this period. Discontented groups sought to influence public policy in accord with their preferences—the farmers, through the Granger movement, the Greenback party, and the Farmer's Alliances, workingmen through the Knights of Labor. But there was truth in the harsh insistence of the hard-headed founder of the American Federation of Labor, Samuel Gompers, that the accumulation and disciplined exercise of economic power would produce greater benefits than moralistic appeals for humanitarian legislation. Groups capable of improving their market position through concerted action— skilled artisans, corporate leaders in many industries, certain professionals, and others—flourished. Less readily organized groups—unskilled workers, small shop-keepers, Negroes, small farmers—fared less well.

In the years between 1850 and 1890 modern America was born. The material achievements of the new society were impressive. Whether the uneasiness, the discontent, the bewildering complexity, and the group conflict it had generated could be satisfactorily dealt with, however, it was left to the future to determine.

# 43

## A Boom Town and the Making of a Millionaire

William Dean Howells, one of the finest novelists of late-nineteenth century America, provides here a vivid sketch of how the discovery of a natural gas field transformed a Midwestern community and one of its residents. Born in a small town in Ohio in 1837, Howells came to Boston shortly after the close of the Civil War and quickly won national eminence as editor of the *Atlantic Monthly* and as a prolific and popular novelist and literary critic. His rise to fame coincided with the birth of modern America. The rise of the city and the factory, the nationalization of American business, and the moral and political challenges these developments posed to older American values were the dominant themes of this era; it was Howells more than any other single figure who saw to it that American writers explored these issues. His philosophy of "literary realism" rejected the romantic, sentimental, and melodramatic and urged that the writer's first task was careful social observation and the realistic portrayal of everyday life. In his most famous work, *The Rise of Silas Lapham* (1885), Howells grappled with the ethical dilemmas confronted by an old-fashioned businessman in an increasingly impersonal and amoral economy. The following scene is drawn from perhaps his finest book, *A Hazard of New Fortunes* (1890), a brilliant critique of the oil tycoon Dryfoos and the class he represented.

### A HAZARD OF NEW FORTUNES
#### *William Dean Howells*

"Yes, yes," said Fulkerson. "Well, the natural-gas country is worth seeing. I don't mean the Pittsburgh gas-fields, but out in Northern Ohio and Indiana around Moffitt—that's the place in the heart of the gas region that they've been booming so. Yes, you ought to see that country. If you haven't got any idea how old the country looks. You remember how the fields used to be all full of stumps?"

From *A Hazard of New Fortunes* (New York, 1911), 92–101.

5

"I should think so."

"Well, you won't see any stumps now. All that country out around Moffitt is just as smooth as a checker-board, and looks as old as England. You know how we used to burn the stumps out; and then somebody invented a stump-extractor, and we pulled them out with a yoke of oxen. Now they just touch 'em off with a little dynamite, and they've got a cellar dug and filled up with kindling ready for housekeeping whenever you want it. Only they haven't got any use for kindling in that country—all gas. I rode along on the cars through those level black fields at corn-planting time, and every once in a while I'd come to a place with a piece of ragged old stove-pipe stickin' up out of the ground, and blazing away like forty, and a fellow ploughing all round it and not minding it any more than if it was spring violets. Horses didn't notice it, either. Well, they've always known about the gas out there; they say there are places in the woods where it's been burning ever since the country was settled.

"But when you come in sight of Moffitt—my, oh, my! Well, you come in smell of it about as soon. That gas out there ain't odorless, like the Pittsburgh gas, and so it's perfectly safe; but the smell isn't bad—about as bad as the finest kind of benzine. Well, the first thing that strikes you when you come to Moffitt is the notion that there has been a good warm, growing rain, and the town's come up overnight. That's in the suburbs, the annexes, and additions. But it ain't shabby—no shantytown business; nice brick and frame houses, some of 'em Queen Anne style, and all of 'em looking as if they had come to stay. And when you drive up from the depot you think everybody's moving. Everything seems to be piled into the street; old houses made over, and new ones going up everywhere. You know the kind of street Main Street always used to be in our section—half plank-road and turnpike, and the rest mud-hole, and a lot of stores and doggeries strung along with false fronts a story higher than the back, and here and there a decent building with the gable end to the public; and a court-house and jail and two taverns and three or four churches. Well, they're all there in Moffitt yet, but architecture has struck it hard, and they've got a lot of new buildings that needn't be ashamed of themselves anywhere; the new court-house is as big as St. Peter's, and the Grand Opera-House is in the highest style of the art. You can't buy a lot on that street for much less than you can buy a lot in New York—or you couldn't when the boom was on; I saw the place just when the boom was in its prime. I went out there to work the newspapers in the syndicate business, and I got one of their men to write me a real bright, snappy account of the gas; and they just took me in their arms and showed me everything. Well, it *was* wonderful, and it was beautiful, too! To see a whole community stirred up like that was—just like a big boy, all hope and high spirits, and no discount on the remotest future; nothing but perpetual boom to the end of time—I tell you it warmed your blood. Why, there were some things about it that made you think what a nice kind of world this would be if people ever took hold together, instead of each fellow fighting it out on his own hook, and devil take the hindmost. They made up their minds at Moffitt that if they wanted their town to grow they'd got to keep their gas public property. So they extended their corporation line so as to take in pretty much the whole gas region round there; and then the city took possession of every well that was put down, and held it for the common good. Anybody that's a mind to come to Moffitt and start any kind of manufacture can have all the gas he wants *free*; and for fifteen dollars a year you can have all the gas you want to heat and light your private house. The people hold on to it for themselves, and, as I say, it's a grand sight to see a whole community hanging together and working for the good of all, instead of splitting up into as many different cut-throats as there are able-bodied citizens. See that fellow?" Fulkerson broke off, and indicated with a twirl of his head a short, dark, foreign-looking man going out of the door. "They say that fellow's a Socialist. I think it's a shame they're allowed to come here. If they don't like the way we manage our affairs let 'em stay at home," Fulkerson continued. "They do a lot of mischief, shooting off their mouths round here. I believe in free speech and all that; but I'd like to see these fellows shut up in jail and left to jaw one another to death. *We* don't want any of their poison."

"Well," Fulkerson resumed, "they took me round everywhere in Moffitt, and showed me their big wells—lit 'em up for a private view, and let me hear them purr with the soft accents of a mass-meeting of locomotives. Why, when they let one of these wells loose in a meadow that they'd piped it into temporarily, it drove the flame away forty feet from the mouth of the pipe and blew it over half an acre of ground. They say when they let one of their big wells burn away all winter before they had learned how to control it, that well kept up a little summer all around it; the grass stayed green, and the flowers bloomed all through the winter. *I* don't know whether it's so or not. But I can believe anything of natural gas. My! but it was beautiful when they turned on the full force of that well and shot a roman candle into the gas—that's the way they light it—and a plume of fire about twenty feet wide and seventy-five feet high, all red and yellow and violet, jumped into the sky, and that big roar shook the ground under your feet! You felt like saying: 'Don't trouble yourself; I'm perfectly convinced. I believe in Moffitt.' We-e-e-ll!" drawled Fulkerson, with a long breath, "that's where I met old Dryfoos."

"Oh yes!—Dryfoos," said March.

"Yes," Fulkerson laughed. "We've got round to Dryfoos again. I thought I could cut a long story short, but I seem to be cutting a short story long. If you're not in a hurry, though—"

"Not in the least. Go on as long as you like."

"I met him there in the office of a real-estate man—speculator, of course; everybody was, in Moffitt; but a first-rate fellow, and public-spirited as all get-out; and when Dryfoos left he told me about him. Dryfoos was an old Pennsylvania Dutch farmer, about three or four miles out of Moffitt, and he'd lived there pretty much all his life; father was one of the first settlers. Everybody knew he had the right stuff in him, but he was slower than molasses in January, like those Pennsylvania Dutch. He'd got together the largest and handsomest farm anywhere around there; and he was making money on it, just like he was in some business somewhere; he was a very intelligent man; he took the papers and kept himself posted; but he was awfully old-fashioned in his ideas. He hung on to the doctrines as well as the dollars of the dads; it was a real thing with him. Well, when the boom

7

began to come he hated it awfully, and he fought it. He used to write communications to the weekly newspaper in Moffitt—they've got three dailies there now—and throw cold water on the boom. He couldn't catch on no way. It made him sick to hear the clack that went on about the gas the whole while, and that stirred up the neighborhood and got into his family. Whenever he'd hear of a man that had been offered a big price for his land and was going to sell out and move into town, he'd go and labor with him and try to talk him out of it, and tell him how long his fifteen or twenty thousand would last him to live on, and shake the Standard Oil Company before him, and try to make him believe it wouldn't be five years before the Standard owned the whole region.

"Of course, he couldn't do anything with them. When a man's offered a big price for his farm, he don't care whether it's by a secret emissary from the Standard Oil or not; he's going to sell and get the better of the other fellow if he can. Dryfoos couldn't keep the boom out of his own family even. His wife was with him. She thought whatever he said and did was just as right as if it had been thundered down from Sinai. But the young folks were sceptical, especially the girls that had been away to school. The boy that had been kept at home because he couldn't be spared from helping his father manage the farm was more like him, but they contrived to stir the boy up with the hot end of the boom, too. So when a fellow came along one day and offered old Dryfoos a cool hundred thousand for his farm, it was all up with Dryfoos. He'd 'a' liked to 'a' kept the offer to himself and not done anything about it, but his vanity wouldn't let him do that; and when he let it out in his family the girls outvoted him. They just *made* him sell.

"He wouldn't sell all. He kept about eighty acres that was off in one piece by itself, but the three hundred that had the old brick house on it, and the big barn—that went, and Dryfoos bought him a place in Moffitt and moved into town to live on the interest of his money. Just what he had scolded and ridiculed everybody else for doing. Well, they say that at first he seemed like he would go crazy. He hadn't anything to do. He took a fancy to that land-agent, and he used to go and set in his office and ask him what he should do. 'I hain't got any horses, I hain't got any cows, I hain't got any pigs, I hain't got any chickens. I hain't got anything to do from sun-up to sun-down.' The fellow said the tears used to run down the old fellow's cheeks, and if he hadn't been so busy himself he believed he should 'a' cried, too. But most o' people thought old Dryfoos was down in the mouth because he hadn't asked more for his farm, when he wanted to buy it back and found they held it at a hundred and fifty thousand. People couldn't believe he was just homesick and heartsick for the old place. Well, perhaps he *was* sorry he hadn't asked more; that's human nature, *too*.

"After a while something happened. That land-agent used to tell Dryfoos to get out to Europe with his money and see life a little, or go and live in Washington, where he could *be* somebody; but Dryfoos wouldn't, and he kept listening to the talk there, and all of a sudden he caught on. He came into that fellow's one day with a plan for cutting up the eighty acres he'd kept into town lots; and he'd got it all plotted out so well, and had so many practical ideas about it, that the fellow was astonished. He went right in with him, as far as Dryfoos would let him, and glad of the chance; and they were working the thing for all it was worth when I struck Moffitt. Old Dryfoos wanted me to go out and see the Dryfoos & Hendry Addition—guess he thought maybe I'd write it up; and he drove me out there himself. Well, it was funny to see a town made: streets driven through; two rows of shade-trees, hard and soft, planted; cellars dug and houses put up—regular Queen Anne style, too, with stained glass—all at once. Dryfoos apologized for the streets because they were hand-made; said they expected their street-making machine Tuesday, and then they intended to *push* things."

Fulkerson enjoyed the effect of his picture on March for a moment, and then went on: "He was mighty intelligent, too, and he questioned me up about my business as sharp as *I* ever was questioned; seemed to kind of strike his fancy; I guess he wanted to find out if there was any money in it. He was making money, hand over hand, then; and he never stopped speculating and improving till he'd scraped together three or four hundred thousand dollars; they said a million, but they like round numbers at Moffitt, and I guess half a million would lay over it comfortably and leave a few thousands to spare, probably. Then he came on to New York."

Fulkerson struck a match against the ribbed side of the porcelain cup that held the matches in the centre of the table, and lit a cigarette, which he began to smoke, throwing his head back with a leisurely effect, as if he had got to the end of at least as much of his story as he meant to tell without prompting.

March asked him the desired question. "What in the world for?"

Fulkerson took out his cigarette and said, with a smile: "To spend his money, and get his daughters into the old Knickerbocker society. Maybe he thought they were all the same kind of Dutch."

"And has he succeeded?"

"Well, they're not social leaders yet. But it's only a question of time—generation or two—especially if time's money, and if *Every Other Week* is the success it's bound to be."

"You don't mean to say, Fulkerson," said March, with a half-doubting, half-daunted laugh, "that *he's* your Angel?"

"That's what I mean to say," returned Fulkerson. "I ran onto him in Broadway one day last summer. If you ever saw anybody in your life, you're sure to meet him in Broadway again, sooner or later. That's the philosophy of the bunco business; country people from the same neighborhood are sure to run up against each other the first time they come to New York. I put out my hand, and I said, 'Isn't this Mr. Dryfoos from Moffitt?' He didn't seem to have any use for my hand; he let me keep it, and he squared those old lips of his till his imperial stuck straight out. Ever see Bernhardt in 'L'Etrangère'? Well, the American husband is old Dryfoos all over; no mustache, and hay-colored chin-whiskers cut slanting from the corners of his mouth. He cocked his little gray eyes at me, and says he: "Yes, young man; my name *is* Dryfoos, and I'm from Moffitt. But I don't want no present of Longfellow's Works, illustrated; and I don't want to taste no fine teas; but I know a policeman that does; and if you're the son of my old friend Squire Strohfeldt, you'd better get out.' 'Well, then,' said I, 'how would you like to go into the newspaper syndicate business?' He

9

gave another look at me, and then he burst out laughing, and he grabbed my hand, and he just froze to it. I never saw anybody so glad.

"Well, the long and the short of it was that I asked him round here to Maroni's to dinner; and before we broke up for the night we had settled the financial side of the plan that's brought you to New York. I can see," said Fulkerson, who had kept his eyes fast on March's face, "that you don't more than half like the idea of Dryfoos. It ought to give you more confidence in the thing than you ever had. You needn't be afraid," he added, with some feeling, "that I talked Dryfoos into the thing for my own advantage."

"Oh, my dear Fulkerson!" March protested, all the more fervently because he was really a little guilty.

"Well, of course not! I didn't mean you were. But I just happened to tell him what I wanted to go into when I could see my way to it, and he caught on of his own accord. The fact is," said Fulkerson, "I guess I'd better make a clean breast of it, now I'm at it. Dryfoos wanted to get something for that boy of his to do. He's in railroads himself, and he's in mines and other things, and he keeps busy, and he can't bear to have his boy hanging round the house doing nothing, like as if he was a girl. I told him that the great object of a rich man was to get his son into just that fix, but he couldn't seem to see it, and the boy hated it himself. He's got a good head, and he wanted to study for the ministry when they were all living together out on the farm; but his father had the old-fashioned ideas about that. You know they used to think that any sort of stuff was good enough to make a preacher out of; but they wanted the good timber for business; and so the old man wouldn't let him. You'll see the fellow; you'll like him; he's no fool, I can tell you; and he's going to be our publisher, nominally at first and actually when I've taught him the ropes a little."

# 44

## The Gospel of Success

Baptist minister Russell Conwell was among the most popular lecturers of his day and one of the leading prophets of the gospel of success. The industrial transformation of America in the latter half of the nineteenth century produced an enormous body of popular literature and speech emphasizing the virtues of aggressive individualism and earnest pursuit of the main chance. Americans had always been committed to self-help, always interested in success, but never before had there been so stark and crude an identification between virtue and money-making. An advertisement for a patent medicine in a newspaper of this period could state quite innocently, "The first object in life with the American people is to get rich; the second how to retain their health. The first can be obtained by energy, honesty, and saving; the second, by using Green's August Flower." The main elements of success creed were summed up well in Conwell's famous "Acres of Diamonds" speech. It was delivered an estimated six thousand times, and netted Conwell a small fortune in lecture fees, part of which he employed to found the Baptist institution, Temple University, in Philadelphia. The version printed here was given in Philadelphia, as several of its remarks indicate. When on the lecture circuit Conwell made a habit of arriving early enough in a new community to obtain local anecdotes consistent with his general theme, which he then inserted where appropriate.

### ACRES OF DIAMONDS
*Russell Conwell*

When going down the Tigris and Euphrates rivers many years ago with a party of English travelers I found myself under the direction of an old Arab guide whom we hired up at Bagdad, and I have often thought how that guide resembled our barbers in certain mental characteristics. He thought that it was not only his duty to guide us down those rivers, and do what he was paid for doing, but also to entertain us with stories curious and weird, ancient and modern, strange and familiar. Many of them I have forgotten, and I am glad I have, but there is one I shall never forget.

Said he, "I will tell you a story now which I reserve for my particular friends." When he emphasized the words "particular friends," I listened, and I have ever been glad I did. I really feel devoutly thankful, that there are 1,674 young men who have been carried through college by this lecture who are also glad that I did listen. The old guide told me that there once lived not far from the River Indus an ancient Persian by the name of Ali Hafed. He said that Ali Hafed owned a very large farm, that he had orchards, grain-fields, and gardens; that he had money at interest, and was a wealthy and contented man. He was contented because he was wealthy, and wealthy because he was contented. One day there visited that old Persian farmer one of those ancient Buddhist priests, one of the wise men of the East. He sat down by the fire and told the old farmer how this world of ours was made. He said that this world was once a mere bank of fog, and that the Almighty thrust His finger into this bank of fog, and began slowly to move His finger around, increasing the speed until at last He whirled this bank of fog into a solid ball of fire. Then it went rolling through the universe, burning its way through other banks of fog, and condensed the moisture without, until it fell in floods of rain upon its hot surface, and cooled the outward crust. Then the internal fires bursting outward through the crust threw up the mountains and hills, the valleys, the plains and prairies of this wonderful world of ours. If this internal molten mass came bursting out and cooled very quickly it became granite; less quickly copper, less quickly silver, less quickly gold, and, after gold, diamonds were made.

Said the old priest, "A diamond is a congealed drop of sunlight." Now that is literally scientifically true, that a diamond is an actual deposit of carbon from the sun. The old priest told Ali Hafed that if he had one diamond the size of his thumb he could purchase the county, and if he had a mine of diamonds he could place his children upon thrones through the influence of their great wealth.

Ali Hafed heard all about diamonds, how much they were worth, and went to his bed that night a poor man. He had not lost anything, but he was poor because he was discontented, and discontented because he feared he was poor. He said, "I want a mine of diamonds," and he lay awake all night.

Early in the morning he sought out the priest. I know by experience that a priest is very cross when awakened early in the morning, and when he shook that old priest out of his dreams, Ali Hafed said to him:

"Will you tell me where I can find diamonds?"

"Diamonds! What do you want with diamonds?" "Why, I wish to be immensely rich." "Well, then, go along and find them. That is all you have to do; go and find them, and then you have them." "But I don't know where to go." "Well, if you will find a river that runs through white sands, between high mountains, in those white sands you will always find diamonds." "I don't believe there is any such river." "Oh yes, there are plenty of them. All you have to do is to go and find them, and then you have them." Said Ali Hafed, "I will go."

So he sold his farm, collected his money, left his family in charge of a neighbor, and away he went in search of diamonds. He began his search, very properly to my mind, at the Mountains of the Moon. Afterward he came around into Palestine, then wandered on into Europe, and at last when his money was all spent and he

12

was in rags, wretchedness, and poverty, he stood on the shore of that bay at Barcelona, in Spain, when a great tidal wave came rolling in between the pillars of Hercules, and the poor, afflicted, suffering, dying man could not resist the awful temptation to cast himself into that incoming tide, and he sank beneath its foaming crest, never to rise in this life again.

When that old guide had told me that awfully sad story he stopped the camel I was riding on and went back to fix the baggage that was coming off another camel, and I had an opportunity to muse over his story while he was gone. I remember saying to myself, "Why did he reserve that story for his 'particular friends'?" There seemed to be no beginning, no middle, no end, nothing to it. That was the first story I had ever heard told in my life, and would be the first one I ever read, in which the hero was killed in the first chapter. I had but one chapter of that story, and the hero was dead.

When the guide came back and took up the halter of my camel, he went right ahead with the story, into the second chapter, just as though there had been no break. The man who purchased Ali Hafed's farm one day led his camel into the garden to drink, and as that camel put its nose into the shallow water of that garden brook, Ali Hafed's successor noticed a curious flash of light from the white sands of the stream. He pulled out a black stone having an eye of light reflecting all the hues of the rainbow. He took the pebble into the house and put it on the mantel which covers the central fires, and forgot all about it.

A few days later this same old priest came in to visit Ali Hafed's successor, and the moment he opened that drawing-room door he saw that flash of light on the mantel, and he rushed up to it, and shouted: "Here is a diamond! Has Ali Hafed returned?" "Oh no, Ali Hafed has not returned, and that is not a diamond. That is nothing but a stone we found right out here in our own garden." "But," said the priest, "I tell you I know a diamond when I see it. I know positively that is a diamond."

Then together they rushed out into that old garden and stirred up the white sands with their fingers, and lo! there came up other more beautiful and valuable gems than the first. "Thus," said the guide to me, and, friends, it is historically true, "was discovered the diamond-mine of Golconda, the most magnificent diamond-mine in all the history of mankind, excelling the Kimberly itself. The Kohinoor, and the Orloff of the crown jewels of England and Russia, the largest on earth, came from that mine."

When that old Arab guide told me the second chapter of his story, he then took off his Turkish cap and swung it around in the air again to get my attention to the moral. Those Arab guides have morals to their stories, although they are not always moral. As he swung his hat, he said to me, "Had Ali Hafed remained at home and dug in his own cellar, or underneath his own wheat-fields, or in his own garden, instead of wretchedness, starvation, and death by suicide in a strange land, he would have had 'acres of diamonds.' For every acre of that old farm, yes, every shovelful, afterward revealed gems which since have decorated the crowns of monarchs."

When he had added the moral to his story I saw why he reserved it for "his

13

particular friends." But I did not tell him I could see it. It was that mean old Arab's way of going around a thing like a lawyer, to say indirectly what he did not dare say directly, that "in his private opinion there was a certain young man then traveling down the Tigris River that might better be at home in America." I did not tell him I could see that, but I told him his story reminded me of one, and I told it to him quick, and I think I will tell it to you.

I told him of a man out in California in 1847, who owned a ranch. He heard they had discovered gold in southern California, and so with a passion for gold he sold his ranch to Colonel Sutter, and away he went, never to come back. Colonel Sutter put a mill upon a stream that ran through that ranch, and one day his little girl brought some wet sand from the raceway into their home and sifted it through her fingers before the fire, and in that falling sand a visitor saw the first shining scales of real gold that were ever discovered in California. The man who had owned that ranch wanted gold, and he could have secured it for the mere taking. Indeed, thirty-eight millions of dollars has been taken out of a very few acres since then. About eight years ago I delivered this lecture in a city that stands on that farm, and they told me that a one-third owner for years and years had been getting one hundred and twenty dollars in gold every fifteen minutes, sleeping or waking, without taxation. You and I would enjoy an income like that—if we didn't have to pay an income tax.

But I need another illustration. I found it in Massachusetts, and I am sorry I did because that is the state I came from. This young man in Massachusetts furnishes just another phase of my thought. He went to Yale College and studied mines and mining, and became such an adept as a mining engineer that he was employed by the authorities of the university to train students who were behind their classes. During his senior year he earned $15 a week for doing that work. When he graduated they raised his pay from $15 to $45 a week, and offered him a professorship, and as soon as they did he went right home to his mother. *If they had raised that boy's pay from $15 to $15.60 he would have stayed and been proud of the place, but when they put it up to $45 at one leap, he said, "Mother, I won't work for $45 a week. The idea of a man with a brain like mine working for $45 a week!* Let's go out in California and stake out gold-mines and silver-mines, and be immensely rich."

Said his mother, "Now, Charlie, it is just as well to be happy as it is to be rich."

"Yes," said Charlie, "but it is just as well to be rich and happy, too." And they were both right about it. As he was an only son and she a widow, of course he had his way. They always do.

They sold out in Massachusetts, and instead of going to California they went to Wisconsin, where he went into the employ of the Superior Copper Mining Company at $15 a week again, but with the proviso in his contract that he should have an interest in any mines he should discover for the company. I don't believe he ever discovered a mine, and if I am looking in the face of any stockholder of that copper company you wish he had discovered something or other. I have friends who are not here because they could not afford a ticket, who did have stock in that company at the time this young man was employed there. This young man went out there, and

I have not heard a word from him. I don't know what became of him, and I don't know whether he found any mines or not, but I don't believe he ever did.

But I do know the other end of the line. He had scarcely gotten out of the old homestead before the succeeding owner went out to dig potatoes. The potatoes were already growing in the ground when he bought the farm, and as the old farmer was bringing in a basket of potatoes it hugged very tight between the ends of the stone fence. You know in Massachusetts our farms are nearly all stone wall. There you are obliged to be very economical of front gateways in order to have some place to put the stone. When that basket hugged so tight he set it down on the ground, and then dragged on one side, and pulled on the other side, and as he was dragging that basket through this farmer noticed in the upper and outer corner of that stone wall, right next the gate, a block of native silver eight inches square. That professor of mines, mining, and mineralogy who knew so much about the subject that he would not work for $45 a week, when he sold that homstead in Massachusetts sat right on that silver to make the bargain. He was born on that homestead, was brought up there, and had gone back and forth rubbing the stone with his sleeve until it reflected his countenance, and seemed to say, "Here is a hundred thousand dollars right down here just for the taking." But he would not take it. It was in a home in Newburyport, Massachusetts, and there was no silver there, all away off—well, I don't know where, and he did not, but somewhere else, and he was a professor of mineralogy.

My friends, that mistake is very universally made, and why should we even smile at him. I often wonder what has become of him. I do not know at all, but I will tell you what I "guess" as a Yankee. I guess that he sits out there by his fireside to-night with his friends gathered around him, and he is saying to them something like this: "Do you know that man Conwell who lives in Philadelphia?" "Oh yes, I have heard of him." "Do you know that man Jones that lives in Philadelphia?" "Yes, I have heard of him, too."

Then he begins to laugh, and shakes his sides, and says to his friends, "Well, they have done just the same thing I did, precisely"—and that spoils the whole joke, for you and I have done the same thing he did, and while we sit here and laugh at him he has a better right to sit out there and laugh at us. I know I have made the same mistakes, but, of course, that does not make any difference, because we don't expect the same man to preach and practise, too.

As I come here to-night and look around this audience I am seeing again what through these fifty years I have continually seen—men that are making precisely that same mistake. I often wish I could see the younger people, and would that the Academy had been filled to-night with our high-school scholars and our grammar-school scholars, that I could have them to talk to. While I would have preferred such an audience as that, because they are most susceptible, as they have not grown up into their prejudices as we have, they have not gotten into any custom that they cannot break, they have not met with any failures as we have; and while I could perhaps do such an audience as that more good than I can do grown-up people, yet I will do the best I can with the material I have. I say to you that you have "acres of diamonds" in Philadelphia right where you now live. "Oh," but you will say,

15

"you cannot know much about your city if you think there are any 'acres of diamonds' here."

But it serves simply to illustrate my thought, which I emphasize by saying if you do not have the actual diamond-mines literally you have all that they would be good for to you. Because now that the Queen of England has given the greatest compliment ever conferred upon American woman for her attire because she did not appear with any jewels at all at the late reception in England, it has almost done away with the use of diamonds anyhow. All you would care for would be the few you would wear if you wish to be modest, and the rest you would sell for money.

Now then, I say again that the opportunity to get rich, to attain unto great wealth, is here in Philadelphia now, within the reach of almost every man and woman who hears me speak to-night, and I mean just what I say. I have not come to this platform even under these circumstances to recite something to you. I have come to tell you what in God's sight I believe to be the truth, and if the years of life have been of any value to me in the attainment of common sense, I know I am right; that the men and women sitting here, who found it difficult perhaps to buy a ticket to this lecture or gathering to-night, have within their reach "acres of diamonds," opportunities to get largely wealthy. There never was a place on earth more adapted than the city of Philadelphia to-day, and never in the history of the world did a poor man without capital have such an opportunity to get rich quickly and honestly as he has now in our city. I say it is the truth, and I want you to accept it as such; for if you think I have come to simply recite something, then I would better not be here. I have no time to waste in any such talk, but to say the things I believe, and unless some of you get richer for what I am saying to-night my time is wasted.

I say that you ought to get rich, and it is your duty to get rich. How many of my pious brethren say to me, "Do you, a Christian minister, spend your time going up and down the country advising young people to get rich, to get money?" "Yes, of course I do." They say, "Isn't that awful! Why don't you preach the gospel instead of preaching about man's making money?" "Because to make money honestly is to preach the gospel." That is the reason. The men who get rich may be the most honest men you find in the community.

"Oh," but says some young man here to-night, "I have been told all my life that if a person has money he is very dishonest and dishonorable and mean and contemptible." My friend, that is the reason why you have none, because you have that idea of people. The foundation of your faith is altogether false. Let me say here clearly, and say it briefly, though subject to discussion which I have not time for here, ninety-eight out of one hundred of the rich men of America are honest. That is why they are rich. That is why they are trusted with money. That is why they carry on great enterprises and find plenty of people to work with them. It is because they are honest men.

Says another young man, "I hear sometimes of men that get millions of dollars dishonestly." Yes, of course you do, and so do I. But they are so rare a thing in fact that the newspapers talk about them all the time as a matter of news until you get the idea that all the other rich men got rich dishonestly.

My friend, you take and drive me—if you furnish the auto—out into the suburbs of Philadelphia, and introduce me to the people who own their homes around this great city, those beautiful homes with gardens and flowers, those magnificent homes so lovely in their art, and I will introduce you to the very best people in character as well as in enterprise in our city, and you know I will. A man is not really a true man until he owns his own home, and they that own their homes are made more honorable and honest and pure, and true and economical and careful, by owning the home.

For a man to have money, even in large sums, is not an inconsistent thing. We preach against covetousness, and you know we do, in the pulpit, and oftentimes preach against it so long and use the terms about "filthy lucre" so extremely that Christians get the idea that when we stand in the pulpit we believe it is wicked for any man to have money—until the collection-basket goes around, and then we almost swear at the people because they don't give more money. Oh, the inconsistency of such doctrines as that!

Money is power, and you ought to be reasonably ambitious to have it. You ought because you can do more good with it than you could without it. Money printed your Bible, money builds your churches, money sends your missionaries, and money pays your preachers, and you would not have many of them, either, if you did not pay them. I am always willing that my church should raise my salary, because the church that pays the largest salary always raises it the easiest. You never knew an exception to it in your life. The man who gets the largest salary can do the most good with the power that is furnished to him. Of course he can if his spirit be right to use it for what it is given to him.

I say, then, you ought to have money. If you can honestly attain unto riches in Philadelphia, it is your Christian and godly duty to do so. It is an awful mistake of these pious people to think you must be awfully poor in order to be pious.

Some men say, "Don't you sympathize with the poor people?" Of course I do, or else I would not have been lecturing these years. I won't give in but what I sympathize with the poor, but the number of poor who are to be sympathized with is very small. To sympathize with a man whom God has punished for his sins, thus to help him when God would still continue a just punishment, is to do wrong, no doubt about it, and we do that more than we help those who are deserving. While we should sympathize with God's poor—that is, those who cannot help them-selves—let us remember there is not a poor person in the United States who was not made poor by his own shortcomings, or by the shortcomings of some one else. It is all wrong to be poor, anyhow. Let us give in to that argument and pass that to one side.

A gentleman gets up back there, and says, "Don't you think there are some things in this world that are better than money?" Of course I do, but I am talking about money now. Of course there are some things higher than money. Oh yes, I know by the grave that has left me standing alone that there are some things in this

17

world that are higher and sweeter and purer than money. Well do I know there are some things higher and grander than gold. Love is the grandest thing on God's earth, but fortunate the lover who has plenty of money. Money is power, money is force, money will do good as well as harm. In the hands of good men and women it could accomplish, and it has accomplished, good.

I hate to leave that behind me. I heard a man get up in a prayer-meeting in our city and thank the Lord he was "one of God's poor." Well, I wonder what his wife thinks about that? She earns all the money that comes into that house, and he smokes a part of that on the veranda. I don't want to see any more of the Lord's poor of that kind, and I don't believe the Lord does. And yet there are some people who think in order to be pious you must be awfully poor and awfully dirty. That does not follow at all. While we sympathize with the poor, let us not teach a doctrine like that.

Yet the age is prejudiced against advising a Christian man (or, as a Jew would say, a godly man) from attaining unto wealth. The prejudice is so universal and the years are far enough back, I think, for me to safely mention that years ago up at Temple University there was a young man in our theological school who thought he was the only pious student in that department. He came into my office one evening and sat down by my desk, and said to me: "Mr. President, I think it is my duty sir, to come in and labor with you." "What has happened now?" Said he, "I heard you say at the Academy, at the Peirce School commencement, that you thought it was an honorable ambition for a young man to desire to have wealth, and that you thought it made him temperate, made him anxious to have a good name, and made him industrious. You spoke about man's ambition to have money helping to make him a good man. Sir, I have come to tell you the Holy Bible says that 'money is the root of all evil.' "

I told him I had never seen it in the Bible, and advised him to go out into the chapel and get the Bible, and show me the place. So out he went for the Bible, and soon he stalked into my office with the Bible open, with all the bigoted pride of the narrow sectarian, or of one who founds his Christianity on some misinterpretation of Scripture. He flung the Bible down on my desk, and fairly squealed into my ear: "There it is, Mr. President; you can read it for yourself." I said to him: "Well, young man, you will learn when you get a little older that you cannot trust another denomination to read the Bible for you. You belong to another denomination. You are taught in the theological school, however, that emphasis is exegesis. Now, will you take that Bible and read it yourself, and give the proper emphasis to it?"

He took the Bible, and proudly read, " 'The love of money is the root of all evil.' "

Then he had it right, and when one does quote aright from that same old Book he quotes the absolute truth. I have lived through fifty years of the mightiest battle that old Book has ever fought, and I have lived to see its banners flying free; for never in the history of this world did the great minds of earth so universally agree that the Bible is true—all true—as they do at this very hour.

So I say that when he quoted right, of course he quoted the absolute truth. "The love of money is the root of all evil." He who tries to attain unto it too quickly, or dishonestly, will fall into many snares, no doubt about that. The love of money. What is that? It is making an idol of money, and idolatry pure and simple everywhere is condemned by the Holy Scriptures and by man's common sense. The man that worships the dollar instead of thinking of the purposes for which it ought to be used, the man who idolizes simply money, the miser that hordes his money in the cellar, or hides it in his stocking, or refuses to invest it where it will do the world good, that man who hugs the dollar until the eagle squeals has in him the root of all evil.

I think I will leave that behind me now and answer the question of nearly all of you who are asking, "Is there opportunity to get rich in Philadelphia?" Well, now, how simple a thing it is to see where it is, and the instant you see where it is it is yours. Some old gentleman gets up back there and says, "Mr. Conwell, have you lived in Philadelphia for thirty-one years and don't know that the time has gone by when you can make anything in this city?" "No, I don't think it is." "Yes, it is; I have tried it." "What business are you in?" "I kept a store here for twenty years, and never made over a thousand dollars in the whole twenty years."

"Well, then, you can measure the good you have been to this city by what this city has paid you, because a man can judge very well what he is worth by what he receives; that is, in what he is to the world at this time. If you have not made over a thousand dollars in twenty years in Philadelphia, it would have been better for Philadelphia if they had kicked you out of the city nineteen years and nine months ago. A man has no right to keep a store in Philadelphia twenty years and not make at least five hundred thousand dollars, even though it be a corner grocery up-town." You say, "You cannot make five thousand dollars in a store now." Oh, my friends, if you will just take only four blocks around you, and find out what the people want and what you ought to supply and set them down with your pencil, and figure up the profits you would make if you did supply them, you would very soon see it. There is wealth right within the sound of your voice.

Some one says: "You don't know anything about business. A preacher never knows a thing about business." Well, then, I will have to prove that I am an expert. I don't like to do this, but I have to do it because my testimony will not be taken if I am not an expert. My father kept a country store, and if there is any place under the stars where a man gets all sorts of experience in every kind of mercantile transactions, it is in the country store. I am not proud of my experience, but sometimes when my father was away he would leave me in charge of the store, though fortunately for him that was not very often. But this did occur many times, friends: A man would come in the store, and say to me, "Do you keep jack-knives?" "No, we don't keep jack-knives," and I went off whistling a tune. What did I care about that man, anyhow? Then another farmer would come in and say, "Do you keep jack-knives?" "No, we don't keep jack-knives." Then I went away and whistled another tune. Then a third man came right in the same door and said, "Do you keep jack-knives?" "No. Why is every one around here asking for jack-knives? Do you suppose we are keeping this store to supply the whole neighborhood with jack-knives?" Do you carry on your store like that in Philadelphia? The difficulty was I had not then learned that the foundation of

19

godliness and the foundation principle of success in business are both the same precisely. The man who says, "I cannot carry my religion into business" advertises himself either as being an imbecile in business, or on the road to bankruptcy, or a thief, one of the three, sure. He will fail within a very few years. He certainly will if he doesn't carry his religion into business. If I had been carrying on my father's store on a Christian plan, godly plan, I would have had a jack-knife for the third man when he called for it. Then I would have actually done him a kindness, and I would have received a reward myself, which it would have been my duty to take.

There are some over-pious Christian people who think if you take any profit on anything you sell that you are an unrighteous man. On the contrary, you would be a criminal to sell goods for less than they cost. You have no right to do that. You cannot trust a man with your money who cannot take care of his own. You cannot trust a man in your family that is not true to his own wife. You cannot trust a man in the world that does not begin with his own heart, his own character, and his own life. It would have been my duty to have furnished a jack-knife to the third man, or the second, and to have sold it to him and actually profited myself. I have no more right to sell goods without making a profit on them than I have to overcharge him dishonestly beyond what they are worth. But I should so sell each bill of goods that the person to whom I sell shall make as much as I make.

The man over there who said he could not make anything in a store in Philadelphia has been carrying on his store on the wrong principle. Suppose I go into your store to-morrow morning and ask, "Do you know neighbor A, who lives one square away, at house No. 1240?" "Oh yes, I have met him. He deals here at the corner store." "Where did he come from?" "I don't know." "How many does he have in his family?" "I don't know." "What ticket does he vote?" "I don't know." "What church does he go to?" "I don't know, and don't care. What are you asking all these questions for?"

If you had a store in Philadelphia would you answer me like that? If so, then you are conducting your business just as I carried on my father's business in Worthington, Massachusetts. You don't know where your neighbor came from when he moved to Philadelphia, and you don't care. If you had cared you would be a rich man now. If you had cared enough about him to take an interest in his affairs, to find out what he needed, you would have been rich. But you go through the world saying, "No opportunity to get rich," and there is the fault right at your own door.

A. T. Stewart, a poor boy in New York, had $1.50 to begin life on. He lost 87½ cents of that on the very first venture. How fortunate that young man who loses the first time he gambles. That boy said, "I will never gamble again in business," and he never did. How come he to lose 87½ cents? You probably all know the story how he lost it—because he bought some needles, threads, and buttons to sell which people did not want, and had them left on his hands, a dead loss. Said the boy, "I will not lose any more money in that way." Then he went around first to the doors and asked the people what they did want. Then when he had found out what they wanted he invested his 62½ cents to supply a known demand. Study it wherever you choose—in business, in your profession, in your housekeeping, whatever your life, that one thing is the secret of success. You must first know the demand. You must first know what people need, and then invest yourself where you are most needed. A. T. Stewart went on that principle until he was worth what amounted afterward to forty millions of dollars, owning the very store in which Mr. Wanamaker carries on his great work in New York. His fortune was made by his losing something, which taught him the great lesson that he must only invest himself or his money in something that people need. When will you salesmen learn it? When will you manufacturers learn that you must know the changing needs of humanity if you would succeed in life? Apply yourselves, all you Christian people, as manufacturers or merchants or workmen to supply that human need. It is a great principle as broad as humanity and as deep as the Scripture itself.

The best illustration I ever heard was of John Jacob Astor. You know that he made the money of the Astor family when he lived in New York. He came across the sea in debt for his fare. But that poor boy with nothing in his pocket made the fortune of the Astor family on one principle. Some young man here to-night will say, "Well, they could make those fortunes over in New York, but they could not do it in Philadelphia!" My friends, did you ever read that wonderful book of Riis (his memory is sweet to us because of his recent death), wherein is given his statistical account of the records taken in 1889 of 107 millionaires of New York. If you read the account you will see that out of the 107 millionaires only seven made their money in New York. Out of the 107 millionaires worth ten million dollars in real estate then, 67 of them made their money in towns of less than 3,500 inhabitants. The richest man in this country to-day, if you read the real-estate values, has never moved away from a town of 3,500 inhabitants. It makes not so much difference where you are as who you are. But if you cannot get rich in Philadelphia you certainly cannot do it in New York.

Now John Jacob Astor illustrated what can be done anywhere. He had a mortgage once on a millinery-store, and they could not sell bonnets enough to pay the interest on his money. So he foreclosed that mortgage, took possession of the store, and went into partnership with the very same people, in the same store, with the same capital. He did not give them a dollar of capital. They had to sell goods to get any money. Then he left them alone in the store just as they had been before, and he went out and sat down on a bench in the park in the shade. What was John Jacob Astor doing out there, and in partnership with people who had failed on his own hands? He had the most important and, to my mind, the most pleasant part of that partnership on his hands. For as John Jacob Astor sat on that bench he was watching the ladies as they went by; and where is the man who would not get rich at that business? As he sat on the bench if a lady passed him with her shoulders back and head up, and looked straight to the front, as if she did not care if all the world did gaze on her, then he studied her bonnet, and by the time it was out of sight he knew the shape of the frame, the color of the trimmings, and the crinklings in the feather. I sometimes try to describe a bonnet, but not always. I would not try to describe a modern bonnet. Where is the man that could describe one? This aggregation of all sorts of driftwood stuck on the back of the head, or the side of the neck, like a rooster with only one tail feather left. But in John Jacob Astor's day there was some art about the millinery business, and he went to the millinery-store and said to them: "Now put into the show-window just such a bonnet as I describe to you, because I have already seen a lady who likes such a bonnet. Don't make up any more until I come back." Then he went out and sat down again, and another lady passed him of a different form, of different complexion, with a different shape and color of bonnet. "Now," said he, "put such a bonnet as that in the show-window." He did not fill his show-window uptown with a lot of hats and bonnets to drive people away, and then sit on the back stairs and bawl because people went to Wanamaker's to trade. He did not have a hat or a bonnet in that show-window but what some lady liked before it was made up. The tide of custom began immediately to turn in, and that has been the foundation of the greatest store in New York in that line, and still exists as one of three stores. Its fortune was made by John Jacob Astor after they had failed in business, not by giving them any more money, but by finding out what the ladies liked for bonnets before they wasted any material in making them up. I tell you if a man could foresee the millinery business he could foresee anything under heaven!

Suppose I were to go through this audience to-night and ask you in this great manufacturing city if there are not opportunities to get rich in manufacturing. "Oh yes," some young man says, "there are opportunities here still if you build with some trust and if you have two or three millions of dollars to begin with as capital." Young man, the history of the breaking up of the trusts by that attack upon "big business" is only illustrating what is now the opportunity of the smaller man. The time never came in the history of the world when you could get rich so quickly manufacturing without capital as you can now.

I spoke thus to an audience in New Britain, Connecticut, and a lady four seats back went home and tried to take off her collar, and the collar-button stuck in the buttonhole. She threw it out and said, "I am going to get up something better than that to put on collars." Her husband said: "After what Conwell said to-night, you see there is a need of an improved collar-fastener that is easier to handle. There is a human need; there is a great fortune. Now, then, get up a collar-button and get rich." He made fun of her, and consequently made fun of me, and that is one of the saddest things which comes over me like a deep cloud of midnight sometimes— although I have worked so hard for more than half a century, yet how little I have ever really done. Notwithstanding the greatness and the handsomeness of your compliment to-night, I do not believe there is one in ten of you that is going to make a million of dollars because you are here to-night; but it is not my fault, it is yours. I say that sincerely. What is the use of my talking if people never do what I advise them to do? When her husband ridiculed her, she made up her mind she would make a better collar-button, and when a woman makes up her mind "she will," and does not say anything about it, she does it. It was that New England woman who invented the snap button which you can find anywhere now. It was first a collar-button with a spring cap attached to the outer side. Any of you who wear modern waterproofs know the button that simply pushes together, and when you unbutton it you simply pull it apart. That is the button to which I refer, and which she invented. She afterward invented several other buttons, and then invested in more, and then was taken into partnership with great factories. Now that woman goes over the sea every summer in her private steamship—yes, and takes her husband with her! If her husband were to die, she would have money enough left now to buy a foreign duke or count or some such title as that at the latest quotations.

Now what is my lesson in that incident? It is this: I told her then, though I did not know her, what I now say to you, "Your wealth is too near to you. You are looking right over it"; and she had to look over it because it was right under her chin.

# 45

## Glimpses
## of a Changing America

After some years as the pilot of a Mississippi River steamboat in the 1850s, Samuel Langhorne Clemens began a brilliant career as a writer, under the pen name Mark Twain. He is best remembered today for his novels of boyhood in pre-Civil War, preindustrial America, *The Adventures of Tom Sawyer* and *Huckleberry Finn,* but he was also a careful observer and critic of the new America that was emerging in his mature years. Both his unabashed enthusiasm for material progress and his underlying nostalgia for an older America are evident in this selection from *Life on the Mississippi*, his account of his trip down the river from St. Louis to New Orleans and back up to Minneapolis in 1882.

## LIFE
## ON THE MISSISSIPPI
### *Mark Twain*

After twenty-one years' absence I felt a very strong desire to see the river again, and the steamboats, and such of the boys as might be left; so I resolved to go out there.

We left per Pennsylvania Railroad, at 8 A.M. April 18.

*Evening*

> Speaking of dress. Grace and picturesqueness drop gradually out of it as one travels away from New York.

I find that among my notes. It makes no difference which direction you take, the fact remains the same. Whether you move north, south, east, or west, no matter: you can get up in the morning and guess how far you have come, by noting what degree of grace and picturesqueness is by that time lacking in the costumes of the new passengers—I do not mean of the women alone, but of both sexes. It may be that *carriage* is at the bottom of this thing; and I think it is; for there are plenty of ladies and gentlemen in the provincial cities whose garments are all made by the best tailors and dressmakers of New York; yet this has no perceptible effect upon the grand fact: the educated eye never mistakes those people for New-Yorkers. No, there is a godless grace and snap and style about a born and bred New-Yorker which mere clothing cannot effect.

From *Life on the Mississippi* (New York, n.d.), 186–188, 253–254, 327–333, 374–376, 461–462, 469–471, 472–475.

*April 19*

This morning struck into the region of full goatees—sometimes accompanied by a mustache, but only occasionally.

It was odd to come upon this thick crop of an obsolete and uncomely fashion; it was like running suddenly across a forgotten acquaintance whom you had supposed dead for a generation. The goatee extends over a wide extent of country, and is accompanied by an iron-clad belief in Adam, and the biblical history of creation, which has not suffered from the assaults of the scientists.

*Afternoon*

At the railway-stations the loafers carry *both* hands in their breeches pockets; it was observable, heretofore, that one hand was sometimes out-of-doors—here, never. This is an important fact of geography.

If the loafers determined the character of a country, it would be still more important, of course.

Heretofore, all along, the station loafer has been often observed to scratch one shin with the other foot; here these remains of activity are wanting. This as an ominous look.

By and by we entered the tobacco-chewing region. Fifty years ago the tobacco-chewing region covered the Union. It is greatly restricted now.

Next, boots began to appear. Not in strong force, however. Later—away from the Mississippi—they became the rule. They disappeared from other sections of the Union with the mud; no doubt they will disappear from the river villages, also, when proper pavements come in.

We were getting down now into the migrating negro region. These poor people could never travel when they were slaves; so they make up for the privation now. They stay on a plantation till the desire to travel seizes them; then they pack up, hail a steamboat, and clear out. Not for any particular place; no, nearly any place will answer; they only want to be moving. The amount of money on hand will answer the rest of the conundrum for them. If it will take them fifty miles, very well; let it be fifty. If not, a shorter flight will do.

During a couple of days we frequently answered these hails. Sometimes there was a group of high-water-stained, tumbledown cabins, populous with colored folk, and no whites visible; with grassless patches of dry ground here and there; a few felled trees, with skeleton cattle, mules, and horses, eating the leaves and gnawing the bark—no other food for them in the flood-wasted land. Sometimes there was a single lonely landing-cabin; near it the colored family that had hailed us; little and big, old and young, roosting on the scant pile of household goods; these consisting of a rusty gun, some bedticks, chests, tinware, stools, a crippled looking-glass, a venerable arm-chair, and six or eight base-born and spiritless yellow curs, attached to the family by strings. They must have their dogs; can't go without their dogs. Yet the dogs are never willing; they always object; so, one after another, in ridiculous procession, they are dragged aboard; all four feet braced and sliding along the stage, head likely to be pulled off; but the tugger marching determinedly forward, bending to his work, with the rope over his shoulder for better purchase. Sometimes a child is forgotten and left on the bank; but never a dog.

I awoke out of a fretted sleep, with a dull confusion of voices in my ears. I listened—two men were talking; subject, apparently, the great inundation. I looked out through the open transom. The two men were eating a late breakfast; sitting opposite each other; nobody else around. They closed up the inundation with a few words—having used it, evidently, as a mere ice-breaker and acquaintanceship-breeder—then they dropped into business. It soon transpired that they were drummers—one belonging in Cincinnati, the other in New Orleans. Brisk men, energetic of movement and speech; the dollar their god, how to get it their religion.

"Now as to this article," said Cincinnati, slashing into the ostensible butter and holding forward a slab of it on his knife-blade, "it's from our house; look at it—smell of it—taste it. Put any test on it you want to. Take your own time—no hurry—make it thorough. There now—what do you say? butter, ain't it? Not by a thundering sight—it's oleomargarine! Yes, sir, that's what it is—oleomargarine. You can't tell it from butter; by George, an *expert* can't! It's from our house. We supply most of the boats in the West; there's hardly a pound of butter on one of them. We are crawling right along—*jumping* right along is the word. We are going to have that entire trade. Yes, and the hotel trade, too. You are going to see the day, pretty soon, when you can't find an ounce of butter to bless yourself with, in any hotel in the Mississippi and Ohio valleys, outside of the biggest cities. Why, we are turning out oleomargarine *now* by the thousands of tons. And we can sell it so dirt-cheap that the whole country has *got* to take it—can't get around it, you see. Butter don't stand any show—there ain't any chance for competition. Butter's had its *day*—and from this out, butter goes to the wall. There's more money in oleomargine than—why, you can't imagine the business we do. I've stopped in every town, from Cincinnati to Natchez; and I've sent home big orders from every one of them."

And so forth and so on, for ten minutes longer, in the same fervid strain. Then New Orleans piped up and said:

"Yes, it's a first-rate imitation, that's a certainty; but it ain't the only one around that's first-rate. For instance, they make olive-oil out of cotton-seed oil, nowadays, so that you can't tell them apart."

"Yes, that's so," responded Cincinnati, "and it was a tip-top business for a while. They sent it over and brought it back from France and Italy, with the United States custom-house mark on it to indorse it for genuine, and there was no end of cash in it; but France and Italy broke up the game—of course they naturally would. Cracked on such a rattling impost that cotton-seed olive-oil couldn't stand the raise; had to hang up and quit."

"Oh, it *did*, did it? You wait here a minute."

Goes to his stateroom, brings back a couple of long bottles, and takes out the corks—says:

"There now, smell them, taste them, examine the bottles, inspect the labels. One of 'm's from Europe, the other's never been out of this country. One's European olive-oil, the other's American cotton-seed olive-oil. Tell 'm apart? 'Course you can't. Nobody can. People that want to, can go to the expense and trouble of shipping their oils to Europe and back—it's their privilege; but our firm knows a trick worth six of that. We turn out the whole thing—clean from the word go—in our factory in New Orleans: labels, bottles, oil, everything. Well, no, not labels: been buying *them* abroad—get them dirt-cheap there. You see there's just one little wee speck, essence, or whatever it is, in a gallon of cotton-seed oil, that gives it a smell, or a flavor, or something—get that out, and you're all right—perfectly easy then to turn the oil into any kind of oil you want to, and there ain't anybody that can detect the true from the false. Well, we know how to get that one little particle out—and we're the only firm that does. And we turn out an olive-oil that is just simply perfect—undetectable! We are doing a ripping trade, too—as I could easily show you by my order-book for this trip. Maybe you'll butter everybody's bread pretty soon, but we'll cotton-seed his salad for him from the Gulf to Canada, that's a dead-certain thing."

Cincinnati glowed and flashed with admiration. The two scoundrels exchanged business-cards, and arose. As they left the table, Cincinnati said:

"But you have to have custom-house marks, don't you? How do you manage that?"

I did not catch the answer.

The Mardi-Gras pageant was the exclusive possession of New Orleans until recently. But now it has spread to Memphis and St. Louis and Baltimore. It has probably reached its limit. It is a thing which could hardly exist in the practical North; would certainly last but a very brief time; as brief a time as it would last in London. For the soul of it is the romantic, not the funny and the grotesque. Take away the romantic mysteries, the kings and knights and big-sounding titles, and Mardi-Gras would die, down there in the South. The very feature that keeps it alive in the South—girly-girly romance—would kill it in the North or in London. *Puck* and *Punch*, and the press universal, would fall upon it and make merciless fun of it, and its first exhibition would be also its last.

Against the crimes of the French Revolution and of Bonaparte may be set two compensating benefactions: the Revolution broke the chains of the *ancien régime* and of the Church, and made a nation of abject slaves a nation of freemen; and Bonaparte instituted the setting of merit above birth, and also so completely stripped the divinity from royalty that, whereas crowned heads in Europe were gods before, they are only men since, and can never be gods again, but only figure-heads, and answerable for their acts like common clay. Such benefactions as these compensate the temporary harm which Bonaparte and the Revolution did, and leave the world in debt to them for these great and permanent services to liberty, humanity, and progress.

Then comes Sir Walter Scott with his enchantments, and by his single might checks this wave of progress, and even turns it back; sets the world in love with dreams and phantoms; with decayed and swinish forms of religion; with decayed and degraded systems of government; with the sillinesses and emptinesses, sham grandeurs, sham gauds, and sham chivalries of a brainless and worthless long-van-ished society. He did measureless harm; more real and lasting harm, perhaps, than any other individual that ever wrote. Most of the world has now outlived good part of these harms, though by no means all of them; but in our South they flourish

27

pretty forcefully still. Not so forcefully as half a generation ago, perhaps, but still forcefully. There, the genuine and wholesome civilization of the nineteenth century is curiously confused and commingled with the Walter Scott Middle-Age sham civilization, and so you have practical common sense, progressive ideas, and progressive works, mixed up with the duel, the inflated speech, and the jejune romanticism of an absurd past that is dead, and out of charity ought to be buried. But for the Sir Walter disease, the character of the Southerner—or Southron, according to Sir Walter's starchier way of phrasing it—would be wholly modern, in place of modern and medieval mixed, and the South would be fully a generation further advanced than it is. It was Sir Walter that made every gentleman in the South a major or a colonel, or a general or a judge, before the war; and it was he, also, that made these gentlemen value these bogus decorations. For it was he that created rank and caste down there, and also reverence for rank and caste, and pride and pleasure in them. Enough is laid on slavery, without fathering upon it these creations and contributions of Sir Walter.

Sir Walter had so large a hand in making Southern character, as it existed before the war, that he is in great measure responsible for the war. It seems a little harsh toward a dead man to say that we never should have had any war but for Sir Walter; and yet something of a plausible argument might, perhaps, be made in support of that wild proposition. The Southerner of the American Revolution owned slaves; so did the Southerner of the Civil War; but the former resembles the latter as an Englishman resembles a Frenchman. The change of character can be traced rather more easily to Sir Walter's influence than to that of any other thing or person.

From St. Louis northward there are all the enlivening signs of the presence of active, energetic, intelligent, prosperous, practical nineteenth-century populations. The people don't dream; they work. The happy result is manifest all around in the substantial outside aspect of things, and the suggestions of wholesome life and comfort that everywhere appear.

La Grange and Canton are growing towns, but I missed Alexandria; was told it was under water, but would come up to blow in the summer.

Keokuk was easily recognizable. I lived there in 1857—an extraordinary year there in real-estate matters. The "boom" was something wonderful. Everybody bought, everybody sold—except widows and preachers; they always hold on; and when the tide ebbs, they get left. Anything in the semblance of a town lot, no matter how situated, was salable, and at a figure which would still have been high if the ground had been sodded with greenbacks.

The town has a population of fifteen thousand now, and is progressing with a healthy growth. It was night, and we could not see details, for which we were sorry, for Keokuk has the reputation of being a beautiful city. It was a pleasant one to live in long ago, and doubtless has advanced, not retrograded, in that respect.

The big towns drop in, thick and fast, now: and between stretch processions of thrifty farms, not desolate solitude. Hour by hour, the boat plows deeper and deeper into the great and populous Northwest; and with each successive section of it which is revealed, one's surprise and respect gather emphasis and increase. Such a people, and such achievements as theirs, compel homage. This is an independent race who think for themselves, and who are competent to do it, because they are educated and enlightened; they read, they keep abreast of the best and newest thought; they fortify every weak place in their land with a school, a college, a library, and a newspaper; and they live under law. Solicitude for the future of a race like this is not in order.

This region is new; so new that it may be said to be still in its babyhood. By what it has accomplished while still teething, one may forecast what marvels it will do in the strength of its maturity. It is so new that the foreign tourist has not heard of it yet; and has not visited it. For sixty years the foreign tourist has steamed up and down the river between St. Louis and New Orleans, and then gone home and written his book; believing he had seen all of the river that was worth seeing or that had anything to see. In not six of all these books is there mention of these Upper-River towns—for the reason that the five or six tourists who penetrated this region did it before these towns were projected. The latest tourist of them all (1878) made the same old regulation trip—he had not heard that there was anything north of St. Louis.

Yet there was. There was this amazing region, bristling with great towns, projected day before yesterday, so to speak, and built next morning. A score of them number from 1,500 to 5,000 people. Then we have Muscatine, 10,000; Winona, 10,000; Moline, 10,000; Rock Island, 12,000; La Crosse, 12,000; Burlington, 25,000; Dubuque, 25,000; Davenport, 30,000; St. Paul, 58,000; Minneapolis, 60,000 and upward.

The foreign tourist has never heard of these; there is no note of them in his books. They have sprung up in the night, while he slept. So new is this region that I, who am comparatively young, am yet older than it is. When I was born St. Paul had a population of three persons; Minneapolis had just a third as many. The then population of Minneapolis died two years ago; and when he died he had seen himself undergo an increase, in forty years, of fifty-nine thousand nine hundred and ninety-nine persons. He had a frog's fertility.

I must explain that the figures set down above, as the population of St. Paul and Minneapolis, are several months old. These towns are far larger now. In fact, I have just seen a newspaper estimate, which gives the former seventy-one thousand and the latter seventy-eight thousand. This book will not reach the public for six or seven months yet; none of the figures will be worth much then.

The majestic bluffs that overlook the river, along through this region, charm one with the grace and variety of their forms, and the soft beauty of their adornment. The steep, verdant slope, whose base is at the water's edge, is topped by a lofty rampart of broken, turreted rocks, which are exquisitely rich and mellow in color—mainly dark browns and dull greens, but splashed with other tints. And then you have the shining river, winding here and there and yonder, its sweep interrupted at intervals by clusters of wooded islands threaded by silver channels; and you have glimpses of distant villages, asleep upon capes; and of stealthy rafts

29

slipping along in the shade of the forest walls; and of white steamers vanishing around remote points. And it is all as tranquil and reposeful as dreamland, and has nothing this-worldly about it—nothing to hang a fret or a worry upon.

Until the unholy train comes tearing along—which it presently does, ripping the sacred solitude to rags and tatters with its devil's war-whoop and the roar and thunder of its rushing wheels—and straightway you are back in this world, and with one of its frets ready to hand for your entertainment: for you remember that this is the very road whose stock always goes down after you buy it, and always goes up again as soon as you sell it. It makes me shudder to this day, to remember that I once came near not getting rid of my stock at all. It must be an awful thing to have a railroad left on your hands.

The locomotive is in sight from the deck of the steamboat almost the whole way from St. Louis to St. Paul—eight hundred miles. These railroads have made havoc with the steamboat commerce.

Up in this region we met massed acres of lumber-rafts coming down—but not floating leisurely along, in the old-fashioned way, manned with joyous and reckless crews of fiddling, song-singing, whisky-drinking, breakdown-dancing rapscallions; no, the whole thing was shoved swiftly along by a powerful stern-wheeler, modern fashion; and the small crews were quiet, orderly men, of a sedate business aspect, with not a suggestion of romance about them anywhere.

# 46

## A New England Girl Confronts the Factory

Lucy Larcom, later a schoolteacher and a highly successful writer for the juvenile market, was forced to work for several years in the gigantic cotton mills of Lowell, Massachusetts, starting at the tender age of eleven. She was a somewhat unusual girl, as this selection from her autobiography makes clear; and it should be noted that she describes a pre-1850 phase of industrial history; late nineteenth-century factory life was more difficult to describe in such rosy terms. The peculiar system of labor recruitment sketched here—the reliance upon farm girls who lived in the strictly controlled company boarding houses and worked for a brief period before departing for marriage—proved difficult to transplant to other cities. By the 1840s, even in Lowell itself, the labor force was becoming more permanent, more heavily immigrant in origin, and less contented; but the values and personal resources upon which Lucy Larcom drew in adjusting to the factory environment were not the exclusive property of New England girls of the Age of Jackson, but a heritage to which many other Americans and Americanized immigrants were exposed.

### A NEW ENGLAND GIRLHOOD
#### Lucy Larcom

During my father's life, a few years before my birth, his thoughts had been turned towards the new manufacturing town growing up on the banks of the Merrimack. He had once taken a journey there, with the possibility in his mind of making the place his home, his limited income furnishing no adequate promise of a maintenance for his large family of daughters. From the beginning, Lowell had a high reputation for good order, morality, piety, and all that was dear to the old-fashioned New Englander's heart.

After his death, my mother's thoughts naturally followed the direction his had taken; and seeing no other opening for herself, she sold her small estate, and moved

From *A New England Girlhood, Outlined from Memory* (Boston, 1889), 145–146, 153–157, 164–165, 167–169, 175–176, 199–201.

to Lowell, with the intention of taking a corporation-house for mill-girl boarders. Some of the family objected, for the Old World traditions about factory life were anything but attractive; and they were current in New England until the experiment at Lowell had shown that independent and intelligent workers invariably give their own character to their occupation. My mother had visited Lowell, and she was willing and glad, knowing all about the place, to make it our home.

Most of my mother's boarders were from New Hampshire and Vermont, and there was a fresh, breezy sociability about them which made them seem almost like a different race of beings from any we children had hitherto known.

We helped a little about the housework, before and after school, making beds, trimming lamps, and washing dishes. The heaviest work was done by a strong Irish girl, my mother always attending to the cooking herself. She was, however, a better caterer than the circumstances required or permitted. She liked to make nice things for the table, and, having been accustomed to an abundant supply, could never learn to economize. At a dollar and a quarter a week for board, (the price allowed for mill-girls by the corporations) great care in expenditure was necessary. It was not in my mother's nature closely to calculate costs, and in this way there came to be a continually increasing leak in the family purse. The older members of the family did everything they could, but it was not enough. I heard it said one day, in a distressed tone, "The children will have to leave school and go into the mill."

There were many pros and cons between my mother and sisters before this was positively decided. The mill-agent did not want to take us two little girls, but consented on condition we should be sure to attend school the full number of months prescribed each year. I, the younger one, was then between eleven and twelve years old.

I listened to all that was said about it, very much fearing that I should not be permitted to do the coveted work. For the feeling had already frequently come to me, that I was the one too many in the overcrowded family nest. Once, before we left our old home, I had heard a neighbor condoling with my mother because there were so many of us, and her emphatic reply had been a great relief to my mind:—

"There isn't one more than I want. I could not spare a single one of my children."

But her difficulties were increasing, and I thought it would be a pleasure to feel that I was not a trouble or burden or expense to anybody. So I went to my first day's work in the mill with a light heart. The novelty of it made it seem easy, and it really was not hard, just to change the bobbins on the spinning-frames every three quarters of an hour or so, with half a dozen other little girls who were doing the same thing. When I came back at night, the family began to pity me for my long, tiresome day's work, but I laughed and said,—

"Why, it is nothing but fun. It is just like play."

And for a little while it was only a new amusement; I liked it better than going to school and "making believe" I was learning when I was not. And there was a great deal of play mixed with it. We were not occupied more than half the time. The intervals were spent frolicking around among the spinning-frames, teasing and talking to the older girls, or entertaining ourselves with games and stories in a corner, or exploring, with the overseer's permission, the mysteries of the carding-room, the dressing-room, and the weaving-room.

I never cared much for machinery. The buzzing and hissing and whizzing of pulleys and rollers and spindles and flyers around me often grew tiresome. I could not see into their complications, or feel interested in them. But in a room below us we were sometimes allowed to peer in through a sort of blind door at the great water-wheel that carried the works of the whole mill. It was so huge that we could only watch a few of its spokes at a time, and part of its dripping rim, moving with a slow, measured strength through the darkness that shut it in. It impressed me with something of the awe which comes to us in thinking of the great Power which keeps the mechanism of the universe in motion. Even now, the remembrance of its large, mysterious movement, in which every little motion of every noisy little wheel was involved, brings back to me a verse from one of my favorite hymns:—

*Our lives through various scenes are drawn,*
 *And vexed by traffic cares,*
*While Thine eternal thought moves on*
 *Thy undisturbed affairs.*

There were compensations for being shut in to daily toil so early. The mill itself had its lessons for us. But it was not, and could not be, the right sort of life for a child, and we were happy in the knowledge that, at the longest, our employment was only to be temporary.

When I took my next three months at the grammar school, everything there was changed, and I too was changed. The teachers were kind, and thorough in their instruction; and my mind seemed to have been ploughed up during that year of work, so that knowledge took root in it easily. It was a great delight to me to study, and at the end of the three months the master told me that I was prepared for the high school.

But alas! I could not go. The little money I could earn—one dollar a week, besides the price of my board—was needed in the family, and I must return to the mill. It was a severe disappointment to me, though I did not say so at home. I did not at all accept the conclusion of a neighbor whom I heard talking about it with my mother. His daughter was going to the high school, and my mother was telling him how sorry she was that I could not.

"Oh," he said, in a soothing tone, "my girl hasn't got any such head-piece as yours has. Your girl doesn't need to go."

Of course I knew that whatever sort of a "head-piece" I had, I did need and want just that very opportunity to study. I think the resolution was then formed, inwardly, that I *would* go to school again, some time, whatever happened. I went back to my work, but now without enthusiasm. I had looked through an open door that I was not willing to see shut upon me.

I began to reflect upon life rather seriously for a girl of twelve or thirteen. What was I here for? What could I make of myself? Must I submit to be carried along with the current, and do just what everybody else did? No: I knew I should not do that, for there was a certain Myself who was always starting up with her own original plan or aspiration before me, and who was quite indifferent as to what people generally thought.

Well, I would find out what this Myself was good for, and that she should be!

It was but the presumption of extreme youth. How gladly would I know now, after these long years, just why I was sent into the world, and whether I have in any degree fulfilled the purpose of my being!

In the older times it was seldom said to little girls, as it always has been said to boys, that they ought to have some definite plan, while they were children, what to be and do when they were grown up. There was usually but one path open before them, to become good wives and housekeepers. And the ambition of most girls was to follow their mother's footsteps in this direction; a natural and laudable ambition. But girls, as well as boys, must often have been conscious of their own peculiar capabilities,—must have desired to cultivate and make use of their individual powers. When I was growing up, they had already begun to be encouraged to do so. We were often told that it was our duty to develop any talent we might possess, or at least to learn to do some one thing which the world needed, or which would make it a pleasanter world.

The gray stone walls of St. Anne's church and rectory made a picturesque spot in the middle of the town, remaining still as a lasting monument to the religious purpose which animated the first manufacturers. The church arose close to the oldest corporation (the "Merrimack"), and seemed a part of it, and a part, also, of the original idea of the place itself which was always a city of worshipers, although it came to be filled with a population which preferred meeting-houses to churches. I admired the church greatly. I had never before seen a real one; never anything but a plain frame meeting-house; and it and its benign, apostolic-looking rector were like a leaf out of an English story-book.

And so, also, was the tiny white cottage nearly opposite, set in the middle of a pretty flower-garden that sloped down to the canal. In the garden there was almost always a sweet little girl in a pink gown and white sunbonnet gathering flowers when I passed that way, and I often went out of my path to do so. These relieved the monotony of the shanty-like shops which bordered the main street. The town had sprung up with a mushroom-rapidity, and there was no attempt at veiling the newness of its bricks and mortar, its boards and paint.

But there were buildings that had their own individuality, and asserted it. One of these was a mud-cabin with a thatched roof, that looked as if it had emigrated bodily from the bogs of Ireland. It had settled itself down into a green hollow by the roadside, and it looked as much at home with the lilac-tinted crane's-bill and yellow buttercups as if it had never lost sight of the shamrocks of Erin.

Now, too, my childish desire to see a real beggar was gratified. Straggling petitioners for "cold victuals" hung around our back yard, always of Hibernian extraction; and a slice of bread was rewarded with a shower of benedictions that lost itself upon us in the flood of its own incomprehensible brogue.

At home I was among children of my own age, for some cousins and other acquaintances had come to live and work with us. We had our evening frolics and entertainments together, and we always made the most of our brief holiday hours. We had also with us now the sister Emilie of my fairy-tale memories, who had grown into a strong, earnest-hearted woman. We all looked up to her as our model, and the ideal of our heroine-worship; for our deference to her in every way did amount to that.

She watched over us, gave us needed reproof and commendation, rarely cosseted us, but rather made us laugh at what many would have considered the hardships of our lot. She taught us not only to accept the circumstances in which we found ourselves, but to win from them courage and strength. When we came in shivering from our work, through a snow-storm, complaining of numb hands and feet, she would say cheerily, "But it doesn't make you any warmer to *say* you are cold"; and this was typical of the way she took life generally, and tried to have us take it. She was constantly denying herself for our sakes, without making us feel that he was doing so. But she did not let us get into the bad habit of pitying ourselves because we were not as "well off" as many other children. And indeed we considered ourselves pleasantly situated; but the best of it all was that we had *her*.

Her theories for herself, and her practice, too, were rather severe; but we tried to follow them, according to our weaker abilities. Her custom was, for instance, to take a full cold bath every morning before she went to her work, even though the water was chiefly broken ice; and we did the same whenever we could be resolute enough. It required both nerve and will to do this at five o'clock on a zero morning, in a room without a fire; but it helped us to harden ourselves, while we formed a good habit. The working-day in winter began at the very earliest daylight, and ended at half-past seven in the evening.

Another habit of hers was to keep always beside her at her daily work something to study or to think about. At first it was "Watts on the Improvement of the Mind," arranged as a textbook, with questions and answers, by the minister of Beverly who had made the thought of the millennium such a reality to his people. She quite wore this book out, carrying it about with her in her working-dress pocket. After that, "Locke on the Understanding" was used in the same way. She must have known both books through and through by heart. Then she read Combe and Abercrombie, and discussed their physics and metaphysics with our girl boarders, some of whom had remarkably acute and well-balanced minds. Her own seemed to have turned from its early bent toward the romantic, her taste being now for serious and practical, though sometimes abstruse, themes.

At this time I had learned to do a spinner's work, and I obtained permission to tend some frames that sood directly in front of the river-windows, with only them and the wall behind me, extending half the length of the mill,—and one young woman beside me, at the farther end of the row. She was a sober, mature person, who scarcely thought it worth her while to speak often to a child like me; and I was, when with strangers, rather a reserved girl; so I kept myself occupied with the river, my work, and my thoughts. And the river and my thoughts flowed on together, the happiest of companions. Like a loitering pilgrim, it sparkled up to me in recognition as it glided along, and bore away my little frets and fatigues on its bosom. When the work "went well," I sat in the window-seat, and let my fancies fly

35

whither they would,—downward to the sea, or upward to the hills that hid the mountain-cradle of the Merrimack.

The printed regulations forbade us to bring books into the mill, so I made my window-seat into a small library of poetry, pasting its side all over with newspaper clippings. In those days we had only weekly papers, and they had always a "poet's corner," where standard writers were well represented, with anonymous ones, also. I was not, of course, much of a critic. I chose my verses for their sentiment, and because I wanted to commit them to memory; sometimes it was a long poem, sometimes a hymn, sometimes only a stray verse. Mrs. Hemans sang with me,—

*Far away, o'er the blue hills far away;*
and I learned and loved her "Better Land," and

*If thou hast crushed a flower,*
and "Kindred Hearts."

We used sometimes to see it claimed, in public prints, that it would be better for all of us mill-girls to be working in families, at domestic service, than to be where we were.

Perhaps the difficulties of modern housekeepers did begin with the opening of the Lowell factories. Country girls were naturally independent, and the feeling that at this new work the few hours they had of every-day leisure were entirely their own was a satisfaction to them. They preferred it to going out as "hired help." It was like a young man's pleasure in entering upon business for himself. Girls had never tried that experiment before, and they liked it. It brought out in them a dormant strength of character which the world did not previously see, but now fully acknowledges. Of course they had a right to continue at that freer kind of work as long as they chose, although their doing so increased the perplexities of the housekeeping problem for themselves even, since many of them were to become, and did become, American house-mistresses.

It would be a step towards the settlement of this vexed and vexing question if girls would decline to classify each other by their occupations, which among us are usually only temporary, and are continually shifting from one pair of hands to another. Changes of fortune come so abruptly that the millionaire's daughter of to-day may be glad to earn her living by sewing or sweeping tomorrow.

It is the first duty of every woman to recognize the mutual bond of universal womanhood. Let her ask herself whether she would like to hear herself or her sister spoken of as a shop-girl, or a factory-girl, or a servant-girl, if necessity had compelled her for a time to be employed in either of the ways indicated. If she would shrink from it a little, then she is a little inhuman when she puts her unknown human sisters who are so occupied into a class by themselves, feeling herself to be somewhat their superior. She is really the superior person who has accepted her work and is doing it faithfully, whatever it is. This designating others by their casual employments prevents one from making real distinctions, from knowing persons as persons. A false standard is set up in the minds of those who classify and of those who are classified.

Perhaps it is chiefly the fault of ladies themselves that the word "lady" has nearly lost its original meaning (a noble one) indicating sympathy and service;—

bread-giver to those who are in need. The idea that it means something external in dress or circumstances has been too generally adopted by rich and poor; and this, coupled with the sweeping notion that in our country one person is just as good as another, has led to ridiculous results, like that of saleswomen calling themselves "salesladies." I have even heard a chambermaid at a hotel introduce herself to guests as "the chamberlady."

I do not believe that any Lowell mill-girl was even absurd enough to wish to be known as a "factory-lady," although most of them knew that "factory-girl" did not represent a high type of womanhood in the Old World. But they themselves belonged to the New World, not to the Old; and they were making their own traditions, to hand down to their Republican descendants,—one of which was and is that honest work has no need to assert itself or to humble itself in a nation like ours, but simply to take its place as one of the foundation-stones of the Republic.

# Religion and the Work Ethic
# on the Missouri Frontier

Edgar Watson Howe, born in Indiana in 1853, traveled in a covered wagon with his family to Fairview,
Missouri, at the age of three. His boyhood life there
provided the raw materials for his autobiographical
novel, *Story of a Country Town* (1882). This excerpt,
a portrait of his father and his father's "old-time religion," gives a vivid sense of frontier life and suggests
some interesting connections between religious attitudes
and economic aspirations. It is obvious that the author
took a different view of the world than his father and
was able to view him with some critical detachment, but
the imprint of his early life upon such fundamental matters as his attitutes toward work was clear and strong.

## STORY
## OF A COUNTRY TOWN
### *Edgar Watson Howe*

My father's religion would have been unsatisfactory without a hell.

It was a part of his hope of the future that worldly men who scoffed at his piety
would be punished, and this was as much a part of his expectation as that those
who were faithful to the end would be rewarded. Everybody saved, to my father's
thinking, was as bad as nobody saved, and in his well-patronized Bible not a
passage for pleasurable contemplation which intimated universal salvation was
marked, if such exists.

The sacrifices he made for religion were tasks, and his reward was a conviction
that those who refused to make them would be punished, for he regarded it as an
injustice of which the Creator was incapable to do as well by His enemies as by His
friends. I believe that he would rather have gone to heaven without the members of
his family than with them, unless they had earned salvation as he had earned it, and
traveled as steadily as himself the hard road marked on his map as leading
heavenward.

One of the best evidences to his mind of a compassionate and loving Saviour
was the belief that all thoughts of unfortunate friends in torment was blotted from
the memory of the redeemed, and the lake of fire he thought of as a remedy for the
great number of disagreeable people with whom he was compelled to come in
contact below, and of whom he would be happily rid above. Religion was a misery

From *Story of a Country Town* (Boston, 1884), Chapter 2.

to be endured on earth, that a reward might be enjoyed after death. A man must spend the ages of his future in a very pleasant place, with comfortable surroundings and pleasant associates, or in a very unpleasant place, with uncomfortable surroundings and all the mean people turned into devils and imps for companions. It was the inevitable law; every man of moderate sense should be able to appreciate the situation at a glance, and do that which would insure his personal safety. If there was a doubt—the thought was too absurd for his contemplation, but admitting a doubt—his future would be equal to that of the worldly man, for one cannot rot more easily than another, or be more comfortable as dust; but if there was no doubt—and all the authorities agree that there was none—then the difference would be in his favor.

It was the best thing offering under the circumstances, and should therefore be accepted without hesitation. If the conditions were hard, he could not help it; he might have suggested changes in the plan of salvation had his judgment been invited, but the plan had been formulated before his time, and there was nothing left for him but obedience. If he thought he deserved credit for all he possessed, the Bible said it came from God. That settled the matter finally and forever—he gave thanks (for a punishment was provided if he did not, and a reward if he did), and pretended to have had nothing to do with accumulating his property.

Religion was a matter of thrift and self-interest as much as laying away money in youth and strength for old age and helplessness, and he called upon sinners to flee the wrath to come because he had been commanded to go out and preach to all the world, for it mattered little to him whether the people were saved or not. They had eyes, therefore let them see; ears, therefore let them hear. The danger was so plain that they ought to save themselves without solicitation.

That which he most desired seldom came to pass; that which he dreaded, frequently, but no matter; he gave thanks to the Lord because it was best to do so, and asked no questions. There were jewels for those who earned them, and as a thrifty man he desired a greater number of these than any other citizen of Fairview. He was the principal man in his neighborhood below, and desired to be a shepherd rather than a sheep above; therefore he was foremost in the church, and allowed no one to be more zealous in doing the service of the hard master he had, after careful thought and study, set out to serve, believing the reward worth the service, and determined to serve well if he served at all, as was his custom in everything else.

If I do him an injustice I do not intend it, but I have thought all my life that he regarded children as troublesome and expensive—a practical sort of punishment for sin, sent from time to time as the case seemed to require; and that he had been burdened with but two was no doubt evidence to his mind that his life had been generally blameless, if, indeed, this opinion was not confirmed by the circumstance that one of them had been taken from him in return for good service in the holy cause. Once they had arrived, however, he accepted the trust to return them to their Maker as nearly like they came as possible, for that was commanded of him.

Because he frequently referred to the road to heaven as narrow and difficult, and the highway in the other direction as broad and easy, I came to believe that but for his religion he would have been a man much given to money getting, and ambitious for distinction, but he put such thoughts aside, and toiled away at his work as if to get out of temptation's way. When he talked of the broad and easy road it was with a relish, as though he could enjoy the pleasant places by the way-side if he dared; and in his preaching I think he described the pleasures of the world so vividly that his hearers were taken with a wish to enjoy them, though it is not probable that he knew anything about them except from hearsay, as he had always been out of temptation's way—in the backwoods during his boyhood, and on the prairie during his maturer years. But when he talked of the narrow and difficult path, his manner changed at once; a frown came upon his face; he looked determined and unforgiving, and at every point he seemed to build signposts marked "Duty!" It has occurred to me since that he thought of his religion as a vigorous, healthy, successful man thinks in his quiet moments of a wife sick since their marriage; although he may deserve a different fate, and desire it, he dares not complain, for the more wearisome the invalid, the louder the call of duty.

I think he disliked the necessity of being religious, and only accepted and taught religion because he believed it to be the best thing to do, for it did not afford him the peace he professed. To all appearances he was a most miserable man, although he taught that only the sinful are miserable, and the few acquaintances he had who were not equally devout (strangers passing through, or those he met at the country town, for all were pious in Fairview) lived an easy and contented life which he seemed to covet, but nobody knew it, for he reproved them with all the more vigor because of his envy.

When not engaged in reading at night, as was his custom, he sat for hours looking steadily into the fire, and was impatient if disturbed. I never knew what occupied his thoughts at these times; it may have been his preaching, or his daily work, but more likely he was seeing glimpses of forbidden pictures; caravans of coveted things passing in procession, or of hopes and ambitions dwarfed by duty. Perhaps in fancy he was out in the world mingling with people of a class more to his taste than Fairview afforded. I believe that during these hours of silent thinking he was tempted and beckoned by the invisible and mysteriously potent forces he pretended to despire, and that he was convinced that, to push them off, his religion must be made more rigorous and pitiless.

That he coveted riches could be easily seen, and but for his fear of conscience he could have easily possessed himself of everything worth owning in Fairview, for with the exception of Theodore Meek, the next best man in the neighborhood, he was about the only one among the people who read books and subscribed for newspapers. None of them was his equal in intelligence or energy, and had he desired he could have traded them out of the little they possessed, and sold it back again at a profit. But, "do unto others as you would have others do unto you," was commanded of him by his inexorable master, and he was called upon to help the weak rather than rob them; therefore he often gave them assistance which he could but poorly afford. This limited him so much that he had no other hope of becoming well-to-do than that the lands which he was constantly buying would finally become valuable by reason of the development and settlement of the country. This he regarded as honorable and fair, and to this work he applied himself with great energy.

I heard little of his father, except that he was noted where he lived as a man of a large family, who provided them all with warm clothes in winter and plenty to eat all the year round. His early history was probably as unimportant and eventless as my own. He seldom mentioned his father to any one, except in connection with a story which he occasionally told, that once, when his house was on fire, he called so loud for help that he was heard a mile. Evidently the son succeeded to this extraordinary pair of lungs, for he sang the religious songs common in that day with such excellence that no man attempted to equal him. While his singing was strong and loud, it was melodious, and he had as great a reputation for that as for piety and thrift. His was a camp-meeting voice, though he occasionally sang songs of little children, as "Moses in the Bulrushes," of which there were thirty-eight verses, and the cradle song commencing, "Hush, my dear, lie still and slumber," written by a noted hymn-writer, otherwise my father would not have patronized him. Besides a thorough familiarity with all the common, long, short, and particular meters, he had a collection of religious songs preserved in a leather-bound book, the notes being written in buckwheat characters on blue paper fast turning yellow with age, and the words on the opposite page. Feeling the necessity of a knowledge of notes once, he had learned the art in a few weeks, in his usual vigorous way, and sang at sight; and after that he preserved his old songs, and all the new ones he fancied, in the book I have mentioned. The songs to which I refer I have never seen in print, and he sang them on special occasions, as at a camp-meeting when a tiresome preacher had allowed the interest to flag. "Behold Paul a Prisoner," a complete history of the Apostle requiring almost an afternoon in its performance, or "Christ in the Garden," nearly as long, never failed to start the interest anew in an emergency, and if the case were very desperate, he called the members of his family into the pulpit, and sang a quartet called "The Glorious Eighth of April," using for the words the first hymn in the book.

This was usually sufficient to start some one to shouting, and after a short prayer he preached as vigorously and loudly as he sang, and with an equally good effect.

Of his brothers and sisters, although he had a great number, he seldom talked, and I scarcely knew the names of the States in which they lived, as they were scattered in every direction. I had heard him mention a Samuel, a Joseph, a Jacob, an Elias, a Rebecca, a Sarah and a Rachel, from which I came to believe that my grandfather was a religious man (his own name was Amos), and I once heard that his children on Sundays carried their shoes to the brook near the meeting-house before putting them on, that they might last the longer, which confirmed the belief that there had been religion in his family as there was in ours.

Of his mother he said nothing at all, and if they had neighbors he never mentioned them. In short, he did not seem proud of his family, which caused us to wonder why he was so much like his father, which we had come to believe without exactly knowing why. We were certain he was like his father in religion; in the hard way in which he worked; in his capacity to mend his own ploughs and wagons; and in the easy manner in which he adapted himself to his surroundings, whatever they were, for in all these particulars he was unlike any other man we had ever known, and different from his neighbors, who spent half a day in asking advice in a matter

41

which could be remedied in half an hour. The people came to our house from miles around to borrow, and to ask the best time to plant and to sow, but the Rev. John Westlock asked advice of no one, and never borrowed. If he needed an extra harrow, he made one of wood to answer until such a time as he could trade to advantage for a better one; if he broke a plough, he managed somehow to mend it until a rainy day came, when he made it as good as new. Even in cases of sickness he usually had a bottle hid away that contained relief, and in all other things was equally capable and thrifty.

If it be to the credit of a man to say that he was a slave to hard work, I cheerfully add this testimony to the greatness of my father, for he went to the field at daylight only to return with the darkness, winter and summer alike; and never in my life have I seen him idle—except on the day oppointed for rest—and even then he devoured the Bible like a man reading at so much per page. He worked hard when he preached, talking rapidly that he might accomplish as much as possible before the people became impatient, and he no sooner finished one song of warning, than he began another.

My father being large and positive, it followed naturally that my mother was small and weak, and thoroughly under his control. He managed his own affairs so well that she was willing he should manage hers, as he had given her good reason to respect his judgment. She probably argued—if she argued the question at all—that as his ideas were good in everything else, he would of course know how to manage a boy, so my bringing up was left entirely to him.

She never corrected me except to say that father would not like what I was doing, and she might find it necessary to call his attention to it, but in the goodness of her heart she forgot it, and never told him unless the offence was a very grave one. While she frequently pleaded with me to be good, and cried in vexation if I would not, she never gave commands which were enforced with punishment, as he did; therefore I am afraid that I did not appreciate her kindness and favor, but rather enjoyed my freedom when under her care as a respite from restraint at other times. She was as quiet and thoughtful as her husband, but seemed sad rather than angry and discontented, as was the case with him, and it will be easily imagined that as a family we were not much given to happiness. While I never heard my father speak harshly to her, he was often impatient, as though he regretted he had not married a wife as ambitious and capable as himself; but if he thought of it, he gave it no other attention than to become more gloomy, and pacified himself by reading far into the night without speaking to any one.

I could find no fault with him except that he never spoke kindly to me, and it annoyed him if I asked him questions concerning what I read in his books. When Jo and I worked with him in the field, which we both began to do very early he always did that which was hardest and most disagreeable, and was not a tyrant in anything save the ungrumbling obedience he exacted to whatever he thought about the matter in hand, without reference to what others thought on the same subject. We had to be at something steadily, because he believed idle boys grew up into idle men. Other boys in the neighborhood built the early fires, and did the early feeding, but he preferred to do these things himself—whether out of consideration for us, or because it was troublesome to drive us to it, I do not know.

42

After starting the fire in the room in which he slept, he stepped to our door and told us to get up, to which command we mumblingly replied and slept on. After returning from the stables, he spoke to us again, but we still paid no attention. Ten minutes later he would start up the stairs with angry strides, but he never caught us, for we knew that was final and hurried on our clothes. Seeing that we were up and dressing when he reached the head of the stairs, he would say, "Well you'd better," and go down again, where we speedily followed. This was his regular custom for years; we always expected it of him, and were never disappointed.

After the morning devotions, which consisted of reading a chapter from the Bible and a prayer always expressed in exactly the same words, he asked a blessing for the meal by this time ready (the blessing was as unvarying as the prayer), and we ate in silence. Then we were warmly clothed, if it were winter, and compelled to go out and work until we were hungry again. I suppose we helped him little enough, but his reasoning convinced him that, to work easily and naturally, work must become a habit, and should be taught from youth up, therefore we went out with him every day and came back only with the darkness.

I think he was kinder with us when at work than at any other time, and we admired him in spite of the hard and exacting tasks he gave us to do—he called them stints—for he was powerful and quick to aid us when we needed it, and tender as a child if we were sick. Sometimes on cold days we walked rather than rode to the timber, where my father went to chop wood while Jo and I corded it. On one of these occasions I became ill while returning home at night—a slight difficulty, it must have been, for I was always stout and robust—and he carried me all the way in his arms. Though I insisted I could walk, and was better, he said I was not heavy, and trudged along like a great giant, holding me so tenderly that I thought for the first time that perhaps he loved me. For weeks after that I tried as hard as I could to please him, and to induce him to commend my work; but he never did, for whether I was good or bad, he was just the same, silent and grave, so that if I became indifferent in my tasks, I fear he was the cause of it.

Other families had their holidays, and owned guns and dogs, which they used in hunting the wild game then abundant; but there was little of this at our house, and perhaps this was the reason why we prospered more than those around us. Usually Jo and I were given the Saturday afternoons to ourselves, when we roamed the country with some of the idle vagabonds who lived in rented houses, visiting turkey roosts a great distance in the woods, and only returning long after night-fall. I do not remember that we were ever idle in the middle of the week, unless we were sent on errands, as buying young stock at low prices of the less thrifty neighbors, or something else in which there was profit; so that we had little time to learn anything except hard work, and if we learned that well it was because we were excellently taught by a competent master. During those years work became such a habit with me that ever since it has clung to me, and perhaps, after all, it was an inheritance for which I have reason to be thankful. I remember my father's saying to me once, as if intimating that I ought to make up by unusual industry for the years of idleness, that I was a positive burden and expense to him until I was seven years old. So it will readily be imagined that I was put to work early, and kept steadily at it.

43

# How the Other Half Lived

Newspaper reporter Jacob Riis, a Danish-born immigrant who had been trapped in destitution in the slums of New York city in the 1870s, won national prominence in 1890 with his biting exposé of New York tenement-house life, *How the Other Half Lives.* Riis was simplistic in his assumption that bad housing conditions were the principal source of social pathology, and that improving the dwellings of poor people without changing other features of their social environment—for example, their low and irregular wages—would transform their lives; nor did he even devise an effective program for upgrading slum housing. He exaggerated what might be accomplished through charitable housing experiments, "philanthropy plus five percent," and he was a victim of the urban renewal fallacy still alive in contemporary America, assuming that tearing down delapidated buildings is itself progress, never asking what would happen to the poor people displaced by demolition. But Riis performed a valuable service in bringing the seamy side of American urban life to public attention, and he made an interesting beginning toward a sociology of immigrant adjustment and assimilation to the urban environment.

## HOW THE OTHER HALF LIVES
### *Jacob Riis*

To-day, what is a tenement? The law defines it as a house "occupied by three or more families, living independently and doing their cooking on the premises; or by more than two families on a floor, so living and cooking and having a common right in the halls, stairways, yards, etc." That is the legal meaning, and includes flats and apartment-houses, with which we have nothing to do. In its narrower sense the typical tenement was thus described when last arraigned before the bar of public justice: "It generally a brick building from four to six stories high on the street, frequently with a store on the first floor which, when used for the sale of liquor, has a side opening for the benefit of the inmates and to evade the Sunday law; four families occupy each floor, and a set of rooms consists of one or two dark

From *How the Other Half Lives: Studies among the Tenements of New York* (New York, 1890), 17–20, 24–27, 43–46, 104–119, 136–141.

closets, used as bedrooms, with a living room twelve feet by ten. The staircase is too often a dark well in the center of the house, and no direct through ventilation is possible, each family being separated from the other by partitions. Frequently the rear of the lot is occupied by another building of three stories high with two families on a floor." The picture is nearly as true to-day as ten years ago, and will be for a long time to come. The dim light admitted by the air-shaft shines upon greater crowds than ever. Tenements are still "good property," and the poverty of the poor man his destruction. A barrack down town where he *has to live* because he is poor brings in a third more rent than a decent flat house in Harlem. The statement once made a sensation that between seventy and eighty children has been found in one tenement. It no longer excites even passing attention, when the sanitary police report counting 101 adults and 91 children in a Crosby Street house, one of twins, built together. The children in the other, if I am not mistaken, numbered 89, a total of 180 for two tenements! Or when a midnight inspection in Mulberry Street unearths a hundred and fifty "lodgers" sleeping on filthy floors in two buildings. Spite of brown-stone trimmings, plate-glass and mosaic vestibule floors, the water does not rise in summer to the second story, while the beer flows unchecked to the all-night picnics on the roof. The saloon with the side-door and the landlord divide the prosperity of the place between them, and the tenant, in sullen submission, foots the bills.

Where are the tenements of to-day? Say rather: where are they not? In fifty years they have crept up from the Fourth Ward slums and the Five Points the whole length of the island, and have polluted the Annexed District to the Westchester line. Crowding all the lower wards, wherever business leaves a foot of ground unclaimed; strung along both rivers, like ball and chain tied to the foot of every street, and filling up Harlem with their restless, pent-up multitudes, they hold within their clutch the wealth and business of New York, hold them at their mercy in the day of mob-rule and wrath. The bullet-proof shutters, the stacks of hand-grenades, and the Gatling guns of the Sub-Treasury are tacit admissions of the fact and of the quality of the mercy expected. The tenements to-day are New York, harboring three-fourths of its population. When another generation shall have doubled the census of our city, and to that vast army of workers, held captive by poverty, the very name of home shall be as a bitter mockery, what will the harvest be?

Cherry Street. Be a little careful, please! The hall is dark and you might stumble over the children pitching pennies back there. Not that it would hurt them: kicks and cuffs are their daily diet. They have little else. Here where the hall turns and dives into utter darkness is a step, and another, another. A flight of stairs. You can feel your way, if you cannot see it. Close? Yes! What would you have? All the fresh air that ever enters these stairs comes from the hall-door that is forever slamming, and from the windows of dark bedrooms that in turn receive from the stairs their sole supply of the elements God meant to be free, but man deals out with such niggardly hand. That was a woman filling her pail by the hydrant you just bumped against. The sinks are in the hallway, that all the tenants may have access—and all be poisoned alike by their summer stenches. Hear the pump squeak! It is the lullaby of tenement-house babes. In summer, when a thousand thirsty throats pant for a cooling drink in this block, it is worked in vain. But the saloon, whose open door you passed in the hall, is always there. The smell of it has followed you up. Here is a door. Listen! That short hacking cough, that tiny, helpless wail—what do they mean? They mean that the soiled bow of white you saw on the door downstairs will have another story to tell—Oh! a sadly familiar story—before the day is at an end. The child is dying with measles. With half a chance it might have lived; but it had none. That dark bedroom killed it.

"It was took all of a suddint," says the mother, smoothing the throbbing little body with trembling hands. There is no unkindness in the rough voice of the man in the jumper, who sits by the window grimly smoking a clay pipe, with the little life ebbing out in his sight, bitter as his words sound: "Hush, Mary! If we cannot keep the baby, need we complain—such as we?"

Such as we! What if the words ring in your ears as we grope our way up the stairs and down from floor to floor, listening to the sounds behind the closed doors—some of quarrelling, some of coarse songs, more of profanity. They are true. When the summer heats come with their suffering they have meaning more terrible than words can tell. Come over here. Step carefully over this baby—it is a baby, spite of its rags and dirt—under these iron bridges called fire-escapes, but loaded down, despite the incessant watchfulness of the firemen, with broken household goods, with wash-tubs and barrels, over which no man could climb from a fire. This gap between dingy brick-walls is the yard. That strip of smoke-colored sky up there is the heaven of these people. Do you wonder the name does not attract them to the churches? That baby's parents live in the rear tenement here. She is at last as clean as the steps we are now climbing. There are plenty of houses with half a hundred such in. The tenement is much like the one in front we just left, only fouler, closer, darker—we will not say more cheerless. The word is a mockery. A hundred thousand people lived in rear tenements in New York last year. Here is a room neater than the rest. The woman, a stout matron with hard lines of care in her face, is at the wash-tub. "I try to keep the childer clean," she says, apologetically, but with a hopeless glance around. The spice of hot soapsuds is added to the air already tainted with the smell of boiling cabbage, of rags and uncleanliness all about. It makes an overpowering compound. It is Thursday, but patched linen is hung upon the pulley-line from the window. There is no Monday cleaning in the tenements. It is wash-day all the week round, for a change of clothing is scarce among the poor. They are poverty's honest badge, these perennial lines of rags hung out to dry, those that are not the washerwoman's professional shingle. The true line to be drawn between pauperism and honest poverty is the clothes-line. With it begins the effort to be clean that is the first and the best evidence of a desire to be honest.

The poorest immigrant comes here with the purpose and ambition to better himself and, given half a chance, might be reasonably expected to make the most of it. To the false plea that he prefers the squalid homes in which his kind are housed there could be no better answer. The truth is, his half chance has too long been wanting, and for the bad result he has been unjustly blamed.

As emigration from east to west follows the latitude, so does the foreign influx in New York distribute itself along certain well-defined lines that waver and break only under the stronger pressure of a more gregarious race or the encroachments of inexorable business. A feeling of dependence upon mutual effort, natural to strangers in a strange land, unacquainted with its language and customs, sufficiently accounts for this.

The Irishman is the true cosmopolitan immigrant. All-pervading, he shares his lodging with perfect impartiality with the Italian, the Greek, and the "Dutchman," yielding only to sheer force of numbers, and objects equally to them all. A map of the city, colored to designate nationalities, would show more stripes than on the skin of a zebra, and more colors than any rainbow. The city on such a map would fall into two great halves, green for the Irish prevailing in the West Side tenement districts, and blue for the Germans on the East Side. But intermingled with these ground colors would be an odd variety of tints that would give the whole the appearance of an extraordinary crazy-quilt. From down in the Sixth Ward, upon the site of the old Collect Pond that in the days of the fathers drained the hills which are no more, the red of the Italian would be seen forcing its way northward along the line of Mulberry Street to the quarter of the French purple on Bleecker Street and South Fifth Avenue, to lose itself and reappear, after a lapse of miles, in the "Little Italy" of Harlem, east of Second Avenue. Dashes of red, sharply defined, would be seen strung through the Annexed District, northward to the city line. On the West Side the red would be seen overrunning the old Africa of Thompson Street, pushing the black of the negro rapidly uptown, against querulous but unavailing protests, occupying his home, his church, his trade and all, with merciless impartiality. There is a church in Mulberry Street that has stood for two generations as a sort of milestone of these migrations. Built originally for the worship of staid New Yorkers of the "old stock," it was engulfed by the colored tide, when the draft-riots drove the negroes out of reach of Cherry Street and the Five Points. Within the past decade the advance wave of the Italian onset reached it, and to-day the arms of United Italy adorn its front. The negroes have made a stand at several points along Seventh and Eighth Avenues; but their main body, still pursued by the Italian foe, is on the march yet, and the black mark will be found overshadowing to-day many blocks on the East Side, with One Hundredth Street as the centre, where colonies of them have settled recently.

Hardly less aggressive than the Italian, the Russian and Polish Jew, having overrun the district between Rivington and Division Streets, east of the Bowery, to the point of suffocation, is filling the tenements of the old Seventh Ward to the river front, and disputing with the Italian every foot of available space in the back alleys of Mulberry Street. The two races, differing hopelessly in much, have this in common: they carry their slums with them wherever they go, if allowed to do it. Little Italy already rivals its parent, the "Bend," in foulness. Other nationalities that begin at the bottom make a fresh start when crowded up the ladder. Happily both are manageable, the one by rabbinical, the other by the civil law. Between the dull gray of the Jew, his favorite color, and the Italian red, would be seen squeezed in on the map a sharp streak of yellow, marking the narrow boundaries of Chinatown. Dovetailed in with the German population, the poor but thrifty

Bohemian might be picked out by the sombre hue of his life as of his philosophy, struggling against heavy odds in the big human bee-hives of the East Side. Colonies of his people extend northward, with long lapses of space, from below the Cooper Institute more than three miles. The Bohemian is the only foreigner with any considerable representation in the city who counts no wealthy man of his race, none who has not to work hard for a living, or has got beyond the reach of the tenement.

Down near the Battery the West Side emerald would be soiled by a dirty stain, spreading rapidly like a splash of ink on a sheet of blotting paper, headquarters of the Arab tribe, that in a single year has swelled from the original dozen to twelve hundred, intent, every mother's son, on trade and barter. Dots and dashes of color here and there would show where the Finnish sailors worship their djumala (God), the Greek pedlars the ancient name of their race, and the Swiss the goddess of thrift. And so on to the end of the long register, all toiling together in the galling fetters of the tenement. Were the question raised who makes the most of life thus mortgaged, who resists most stubbornly its levelling tendency—knows how to drag even the barracks upward a part of the way at least toward the ideal plane of the home—the palm must be unhesitatingly awarded the Teuton. The Italian and the poor Jew rise only by compulsion. The Chinaman does not rise at all; here, as at home, he simply remains stationary. The Irishman's genius runs to public affairs rather than domestic life; wherever he is mustered in force the saloon is the gorgeous centre of political activity. The German struggles vainly to learn his trick; his Teutonic wit is too heavy, and the political ladder he raises from his saloon usually too short or too clumsy to reach the desired goal. The best part of his life is lived at home, and he makes himself a home independent of the surroundings, giving the lie to the saying, unhappily become a maxim of social truth, that pauperism and drunkenness naturally grow in the tenements. He makes the most of his tenement, and it should be added that whenever and as soon as he can save up money enough, he gets out and never crosses the threshold of one again.

The tenements grow taller, and the gaps in their ranks close up rapidly as we cross the Bowery and, leaving Chinatown and the Italians behind, invade the Hebrew quarter. Baxter Street, with its interminable rows of old clothes shops and its brigades of pullers-in—nicknamed "the Bay" in honor, perhaps, of the tars who lay to there after a cruise to stock up their togs, or maybe after the "schooners" of beer plentifully bespoke in that latitude—Bayard Street, with its synagogues and its crowds, gave us a foretaste of it. No need of asking here where we are. The jargon of the street, the signs of the sidewalk, the manner and dress of the people, their unmistakable physiognomy, betray their race at every step. Men with queer skull-caps, venerable beard, and the outlandish long-skirted kaftan of the Russian Jew, elbow the ugliest and the handsomest women in the land. The contrast is startling. The old women are hags; the young, houris. Wives and mothers at sixteen, at thirty they are old. So thoroughly has the chosen people crowded out the Gentiles in the Tenth Ward that, when the great Jewish holidays come around every year, the public schools in the district have practically to close up. Of their thousands of pupils scarce a handful come to school. Nor is there any suspicion that the rest are playing hookey. They stay honestly home to celebrate. There is no mistaking it: we are in Jewtown.

It is said that nowhere in the world are so many people crowded together on a square mile as here. The average five-story tenement adds a story or two to its stature in Ludlow Street and an extra building on the rear lot, and yet the sign "To Let" is the rarest of all there. Here is one seven stories high. The sanitary policeman whose beat this is will tell you that it contains thirty-six families, but the term has a widely different meaning here and on the avenues. In this house, where a case of small-pox was reported, there were fifty-eight babies and thirty-eight children that were over five years of age. In Essex Street two small rooms in a six-story tenement were made to hold a "family" of father and mother, twelve children, and six boarders. The boarder plays as important a part in the domestic economy of Jewtown as the lodger in the Mulberry Street Bend. These are samples of the packing of the population that has run up the record here to the rate of three hundred and thirty thousand per square mile. The densest crowding of Old London, I pointed out before, never got beyond a hundred and seventy-five thousand. Even the alley is crowded out. Through dark hallways and filthy cellars, crowded, as is every foot of the street, with dirty children, the settlements in the rear are reached. Thieves know how to find them when pursued by the police, and the tramps that sneak in on chilly nights to fight for the warm spot in the yard over some baker's oven. They are out of place in this hive of busy industry, and they know it. It has nothing in common with them or with their philosophy of life, that the world owes the idler a living. Life here means the hardest kind of work almost from the cradle. The world as a debtor has no credit in Jewtown. Its promise to pay wouldn't buy one of the old hats that are hawked about Hester Street, unless backed by security representing labor done at lowest market rates. But this army of workers must have bread. It is cheap and filling, and bakeries abound. Wherever they are in the tenements the tramp will skulk in, if he can. There is such a tramps' roost in the rear of a tenement near the lower end of Ludlow Street, that is never without its tenants in winter. By a judicious practice of flopping over on the stone pavement at intervals, and thus warming one side at a time, and with an empty box to put the feet in, it is possible to keep reasonably comfortable there even on a rainy night. In summer the yard is the only one in the neighborhood that does not do duty as a public dormitory.

Thrift is the watchword of Jewtown, as of its people the world over. It is at once its strength and its fatal weakness, its cardinal virtue and its foul disgrace. Become an over-mastering passion with these people who come here in droves from Eastern Europe to escape persecution, from which freedom could be bought only with gold, it has enslaved them in bondage worse than that from which they fled. Money is their God. Life itself is of little value compared with even the leanest bank account. In no other spot does life wear so intensely bald and materialistic an aspect as in Ludlow Street. Over and over again I have met with instances of these Polish or Russian Jews deliberately starving themselves to the point of physical exhaustion, while working night and day at a tremendous pressure to save a little money. An avenging Nemesis pursues this headlong hunt for wealth; there is no worse paid class anywhere. I once put the question to one of their own people, who, being a pawnbroker, and an unusually intelligent and charitable one, certainly enjoyed the advantage of a practical view of the situation: "Whence the many

49

wretchedly poor people in such a colony of workers, where poverty, from a misfortune, has become a reproach, dreaded as the plague?"

"Immigration," he said, "brings us a lot. In five years it has averaged twenty-five thousand a year, of which more than seventy per cent, have stayed in New York. Half of them require and receive aid from the Hebrew Charities from the very start, lest they starve. That is one explanation. There is another class than the one that cannot get work: those who have had too much of it; who have worked and hoarded and lived, crowded together like pigs, on the scantiest fare and the worst to be got, bound to save whatever their earnings, until, worn out, they could work no longer. Then their hoards were soon exhausted. That is their story." And I knew that what he said was true.

Penury and poverty are wedded everywhere to dirt and disease, and Jewtown is no exception. It could not well be otherwise in such crowds, considering especially their low intellectual status. The managers of the Eastern Dispensary, which is in the very heart of their district, told the whole story when they said: "The diseases these people suffer from are not due to intemperance or immorality, but to ignorance, want of suitable food, and the foul air in which they live and work." The homes of the Hebrew quarter are its workshops also. Reference will be made to the economic conditions under which they work in a succeeding chapter. Here we are concerned simply with the fact. You are made fully aware of it before you have travelled the length of a single block in any of these East Side streets, by the whir of a thousand sewing-machines, worked at high pressure from earliest dawn till mind and muscle give out together. Every member of the family, from the youngest to the oldest, bears a hand, shut in the qualmy rooms, where meals are cooked and clothing washed and dried besides, the live-long day. It is not unusual to find a dozen persons—men, women, and children—at work in a single small room. The fact accounts for the contrast that strikes with wonder the observer who comes across from the Bend. Over there the entire population seems possessed of an uncontrollable impulse to get out into the street; here all its energies appear to be bent upon keeping in and away from it. Not that the streets are deserted. The overflow from these tenements is enough to make a crowd anywhere. The children alone would do it. Not old enough to work and no room for play, that is their story. In the home the child's place is usurped by the lodger, who performs the service of the Irishman's pig—pays the rent. In the street the army of hucksters crowd him out. Typhus fever and small-pox are bred here, and help solve the question what to do with him. Filth diseases both, they sprout naturally among the hordes that bring the germs with them from across the sea, and whose first instinct is to hide their sick lest the authorities carry them off to the hospital to be slaughtered, as they firmly believe. The health officers are on constant and sharp lookout for hidden fever-nests. Considering that half of the ready-made clothes that are sold in the big stores, if not a good deal more than half, are made in these tenement rooms, this is not excessive caution. It has happened more than once that a child recovering from small-pox, and in the most contagious stage of the disease, has been found crawling among heaps of half-finished clothing that the next day would be offered for sale on the counter of a Broadway store; or that a typhus fever patient has been discovered in a room whence perhaps a hundred coats had been sent home that week, each one with the wearer's death-warrant, unseen and unsuspected, basted in the lining.

Attached to many of the synagogues, which among the poorest Jews frequently consist of a scantily furnished room in a rear tenement, with a few wooden stools or benches for the congregation, are Talmudic schools that absorb a share of the growing youth. The school-master is not rarely a man of some attainments who has been stranded there, his native instinct for money-making having been smothered in the process that has made of him a learned man. It was of such a school in Eldridge Street that the wicked Isaac Iacob, who killed his enemy, his wife, and himself in one day, was janitor. But the majority of the children seek the public schools, where they are received sometimes with some misgivings on the part of the teachers, who find it necessary to inculcate lessons of cleanliness in the worst cases by practical demonstration with wash-bowl and soap. "He took hold of the soap as if it were some animal," said one of these teachers to me after such an experiment upon a new pupil, "and wiped three fingers across his face. He called that washing." In the Allen Street public school the experienced principal has embodied among the elementary lessons, to keep constantly before the children the duty that clearly lies next to their hands, a characteristic exercise. The question is asked daily from the teacher's desk: "What must I do to be healthy?" and the whole school responds:

*I must keep my skin clean,*
*Wear clean clothes,*
*Breathe pure air,*
*And live in the sunlight.*

It seems little less than biting sarcasm to hear them say it, for to not a few of them all these things are known only by name. In their everyday life there is nothing even to suggest any of them. Only the demand of religious custom has power to make their parents clean up at stated intervals, and the young naturally are no better. As scholars, the children of the most ignorant Polish Jew keep fairly abreast of their more favored playmates, until it comes to mental arithmetic, when they leave them behind with a bound. It is surprising to see how strong the instinct of dollars and cents is in them. They can count, and correctly, almost before they can talk.

Thursday night and Friday morning are bargain days in the "Pig-market." Then is the time to study the ways of this peculiar people to the best advantage. A common pulse beats in the quarters of the Polish Jews and in the Mulberry Bend, though they have little else in common. Life over yonder in fine weather is a perpetual holiday, here a veritable tread-mill of industry. Friday brings out all the latent color and picturesqueness of the Italians, as of these Semites. The crowds and the common poverty are the bonds of sympathy between them. The Pig-market is in Hester Street, extending either way from Ludlow Street, and up and down the side streets two or three blocks, as the state of trade demands. The name was given to it probably in derision, for pork is the one ware that is not on sale in the Pig-market. There is scarcely anything else that can be hawked from a wagon that is not to be found, and at ridiculously low prices. Bandannas and tin cups at two

51

cents, peaches at a cent a quart, "damaged" eggs for a song, hats for a quarter, and spectacles, warranted to suit the eye, at the optician's who has opened shop on a Hester Street door-step, for thirty-five cents; frowsy-looking chickens and half-plucked geese, hung by the neck and protesting with wildly strutting feet even in death against the outrage, are the great staple of the market. Half or a quarter of a chicken can be bought here by those who cannot afford a whole. It took more than ten years of persistent effort on the part of the sanitary authorities to drive the trade in live fowl from the streets to the fowl-market on Gouverneur Slip, where the killing is now done according to Jewish rite by priests detailed for the purpose by the chief rabbi. Since then they have had a characteristic rumpus, that involved the entire Jewish community, over the fees for killing and the mode of collecting them. Here is a woman churning horse-radish on a machine she has chained and padlocked to a tree on the sidewalk, lest someone steal it. Beside her a butcher's stand with cuts at prices the avenues never dreamed of. Old coats are hawked for fifty cents, "as good as new," and "pants"—there are no trousers in Jewtown, only pants—at anything that can be got. There is a knot of half a dozen "pants" pedlars in the middle of the street, twice as many men of their own race fingering their wares and plucking at the seams with the anxious scrutiny of would-be buyers, though none of them has the least idea of investing in a pair. Yes, stop! This baker, fresh from his trough, bare-headed and with bare arms, has made an offer: for this pair thirty cents; a dollar and forty was the price asked. The pedlar shrugs his shoulders, and turns up his hands with a half pitying, wholly indignant air. What does the baker take him for? Such pants—. The baker has turned to go. With a jump like a panther's, the man with the pants has him by the sleeve. Will he give eighty cents? Sixty? Fifty? So help him, they are dirt cheap at that. Lose, will he, on the trade, lose all the profit of his day's peddling. The baker goes on unmoved. Forty then? What, not forty? Take them then for thirty, and wreck the life of a poor man. And the baker takes them and goes, well knowing that at least twenty cents of the thirty, two hundred per cent., were clear profit, if indeed the "pants" cost the pedlar anything.

The suspender pedlar is the mystery of the Pig-market, omnipresent and unfathomable. He is met at every step with his wares dangling over his shoulder, down his back, and in front. Millions of suspenders thus perambulate Jewtown all day on a sort of dress parade. Why suspenders, is the puzzle, and where do they all go to? The "pants" of Jewtown hang down with a common accord, as if they had never known the support of suspenders. It appears to be as characteristic a trait of the race as the long beard and the Sabbath silk hat of ancient pedigree. I have asked again and again. No one has ever been able to tell me what becomes of the suspenders of Jewtown. Perhaps they are hung up as bric-à-brac in its homes, or laid away and saved up as the equivalent of cash. I cannot tell. I only know that more suspenders are hawked about the Pig-market every day than would supply the whole of New York for a year, were they all bought and turned to use.

The crowds that jostle each other at the wagons and about the sidewalk shops, where a gutter plank on two ash-barrels does duty for a counter! Pushing, struggling, babbling, and shouting in foreign tongues, a veritable Babel of confusion. An English word falls upon the ear almost with a sense of shock, as something unexpected and strange. In the midst of it all there is a sudden wild scattering, a hustling of things from the street into dark cellars, into back-yards and by-ways, a slamming and locking of doors hidden under the improvised shelves and counters. The health officers' cart is coming down the street, preceded and followed by stalwart policemen, who shovel up with scant ceremony the eatables—musty bread, decayed fish and stale vegetables—indifferent to the curses that are showered on them from stoops and windows, and carry them off to the dump. In the wake of the wagon, as it makes its way to the East River after the raid, follow a line of despoiled hucksters shouting defiance from a safe distance. Their clamor dies away with the noise of the market. The endless panorama of the tenements, rows upon rows, between stony streets, stretches to the north, to the south, and to the west as far as the eye reaches.

Evil as the part is which the tenement plays in Jewtown as the pretext for circumventing the law that was made to benefit and relieve the tenant, we have not far to go to find it in even a worse role. If the tenement is here continually dragged into the eye of public condemnation and scorn, it is because in one way or another it is found directly responsible for, or intimately associated with, three-fourths of the miseries of the poor. In the Bohemian quarter it is made the vehicle for enforcing upon a proud race a slavery as real as any that ever disgraced the South. Not content with simply robbing the tenant, the owner, in the dual capacity of landlord and employer, reduces him to virtual serfdom by making his becoming *his* tenant, on such terms as he sees fit to make, the condition of employment at wages likewise of his own making. It does not help the case that this landlord employer, almost always a Jew, is frequently of the thrifty Polish race just described.

Probably more than half of all the Bohemians in this city are cigarmakers, and it is the herding of these in great numbers in the so-called tenement factories, where the cheapest grade of work is done at the lowest wages, that constitutes at once their greatest hardship and the chief grudge of other workmen against them. The manufacturer who owns, say, from three or four, to a dozen or more tenements contiguous to his shop, fills them up with these people, charging them outrageous rents, and demanding often even a preliminary deposit of five dollars "key money;" deals them out tobacco by the week, and devotes the rest of his energies to the paring down of wages to within a peg or two of the point where the tenant rebels in desperation. When he does rebel, he is given the alternative of submission, or eviction with entire loss of employment. His needs determine the issue. Usually he is not in a position to hesitate long. Unlike the Polish Jew, whose example of untiring industry he emulates, he has seldom much laid up against a rainy day. He is fond of a glass of beer, and likes to live as well as his means will permit. The shop triumphs, and fetters more galling than ever are forged for the tenant. In the opposite case, the newspapers have to record the throwing upon the street of a small army of people, with pitiful cases of destitution and family misery.

Men, women and children work together seven days in the week in these cheerless tenements to make a living for the family, from the break of day till far into the night. Often the wife is the original cigarmaker from the old home, the husband having adopted her trade here as a matter of necessity, because, knowing no word of English, he could get no other work. As they state the cause of the bitter hostility of the trades unions, she was the primary bone of contention in the day of the early Bohemian immigration. The unions refused to admit the women, and, as the support of the family depended upon her to a large extent, such terms as were offered had to be accepted. The manufacturer has ever since industriously fanned the antagonism between the unions and his hands, for his own advantage. The victory rests with him, since the Court of Appeals decided that the law, passed a few years ago, to prohibit cigarmaking in tenements was unconstitutional, and thus put an end to the struggle.

The sore grievances I found were the miserable wages and the enormous rents exacted for the minimum of accommodation. And surely these stand for enough of suffering. Take a row of houses in East Tenth Street as an instance. They contained thirty-five families of cigarmakers, with probably not half a dozen persons in the whole lot of them, outside of the children, who could speak a word of English, though many had been in the country half a lifetime. This room with two windows giving on the street, and a rear attachment without windows, called a bedroom by courtesy, is rented at $12.25 a month. In the front room man and wife work at the bench from six in the morning till nine at night. They make a team, stripping the tobacco leaves together; then he makes the filler, and she rolls the wrapper on and finishes the cigar. For a thousand they receive $3.75, and can turn out together three thousand cigars a week. The point has been reached where the rebellion comes in, and the workers in these tenements are just now on a strike, demanding $5.00 and $5.50 for their work. The manufacturer having refused, they are expecting hourly to be served with notice to quit their homes, and the going of a stranger among them excites their resentment, until his errand is explained. While we are in the house, the ultimatum of the "boss" is received. He will give $3.75 a thousand, not another cent. Our host is a man of seeming intelligence, yet he has been nine years in New York and knows neither English nor German. Three bright little children play about the floor.

His neighbor on the same floor has been here fifteen years, but shakes his head when asked if he can speak English. He answers in a few broken syllables when addressed in German. With $11.75 rent to pay for like accommodation, he has the advantage of his oldest boy's work besides his wife's at the bench. Three properly make a team, and these three can turn out four thousand cigars a week, at $3.75. This Bohemian has a large family; there are four children, too small to work, to be cared for. A comparison of the domestic bill of fare between Tenth and Ludlow Streets results in the discovery that this Bohemian's butcher's bill for the week, with meat at twelve cents a pound as in Ludlow Street, is from two dollars and a half to three dollars. The Polish Jew fed as big a family on one pound of meat a day. The difference proves to be typical.

# 49

## The Making of a Monopoly

In this early essay published in the *Atlantic Monthly* in 1881, Henry Demerast Lloyd, later to win fame for his fiery denunciation of big business, *Wealth Against Commonwealth* (1894), provides a bitter description of some of the methods by which John D. Rockefeller's Standard Oil Company achieved for a time a monopoly over oil refining. Lloyd was insufficiently appreciative of the increased efficiency Rockefeller brought to the chaotic oil industry, but his sense of moral outrage at the devious techniques pictured here and his fear of the concentration of so much power in one organization were widely shared by Americans of his day. By the 1890s Lloyd was less inclined to look back in nostalgia toward an economy of intensely competitive small producers, and had come to favor public ownership of the great corporations; but most of his countrymen were slow to abandon their faith in free competition and their distrust of government.

## STORY OF A GREAT MONOPOLY
### *Henry Demarest Lloyd*

When Commodore Vanderbilt began the world he had nothing, and there were no steamboats or railroads. He was thirty-five years old when the first locomotive was put into use in America. When he died, railroads had become the greatest force in modern industry, and Vanderbilt was the richest man of Europe or America, and the largest owner of railroads in the world. He used the finest business brains of his day and the franchise of the state to build up a kingdom within the republic, and like a king he bequeathed his wealth and power to his eldest son. Bancroft's History of the United States and our railroad system were begun at the same time. The history is not yet finished, but the railroads owe on stocks and bonds $4,600,000,000, more than twice our national debt of $2,220,000,000, and tax the people annually $490,000,000, one and a half times more than the government's revenue last year of $274,000,000. More than any other class, our railroad men have developed the country, and tried its institutions. The evasion of almost all taxes by the New York Central Railroad has thrown upon the people of New York State more than a fair share of the cost of government, and illustrates some of the methods by which the rich are making the poor poorer. Violations of trust by Credit Mobiliers, Jay Gould's wealth and the poverty of Erie stockholders, such

From "Story of a Great Monopoly," *Atlantic Monthly*, March, 1881.

corruption of legislatures as gave the Pacific Mail its subsidies, and nicknamed New Jersey "The State of Camden and Amboy," are sins against public and private faith on a scale impossible in the early days of republics and corporations. A lawsuit still pending, though begun ten years ago by a citizen of Chicago, to recover the value of baggage destroyed by the Pennsylvania Railroad; Judge Barnard's midnight orders for the Erie ring; the surrender of its judicial integrity by the supreme court of Pennsylvania at the bidding of the Pennsylvania Railroad, as charged before Congress by President Gowen, of the Reading Railroad; the veto by the Standard Oil Company of the enactment of a law by the Pennsylvania legislature to carry out the provision of the constitution of the State that every one should have equal rights on the railroads,—these are a few of the many things that have happened to kill the confidence of our citizens in the laws and the administration of justice. No other system of taxation has borne as heavily on the people as those extortions and inequalities of railroad charges which caused the granger outburst in the West, and the recent uprising in New York. In the actual physical violence with which railroads have taken their rights of way through more than one American city, and in the railroad strikes of 1876 and 1877 with the anarchy that came with them, there are social disorders we hoped never to see in America. These incidents in railroad history show most of the points where we fail, as between man and man, employer and employed, the public and the corporation, the state and the citizen, to maintain the equities of "government"—and employ-ment—"of the people, by the people, for the people."

Our treatment of "the railroad problem" will show the quality and calibre of our political sense. It will go far in foreshadowing the future lines of our social and political growth. It may indicate whether the American democracy, like all the democratic experiments which have preceded it, is to become extinct because the people had not wit enough or virtue enough to make the common good supreme.

The remarkable series of eight railroad strikes, which began during the Centennial Exposition of the prosperity of our first century and the perfection of our institutions, culminated on July 16, 1877, in the strike on the Baltimore and Ohio Railroad at Martinsburg, West Virginia. This spread into the greatest labor disturbance on record. For a fortnight there was an American Reign of Terror. We have forgotten it,—that is, it has taught us nothing; but if Freeman outlives us to finish his History of Federal Government from the Achaian League to the Disruption of the United States, he will give more than one chapter to the labor rising of 1877. The strike at Martinsburg was instantly felt at Chicago and Baltimore in the stoppage of shipments. In a few hours the Baltimore and Ohio, one of the chief commercial arteries of Maryland, Virginia, West Virginia, Ohio, Indiana, and Illinois, was shut up. The strike spread to the Pennsylvania, the Erie and the New York Central railroads, and to the Great Western lines, with their countless branches, as far west as Omaha and Topeka, and as far south as the Ohio River and the Texas Pacific. The feeling of the railroad employés all over the country was expressed by the address of those of the Pennsylvania Railroad to its stockholders. The stockholders were reminded that "many of the railroad's men did not average wages of more than seventy-five cents a day;" that "the influence of the road had been used to destroy the business of its best customers, the oil producers, for the purpose of building up individual interests." "What is the result? The traffic has almost disappeared from the Pennsylvania Railroad, and in place of $7,-000,000 revenue this year, although shipments are in excess of last year, your road will receive scarcely half the amount. This alone would have enabled your company to pay us enough for a living." The address also refers pointedly to the abuses of fast freight lines, rolling-stock companies, and other railroad inventions for switching business into private pockets. Other workingmen followed the example of the railroad employés. At Zanesville, Ohio, fifty manufactories stopped work. Baltimore ceased to export petroleum. The rolling mills, foundries, and refineries of Cleveland were closed. Chicago, St. Louis, Cincinnati, all the cities large and small, had the same experience. At Indianapolis, next to Chicago the largest point for the eastward shipment of produce, all traffic was stopped except on the two roads that were in the hands of the national government. At Erie, Pa., the railroad struck, and notwithstanding the remonstrance of the employés refused to forward passengers or the United States mails. The grain and cattle of the farmer ceased to move to market, and the large centres of population began to calculate the chances of famine. New York's supply of Western cattle and grain was cut off. Meat rose three cents a pound in one day, while Cleveland telegraphed that hogs, sheep, beeves, and poultry billed for New York were dying on the side-tracks there. Merchants could not sell, manufacturers could not work, banks could not lend. The country went to the verge of panic, for the banks, in the absence of remittances, had resolved to close if the blockade lasted a few days longer. President Garrett, of the Baltimore and Ohio Railroad, wrote that his "great national highway could be restored to public use only by the interposition of the United States army." President Scott, of the Pennsylvania Railroad, telegraphed the authorities at Washington, "I fear that unless the general government will assume the responsibility of order throughout the land, the anarchy which is now present will become more terrible than has ever been known in the history of the world." The governors of ten States—West Virginia, Maryland, New Jersey, New York, Pennsylvania, Ohio, Illinois, Wisconsin, Missouri, and Kentucky—issued dispersing proclamations which did not disperse. The governors of four of them—West Virginia, Maryland, Pennsylvania, and Illinois—appealed to the national government for help against domestic insurrection, which the State could not suppress. The president of the United States issued two national proclamations to the insurgents. The state troops were almost useless, as in nearly all cases they fraternized with the strikers. All the national troops that could be spared from the Indian frontier and the South were ordered back to the centres of civilization. The regulars were welcomed by the frightened people of Chicago with cheers which those who heard will never forget. Armed guards were placed at all the public buildings of Washington, and ironclads were ordered up for the protection of the national capital. Cabinet meetings were continuous. General Winfield S. Hancock was sent to Baltimore to take command, General Sherman was called back from the West, and General Schofield was ordered from West Point into active service. Barricades, in the French style, were thrown up by the voters of Baltimore. New York and Philadelphia were heavily

57

garrisoned. In Philadelphia every avenue of approach to the Pennsylvania Railroad was patrolled, and the city was under a guard of six thousand armed men, with eight batteries of artillery. There were encounters between troops and voters, with loss of life, at Martinsburg, Baltimore, Pittsburg, Chicago, Reading, Buffalo, Scranton, and San Francisco. In the scene at Pittsburg, there was every horror of revolution. Citizens and soldiers were killed, the soldiers were put to flight, and the town left at the mercy of the mob. Railroad cars, depots, hotels, stores, elevators, private houses, were gutted and burned. The city has just compromised for $1,810,000 claims for damages to the amount of $2,938,460, and has still heavy claims to settle. The situation was described at this point by a leading newspaper as one of "civil war with the accompanying horrors of murder, conflagration, rapine, and pillage." These were days of greater bloodshed, more actual suffering, and wider alarm in the North than that part of the country experienced at any time during the civil war, except when Lee invaded Pennsylvania. As late as August 3d, the beautiful valley of the Wyoming, in Pennsylvania, was a military camp, traversed by trains loaded with Gatling guns and bayonets, and was guarded by Governor Hartranft in person with five thousand soldiers. These strikes, penetrating twelve States and causing insurrections in ten of them, paralyzed the operation of twenty thousand miles of railroad, and directly and indirectly threw one million men temporarily out of employment. While they lasted they caused greater losses than any blockade which has been made by sea or land in the history of war. Non-sensational observers, like the Massachusetts Board of Railroad Commissioners, look to see the outburst repeated, possibly to secure a rise of wages. The movement of the railroad trains of this country is literally the circulation of its blood. Evidently, from the facts we have recited, the States cannot prevent its arrest by the struggle between these giant forces within society, outside the law.

Kerosene has become, by its cheapness, the people's light the world over. In the United States we used 220,000,000 gallons of petroleum last year. It has come into such demand abroad that our exports of it increased from 79,458,888 gallons in 1868, to 417,648,544 in 1879. It goes all over Europe, and to the far East. The Oriental demand for it is increasing faster than any other. We are assured by the eloquent petroleum editor of the New York Shipping List that "it blazes across the ruins of Babylon and waste Persepolis," and that "all over Polynesia, and Far Cathay, in Burmah, in Siam, in Java, the bronzed denizens toil and dream, smoke opium and swallow hasheesh, woo and win, love and hate, and sicken and die under the rays of this wonderful product of our fruitful caverns." However that may be, it is statistically true that China and the East Indies took over 10,000,000 gallons in 1877, and nearly 25,000,000 gallons in 1878. After articles of food, this country has but one export, cotton, more valuable than petroleum. It was worth $61,789,438 in our foreign trade in 1877; $46,574,974 in 1878; and $18,546,642 in the five months ending November 30, 1879. In the United States, in the cities as well as the country, petroleum is the general illuminator. We use more kerosene lamps than Bibles. The raw material of this world's light is produced in a territory beginning with Cattaraugus County in New York, and extending southwesterly through eight or nine counties of Pennsylvania, making a belt about one hundred and fifty miles long, and twelve or fifteen miles wide, and then, with an interval, running into West Virginia, Kentucky, and Tennessee, where the yield is unimportant. The bulk of the oil comes from two counties, Cattaraugus in New York, and McKean in Pennsylvania. There are a few places elsewhere that produce rock oil, such as the shales of England, Wales, and Scotland, but the oil is so poor that American kerosene, after being carried thousands of miles, can undersell it. Very few of the forty millions of people in the United States who burn kerosene know that its production, manufacture, and export, its price at home and abroad, have been controlled for years by a single corporation,—the Standard Oil Company. This company began in a partnership, in the early years of the civil war, between Samuel Andrews and John Rockefeller in Cleveland. Rockefeller had been a bookkeeper in some interior town in Ohio, and had afterwards made a few thousand dollars by keeping a flour store in Cleveland. Andrews had been a day laborer in refineries, and so poor that his wife took in sewing. He found a way of refining by which more kerosene could be got out of a barrel of petroleum than by any other method, and set up for himself a ten-barrel still in Cleveland, by which he cleared $500 in six months. Andrews' still and Rockefeller's savings have grown into the Standard Oil Company. It has a capital, nominally $3,500,000, but really much more, on which it divides among its stockholders every year millions of dollars of profits. It has refineries at Cleveland, Baltimore, and New York. Its own acid works, glue factories, hardware stores, and barrel shops supply it with all the accessories it needs in its business. It has bought land at Indianapolis on which to erect the largest barrel factory in the country. It has drawn its check for $1,000,000 to suppress a rival. It buys 30,000 to 40,000 barrels of crude oil a day, at a price fixed by itself, and makes special contracts with the railroads for the transportation of 13,000,000 to 14,000,000 barrels of oil a year. The four quarters of the globe are partitioned among the members of the Standard combinations. One has the control of the China trade; another that of some country of Europe; another that of the United States. In New York, you cannot buy oil for East Indian export from the house that has been given the European trade; reciprocally, the East Indian house is not allowed to sell for export to Europe. The Standard produces only one fiftieth or sixtieth of our petroleum, but dictates the price of all, and refines nine tenths. Circulars are issued at intervals by which the price of oil is fixed for all the cities of the country, except New York, where a little competition survives. Such is the indifference of the Standard Oil Company to railroad charges that the price is made the same for points so far apart as Terre Haute, Chicago, and Keokuk. There is not to-day a merchant in Chicago, or in any other city in the New England, Western, or Southern States, dealing in kerosene, whose prices are not fixed for him by the Standard. In all cases these prices are graded so that a merchant in one city cannot export to another. Chicago, Cincinnati, or Cleveland is not allowed to supply the tributary towns. That is done by the Standard itself, which runs oil in its own tank cars to all the principal points of distribution. This corporation has driven into bankruptcy, or out of business, or into union with itself, all the petroleum refineries of the country except five in New York, and a few of little consequence in Western Pennsylvania. Nobody knows how many millions Rockefeller is worth. Current gossip among his business acquaintance in Cleveland puts his income last year at a figure second only, if second at all, to that of Vanderbilt. His partner, Samuel Andrews, the poor English day laborer, retired years ago with millions. Just who the Standard Oil Company are, exactly what their capital is, and what are their relations to the railroads, nobody knows except in part. Their officers refused to testify before the supreme court of Pennsylvania, the last New York Railroad Investigating Committee, and a committee of Congress. The New York committee found there was nothing to be learned from them, and was compelled to confess its inability to ascertain as much as it desired to know "of this mysterious organization, whose business and transactions are of such a character that its members declined giving a history or description, lest their testimony be used to convict them of crime."

Their great business capacity would have insured the managers of the Standard success, but the means by which they achieved monopoly was by conspiracy with the railroads. Mr. Simon Sterne, counsel for the merchants of New York in the New York investigation, declared that the relations of the railroads to the Standard exhibited "the most shameless perversion of the duties of a common carrier to private ends that has taken place in the history of the world." The Standard killed its rivals, in brief, by getting the great trunk lines to refuse to give them transportation. Commodore Vanderbilt is reported to have said that there was but one man—Rockefeller—who could dictate to him. Whether or not Vanderbilt said it, Rockefeller did it. The Standard has done everything with the Pennsylvania legislature, except refine it. In 1876 its organization was brought before Congress, and referred to a committee. A prominent member of the Standard, not a member of Congress, conducted the farce of inquiry from behind the seat of the chairman. Another member of the company, who was a member of Congress, came with the financial officer of the company before the committee, and sustained him in his refusal to testify about the organization, its members, or its relations with the railroads. The committee never reported. The facts they suppressed must be hunted out through newspaper articles, memorials from the oil producers and refiners, records of lawsuits, reports of chambers of commerce and of legislative investigating committees, and other miscellaneous sources of information.

The contract is in print by which the Pennsylvania Railroad agreed with the Standard, under the name of the South Improvement Company, to double the freights on oil to everybody, but to repay the Standard one dollar for every barrel of oil it shipped, and one dollar for every barrel any of its competitors shipped. This contract was produced in Congress, and was stigmatized by Representative Conger as "the most damnable and startling evidence yet produced of the possibility of railroad monopoly." Ostensibly this contract was given up, in deference to the whirlwind of indignation it excited. But Rockefeller, the manager of the Standard, was a man who could learn from defeat. He made no more tell-tale contracts that could be printed. He effected secret arrangements with the Pennsylvania, the New York Central, the Erie, and the Atlantic and Great Western. What influences he used to make the railroad managers pliable may probably be guessed from the fact that one quarter of the stock of the Acme Oil Company, a partner in the Standard combination, on which heavy monthly dividends are paid, is owned by persons whose names Rockefeller would never reveal, which Mr. Archbold, the president of the company, said under oath he had not been told, and which the supreme court of Pennsylvania has not yet been able to find out. The Standard succeeded in getting from Mr. Vanderbilt free transportation for its crude oil from the wells in Pennsylvania, one hundred and fifty miles, to the refineries at Cleveland, and back. This stamped out competing refineries at Pittsburgh, and created much of the raw material of the riots of July, 1877. Vanderbilt signed an agreement, March 25, 1872, that "all agreements for the transportation of oil after this date shall be upon a basis of perfect equality," and ever since has given the Standard special rates and privileges. He has paid it back in rebates millions of dollars, which have enabled it to crush out all competitors, although many of them, like the Octave Oil Company and the Titusville refiners, had done all their business over his road till they went into bankruptcy, broken by his contracts with the Standard. He united with the Erie in a war on the Pennsylvania Railroad, to force it to sell to the Standard all its refineries, and the great pipe lines by which the oil, like Croton water in the mains, was carried from the wells to the railroads. He then joined with the Erie and the Pennsylvania in a similar attack on the Baltimore and Ohio, which had to sell out to the Standard. So the Standard obtained the control of all the pipe lines and of the transportation, of everything, in fact, as a witness said before the New York Railroad Investigating Committee, except the bodies of the producers. Mr. Vanderbilt began, as did the Erie and Pennsylvania railroad kings, with paying back to the Standard, but to no other shipper, ten per cent. of its freight bills. He continued making one concession after another, till when he was doing the business for other shippers at $1.40 and $1.25 a barrel, he charged the Standard only eighty and eighty-one cents, and this was afterwards reduced to sixty cents a barrel. During the war against the Pennsylvania road to make it sell out to the Standard, the New York Central carried oil for less than nothing. Besides the other allowances, Mr. Vanderbilt paid the Standard through its alias, the American Transfer Company, a rebate of thirty-five cents a barrel on all the crude oil shipped by it or its competitors. When the oil producers, whom the Standard had cut off from all access to the world except through it, sought an exit through an out-of-the-way railroad and the Erie Canal, or down the Ohio River hundreds of miles to Huntingdon, thence by the Chesapeake and Ohio Railroad to Richmond, and so to the sea, Mr. Vanderbilt lowered his rates to the Standard so that it could undersell any one who used these devious routes. When the producers, June, 1879, completed their own tidewater pipe line, 104 miles long, to a junction with the Reading Railroad, obtaining in this way a direct connection with the seaboard, Mr. Vanderbilt reduced his rate to the public from $1.40 to $1.25 a barrel to thirty-five and twenty-five cents, and charged the Standard twenty, fifteen, finally but ten cents. For ten cents Mr. Vanderbilt hauled for the Standard a barrel weighing 390 pounds over 400 miles, and hauled back the empty cars, at the same time that he charged forty-five cents for hauling a can of milk weighing ninety pounds for sixty miles. So closely had the Standard octopus gripped itself about Mr. Vanderbilt that even at the outside rates its competitors could not get transportation from him. He

61

allowed the Standard to become the owner of all the oil cars run over his road, and of all his terminal facilities for oil. As the Standard owned all but 200 of the oil cars run on the Erie, and leased all that road's terminal facilities, it could charge its rivals anything it pleased for the privileges of New York harbor. When Mr. Vanderbilt was questioned by Mr. Simon Sterne, of the New York committee, about these and other things, his answers were, "I don't know," "I forget," "I don't remember," to 116 questions out of 249 by actual count. At a time when the Standard Oil Company through its other self, the American Transfer Company, was receiving from the New York Central thirty-five cents a barrel on all oil shipped by itself or its competitors, and was getting other rebates which cost the New York Central over $2,000,000 from October 17, 1877, to March 31, 1879, Mr. Vanderbilt testified positively before the New York Investigating Committee that he knew nothing whatever about the American Transfer Company, its officers, or the payments to it.

# 50

## The Impulse
## toward Labor Organization

In his testimony before the United States Industrial Commission investigating "the relations between labor and capital" in 1900, Samuel Gompers expounds the philosophy of disciplined struggle that allowed his American Federation of Labor to triumph over its rival the Knights of Labor in the 1880s. Unlike the Knights of Labor, the American Federation of Labor was the organ of the skilled elite of American labor, and the great mass of unskilled, semiskilled, and service workers remained outside its ranks. But Gompers was probably correct in his belief that at a time when the presuppositions of employers, and indeed of most middle-class Americans, were hostile to union organization, it was necessary to concentrate on the task of building strength among workers who had special skills and hence market power.

### TESTIMONY BEFORE THE U.S.
### INDUSTRIAL COMMISSION
#### Samuel Gompers

Gompers.   It is the purpose of organized labor to bring the number of strikes down to a minimum, and in order to accomplish that we try to be better prepared for them.

Q.   What is the result in the last 10 years? Have strikes decreased or increased—that is, compared with the increase of organized labor?—A.   During the first year of organizations, as a rule, there are strikes. When workmen remain organized for any considerable length of time, strikes are reduced in number. It is a peculiar fact that when workmen are unorganized they imagine their employers are almighty and themselves absolutely impotent. When workmen organize for the first time, this transformation takes place: they imagine their employers absolutely impotent and themselves almighty, and the result of it is there is conflict. The employer, so far as strikes begun in his establishment are concerned, resents immediately the assumption of the workmen to appear by committee. He has been accustomed to look upon himself, as to his factory or his establishment, as "monarch of all he surveys" with undisputed sway, and the fact that his employees have an entity as an organization, to be represented by a committee, is something

From *Report of the U.S. Industrial Commission on the Relations and Conditions of Capital and Labor* (Washington, D.C., 1901), VII: 606–608, 617–618, 642–646, 655.

unheard of by him and absolutely intolerable. He imagines immediately that it is a question as to his right to his property: imagines immediately that his property is threatened, and surrounds himself with such safeguards—as the lamented Gladstone once said, "The entire resources of civilization had not yet been exhausted"—arms everybody who swears loyalty to the company, and often surrounds himself with a mercenary armed force, and all the wiles and devices that the acumen of our legal friends can suggest are always employed to overcome, overawe these "mutineers" against his authority.

Q.   To what extent, if any, is the employer, in your judgment, responsible for that condition of affairs?—A.   To the same extent that the bourgeois of France, the royalists of France, were responsible in cowing the people of France, which resulted in the revolution and the brutality manifested by the people when they got power. The employers have simply cut wages whenever they thought it convenient. They looked upon their employees as part of the machinery; to exhibit, perhaps, some little sympathy when one was very critically injured or suffering, and then expected the worship of them all; the cutting of wages time and again, in season and out of season; the discharge of a man who proposed to exercise his right as a man, whether it was as a workman or as a citizen; and so on, driving practically the courage and heart out of the man; and when, through some incident, of which there are thousands, the men are organized of their own volition, quite frequently they touch shoulders for the first time outside of the shop—they touch shoulders, and the thrill simply enthuses them and intoxicates them with new-found power. It is only after the organization has administered a very costly lesson to the employer, and it is only after the workmen themselves have felt the pangs of hunger, perhaps, or other sacrifices resultant from strikes they suffer when unprepared, unorganized, that they are more careful of each other—both sides. They organize and try to meet each other and discuss with each other, and the better the workmen are organized the more able are they to convince the employer that there is an ethical side to the demands of labor. It required 40,000 people in the city of New York in my own trade in 1877 to demonstrate to the employers that we had a right to be heard in our own defense of our trade, and an opportunity to be heard in our own interests. It cost the miners of the country, in 1897, 16 weeks of suffering to secure a national conference and a national agreement. It cost the railroad brotherhoods long months of suffering, many of them sacrificing their positions, in the railroad strike of 1877, and in the Chicago, Burlington and Quincy strike, of the same year, to secure from the employers the right to be heard through committees, their representatives—that is, their committees of the organization to secure these rights. Workmen have had to stand the brunt of the suffering. The American Republic was not established without some suffering, without some sacrifice, and no tangible right has yet been achieved in the interest of the people unless it has been secured by sacrifices and persistency. After a while we become a little more tolerant to each other and recognize all have rights; get around the table and chaff each other; all recognize that they were not so reasonable in the beginning. Now we propose to meet and discuss our interests, and if we can not agree we propose in a more reasonable way to conduct our contests, each to decide how to hold out and bring the other one to terms. A strike, too, is to industry as the right that the British people contended for in placing in the House of Commons the power to close the purse strings to the Government. The rights of the British people were secured in two centuries—between 1500 and 1600—more than ever before, by the securing of that power to withhold the supplies; tied up the purse strings and compelled the Crown to yield. A strike on the part of workmen is to close production and compel better terms and more rights to be acceded to the producers. The economic results of strikes to workers have been advantageous. Without strikes their rights would not have been considered. It is not that workmen or organized labor desires the strike, but it will tenaciously hold to the right to strike. We recognize that peaceful industry is necessary to successful civilized life, but the right to strike and the preparation to strike is the greatest preventive to strikes. If the workmen were to make up their minds to-morrow that they would under no circumstances strike, the employers would do all the striking for them in the way of lesser wages and longer hours of labor.

Q.   The whole philosophy is contest and conquest?—A.   Except when there be like power on both sides; then it becomes reason, by the power on both sides; it then comes to reason rather than contest and conquest. It becomes a matter then of reason; and, as I tried to say in the earlier part of my testimony, no matter how just a cause is, unless that cause is backed up with power to enforce it, it is going to be crushed and annihilated. I tried to illustrate some time ago this proposition by the fact that when England has a dispute with the Afghanistans she immediately proceeds to bombard them unless they acquiesce in her demands; and she would have done the same thing in Venezuela; but when England has a dispute with the United States, she says, "Let us arbitrate" this question; and I think the United States in this regard, or any other nation, is not any different in that regard at all; and the employers are practically in the same position. When the strike occurred at Pullman, Mr. Pullman said he had nothing to arbitrate. His people were unorganized, but he met the committees; not now; he don't meet anyone now; but he used to meet the committees of his unorganized workmen; and the railroad managers—they simply throw their unorganized workmen into the streets if they have any grievances or supposed grievances, but when it comes to organized engineers, firemen, or conductors, or trainmen, who have fairly well organized unions, why, they meet them in conference, pat them on the back sometimes, and say they are jolly good fellows. The economic results to the workers have been invariably beneficial. Even strikes which have been lost have had their good, beneficial results upon the workers. For after all the question must be looked upon in a comprehensive, in a broad way. If the workers, say, have struck for an increase in wages, and the employers refuse to concede them, and finally defeat the workmen, yet as a matter of fact it is almost invariably the case that those who have taken the places of the men who went on strike were themselves receiving less wages before doing so. It is seldom, if ever, that a workman will go from a position where he receives higher wages to take the place of a striker at lower wages. It therefore shows that those who take the places of the strikers improve their material position in the matter of wages. It is asserted that those who strike are compelled to look out for other positions, which is naturally true; but in only isolated cases do they accept positions which pay them less than those they struck

65

against; so that in the sum total of it there is an economic and social advantage. Strikes have convinced the employers of the economic advantage of reduced hours of labor; strikes have rid many a trade of the "jerry builder;" of the fraudulent employer who won't pay wages; strikes have enforced lien laws for wages, where laws have been previously unable to secure the payment; strikes have organized employers as well as employees; strikes have made strong and independent men who were for a long period of years cowards; strikes have made a more independent citizenship of men who often voted simply because it pleased the boss; strikes have given men greater lease of life; strikes have resulted in higher wages, better homes, and demand for better things; strikes have organized wage-earners, too. The strike has taken the place of the barbarous weapons of the dirk and bludgeon. Strikes in the modern sense can occur only in civilized countries.

Q.   Does the community at large suffer from strikes?—A.   Seldom, if any, except temporarily. It is alleged by some that strikes diminish the wealth of a community and do irreparable injury. If a strike takes place and is not adjusted, it is the very best evidence, of itself, that the community is not suffering for the want of that article. If the community would begin to suffer for that article, employers would immediately concede the demand of the strikers, and the time which is lost in the strike is always made up in a greater continuity of industry after the strike is closed. It is seldom, if ever, workmen are continually employed throughout the entire year. A strike is simply a transferring of the time when idleness shall occur from the advantage of the employer to the advantage of the employees.

Q.   So that you would say that the introduction of new machinery does not make a permanent displacement of labor?—A.   It would, were it not for the extent of the movement of the wage earners to reduce the hours of labor. When the wage earners do not reduce their hours of labor in proportion to the progress made in the introduction of machinery, new tools, and the division and subdivision of labor, then there is a greater number who are unemployed.

Q.   When you say that new machinery, bringing in more rapid processes of production, has lightened the toil of the operatives?—A.   No. The organizations of labor have lightened the toil of the workingman, if the toil has been lightened. As a matter of fact, the velocity with which machinery is now run calls forth the expenditure of nearly all the physical and mental force which the wage-earner can give to industry. In substantiation of my negative answer to your question, I would call attention to the fact that after the introduction of machinery, machinery propelled by the motive power of steam, the hours of labor of the working people were from sunup to sundown, and the machinery, which was costly, was not of advantage to the possessor unless it could be operated for a longer period than from sunup to sundown, and it was in that case as perhaps in all, that necessity, being the mother of invention, that which was absent was forthcoming; that was, artificial light to take the place of the rays of the sun after it had set for the day, and with the introduction of artificial light, gas, came the lengthening of the hours of labor of the working people both of the United States and continental Europe. Wherever machinery was at all introduced the object was to have the machinery operated as long as possible, and with the aid of gas the opportunity came. The organizations of the working people were very fragmentary, and few and weak. The hours of labor were lengthened until lives were destroyed by the thousands; and then came the introduction of woman and child labor. There was no restrictive legislation for them; and then came the efforts of the organizations of labor that called forth a yearning and cry of the whole human family against the slaughter of the innocents in the factories of Great Britain particularly, and subsequently in the United States. And it was the power of organized labor—first in feeling that its cause was right, that men and women were being cut down in their manhood and womanhood and childhood, dwarfed or killed, that in a few generations the working people were bound to deteriorate physically, mentally, and morally; that they were deteriorating physically, mentally, and morally; and their ability as producers of wealth would have been destroyed in a few generations had the possessors of machines at that time continued in full sway—it was the efforts of the trade unions of Great Britain, first in their protests, second, in their strikes, and third in their appeals to the public conscience which called forth the factory legislation which limited the hours of labor of women and children in certain industries. Only a few years ago the counsel for the Arkwright Club of Massachusetts said, in a hearing before the labor committee of the Massachusetts legislature in opposition to a bill to limit hours of labor: "If you take the women and children out of the industry, why you take the very heart out of it." And regardless of the brutality of the remark, it was held that if the law limited the hours of labor of the women and children the mill owners would close down the mill and thus close it for men, too. It is for that reason I call attention to the attorney's remark—that with the factory legislation of Great Britain limiting the hours of labor of women and children in several of the industries, it practically secured a reduction in the hours of labor of the male adults also.

Q. In this year of combinations and consolidations and so-called trusts, part of the press and some public men have classified labor associations as connected with and a part of this trust body. What do you say to that classification of labor organizations with capitalistic trusts?—A. I think it is unjustifiable to make that charge against organized labor. Organized labor's efforts are directed to bring within the fold of the organization everyone who works at the trade, everyone who works for wages. The effort is to extend the organization to everyone. You can not break into a trust, and it is our effort to try to make it unprofitable for the workers to break out or longer remain out of the union. One is a close corporation, and the other is an organization world-wide in its effect and influence for good, and the effort is to have the entire body of workers members of the organization.

Q. Is it general that these unions invite the cooperation and the membership of good workmen who have not been associated in labor before?—A. The testimony I gave last April before your commission covers that question partly, but I would say that while we then had 475 general organizers, we now have 550. Where we then had 3 special paid organizers for the American Federation of Labor, we now have 15. There is not a national union in the entire country that has not from 3 to 10 special traveling organizers, whose sole duty it is to try and bring the unorganized workmen within the fold of the union, and to share the benefits of organized effort.

Q. So you would say that the trades union itself is not particularly a selfish organization, for the benefit of those who are first incorporated into it, and to the immediate membership that is attached to it locally: that its influence is wider?—A. Decidedly wider. There is a difference between the contracted selfishness and the broad selfishness that finds one's good served by serving others; by benefiting others. We know that our movement is largely hampered, our progress is hindered, by the large number of unorganized men, and to bring the unorganized within the pale of the organization would make our effort all the more successful and the struggle less intense.

Q. What effect do you think these combinations of capital, or so-called trusts, will have, so far as the interests of organized labor are concerned, for good or for evil?—A. I should prefer that the future shall determine that. Our attitude toward the trusts, I should say, would be largely determined by the attitude of the trusts toward organized labor. It can't be taken as a general proposition. There have been some trusts where, in absorbing, say, some nonunion establishment, and the organization of labor of that trade has had contracts with the different union establishments before the trust was formed, the result of the trust in that particular case has been that the nonunion establishment, paying way below the scale, became part of the trust, became unionized, and an agreement reached increasing wages, reducing hours, and recognizing union conditions. On the other hand, again, there have been trusts where union establishments have been absorbed, and they have become nonunion, so there is no real hard and fast rule by which this question can be determined from our standpoint. We view the trust from the standpoint that they are our employers, and the employer who is fair to us, whether an individual, or a collection of individuals, an aggregation of individuals in the form of a corporation or a trust, matters little to us so long as we obtain the fair conditions—that condition that we regard as fair compensation or reward for our labor.

Q. So far as the whole body of workmen of the United States are concerned, organized or unorganized, do you think that those consolidated bodies where they reach a capitalization of say one hundred, one hundred and fifty, or two hundred millions are really abnormal in the conduct of our business, and are they not, through the great control they have of capital and influence, through legislation and otherwise, rather a menace to the welfare of the country at large?—A. Yes; from some of the causes I have tried to indicate; not necessarily the possession of the wealth, but it is the abuse of the possession.

Q. In other words, you are not particularly afraid, as the head of a great organization, of the large accumulations of wealth, provided that, either through legislation or public opinion, the abuses of that wealth can be regulated?—A. I believe that as time goes on the wage-earners will continue to become larger sharers per dollar of the wealth produced. I have no fear as to the future of organized labor. I have no fear as to the future of labor. This morning I indicated the fact that there is a constant struggle which has been going on from time immemorial between the wealth possessors and those who produce wealth, and that struggle has manifested itself in different forms, at different times, in different countries. That struggle has continued up to date, and will continue so long as there are divers interests between the two. Now, if the wealth possessors, now in form of trusts, make their attitude more unbearable to labor, become more oppressive than ever to labor, it may make the struggle more intense and more bitter; but the struggle is to be met, and will be met; it is only a question whether it shall manifest itself in the power of organization of labor on the one hand and the power of organized wealth on the other, within the bounds of reason, making material concessions, and realizing the development that is continually going on, and the natural desire and the natural right of labor to be continually sharing larger in the product of labor, the social evolution taking place, or whether the trusts, through the intense antagonism that they may manifest toward labor, make that fight all the more bitter, all the more intense. I have not any fear as to the future. My only fear is—and there is something I want to obviate, that I am trying to give my life's work to obviate, that the struggle shall not be so bitter and costly.

Q.  Suppose it is thought best on the part of capital to call in as a cooperative factor the forces of labor organized, especially in the profit sharing, or cooperative, or other form of just division of profits in the wealth producers, and wealth itself, would you say that organized labor would accept conditions of that kind in preference to the wage system that they have now?—A.  I would say that judging from the history of such efforts in the past, I would look upon such propositions with a very great deal of suspicion. There have been few, if any, of these concerns that have been even comparatively fair to their employees. The average employer who has indulged in this single-handed scheme to solve the social problem has gotten out of the workers all that there was in them and all their vitality, and made the mold prematurely, to the tune of 5 or 10 years of their lives. They made the worker work harder, longer hours, and when the employees of other concerns in the same line of trade were enjoying increased wages, shorter hours of labor, and other improvements, tending to the material progress of the worker, the employees of the concern where so-called profit sharing was the system at the end of the year found themselves receiving lower wages for harder work than were those who were not under that beneficent system.

Q.  Then you would say that practically attempts made in this country in the line of profit sharing, and mutuality between the employer and employee in the sharing of profits of the production, have been failures?—A. There are few exceptions. So long as our present social system shall last, it is positively ludicrous for any concern or few concerns to attempt to solve the social problem for themselves. It is just as ludicrous and ridiculous as it is for a number of well-meaning people, well-meaning workmen, to make up their minds to enter upon a colonization scheme of cooperation. They isolate themselves from the world— even if their purpose is a success, if their scheme is a success, they have simply emancipated themselves from the world, and are contributing nothing toward the solution of the struggle; yes, they have hindered the struggle, for, as a rule, these people are discontented with the wrongs that exist, but, though manifesting some little thought and ability, deprive the people who are struggling from the benefits of that knowledge and discontent; so in the sum total, it is depriving the movement for social improvement, economic advancement, of the intelligence, and independence, and manhood, and character of these people who isolate themselves from the rest of

69

the world. And so it is with those profit-sharing concerns, perhaps prompted by no other cause than that of philanthropy or desire to solve the problem. That is not the way it must be solved; you can not solve the social problem without taking into consideration the human family. There is no such thing as solving the social problem without incorporating the whole human family.

Q.   Would the general proposition be that the worker should be a sharer in the profits of production? Then ought he to be a sharer in the losses of production?—A.   We have so little that we can afford to do with nothing less than what we have.

Q.   In other words you think the wage-scale system is on a minimum?—A. The wage scale, sliding often—but there is a minimum or a life line, below which we object it shall go. If an employer of labor can not conduct business by paying a minimum and living wage let him get out of business and make room for someone else who can pay it. We contend that it is a libel upon the human family to say that any industry, to be successfully conducted, can not afford to pay a living wage to the producers of the article in that industry.

Q.   You believe in the wage system then, rather than in partnership?—A.   I can not assent to that. I know that we are operating under the wage system. As to what system will ever come to take its place I am not prepared to say. I have given this subject much thought; I have read the works of the most advanced economists, competent economists in all schools of thought—the trade unionist, the socialist, the anarchist, the single taxer, the cooperationist, etc. I am not prepared to say, after having read, and with an honest endeavor to arrive at a conclusion—I am not prepared to say that either of their propositions are logical, scientific, or natural. I know that we are living under the wage system, and so long as that lasts, it is our purpose to secure a continually larger share for labor, for the wealth producers. Whether the time shall come, as this constantly increasing share to labor goes on, when profits shall be entirely eliminated, and the full product of labor, the net result of production, go to the laborer, thus abolishing the wage system; or whether, on the other hand, through the theory of the anarchist, there should be an abolition of all title in land other than its occupation and use, the abolition of the monopoly of the private issuance of money, the abolition of the patent system—whether we will return to the first principles; or whether, under the single tax, taxing the land to the full value of it—I am perfectly willing that the future shall determine and work out. I know that as the workers more thoroughly organize, and continually become larger sharers in the product of their toil, they will have the better opportunities for their physical and mental cultivation instilled into them, higher hopes and aspirations, and they will be the better prepared to meet the problems that will then confront them. For the present it is our purpose to secure better conditions and instill a larger amount of manhood and independence into the hearts and minds of the workers, and to broaden their mental sphere and the sphere of their affections.

Q.   Is it not true that for many years, the tendency to improved condition of the working people of this country has been very marked, and that to-day they are larger sharers in their product than ever before?—A.   That is true; yes, and it is wholly due to the efforts of their own organization.

Q.   You would not agree to the statement sometimes made that the conditions of the working man are growing worse and worse?—A.   Oh, that is perfectly absurd.

Q.   Of course you lay the improved conditions to the organization of labor?—A.   Yes. That can be easily proven, for, as a matter of fact, where the workers remain unorganized, as a rule they have not shared in the great improvements that the working people have who have been organized, and, judging from cause and effect, one can easily determine that that for which I contend is a fact. During the entire industrial revival of industry of 1884 to 1886 and 1887, the textile workers in Cohoes, N.Y., I think, were the only body of working people in the country who suffered a reduction of wages, despite the revival of industry. They were unorganized. But, of course, I want to say this in connection with this matter: In our present economic condition of society we have with a very great degree of regularity a period of these industrial panics that the student can determine almost with the exactness that an astronomer does of the comets, the coming of these periods of industrial crises. Quite a number do not observe this economic phenomena. The worker knows that during these industrial panics he is out of a job; and you might have all the philosophy in the world, all the facts in the world to demonstrate the truthfulness of your position, but he is out of a job, and he can not understand that there has been any social improvement, not even that he has improved beyond the condition of his forefathers 10 centuries age; he knows he is out of a job, and he is hungry, and the prospects of something in the future are very remote, and to him the world has been growing worse all the time; the world is in an awful condition, and it is in an awful condition truly, and we must remember this, when we consider the social progress; we must not compare this year with the last, or last year with the year before, but compare it for a century by decades, then the marvelous progress can be easily observed. One, of course, can not—unless he is as old as my friend, Major Farquhar—go back a century, but most of us young men can go back 20 or 30 years; we can mark the condition, and that which we do not know of our own knowledge we can ascertain of truthful recorders.

Q.   To what do you attribute the vastly superior condition of the American workingmen over the European; the social condition; the advanced, you might say, scale of wages paid in America over the European condition?—A.   First, the working people of Europe have emerged from a condition of slavery and serfdom to that of wage laborers. The workingmen of America have not had this hereditary condition of slavery and serfdom. There has been no special status for them as slaves or serfs, and in theory, at least, they were supposed to be equals to all others.

Another reason is the climatic conditions that obtain in our country. The changes from extreme heat to extreme cold make the people more active, more nervous; accelerates their motion, accelerates their thought; again, the vast domain of land, rich soil, that even to-day is beyond speculation, much less the knowledge of our own people—all these things have contributed to a better material condition for the working people of our country. I should add, I think, that the climate conditions, requiring better food, more nutritious food, better clothing, more comfortable clothing, better houses, better homes, have all been contributing factors for the workers to insist upon receiving—to secure these things in the shape of higher wages.

Q. He demands higher wages and gets them?—A. Yes.

Q. Comparatively higher wages?—A. He gets higher wages; comparatively higher wages.

Then again I will say that the productivity of the American laborer is far greater than that of his brother workman in any part of the wcrld.

Q. How do you rate that?—A. I can not begin to tell you. I can say, however, that in every mechanical trade, when European workmen come over to this country and stand beside their American fellow workingmen it simply dazes them—the velocity of motion, the deftness, the quickness, the constant strain. The European bricklayer, the European carpenter, the European compositor-printer, the European tailor comes over here and works in the shop, or factory, or office, and he is simply intoxicated by the rapidity of the movements of the American workingman, and it is some months, with the greatest endeavor, before he can at all come near the production of the American workingman. He must do it in time or he will go without a job.

Q. The capital that is employed in productive industry sustains very close relation with labor, so there ought to be a very great harmony of interests between the owners of that capital and the owners of labor?—A. There has never yet existed identity of interests between buyer and seller of an article. If you have anything to sell and I want to buy it your interest and mine are not identical

Q. Is there not a possibility that the day will come when they will be substantially identical, when they recognize each other's rights?—A. I should regard that upon the same plan as I would the panaceas that are offered by our populists, socialists, anarchists, and single-tax friends, as very remote and very far removed, if that time should ever come. I am perfectly satisfied to fight the battles of to-day, of those here, and those that come to-morrow, so their conditions may be improved, and they may be better prepared to fight in the contests or solve the problems that may be presented to them. The hope for a perfect millennium—well, it don't come every night; it don't come with the twinkling of the eye; it is a matter which we have got to work out, and every step that the workers make or take, every vantage point gained, is a solution in itself. I have often inquired of men who have ready-made patent solutions of this social problem, and I want to say to you, sir, that I have them offered to me on an average of two or three a week, and they are all equally unsatisfactory. I maintain that we are solving the problem every day; we are solving the problems as they confront us. One would imagine by what is often considered as the solution of the problem that it is going to fall among us, that a world cataclysm is going to take place; that there is going to be a social revolution; that we will go to bed one night under the present system and the morrow morning wake up with a revolution in full blast, and the next day organize a Heaven on earth. That is not the way that progress is made; that is not the way the social evolution is brought about; that is not the way the human family are going to have interests advanced. We are solving the problem day after day. As we get an hour's more leisure every day it means millions of golden hours, of opportunities, to the human family. As we get 25 cents a day wages increase it means another solution, another problem solved, and brings us nearer the time when a greater degree of justice and fair dealing will obtain among men.

# In Defense
# of the Status Quo

In the last third of the nineteenth century Yale professor William Graham Sumner skillfully turned Charles
Darwin's conception of "the survival of the fittest" to
the defense of rugged individualism and laissez-faire
political economy. While his essay "The Absurd Effort to Make the World Over" was published a few
years after 1890, the terminal date of the present
section, it summed up arguments he had widely dissem-
inated in the 1870s and 1880s. Popular discontent with
the workings of the economy was growing steadily, and
a diverse band of critics and reformers—Henry George,
Edmund Bellamy, Howells, Riis, Lloyd, and others—was finding a wider audience. In response Sumner
offered a thoughtful defense of the status quo and a
sharp critique of the assumptions of reformers. His
emphasis upon the inexorable evolution of modern
society toward greater organization, however, could
have been used to justify the program of a Samuel
Gompers as well as a John D. Rockefeller, and soon
"Reform Darwinist" thinkers like sociologist Lester
Frank Ward were to do just that.

## THE ABSURD EFFORT
## TO MAKE THE WORLD OVER
### *William Graham Sumner*

It will not probably be denied that the burden of proof is on those who affirm that
our social condition is utterly diseased and in need of radical regeneration. My task
at present, therefore, is entirely negative and critical: to examine the allegations of
fact and the doctrines which are put forward to prove the correctness of the
diagnosis and to warrant the use of the remedies proposed

The propositions put forward by social reformers nowadays are chiefly of two
kinds. There are assertions in historical form, chiefly in regard to the comparison of
existing with earlier social states, which are plainly based on defective historical
knowledge, or at most on current stock historical dicta which are uncritical and
incorrect. Writers very often assert that something never existed before because
they do not know that it ever existed before, or that something is worse than ever

From *War and Other Essays* (New Haven, Conn., 1911), 195–210.

before because they are not possessed of detailed information about what has existed before. The other class of propositions consists of dogmatic statements which, whether true or not, are unverifiable. This class of propositions is the pest and bane of current economic and social discussion. Upon a more or less superficial view of some phenomenon a suggestion arises which is embodied in a philosophical proposition and promulgated as a truth. From the form and nature of such propositions they can always be brought under the head of "ethics." This word at least gives them an air of elevated sentiment and purpose, which is the only warrant they possess. It is impossible to test or verify them by any investigation or logical process whatsoever. It is therefore very difficult for anyone who feels a high responsibility for historical statements, and who absolutely rejects any statement which is unverifiable, to find a common platform for discussion or to join issue satisfactorily in taking the negative.

When anyone asserts that the class of skilled and unskilled manual laborers of the United States is worse off now in respect to diet, clothing, lodgings, furniture, fuel, and lights; in respect to the age at which they can marry; the number of children they can provide for; the start in life which they can give to their children, and their chances of accumulating capital, than they ever have been at any former time, he makes a reckless assertion for which no facts have been offered in proof. Upon an appeal to facts, the contrary of this assertion would be clearly established. It suffices, therefore, to challenge those who are responsible for the assertion to make it good.

If it is said that the employed class are under much more stringent discipline than they were thirty years ago or earlier, it is true. It is not true that there has been any qualitative change in this respect within thirty years, but it is true that a movement which began at the first settlement of the country has been advancing with constant acceleration and has become a noticeable feature within our time. This movement is the advance in the industrial organization. The first settlement was made by agriculturists, and for a long time there was scarcely any organization. There were scattered farmers, each working for himself, and some small towns with only rudimentary commerce and handicrafts. As the country has filled up, the arts and professions have been differentiated and the industrial organization has been advancing. This fact and its significance has hardly been noticed at all; but the stage of the industrial organization existing at any time, and the rate of advance in its development, are the absolutely controlling social facts. Nine-tenths of the socialistic and semi-socialistic, and sentimental or ethical, suggestions by which we are overwhelmed come from failure to understand the phenomena of the industrial organization and its expansion. It controls us all because we are all in it. It creates the conditions of our existence, sets the limits of our social activity, regulates the bonds of our social relations, determines our conceptions of good and evil, suggests our life-philosophy, molds our inherited political institutions, and reforms the oldest and toughest customs, like marriage and property. I repeat that the turmoil of heterogeneous and antagonistic social whims and speculations in which we live is due to the failure to understand what the industrial organization is and its all-pervading control over human life, while the traditions of our school of philosophy lead us always to approach the industrial organization, not from the side of objective study, but from that of philosophical doctrine. Hence it is that we find that the method of measuring what we see happening by what are called ethical standards, and of proposing to attack the phenomena by methods thence deduced, is so popular.

The advance of a new country from the very simplest social coordination up to the highest organization is a most interesting and instructive chance to study the development of the organization. It has of course been attended all the way along by stricter subordination and higher discipline. All organization implies restriction of liberty. The gain of power is won by narrowing individual range. The methods of business in colonial days were loose and slack to an inconceivable degree. The movement of industry has been all the time toward promptitude, punctuality, and reliability. It has been attended all the way by lamentations about the good old times; about the decline of small industries; about the lost spirit of comradeship between employer and employee; about the narrowing of the interests of the workman; about his conversion into a machine or into a "ware," and about industrial war. These lamentations have all had reference to unquestionable phenomena attendant on advancing organization. In all occupations the same movement is discernible—in the learned professions, in schools, in trade, commerce, and transportation. It is to go on faster than ever, now that the continent is filled up by the first superficial layer of population over its whole extent and the intensification of industry has begun. The great inventions both make the intension of the organization possible and make it inevitable, with all its consequences, whatever they may be. I must expect to be told here, according to the current fashions of thinking, that we ought to control the development of the organization. The first instinct of the modern man is to get a law passed to forbid or prevent what, in his wisdom, he disapproves. A thing which is inevitable, however, is one which we cannot control. We have to make up our minds to it, adjust ourselves to it, and sit down to live with it. Its inevitableness may be disputed, in which case we must re-examine it; but if our analysis is correct, when we reach what is inevitable we reach the end, and our regulations must apply to ourselves, not to the social facts.

Now the intensification of the social organization is what gives us greater social power. It is to it that we owe our increased comfort and abundance. We are none of us ready to sacrifice this. On the contrary, we want more of it. We would not return to the colonial simplicity and the colonial exiguity if we could. If not, then we must pay the price. Our life is bounded on every side by conditions. We can have this if we will agree to submit to that. In the case of industrial power and product the great condition is combination of force under discipline and strict coordination. Hence the wild language about wage-slavery and capitalistic tyranny.

In any state of society no great achievements can be produced without great force. Formerly great force was attainable only by slavery aggregating the power of great numbers of men. Roman civilization was built on this. Ours has been built on steam. It is to be built on electricity. Then we are all forced into an organization around these natural forces and adapted to the methods or their application; and

75

although we indulge in rhetoric about political liberty, nevertheless we find ourselves bound tight in a new set of conditions, which control the modes of our existence and determine the directions in which alone economic and social liberty can go.

If it is said that there are some persons in our time who have become rapidly and in a great degree rich, it is true; if it is said that large aggregations of wealth in the control of individuals is a social danger, it is not true.

The movement of the industrial organization which has just been described has brought out a great demand for men capable of managing great enterprises. Such have been called "captains of industry." The analogy with military leaders suggested by this name is not misleading. The great leaders in the development of the industrial organization need those talents of executive and administrative skill, power to command, courage, and fortitude, which were formerly called for in military affairs and scarcely anywhere else. The industrial army is also as dependent on its captains as a military body is on its generals. One of the worst features of the existing system is that the employees have a constant risk in their employer. If he is not competent to manage the business with success, they suffer with him. Capital also is dependent on the skill of the captain of industry for the certainty and magnitude of its profits. Under these circumstances there has been a great demand for men having the requisite ability for this function. As the organization has advanced, with more impersonal bonds of coherence and wider scope of operations, the value of this functionary has rapidly increased. The possession of the requisite ability is a natural monopoly. Consequently, all the conditions have concurred to give to those who possessed this monopoly excessive and constantly advancing rates of remuneration.

Another social function of the first importance in an intense organization is the solution of those crises in the operation of it which are called the conjuncture of the market. It is through the market that the lines of relation run which preserve the system in harmonious and rhythmical operation. The conjuncture is the momentary sharper misadjudgment of supply and demand which indicates that a redistribution of productive effort is called for. The industrial organization needs to be insured against these conjunctures, which, if neglected, produce a crisis and catastrophe; and it needs that they shall be anticipated and guarded against as far as skill and foresight can do it. The rewards of this function for the bankers and capitalists who perform it are very great. The captains of industry and the capitalists who operate on the conjuncture, therefore, if they are successful, win, in these days, great fortunes in a short time. There are no earnings which are more legitimate or for which greater services are rendered to the whole industrial body. The popular notions about this matter really assume that all the wealth accumulated by these classes of persons would be here just the same if they had not existed. They are supposed to have appropriated it out of the common stock. This is so far from being true that, on the contrary, their own wealth would not be but for themselves; and besides that, millions more of wealth, many-fold greater than their own, scattered in the hands of thousands, would not exist but for them.

Within the last two years I have traveled from end to end of the German

Empire several times on all kinds of trains. I reached the conviction, looking at the matter from the passenger's standpoint, that, if the Germans could find a Vanderbilt and put their railroads in his hands for twenty-five years, letting him reorganize the system and make twenty-five million dollars out of it for himself in that period, they would make an excellent bargain.

But it is repeated until it has become a commonplace which people are afraid to question, that there is some social danger in the possession of large amounts of wealth by individuals. I ask, Why? I heard a lecture two years ago by a man who holds perhaps the first chair of political economy in the world. He said, among other things, that there was great danger in our day from great accumulations; that this danger ought to be met by taxation, and he referred to the fortune of the Rothschilds and to the great fortunes made in America to prove his point. He omitted, however, to state in what the danger consisted or to specify what harm has ever been done by the Rothschild fortunes or by the great fortunes accumulated in America. It seemed to me that the assertions he was making, and the measures he was recommending, ex-cathedra, were very serious to be thrown out so recklessly. It is hardly to be expected that novelists, popular magazinists, amateur economists, and politicians will be more responsible. It would be easy, however, to show what good is done by accumulations of capital in a few hands—that is, under close and direct management, permitting prompt and accurate application; also to tell what harm is done by loose and unfounded denunciations of any social component or any social group. In the recent debates on the income tax the assumption that great accumulations of wealth are socially harmful and ought to be broken down by taxation was treated as an axiom, and we had direct proof how dangerous it is to fit out the average politician with such unverified and unverifiable dogmas as his warrant for his modes of handling the direful tool of taxation.

Great figures are set out as to the magnitude of certain fortunes and the proportionate amount of the national wealth held by a fraction of the population, and eloquent exclamation-points are set against them. If the figures were beyond criticism, what would they prove? Where is the rich man who is oppressing anybody? If there was one, the newspapers would ring with it. The facts about the accumulation of wealth do not constitute a plutocracy, as I will show below. Wealth, in itself considered, is only power, like steam, or electricity, or knowledge. The question of its good or ill turns on the question how it will be used. To prove any harm in aggregations of wealth it must be shown that great wealth is, as a rule, in the ordinary course of social affairs, put to a mischievous use. This cannot be shown beyond the very slightest degree, if at all.

Therefore, all the allegations of general mischief, social corruption, wrong, and evil in our society must be referred back to those who make them for particulars and specifications. As they are offered to us we cannot allow them to stand, because we discern in them faulty observation of facts, or incorrect interpretation of facts, or a construction of facts according to some philosophy, or misunderstanding of phenomena and their relations, or incorrect inferences, or crooked deductions.

Assuming, however, that the charges against the existing "capitalistic"—that is, industrial—order of things are established, it is proposed to remedy the ill by

77

reconstructing the industrial system on the principles of democracy. Once more we must untangle the snarl of half ideas and muddled facts.

Democracy is, of course, a word of conjure with. We have a democratic-republican political system, and we like it so well that we are prone to take any new step which can be recommended as "democratic" or which will round some "principle" of democracy to a fuller fulfillment. Everything connected with this domain of political thought is crusted over with false historical traditions, cheap philosophy, and undefined terms, but it is useless to try to criticize it. The whole drift of the world for five hundred years has been toward democracy. That drift, produced by great discoveries and inventions, and by the discovery of a new continent, has raised the middle class out of the servile class. In alliance with the crown they crushed the feudal classes. They made the crown absolute in order to do it. Then they turned against the crown and, with the aid of the handicraftsmen and peasants, conquered it. Now the next conflict which must inevitably come is that between the middle capitalist class and the proletariat, as the word has come to be used. If a certain construction is put on this conflict, it may be called that between democracy and plutocracy, for it seems that industrialism must be developed into plutocracy by the conflict itself. That is the conflict which stands before civilized society to-day. All the signs of the times indicate its commencement, and it is big with fate to mankind and to civilization.

Although we cannot criticize democracy profitably, it may be said of it, with reference to our present subject, that up to this time democracy never has done anything, either in politics, social affairs, or industry, to prove its power to bless mankind. If we confine our attention to the United States, there are three difficulties with regard to its alleged achievements, and they all have the most serious bearing on the proposed democratization of industry.

1. The time during which democracy has been tried in the United States is too short to warrant any inferences. A century or two is a very short time in the life of political institutions, and if the circumstances change rapidly during the period the experiment is vitiated.

2. The greatest question of all about American democracy is whether it is a cause or a consequence. It is popularly assumed to be a cause, and we ascribe to its beneficent action all the political vitality, all the easiness of social relations, all the industrial activity and enterprise which we experience and which we value and enjoy. I submit, however, that, on a more thorough examination of the matter, we shall find that democracy is a consequence. There are economic and sociological causes for our political vitality and vigor, for the ease and elasticity of our social relations, and for our industrial power and success. Those causes have also produced democracy, given it success, and have made its faults and errors innocuous. Indeed, in any true philosophy, it must be held that in the economic forces which control the material prosperity of a population lie the real causes of its political institutions, its social class-adjustments, its industrial prosperity, its moral code, and its world-philosophy. If democracy and the industrial system are both products of the economic conditions which exist, it is plainly absurd to set democracy to defeat those conditions in the control of industry. If, however, it is

not true that democracy is a consequence, and I am well aware that very few people believe it, then we must go back to the view that democracy is a cause. That being so, it is difficult to see how democracy, which has had a clear field here in America, is not responsible for the ills which Mr. Bellamy and his comrades in opinion see in our present social state, and it is difficult to see the grounds of asking us to intrust it also with industry. The first and chief proof of success of political measures and systems is that, under them, society advances in health and vigor and that industry develops without causing social disease. If this has not been the case in America, American democracy has not succeeded. Neither is it easy to see how the masses, if they have undertaken to rule, can escape the responsibilities of ruling, especially so far as the consequences affect themselves. If, then, they have brought all this distress upon themselves under the present system, what becomes of the argument for extending the system to a direct and complete control of industry?

3. It is by no means certain that democracy in the United States has not, up to this time, been living on a capital inherited from aristocracy and industrialism. We have no pure democracy. Our democracy is limited at every turn by institutions which were developed in England in connection with industrialism and aristocracy, and these institutions are of the essence of our system. While our people are passionately democratic in temper and will not tolerate a doctrine that one man is not as good as another, they have common sense enough to know that he is not; and it seems that they love and cling to the conservative institutions quite as strongly as they do to the democratic philosophy. They are, therefore, ruled by men who talk philosophy and govern by the institutions. Now it is open to Mr. Bellamy to say that the reason why democracy in America seems to be open to the charge made in the last paragraph, of responsibility for all the ill which he now finds in our society, is because it has been infected with industrialism (capitalism); but in that case he must widen the scope of his proposition and undertake to purify democracy before turning industry over to it. The socialists generally seem to think that they make their undertakings easier when they widen their scope, and make them easiest when they propose to remake everything; but in truth social tasks increase in difficulty in an enormous ratio as they are widened in scope.

The question, therefore, arises, if it is proposed to reorganize the social system on the principles of American democracy, whether the institutions of industrialism are to be retained. If so, all the virus of capitalism will be retained. It is forgotten, in many schemes of social reformation in which it is proposed to mix what we like with what we do not like, in order to extirpate the latter, that each must undergo a reaction from the other, and that what we like may be extirpated by what we do not like. We may find that instead of democratizing capitalism we have capitalized democracy—that is, have brought in plutocracy. Plutocracy is a political system in which the ruling force is wealth. The denunciation of capital which we hear from all the reformers is the most eloquent proof that the greatest power in the world to-day is capital. They know that it is, and confess it most when they deny it most strenuously. At present the power of capital is social and industrial, and only in a small degree political. So far as capital is political, it is on account of political abuses, such as tariffs and special legislation on the one hand and legislative strikes on the other. These conditions exist in the democracy to which it is proposed to transfer the industries. What does that mean except bringing all the power of capital once for all into the political arena and precipitating the conflict of democracy and plutocracy at once? Can anyone imagine that the masterfulness, the overbearing disposition, the greed of gain, and the ruthlessness in methods, which are the faults of the master of industry at his worst, would cease when he was a functionary of the State, which had relieved him of risk and endowed him with authority? Can anyone imagine that politicians would no longer be corruptly fond of money, intriguing, and crafty when they were charged, not only with patronage and government contracts, but also with factories, stores, ships, and railroads? Could we expect anything except that, when the politician and the master of industry were joined in one, we should have the vices of both unchecked by the restraints of either? In any socialistic state there will be one set of positions which will offer chances of wealth beyond the wildest dreams of avarice; *viz.*, on the governing committees. Then there will be rich men whose wealth will indeed be a menace to social interests, and instead of industrial peace there will be such war as no one has dreamed of yet: the war between the political ins and outs—that is, between those who are on the committee and those who want to get on it.

We must not drop the subject of democracy without one word more. The Greeks already had occasion to notice a most serious distinction between two principles of democracy which lie at its roots. Plutarch says that Solon got the archonship in part by promising equality, which some understood of esteem and dignity, others of measure and number. There is one democratic principle which means that each man should be esteemed for his merit and worth, for just what he is, without regard to birth, wealth, rank, or other adventitious circumstances. The other principle is that each one of us ought to be equal to all the others in what he gets and enjoys. The first principle is only partially realizable, but, so far as it goes, it is elevating and socially progressive and profitable. The second is not capable of an intelligible statement. The first is a principle of industrialism. It proceeds from and is intelligible only in a society built on the industrial virtues, free endeavor, security of property, and repression of the baser vices; that is, in a society whose industrial system is built on labor and exchange. The other is only a rule of division for robbers who have to divide plunder or monks who have to divide gifts. If, therefore, we want to democratize industry in the sense of the first principle, we need only perfect what we have now, especially on its political side. If we try to democratize it in the sense of the other principle, we corrupt politics at one stroke; we enter upon an industrial enterprise which will waste capital and bring us all to poverty, and we set loose greed and envy as ruling social passions.

If this poor old world is as bad as they say, one more reflection may check the zeal of the headlong reformer. It is at any rate a tough old world. It has taken its trend and curvature and all its twists and tangles from a long course of formation. All its wry and crooked gnarls and knobs are therefore stiff and stubborn. If we puny men by our arts can do anything at all to straighten them, it will only be by modifying the tendencies of some of the forces at work, so that, after a sufficient time, their action may be changed a little and slowly the lines of movement may be modified. This effort, however, can at most be only slight, and it will take a long time. In the meantime spontaneous forces will be at work, compared with which our efforts are like those of a man trying to deflect a river, and these forces will have changed the whole problem before our interferences have time to make themselves felt. The great stream of time and earthly things will sweep on just the same in spite of us. It bears with it now all the errors and follies of the past, the wreckage of all the philosophies, the fragments of all the civilizations, the wisdom of all the abandoned ethical systems, the debris of all the institutions, and the penalties of all the mistakes. It is only in imagination that we stand by and look at and criticize it and plan to change it. Everyone of us is a child of his age and cannot get out of it. He is in the stream and is swept along with it. All his sciences and philosophy come to him out of it. Therefore the tide will not be changed by us. It will swallow up both us and our experiments. It will absorb the efforts at change and take them into itself as new but trivial components, and the great movement of tradition and work will go on unchanged by our fads and schemes. The things which will change it are the great discoveries and inventions, the new reactions inside the social organism, and the changes in the earth itself on account of changes in the cosmical forces. These causes will make of it just what, in fidelity to them, it ought to be. The men will be carried along with it and be made by it. The utmost they can do by their cleverness will be to note and record their course as they are carried along, which is what we do now, and is that which leads us to the vain fancy that we can make or guide the movement. That is why it is the greatest folly of which a man can be capable, to sit down with a slate and pencil to plan out a new social world.

## PART SEVEN

# The Thrust of Progress, 1890–1912

Describing the ferment of reform in the first decade of the twentieth century, Theodore Roosevelt found "a condition of excitement and irritation in the public mind." In the twenty-two years between 1890 and 1912, many Americans began to question the political and social justice of their society. The sources for this era of reform were varied, and their origins were old; but in the scope and variety of evils attacked, the era was unprecedented, provoked by a restless urge to re-examine the nature of the American dream.

Economic distress caused some of the excitement. American farmers were learning that hard work and technical success were not enough. Despite their immense acreages of wheat, corn, and cotton, despite the growing market for their cattle and grain in the huge cities of the Eastern seaboard and across the ocean in Europe, farm prices had not kept pace with the wants and needs of American farmers. Angered by the rising costs of transportation, dismayed by the obvious contrasts between their own living styles and those of the rising businessmen and professionals, many farmers turned to political action. The targets of their denunciations varied, but in the early 1890s many farmers hoped that government manipulation of currency, principally increasing the monetization of silver, would solve their problems. The formation of the Populist Party represented the peak of agrarian political action, and even though it was unsuccessful, the bitterness and despair that its rhetoric recorded aroused other Americans to reconsider inequities in the nation's economic life.

Farmers were not alone in searching for radical methods to re-establish their position. Rapid industrialization had concentrated thousands of ill-paid and resentful workers in the great new factories and coal mines which were powering America's enormous growth. Industrialists were frequently ignorant of or unsympathetic toward their employees' problems. When strikers sought to gain reduced hours or higher wages through collective action, magnates turned to the police powers of the state to protect their private interests, or else relied on armies of mercenaries to force labor into a more compromising mood. The 1880s and 1890s witnessed a series of savage strikes in the United States, which destroyed unions without producing an alternative way of solving the basic conflicts dividing management and labor. Many Americans brooded about the consequences of a clash they saw as inevitable and bloody. Under the spur of larger profits, firms began to combine and multiply in size, until their working forces were enormous. The huge and increasingly impersonal corporations were an object of fear, not only to workers, but to consumers and small businessmen who worried that in the race toward bigness older freedoms and opportunities that had been regarded as distinctively American were being lost.

The perils of size were nowhere more apparent than in the enormous new cities created by migration from the farms and from Europe. In the city the contrasts of civilized life were shockingly exposed. Journalists, economists, social workers, and clergymen returned from voyages of exploration to the slums and sweatshops with a sense of horror and outrage. Technological inventions like the automobile and electric traction, bridge-building and subway construction, structural steel skyscrapers and high-speed elevators, were helping to meet the city's most elementary problems of communication and transport, but the social disasters of inadequate housing, delinquency, epidemic disease, prostitution, and family desertion seemed larger than ever before. Groups of clergymen sought to return their churches to a role in the life of the masses by becoming involved in causes for social justice, and expanding their religious activities to include entertainment, recreation, and socializing. Members of Protestant sects, uneasy and sometimes afraid of the alien religious heritage that urban immigrants carried with them from the Old World, launched aggressive revival campaigns to convert the new Americans to their faith and social values.

The city was also discovered by lay reformers, disturbed by the breakdown of community institutions and anxious to provide surrogates for them. The settlement-house movement was probably the most memorable of these efforts to restore some sense of order and belonging to the fragmented and fast-moving life of the great cities. Immigrant families, caught between nostalgia for older ways and a desire to adjust rapidly to new demands, coped painfully with the novel independence of their children. Settlements offered club life and music, art classes and dances, remedial instruction and sports to ease the entrance of these youngsters into an alien world, and to restore some unity and purpose to the disrupted living patterns of their parents. Older ethnic traditions, church life and village associations, native theater and foreign language newspapers added vitality to urban culture, while they also gave some structure to the daily lives of former peasants and village artisans.

The wealthy were also seeking structure for their lives, and ways of expressing their newly won fortunes and prestige. Private schools, country clubs, opera houses, and museums testified to their desire for isolation from the masses, on the one hand, and their interest in display, on the other. The high arts of music, drama, painting, and sculpture were patronized by rich Americans with industry and often with taste, but their pretensions and ignorance frequently called down the contempt and anger of working people, whose own culture and values they ignored. The resulting lack of communication would be bridged, to a slight extent, by the appearance of the infant motion-picture industry, but in these years social reformers worried about the melodrama and cheap violence of popular entertainments and sought ways of countering them in community-sponsored recreation programs.

Immigrants and aristocrats were not the only groups divided by cultural preferences. In these years the first massive migrations northward by Southern Negroes brought new groups to American cities. Increasingly severe segregation laws and practical disenfranchisement in the South posed a dilemma for Negro leadership. Followers of Booker T. Washington's gradualist program, which emphasized the acquisition of occupational skills, clashed with more determined radicals led by W. E. B. DuBois, who advocated more militancy and aggressiveness in demanding political equality. Despite its gravity, however, the problem of integrating American Negroes into the life of the country did not receive the sustained attention of many reformers, whose energy was focused instead on relieving the problems of the cities, and stating the objections of the middle classes to the curse of bigness.

Many of these reform leaders, coming out of educated, reasonably comfortable Protestant backgrounds, were aroused by the spectacle of corrupt municipal governments and underhanded business practices; both seemed to produce wasteful and constraining results, increasing the costs that taxpayers and consumers were forced to pay, without increasing the services and benefits they received. Urban journalists like Lincoln Steffens, magazine contributors like Ida Tarbell and David Graham Phillips, earned for themselves the sobriquet of "muckrakers" for their delight in exposing the grimy and suspect aspects of business and government; but the man who gave them that title, Theodore Roosevelt, became himself a hero to reformers of this generation, a gifted publicist who brought to the White House a sense of drama and excitement that had been missing for forty years. Roosevelt's friends and appointees helped bring a new sense of purpose to the activities of the federal government, so long dwarfed by the giant operations of big business. Under the prodding of progressives the first efforts were made to bring social security to millions of laborers, through experimental workmen's compensation programs, new minimum wage and maximum hour laws, and renewed attacks on the attempts of large corporations to fix prices and restrain trade for their own profit. Roosevelt's efforts in the field of conservation were particularly attractive to the middle-class activists who supported him; humanitarianism combined with efficiency in stimulating them to political involvement, and programs that promised to conserve more effectively the nation's resources, even while they curbed the rapacious practices of private industry, were sure to win their applause.

Roosevelt's reform commitments were not total or radical. His nostalgia was for older value systems, not for the small-scale individualistic America of the midnineteenth century. He accepted the responsibility of size, in foreign as well as domestic relations, and was an active supporter of a more aggressive diplomacy, particularly since the Spanish-American War, in which he participated, had brought a sense of imperial destiny to millions of Americans. The issue of annexing territories was bitterly debated, with participants acting from a variety of motives. Anti-imperialists feared not only the regimenting effects of overseas expansion but they brooded also about the social dangers of amalgamating alien racial groups. Already the millions of immigrants from eastern and central Europe were deemed a menace to older values by conservative leaders, who argued that if the policy of unlimited immigration were continued, Americans would be committing race suicide. Though their efforts were still unsuccessful by 1912, they had scored impressive gains and had attracted wide support. Doctrines of eugenic improvement and racial inferiority illustrated the paradoxes that seemingly scientific research could bring along with it.

But the ugly side of foreign expansion and American self-confidence was counterbalanced by the undeniable energy and originality of the Progressive Idea. Lawyers, professors, journalists, and clergymen were joining together to find new ways of purging government of its political insensitivities and bringing to the dependent and the deprived at least a taste of the promise of American life. Political experiments like the primary, the initiative, and the referendum sought to restore a sense of contact and meaning to the individual's relationship with government. Governors, mayors, and Congressmen dramatized efforts to revise old municipal codes, to discover more equitable methods of taxation, to beautify an increasingly ugly physical environment, to use the resources of government to inspect and standardize foods and drugs, to improve the vitality of public-school systems and toy with expanding the curricula, to control the vast transportation and communications networks whose franchises were often bought with bribery and extortion, and to extend the protection of the state to women and children victimized by the demands of the industrial system. Many of these efforts left basic problems untouched and were far from solving the misery of millions of toiling farmers and workers; but they had indicated the possibilities of collective action and introduced a new generation to the excitement of political reform.

Above all, the urge for improvement that dominated the politics and social life of the first decade of the century led many Americans to reconsider the purposes of their national life, to examine the costs that growth carried with it. Old ideas of mission and special purpose, which had characterized the American experiment in previous centuries, were expressed now in a new language, suited to the complexities of the twentieth century. In rhetoric that was both flamboyant and inspiring, political leaders sought to reassure their troubled countrymen that the possibilities of power were good as well as dangerous and that the people could again become their own masters. Artists and writers, as well as politicians, were discovering new patterns of beauty and new possibilities of order in the vast commercial and technological monuments being erected across the nation. This sense of optimism and energy was no substitute for answers to the problems and frequently was marred by nostalgia and moral narrowness. Nonetheless the thrust of progress had finally brought with it a self-consciousness and insight that was indispensable for future national development. Material growth alone was no longer sufficient to guarantee the country's safety, and, by expressing their hopes as well as fears, Progressive leaders articulated modern versions of an older dream of dignity.

# 52

## Social Division

The great strikes of the last third of the nineteenth century were frightening in their violence and bitterness. Every decade seemed to have its own crisis. There were the railroad strikes of 1877, the Haymarket Massacre of 1886, and in 1892 the battle between three hundred imported Pinkerton detectives in Homestead, Pennsylvania, and striking steelworkers. When state police finally succeeded in restoring order, the strike was broken and the union destroyed.

By the 1890s reactions to these strikes took more complex forms than they had earlier. There were some who panicked and condemned totally the aggressiveness of the laboring force. But others, more sympathetic to the demands of the workers, brooded about a society that permitted private armies in the name of individualism and free enterprise. It seemed a devolution back hundreds of years, with the state as a powerless umpire, helpless to regulate basic needs. *The Forum* was one of the journals of the decade that aired these doubts and helped prepare Americans for those new conceptions of state power that would mark the reforms of the Progressive Era.

### THE LESSON OF HOMESTEAD:
### A REMEDY FOR LABOR TROUBLES
#### *Chauncey F. Black*

The disturbance occasioned by the differences between the Carnegie companies and the large bodies of organized workingmen employed by them has extended to the whole country. It has been felt not merely in the derangement of dependent industries and of business in general, but as a menace of the common peace. A great Commonwealth has had its entire available military force on duty at large expense to the men and the State, for a long period, and at every passing moment the general Government has been liable to be called upon, as it actually was in a similar but less stubborn affair in Idaho. It, with some of its specially dramatic and significant incidents, such as the strange battle between the private armed forces of the respective parties, the attempted assassination of the chairman of the Carnegie companies, and the unusual punishment of a private soldier for the utterance of a

From "The Lesson of Homestead: A Remedy for Labor Troubles," *The Forum*, XIV (September, 1892), 14–25.

mere sentiment, unaccompanied by any act, has attracted the most profound and anxious attention of the entire civilized world. Occurring, as it did, in this well-ordered Republic, regulated by law, in a land where the people themselves are supposed to be sovereign and to possess the power to right their own wrongs, it is necessarily accepted as a sign or symptom of a fatal vice in our system of government, or in the laws relating to such matters, which promises even wider disaster unless a remedy shall be found.

The question raised by the bloody encounter between the organized workingmen and the embodied Pinkertons on the Monongahela is one which cannot be put aside until there shall be found a satisfactory answer to it. It is but a single incident of a long and terrible warfare, whose persistent barbarity is the darkest reproach of the otherwise peaceful age in which we live. For the settlement of all ordinary private disputes, legal and effectual methods are duly provided. Murder, arson, pillage, and rapine in all other shapes are repressed and punished without any draft upon the reserved forces of the State and without a general disturbance of peaceful communities. Even war is prevented by a gradually crystallizing system of arbitration, which, sustained by enlightened public opinon the world over, has acquired almost the authority of public law. Here, only, in the controversies between large employers and great masses of workingmen, in those controversies which in the last quarter of a century have reddened the streets of every great European city with blood, and which have shamed this country in many instances, the state stands practically aloof, permitting each separate difference to degenerate, it may be, into a cruel and unequal combat between the capitalist and the workingman, until the moment arrives to crush the latter down in his tracks, to take away his arms, to evict him from his home, and to set his family in the road, in the name of law and order!

Let us look more particularly at the case at Homestead. There was little or no reason to anticipate such an outbreak at the time it took place. The intelligence of organized labor, realizing the futility of strikes, discouraged them; and the intelligence of the capitalist class, summing up the inevitable losses of such conflicts and finding a certain degree of security in dealing with the responsible officials of associated labor, was apparently more inclined to justice and moderation. It seemed as if the time was approaching when the antagonists in struggles of this nature would find a way to prevent them, out of mere respect for the colossal power of one another. The Missouri-Pacific strike, the New York Central strike, even the portentous riots of 1877, when we narrowly escaped universal collision between the forces of organized society and the aggrieved classes, had been forgotten, and we were drifting calmly along, complacently estimating the increase of our National wealth, counting the deposits in the banks, pointing to the "poor boys" who were becoming millionaires by the hundreds as the best evidence of our wonderful prosperity, felicitating ourselves upon the prospect of another good crop and the possibility of a small percentage of the mortgages being paid, when the red sky above Homestead, in the very heart of this hollow prosperity, where the "poor boys" were rolling up, more rapidly than anywhere else, the millions afforded them by tariff bounties, summoned us to look not merely upon a local scene of blood and misery, present and anticipated, but to go to the bottom of our paternal industrial system, to consider the cause of the man whose brawny hands were on the machines turning out the vast product of which we were so proud, and to determine whether or not he also was worthy of the protection of the law.

Has the workman made this situation at Homestead in pure wantonness? Has he imperilled the livelihood of wife and child for any light or trivial reason? Had he any legal recourse for the settlement of what he deemed his wrongs? What had he, then, done which put him beyond the pale of law when his request for reasonable concession in wages was refused; when he was shut out; when he was told that he must abandon the right of association, which he held most sacred, and which alone in all the controversies of the past had secured him any consideration, and must thereby disarm himself of all power of self-protection if he would keep his home and work at that place and in the only trade he knew? Where was he, with the thousands like him and in the same evil case, to turn for legal relief? To what tribunal was he to resort for the adjustment of his rights and the redress of his wrongs? Was there any adequate tribunal provided by the highly civilized state, which owed him peace and security as much as it owed them to the proprietors of the fortified mills, to the service of which he had adapted his life and his labor? Shall the complaints of men in his condition be met forever only with the policeman's bludgeon or the militiaman's musket?

The very spot is sanguinary. At or near Homestead Braddock crossed to slaughter in the tangled thickets where the Edgar Thompson steel works stand to-day. The latter place, in full view of Homestead, was the rendezvous of the so-called "Whiskey Insurgents" army; and it was here, all along the banks of this romantic river, that Alexander Hamilton's brutal expedient of "terror" as a principal means of "strong government" was put in practice, and bands of military marauders were sent out at midnight to raid the peaceful farmsteads, to kidnap unoffending citizens amid the shrieks of their families, and hale them, with blows and sabre-cuts, before a lawless mixed commission. Both Homestead and Braddock's were lighted up by the fierce glare of the fires kindled by the riots of '77, and heard the musketry which did the slaughter of that day. And now again it became the scene of a conflict more portentous than any of them.

Homestead is but one of the great establishments of the Carnegie companies. Opposite is Braddock's, to which must be added Duquesne, Beaver Falls, and others. With the business of the steel companies has recently been incorporated Mr. Frick's more or less complete monopoly of coke-production in the bituminous-coal regions near by; and that gentleman has become the omnipotent single manager of the whole, employing from thirteen thousand to twenty thousand men. The original plant has grown to unprecedented proportions, until the fortunes of the proprietors, united with the fortunes of a few others like themselves, actually constitute a menace to the free institutions of the country, contributing as they do fabulous sums for election purposes in order to keep in power a party which shapes public policies in their interests as against the interests of all other classes. Nobody disputes their title to this wealth or their right to use it as they see fit, within the limits of the general public safety. It is certain, however, that the greater part of it is but the tribute which iniquitous tariff laws have enabled them to levy upon the domestic consumption of their product. They have, during a long period, enjoyed an enormously profitable monopoly. The State has stood over their vast accumulations and their huge operations with all its police power affording them every possible security. But neither the Union, which granted them the unconstitutional bounties, nor the Commonwealth, which gives them its peace, has imposed upon them any obligation to share with their unskilled laborers or even their operatives ever so small a proportion of the joint earnings of the capital and labor employed in the business. Accordingly when the men look out upon these vast establishments and note the swelling millions rolling into the account of the proprietors under favor of government, they feel that they have a strong moral right to an adjustment of wages which shall not be dictated entirely from the employers' side. And moral right in the common mind is very readily transmuted into legal right.

At Homestead the men were grievously discontented with certain new arrangements proposed by the company. They belonged to the "Amalgamated Association of Iron and Steel Workers," one of the most conservative of the labor organizations. The company refused to sign the scale presented by the association, but announced, instead, an arbitrary reduction of wages, on the ground that new machinery increased the earning power of the men, thus taking to itself all the advantage of invention and experience, while denying it to the other side. When the men came to remonstrate, through their usual committees and in their usual orderly manner, they were met with the ultimatum: Accept the reduction, abandon your organization, and submit yourselves in every particular to the arrangements which our interests shall suggest, and you may work in these mills, but upon no other terms whatever! There was no strike; no time was given for a strike. Going about consulting and planning with their officers and committees, seeking conferences with the company, and otherwise anxiously endeavoring to strengthen their position in the controversy, though doubtless contemplating a strike as a last resort, the gates were suddenly shut in their faces, and instead of a strike on the part of the men, there was a lock-out on the part of the company. What followed might readily have been anticipated. It is reasonable to suppose that the company did both anticipate and desire it. The doom thus pronounced upon three thousand men and their families could not fail to alarm and exasperate the victims beyond peaceable endurance. It meant practical slavery in those mills, or migration, with all that migration implies. But they did only what their fellows in the absence of just and legal methods of settlement have done elsewhere. They resisted as best they could the introduction of non-union labor into the works from which they had been locked out and which had been insultingly fortified against them in advance. It was not wonderful that non-union men, however urgent their necessities, feared to venture in, or that the sheriff of Allegheny County was unable to raise a *posse* to protect them. Not only everybody in Homestead, but almost everybody in Allegheny County sympathized with the locked-out men.

But the situation was not an especially threatening one. Many such have existed for a long time without serious injury to life or property and without other loss than that occasioned by the idleness of men and machinery. But the class of "protected gentlemen" to which Messrs. Carnegie and Frick belong appear to be, of all human beings, the most impressed with the awful sanctity of their individual right to "do as they please with their own." These gentlemen have been apparently, throughout this trouble, unable to apprehend any other principle. It seems to be not only uppermost in their minds, but to fill their minds wholly, to the exclusion of any other consideration. To all appeals for accommodation; to all remonstrance and argument; to the county of Allegheny, looking forward to an enormous bill of damages; to the Commonwealth of Pennsylvania, hurrying eight thousand soldiers from their daily avocations to protect them, at a cost of twenty-five thousand dollars a day; to the people of the United States, who gave them their monopoly and stuffed their pockets with unearned money, to the three thousand operatives at Homestead; and to the women and children whose homes are practically confiscated over their heads and who must follow their husbands and fathers into exile, they answer only that they will do as they like with their own. They will have their pound of flesh; they will take it next the heart, they will crush the "Amalgamated"; they will employ no union men; they will pocket the largest profits—but they will pay the wages that please them and entertain no question about them.

But how was this programme to be excuted? There was no disorder at the mills. The locked-out men lay quietly around them, and the barbed-wire fences and the electric batteries and the hot-water pipes were all useless. There was a dead calm over the whole place. But no non-union man would go near. The sheriff was powerless; and the public opinion of the county, of the State, and of the world was against the proposition of the private owners to use their own—as the sultan of Muscat or the king of Dahomey or an Apache Indian might use his—without the smallest regard to common humanity. In this emergency they turned to a power beyond the territory and unknown to the laws of the State.

The Pinkertons have been compared to the Hessians, but the comparison is unfair to the latter. They resemble more the free companies of the middle ages, recruited by freebooters for freebooting and their services sold to the highest bidder. The agency is a natural outgrowth of existing conditions. It, more than anything else, illustrates the barbarity of our methods, or rather our lack of methods, in such contingencies. We encourage the association of capital; we foster manufacturing monopolies with subsidies; we permit railways to discriminate in their favor; we allow them to combine in trusts; we drive masses of men, skilled and unskilled, to these centres of work; we induce them by public policy, as exhibited in discriminating laws, to adapt their lives and their labor to these favored industries—and then, when disputes arise between the capitalists engaged in semi-public enterprises and the men employed by them, we allow the fight to go on as it will until the general peace is endangered, and finally turn in the power of the State to crush the weaker. But in intermediate stages of the contest the employer must rely upon his own or hired force if he chooses to employ force. It is therefore much to his convenience and frequently to his pleasure to be able to make a draft upon a private standing army duly disciplined and weaponed and open for engagement in any quarrel, and so to make private war on his own account and in his own way. This was what was done when three hundred Pinkertons, armed with

Winchester rifles, were secretly sent up the Monongahela, but the sheriff of Allegheny was left as powerless as ever, and the calm at Homestead after the battle was deeper and more ominous than before.

The governor had held off as long as he dared. Any action whatever on his part must necessarily determine the contest, and determine it against the men. But it was a strained and painful situation. Another onset of the Pinkertons, which might be expected at any moment, would doubtless cause the loss of many lives and widen the breach instead of closing it. For how much of the blood thus shed and of the injury thus inflicted would he be accountable if he should fail to interpose in time? He seemed to have no alternative, after the formal demand of the sheriff, except to call out the troops, and, as a matter of fact, this unavoidable action of the Executive settled the particular dispute between the locked-out Homestead men and their recent employers; and thenceforward the latter could do as they would with their own. The non-union men would go in if they chose, and the armed Pinkertons would follow them if it pleased the company and the governor of Pennsylvania should permit it. The men at Homestead were helpless and hopeless. There was but one quarter to which they could look for lawful succor. Their fellows in the other Carnegie mills, numbering many thousands, might go out of their own volition, instead of being locked out, as was the case with the Homesteaders, and thus reduce the contest to a question of endurance on a larger scale, as it was at Homestead before the disastrous appearance of the Pinkertons and the fateful arrival of the troops.

The Homestead situation is liable to be reproduced at any other place in the country where multitudes of men are assembled in the conduct of large enterprises. The people of the United States and their governments, State and Federal, are in danger of being plunged into violent conflicts, not of their own making, and in which they have no interest other than the maintenance of the public peace. As to the duty of the State in regard to them, their prevention and repression, or the restraint and punishment of those who cause them, even enlightened opinions seem to differ very widely. The governor of Pennsylvania has shown by his action what he deems the duty of that State under the circumstances and in the present state of the law. He had no choice but to enforce the laws as he found them on the statute-book, and no power with which to do it, in the face of a turbulent community, less warlike than the militia. He might—I believe that he should—have preceded, or at least have accompanied, the order to the militia by a proclamation warning the discontented men to obey the letter of the law, reciting the personal consequences of further disobedience and the necessity of stern enforcement, and at the same time commanding the armed Pinkerton forces and all other armed bodies, except only the sheriff's *posse*, to disperse or to retire instantly beyond the limits of the Commonwealth, whose peace they threatened. Such a proclamation might have prevented further conflicts between the Pinkertons and the Homestead men, and it might have saved the people of the State the expense and peril of military operations. But the governor doubtless had better information, and he may have been well assured that only the actual presence of an overwhelming force would restore peace and prevent bloodshed. He could not pause to consider the merits of

93

the dispute on either side or to weigh the hardships which might ensue to one or the other.

But the duty of the State in the large sense is not limited to the suppression of mobs. It is confronted by the higher duty of preventing mobs, of depriving mobs of all decent excuse for existence, and of removing the grievances which in labor controversies are alleged as their occasion. Whether these grievances exist or not must be submitted to some other arbitrament than that of clubs and guns, hot water, electric batteries, and dynamite, in the very near future, if any peace is to be kept in the land. The steadily increasing concentration of workingmen in large numbers in mills and mines and at railway terminals has changed all previous conditions. Capital massed on one side and men massed on the other make a situation to which neither the common law nor the statute law of our foregoers is at all adequate. The principles of those laws are as applicable and as effectual to-day as ever, but they need elaboration and the support of new machinery. A dispute between an employer and eighteen thousand men—the number said to be in the service of the Carnegie companies—who with their families make sixty or seventy thousand souls, cannot be satisfactorily disposed of by ordinary judicial procedure. While executives, courts, and juries are confessedly unable or unwilling to cope with unlawful combinations of capital, how can we expect them to deal promptly, successfully, and justly with vast multitudes of aggrieved laborers, too often technically at fault? Is the spectacle of trusts and gigantic conspiracies of corporations overriding constitutions and laws unchecked and practically unop- posed calculated to encourage scrupulously legal and orderly conduct on the part of men situated as were these at Homestead? The danger and the damage to the community and ultimately to the individual citizens who are oppressed and pillaged by such combinations are infinitely greater than any to be apprehended from the disorders of which workingmen, organized or unorganized, have ever been guilty. But in the one case the State defends itself with writs and bills in equity; in the other with its rifles. Why not the writs in both or the rifles in both? Why the summary suppression here and the tender toleration there? Because the corporate offenders are powerful, often more powerful to command and to corrupt than a weakly-officered State to resist, and do not hesitate to employ special privileges to harass and plunder the very people who granted them. Ambitious politicians too frequently prefer to find a specious way to serve them rather than to oppose them; and the workingmen clearly understand the difference in the treatment of the two kinds of law-breaking and the reason of it.

Overgrown and transgressing corporations thus offending against the public, which created and protects them, should be driven back within the strictest limits of their charters, or their charters forfeited, and at the same time a new class of corporations in the interests of labor might be invited and encouraged in American States. Suppose, for instance, that the "Amalgamated Association," or, to present a smaller subdivision, the iron and steel workers of Homestead, incorporated for the purpose of furnishing labor. The men, who lately imagined themselves efficiently organized for all proper purposes, and who have been so rudely undeceived, are members of it. This corporation contracts with Mr. Frick for a given amount of work of a given character. The corporation deals with the men; Mr. Frick does not. It collects wages and in turn pays dividends. It employs and dismisses, or admits to its membership and expels. It hears and redresses grievances. Its existence manifestly renders such outbreaks as the one under consideration almost an impossibility, since the men manage their own corporation and their own business in their own way. It is a counterpart of the capitalist corporation which confronts it. It will sue and be sued; it will collect damages or pay them. It will prosper or not, as other corporations do.

Would such a thing be feasible? Of course not while our one-sided laws remain as they are, while the aggressions of a moneyed corporation are unrestrained and those of a labor association are crushed out in blood. But the State can make it feasible. It can make this labor corporation for all the purposes of its creation quite as responsible as the Carnegie companies, and it can regulate the conduct of both classes of corporations and provide methods for the settlement of disputes which would relieve the sheriff and the militia of a large part, if not the whole, of their disagreeable duties.

The first objection to this corporation is that it would have no means wherewith to answer in damages for breaches of its contracts. But it can be given means by a provision in its charter requiring that a sufficient percentage of its whole earnings shall be withheld from distribution and invested in public securities, never to be disturbed or expended except for that purpose. The second objection is that its membership would be fitful and shifting. But would it be necessarily more so than the stockholders of other corporations? The latter usually, it is true, pay in money; but the former would pay in solid labor, of which money is but a measure. Such a corporation, if managed with one-half the conservative skill and judgment that have marked the administration of the affairs of the "Amalgamated Association," could well be trusted to arrange the details of its business satisfactorily to all its components and to those with whom it might contract.

But the State has not discharged its duty by merely granting a charter to a labor corporation, with even the most careful and elaborate provisions for its safe management. It must also provide for the peaceful settlement of disputes between the aggregations of capital on the one side and the aggregations of men on the other. It must do this not only in justice to the parties immediately concerned, but in justice to itself. Provisions for arbitration, provisions for speedy litigation in default of arbitration, provisions for preserving conditions against radical changes while the legal settlement is in progress, provisions against call-outs, lock-outs, and strikes in the interim, and, above all, provisions against evictions of workmen and the introduction of armed forces—these are the outlines which the wisdom of a legislature bent upon a fair solution of the most difficult problem and the removal of the gravest danger of modern times might be expected to fill in with details that would not defeat the great object in view.

Many large employers prefer to deal with labor organizations, loose as they are, under present conditions, rather than with the individual men; and some of the associations have been of incalculable benefit in preserving agreeable and profitable relations between employers and employed. The "Amalgamated Association" has been one of these, and its management has in an unusual degree commanded the confidence of the public and of all those having business with it. The labor corporation suggested would be that perfection of organization which would best serve the rights and interests of all concerned. It would bring to the front the best character and the highest talents on the labor side, and the responsible manufacturing or mining corporation would be able to buy its labor from an equally responsible corporation having it to sell, and to carry on its business with an almost absolute certainty that the contracts between them would be faithfully and voluntarily observed, and, if not, would be readily enforced. This, with the obligation upon each not to strike or to lock out or to evict until a question properly raised and pending should be judicially determined, would probably save the public from these gigantic disturbances, which shake the whole State and therefore sternly demand the public intervention of the State for their suppression.

Is it worth trying? Is the public peace worth maintaining? Is it better that American operatives and miners and other classes of laborers too numerous to mention should go on, their hearts swelling with a bitter sense of wrong and continuously on the very verge of turbulent outbreak; or that they should have legal justice, with appropriate tribunals as wide open to them as to those whom they too frequently are compelled to regard as their conscienceless adversaries? Shall we go on forever in this brutish old way, standing off from these dangerous disputes until they degenerate into lock-outs and strikes and riots, only to interpose with the crushing power of the State when it is too late to consider the merits of any of the questions involved, and the naked and cruel letter of the deficient law must be enforced without inquiry and without mercy?

It is true that some of the greater employers, and among them those most highly "protected," deny the right of the public to regulate their business in any way whatever. They would naturally prefer to pursue unmolested the course which has so marvellously enriched them at the common expense of consumers and workingmen. They have cultivated the feudal spirit until it has become the master-passion. They will be naturally reluctant, like the barons—which in many respects they are—to yield the privilege of private warfare. They will, beyond question, prefer the Pinkertons and the soldiers to the milder and fairer methods of the proposed law. They will insist upon their alleged right to use their property precisely as they see fit and to make any contract which seems to them good. They are doubtless perfectly sincere and conscientious in this remarkable claim, and the almost ludicrous solemnity with which it is made and repeated seems to have imposed upon some minds besides their own. But it will not stand a moment's examination.

They are utterly mistaken in their first and fundamental assumption. No man in civilized society can do what he pleases with his own. He cannot do what he likes with his own skin if a public necessity requires a different disposition of it. His blood and his bones belong to his country. They are taken when his country needs them. His property, no less than his life, is held at the call of the State. But recently eight thousand men were taken bodily from their daily avocations and their comfortable homes and encamped upon the hills about Homestead, without in the least consulting their individual pleasure. Mr. Carnegie's business and the business of other men situated like him challenge public regulation by reason of their very immensity, to say nothing of the public contributions to them by the unjust operation of monopoly tariff laws. If not as clearly subject to such regulation as common carrying, they are certainly as plainly so as money-lending, education of children, poison-vending, powder-making, and hundreds of others. If the law can prohibit Mr. Carnegie from running a "pluck-me store" in connection with his business, it can prohibit him from doing anything else which is unjust and unreasonable, and especially anything which provokes or tends toward a breach of the peace. If the State chooses to say him nay and to lay down the limits of his freedom, he can have no right whatever to go on dealing with three thousand men here, and five thousand men there, and ten thousand men elsewhere, according to his private impulses. All private property is held and enjoyed subject to the public safety; and the contention that great plants like that of the Carnegie companies, built up mainly by public bounties, are exempt from the rule would be nothing short of monstrous.

To this proposed regulation, therefore, of the transactions between employers and their workingmen there could be no reasonable opposition. The State, which upon all established theories of our free institutions is supreme, can never be said to have discharged its sovereign duty until it has opened the way to peaceable and orderly settlement of such disputes and compelled all parties concerned to walk in it.

# 53

## The Omaha Convention
## of 1892

The farmer's revolt against the inequities of American life reached a political climax in the summer of 1892 when the People's Party met in Omaha to nominate a Presidential candidate. For years farmers had been complaining about the low prices of their crops, and the high prices of railroads, telephones, storaging, and servicing, which had cut their profit margins almost to a vanishing point. With the two major political parties apparently impervious to their demands, the protestors decided to organize their own vehicle, and in Omaha they nominated an old Greenbacker and Civil War veteran, James B. Weaver, as their candidate on a platform aimed at monopolies and wealthy interests. The Convention was a picturesque assemblage of men and women who felt outside the mainstream of recent American events. They sought to purify American life with an almost evangelical fervor. Some of the flavor of their rhetoric, as well as the substance of their program, is contained in the following account, published by the Populist's that same year.

### THE LIFE AND PUBLIC SERVICES
### OF JAMES BAIRD WEAVER
#### E. A. Allen

The National Convention of the People's Party convened in Omaha at 10 o'clock, Saturday, July 2d, 1892. Long before the hour of gathering the vast hall was crowded with visitors. The scene presented characteristics of a great National Convention. There was one significant difference between the gathering and the national conclaves of the Democratic and Republican Parties held a few days ago.

In the Convention the politician was conspicuously absent. Tactics and subterfuge gave place to open declarations, and all there was of politics at this Convention was on the surface and was plainly manifested in every demonstration that occasion afforded. Indeed, there was little of that competition for factional advantage that is typical of all other National Conventions. Everybody seemed to be in a congratulatory mood over the large attendance to the Convention, and there was a general determination that harmony should be preserved on all questions, and

From *The Life and Public Services of James Baird Weaver* (n.p., 1892), 53–66, 75–77, 96–101.

that the most available man should be selected to lead the fight in the coming campaign.

Even in the Convention, the People's Party would seem anxious to preserve an individuality and to set at defiance an example of two great Parties whose National Conventions have been held.

By 11 o'clock the part of the hall allotted to delegates was fairly well filled, most of the delegates being present, but in much confusion.

The general remark was that it was a fine looking body of men. Strong and striking physiognomies were present. Cranks and odd creatures, however, were occasionally seen. Before the Convention was called to order straw hats predominated. Compared with the Minneapolis and Chicago Conventions the Omaha Convention was not so well dressed, though it appeared by no means poverty stricken.

The extensive preparations made by the Democrats at the Wigwam at Chicago, and by the Republicans at Minneapolis, are noted by their absence at the Coliseum at Omaha. Nevertheless, the building presented a gay and inviting appearance, as the delegates began to assemble, and as the hour for the meeting approached an exhibition of enthusiasm was added to this sprightliness, which could not be exceeded if the hall would contain 100,000 instead of one-tenth that number.

The circular building had been arranged in terraces, with a number of outlets, which prevented anything approaching confusion. Flags and banners floated from every pillar and arch, and the display of evergreens is something in the nature of triumphal arches, not the less inviting because of their scarcity, adding a degree of freshness to the scene. The delegates were slow in arriving. The press were first to enter, and delegation after delegation followed, and the hall became full of industrial leaders in straw hats and breezy attire, in keeping with the day.

There was a slight lull as Chairman Taubeneck, of the National Committee, announced that the first National Convention of the People's Party was now convened in regular session. Then followed a burst of applause. Prayer was offered by Rev. Diffenbacher, a well known Alliance man. Mayor Bemis, of Omaha, heartily welcomed the delegates, and then Ben Terrell, of Texas, was introduced as "the hero of the Alliance movement from its earliest day."

Prolonged cheers greeted Mr. Terrell's appearance. Mr. Terrell paid a graceful tribute to Omaha's Mayor and continued: "This Convention is indeed a protest against present conditions. It is utterly impossible to stay the movement. If every leader of this movement, I care not who he is, be he Powderly (cheers) or Weaver, that we trust above all men as a patriotic man, or whoever you may name—if they were to-day to put themselves in opposition the movement would sweep over them and their names be forgotten. (Applause.)

"Never before in this country has such a Convention been assembled. I believe there is no man here seeking position. I have never before attended a Convention where every man desired success to everything and was perfectly willing to lay down personal ambition to secure it.

"As to the South, I want to say it is imbued with the same spirit you are. (Cheers.) The South will vote for the man who stands on the St. Louis platform, be he who he may, and the man from the South who does not share this spirit had better leave the hall." (Cheers.) The speaker then declared that the People's Party had ended sectionalism, and for that alone was entitled to the gratitude of the people.

C. H. Ellington, of Georgia, was introduced as temporary Chairman, and in his speech of acceptance he said: "Ladies and gentlemen, fellow-countrymen and brethren—I salute you. From far-off Georgia, the great Empire State of the South, I come to greet you. Language fails me. It is impossible to tell my high appreciation of the honor this greatest of Conventions has conferred upon me by electing me to the Temporary Chairmanship. But when my mind turns to the great purpose for which we have met—its mighty depth, length, breadth, its wonderful conception, all that is wrapped up in what it means to us to be defeated and what it would mean should victory crown our efforts—all these things crowd upon me, and I long for the tongue of Gabriel, whose trumpet tones shall reach to the farthest end of the globe, rousing and convening the people wherever its sound shall fall upon them.

"In all the history of this country, the land of the free, the home of the brave, there has never been another such gathering of people. (Applause.) North, South, East or West are to-day mingling their hosts together in a sense and for a purpose never before realized in this country. (Applause.) When, in the early days of this new country, our forefathers fought for their liberty and won, it was with a different foe and by use of different means. The battlefield which settled the fight was a long, bloody one. Again, when we fought in the late rivalry, though between brother and brother, between those who were bone of the same bone and flesh of the same flesh, the fight was a bloody one, and now, for the first time, the classes in these United States are marching and marshaling their armies for the greatest struggle the world ever saw. (Cheers.) A mortal combat is on, and the ballot will be the weapon of war. (Cheers.)

"The eyes of the world are upon us. Some are looking at us with hate and fear in their hearts, while others are watching us prayerfully, anxiously and hopefully. Nothing would give more joy to our opponents than to see this vast assemblage disagree. They want us to bicker and wrangle. Hundreds of pens stand ready to note the first word of discord, and in every direction the wires are waiting to transmit the hoped-for news. Brethren, friends, let us disappoint them and from the very beginning shake hands upon this one point that harmony, unity and good will shall prevail. (Cheers.) Let us lay aside all selfish individual feeling, all personal ambition that may by any possibility tend to disharmonize, and coming together in the spirit of pure fractional feeling, determined that the dominant principle shall be patriotism, pure and simple, and the desire for the general and permanent prosperity of the people. (Cheers.) I believe it is possible for this representative body to meet, counsel, perform its work and adjourn without one single word of discord, one atom of hateful strife to mar and deface its glorious record. To this end I am absolutely, untiringly at your service. We have reached the crisis in our history, and this meeting will show, whether or not we measure up the responsibilities of the hour.

"The subscribers here desire to tender you our utmost thanks. Nothing would please us better than to meet with you, that we might clasp hands and exchange with you words of encouragement as the co-workers in the great struggle now going on between the people and those who live and fatten through class laws and the violation of the law. But, however pleasant it might be for us to meet and enjoy a general hand-shaking, yet in our opinion those of us who are not delegates should remain here to watch the work which the people have given us to do.

"The two Wall Street Parties have held their Conventions. They have nominated their canditates and are marshalling their hosts. One side is engaged in 'putting the rascals out,' the other in 'keeping them in.' They have no aims or objects but the spoils of office, while the people are sinking from affluence to penury, and laborers in the cities, factories, shops and mines are dying of starvation and by Pinkerton bullets. It is the mission of our new party, then, to restore to the people their God-given rights and the scepter of the Government; to restore the people their lands and their confiscated highways, and to wrest from corporations and money kings the control of the people's money and all the other appliances of commerce and of our Christian civilization. We have full faith in your united wisdom. We believe you will select for our great party of the people standard-bearers who are worthy of the times and the occasion, and you will arrange the necessary details for a vigorous and successful campaign. The times are auspicious. Men are everywhere surrendering their party predjudices and trampling under foot old party lines. They are crying out on all sides—North, South, East and West—'What must we do to be saved.' Let us on with the work so nobly begun by our patriotic fathers, that the Government of the people, by the people, and for the people shall not perish from the earth.

"Accept, gentlemen, our fraternal regards, and may the great Ruler of Nations guide your councils."

*W. A. Peffer, U. S. Senate*

Ignatius Donnelly, of Minnesota, was introduced, pending the Committee's report, and spoke at length on the issues of the People's party:

"I do not mean," said Mr. Donnelly, "to indulge in any words of idle compliments—for the dignity of the occasion forbids it—when I say that no greater body of men has ever assembled upon this continent than those who sit here to-day, since those men met who formulated the immortal Declaration of Independence.

"It is in many respects the most astonishing gathering this country has ever seen—a Convention without a single tool or instrument of monopoly in its midst; a Convention whose every man has paid the expenses of his journey thither and his return, or which have been paid by a man as poor as himself. (Cheers.)

"There is not in this gathering a single President of a railroad (cheers); there is not a single representative of an army or rings which are robbing and sucking the life blood out of the American people. (Cheers.)

"I can not help but think of the astounding contrast this body presents to the Conventions which have recently met in Minneapolis and Chicago. One little point emphasizes the difference, and should be sufficient in itself to show the American people who are its friends.

"There are in this Convention delegates from the distant State of California,

101

and they could not obtain the same railroad concessions that are granted to the National Conventions. They are here at a cost, as I am informed, of $150 to each of them. I am told that there are delegates here from Wyoming who traveled 300 miles in farm-wagons to reach the nearest depot where they could take the train for Omaha. (Cries of "Hurrah for Wyoming.")

"One hundred and sixteen years of national life under the management of two great parties has given us, according to the different estimates, from 8,000 to 30,000 millionaires, and 1,500,000 tramps, while the whole land is blistered with mortgages and the whole people are steeped to the lips in poverty. My friends, every great fight that was ever made in the past for right and liberty culminates in this present gathering. Every battlefield of the past fought to make men more free, more happy and more prosperous, has shed the fruits of victory upon this great assemblage. (Cheers.) What a contrast to that Minneapolis Convention. The leading man of that body, the man most petted, and dined and wined, was Chauncey M. Depew, twenty times a millionaire, President of two railroad companies and representative of the Vanderbilt's $200,000,000. Why he could not sneeze but the Republican papers had pictures of him in every point of the process. (Laughter and cheers.) I had a debate the other day in Minnesota, with a representative speaker of the Republican party, and I challenged him to point to a man in the great Convention who could be mentioned in one breath with the great philanthropist and humanitarian who founded the Republican party. Where is your Horace Greeley, your Charles Sumner, your Wendell Phillips, your Abraham Lincoln? I asked him to point me out a single friend of labor in the Convention, a single friend of the farmer, a single friend of the mechanic; what was the answer? I was given as an example of the philanthropist, Fred Douglass. (Cheers.) 'Why,' I replied, 'you have to go out of your own color to find an example.' (Cheers.)

"And when I asked for another name, I was given the name of William McKinley, Jr., (laughter) a man who put up the tariff for the benefit of the protectionist manufacturers to increase burdens of the people. That is Republican philanthropy. It would be a miracle if the American people had not by this time appreciated Bill McKinley's philanthropy. I want it understood that I am not saying anything against the rank and fame of either of these parties. (Cries of "Good.") The whole American people have been in one or the other of these parties, and as the American people are, in my judgment, the best and noblest people on the face of the earth, it would not become me to accuse either of them, but the leaders, the politics and the Conventions of these parties, are legitimate subjects for comment. They point in the direction of this terrible power of pleutocracy that has got the whole country by the throat."

In conclusion Mr. Donnelly said: "I am willing that the Southern delegates to this Convention should meet and agree upon a candidate for President, and I will pledge for the man so nominated the unanimous support of Minnesota; I can promise you the solid Electoral vote of Minnesota for the People's Party. I believe that I can promise that Nebraska will go the same way, and North and South Carolina and Georgia. I know that we can count on Kansas. I tell you, there is no such word as fail, so far as this movement is concerned."

It was the desire of the People's Party delegates to set an example for sobriety and the observance of the Sabbath Day for the other political parties. The necessity for such a course may be better understood by reading the following, taken from a prominent Chicago paper:

"The Democrats do not mean to be outdone by the Republicans. The drunkenness and debauchery that characterized the Minneapolis Convention have been equaled, if not surpassed, by the Democrats in session in Chicago. With the first arrival of delegations and boomers the carnival of drink began. Saturday night squads of drunken men could be seen reeling from saloon to saloon. Sunday matters got worse. Sunday night a mob of yelling, half-drunken men crowded the lobby of the Palmer House, and in nearly every saloon within a mile of the center of the city crowds of men could be found drinking, fighting, cursing, and shouting for Cleveland, Hill, Boies, Gorman, or some other candidate. The dens of the 'levee' were crowded with men wearing badges indicating their choice for President. A little after midnight Sunday the Calumet Club, of Maryland, arrived, and, headed by a brass band, marched up to the Tremont House. Five minutes after breaking ranks they lined up four deep before the long bar of the Tremont House, waiting for drinks. The bar rooms and saloons had made great preparations. Chicago's capacity in a saloon line is very large under ordinary circumstances. There are hundreds of dens and gin shops within a radius of a mile of the court-house. On Sunday night they all did a tremendous business. Their capacity was taxed to its utmost. Monday night was even worse. More delegates and boomers had arrived. The crowds were large. Vice and drunkenness did not abate in the least, but grew visible. At midnight carriages were rolling down the streets, filled with drunken, shouting men. The yells of intoxicated men resounded through the streets and pandemonium broke loose. Down on the dark avenues, where vice reigns supreme, was a terrible scene. The streets were filled with carriages carrying enthusiastic delegates from place to place. Wine, beer, and whisky flowed like water, and the shouts of the revelers could be heard on every side. Crowds of men filed out of one gilded gin-shop and den only to enter another a few doors away. The scenes that were enacted were too disgraceful to print.

"Not until the gray light of morning appeared did the shouts of the revelers die away. One by one, overcome by liquor and tired out with the night's debauch, they fell into a drunken sleep. The saloon-keepers and den-owners counted over the harvest they had reaped, safely stowed away their ill-gotten gains, and congratulated themselves on the character of the representatives of the great political party that had gathered in this city.

"These men were to assemble a few hours later to help select the candidates of one of the large parties for the highest offices in our nation. They were to frame a platform of principles to guide the legislation of the United States. They were preparing for this task in a manner which should strike terror to the hearts of the patriotic, sober manhood of this country. And their preparation for this important service was a drunken debauch! Is it possible that Christian men can train and vote with a party which is represented by so many of this class of citizens?"

## People's Party Platform

ADOPTED AT OMAHA, NEB., JULY 4, 1892

*Preamble*

Assembled upon the one hundred and sixteenth anniversary of the Declaration of Independence, the People's party of America, in their first National Convention, invoking upon their action the blessing of Almighty God, puts forth, in the name and on behalf of the people of this country, the following preamble and declaration of principles:

The conditions which surround us best justify our cooperation. We meet in the midst of a nation brought to the verge of political and material ruin; corruption dominates the ballot-box, the Legislature, the Congress, and touching even the ermine of the bench. The people are demoralized; most of the States have been compelled to isolate the voters at the polling places to prevent universal intimidation or bribery. The newspapers are subsidized or muzzled; public opinion silenced; business prostrated; our homes covered with mortgages, labor impoverished, and the land concentrating in the hands of the capitalists.

The urban workmen are denied the rights of organization for self protection; imported, pauperized labor beats down their wages; a hireling standing army, unrecognized by our laws, is established to shoot them down, and they are rapidly degenerating into European conditions. The fruits of the toil of millions are boldly stolen to build up colossal fortunes for a few, unprecedented in the history of mankind; and the possessors of these, in turn, despise the republic and endanger liberty. From the same prolific womb of governmental injustice we breed the two great classes—tramps and millionaires. The national power to create money is appropriated to enrich bond-holders; a vast public debt, payable in legal tender currency, has been funded into gold-bearing bonds, thereby adding millions to the burdens of the people.

Silver which has been used as coin since the dawn of history, has been demonetized to add to the purchasing power of gold by decreasing the value of all forms of property as well as human labor, and the supply of currency is purposely abridged to fatten usurers, bankrupt enterprise and enslave industry. A vast conspiracy against mankind has been organized on two continents, and is rapidly taken possession of the world. If not met and overthrown at once it forbodes terrible social convultions, the destruction of civilization or the establishment of an absolute despotism.

We have witnessed for more than a quarter of a century the struggles of the two great political parties for power and plunder, while grievous wrongs have been inflicted on the suffering people. We charge that the controlling influences dominating both these parties have permitted the existing dreadful conditions to develop without serious effort to prevent or restrain them. Neither do they promise any substantial reform. They have agreed together to ignore, in the coming campaign, every issue but one. They propose to drown the outcries of a plundered people with the uproar of a sham battle over the tariff, so that capitalists, corporations, national banks, trusts, watered stock, the demonetization of silver and the oppression of the usurers may all be lost sight of. They propose to sacrifice our homes, lives and children on the altar of Mammon; to destroy the multitude in order to secure corruption funds from the millionaires.

Assembled on the anniversary of the birth of our nation, and filled with the spirit of the grand generation who established our independence, we seek to restore the government of the Republic to the hands of the "plain people," with whose class it originated. We assert our purpose to be identical with the purposes of the national constitution: To form a more perfect union, establish justice, insure domestic tranquility, provide for the common defense, promote the general welfare, and secure the blessing of liberty for ourselves and our posterity.

We declare that this republic can only endure as a free government while built upon the love of the whole people for each other and for the nation; that it cannot be pinned together by bayonets; that the civil war is over, and that every passion and resentment which grew out of it must die with it, and that we must be in fact, as we are in name, one united brotherhood of free men.

Our country finds itself confronted by conditions for which there is no precedent in the history of the world; our annual agricultural productions amount to billions of dollars in value, which must within a few weeks perhaps be exchanged for billions of dollars of commodities consumed in their production; the existing currency supply is wholly inadequate to make this exchange. The results are falling prices, the formation of combines and rings, the impoverishment of the producing class. We pledge ourselves that if given power we will labor to correct these evils by wise and reasonable legislation in accordance with the terms of our platform.

We believe that the powers of government should be expanded as in the case of the postal service, as rapidly and as far as the good sense of an intelligent people and the teachings of experience shall justify, to the end that oppression, injustice and poverty shall eventually cease in the land.

While our sympathies, as a party of reform, are naturally upon the side of every proposition that will tend to make men intelligent, virtuous and temperate, we nevertheless regard these questions, important as they are, subordinate to the great issues now pressing for solution, and upon which not only our individual prosperity, but the very existence of free institutions depends; and we ask all men to first help us determine whether we are to have a republic to administer before we differ as to the condition upon which it is to be administered, believing that the forces of reform this day organized will never cease to move forward until every wrong is remedied and the equal rights and equal privileges securely established for all the men and women of the country. We declare therefore,

1. That the union of the labor forces of the United States, this day consummated shall be permanent and perpetual. May its spirit come into all hearts for the salvation of the republic and the uplifting of mankind.

2. Wealth belongs to him who creates it, and every dollar taken from industry, without an equivalent, is robbery. "If any will not work, neither shall he eat." The interests of rural and civic labor are the same; their enemies are identical.

We believe that the time has come when the railroad corporations will either own the people or the people must own the railroads, and should the government enter upon the work of owning the managing any or all railroads, we should favor an amendment to the constitution by which all persons engaged in the government service shall be placed under civil service regulation of the most rigid character, so as to prevent the increase of the power of the national administration by the use of such additional government employes.

*Finance. First*

We demand a national currency, safe, sound and flexible, issued by the general government only, a full legal tender for all debts, public and private; and that without the use of banking corporations, a just, equitable and efficient means of distribution direct to the people at a tax not to exceed 2 per cent to be provided as set forth in the subtreasury plan of the Farmers' Alliance, or some better system; also by payment in discharge of its obligations for public improvements.

*a.* We demand the free and unlimited coinage of silver.

*b.* We demand that the amount of circulating medium be speedily increased to not less than $50 per capita.

*c.* We demand a graduated income tax.

*d.* We believe that the money of the country should be kept as much as possible in the hands of the people, and hence we demand all national and State revenue shall be limited to the necessary expenses of the government economically and honestly administered.

*e.* We demand that postal savings banks be established by the government for the safe deposit of the earnings of the people and to facilitate exchange.

*Land. Second*

The land, including all the natural resources of wealth, is the heritage of all the people and should not be monopolized for speculative purposes, and alien ownership of land should be prohibited. All land now held by railroads and other corporations in excess of their actual needs, and all lands now owned by aliens, should be reclaimed by the government, and held for actual settlers only.

*Transportation. Third*

Transportation being a means of exchange and a public necessity, the government should own and operate the railroads in the interest of the people.

*a.* The telegraph and telephone, like the post-office system, being a necessity for the transmission of news, should be owned and operated by the government in the interest of the people.

The reading of nearly every plank of the platform proper was received with some applause. The free silver plank was enthusiastically greeted with cheers, and the Government ownership of the railroads plank again got a tumultous greeting, in which it was noticeable that Nebraska, Georgia, Kansas and Texas led. Applause and cries of "Amen" from all parts of the house was the reception accorded the paragraph favoring Government control of the telephone and telegraph lines. A regular Baptist camp-meeting chorus greeted the land plank.

The conclusion of the reading of the platform was warmly greeted. Its adoption was instantly moved, and, though a Missouri delegate was striving for some unknown purpose to get recognition, it was put through by unanimous consent, the whole Convention rising in advance of the Chair and adopting the platform almost before he could move its adoption.

At once on the adoption of the platform the Convention broke over all restraint and went wild in a demonstration that had a likeness to description of enthusiastic Bastile demonstrations in France. The whole Convention, delegates and audience, rose to their feet and the first platform of the People's party was ushered into the world with a scene of enthusiasm, though not in absolute length, almost equal to the cyclonic ovation which greeted the mention of the name of James G. Blaine, at Minneapolis. That scene lasted thirty-one minutes, and this scene between twenty and twenty-five minutes.

It began by the Convention rising in their chairs, cheering, swinging coats, which had been taken off on account of the heat, waving hats and fans, and throwing things in the air. All the delegates were on their feet and the stage was crowded with members of the Committee on Resolutions. Several delegates seized Branch, of Georgia, Chairman, and trotted him up and down the main aisle on their shoulders.

The uproar continued tremendously. As if by a flash a number of delegates seized the uprights used to hold the placards designating the place of State delegations in the hall, and rushed with them to the platform, forming a cordon about the whole platform. Banners were also borne there. The New Yorkers seized old man Lloyd, of New York, whose beaming, ruddy, face, long, white locks and beard gave him a Rip Van Winkle aspect, and, bearing him on their shoulders, placed him in the very front of the phalanx on the stage, where he was handed a baton, and enthusiastically beat time to the wild cheering of the crowd.

# 54

## The Church's Role

Josiah Strong (1847–1916), a Congregational clergy-
man and social reformer, began his career in Wyoming
and spent several decades preaching and doing mission
work in the Midwest. In 1885 he published *Our
Country,* an impassioned attack on the menaces of
urbanization, immigration, and industrial concentration,
and a plea for Protestant churches to meet the challenge of modernization by confronting the grave social
problems of the day. In the years that followed Strong
became a world-famous evangelical leader, seeking in
his books and from positions of executive leadership to
recover for the churches the allegiance of the working
masses by taking an interest in labor conditions and
demonstrating the ministry's concern with the material
conditions of life. Strong helped establish a number of
institutions that carried out this work, including the
Federal Council of the Churches of Christ in America,
and he traveled to Europe and South America to aid
burgeoning Protestant social service movements there.
His sermons, pamphlets, and many books all concentrated on the need for the church to play a part in the
solution of civic and industrial dilemmas, by expanding
its organization and uniting contending sects in an
evangelical alliance.

## THE NEW ERA
### *Reverend Josiah Strong*

A generation ago Professor Francis Lieber, I think it was, said that the city was
"the most difficult and perplexing problem of modern times." And more than forty
years ago Alexis De Tocqueville, whom Mr. Gladstone calls the Edmund Burke of
his generation, wrote: "I look upon the size of certain American cities, and
especially upon the nature of their population, as a real danger which threatens the
security of the democratic republics of the New World." If the judgment and fears
of Lieber and De Tocqueville were well founded, the problem of the city is now
much more perplexing and the necessity of its solution far more urgent, for our
urban population is to-day six times as large as it was forty years ago, and more

From *The New Era or The Coming Kingdom* (New York, 1893), 178–180, 184–196, 198, 201–
204, 210–211, 218, 220–221, 237–241, 244–247, 251.

than twice as large relatively. In 1850 one eighth of our population lived in cities of 8000 and over; now considerably more than one fourth.

The government of the city is by a "boss," who is skilful in the manipulation of the "machine," and who holds no political principles "except for revenue only."

The "boss" is the natural product of a vicious political partisanship, together with a large foreign population which has not sufficient character and intelligence for independent or individual judgment and action. While in the aggregate there are many foreigners to whom this remark does not apply, we still have the "Irish vote," the "German vote," the "Roman Catholic vote," and the like, which by appeals to race or religious prejudice or for "value received" may be cast in great blocks— which of course constitutes the city the demagogue's Paradise.

Most of these foreigners have little understanding of our political issues and less of our institutions. They see nothing to be gained by independent action at the polls and much to be gained by concerted action. They accordingly follow their leaders, and are led into whatever camp bids highest in patronage or plunder. Doubtless in every city the good citizens who want honest government are in a majority, but with fatal folly they divide on political questions which have no more to do with municipal government than with the moon; and this division enables the "bosses" to hold the balance of power and dictate their terms. The perfectly natural result is a debauched city government.

This unspeakable folly is all but universal. Occasionally outraged citizens become sufficiently indignant to rebel against party leaders and, in a moment of sanity, set up an independent candidate. But usually a partisan press succeeds in whipping enough good men back into line to defeat the reform movement. Returns from 127 cities show only *one* independent or non-political mayor. Politics is thoroughly rooted in our system of municipal government, and has so vitiated that system that its failure has become notorious. "There is no denying," says Mr. Bryce, "that the government of cities is the one conspicuous failure of the United States." Mr. Andrew D. White, who has enjoyed exceptional opportunities of observation, says: "Without the slightest exaggeration we may assert that, with very few exceptions, the city governments of the United States are the worst in Christendom—the most expensive, the most inefficient, and the most corrupt."

Let us consider now the significance of this fact. It means that the social structure is weakest at the precise point where it ought to be strongest, viz., where it suffers the severest strain. Because the city is the microcosm of the civilization which has produced it, it gathers into itself representatives of all classes of society; and because it is the point of most intense activity, every maladjustment of society produces the greatest friction and soreness there. It is there that riots occur; it is there chiefly that the unnatural duel between capital and labor is fought; it is there that social extremes are found in sharpest contrast and the deepest jealousies are felt; it is there that haters of society gather, men who are the implacable enemies of all order.

Of course there can be no government without law. The less popular respect for it there is, the more centralized must the government be to prevent anarchy. Such a government may control lawless people, but how shall lawless people control themselves? The fact is that here in the United States those classes which most need to be controlled are themselves very generally in control of the city.

And this fact has far more than local significance. Our political fabric rests on two fundamental principles, that of local self-government and that of federation. The latter was at stake during our civil war; and South and North are now alike agreed that this principle is settled for all time. *The former principle is to-day at stake in the government of the city.* This principle is as vitally essential as the other; its subversion would involve national destruction as surely as the dismemberment of the Union.

When the population of the city exceeds that of the country, it will be able to dominate both the state and the nation. And if our municipal government is a failure *then,* the governments of state and nation, controlled by the city, will also be failures, and our free institutions will fail.

The peril to the republic through the threatened failure of one of our two fundamental principles is as real as when the government was shaken by the shock of civil strife. And perhaps the peril is all the greater because the crisis is less imminent and to many gives no warning. Men are not apt to sleep when the drum beats the nation to battle. A generation ago men were awake to the peril of the hour, their patriotism was aroused, and no sacrifice of blood or treasure was too precious to lay on the altar of country when the principle of federation was endangered. But the peril which now threatens the no less fundamental principle of local self-government is insidious. It beats no drum, it fires no cannon, it does not solidify a public sentiment against itself, it kindles no patriotism, and inspires no sacrifice in its opposition; but it is slowly, secretly, and surely undermining one of the two foundations on which rests the arch of our free institutions.

Touching municipal government, the problem of the city is to make it capable of governing itself; and this problem must be solved speedily before it assumes national proportions, before the city dominates the country, for if it remains unsolved, it will then involve our republican institutions in national ruin.

Turn now to the problem of city evangelization. Not only must the city be made a safe factor in our civilization; it must be saved.

One of the most important factors of this problem is the *composition* of the city, which is thoroughly heterogeneous. What mosaics of living stones our city populations are, representing all colors, shades, and climes! In New York one would scarcely look in vain for a representative of any people. There may be heard a babel of all tongues. It is said that seventeen languages were spoken there before the Revolution, when the population was less than 22,000.

If the foreigners were scattered among the native population, our language would be a necessity to them, and they would soon become acquainted and assimilated; but segregated they simply live the old country life on our soil. They are like unmasticated food. Mastication is a process of *separating,* without which digestion is a slow and painful process.

Not only different languages but also different ideas and habits of life combine to make the evangelization of these peoples more difficult. Their presence has very noticeably and lamentably lowered the standard of Sabbath observance and impaired habits of sobriety in the cities.

I bring no sweeping accusation against foreigners. Many of those who come to us—perhaps more than we commonly suppose—are Christian in fact as well as in name, while not a few have rendered eminent service to religion, morals, literature, and political reform. Still we are compelled to recognize facts, and the facts are that a majority of immigrants believe either in a perverted and superstitious form of Christianity or in none at all. A great majority were peasants, whose lives, in many instances, have been subjected to spoliation and wrong, and who have learned, therefore, to associate law with tyranny, and conceive of freedom as freedom from law, or, in one word, license. We must not wonder, therefore, that the foreign element produces far more than its due proportion of criminals, and heterogeneous as is the city in the nationality of its people, it is of course no less so in their character. It gathers the good and the bad, and contains that which is fairest and foulest in our civilization.

Another most important factor in the problem is *environment,* which in the slums is such as to discourage everything except a divine faith and love.

The crowded tenement is the hot-house of physical and moral disease. As the compression of matter develops heat, so the compacting of populations produces a sort of fever heat which manifests itself in morbid passions and appetites. In a single square there are crowded together two, three, and even four thousand souls, as many as in the country might be found occupying twenty-five or fifty square miles. Mrs. Ballington Booth finds seven families huddled together in one room. In a room not more than ten by twelve feet, Dr. A. T. Pierson finds eighteen people, men, women, and children, black and white, eating, sleeping, living. Sometimes as many as forty-five people sleep in a single room.

We read of fifty-eight babies in one tenement. Think of the thousands born of drunkenness and lust, whose welcome into the world is a curse, whose lullabies are blasphemies, whose admonitions are kicks, whose examples are vice and crime! How many children of the slums by an awful heritage from both father and mother are indeed "damned into the world," receive their life and live it under conditions that make disease of body and soul as certain as natural law! What a mistake many children make in being born humans instead of wild beasts!

The city cannot be saved while such conditions exist. The people cannot be elevated while their environment remains unchanged. A much more robust virtue than exists in the slums would yield to the conditions which there prevail. On the other hand, we cannot very materially change the environment while the people remain unchanged. Both must be transformed together; while moral and spiritual influences are brought to bear on the people, the physical causes of their degradation must be removed.

Another factor of the dark problem before us is the *isolation* of the city, which is no less real than that of the country.

Where men are most crowded together they are farthest apart. In the village or out in the country everybody knows everybody else, and personal acquaintance makes personal interest and influence easy. Misfortune becomes quickly known and brings with it helpful sympathy. Moreover, the fact that a man is known and that something is expected of him helps wonderfully to keep him up to the mark. We know to what an extent reputation is dependent on character, but do we appreciate to how great an extent character depends on reputation? Every man has some sort of standing where he is known, and until he has lost all self-respect desires to sustain whatever good reputation he possesses. Let him go among strangers, and this external restraint is lost.

This suggests one of the reasons, and possibly the principal one, why there is so much more of pauperism and crime in a city of 500,000 than among an equal number of people scattered in small towns and villages. In the city there is little or no sense of neighborhood. You may be separated from your next neighbor by only a few inches, and yet for years never see his face or learn his name. Mere proximity does not imply social touch. Association is determined by wealth, occupation, intelligence, taste, nationality, church connection, and a dozen other conditions. Society is, therefore, divided into classes, which are again subdivided into groups; and between these there is no intercourse unless it be of a business character.

And classes are not only separated socially but also geographically, which is an added obstacle to city evangelization. Water communication has been a very important factor in the development of American cities. Nearly all of our large cities have an ocean, lake, or river front, which limits their expansion in one or more directions. Wealthy residences and churches retire before advancing business, while the poorer classes must remain near their work; so that there come to be an "up-town" and "down-town," an "east side" and "west side," which are far separated geographically, and vastly farther socially.

There are still other causes of isolation, which are peculiarly operative in American cities. The three great natural bonds which bind men together into nationalities and social organizations are identity of race, of language, and of religion. In England, however widely classes may be separated socially, they are generally bound together by these three bonds. The lord and the peasant boast the same national history, speak the same tongue, and presumably they are both Protestants. But the great heterogeneous masses of our cities are separated by differences of blood, of language, and of religion. Only slowly can they evolve the conditions which make it possible for them to enter into a common national life, to say nothing of closer social relations.

Thus many different lines of cleavage run through our cities, dividing them into isolated fragments, making it very difficult, if not quite impossible, for influences which would otherwise be generally pervasive to reach and mould these varied elements and greatly complicating the problem of evangelization.

Without doubt the city is soon to control the nation by the dominance of numbers. It is now, as it has always been, the centre of civilization, and the source of moulding influences. As civilization grows less martial and more industrial, wealth becomes an increasingly important factor, and wealth is being massed more and more in the city. With the increase of popular intelligence, the press is exerting an ever-widening influence. And this tree of the knowledge of good and evil, whose leaves are not altogether for the *healing* of the nations, grows in the city. The city is already, and is to become increasingly, the source of determinative influences, bad as well as good. It becomes, then, a question of vital importance whether the growth of the Christian church in the city is keeping pace with the rapid strides of population.

The accompanying table, giving the relative increase in the number of churches and the population, would seem to indicate that the growth of the city has generally been far in excess of church provision. If all our large cities had been included in the investigation, there is no reason to think the result would have been substantially different.

### NUMBER OF PROTESTANT CHURCHES TO POPULATION

|      | *Boston* | *Brooklyn* | *Buffalo* | *Chicago* |
|------|----------|------------|-----------|-----------|
|      |          |            |           | In 1836 |
| 1840 | 1 to 1,228 souls | 1 to 1,294 souls | 1 to 1,069 souls | 1 to 1,042 souls |
|      |          |            |           | In 1851 |
| 1850 | " 1,200 " | " 2,105 " | " 1,509 " | 1 to 1,577 souls |
| 1860 | " 1,368 " | " 2,051 " | " 1,690 " | " 1,820 " |
| 1870 | " 1,898 " | " 2,052 " | " 2,402 " | " 2,433 " |
| 1880 | " 2,311 " | " 2,442 " | " 2,216 " | " 3,062 " |
| 1890 | " 2,581 " | " 2,800 " | " 2,650 " | " 3,601 " |

Thus we have seen that while our civilization is suffering a greater strain in the city than elsewhere, the two great conservative institutions of society, the church and the home, are weaker in the city than anywhere else. And as the city grows larger and the strain becomes more severe, the home and the church are growing relatively weaker.

We see then the existing situation and tendencies—a mottled population, containing the worst elements of society, far removed from saving Christian influences and peculiarly difficult to reach with them, growing rapidly in numbers, political influence, and commercial importance, while church provision is steadily becoming more inadequate.

What is to be the outcome? One of three things. Present tendencies will continue until our cities are literally heathenized, or their arrested growth will enable the churches to regain lost ground, or the churches will awake to their duty and their opportunity. To accept the first alternative is to despair of our country and of the Kingdom: to entertain the thought for a moment would be disloyalty to Christ. Any hope of escape by the second alternative must be based on ignorance of the causes of this great world movement toward the cities. The third alternative, then, is the only one that can be accepted. *The churches will awake.*

The first city was built by the first murderer, and crime and wretchedness have dwelt in the city ever since, but the city is to be redeemed. Every generation might have said with the Psalmist, "for I have seen violence and strife in the city; mischief also and sorrow are in the midst of it;" but when John in apocalyptic vision sees a perfected society, a heaven on earth, it is a *holy city* which inspires his prophecy. "And there shall in no wise enter into it anything that defileth, neither, whatsoever worketh abomination, or maketh a lie;" and in it there shall be "neither sorrow nor crying, neither shall there be any more pain, for the former things are passed away."

CHAPTER X

THE SEPARATION OF THE MASSES FROM THE CHURCH

"How to reach the masses" has been a standing challenge to the wisdom of religious convention for several years. The fact of a separation between the masses and the church has thus been generally assumed. It has, however, been questioned by a few on the ground that church membership is increasing more rapidly than the population. It is true that according to the best available statistics the Evangelical communicants in the United States in 1800 were 7 per cent of the population. In 1880 they had risen to 20.07 per cent; and in 1890 to 21.42.

Thus, the proportion of Evangelical church members to the population was three times as large in 1890 as in 1800. It does not follow, however, that the proportion of the population attending church has increased in like ratio, nor indeed that it has not decreased.

The proportion of attendants who are non-communicants has been greatly reduced, until now it is a very narrow margin. The great body of church attendants to-day are communicants or the children of communicants, most of whom in due time will become members of the church. The gospel has brought nearly all to acknowledge its claims who have come statedly within the sphere of the pulpit's influence.

Thus, it has been quite possible for the church to grow more rapidly than the population while at the same time it was losing its hold on the multitude. We have been known as a church-going people. De Tocqueville was greatly impressed by our Sabbath observance and church attendance. Few appreciate to what extent we have now become a non-church-going people. Mr. Moody said a few years ago: "The gulf between the church and the masses is growing deeper, wider, and darker every hour." The reality of such a gulf is not a matter of opinion. Careful investigations have been made in city and country which give us definite knowlegde. From these investigations, made in some hundreds of towns in several different states, it appears that somewhat less than one half of the people profess to attend church; and it should be remembered that many claim to be attendants who are shown by a little cross-questioning not to have been inside a church for years.

When we ask after the causes of this separation between the church and the masses, we find at once that they are many and complex.

1. Ideas of duty are not so strict now as formerly, and men, therefore, more readily yield to inclination. The present generation of young people have had a training very different from that which their grandparents or even their parents received. In most families the rod, like Aaron's rod, has budded and brought forth

almonds and sugar-plums of all sorts. Children are hired and coaxed instead of being commanded and required, and accordingly grow up to consult inclination rather than obligation. Attending church is not now commonly considered a sacred duty. People go, if they feel like it: and for a great variety of reasons most people do not feel like it.

2. Prevalence of the Continental ideas of the Sabbath, which have come to us with immigration, have helped to reduce church attendance.

3. The rush which characterizes modern, and especially American, living brings a Sunday lassitude which affords an excuse quite sufficient to placate many an easy conscience for neglecting the sanctuary.

4. The pulpit once afforded the people most of their intellectual, as well as spiritual, stimulus. Now it must compete with books, magazines, and papers, and especially with the Sunday-morning newspaper.

5. The Sunday-school, notwithstanding all the good it has done and is doing, by being considered "the children's church," has interfered with the formation of church-going habits on the part of many children, and so has eventually contributed not a few to the non-church-going class.

6. Our almost nomadic habits of life break up church relationships, which often are not renewed among strangers.

7. A wrong conception of the Christian life has led laymen to hire the minister to do their Christian work for them. In the cities, where churches are more apt to be large, the minister is fully occupied with his duties to his congregation, so that the non-church-goers are not looked after at all, except as this duty is occasionally laid on a lonesome city-missionary.

8. Private ownership in church pews has an influence, though it is probably more of an excuse than a reason.

9. Church dress also is a deterrent to workingmen and their families, when Sunday best, if they are fortunate enough to have any, is such as to make them conspicuous for their plain appearance.

10. But more important than any of these causes is an indifference which too often rises into a positive class antipathy—an indifference on the part both of church-goers and of non-church-goers.

There are in every church choice men and women, just the material to make a heaven of, who believe that Jesus Christ died for every man, and who see in every man, however degraded or besotted in sin and ignorance, the possibility of glorious likeness to Christ; men and women who long and labor to see this possible likeness become actual. But I fear that a very large proportion are indifferent or worse than indifferent in regard to reaching the masses with Christian influence, under the impression that the church is a kind of religious coterie or "steepled club," existing expressly for "our sort of folks." They are under the impression that "our sort of folks" would pretty nearly exhaust the list of the elect; they are willing that the masses should be saved, but not in their church or by their instrumentality.

The workingman, even though he never goes to church, knows that Christ taught the duty of loving our neighbor as we love ourselves. He does not see this duty exemplified by the church, and perhaps makes a sweeping charge of insincerity or at least of inconsistency against its members. He misjudges the church because he does not know it. Almost the only contact between the artisan class and well-to-do church members is contact in business, and business which is intensely competitive, i.e., selfish. How could men whose knowledge of Christians is gained by such contact avoid wrong impressions of the church? They do not know how much of genuine Christian love there is in it. To be sure, if there were all there ought to be, no one could help knowing it. But as a matter of fact there is a great deal which finds but little *personal* expression. The average Christian to-day is hiring his Christian work done by proxy—by societies, institutions, the minister, the city missionary. He is so very busy that he would rather give his money than his time. His interest in his fellow-men, therefore, is expressed through various organizations which make a business of philanthropy. Thus our Christian work has become largely *institutional* instead of *personal,* and, therefore, largely mechanical instead of vital.

There is an enormous amount of good done by Christian organizations and institutions, and a great deal of Christian self-denial exercised in their support, but they appeal very little to the average non-church-goer. The dissatisfied classes, who believe that they are not receiving their just dues, that they are wronged by the capitalist class, look on charitable institutions not as an expression of Christian love, but as a mere sop to Cerberus.

There is a great discontented class; there is a great non-church-going class. Let us now weigh the fact that *these two classes are substantially one and the same.* It is the masses who are discontented; it is the masses who rule and who will determine our future; it is the masses who constitute the non-church-goers.

Let us again remind ourselves that in this country the masses are the sources of power, the arbiters of destiny, the supreme judicature. We are concerned not with aristocracies or kings, but with the people. And when we say that the people rule, that means that mere numbers rule, that the complex and difficult questions of government and statesmanship, questions on whose answers may depend the rights and well-being of millions and even the future of civilization—that such questions are settled ultimately not by the intelligence and conscience of the wisest and best, but by *mere majorities.*

Not only do we find industrious, intelligent and law-abiding workingmen and farmers among the non-church-goers, but also the criminal classes, the army of tramps and vagrants and a larger army of saloon keepers, the illiterate, the venders of votes and the anarchists, who at the last presidential election cast twice as many votes in New York City as did the prohibitionists. The dangerous elements in general are found in the non-church-going multitude.

Evidently, if the church is to purify society, if she is to solve the great problems of the times, if she is to mould the civilization of the future, if she is to accomplish her mission by ushering in the full coming of Christ's kingdom, then the great body of her work, yet to be done, is to be found in the non-church-going class, and she is separated from her greatest and most urgent work by a deep and wide chasm.

She is spending her energies on the *best* elements of society, her time is given to teaching the most *intelligent,* she is medicating the *healthiest,* she is salting the *salt,* while the determining masses, which include the most ignorant and vicious, the poorest and most degraded, are alike beyond her influence and her effort.

The church ought always to have been the first to recognize and relieve human needs and to right human wrongs. But with a narrow conception of her mission she has sat with folded hands while a thousand organizations have sprung up at her side to do her proper work. No benevolent work or reform inspired by a Christian spirit should ever have been forced to go outside the Christian church for organization. The Young Men's Christian Association, the Woman's Christian Temperance Union, the Charity Organization Societies, the Red Cross, the White Cross, and scores of similar organizations are all doing the proper work of the church. I rejoice greatly in the manifold fruits of their work. I do not see how the dreariest pessimist could acquaint himself with them and not be converted to a good hope for humanity. I rejoice that when these organizations became necessary they appeared; but if the church had fully recognized her relations to society, if she had appreciated the largeness of her mission, they would never have been needed.

All of these organizations draw their life, their inspiration, and most of their members from the church; but their success is not her success, their influence and their honors are not hers, and some of them contribute little or nothing to her upbuilding. There is a law in nature that the tree's fruit shall contain the seed which reproduces the tree. There are a thousand beautiful charities and blessed reforms which are the fruit of Christianity, but which contain no seed for the reproduction and increase of the church because they were not produced by the church.

We are living in the sociological age of the world, the distinctive problems of which spring from the relations of man to his fellow. When civilization is brought face to face with an age problem it constitutes a race emergency. If a religion is to prove itself thoroughly adapted to human nature and destined to be final, it must show itself equal to the great emergencies of the race, and able to meet the peculiar demands of every age.

Here is the most serious question of our times: Is Christianity able to establish right relations between man and man? The skepticism which is most dangerous to Christianity to-day is not doubt as to the age or authenticity or genuineness of its sacred books or distrust of time-honored doctrines, but *loss of faith in its vitality*. Is it equal to living issues, can it inform our developing civilization and determine its character, can it reconcile classes and conflicting interests, can it right existing wrongs, can it purify politics, can it command the public conscience, can it lay the industrial world under its law of love to one's neighbor, thus putting an end to the unnatural duel between capital and labor, can it fit men for earth as well as heaven?

This leads us to institutional methods of church work, or to what some prefer to call the institutional church, which is a natural outgrowth of a larger conception of the mission of the church.

The church that adopts these methods recognizes its duty to the whole man. It aims to cultivate body and mind as well as heart. The need of these methods is naturally felt by "down-town" churches, which are surrounded by people whose homes have few attractions; to whom, therefore, saloons and places of amusement

117

appeal strongly. In order to compete successfully with these demoralizing attractions, the church emphasizes its social features and keeps its doors open seven days and nights in the week.

The gymnasium, the reading-room, industrial training, the cooking-school, popular lectures, concerts, recreation-rooms, bath-rooms, games, and clubs are prominent features, though not all of these necessarily are employed by the same church. These churches are earnestly evangelistic in spirit, preaching a simple gospel, and pressing men to an immediate decision. The people are not only attracted to the church, but are also frequently visited in their homes.

What of the success of these methods? They seem in every instance to win the people, especially the young men and boys. Dr. Scudder reports that twelve hundred patronize the gymnasium weekly, that the weekly visits to the recreation-rooms run from fifteen hundred to two thousand. He says: "No need of talking about reaching the masses any longer. . . . We have more masses than we know what to do with. When we opened our Boys' Club we had five hundred and seventy applications in less than a week and then we quit giving out any more, for fear of a Johnstown flood of juvenile humanity. We could not accommodate all who want to come, if we had four times the room."

When we remember that this success has been won in localities where churches working along the old lines have become enfeebled and have died or moved away, we can better appreciate its significance.

At this point an objection is interposed. Some will fear that this is turning the churches aside from their proper spiritual work to caring for bodily and temporal things.

If the result were to subordinate the spiritual to the physical, if it practically led to the belief that religion *consists* in the service of man and in perfecting the life that now is, this extreme would be a worse error than the opposite. While Christ had much more to say concerning this life than the next, he left no room for misapprehension as to their relative importance. "Be not afraid of them that kill the body, and after that have no more that they can do. But I will forewarn you whom ye shall fear: Fear him, which after he hath killed hath power to cast into hell; yea, I say unto you, Fear him." Christ taught with entire distinctness that the spiritual is more important than the physical, but he did not, therefore, fall into the narrow-minded error of depreciating the body. He was mindful of bodily needs and tenderly compassionate of bodily sufferings; and surely his care for men's bodies gave him no less influence over men's souls. So far as the Great Teacher "turned aside" from preaching the Gospel in order to give sight to the blind, health to the sick, and food to the hungry, it is quite safe for the church to follow his example. Had his *words* of love any less meaning because of his *works* of love? If the church *lived* the Gospel as well as she *preaches* it, the multitude would have less doubt of the love which she professes.

The world in this sociological age needs a new social ideal to direct the progress of civilization. Let the church fully accept her mission and she will furnish this needed ideal, viz., her Master's conception of the kingdom of God come upon earth.

# 55

# The Spanish-American War

Stephen Crane (1871–1900) grew up in New York and New Jersey, attending several colleges, playing baseball, doing newspaper work, all while in his teens. After 1890 he moved to New York City, writing occasionally for newspapers and working on his first novel, *Maggie*, a naturalistic view of life in the slums of a great city. This was followed by Crane's great picture of battle experience, *The Red Badge of Courage*, which for many became the greatest literary work inspired by the Civil War. Other stories and poems followed, and Crane saw much of the world as a newspaper correspondent. In 1898 Crane sailed for Cuba, to cover the war for the New York *World*. His battlefield descriptions, sometimes written under great danger and with increasingly precarious health, evoked some of the quieter heroisms and secret ironies of a war that seemed like a splendid lark to those at home. Less than two years after penning these dispatches, Crane was dead of tuberculosis, at the age of twenty-nine.

### DISPATCHES FROM THE
### SPANISH-AMERICAN WAR
#### Stephen Crane

1    **In Front of Santiago, July 4,
     via Old Point Comfort, Va.**

*July 13*

The action at San Juan on July 1 was, particularly speaking, a soldier's battle. It was like Inkerman, where the English fought half leaderless all day in a fog. Only the Cuban forest was worse than any fog.

No doubt when history begins to grind out her story we will find that many a thundering, fine, grand order was given for that day's work; but after all there will be no harm in contending that the fighting line, the men and their regimental officers, took the hill chiefly because they knew they could take it, some having no orders and others disobeying whatever orders they had.

In civil life the newspapers would have called it a grand, popular movement. It will never be forgotten as long as America has a military history.

A line of intrenched hills held by men armed with a weapon like a Mauser is

These three dispatches from the New York *World*, July 14, 1898, July 8, 1898, and July 20, 1898, are reprinted in R. W. Stallman and E. R. Hagemann, eds., *The War Dispatches of Stephen Crane* (New York, 1964), 172–190.

not to be taken by a front attack of infantry unless the trenches have first been heavily shaken by artillery fire. Any theorist will say that it is impossible, and prove it to be impossible. But it was done, and we owe the success to the splendid gallantry of the American private soldier.

As near as one can learn, headquarters expected little or no fighting on the 1st. Lawton's division was to go by the Caney road, chase the Spaniards out of that interesting village, and then, wheeling half to the left, march down to join the other divisions in some kind of attack on San Juan at daybreak on the 2d.

But somebody had been entirely misinformed as to the strength and disposition of the Spanish forces at Caney, and instead of taking Lawton six minutes to capture the town it took him nearly all day, as well it might.

The other divisions lying under fire, waiting for Lawton, grew annoyed at a delay which was, of course, not explained to them, and suddenly arose and took the formidable hills of San Juan. It was impatience suddenly exalted to one of the sublime passions.

The marching was of necessity very slow, and even then the narrow road was often blocked. The men, weighted with their packs, cartridge belts and rifles, forded many streams, climbed hills, slid down banks and forced their way through thickets.

Suddenly there was a roar of guns just ahead and a little to the left. This was Grimes's battery going into action on the hill which is called El Pasco. Then, all in a moment, the quiet column moving forward was opposed by men carrying terrible burdens. Wounded Cubans were being carried to the rear. Most of them were horribly mangled.

The second brigade of dismounted American cavalry had been in support of the battery, its position being directly to the rear. Some Cubans had joined there. The Spanish shrapnel fired at the battery was often cut too long, and, passing over, burst amid the supports and the Cubans.

The loss of the battery, the cavalry and the Cubans from this fire was forty men killed and wounded, the First regular cavalry probably suffering most grievously. Presently there was a lull in the artillery fire, and down through spaces in the trees we could see the infantry still plodding with its packs steadily toward the front.

The artillerymen were greatly excited. Some showed with glee fragments of Spanish shells which had come dangerously near their heads. They had gone through their ordeal and were talking over it lightly.

In the mean time Lawton's division, some three miles away, was making plenty of noise. Caney is just at the base of a high willow-green, crinkled mountain, and Lawton was making his way over little knolls which might be termed foothills. We could see the great white clouds of smoke from Capron's guns and hear their roar punctuating the incessant drumming of the infantry. It was plain even then that Lawton was having considerably more of a fete than anybody had supposed previously.

[GRIMES SMASHED THEM]

At 11.25 our artillery reopened on the central block-house and intrenchments. The Spanish fire had been remarkably fine, but it was our turn now. Grimes had his ranges to a nicety. After the great "shout of the gun" came the broad, windy, diminishing noise of the flung shell; then a fainter boom and a cloud of red debris out of the block-house or up from the ground near the trenches.

The Spanish infantry in the trenches fired a little volley immediately after every one of the American shells. It puzzled many to decide at what they could be firing, but it was finally resolved that they were firing just to show us that they were still there and were not afraid.

It must have been about 2 o'clock when the enemy's battery again retorted.

The cruel thing about this artillery duel was that our battery had nothing but old-fashioned powder, and its position was always as clearly defined as if it had been the Chicago fire. There is no secrecy about a battery that uses that kind of powder. The great billowy white smoke can be seen for miles. On the other hand, the Spaniards were using the best smokeless. There is no use groaning over what was to be, but!—

However, fate elected that the Spanish shooting should be very bad. Only two-thirds of their shells exploded in this second affair. They all whistled high, and those that exploded raked the ground long since evacuated by the supports and the timbers. No one was hurt.

From El Paso to San Juan there is a broad expanse of dense forest, spotted infrequently with vividly green fields. It is traversed by a single narrow road which leads straight between the two positions, fording two little streams. Along this road had gone our infantry and also the military balloon. Why it was ever taken to such a position nobody knows, but there it was—huge, fat, yellow, quivering—being dragged straight into a zone of fire that would surely ruin it.

There were two officers in the car for the greater part of the way, and there surely were never two men who valued their lives less. But they both escaped unhurt, while the balloon sank down, torn to death by the bullets that were volleyed at it by the nervous Spaniards, who suspected dynamite. It was never brought out of the woods where it recklessly met its fate.

In these woods, unknown to some, including the Spaniards, was fulminated the gorgeous plan of taking an impregnable position.

One saw a thin line of black figures moving across a field. They disappeared in the forest. The enemy was keeping up a terrific fire. Then suddenly somebody yelled, "By God, there go our boys up the hill!"

There is many a good American who would give an arm to get the thrill of patriotic insanity that coursed through us when we heard that yell.

Yes, they were going up the hill, up the hill. It was the best moment of anybody's life. An officer said to me afterward: "If we had been in that position and the Spaniards had come at us, we would have piled them up so high the last man couldn't have climbed over." But up went the regiments with no music save that ceaseless, fierce crashing of rifles.

The foreign attaches were shocked. "It is very gallant, but very foolish," said one sternly.

"Why, they can't take it, you know. Never in the world," cried another, much agitated. "It is slaughter, absolute slaughter."

The little Japanese shrugged his shoulders. He was one who said nothing.

The road from El Paso to San Juan was now a terrible road. It should have a tragic fame like the sunken road at Waterloo. Why we did not later hang some of the gentry who contributed from the trees to the terror of this road is not known.

The wounded were stringing back from the front, hundreds of them. Some walked unaided, an arm or a shoulder having been dressed at a field station. They stopped often enough to answer the universal hail "How is it going?" Others hobbled or clung to a friend's shoulders. Their slit trousers exposed red bandages. A few were shot horribly in the face and were led, bleeding and blind, by their mates.

And then there were the slow pacing stretcher-bearers with the dying, or the insensible, the badly wounded, still figures with blood often drying brick color on their hot bandages.

Prostrate at the roadside were many, others who had made their way thus far and were waiting for strength. Everywhere moved the sure-handed, invaluable Red Cross men.

Over this scene was a sort of haze of bullets. They were of two kinds. First, the Spanish lines were firing just a trifle high. Their bullets swept over our firing lines and poured into this devoted roadway, the single exit, even as it had been the single approach. The second fire was from guerillas concealed in the trees and in the thickets along the trail. They had come in under the very wings of our strong advance, taken good positions on either side of the road and were peppering our line of communication whenever they got a good target, no matter, apparently, what the target might be.

Red Cross men, wounded men, sick men, correspondents and attaches were all one to the guerilla. The move of sending an irregular force around the flanks of the enemy as he is making his front attack is so legitimate that some of us could not believe at first that the men hidden in the forest were really blazing away at the non-combatants or the wounded. Viewed simply as a bit of tactics, the scheme was admirable. But there is no doubt now that they intentionally fired at anybody they thought they could kill.

You can't mistake an ambulance driver when he is driving his ambulance. You can't mistake a wounded man when he is lying down and being bandaged. And when you see a field hospital you don't mistake it for a squadron of cavalry or a brigade of infantry.

As we went along the road we suddenly heard a cry behind us. "Oh, come quick! Come quick!" We turned and saw a young soldier spinning around frantically and grabbing at his leg. Evidently he had been going to the stream to fill his canteen, but a guerilla had barred him from that drink. Two Red Cross men rushed for him.

At the last ford, in the shelter of the muddy bank, lay a dismal band, forty men on their backs with doctors working at them and bullets singing in flocks over their heads. They rolled their eyes quietly at us. There was no groaning. They exhibited that profound patience which has been the marvel of every one.

After the ford was passed the woods cleared. The road passed through lines of barbed wire. There were, in fact, barbed wire fences running in almost every direction.

The mule train, galloping like a troop of cavalry, dashed up with a reinforcement of ammunition, every mule on the jump, the cowboys swinging their whips. They were under a fairly strong fire, but up they went.

One does not expect gallantry in a pack train, but incidentally it may be said that this charge, led by the bell mare, was one of the sights of the day.

To the rear, over the ground that the army had taken, a breeze was gently stirring the long grass and ruffling the surface of a pool that lay in a sort of meadow. The army took its glory calmly. Having nothing else to do, the army sat down and looked tranquilly at the scenery. There was not that exuberance of enthusiasm which surrounds the vicinity of a candidate for the Assembly.

The army was dusty, dishevelled, its hair matted to its forehead with sweat, its shirts glued to its back with the same, and indescribably dirty, thirsty, hungry, and a-weary from its bundles and its marches and its fights. It sat down on the conquered crest and felt satisfied.

"Well, hell! here we are."

The road to the rear increased its terrors in the darkness. The wounded men, stumbling along in the mud, a miasmic mist from the swampish ground filling their nostrils, heard often in the air the whiplash sound of a bullet that was meant for them by the lurking guerillas. A mile, two miles, two miles and a half to the rear, great populous hospitals had been formed.

The long lines of the hill began to intrench under cover of night, each regiment for itself, still, however, keeping in touch on the flanks. Each regiment dug in the ground that it had taken by its own valor. Some commands had two or three shovels, an axe or two, maybe a pick. Other regiments dug with their bayonets and shovelled out the dirt with their meat ration cans.

When the day was in full bloom Lawton's division, having marched all night, appeared in the road. The long, long column wound around the base of the ridge and disappeared among the woods and knolls on the right of Wheeler's line. The army was now concentrated in a splendid position.

[CUBANS HELD IN CONTEMPT]

It becomes necessary to speak of the men's opinion of the Cubans. To put it shortly, both officers and privates have the most lively contempt for the Cubans. They despise them. They came down here expecting to fight side by side with an ally, but this ally has done little but stay in the rear and eat army rations, manifesting an indifference to the cause of Cuban liberty which could not be exceeded by some one who had never heard of it.

In the great charge up the hills of San Juan the American soldiers who, for their part, sprinkled a thousand bodies in the grass, were not able to see a single Cuban assisting in what might easily turn out to be the decisive battle for Cuban freedom.

At Caney a company of Cubans came into action on the left flank of one of the American regiments just before the place was taken. Later they engaged a blockhouse at 2,000 yards and fired away all their ammunition. They sent back to the American commander for more, but they got only a snort of indignation.

As a matter of fact, the Cuban soldier, ignorant as only such isolation as has been his can make him, does not appreciate the ethics of the situation.

This great American army he views as he views the sky, the sea, the air; it is a natural and most happy phenomenon. He will go to sleep while this flood drowns the Spaniards.

The American soldier, however, thinks of himself often as a disinterested benefactor, and he would like the Cubans to play up to the ideal now and then. His attitude is mighty human. He does not really want to be thanked, and yet the total absence of anything like gratitude makes him furious. He is furious, too, because the Cubans apparently consider themselves under no obligation to take part in an engagement; because the Cubans will stay at the rear and collect haversacks, blankets, coats and shelter tents dropped by our troops.

The average Cuban here will not speak to an American unless to beg. He forgets his morning, afternoon or evening salutation unless he is reminded. If he takes a dislike to you he talks about you before your face, using a derisive undertone.

### [DEMORALIZED BY AID]

The truth probably is that the food, raiment and security furnished by the Americans have completely demoralized the insurgents. When the force under Gomez came to Guantanamo to assist the marines they were a most efficient body of men. They guided the marines to the enemy and fought with them shoulder to shoulder, not very skilfully in the matter of shooting, but still with courage and determination.

After this action there ensued at Guantanamo a long peace. The Cubans built themselves a permanent camp and they began to eat, eat much, and to sleep long, day and night, until now, behold, there is no more useless body of men anywhere! A trifle less than half of them are on Dr. Edgar's sick list, and the others are practically insubordinate. So much food seems to act upon them like a drug.

Here with the army the demoralization has occurred on a big scale. It is dangerous, too, for the Cuban. If he stupidly, drowsily remains out of these fights, what weight is his voice to have later in the final adjustments? The officers and men of the army, if their feeling remains the same, will not be happy to see him have any at all. The situation needs a Gomez. It is more serious than these bestarred machete bearers know how to appreciate, and it is the worst thing for the cause of an independent Cuba that could possibly exist.

At Caney about two hundred prisoners were taken. Two big squads of them were soldiers of the regular Spanish infantry in the usual blue-and-white pajamas. The others were the rummiest-looking set of men one could possibly imagine. They were native-born Cubans, reconcentrados, traitors, guerillas of the kind that bushwacked us so unmercifully. Some were doddering old men, shaking with the palsy of their many years. Some were slim, dirty, bad-eyed boys. They were all of a lower class than one could find in any United States jail.

At first they had all expected to be butchered. In fact, to encourage them to fight, their officers had told them that if they gave in they need expect no mercy from the dreadful Americans.

Our great, good, motherly old country has nothing in her heart but mercy, and nothing in her pockets but beef, hard-tack and coffee for all of them—lemon-colored refugee from Santiago, wild-eyed prisoner from the trenches, Spanish guerilla from out the thickets, half-naked insurgent from the mountains—all of them.

## 2    El Caney, July 5, via Port Antonio, Jamaica

*July 7*

During to-day's lull in the hostilities a steady stream of refugees has poured into our lines from the beleaguered city of Santiago. Women, by far, have been in the majority. Men, strong and able-bodied, have been few indeed. Spain has urgent need of such, wherefore Santiago has given up few more than wrecked and helpless creatures, too far upon the road to death to aid in staying our advance.

Yet, as the truce advanced, it changed the number and the character of these refugees. More men flocked in, young men and strong men. Certainly among them were deserters. There was the air of the true Spaniard about them. They had cast aside their distinguishing uniforms, to be sure, but they could not so easily disguise the ways and bearing of the soldier. Undoubtedly they were renegades. But, then—what matter? They were permitted within the lines, the one place where they would find safety from the impending avalanche of death soon to roll down upon Santiago from the hillside.

One saw in this great, gaunt assemblage the true horror of war. The sick, the lame, the halt and the blind were there. Women and men, tottering upon the verge of death, plodded doggedly onward. Beyond were our lines and safety. But so long had this same horror of war been before them that no longer could they feel its horridness. Their air was stolid and indifferent. It was a forlorn hope at the best. If this was safety, well and good. If death, what difference how it came.

Again, in the throng toiling on to safety were men and women carried in chairs and litters, some even in cot-beds. Our ambulances went forth to meet them. Then when these stolid, hopeless, unimpassioned ones found the dreaded enemy receiving and aiding them with kindness they showed, for the first time, some trace of feeling. What! Should these mad, despised Americanos spend time aiding the weak and aged! This was a wonder, indeed.

But, though the Americans' hands were turned to doing gentleness, it was otherwise with those Spanish miserables, Spain's ignoble pride, the guerillas. They lurked along the roadsides, eager and ready for bloodshed, plunder and unnameable wickedness. To drive them back the American cavalry patrolled the road of the refugees, whereupon the guerillas withdrew.

At the church in Caney the American surgeons were laboring among the enemy's sorely wounded. Here fifty-two Spanish were under treatment. Their amazement was profound. In the centre of the church lies one of the Spanish commanders, sorely wounded. There never was a more astonished man than he. Like the others, he believed his position impregnable. How any mortal could cross the zone of fire and survive was a matter beyond his ken. By the saints, it was a miracle! Three thousand Mausers, he knew to his own knowledge, were trained down the one slope he guarded. Yet had the Americans plunged through the rain of death and driven all before them.

Almost as great was his amazement at our treatment of himself and his wounded men. Why should we waste time upon them, when so many of ours had been stricken? Why this kindness? They had expected to lie where they had fallen, waiting but to die. It was the fortune of war. Why should it not be?

Our course of all at Caney has been moderation. Sometimes we have been too kind. Everybody knows the story of the road from the battle-field—the guerillas hanging to the flanks of the long line of wounded going to the rear. Though these men of ours could fight no longer, though they were in sore distress, these fiends incarnate fired upon them. They picked off, where they were able, the ambulance men, the bearers of the Red Cross flag and the surgeons at their work. They bowled them over at every chance. Yet three of these miscreants, caught among the trees, wearing clothes stripped from our dead, have been set to work about headquarters.

### 3    Siboney, July 9

Of course people all over the United States are dying to hear the names of the men who are conspicuous for bravery in Shafter's army. But as a matter of fact nobody with the army is particularly conspicuous for bravery. The bravery of an individual here is not a quality which causes him to be pointed out by his admiring fellows; he is, rather, submerged in the general mass. Now, cowardice—that would make a man conspicuous. He would then be pointed out often enough, but—mere bravery—that is no distinction in the Fifth Corps of the United States Army.

The main fact that has developed in this Santiago campaign is that the soldier of the regular army is the best man standing on two feet on God's green earth. This fact is put forth with no pretense whatever of interesting the American public in it. The public doesn't seem to care very much for the regular soldier.

The public wants to learn of the gallantry of the Reginald Marmaduke Maurice Montmorenci Sturtevant, and for goodness sake how the poor old chappy endures that dreadful hard-tack and bacon. Whereas, the name of the regular soldier is probably Michael Nolan and his life-sized portrait was not in the papers in celebration of his enlistment.

Just plain Private Nolan, blast him—he is of no consequence. He will get his name in the paper—oh, yes, when he is "killed." Or when he is "wounded." Or when he is "missing." If some good Spaniard shoots him through he will achieve a temporary notoriety, figuring in the lists for one brief moment in which he will appear to the casual reader mainly as part of a total, a unit in the interesting sum of men slain.

In fact, the disposition to leave out entirely all lists of killed and wounded regulars is quite a rational one since nobody cares to read them, anyhow, and their omission would allow room for oil paintings of various really important persons, limned as they were in the very act of being at the front, proud young men riding upon horses, the horses being still in Tampa and the proud young men being at Santiago, but still proud young men riding upon horses.

The three shining points about the American regular are his illimitable patience under anything which he may be called upon to endure, his superlative marksmanship and his ability in action to go ahead and win without any example or leading or jawing or trumpeting whatsoever. He knows his business, he does.

He goes into battle as if he had been fighting every day for three hundred years. If there is heavy firing ahead he does not even ask a question about it. He doesn't even ask whether the Americans are winning or losing. He agitates himself over no extraneous points. He attends exclusively to himself. In the Turk or Cossack this is a combination of fatalism and wooden-headedness. It need not be said that these qualities are lacking in the regular.

After the battle, at leisure—if he gets any—the regular's talk is likely to be a complete essay on practical field operations. He will be full of views about the management of such and such a brigade, the practice of this or that battery, and be admiring or scornful in regard to the operations of the right flank. He will be a tireless critic, bolstering his opinions with technical information procured heaven only knows where. In fact, he will alarm you. You may say: "This man gabbles too much for to be a soldier."

Then suddenly the regular becomes impenetrable, enigmatic. It is a question of Orders. When he hears the appointed voice raised in giving an Order, he is a changed being. When an Order comes he has no more to say; he simply displays as fine a form of unquestioning obedience as there is to be seen anywhere. It is his sacred thing, his fetich, his religion. Nothing now can stop him but a bullet.

In speaking of Reginald Marmaduke Maurice Montmorenci Sturtevant and his life-sized portraits, it must not be supposed that the unfortunate youth admires that sort of thing. He is a man and a soldier, although not so good either as man or soldier as Michael Nolan. But he is in this game honestly and sincerely; he is playing it gallantly; and, if from time to time he is made to look ridiculous, it is not his fault at all. It is the fault of the public.

We are as a people a great collection of the most arrant kids about anything that concerns war, and if we can get a chance to perform absurdly we usually seize it. It will probably take us three more months to learn that the society reporter, invaluable as he may be in times of peace, has no function during the blood and smoke of battle.

And shame, deep shame, on those who, because somebody once led a cotillion can seem to forget Nolan—Private Nolan of the regulars—shot through, his half-bred terrier masterless at Reno and his sister being chambermaid in a hotel in Omaha; Nolan, no longer sweating, swearing, overloaded, hungry, thirsty, sleepless, but merely a corpse, attired in about 40 cents' worth of clothes. Here's three volleys and taps to one Nolan, of this regiment or that regiment, and maybe some day, in a fairer, squarer land, he'll get his picture in the paper, too.

# 56

## The Negro's Strategy

However bright the promise of the Progressive Era seemed to many reformers, the American Negro continued to experience degradation and repression, North and South. Lynchings, segregation, economic deprivation, and legal discrimination of all sorts made life bleak for millions of black Americans.

Solutions to the problem varied. One of the most influential programs was offered by Booker T. Washington (1856–1915), born a slave in Virginia. After emancipation, Washington managed to attend school, and in 1872 he entered Hampton Institute, where he worked his way through as a janitor. Some years later Washington was asked to take charge of a newly established Negro normal school (for training teachers) in Tuskegee, Alabama. Washington developed there a nationally famous educational center, and established a world-wide reputation as a spokesman for the American Negro. His program of industrial progress, self-help, personal discipline, and political moderation was epitomized in his famous 1893 address in Atlanta, the text of which follows.

Washington was willing to sacrifice immediate political equality for economic advances; others angrily refused to do so. W. E. B. DuBois (1868–1963), a Harvard-trained sociologist, expressed a more radical view. As the twentieth century proceeded, his objectives gained greater support, and DuBois went on to help found the NAACP, carrying forth an active career of political leadership and creative scholarship.

### UP FROM SLAVERY
*Booker T. Washington*

In my early life I used to cherish a feeling of ill will toward any one who spoke in bitter terms against the Negro, or who advocated measures that tended to oppress the black man or take from him opportunities for growth in the most complete manner. Now, whenever I hear any one advocating measures that are meant to curtail the development of another, I pity the individual who would do this. I know that the one who makes this mistake does so because of his lack of opportunity for

From *Up from Slavery, An Autobiography* (New York, 1901), 203–204, 206, 208–213, 215–226, 229–230, 234–237.

the highest kind of growth. I pity him because I know that he is trying to stop the progress of the world, and because I know that in time the development and the ceaseless advance of humanity will make him ashamed of his weak and narrow position. One might as well try to stop the progress of a mighty railroad train by throwing his body across the track, as to try to stop the growth of the world in the direction of giving mankind more intelligence, more culture, more skill, more liberty, and in the direction of extending more sympathy and more brotherly kindness.

I now come to that one of the incidents in my life which seems to have excited the greatest amount of interest, and which perhaps went farther than anything else in giving me a reputation that in a sense might be called National. I refer to the address which I delivered at the opening of the Atlanta Cotton states and International Exposition, at Atlanta, Ga., September 18, 1895.

The directors of the Exposition decided that it would be a fitting recognition of the coloured race to erect a large and attractive building which should be devoted wholly to showing the progress of the Negro since freedom. It was further decided to have the building designed and erected wholly by Negro mechanics. This plan was carried out. In design, beauty, and general finish the Negro Building was equal to the others on the grounds.

As the day for the opening of the Exposition drew near, the Board of Directors began preparing the programme for the opening exercises. In the discussion from day to day of the various features of this programme, the question came up as to the advisability of putting a member of the Negro race on for one of the opening addresses, since the Negroes had been asked to take such a prominent part in the Exposition. It was argued, further, that such recognition would mark the good feeling prevailing between the two races. After the question had been canvassed for several days, the directors voted unanimously to ask me to deliver one of the opening-day addresses, and in a few days after that I received the official invitation.

The receiving of this invitation brought to me a sense of responsibility that it would be hard for any one not placed in my position to appreciate. What were my feelings when this invitation came to me? I remembered that I had been a slave; that my early years had been spent in the lowest depths of poverty and ignorance, and that I had had little opportunity to prepare me for such a responsibility as this. It was only a few years before that time that any white man in the audience might have claimed me as his slave; and it was easily possible that some of my former owners might be present to hear me speak.

I knew, too, that this was the first time in the entire history of the Negro that a member of my race had been asked to speak from the same platform with white Southern men and women on any important National occasion. I was asked now to speak to an audience composed of the wealth and culture of the white South, the representatives of my former masters. I knew, too, that while the greater part of my audience would be composed of Southern people, yet there would be present a large number of Northern whites, as well as a great many men and women of my own race.

I was determined to say nothing that I did not feel from the bottom of my heart

129

to be true and right. When the invitation came to me, there was not one word of intimation as to what I should say or as to what I should omit. In this I felt that the Board of Directors had paid a tribute to me. They knew that by one sentence I could have blasted, in a large degree, the success of the Exposition. I was also painfully conscious of the fact that, while I must be true to my own race in my utterances, I had it in my power to make such an ill-timed address.

On the morning of September 17, together with Mrs. Washington and my three children, I started for Atlanta. I felt a good deal as I suppose a man feels when he is on his way to the gallows. In passing through the town of Tuskegee I met a white farmer who lived some distance out in the country. In a jesting manner this man said: "Washington, you have spoken before the Northern white people, the Negroes in the South, and to us country white people in the South; but in Atlanta, to-morrow, you will have before you the Northern whites, the Southern whites, and the Negroes all together. I am afraid that you have got yourself into a tight place." This farmer diagnosed the situation correctly, but his frank words did not add anything to my comfort.

Early in the morning a committee called to escort me to my place in the procession which was to march to the Exposition grounds. In this procession were prominent coloured citizens in carriages, as well as several Negro military organizations. I noted that the Exposition officials seemed to go out of their way to see that all of the coloured people in the procession were properly placed and properly treated.

The room was very large, and well suited to public speaking. When I entered the room, there were vigorous cheers from the coloured portion of the audience, and faint cheers from some of the white people. I had been told, while I had been in Atlanta, that while many white people were going to be present to hear me speak, simply out of curiosity, and that others who would be present would be in full sympathy with me, there was a still larger element of the audience which would consist of those who were going to be present for the purpose of hearing me make a fool of myself, or, at least, of hearing me say some foolish thing, so that they could say to the officials who had invited me to speak, "I told you so!"

When I arose to speak, there was considerable cheering, especially from the coloured people. As I remember it now, the thing that was uppermost in my mind was the desire to say something that would cement the friendship of the races and bring about hearty coöperation between them. So far as my outward surroundings were concerned, the only thing that I recall distinctly now is that when I got up, I saw thousands of eyes looking intently into my face. The following is the address which I delivered:—

**Mr. President and Gentlemen
of the Board of Directors and Citizens**

One-third of the population of the South is of the Negro race. No enterprise seeking the material, civil, or moral welfare of this section can disregard this element of our population and reach the highest success. I but convey to you, Mr.

President and Directors, the sentiment of the masses of my race when I say that in no way have the value and manhood of the American Negro been more fittingly and generously recognized than by the managers of this magnificent Exposition at every stage of its progress. It is a recognition that will do more to cement the friendship of the two races than any occurrence since the dawn of our freedom.

Not only this, but the opportunity here afforded will awaken among us a new era of industrial progress. Ignorant and inexperienced, it is not strange that in the first years of our new life we began at the top instead of at the bottom; that a seat in Congress or the state legislature was more sought than real estate or industrial skill; that the political convention of stump speaking had more attractions than starting a dairy farm or truck garden.

A ship lost at sea for many days suddenly sighted a friendly vessel. From the mast of the unfortunate vessel was seen a signal, "Water, water: we die of thirst!" The answer from the friendly vessel at once came back, "Cast down your bucket where you are." A second time the signal, "Water, water; send us water!" ran up from the distressed vessel, and was answered, "Cast down your bucket where you are." And a third and fourth signal for water was answered, "Cast down your bucket where you are." The captain of the distressed vessel, at last heeding the injunction, cast down his bucket, and it came up full of fresh, sparkling water from the mouth of the Amazon River. To those of my race who depend on bettering their condition in a foreign land or who underestimate the importance of cultivating friendly relations with the Southern white man, who is their next-door neighbour, I would say: "Cast down your bucket where you are"—cast it down in making friends in every manly way of the people of all races by whom we are surrounded.

Cast it down in agriculture, mechanics, in commerce, in domestic service, and in the professions. And in this connection it is well to bear in mind that whatever other sins the South may be called to bear, when it comes to business, pure and simple, it is in the South that the Negro is given a man's chance in the commercial world, and in nothing is this Exposition more eloquent than in emphasizing this chance. Our greatest danger is that in the great leap from slavery to freedom we may overlook the fact that the masses of us are to live by the productions of our hands, and fail to keep in mind that we shall prosper in proportion as we learn to dignify and glorify common labour and put brains and skill into the common occupations of life; shall prosper in proportion as we learn to draw the line between the superficial and the substantial, the ornamental gewgaws of life and the useful. No race can prosper till it learns that there is as much dignity in tilling a field as in writing a poem. It is at the bottom of life we must begin, and not at the top. Nor should we permit our grievances to overshadow our opportunities.

To those of the white race who look to the incoming of those of foreign birth and strange tongue and habits for the prosperity of the South, were I permitted I would repeat what I say to my own race, "Cast down your bucket where you are." Cast it down among the eight millions of Negroes whose habits you know, whose fidelity and love you have tested in days when to have proved treacherous meant the ruin of your firesides. Cast down your bucket among these people who have, without strikes and labour wars, tilled your fields, cleared your forests, builded your

131

railroads and cities, and brought forth treasures from the bowels of the earth, and helped make possible this magnificent representation of the progress of the South. Casting down your bucket among my people, helping and encouraging them as you are doing on these grounds, and to education of head, hand, and heart, you will find that they will buy your surplus land, make blossom the waste places in your fields, and run your factories. While doing this, you can be sure in the future, as in the past, that you and your families will be surrounded by the most patient, faithful, law-abiding, and unresentful people that the world has seen. As we have proved our loyalty to you in the past, in nursing your children, watching by the sick-bed of your mothers and fathers, and often following them with tear-dimmed eyes to their graves, so in the future, in our humble way, we shall stand by you with a devotion that no foreigner can approach, ready to lay down our lives, if need be, in defence of yours, interlacing our industrial, commercial, civil, and religious life with yours in a way that shall make the interests of both races one. In all things that are purely social we can be as separate as the fingers, yet one as the hand in all things essential to mutual progress.

There is no defence or security for any of us except in the highest intelligence and development of all. If anywhere there are efforts tending to curtail the fullest growth of the Negro, let these efforts be turned into stimulating, encouraging, and making him the most useful and intelligent citizen. Effort or means so invested will pay a thousand per cent interest. These efforts will be twice blessed—"blessing him that gives and him that takes."

There is no escape through law of man or God from the inevitable:—

*The laws of changeless justice bind*
  *Oppressor with oppressed;*
*And close as sin and suffering joined*
  *We march to fate abreast.*

Nearly sixteen millions of hands will aid you in pulling the load upward, or they will pull against you the load downward. We shall constitute one-third and more of the ignorance and crime of the South, or one-third its intelligence and progress; we shall contribute one-third to the business and industrial prosperity of the South, or we shall prove a veritable body of death, stagnating, depressing, retarding every effort to advance the body politic.

Gentlemen of the Exposition, as we present to you our humble effort at an exhibition of our progress, you must not expect overmuch. Starting thirty years ago with ownership here and there in a few quilts and pumpkins and chickens (gathered from miscellaneous sources), remember the path that has led from these to the inventions and production of agricultural implements, buggies, steam-engines, newspapers, books, statuary, carving, paintings, the management of drug-stores and banks, has not been trodden without contact with thorns and thistles. While we take pride in what we exhibit as a result of our independent efforts, we do not for a moment forget that our part in this exhibition would fall far short of your expectations but for the constant help that has come to our educational life, not only from the Southern states, but especially from Northern philanthropists, who have made their gifts a constant stream of blessing and encouragement.

The wisest among my race understand that the agitation of questions of social equality is the extremest folly, and that progress in the enjoyment of all the privileges that will come to us must be the result of severe and constant struggle rather than of artificial forcing. No race that has anything to contribute to the markets of the world is long in any degree ostracized. It is important and right that all privileges of the law be ours, but it is vastly more important that we be prepared for the exercises of these privileges. The opportunity to earn a dollar in a factory just now is worth infinitely more than the opportunity to spend a dollar in an opera-house.

In conclusion, may I repeat that nothing in thirty years has given us more hope and encouragement, and drawn us so near to you of the white race, as this opportunity offered by the Exposition; and here bending, as it were, over the altar that represents the results of the struggles of your race and mine, both starting practically empty-handed three decades ago. I pledge that in your effort to work out the great and intricate problem which God has laid at the doors of the South, you shall have at all times the patient, sympathetic help of my race; only let this be constantly in mind, that, while from representations in these buildings of the product of field, of forest, of mine, of factory, letters, and art, much good will come, yet far above and beyond material benefits will be that higher good, that, let us pray God, will come, in a blotting out of sectional differences and racial animosities and suspicions, in a determination to administer absolute justice, in a willing obedience among all classes to the mandates of law. This, then, coupled with our material prosperity, will bring into our beloved South a new heaven and a new earth.

The first thing that I remember, after I had finished speaking, was that Governor Bullock rushed across the platform and took me by the hand, and that others did the same. I received so many and such hearty congratulations that I found it difficult to get out of the building. I did not appreciate to any degree, however, the impression which my address seemed to have made, until the next morning, when I went into the business part of the city. As soon as I was recognized, I was surprised to find myself pointed out and surrounded by a crowd of men who wished to shake hands with me. This was kept up on every street on to which I went, to an extent which embarrassed me so much that I went back to my boarding-place. The next morning I returned to Tuskegee. At the station in Atlanta, and at almost all of the stations at which the train stopped between that city and Tuskegee, I found a crowd of people anxious to shake hands with me.

The papers in all parts of the United States published the address in full, and for months afterward there were complimentary editorial references to it. Mr. Clark Howell, the editor of the Atlanta *Constitution,* telegraphed to a New York paper, among other words, the following, "I do not exaggerate when I say that Professor Booker T. Washington's address yesterday was one of the most notable speeches, both as to character and as to the warmth of its reception, ever delivered to a

Southern audience. The address was a revelation. The whole speech is a platform upon which blacks and whites can stand with full justice to each other."

The coloured people and the coloured newspapers at first seemed to be greatly pleased with the character of my Atlanta address, as well as with its reception. But after the first burst of enthusiasm began to die away, and the coloured people began reading the speech in cold type, some of them seemed to feel that they had been hypnotized. They seemed to feel that I had been too liberal in my remarks toward the Southern whites, and that I had not spoken out strongly enough for what they termed the "rights" of the race. For a while there was a reaction, so far as a certain element of my own race was concerned, but later these reactionary ones seemed to have been won over to my way of believing and acting.

I am often asked to express myself more freely than I do upon the political condition and the political future of my race. These recollections of my experience in Atlanta give me the opportunity to do so briefly. My own belief is, although I have never before said so in so many words, that the time will come when the Negro in the South will be accorded all the political rights which his ability, character, and material possessions entitle him to. I think, though, that the opportunity to freely exercise such political rights will not come in any large degree through outside or artificial forcing, but will be accorded to the Negro by the Southern white people themselves, and that they will protect him in the exercise of those rights. Just as soon as the South gets over the old feeling that it is being forced by "foreigners," or "aliens," to do something which it does not want to do, I believe that the change in the direction that I have indicated is going to begin. In fact, there are indications that it is already beginning in a slight degree.

I believe it is the duty of the Negro—as the greater part of the race is already doing—to deport himself modestly in regard to political claims, depending upon the slow but sure influences that proceed from the possession of property, intelligence, and high character for the full recognition of his political rights. I think that the according of the full exercise of political rights is going to be a matter of natural, slow growth, not an over-night, gourd-vine affair. I do not believe that the Negro should cease voting, for a man cannot learn the exercise of self-government by ceasing to vote any more than a boy can learn to swim by keeping out of the water, but I do believe that in his voting he should more and more be influenced by those of intelligence and character who are his next-door neighbours.

I know coloured men who, through the encouragement, help, and advice of Southern white people, have accumulated thousands of dollars' worth of property, but who, at the same time, would never think of going to those same persons for advice concerning the casting of their ballots. This, it seems to me, is unwise and unreasonable, and should cease. In saying this I do not mean that the Negro should truckle, or not vote from principle, for the instant he ceases to vote from principle he loses the confidence and respect of the Southern white man even.

As a rule, I believe in universal, free suffrage, but I believe that in the South we are confronted with peculiar conditions that justify the protection of the ballot in many of the states, for a while at least, either by an educational test, a property test, or by both combined; but whatever tests are required, they should be made to apply with equal and exact justice to both races.

# THE SOULS OF BLACK FOLK
## *W. E. B. DuBois*

Mr. Washington represents in Negro thought the old attitude of adjustment and submission; but adjustment at such a peculiar time as to make his programme unique. This is an age of unusual economic development, and Mr. Washington's programme naturally takes an economic cast, becoming a gospel of Work and Money to such an extent as apparently almost completely to overshadow the higher aims of life. Moreover, this is an age when the more advanced races are coming in closer contact with the less developed races, and the race-feeling is therefore intensified; and Mr. Washington's programme practically accepts the alleged inferiority of the Negro races. Again, in our own land, the reaction from the sentiment of war time has given impetus to race-prejudice against Negroes, and Mr. Washington withdraws many of the high demands of Negroes as men and American citizens. In other periods of intensified prejudice all the Negro's tendency to self-assertion has been called forth; at this period a policy of submission is advocated. In the history of nearly all other races and peoples the doctrine preached at such crises has been that manly self-respect is worth more than lands and houses, and that a people who voluntarily surrender such respect, or cease striving for it, are not worth civilizing.

In answer to this, it has been claimed that the Negro can survive only through submission. Mr. Washington distinctly asks that black people give up, at least for the present, three things,—

First, political power,

Second, insistence on civil rights,

Third, higher education of Negro youth,—

and concentrate all their energies on industrial education, the accumulation of wealth, and the conciliation of the South. This policy has been courageously and insistently advocated for over fifteen years, and has been triumphant for perhaps ten years. As a result of this tender of the palm-branch, what has been the return? In these years there have occurred:

1. The disfranchisement of the Negro.

2. The legal creation of a distinct status of civil inferiority for the Negro.

3. The steady withdrawal of aid from institutions for the higher training of the Negro.

These movements are not, to be sure, direct results of Mr. Washington's teachings; but his propaganda has, without a shadow of doubt, helped their speedier accomplishment. The question then comes: Is it possible, and probable, that nine millions of men can make effective progress in economic lines if they are deprived of political rights, made a servile caste, and allowed only the most meagre

From *The Souls of Black Folk* (Chicago, 1904), 50–59.

chance for developing their exceptional men? If history and reason give any distinct answer to these questions, it is an emphatic *No*. And Mr. Washington thus faces the triple paradox of his career:

1. He is striving nobly to make Negro artisans business men and property-owners; but it is utterly impossible, under modern competitive methods, for workingmen and property-owners to defend their rights and exist without the right of suffrage.

2. He insists on thrift and self-respect, but at the same time counsels a silent submission to civic inferiority such as is bound to sap the manhood of any race in the long run.

3. He advocates common-school and industrial training, and depreciates institutions of higher learning; but neither the Negro common-schools, nor Tuskegee itself, could remain open a day were it not for teachers trained in Negro colleges, or trained by their graduates.

In failing thus to state plainly and unequivocally the legitimate demands of their people, even at the cost of opposing an honored leader, the thinking classes of American Negroes would shirk a heavy repsonsibility,—a responsibility to themselves, a responsibility to the struggling masses, a responsibility to the darker races of men whose future depends so largely on this American experiment, but especially a responsibility to this nation,—this common Fatherland. It is wrong to encourage a man or a people in evil-doing; it is wrong to aid and abet a national crime simply because it is unpopular not to do so. The growing spirit of kindliness and reconciliation between the North and South after the frightful difference of a generation ago ought to be a source of deep congratulation to all, and especially to those whose mistreatment caused the war; but if that reconciliation is to be marked by the industrial slavery and civic death of those same black men, with permanent legislation into a position of inferiority, then those black men, if they are really men, are called upon by every consideration of patriotism and loyalty to oppose such a course by all civilized methods, even though such opposition involves disagreement with Mr. Booker T. Washington. We have no right to sit silently by while the inevitable seeds are sown for a harvest of disaster to our children, black and white.

It would be unjust to Mr. Washington not to acknowledge that in several instances he has opposed movements in the South which were unjust to the Negro; he sent memorials to the Louisiana and Alabama constitutional conventions, he has spoken against lynching, and in other ways has openly or silently set his influence against sinister schemes and unfortunate happenings. Notwithstanding this, it is equally true to assert that on the whole the distinct impression left by Mr. Washington's propaganda is, first, that the South is justified in its present attitude toward the Negro because of the Negro's degradation; secondly, that the prime cause of the Negro's failure to rise more quickly is his wrong education in the past; and, thirdly, that his future rise depends primarily on his own efforts. Each of these propositions is a dangerous half-truth. The supplementary truths must never be lost sight of: first, slavery and race-prejudice are potent if not sufficient causes of the Negro's position; second, industrial and common-school training were necessarily slow in planting because they had to await the black teachers trained by higher institutions,—it being extremely doubtful if any essentially different development was possible, and certainly a Tuskegee was unthinkable before 1880; and, third, while it is a great faith to say that the Negro must strive and strive mightily to help himself, it is equally true that unless his striving be not simply seconded, but rather aroused and encouraged, by the initiative of the richer and wiser environing group, he cannot hope for great success.

In his failure to realize and impress this last point, Mr. Washington is especially to be criticised. His doctrine has tended to make the whites, North and South, shift the burden of the Negro problem to the Negro's shoulders and stand aside as critical and rather pessimistic spectators; when in fact the burden belongs to the nation, and the hands of none of us are clean if we bend not our energies to righting these great wrongs.

The South ought to be led, by candid and honest criticism, to assert her better self and do her full duty to the race she has cruelly wronged and is still wronging. The North—her co-partner in guilt—cannot salve her conscience by plastering it with gold. We cannot settle this problem by diplomacy and suaveness, by "policy" alone. If worse come to worst, can the moral fibre of this country survive the slow throttling and murder of nine millions of men?

The black men of America have a duty to perform, a duty stern and delicate,— a forward movement to oppose a part of the work of their greatest leader. So far as Mr. Washington preaches Thrift, Patience, and Industrial Training for the masses, we must hold up his hands and strive with him, rejoicing in his honors and glorying in the strength of this Joshua called of God and of man to lead the headless host. But so far as Mr. Washington apologizes for injustice, North or South, does not rightly value the privilege and duty of voting, belittles the emasculating effects of caste distinctions, and opposes the higher training and ambition of our brighter minds,—so far as he, the South, or the Nation, does this—we must unceasingly and firmly oppose them. By every civilized and peaceful method we must strive for the rights which the world accords to men, clinging unwaveringly to those great words which the sons of the Fathers would fain forget: "We hold these truths to be self-evident: That all men are created equal; that they are endowed by their Creator with certain unalienable rights; that among these are life, liberty, and the pursuit of happiness."

# 57

## The House of Dreams

Jane Addams (1860–1935) was one of the great social reformers of her era. The daughter of an Illinois miller and state senator, she graduated from college intending to become a physician, but after her health failed she abandoned her plans and spent some years traveling in Europe. During a second trip there she was inspired by the work of Toynbee Hall, a settlement in London, and returned to America to begin the country's first great settlement house, Hull House, in Chicago. There she gathered artists, educators, and social workers to help repair the social damage caused by immigration, urbanization, and industrialization. Through nurseries, women's clubs, lectures, theater groups, gymnasiums, she sought to restore a sense of community participation and generational understanding to the people of her neighborhood.

The tact and energy of Miss Addams were matched by her writing skills; in a series of notable books she popularized the causes of social work, community reconstruction, women's rights, and peace. Her works were tied together by a desire to reassert older moral and ethical values in a vocabulary that made them meaningful to victims of rapid change. In 1931, several years before her death, she received the Nobel Peace Prize.

### THE HOUSE OF DREAMS
*Jane Addams*

To the preoccupied adult who is prone to use the city street as a mere passageway from one hurried duty to another, nothing is more touching than his encounter with a group of children and young people who are emerging from a theater with the magic of the play still thick upon them. They look up and down the familiar street scarcely recognizing it and quite unable to determine the direction of home. From a tangle of "make believe" they gravely scrutinize the real world which they are so reluctant to reënter, reminding one of the absorbed gaze of a child who is groping his way back from fairy-land whither the story has completely transported him.

"Going to the show" for thousands of young people in every industrial city is the only possible road to the realm of mystery and romance; the theater is the only

From *The Spirit of Youth and the City Streets* (New York, 1905), 75–103.

place where they can satisfy that craving for a conception of life higher than that which the actual world offers them. In a very real sense the drama and the drama alone performs for them the office of art as is clearly revealed in their blundering demand stated in many forms for "a play unlike life." The theater becomes to them a "veritable house of dreams" infinitely more real than the noisy streets and the crowded factories.

This first simple demand upon the theater for romance is closely allied to one more complex which might be described as a search for solace and distraction in those moments of first awakening from the glamour of a youth's interpretation of life to the sterner realities which are thrust upon his consciousness. These perceptions which inevitably "close around" and imprison the spirit of youth are perhaps never so grim as the case of the wage-earning child. We can all recall our own moments of revolt against life's actualities, our reluctance to admit that all life was to be as unheroic and uneventful as that which we saw about us, it was too unbearable that "this was all there was" and we tried every possible avenue of escape. As we made an effort to believe, in spite of what we saw, that life was noble and harmonious, as we stubbornly clung to poesy in contradiction to the testimony of our senses, so we see thousands of young people thronging the theaters bent in their turn upon the same quest. The drama provides a transition between the romantic conceptions which they vainly struggle to keep intact and life's cruelties and trivialities which they refuse to admit. A child whose imagination has been cultivated is able to do this for himself through reading and reverie, but for the overworked city youth of meager education, perhaps nothing but the theater is able to perform this important office.

The theater also has a strange power to forecast life for the youth. Each boy comes from our ancestral past not "in entire forgetfulness," and quite as he unconsciously uses ancient war-cries in his street play, so he longs to reproduce and to see set before him the valors and vengeances of a society embodying a much more primitive state of morality than that in which he finds himself. Mr. Patten has pointed out that the elemental action which the stage presents, the old emotions of love and jealousy, of revenge and daring take the thoughts of the spectator back into deep and well worn channels in which his mind runs with a sense of rest afforded by nothing else. The cheap drama brings cause and effect, will power and action, once more into relation and gives a man the thrilling conviction that he may yet be master of his fate. The youth of course, quite unconscious of this psychology, views the deeds of the hero simply as a forecast of his own future and it is this fascinating view of his own career which draws the boy to "shows" of all sorts. They can scarcely be too improbable for him, portraying, as they do, his belief in his own prowess. A series of slides which has lately been very popular in the five-cent theaters of Chicago, portrayed five masked men breaking into a humble dwelling, killing the father of the family and carrying away the family treasure. The golden-haired son of the house, aged seven, vows eternal vengeance on the spot, and follows one villain after another to his doom. The execution of each is shown in lurid detail, and the last slide of the series depicts the hero, aged ten, kneeling upon his father's grave counting on the fingers of one hand the number of men that

139

he has killed, and thanking God that he has been permitted to be an instrument of vengeance.

In another series of slides, a poor woman is wearily bending over some sewing, a baby is crying in the cradle, and two little boys of nine and ten are asking for food. In despair the mother sends them out into the street to beg, but instead they steal a revolver from a pawn shop and with it kill a Chinese laundryman, robbing him of $200. They rush home with the treasure which is found by the mother in the baby's cradle, wereupon she and her sons fall upon their knees and send up a prayer of thankfulness for this timely and heaven-sent assistance.

Is it not astounding that a city allows thousands of its youth to fill their impressionable minds with these absurdities which certainly will become the foundation for their working moral codes and the data from which they will judge the proprieties of life!

It is as if a child, starved at home, should be forced to go out and search for food, selecting, quite naturally, not that which is nourishing but that which is exciting and appealing to his outward sense, often in his ignorance and foolishness blundering into substances which are filthy and poisonous.

Out of my twenty years' experience at Hull-House I can recall all sorts of pilfering, petty larcenies, and even burglaries, due to that never ceasing effort on the part of boys to procure theater tickets. I can also recall indirect efforts towards the same end which are most pitiful. I remember the remorse of a young girl of fifteen who was brought into the Juvenile Court after a night spent weeping in the cellar of her home because she had stolen a mass of artificial flowers with which to trim a hat. She stated that she had taken the flowers because she was afraid of losing the attention of a young man whom she had heard say that "a girl has to be dressy if she expects to be seen." This young man was the only one who had ever taken her to the theater and if he failed her, she was sure that she would never go again, and she sobbed out incoherently that she "couldn't live at all without it." Apparently the blankness and grayness of life itself had been broken for her only by the portrayal of a different world.

One boy whom I had known from babyhood began to take money from his mother from the time he was seven years old, and after he was ten she regularly gave him money for the play Saturday evening. However, the Saturday performance, "starting him off like," he always went twice again on Sunday, procuring the money in all sorts of illicit ways. Practically all of his earnings after he was fourteen were spent in this way to satisfy the insatiable desire to know of the great adventures of the wide world which the more fortunate boy takes out in reading Homer and Stevenson.

In talking with his mother, I was reminded of my experience one Sunday afternoon in Russia when the employees of a large factory were seated in an open-air theater, watching with breathless interest the presentation of folk stories. I was told that troupes of actors went from one manufacturing establishment to another presenting the simple elements of history and literature to the illiterate employees. This tendency to slake the thirst for adventure by viewing the drama is, of course, but a blind and primitive effort in the direction of culture; for "he who makes himself its vessel and bearer thereby acquires a freedom from the blindness and soul poverty of daily existence."

It is partly in response to this need that more sophisticated young people often go to the theater, hoping to find a clue to life's perplexities. Many times the bewildered hero reminds one of Emerson's description of Margaret Fuller, "I don't know where I am going, follow me"; nevertheless, the stage is dealing with the moral themes in which the public is most interested.

And while many young people go to the theater if only to see represented, and to hear discussed, the themes which seem to them so tragically important, there is no doubt that what they hear there, flimsy and poor as it often is, easily becomes their actual moral guide. In moments of moral crisis they turn to the sayings of the hero who found himself in a similar plight. The sayings may not be profound, but at least they are applicable to conduct. In the last few years scores of plays have been put upon the stage whose titles might be easily translated into proper headings for sociological lectures or sermons, without including the plays of Ibsen, Shaw and Hauptmann, which deal so directly with moral issues that the moralists themselves wince under their teachings and declare them brutal. But it is this very brutality which the over-refined and complicated city dwellers often crave. Moral teaching has become so intricate, creeds so metaphysical, that in a state of absolute reaction they demand definite instruction for daily living. Their whole-hearted acceptance of the teaching corroborates the statement recently made by an English playwright that "The theater is literally making the minds of our urban populations today. It is a huge factory of sentiment, of character, of points of honor, of conceptions of conduct, of everything that finally determines the destiny of a nation. The theater is not only a place of amusement, it is a place of culture, a place where people learn how to think, act, and feel." Seldom, however, do we associate the theater with our plans for civic righteousness, although it has become so important a factor in city life.

One Sunday evening last winter an investigation was made of four hundred and sixty six theaters in the city of Chicago, and it was discovered that in the majority of them the leading theme was revenge; the lover following his rival; the outraged husband seeking his wife's paramour; or the wiping out by death of a blot on a hitherto unstained honor. It was estimated that one sixth of the entire population of the city had attended the theaters on that day. At that same moment the churches throughout the city were preaching the gospel of good will. Is not this a striking commentary upon the contradictory influences to which the city youth is constantly subjected!

This discrepancy between the church and the stage is at times apparently recognized by the five-cent theater itself, and a blundering attempt is made to suffuse the songs and moving pictures with piety. Nothing could more absurdly demonstrate this attempt than a song, illustrated by pictures, describing the adventures of a young man who follows a pretty girl through street after street in the hope of "snatching a kiss from her ruby lips." The young man is overjoyed when a sudden wind storm drives the girl to shelter under an archway, and he is about to succeed in his attempt when the good Lord, "ever watchful over innocence," makes the same wind "blow a cloud of dust into the eyes of the rubberneck," and "his foul purpose is foiled." This attempt at piety is also shown in a series of films depicting Bible stories and the Passion Play at Oberammergau, forecasting the time when the moving film will be viewed as a mere mechanical device for the use of the church, the school and the library, as well as for the theater.

At present, however, most improbable tales hold the attention of the youth of the city night after night, and feed his starved imagination as nothing else succeeds in doing. In addition to these fascinations, the five-cent theater is also fast becoming the general social center and club house in many crowded neighborhoods. It is easy of access from the street, the entire family of parents and children can attend for a comparatively small sum of money, and the performance lasts for at least an hour; and, in some of the humbler theaters, the spectators are not disturbed for a second hour.

The room which contains the mimic stage is small and cozy, and less formal than the regular theater, and there is much more gossip and social life as if the foyer and pit were mingled. The very darkness of the room, necessary for an exhibition of the films, is an added attraction to many young people, for whom the space is filled with the glamour of love making.

Hundreds of young people attend these five-cent theaters every evening in the week, including Sunday, and what is seen and heard there becomes the sole topic of conversation, forming the ground pattern of their social life. That mutual understanding which in another social circle is provided by books, travel and all the arts, is here compressed into the topics suggested by the play.

The young people attend the five-cent theaters in groups, with something of the "gang" instinct, boasting of the films and stunts in "our theater." They find a certain advantage in attending one theater regularly, for the *habitués* are often invited to come upon the stage on "amateur nights," which occur at least once a week in all the theaters. This is, of course, a most exciting experience. If the "stunt" does not meet with the approval of the audience, the performer is greeted with jeers and a long hook pulls him off the stage; if, on the other hand, he succeeds in pleasing the audience, he may be paid for his performance and later register with a booking agency, the address of which is supplied by the obliging manager, and thus he fancies that a lucrative and exciting career is opening before him. Almost every night at six o'clock a long line of children may be seen waiting at the entrance of these booking agencies, of which there are fifteen that are well known in Chicago.

Thus, the only art which is constantly placed before the eyes of "the temperamental youth" is a debased form of dramatic art, and a vulgar type of music, for the success of a song in these theaters depends not so much upon its musical rendition as upon the vulgarity of its appeal. In a song which held the stage of a cheap theater in Chicago for weeks, the young singer was helped out by a bit of mirror from which she threw a flash of light into the faces of successive boys whom she selected from the audience as she sang the refrain, "You are my Affinity." Many popular songs relate the vulgar experiences of a city man wandering from amusement park to bathing beach in search of flirtations. It may be that these "stunts" and recitals of city adventure contain the nucleus of coming poesy and romance, as the songs and recitals of the early minstrels sprang directly from the life of the people, but all the more does the effort need help and direction, both in the development of its technique and the material of its themes.

The few attempts which have been made in this direction are astonishingly rewarding to those who regard the power of self-expression as one of the most precious boons of education. The Children's Theater in New York is the most successful example, but every settlement in which dramatics have been systematically fostered can also testify to a surprisingly quick response to this form of art on the part of young people. The Hull-House Theater is constantly besieged by children clamoring to "take part" in the plays of Schiller, Shakespeare, and Molière, although they know it means weeks of rehearsal and the complete memorizing of "stiff" lines. The audiences sit enthralled by the final rendition and other children whose tastes have supposedly been debased by constant vaudeville, are pathetically eager to come again and again. Even when still more is required from the young actors, research into the special historic period, copying costumes from old plates, hours of labor that the "th" may be restored to its proper place in English speech, their enthusiasm is unquenched. But quite aside from its educational possibilities one never ceases to marvel at the power of even a mimic stage to afford to the young a magic space in which life may be lived in efflorescence, where manners may be courtly and elaborate without exciting ridicule, where the sequence of events is impressive and comprehensible. Order and beauty of life is what the adolescent youth craves above all else as the younger child indefatigably demands his story. "Is this where the most beautiful princess in the world lives?" asks a little girl peering into the door of the Hull-House Theater, or "Does Alice in Wonderland always stay here?" It is much easier for her to put her feeling into words than it is for the youth who has enchantingly rendered the gentle poetry of Ben Jonson's "Sad Shepherd," or for him who has walked the boards as Southey's Wat Tyler. His association, however, is quite as clinging and magical as in the child's although he can only say, "Gee, I wish I could always feel the way I did that night. Something would be doing then." Nothing of the artist's pleasure, nor of the revelation of that larger world which surrounds and completes our own, is lost to him because a careful technique has been exacted,—on the contrary this has only dignified and enhanced it. It would also be easy to illustrate youth's eagerness for artistic expression from the recitals given by the pupils of the New York Music School Settlement, or by those of the Hull-House Music School. These attempts also combine social life with the training of the artistic sense and in this approximate the fascinations of the five-cent theater.

This spring a group of young girls accustomed to the life of a five-cent theater, reluctantly refused an invitation to go to the country for a day's outing because the return on a late train would compel them to miss one evening's performance. They found it impossible to tear themselves away not only from the excitements of the theater itself but from the gaiety of the crowd of young men and girls invariably gathered outside discussing the sensational posters.

143

A steady English shopkeeper lately complained that unless he provided his four daughters with the money for the five-cent theaters every evening they would steal it from his till, and he feared that they might be driven to procure it in even more illicit ways. Because his entire family life had been thus disrupted he gloomily asserted that "this cheap show had ruined his home and was the curse of America." This father was able to formulate the anxiety of many immigrant parents who are absolutely bewildered by the keen absorption of their children in the cheap theater. This anxiety is not, indeed, without foundation. An eminent alienist of Chicago states that he has had a number of patients among neurotic children whose emotional natures have been so over-wrought by the crude appeal to which they had been so constantly subjected in the theaters, that they have become victims of hallucination and mental disorder. The statement of this physician may be the first note of alarm which will awaken the city to its duty in regard to the theater, so that it shall at least be made safe and sane for the city child whose senses are already so abnormally developed.

This testimony of a physician that the conditions are actually pathological, may at last induce us to bestir ourselves in regard to procuring a more wholesome form of public recreation. Many efforts in social amelioration have been undertaken only after such exposures; in the meantime, while the occasional child is driven distraught, a hundred children permanently injure their eyes watching the moving films, and hundreds more seriously model their conduct upon the standards set before them on this mimic stage.

Three boys, aged nine, eleven and thirteen years, who had recently seen depicted the adventures of frontier life including the holding up of a stage coach and the lassoing of the driver, spent weeks planning to lasso, murder, and rob a neighborhood milkman, who started on his route at four o'clock in the morning. They made their headquarters in a barn and saved enough money to buy a revolver, adopting as their watchword the phrase "Dead Men Tell no Tales." One spring morning the conspirators, with their faces covered with black cloth, lay "in ambush" for the milkman. Fortunately for him, as the lariat was thrown the horse shied, and, although the shot was appropriately fired, the milkman's life was saved. Such a direct influence of the theater is by no means rare, even among older boys. Thirteen young lads were brought into the Municipal Court in Chicago during the first week that "Raffles, the Amateur Cracksman" was upon the stage, each one with an outfit of burglar's tools in his possession, and each one shamefacedly admitting that the gentlemanly burglar in the play had suggested to him a career of similar adventure.

In so far as the illusions of the theater succeed in giving youth the rest and recreation which comes from following a more primitive code of morality, it has a close relation to the function performed by public games. It is, of course, less valuable because the sense of participation is largely confined to the emotions and the imagination, and does not involve the entire nature.

We might illustrate by the "Wild West Show" in which the onlooking boy imagines himself an active participant. The scouts, the Indians, the bucking ponies, are his real intimate companions and occupy his entire mind. In contrast with this we have the omnipresent game of tag which is, doubtless, also founded upon the chase. It gives the boy exercise and momentary echoes of the old excitement, but it is barren of suggestion and quickly degenerates into horse-play.

Well considered public games easily carried out in a park or athletic field, might both fill the mind with the imaginative material constantly supplied by the theater, and also afford the activity which the cramped muscles of the town dweller so sorely need. Even the unquestioned ability which the theater possesses to bring men together into a common mood and to afford them a mutual topic of conversation, is better accomplished with the one national game which we already possess, and might be infinitely extended through the organization of other public games.

The theater even now by no means competes with the baseball league games which are attended by thousands of men and boys who, during the entire summer, discuss the respective standing of each nine and the relative merits of every player. During the noon hour all the employees of a city factory gather in the nearest vacant lot to cheer their own home team in its practice for the next game with the nine of a neighboring manufacturing establishment and on a Saturday afternoon the entire male population of the city betakes itself to the baseball field; the ordinary means of transportation are supplemented by gay stage-coaches and huge automobiles, noisy with blowing horns and decked with gay pennants. The enormous crowd of cheering men and boys are talkative, good-natured, full of the holiday spirit, and absolutely released from the grind of life. They are lifted out of their individual affairs and so fused together that a man cannot tell whether it is his own shout or another's that fills his ears; whether it is his own coat or another's that he is wildly waving to celebrate a victory. He does not call the stranger who sits next to him his "brother" but he unconsciously embraces him in an overwhelming outburst of kindly feeling when the favorite player makes a home run. Does not this contain a suggestion of the undoubted power of public recreation to bring together all classes of a community in the modern city unhappily so full of devices for keeping men apart?

Already some American cities are making a beginning toward more adequate public recreation. Boston has its municipal gymnasiums, cricket fields, and golf grounds. Chicago has seventeen parks with playing fields, gymnasiums and baths, which at present enroll thousands of young people. These same parks are provided with beautiful halls which are used for many purposes, rent free, and are given over to any group of young people who wish to conduct dancing parties subject to city supervision and chaperonage. Many social clubs have deserted neighboring saloon halls for these municipal drawing rooms beautifully decorated with growing plants supplied by the park greenhouses, and flooded with electric lights supplied by the park power house. In the saloon halls the young people were obliged to "pass money freely over the bar," and in order to make the most of the occasion they usually stayed until morning. At such times the economic necessity itself would override the counsels of the more temperate, and the thrifty door keeper would not insist upon invitations but would take in any one who had the "price of a ticket."

145

The free rent in the park hall, the good food in the park restaurant, supplied at cost, have made three parties closing at eleven o'clock no more expensive than one party breaking up at daylight, too often in disorder.

Is not this an argument that the drinking, the late hours, the lack of decorum, are directly traceable to the commercial enterprise which ministers to pleasure in order to drag it into excess because excess is more profitable? To thus commercialize pleasure is as monstrous as it is to commercialize art. It is intolerable that the city does not take over this function of making provision for pleasure, as wise communities in Sweden and South Carolina have taken the sale of alcohol out of the hands of enterprising publicans.

We are only beginning to understand what might be done through the festival, the street procession, the band of marching musicians, orchestral music in public squares or parks, with the magic power they all possess to formulate the sense of companionship and solidarity. The experiments which are being made in public schools to celebrate the national holidays, the changing seasons, the birthdays of heroes, the planting of trees, are slowly developing little ceremonials which may in time work out into pageants of genuine beauty and significance. No other nation has so unparalleled an opportunity to do this through its schools as we have, for no other nation has so wide-spreading a school system, while the enthusiasm of children and their natural ability to express their emotions through symbols, gives the securest possible foundation to this growing effort.

The city schools of New York have effected the organization of high school girls into groups for folk dancing. These old forms of dancing which have been worked out in many lands and through long experiences, safeguard unwary and dangerous expression and yet afford a vehicle through which the gaiety of youth may flow. Their forms are indeed those which lie at the basis of all good breeding, forms which at once express and restrain, urge forward and set limits.

One may also see another center of growth for public recreation and the beginning of a pageantry for the people in the many small parks and athletic fields which almost every American city is hastening to provide for its young. These small parks have innumerable athletic teams, each with its distinctive uniform, with track meets and match games arranged with the teams from other parks and from the public schools; choruses of trade unionists or of patriotic societies fill the park halls with eager listeners. Labor Day processions are yearly becoming more carefully planned and more picturesque in character, as the desire to make an overwhelming impression with mere size gives way to a growing ambition to set forth the significance of the craft and the skill of the workman. At moments they almost rival the dignified showing of the processions of the German Turn Vereins which are also often seen in our city streets.

The many foreign colonies which are found in all American cities afford an enormous reserve of material for public recreation and street festival. They not only celebrate the feasts and holidays of the fatherland, but have each their own public expression for their mutual benefit societies and for the observance of American anniversaries. From the gay celebration of the Scandinavians when war was averted and two neighboring nations were united, to the equally gay celebration of the centenary of Garibaldi's birth; from the Chinese dragon cleverly trailing its way through the streets, to the Greek banners flung out in honor of immortal heroes, there is an infinite variety of suggestions and possibilities for public recreation and for the corporate expression of stirring emotions. After all, what is the function of art but to preserve in permanent and beautiful form those emotions and solaces which cheer life and make it kindlier, more heroic and easier to comprehend; which lift the mind of the worker from the harshness and loneliness of his task, and, by connecting him with what has gone before, free him from a sense of isolation and hardship?

Were American cities really eager for municipal art, they would cherish as genuine beginnings the tarentella danced so interminably at Italian weddings; the primitive Greek pipe played throughout the long summer nights; the Bohemian theaters crowded with eager Slavophiles; the Hungarian musicians strolling from street to street; the fervid oratory of the young Russian preaching social righteousness in the open square.

Many Chicago citizens who attended the first annual meeting of the National Playground Association of America, will never forget the long summer day in the large playing field filled during the morning with hundreds of little children romping through the kindergarten games, in the afternoon with the young men and girls contending in athletic sports; and the evening light made gay by the bright colored garments of Italians, Lithuanians, Norwegians, and a dozen other nationalities, reproducing their old dances and festivals for the pleasure of the more stolid Americans. Was this a forecast of what we may yet see accomplished through a dozen agencies promoting public recreation which are springing up in every city of America, as they already are found in the large towns of Scotland and England?

Let us cherish these experiments as the most precious beginnings of an attempt to supply the recreational needs of our industrial cities. To fail to provide for the recreation of youth, is not only to deprive all of them of their natural form of expression, but is certain to subject some of them to the overwhelming temptation of illicit and soul-destroying pleasures. To insist that young people shall forecast their rose-colored future only in a house of dreams, is to deprive the real world of that warmth and reassurance which it so sorely needs and to which it is justly entitled; furthermore, we are left outside with a sense of dreariness, in company with that shadow which already lurks only around the corner for most of us—a skepticism of life's value.

# 58

## Mr. Dooley on Culture

Martin Dooley, the "Sage of Archer Avenue," was the creation of a Chicago journalist and humorist, Finley Peter Dunne (1867–1936). Dunne, who worked on a series of Chicago newspapers, introduced his alter ego, an Irish saloon-keeper, in 1893. For the next twenty-five years, in newspaper columns, magazines, and books, Mr. Dooley, in a rich native brogue, gave his comments on the great events and personages of the day. Generally on the side of the underdog, an enemy to pretense and pomposity of all sorts, Mr. Dooley punctured a whole series of sacred cows. Imperialism, immigration restrictionists, racial bigots, and trusts were among his targets, but his more general subject was the human condition itself.

"Oh, well," said Mr. Hennessy, "we are as th' Lord made us."

"No," said Mr. Dooley, "lave us be fair. Lave us take some iv th' blame oursilves."

### ART PATRONAGE

"I see in this pa-aper," said Mr. Dooley, "they'se a fellow kickin' because an American painther ain't got anny chanst again' foreign compytition."

"Sure," said Mr. Hennessy; "he's aisy displaced. I niver knew th' business to be betther. Wages is high an' 'tis a comfortable thrade barrin' colic."

"I don't mane that kind iv painthers," said Mr. Dooley. "I don't mane th' wans that paint ye'er barn, but th' wans that paints a pitcher iv ye'er barn an' wants to sell it to ye f'r more thin th' barn is worth. This man says no matther how industhrees an American painther is, no matther if he puts on his overalls arly in th' mornin' an' goes out with a laddher an' whales away all day long, he can hardly arn a livin', while th' pauper artists iv Europe is fairly rowlin' in th' lap iv luxury. Manny a la-ad that started in life with th' intintion iv makin' th' wurruld f'rget that what's his name—Hogan's frind—ye know who I mane—Michael Angelo—ever lived, is now glad to get a job decoratin' mountain scenery with th' latest news about th' little liver pills.

"Ye see, Hinnissy, whin a man gets hold iv a large hatful iv money, wan iv th' first things he does is to buy some art. Up to th' time whin th' top blew off th' stock market, he bought his art out iv th' front window iv a news an' station'ry shop or

From [Finley Peter Dunne] "Art Patronage," *Observations by Mr. Dooley* (New York and London, 1906), 41–46.

had it put in be th' paperhanger. He took th' Sundah pa-apers that ar-re a gr-reat help if ye're collectin' art, an' he had some pitchers iv fruit that looks nachral enough to ate, d'ye mind, a paintin' iv a deer like th' wan he shot at in th' Manotowish counthry in Eighty-eight, an' a livin' likeness iv a Lake Supeeryor white fish on a silver plate. That was th' peeryod, mind ye, whin th' iron dogs howled on his lawn an' people come miles an' miles f'r to see a grotto made out iv relics iv th' Chicago fire.

"Manetime his daughter was illustratin' suspinders an' illuminatin' china plates an' becomin' artistic, an' afther awhile whin th' time come that he had to keep a man at th' dure to sweep out th' small bills, she give him a good push to'rd betther things. Besides, his pardner down th' sthreet had begun collectin' pitchers, an' ivry time he wint abroad th' mannyfacthrers iv pitcher frames bought new autymobills f'r th' Champs All Easy. So 'twas a soft matther f'r our frind Higbie to be persuaded that he ought to be a pathron iv art, an' he wint abroad determined to buy a bunch iv chromos that'd make people come out iv th' gallery iv his pardner down th' sthreet stiflin' their laughter in their hands.

"Now ye'd think seein' that he made his money in this counthry, he'd pathronize American art. Ye'd believe he'd sind wurrud down to his agent f'r to secure forty feet iv Evansville be moonlight an' be con-tint. But he don't.

"Ye don't catch Higbie changin' iv anny iv his dividends on domestic finished art. He jumps on a boat an' goes sthraight acrost to th' centhral deepo. The first thing he gets is a porthrait iv himsilf be wan iv th' gr-reat modhren masthers, Sargent be name. This here Sargent, Hogan tells me, used to live in this counthry, an' faith, if he'd stayed here ye might see him to-day on a stagin'. But he had a mind in his head an' he tore off f'r Europe th' way a duck hunter goes f'r a rice swamp. Afther awhile, Higbie shows up, an' says he: 'I'm Higbie iv th' Non-Adhesive Consolidated Glue Company,' he says. 'Can ye do me?' 'I can an' will,' says Sargent. 'I'll do ye good. How much have ye got?' he says. 'Get some more an' come around,' he says. An' Higbie puts on his Prince Albert coat an' laves it open so that ye can see his watch charm—th' crown iv Poland with th' Kohinoor in th' top iv it— an' me frind Sargent does him brown an' red. He don't give him th' pitcher iv coorse. If ye have ye'er porthrait painted be a gr-reat painther, it's ye'er porthrait but 'tis his pitcher, an' he keeps it till ye don't look that way anny more. So Higbie's porthrait is hung up in a gallery an' th' doctors brings people to see it that ar-re sufferin' fr'm narvous dyspepsia to cheer thim up. Th' pa-apers says 'tis fine. 'Number 108 shows Sargent at his best. There is the same marvellous ticknick that th' great master displayed in his cillybrated take-off on Mrs. Maenheimer in last year's gallery. Th' skill an' ease with which th' painther has made a monkey iv his victim are beyond praise. Sargent has torn th' sordid heart out iv th' wretched crather an' exposed it to th' wurruld. Th' wicked, ugly little eyes, th' crooked nose, th' huge graspin' hands, tell th' story iv this miscreant's character as completely as if they were written in so manny wurruds, while th' artist, with wondherful malice, has painted onto th' face a smile iv sickenin' silf-complacency that is positively disgustin'. No artist iv our day has succeeded so well in showin' up th' maneness iv th' people he has mugged. We ondershtand that th' atrocious Higbie paid wan

149

hundherd thousan' dollars f'r this comic valentine. It is worth th' money to ivrybody but him.'

"But Higbie don't see th' pa-aper. He's over in Paris. Th' chimes are rung, bonefires are lighted in th' sthreets an' th' Pannyma Comp'ny declares a dividend whin he enters th' city. They'se such a demand f'r paint that th' supply runs out an' manny gr-reat imprishonist pitcher facthries is foorced to use bluein'. Higbie ordhers paintin's be th' ton, th' r-runnin' foot, th' foot pound, th' car load. He insthructs th' pitcher facthries to wurruk night an' day till his artistic sowl is satisfied. We follow his coorse in th' pa-apers. 'Th' cillybrated Gainsborough that niver wud be missed has been captured be Misther Higbie, th' American millyionaire. Th' price paid is said to be wan hundherd thousan' dollars. Th' pitcher riprisints a lady in a large hat fondlin' a cow. It is wan iv th' finest Gainsboroughs painted be th' Gainsborough Mannyfacthrin' comp'ny iv Manchester. At th' las' public sale, it was sold f'r thirty dollars. Misther Higbie has also purchased th' cillybrated Schmartzmeister Boogooroo, wan iv th' mos' horrible examples iv this delightful painther's style. He is now negotyatin' with th' well-known dealer Moosoo Mortheimer f'r th' intire output iv th' Barabazah School. Yisterdah in a call on th' janial dealer, th' name iv th' cillybrated painther Mooney was mintioned. "How manny pitchers has he painted?" "Four hundherd and forty-three thousan' at ilivin o'clock to-day," says th' dealer. "But four hundherd thousan' iv thim ar-re in America." "Get th' r-est iv thim f'r me," says th' connysoor. "What did ye say th' gintleman's name was?" We ondershtand that Misther Mooney has had to put in two new four-deck machines to meet th' ordhers, which include thirty green an' mauve haystacks, forty blue barns or childher at play, an' no less thin ninety riprisitations iv mornin' at sea, moonlight avenin', flock iv sheep, or whativer ye may call thim.'

"An whin he comes home, he hangs thim in his house, so that his friends can't turn around without takin' off a pasthral scene on their coats, an' he pastes th' price on th' frame, an' whin he dies, he laves his pitcher to some definceless art museem. An' there ye ar-re.

"So I tell ye, Hinnissy, if I was a young an' ambitious American painther, I'd go to Europe. Whin Hannigan was over there, he met a young man that painted that fine head iv Murphy that looks so much like Casey that hangs in Schwartzmeister's back room. 'Ar-re ye still at th' art?' says Hannigan. 'I am,' says th' young man. 'How does it go?' asks Hannigan. 'I've more thin I can do,' says th' young man. 'Since steel rails got so high, I've had to hire an assistant. Ye see, I didn't get on in Chicago. Me "Bridgepoort in a Fog" was th' on'y pitcher I sold, an' a sausage mannyfacthrer bought that because his facthry was in it. I come over here, an' so's me pitchers will have a fair show, I sign annywan's name ye want to thim. Ye've heerd iv Michael Angelo? That's me. Y've heerd iv Gainsborough? That's me. Ye've heerd iv Millet, th' boy that painted th' pitcher give away with th' colored supplimint iv th' Sundah Howl? That's me. Yis, sir, th' rale name iv near ivry distinguished painther iv modhren times is Remsen K. Smith. Whin ye go home, if ye see a good painther an' glazier that'd like a job as assistant Rimbrandt f'r th'

American thrade, sind him to me. F'r,' he says, 'th' on'y place an American artist can make a livin' is here. Charity f'r artists,' he says, 'begins abroad,' he says."

"Well," said Mr. Hennessy, "perhaps a bum Europeen pitcher is betther thin a good American pitcher."

"Perhaps so," said Mr. Dooley. "I think it is so. Annyhow, no matther how bad a painther he is, annywan that can get money out iv an American millyionaire is an artist an' desarves it. There's th' rale art. I wish it was taught in th' schools. I'd like to see an exhibition at th' Museem with 'Check iv American Gintleman, dhrawn fr'm life,' hung on th' wall."

## THE CARNEGIE LIBRARIES

"Has Andhrew Carnaygie given ye a libry yet?" asked Mr. Dooley.

"Not that I know iv," said Mr. Hennessy.

"He will," said Mr. Dooley. "Ye'll not escape him. Befure he dies he hopes to crowd a libry on ivry man, woman, an' child in th' counthry. He's given thim to cities, towns, villages, an' whistlin' stations. They're tearin' down gas-houses an' poor-houses to put up libries. Befure another year, ivry house in Pittsburg that ain't a blast-furnace will be a Carnaygie libry. In some places all th' buildin's is libries. If ye write him f'r an autygraft he sinds ye a libry. No beggar is iver turned impty-handed fr'm th' dure. Th' pan-handler knocks an' asts f'r a glass iv milk an' a roll. 'No, sir,' says Andhrew Carnaygie. 'I will not pauperize this onworthy man.' Nawthin is worst f'r a beggar-man thin to make a pauper iv him. Yet it shall not be said iv me that I give nawthin' to th' poor. Saunders, give him a libry, an' if he still insists on a roll tell him to roll th' libry. F'r I'm humorous as well as wise,' he says."

"Does he give th' books that go with it?" asked Mr. Hennessy.

"Books?" said Mr. Dooley. "What ar-re ye talkin' about? D'ye know what a libry is? I suppose ye think it's a place where a man can go, haul down wan iv his fav'rite authors fr'm th' shelf, an' take a nap in it. That's not a Carnaygie libry. A Carnaygie libry is a large, brown-stone, impenethrible buildin' with th' name iv th' maker blown on th' dure. Libry, fr'm th' Greek wurruds, libus, a book, an' ary, sildom,—sildom a book. A Carnaygie libry is archytechoor, not lithrachoor. Lithrachoor will be riprisinted. Th' most cillybrated dead authors will be honored be havin' their names painted on th' wall in distinguished comp'ny, as thus: Andhrew Carnaygie, Shakespeare; Andhrew Carnaygie, Byron; Andhrew Carnaygie, Bobby Burns; Andhrew Carnaygie, an' so on. Ivry author is guaranteed a place next to pure readin' matther like a bakin' powdher advertisemint, so that whin a man comes along that niver heerd iv Shakespeare he'll know he was somebody, because there he is on th' wall. That's th' dead authors. Th' live authors will stand outside an' wish they were dead.

From [Finley Peter Dunne] "The Carnegie Libraries," *Dissertations by Mr. Dooley* (New York and London, 1906), 177–182.

"He's havin' gr-reat spoort with it. I r-read his speech th' other day, whin he laid th' corner-stone iv th' libry at Pianola, Ioway. Th' entire popylation iv this lithry cinter gathered to see an' hear him. There was th' postmaster an' his wife, th' blacksmith an' his fam'ly, the station agent, mine host iv th' Farmers' Exchange, an' some sthray live stock. 'Ladies an' gintlemen,' says he. 'Modesty compels me to say nawthin' on this occasion, but I am not be be bulldozed,' he says. 'I can't tell ye how much pleasure I take in disthributin' monymints to th' humble name around which has gathered so manny hon'rable associations with mesilf. I have been a very busy little man all me life, but I like hard wurruk, an' givin' away me money is th' hardest wurruk I iver did. It fairly makes me teeth ache to part with it. But there's wan consolation. I cheer mesilf with th' thought that no matther how much money I give it don't do anny particular person anny good. Th' worst thing ye can do f'r anny man is to do him good. I pass by th' organ-grinder on th' corner with a savage glare. I bate th' monkey on th' head whin he comes up smilin' to me window, an' hurl him down on his impecyoonyous owner. None iv me money goes into th' little tin cup. I cud kick a hospital, an' I lave Wall Sthreet to look afther th' widow an' th' orphan. Th' submerged tenth, thim that can't get hold iv a good chunk iv th' goods, I wud cut off fr'm th' rest iv th' wurruld an' prevint fr'm bearin' th' haughty name iv papa or th' still lovelier name iv ma. So far I've got on'y half me wish in this matther.

" 'I don't want poverty an' crime to go on. I intind to stop it. But how? It's been holdin' its own f'r cinchries. Some iv th' gr-reatest iv former minds has undertook to prevint it an' has failed. They didn't know how. Modesty wud prevint me agin fr'm sayin' that I know how, but that's nayether here nor there. I do. Th' way to abolish poverty an' bust crime is to put up a brown-stone buildin' in ivry town in th' counthry with me name over it. That's th' way. I suppose th' raison it wasn't thried befure was that no man iver had such a name. 'Tis thrue me efforts is not appreciated ivrywhere. I offer a city a libry, an' oftentimes it replies an' asks me f'r something to pay off th' school debt. I rayceive degraded pettyshuns fr'm so-called proud methropolises f'r a gas-house in place iv a libry. I pass thim by with scorn. All I ask iv a city in rayturn f'r a fifty-thousan'-dollar libry is that it shall raise wan millyon dollars to maintain th' buildin' an' keep me name shiny, an' if it won't do that much f'r lithrachoor, th' divvle take it, it's onworthy iv th' name iv an American city. What ivry community needs is taxes an' lithrachoor. I give thim both. Three cheers f'r a libry an' a bonded debt! Lithrachoor, taxation, an' Andhrew Carnaygie, wan an' insiprable, now an' foriver! They'se nawthin' so good as a good book. It's betther thin food; it's betther thin money. I have made money an' books, an' I like me books betther thin me money. Others don't, but I do. With these few wurruds I will con-clude. Modesty wud prevint me fr'm sayin' more, but I have to catch a thrain, an' cannot go on. I stake ye to this libry, which ye will have as soon as ye raise th' money to keep it goin'. Stock it with useful readin', an' some day ye're otherwise pauper an' criminal childher will come to know me name whin I am gone an' there's no wan left to tell it thim.'

"Whin th' historyan comes to write th' histhry iv th' West he'll say: 'Pianola, Ioway, was a prosperous town till th' failure iv th' corn crop in nineteen hundherd an' wan, an' th' Carnaygie libry in nineteen hundherd an' two. Th' govermint ast f'r thirty dollars to pave Main Sthreet with wooden blocks, but th' gr-reat philanthropist was firm, an' the libry was sawed off on th' town. Th' public schools, th' wurruk-house, th' wather wurruks, an' th' other penal instichoochions was at wanst closed, an' th' people begun to wurruk to support th' libry. In five years th' popylation had deserted th' town to escape taxation, an' now, as Mr. Carnaygie promised, poverty an' crime has been abolished in th' place, th' janitor iv th' buildin' bein' honest an' well paid.'

"Isn't it good f'r lithrachoor, says ye? Sure, I think not, Hinnissy. Libries niver encouraged lithrachoor anny more thin tombstones encourage livin'. No wan iver wrote annythin' because he was tol' that a hundherd years fr'm now his books might be taken down fr'm a shelf in a granite sepulcher an' some wan wud write 'Good' or 'This man is crazy' in th' margin. What lithrachoor needs is fillin' food. If Andhrew wud put a kitchen in th' libries an' build some bunks or even swing a few hammocks where livin' authors cud crawl in at night an' sleep while waitin' f'r this enlightened nation to wake up an' discover th' Shakespeares now on th' turf, he wud be givin' a rale boost to lithrachoor. With th' smoke curlin' fr'm th' chimbley, an' hundherds iv potes settin' aroun' a table loaded down with pancakes an' talkin' pothry an' prize-fightin', with hundherds iv other potes stacked up nately in th' sleepin'-rooms an' snorin' in wan gran' chorus, with their wives holdin' down good-payin' jobs as libraryans or cooks, an' their happy little childher playin' through th' marble corrydors, Andhrew Carnaygie wud not have lived in vain. Maybe that's th' on'y way he knows how to live. I don't believe in libries. They pauperize lithrachoor. I'm f'r helpin' th' boys that's now on th' job. I know a pote in Halsted Sthreet that wanst wrote a pome beginnin', 'All th' wealth iv Ind,' that he sold to a magazine f'r two dollars, payable on publycation. Lithrachoor don't need advancin'. What it needs is advances f'r th' lithrachoors. Ye can't shake down posterity f'r th' price.

"All th' same, I like Andhrew Carnaygie. Him an' me ar-re agreed on that point. I like him because he ain't shamed to give publicly. Ye don't find him puttin' on false whiskers an' turnin' up his coat-collar whin he goes out to be benivolent. No, sir. Ivry time he dhrops a dollar it makes a noise like a waither fallin' down-stairs with a tray iv dishes. He's givin' th' way we'd all like to give. I niver put annything in th' poor-box, but I wud if Father Kelly wud rig up like wan iv thim slot-machines, so that whin I stuck in a nickel me name wud appear over th' altar in red letters. But whin I put a dollar in th' plate I get back about two yards an' hurl it so hard that th' good man turns around to see who done it. Do good be stealth, says I, but see that th' burglar-alarm is set. Anny benivolent money I hand out I want to talk about me. Him that giveth to th' poor, they say, lindeth to th' Lord; but in these days we look f'r quick returns on our invistmints. I like Andhrew Carnaygie, an', as he says, he puts his whole soul into th' wurruk."

"What's he mane be that?" asked Mr. Hennessy.

"He manes," said Mr. Dooley, "that he's gin'rous. Ivry time he gives a libry he gives himsilf away in a speech."

# 59

# The Melting Pot

Two hundred and fifty years after the first settlements, millions of immigrants were still making their way from Europe to the New World. Between 1890 and 1912 many of them came from southern and eastern Europe, escaping conditions of great poverty and oppression. Like the seventeenth-century colonists, these immigrants had to make great adjustments, but their difficulties were compounded by special religious and linguistic traditions, and the need to come to terms with a national history that was already more than a century old.

Mary Antin (1881–1949) was one who managed the adjustments and exploited her handicaps to brilliant advantage. Brought to Boston from Russian Poland in 1894, she showed great precocity as a child, writing poems printed in local newspapers. As a child she also wrote, in Yiddish, a moving account of her long journey, *From Polotzk to Boston*; but her mastery of English was equally impressive, as revealed in the pages of *The Promised Land*. This account of growing up in a new country, searching for the meaning of citizenship and liberty even while trying to retain some older memories and values, was unusual for its eloquence if not for its contents. In articulating her own passage to adulthood, Mary Antin was describing the experience of a generation.

## THE PROMISED LAND
### *Mary Antin*

Memory may take a rest while I copy from a contemporaneous document the story of the great voyage. In accordance with my promise to my uncle, I wrote, during my first months in America, a detailed account of our adventures between Polotzk and Boston. Ink was cheap, and the epistle, in Yiddish, occupied me for many hot summer hours.

On a gray wet morning in early April we set out for the frontier. This was the real beginning of our journey, and all my faculties of observation were alert. I took note of everything,—the weather, the trains, the bustle of railroad stations, our fellow passengers, and the family mood at every stage of our progress.

From *The Promised Land* (Boston and New York, 1912), 169–170, 172, 175–179, 222–228, 270–275.

The bags and bundles which composed our travelling outfit were much more bulky than valuable. A trifling sum of money, the steamer ticket, and the foreign passport were the magic agents by means of which we hoped to span the five thousand miles of earth and water between us and my father. The passport was supposed to pass us over the frontier without any trouble, but on account of the prevalence of cholera in some parts of the country, the poorer sort of travellers, such as emigrants, were subjected, at this time, to more than ordinary supervision and regulation.

The phrases "we were told to do this" and "told to do that" occur again and again in my narrative, and the most effective handling of the facts could give no more vivid picture of the proceedings. We emigrants were herded at the stations, packed in the cars, and driven from place to place like cattle.

We arrived in Hamburg early one morning, after a long night in the crowded cars. We were marched up to a strange vehicle, long and narrow and high, drawn by two horses and commanded by a mute driver. We were piled up on this wagon, our baggage was thrown after us, and we started on a sight-seeing tour across the city of Hamburg.

The smiles and shivers fairly crowded each other in some parts of our career.

Suddenly, when everything interesting seemed at an end, we all recollected how long it was since we had started on our funny ride. Hours, we thought, and still the horses ran. Now we rode through quieter streets where there were fewer shops and more wooden houses. Still the horses seemed to have just started. I looked over our perch again. Something made me think of a description I had read of criminals being carried on long journeys in uncomfortable things—like this? Well, it was strange—this long, long drive, the conveyance, no word of explanation; and all, though going different ways, being packed off together. We were strangers; the driver knew it. He might take us anywhere—how could we tell?

Yes, we are frightened. We are very still. Some Polish women over there have fallen asleep, and the rest of us look such a picture of woe, and yet so funny, it is a sight to see and remember.

Our mysterious ride came to an end on the outskirts of the city, where we were once more lined up, cross-questioned, disinfected, labelled, and pigeonholed.

This last place of detention turned out to be a prison. "Quarantine" they called it, and there was a great deal of it—two weeks of it. Two weeks within high brick walls, several hundred of us herded in half a dozen compartments,—numbered compartments,—sleeping in rows, like sick people in a hospital; with roll-call morning and night, and short rations three times a day; with never a sign of the free world beyond our barred windows; with anxiety and longing and homesickness in our hearts, and in our ears the unfamiliar voice of the invisible ocean, which drew and repelled us at the same time. The fortnight in quarantine was not an episode; it was an epoch, divisible into eras, periods, events.

Our turn came at last. We were conducted through the gate of departure, and after some hours of bewildering manœuvres, described in great detail in the report to my uncle, we found ourselves—we five frightened pilgrims from Polotzk—on the deck of a great big steamship afloat on the strange big waters of the ocean.

For sixteen days the ship was our world. My letter dwells solemnly on the details of the life at sea, as if afraid to cheat my uncle of the smallest circumstance. It does not shrink from describing the torments of seasickness; it notes every change in the weather. A rough night is described, when the ship pitched and rolled so that people were thrown from their berths; days and nights when we crawled through dense fogs, our foghorn drawing answering warnings from invisible ships. The perils of the sea were not minimized in the imagination of us inexperienced voyagers. The captain and his officers ate their dinners, smoked their pipes and slept soundly in their turns, while we frightened emigrants turned our faces to the wall and awaited our watery graves.

All this while the seasickness lasted. Then came happy hours on deck, with fugitive sunshine, birds atop the crested waves, band music and dancing and fun. I explored the ship, made friends with officers and crew, or pursued my thoughts in quiet nooks. It was my first experience of the ocean, and I was profoundly moved.

Oh, what solemn thoughts I had! How deeply I felt the greatness, the power of the scene! The immeasurable distance from horizon to horizon; the huge billows for-ever changing their shapes—now only a wavy and rolling plain, now a chain of great mountains, coming and going farther away; then a town in the distance, perhaps, with spires and towers and buildings of gigantic dimensions; and mostly a vast mass of uncertain shapes, knocking against each other in fury, and seething and foaming in their anger; the gray sky, with its mountains of gloomy clouds, flying, moving with the waves, as it seemed, very near them; the absence of any object besides the one ship; and the deep, solemn groans of the sea, sounding as if all the voices of the world had been turned into sighs and then gathered into that one mournful sound—so deeply did I feel the presence of these things, that the feeling became one of awe, both painful and sweet, and stirring and warming, and deep and calm and grand.

I would imagine myself all alone on the ocean, and Robinson Crusoe was very real to me. I was alone sometimes. I was aware of no human presence; I was con-scious only of sea and sky and something I did not understand. And as I listened to its solemn voice, I felt as if I had found a friend, and knew that I loved the ocean. It seemed as if it were within as well as without, part of myself; and I wondered how I had lived without it, and if I could ever part with it.

And so suffering, fearing, brooding, rejoicing, we crept nearer and nearer to the coveted shore, until, on a glorious May morning, six weeks after our departure from Polotzk, our eyes beheld the Promised Land, and my father received us in his arms.

The public school has done its best for us foreigners, and for the country, when it has made us into good Americans. I am glad it is mine to tell how the miracle was wrought in one case. You should be glad to hear of it, you born Americans; for it is the story of the growth of your country; of the flocking of your brothers and sisters from the far ends of the earth to the flag you love; of the recruiting of your armies of workers, thinkers, and leaders. And you will be glad to hear of it, my comrades in adoption; for it is a rehearsal of your own experience, the thrill and wonder of which your own hearts have felt.

How long would you say, wise reader, it takes to make an American? By the middle of my second year in school I had reached the sixth grade. When, after the Christmas holidays, we began to study the life of Washington, running through a summary of the Revolution, and the early days of the Republic, it seemed to me that all my reading and study had been idle until then. The reader, the arithmetic, the song book, that had so fascinated me until now, became suddenly sober exercise books, tools wherewith to hew a way to the source of inspiration. When the teacher read to us out of a big book with many bookmarks in it, I sat rigid with attention in my little chair, my hands tightly clasped on the edge of my desk; and I painfully held my breath, to prevent sighs of disappointment escaping, as I saw the teacher skip the parts between bookmarks. When the class read, and it came my turn, my voice shook and the book trembled in my hands. I could not pronounce the name of George Washington without a pause. Never had I prayed, never had I chanted the songs of David, never had I called upon the Most Holy, in such utter reverence and worship as I repeated the simple sentences of my child's story of the patriot. I gazed with adoration at the portraits of George and Martha Washington, till I could see them with my eyes shut. And whereas formerly my self-consciousness had bordered on conceit, and I thought myself an uncommon person, parading my schoolbooks through the streets, and swelling with pride when a teacher detained me in conversation, now I grew humble all at once, seeing how insignificant I was beside the Great.

As I read about the noble boy who would not tell a lie to save himself from punishment, I was for the first time truly repentant of my sins. Formerly I had fasted and prayed and made sacrifice on the Day of Atonement, but it was more than half play, in mimicry of my elders. I had no real horror of sin, and I knew so many ways of escaping punishment. I am sure my family, my neighbors, my teachers in Polotzk—all my world, in fact—strove together, by example and precept, to teach me goodness. Saintliness had a new incarnation in about every third person I knew. I did respect the saints, but I could not help seeing that most of them were a little bit stupid, and that mischief was much more fun than piety. Goodness, as I had known it, was respectable, but not necessarily admirable. The people I really admired, like my Uncle Solomon, and Cousin Rachel, were those who preached the least and laughed the most. My sister Frieda was perfectly good, but she did not think the less of me because I played tricks. What I loved in my friends was not inimitable. One could be downright good if one really wanted to. One could be learned if one had books and teachers. One could sing funny songs and tell anecdotes if one travelled about and picked up such things, like one's uncles and cousins. But a human being strictly good, perfectly wise, and unfailingly valiant, all at the same time, I had never heard or dreamed of. This wonderful George Washington was as inimitable as he was irreproachable. Even if I had never, never told a lie, I could not compare myself to George Washington; for I was not brave—I was afraid to go out when snowballs whizzed—and I could never be the First President of the United States.

So I was forced to revise my own estimate of myself. But the twin of my new-born humility, paradoxical as it may seem, was a sense of dignity I had never known before. For if I found that I was a person of small consequence, I discovered at the same time that I was more nobly related than I had ever supposed. I had relatives and friends who were notable people by the old standards,—I had never been ashamed of my family,—but this George Washington, who died long before I was born, was like a king in greatness, and he and I were Fellow Citizens. There was a great deal about Fellow Citizens in the patriotic literature we read at this time; and I knew from my father how he was a Citizen, through the process of naturalization, and how I also was a citizen, by virtue of my relation to him. Undoubtedly I was a Fellow Citizen, and George Washington was another. It thrilled me to realize what sudden greatness had fallen on me; and at the same time it sobered me, as with a sense of responsibility. I strove to conduct myself as befitted a Fellow Citizen.

Before books came into my life, I was given to star-gazing and daydreaming. When books were given me, I fell upon them as a glutton pounces on his meat after a period of enforced starvation. I lived with my nose in a book, and took no notice of the alternations of the sun and stars. But now, after the advent of George Washington and the American Revolution, I began to dream again. I strayed on the common after school instead of hurrying home to read. I hung on fence rails, my pet book forgotten under my arm, and gazed off to the yellow-streaked February sunset, and beyond, and beyond. I was no longer the central figure of my dreams; the dry weeds in the lane crackled beneath the tread of Heroes.

What more could America give a child? Ah, much more! As I read how the patriots planned the Revolution, and the women gave their sons to die in battle, and the heroes led to victory, and the rejoicing people set up the Republic, it dawned on me gradually what was meant by *my country*. The people all desiring noble things, and striving for them together, defying their oppressors, giving their lives for each other—all this it was that made *my country*. It was not a thing that I *understood*; I could not go home and tell Frieda about it, as I told her other things I learned at school. But I knew one could say "my country" and *feel* it, as one felt "God" or "myself." My teacher, my schoolmates, Miss Dillingham, George Washington himself could not mean more than I when they said "my country," after I had once felt it. For the Country was for all the Citizens, and *I was a Citizen*. And when we stood up to sing "America," I shouted the words with all my might. I was in very earnest proclaiming to the world my love for my new-found country.

*I love thy rock and rills,*
*Thy woods and templed hills.*

Boston Harbor, Crescent Beach, Chelsea Square—all was hallowed ground to me. As the day approached when the school was to hold exercises in honor of Washington's Birthday, the halls resounded at all hours with the strains of patriotic songs; and I, who was a model of the attentive pupil, more than once lost my place in the lesson as I strained to hear, through closed doors, some neighboring class rehearsing "The Star-Spangled Banner." If the doors happened to open, and the chorus broke out unveiled—

*O! say, does that Star-Spangled Banner yet wave*
*O'er the land of the free, and the home of the brave?*—

delicious tremors ran up and down my spine, and I was faint with suppressed enthusiasm.

Where had been my country until now? What flag had I loved? What heroes had

I worshipped? The very names of these things had been unknown to me. Well I knew that Polotzk was not my country. It was *goluth*—exile. On many occasions in the year we prayed to God to lead us out of exile. The beautiful Passover service closed with the words, "Next year, may we be in Jerusalem." On childish lips, indeed, those words were no conscious aspiration; we repeated the Hebrew syllables after our elders, but without their hope and longing. Still not a child among us was too young to feel in his own flesh the lash of the oppressor. We knew what it was to be Jews in exile, from the spiteful treatment we suffered at the hands of the smallest urchin who crossed himself; and thence we knew that Israel had good reason to pray for deliverance. But the story of the Exodus was not history to me in the sense that the story of the American Revolution was. It was more like a glorious myth, a belief in which had the effect of cutting me off from the actual world, by linking me with a world of phantoms. Those moments of exaltation which the contemplation of the Biblical past afforded us, allowing us to call ourselves the children of princes, served but to tinge with a more poignant sense of disinheritance the long humdrum stretches of our life. In very truth we were a people without a country. Surrounded by mocking foes and detractors, it was difficult for me to realize the persons of my people's heroes or the events in which they moved. Except in moments of abstraction from the world around me, I scarcely understood that Jerusalem was an actual spot on the earth, where once the Kings of the Bible, real people, like my neighbors in Polotzk, ruled in puissant majesty. For the conditions of our civil life did not permit us to cultivate a spirit of nationalism. The freedom of worship that was grudgingly granted within the narrow limits of the Pale by no means included the right to set up openly any ideal of a Hebrew State, any hero other than the Czar. What we children picked up of our ancient political history was confused with the miraculous story of the Creation, with the supernatural legends and hazy associations of Bible lore.

So it came to pass that we did not know what *my country* could mean to a man. And as we had no country, so we had no flag to love. It was by no far-fetched symbolism that the banner of the House of Romanoff became the emblem of our latter-day bondage in our eyes. Even a child would know how to hate the flag that we were forced, on pain of severe penalties, to hoist above our housetops, in celebration of the advent of one of our oppressors. And as it was with country and flag, so it was with heroes of war. We hated the uniform of the soldier, to the last brass button. On the person of a Gentile, it was the symbol of tyranny; on the person of a Jew, it was the emblem of shame.

So a little Jewish girl in Polotzk was apt to grow up hungry-minded and empty-hearted; and if, still in her outreaching youth, she was set down in a land of outspoken patriotism, she was likely to love her new country with a great love, and to embrace its heroes in a great worship. Naturalization, with us Russian Jews, may mean more than the adoption of the immigrant by America. It may mean the adoption of America by the immigrant.

It was characteristic of the looseness of our family discipline at this time that nobody was seriously interested in our visits to Morgan Chapel. Our time was our

159

own, after school duties and household tasks were done. Joseph sold newspapers after school; I swept and washed dishes; Dora minded the baby. For the rest, we amused ourselves as best we could. Father and mother were preoccupied with the store day and night; and not so much with weighing and measuring and making change as with figuring out how long it would take the outstanding accounts to ruin the business entirely. If my mother had scruples against her children resorting to a building with a cross on it, she did not have time to formulate them. If my father heard us talking about Morgan Chapel, he dismissed the subject with a sarcastic characterization, and wanted to know if we were going to join the Salvation Army next; but he did not seriously care, and he was willing that the children should have a good time. And if my parents had objected to Morgan Chapel, was the sidewalk in front of the saloon a better place for us children to spend the evening? They could not have argued with us very long, so they hardly argued at all.

In Polotzk we had been trained and watched, our days had been regulated, our conduct prescribed. In America, suddenly, we were let loose on the street. Why? Because my father having renounced his faith, and my mother being uncertain of hers, they had no particular creed to hold us to. The conception of a system of ethics independent of religion could not at once enter as an active principle in their life; so that they could give a child no reason why to be truthful or kind. And as with religion, so it fared with other branches of our domestic education. Chaos took the place of system; uncertainty, inconsistency undermined discipline. My parents knew only that they desired us to be like American children; and seeing how their neighbors gave their children boundless liberty, they turned us also loose, never doubting but that the American way was the best way. In public deportment, in etiquette, in all matters of social intercourse, they had no standards to go by, seeing that America was not Polotzk. In their bewilderment and uncertainty they must trust us children to learn from such models as the tenements afforded. More than this, they must step down from their throne of parental authority, and take the law from their children's mouths; for they had no other means of finding out what was good American form. The result was that laxity of domestic organization, that inversion of normal relations which makes for friction, and which sometimes ends in breaking up a family that was formerly united and happy.

This sad process of disintegration of home life may be observed in almost any immigrant family of our class and with our traditions and aspirations. It is part of the process of Americanization; an upheaval preceding the state of repose. It is the cross that the first and second generations must bear, an involuntary sacrifice for the sake of the future generations. These are the pains of adjustment, as racking as the pains of birth. And as the mother forgets her agonies in the bliss of clasping her babe to her breast, so the bent and heart-sore immigrant forgets exile and homesickness and ridicule and loss and estrangement, when he beholds his sons and daughters moving as Americans among Americans.

On Wheeler Street there were no real homes. There were miserable flats of three or four rooms, or fewer, in which families that did not practise race suicide cooked, washed, and ate; slept from two to four in a bed, in windowless bedrooms;

quarrelled in the gray morning, and made up in the smoky evening; tormented each other, supported each other, saved each other, drove each other out of the house. But there was no common life in any form that means life. There was no room for it, for one thing. Beds and cribs took up most of the floor space, disorder packed the interspaces. The centre table in the "parlor" was not loaded with books. It held, invariably, a photograph album and an ornamental lamp with a paper shade; and the lamp was usually out of order. So there was as little motive for a common life as there was room. The yard was only big enough for the perennial rubbish heap. The narrow sidewalk was crowded. What were the people to do with themselves? There were the saloons, the missions, the libraries, the cheap amusement places, and the neighborhood houses. People selected their resorts according to their tastes. The children, let it be thankfully recorded, flocked mostly to the clubs; the little girls to sew, cook, dance, and play games; the little boys to hammer and paste, mend chairs, debate, and govern a toy republic. All these, of course, are forms of baptism by soap and water.

Our neighborhood went in search of salvation to Morgan Memorial Hall, Barnard Memorial, Morgan Chapel aforementioned, and some other clean places that lighted a candle in their window. My brother, my sister Dora, and I were introduced to some of the clubs by our young neighbors, and we were glad to go. For our home also gave us little besides meals in the kitchen and beds in the dark. What with the six of us, and the store, and the baby, and sometimes a "greener" or two from Polotzk, whom we lodged as a matter of course till they found a permanent home—what with such a company and the size of our tenement, we needed to get out almost as much as our neighbors' children. I say almost; for our parlor we managed to keep pretty clear, and the lamp on our centre table was always in order, and its light fell often on an open book. Still, it was part of the life of Wheeler Street to belong to clubs, so we belonged.

I didn't care for sewing or cooking, so I joined a dancing-club; and even here I was a failure. I had been a very good dancer in Russia, but here I found all the steps different, and I did not have the courage to go out in the middle of the slippery floor and mince it and toe it in front of the teacher. When I retired to a corner and tried to play dominoes, I became suddenly shy of my partner; and I never could win a game of checkers, although formerly I used to beat my father at it. I tried to be friends with a little girl I had known in Chelsea, but she met my advances coldly. She lived on Appleton Street, which was too aristocratic to mix with Wheeler Street. Geraldine was studying elocution, and she wore a scarlet cape and hood, and she was going on the stage by and by. I acknowledged that her sense of superiority was well-founded, and retired farther into my corner, for the first time conscious of my shabbiness and lowliness.

I looked on at the dancing until I could endure it no longer. Overcome by a sense of isolation and unfitness, I slipped out of the room, avoiding the teacher's eye, and went home to write melancholy poetry.

What had come over me? Why was I, the confident, the ambitious, suddenly grown so shy and meek? Why was the candidate for encyclopædic immortality overawed by a scarlet hood? Why did I, a very tomboy yesterday, suddenly find my playmates stupid, and hide-and-seek a bore? I did not know why. I only knew that I was lonely and troubled and sore; and I went home to write sad poetry.

I shall never forget the pattern of the red carpet in our parlor,—we had achieved a carpet since Chelsea days,—because I lay for hours face down on the floor, writing poetry on a screechy slate. When I had perfected my verses, and copied them fair on the famous blue-lined note paper, and saw that I had made a very pathetic poem indeed, I felt better. And this happened over and over again. I gave up the dancing-club, I ceased to know the rowdy little boys, and I wrote melancholy poetry oftener, and felt better. The centre table became my study. I read much, and mooned between chapters, and wrote long letters to Miss Dillingham.

For some time I wrote to her almost daily. That was when I found in my heart such depths of woe as I could not pack into rhyme. And finally there came a day when I could utter my trouble in neither verse nor prose, and I implored Miss Dillingham to come to me and hear my sorrowful revelations. But I did not want her to come to the house. In the house there was no privacy; I could not talk. Would she meet me on Boston Common at such and such a time?

Would she? She was a devoted friend, and a wise woman. She met me on Boston Common. It was a gray autumn day—was it not actually drizzling?—and I was cold sitting on the bench; but I was thrilled through and through with the sense of the magnitude of my troubles, and of the romantic nature of the rendezvous.

Who that was even half awake when he was growing up does not know what all these symptoms betokened? Miss Dillingham understood, and she wisely gave me no inkling of her diagnosis. She let me talk and kept a grave face. She did not belittle my troubles—I made specific charges against my home, members of my family, and life in general; she did not say that I would get over them, that every growing girl suffers from the blues; that I was, in brief, a little goose stretching my wings for flight. She told me rather that it would be noble to bear my sorrows bravely, to soothe those who irritated me, to live each day with all my might. She reminded me of great men and women who have suffered, and who overcame their troubles by living and working. And she sent me home amazingly comforted, my pettiness and self-consciousness routed by the quiet influence of her gray eyes searching mine. This, or something like this, had to be repeated many times, as anybody will know who was present at the slow birth of his manhood. From now on, for some years, of course, I must weep and laugh out of season, stand on tiptoe to pluck the stars in heaven, love and hate immoderately, propound theories of the destiny of man, and not know what is going on in my own heart.

# 60

## A Visitor's America

Like many other foreigners, English men of letters took great interest in the development of American society. What distinguished their concern was the stream of books they issued to acquaint the world with their conclusions. Dickens, Thackeray, Anthony Trollope, Matthew Arnold, and Oscar Wilde all visited the United States and recorded their impressions. In 1912 the novelist Arnold Bennett (1867–1931) joined this list, spending several weeks in America before returning home to pen his observations. A versatile and accomplished writer who catered to many levels of taste, Bennett caught something of the energy and concentration of American life, in the days just preceding World War I. Present-day problems and prejudices, as well as distinctive features of the prewar era, are embedded in Bennett's picture of the new technology and the world of business.

## YOUR UNITED STATES
### *Arnold Bennett*

What strikes and frightens the backward European as much as anything in the United States is the efficiency and fearful universality of the telephone. Just as I think of the big cities as agglomerations pierced everywhere by elevator-shafts full of movement, so I think of them as being threaded, under pavements and over roofs and between floors and ceilings and between walls, by millions upon millions of live filaments that unite all the privacies of the organism—and destroy them in order to make one immense publicity! I do not mean that Europe has failed to adopt the telephone, nor that in Europe there are no hotels with the dreadful curse of an active telephone in every room. But I do mean that the European telephone is a toy, and a somewhat clumsy one, compared with the inexorable seriousness of the American telephone. Many otherwise highly civilized Europeans are as timid in addressing a telephone as they would be in addressing a royal sovereign. The average European middle-class householder still speaks of his telephone, if he has one, in the same falsely casual tone as the corresponding American is liable to speak of his motor-car. It is naught—a negligible trifle—but somehow it comes into the conversation!

"How odd!" you exclaim. And you are right. It is we Europeans who are wrong, through no particular fault of our own.

The American is ruthlessly logical about the telephone. The only occasion on

From *Your United States* (New York and London, 1912), 73–98.

which I was in really serious danger of being taken for a madman in the United States was when, in a Chicago hotel, I permanently removed the receiver from the telephone in a room designed (doubtless ironically) for slumber. The whole hotel was appalled. Half Chicago shuddered. In response to the prayer of a deputation from the management I restored the receiver. On the horrified face of the deputation I could read the unspoken query: "Is it conceivable that you have been in this country a month without understanding that the United States is primarily nothing but a vast congeries of telephone-cabins?" Yes, I yielded and admired! And I surmise that on my next visit I shall find a telephone on every table of every restaurant that respects itself.

It is the efficiency of the telephone that makes it irresistible to a great people whose passion is to "get results"—the instancey with which the communication is given, and the clear loudness of the telephone's voice in reply to yours: phenomena utterly unknown in Europe. Were I to inhabit the United States, I too should become a victim of the telephone habit, as it is practised in its most advanced form in those suburban communities to which I have already incidentally referred at the end of the previous chapter. There a woman takes to the telephone as women in more decadent lands take to morphia. You can see her at morn at her bedroom window, pouring confidences into her telephone, thus combining the joy of an innocent vice with the healthy freshness of breeze and sunshine. It has happened to me to sit in a drawing-room, where people gathered round the telephone as Europeans gather around a fire, and to hear immediately after the ejaculation of a number into the telephone a sharp ring from outside through the open window, and then to hear in answer to the question, "What are you going to wear to-night?" two absolutely simultaneous replies, one loudly from the telephone across the room, and the other faintlier from a charming human voice across the garden: "I don't know. What are you?" Such may be the pleasing secondary scientific effect of telephoning to the lady next door on a warm afternoon.

Now it was obvious that behind the apparently simple exterior aspects of any telephone system there must be an intricate and marvelous secret organization. In Europe my curiosity would probably never have been excited by the thought of that organization—at home one accepts everything as of course!—but, in the United States, partly because the telephone is so much more wonderful and terrible there, and partly because in a foreign land one is apt to have strange caprices, I allowed myself to become the prey of a desire to see the arcanum concealed at the other end of all the wires; and thus, one day, under the high protection of a demigod of the electrical world, I paid a visit to a telephone-exchange in New York, and saw therein what nine hundred and ninety-nine out of every thousand of the most ardent telephone-users seldom think about and will never see.

A murmuring sound, as of an infinity of scholars in a prim school conning their lessons, and a long row of young women seated in a dim radiance on a long row of precisely similar stools, before a long apparatus of holes and pegs and pieces of elastic cord, all extremely intent: that was the first broad impression. One saw at once that none of these young women had a single moment to spare; they were all involved in the tremendous machine, part of it, keeping pace with it and in it, and not daring to take their eyes off it for an instant, lest they should sin against it. What they were droning about it was impossible to guess; for if one stationed oneself close to any particular rapt young woman, she seemed to utter no sound, but simply and without ceasing to peg and unpeg holes at random among the thousands of holes before her, apparently in obedience to the signaling of faint, tiny lights that in thousands continually expired and were rekindled. (It was so that these tiny lights should be distinguishable that the illumination of the secret and finely appointed chamber was kept dim.) Throughout the whole length of the apparatus the colored elastic cords to which the pegs were attached kept crossing one another in fantastic patterns.

We who had entered were ignored. We might have been ghosts, invisible and inaudible. Even the supervisors, less-young women set in authority, did not turn to glance at us as they moved restlessly peering behind the stools. And yet somehow I could hear the delicate shoulders of all the young women saying, without speech: "Here come these tyrants and taskmasters again, who have invented this exercise which nearly but not quite cracks our little brains for us! They know exactly how much they can get out of us, and they get it. They are cleverer than us and more power than us; and we have to submit to their discipline. But—" And afar off I could hear: "What are you going to wear to-night?" "Will you dine with me to-night?" "I want two seats." "Very well, thanks, and how is Mrs. . . . ?" "When can I see you to-morrow?" "I'll take your offer for those bonds." . . . And I could see the interiors of innumerable offices and drawing-rooms. . . . But of course I could hear and see nothing really except the intent drone and quick gesturing of those completely absorbed young creatures in the dim radiance, on stools precisely similar.

I understood why the telephone service was so efficient. I understood not merely from the demeanor of the long row of young women, but from everything else I had seen in the exact and diabolically ingenious ordering of the whole establishment.

We were silent for a time, as though we had entered a church. We were, perhaps unconsciously, abashed by the intensity of the absorption of these neat young women. After a while one of the guides, one of the inscrutable beings who had helped to invent and construct the astounding organism, began in a low voice on the forlorn hope of making me comprehend the mechanism of a telephone-call and its response. And I began on the forlorn hope of persuading him by intelligent acting that I did comprehend. We each made a little progress. I could not tell him that, though I genuinely and humbly admired his particular variety of genius, what interested me in the affair was not the mechanics, but the human equation. As a professional reader of faces, I glanced as well as I could sideways at those bent girls' faces to see if they were happy. An absurd inquiry! Do *I* look happy when I'm at work, I wonder! Did they then look reasonably content? Well, I came to the conclusion that they looked like most other faces—neither one thing nor the other. Still, in a great establishment, I would sooner search for sociological information in the faces of the employed than in the managerial rules.

165

"What do they earn?" I asked, when we emerged from the ten-atmosphere pressure of that intense absorption. (Of course I knew that no young women could possibly for any length of time be as intensely absorbed as these appeared to be. But the illusion was there, and it was effective.)

I learned that even the lowest beginner earned five dollars a week. It was just the sum I was paying for a pair of clean sheets every night at a grand hotel. And that the salary rose to six, seven, eight, eleven, and even fourteen dollars for supervisors, who, however, had to stand on their feet seven and a half hours a day, as shopgirls do ten hours a day; and that in general the girls had thirty minutes for lunch, and a day off every week, and that the Company supplied them gratuitously with tea, coffee, sugar, couches, newspapers, arm-chairs, and fresh air, of which last fifty fresh cubic feet were pumped in for every operator every minute.

Said the demigod of the electrical world, condescendingly: "All this telephone business is done on a mere few hundred horse-power. Come away, and I'll show you electricity in bulk."

And I went away with him, thoughtful. In spite of the inhuman perfection of its functioning, that exchange was a very human place indeed. It brilliantly solved some problems; it raised others. Excessively difficult to find any fault whatever in it! A marvelous service, achieved under strictly hygienic conditions—and young women must make their way through the world! And yet—Yes, a very human place indeed!

The demigods of the electric world do not condescend to move about in petrol motor-cars. In the exercise of a natural and charming coquetry they insist on electrical traction, and it was in the most modern and soundless electric brougham that we arrived at nightfall under the overhanging cornice-eaves of two gigantic Florentine palaces—just such looming palaces, they appeared in the dark, as may be seen in any central street of Florence, with a cinema-show blazing its signs on the ground floor, and Heaven knows what remnants of Italian aristocracy in the mysterious upper stories. Having entered one of the palaces, simultaneously with a tornado of wind, we passed through long, deserted, narrow galleries, lined with thousands of small, caged compartments containing "transformers," and on each compartment was a label bearing always the same words: "Danger, 6,600 volts." "Danger, 6,600 volts." "Danger, 6,600 volts." A wondrous relief when we had escaped with our lives from the menace of those innumerable volts! And then we stood on a high platform surrounded by handles, switches, signals—apparatus enough to put all New York into darkness, or to annihilate it in an instant by the unloosing of terrible cohorts of volts!—and faced an enormous white hall, sparsely peopled by a few colossal machines that seemed to be revolving and oscillating about their business with the fatalism of conquered and resigned leviathans. Immaculately clean, inconceivably tidy, shimmering with brilliant light under its lofty and beautiful ceiling, shaking and roaring with the terrific thunder of its own vitality, this hall in which no common voice could make itself heard produced nevertheless an effect of magical stillness, silence, and solitude. We were alone in it, save that now and then in the far-distant spaces a figure might flit and disappear between the huge glinting columns of metal. It was a hall enchanted and inexplicable. I understood nothing of it. But I understood that half the electricity of New York was being generated by its engines of a hundred and fifty thousand horse-power, and that if the spell were lifted the elevators of New York would be immediately paralyzed, and the twenty million lights expire beneath the eyes of a startled population. I could have gazed at it to this day, and brooded to this day upon the human imaginations that had perfected it; but I was led off, hypnotized, to see the furnaces and boilers under the earth. And even there we were almost alone, to such an extent had one sort of senseless matter been compelled to take charge of another sort of senseless matter. The odyssey of the coal that was lifted high out of ships on the tide beyond, to fall ultimately into the furnaces within, scarcely touched by the hand-wielded shovel, was by itself epical. Fresh air pouring in at the rate of twenty-four million cubic feet per hour cooled the entire palace, and gave to these stoke-holes the uncanny quality of refrigerators. The lowest horror of the steamship had been abolished here.

I was tempted to say: "This alone is fit to be called the heart of New York!"

But was it necessary to come to America in order to see and describe telephone-exchanges and electrical power-houses? Do not these wonders exist in all the cities of earth? They do, but not to quite the same degree of wondrousness. Hat-shops, and fine hat-shops, exist in New York, but not to quite the same degree of wondrousness as in Paris. People sing in New York, but not with quite the same natural lyricism as in Naples. The great civilizations all present the same features; but it is just the differences in degree between the same feature in this civilization and in that—it is just these differences which together constitute and illustrate the idiosyncrasy of each. It seems to me that the brains and the imagination of America shone superlatively in the conception and ordering of its vast organizations of human beings, and of machinery, and of the two combined. By them I was more profoundly attracted, impressed, and inspired than by any other non-spiritual phenomena whatever in the United States. For me they were the proudest material achievements, and essentially the most poetical achievements, of the United States. And that is why I am dwelling on them.

Further, there are business organizations in America of a species which do not flourish at all in Europe. For example, the "mail-order house," whose secrets were very generously displayed to me in Chicago—a peculiar establishment which sells merely everything (except patent-medicines)—on condition that you order it by post. Go into that house with money in your palm, and ask for a fan or a flail or a fur-coat or a fountain-pen or a fiddle, and you will be requested to return home and write a letter about the proposed purchase, and stamp the letter and drop it into a mail-box, and then to wait till the article arrives at your door. That house is one of the most spectacular and pleasing proofs that the inhabitants of the United States are thinly scattered over an enormous area, in tiny groups, often quite isolated from stores. On the day of my visit sixty thousand letters had been received, and every executable order contained in these was executed before closing time, by the co-ordinated efforts of over four thousand female employees and over three thousand males. The conception would make Europe dizzy. Imagine a merchant in Moscow trying to inaugurate such a scheme!

A little machine no bigger than a soup-plate will open hundreds of envelopes at once. They are all the same, those envelopes; they have even less individuality than sheep being sheared, but when the contents of one—any one at random—are put into your hand, something human and distinctive is put into your hand. I read the caligraphy on a blue sheet of paper, and it was written by a woman in Wyoming, a neat, earnest, harassed, and possibly rather harassing woman, and she wanted all sorts of things and wanted them intensely—I could see that with clearness. This complex purchase was an important event in her year. So far as her imagination went, only one mail-order would reach the Chicago house that morning, and the entire establishment would be strained to meet it.

Then the blue sheet was taken from me and thrust into the system, and therein lost to me. I was taken to a mysteriously rumbling shaft of broad diameter, that pierced all the floors of the house and had trap-doors on each floor. And when one of the trap-doors was opened I saw packages of all descriptions racing after one another down spiral planes within the shaft. There were several of these great shafts—with divisions for mail, express, and freight traffic—and packages were ceaselessly racing down all of them, laden with the objects desired by the woman of Wyoming and her fifty-nine-thousand-odd fellow-customers of the day. At first it seemed to me impossible that that earnest, impatient woman in Wyoming should get precisely what she wanted; it seemed to me impossible that some mistake should not occur in all that noisy fever of rushing activity. But after I had followed an order, and seen it filled and checked, my opinion was that a mistake would be the most miraculous phenomenon in that establishment. I felt quite reassured on behalf of Wyoming.

And then I was suddenly in a room where six hundred billing-machines were being clicked at once by six hundred young women, a fantastic aural nightmare, though none of the young women appeared to be conscious that anything bizarre was going on. . . . And then I was in a printing-shop, where several lightning machines spent their whole time every day in printing the most popular work of reference in the United States, a bulky book full of pictures, with an annual circulation of five and a half million copies—the general catalogue of the firm. For the first time I realized the true meaning of the word "popularity"—and sighed. . . .

And then it was lunch-time for about a couple of thousand employees, and in the boundless restaurant I witnessed the working of the devices which enabled these legions to choose their meals, and pay for them (cost price) in a few moments, and without advanced mathematical calculations. The young head of the restaurant showed me, with pride, a menu of over a hundred dishes—Austrian, German, Hungarian, Italian, Scotch, French, and American; at prices from one cent up as high as ten cents (prime roast-beef)—and at the foot of the menu was his personal appeal: "*I* desire to extend to you a cordial invitation to inspect," etc. "*My* constant aim will be," etc. Yet it was not *his* restaurant. It was the firm's restaurant. Here I had a curious illustration of an admirable characteristic of American business methods that was always striking me—namely, the real delegation of responsibility. An American board of direction will put a man in charge of a department, as a viceroy over a province, saying, as it were: "This is yours. Do as you please with it. We will watch the results." A marked contrast this with the centralizing of authority which seems to be ever proceeding in Europe, and which breeds in all classes at all ages—especially in France—a morbid fear and horror of accepting responsibility.

Later, I was on the ground level, in the midst of an enormous apparent confusion—the target for all the packages and baskets, big and little, that shot every instant in a continuous stream from those spiral planes, and slid dangerously at me along the floors. Here were the packers. I saw a packer deal with a collected order, and in this order were a number of tiny cookery utensils, a four-cent curling-iron, a brush, and two incredibly ugly pink china mugs, inscribed in cheap gilt respectively with the words "Father" and "Mother." Throughout my stay in America no moment came to me more dramatically than this moment, and none has remained more vividly in my mind. All the daily domestic life of the small communities in the wilds of the West and the Middle West, and in the wilds of the back streets of the great towns, seemed to be revealed to me by the contents of that basket, as the packer wrapped up and protected one article after another. I had been compelled to abandon a visitation of the West and of the small communities everywhere, and I was sorry. But here in a microcosm I thought I saw the simple reality of the backbone of all America, a symbol of the millions of the little plain people, who ultimately make possible the glory of the world-renowned streets and institutions in dazzling cities.

There was something indescribably touching in that curling-iron and those two mugs. I could see the table on which the mugs would soon proudly stand, and "father" and "mother" and children there at, and I could see the hand heating the curling-iron and applying it. I could see the whole little home and the whole life of the little home. . . . And afterward, as I wandered through the warehouses—pyramids of the same chair, cupboards full of the same cheap violin, stacks of the same album of music, acres of the same carpet and wallpaper, tons of the same gramophone, hundreds of tons of the same sewing-machine and lawn-mower—I felt as if I had been made free of the secrets of every village in every State of the Union, and as if I had lived in every little house and cottage thereof all my life! Almost no sense of beauty in those tremendous supplies of merchandise, but a lot of honesty, self-respect, and ambition fulfilled. I tell you I could hear the engaged couples discussing ardently over the pages of the catalogue what manner of bedroom suite they would buy, and what design of sideboard. . . .

Finally, I arrived at the firm's private railway station, where a score or more trucks were being laden with the multifarious boxes, bales, and parcels, all to leave that evening for romantic destinations such as Oregon, Texas, and Wyoming. Yes, the package of the woman of Wyoming's desire would ultimately be placed somewhere in one of those trucks! It was going to start off toward her that very night!

Impressive as this establishment was, finely as it illustrated the national genius for organization, it yet lacked necessarily, on account of the nature of its activity, those outward phenomena of splendor which charm the stranger's eye in the great central houses of New York, and which seem designed to sum up all that is most characteristic and most dazzling in the business methods of the United States. These central houses are not soiled by the touch of actual merchandise. Nothing more squalid than ink ever enters their gates. They traffic with symbols only, and the symbols, no matter what they stand for, are never in themselves sordid. The men who have created these houses seem to have realized that, from their situation and their importance, a special effort toward representative magnificence was their pleasing duty, and to have made the effort with a superb prodigality and an astounding ingenuity.

Take, for a good, glorious example, the very large insurance company, conscious that the eyes of the world are upon it, and that the entire United States is expecting it to uphold the national pride. All the splendors of all the sky-scrapers are united in its building. Its foyer and grand staircase will sustain comparison with those of the Paris Opéra. You might think you were going into a place of entertainment! And, as a fact, you are! This affair, with nearly four thousand clerks, is the huge toy and pastime of a group of millionaires who have discovered a way of honestly amusing themselves while gaining applause and advertisement. Within the foyer and beyond the staircase, notice the outer rooms, partitioned off by bronze grilles, looming darkly gorgeous in an eternal windowless twilight studded with the beautiful glowing green disks of electric-lamp shades; and under each disk a human head bent over the black-and-red magic of ledgers! The desired effect is at once obtained, and it is wonderful. Then lose yourself in and out of the ascending and descending elevators, and among the unending multitudes of clerks, and along the corridors of marble (total length exactly measured and recorded). You will be struck dumb. And immediately you begin to recover your speech you will be struck dumb again. . . .

Other houses, as has been seen, provide good meals for their employees at cost price. This house, then, will provide excellent meals, free of charge! It will install the most expensive kitchens and richly spacious restaurants. It will serve the delicate repasts with dignity. "Does all this lessen the wages?" No, not in theory. But in practice, and whether the management wishes or not, it must come out of the wages. "Why do you do it?" you ask the department chief, who apparently gets far more fun out of the contemplation of these refectories than out of the contemplation of premiums received and claims paid. "It is better for the employees," he says. "But we do it because it is better for us. It pays us. Good food, physical comfort, agreeable environment, scientific ventilation—all these things pay us. We get results from them." He does not mention horses, but you feel that the comparison is with horses. A horse, or a clerk, or an artisan—it pays equally well to treat all of them well. This is one of the latest discoveries of economic science, a discovery not yet universally understood.

I say you do not mention horses, and you certainly must not hint that the men in authority may have been actuated by motives of humanity. You must believe what you are told—that the sole motive is to get results. The eagerness with which all heads of model establishments would disavow to me any thought of being humane was affecting in its *naiveté*; it had that touch of ingenuous wistfulness which I remarked everywhere in America—and nowhere more than in the demeanor of many mercantile highnesses. (I hardly expect Americans to understand just what I mean here.) It was as if they would blush at being caught in an act of humanity, like school-boys caught praying. Still, to my mind, the white purity of their desire to get financial results was often muddied by the dark stain of a humane motive. I may be wrong (as people say), but I know I am not (as people think).

The further you advance into the penetralia of this arch-exemplar of American organization and profusion, the more you are amazed by the imaginative perfection of its detail: as well in the system of filing for instant reference fifty million separate documents, as in the planning of a concert-hall for the diversion of the human machines.

As we went into the immense concert-hall a group of girls were giving an informal concert among themselves. When lunch is served on the premises with chronographic exactitude, the thirty-five minutes allowed for the meal give an appreciable margin for music and play. A young woman was just finishing a florid song. The concert was suspended, and the whole party began to move humbly away at this august incursion.

"Sing it again; do, please!" the departmental chief suggested. And the florid song. The concert was suspended, and the whole party began to move humbly away the group fled, the thirty-five minutes being doubtless up. The departmental chief looked at me in silence, content, as much as to say: "This is how we do business in America." And I thought, "Yet another way of getting results!"

But sometimes the creators of the organization, who had provided everything, had been obliged to confess that they had omitted from their designs certain factors of evolution. Hat-cupboards were a feature of the women's offices—delightful specimens of sound cabinetry. And still, millinery was lying about all over the place, giving it an air of feminine occupation that was extremely exciting to a student on his travels. The truth was that none of those hats would go into the cupboards. Fashion had worsted the organization completely. Departmental chiefs had nothing to do but acquiesce in this startling untidiness. Either they must wait till the circumference of hats lessened again, or they must tear down the whole structure and rebuild it with due regard to hats.

Finally, we approached the sacred lair and fastness of the president, whose massive portrait I had already seen on several walls. Spaciousness and magnificence increased. Ceilings rose in height, marble was softened by the thick pile of carpets. Mahogany and gold shone more luxuriously. I was introduced into the vast ante-chamber of the presidential secretaries, and by the chief of them inducted through polished and gleaming barriers into the presence-chamber itself: a noble apartment, an apartment surpassing dreams and expectations, conceived and executed in a spirit of majestic prodigality. The president had not been afraid. And his costly audacity was splendidly justified of itself. This man had a sense of the romantic, of the dramatic, of the fit. And the qualities in him and his *état major* which had commanded the success of the entire enterprise were well shown in the brilliant symbolism of that room's grandiosity. . . . And there was the president's portrait again, gorgeously framed.

He came in through another door, an old man of superb physique, and after a little while he was relating to me the early struggles of his company. "My wife used to say that for ten years she never saw me," he remarked.

I asked him what his distractions were, now that the strain was over and his ambitions so gloriously achieved. He replied that occasionally he went for a drive in his automobile.

"And what do you do with yourself in the evenings?" I inquired.

He seemed a little disconcerted by this perhaps unaccustomed bluntness.

"Oh," he said, casually, "I read insurance literature."

He had the conscious mien and manners of a reigning prince. His courtesy and affability were impeccable and charming. In the most profound sense this human being had succeeded, for it was impossible to believe that, had he to live his life again, he would live it very differently.

Such a type of man is, of course, to be found in nearly every country; but the type flourishes with a unique profusion and perfection in the United States; and in its more prominent specimens the distinguishing idiosyncrasy of the average American successful man of business is magnified for our easier inspection. The rough, broad difference between the American and the European business man is that the latter is anxious to leave his work, while the former is anxious to get to it. The attitude of the American business man toward his business is pre-eminently the attitude of an artist. You may say that he loves money. So do we all—artists particularly. No stock-broker's private journal could be more full of dollars than Balzac's intimate correspondence is full of francs. But whereas the ordinary artist loves money chiefly because it represents luxury, the American business man loves it chiefly because it is the sole proof of success in his endeavor. He loves his business. It is not his toil, but his hobby, passion, vice, monomania—any vituperative epithet you like to bestow on it! He does not look forward to living in the evening; he lives most intensely when he is in the midst of his organization. His instincts are best appeased by the hourly excitements of a good, scrimmaging commercial day. He needs these excitements as some natures need alcohol. He cannot do without them.

On no other hypothesis can the unrivaled ingenuity and splendor and ruthlessness of American business undertakings be satisfactorily explained. They surpass the European, simply because they are never out of the thoughts of their directors, because they are adored with a fine frenzy. And for the same reason they are decked forth in magnificence. Would a man enrich his office with rare woods and stuffs and marbles if it were not a temple? Would he bestow graces on the environment if while he was in it the one idea at the back of his head was the anticipation of leaving it? Watch American business men together, and if you are a European you will clearly perceive that they are devotees. They are open with one another, as intimates are. Jealousy and secretiveness are much rarer among them than in Europe. They show off their respective organizations with pride and with candor. They admire one another enormously. Hear one of them say enthusiastically of another: "It was a great idea he had—connecting his New York and his Philadelphia places by wireless—a great idea!" They call one another by their Christian names, fondly. They are capable of wonderful friendships in business. They are cemented by one religion—and it is not golf. For them the journey "home" is often not the evening journey, but the morning journey. Call this a hard saying if you choose: it is true. Could a man be happy long away from a hobby so entrancing, a toy so intricate and marvelous, a setting so splendid? Is it strange that, absorbed in that wondrous satisfying hobby, he should make love with the nonchalance of an animal? At which point I seem to have come dangerously near to the topic of the singular position of the American woman, about which everybody is talking.

# 61

# Persisting Ideals

Woodrow Wilson (1856–1924) was elected President of the United States on November 5, 1912, only the second Democrat to serve in the White House since the Civil War. His campaign speeches against William Howard Taft and Theodore Roosevelt revealed his anxiety over the power certain "interests" had attained in American life and his desire to restore the meaningful competition and sense of participation that the previous decades of industrial concentration had helped erode.

A student of American history and government, from his graduate days at Johns Hopkins and his teaching at Wesleyan and Princeton, Wilson used the public forum as a means of inspiring men to share his version of the possibilities of democracy. His first inaugural, coming on the eve of dramatic reforms in the nation's financial structure, summed up with a religious intensity his assessment of the meaning of American life, and the wrongs that needed righting. As a statement of purposes and a declaration of mission, it stands in a long line of eloquent American testaments, going back, perhaps, to John Winthrop's famous exhortation on board the *Arbella* in 1630.

## THE FIRST INAUGURAL
### *Woodrow Wilson*

*My Fellow Citizens:*

There has been a change of government. It began two years ago, when the House of Representatives became Democratic by a decisive majority. It has now been completed. The Senate about to assemble will also be Democratic. The offices of President and Vice-President have been put into the hands of Democrats. What does the change mean? That is the question that is uppermost in our minds to-day. That is the question I am going to try to answer, in order, if I may, to interpret the occasion.

It means much more then the mere success of a party. The success of a party means little except when the Nation is using that party for a large and definite purpose. No one can mistake the purpose for which the Nation now seeks to use

From *Inaugural Addresses of the Presidents of the United States*, U.S. 82nd Congress, 2nd Session, House Document 540 (1952), 189–192.

the Democratic Party. It seeks to use it to interpret a change in its own plans and point of view. Some old things with which we had grown familiar, and which had begun to creep into the very habit of our thought and of our lives, have altered their aspect as we have latterly looked critically upon them, with fresh, awakened eyes; have dropped their disguises and shown themselves alien and sinister. Some new things, as we look frankly upon them, willing to comprehend their real character, have come to assume the aspect of things long believed in and familiar, stuff of our own convictions. We have been refreshed by a new insight into our own life.

We see that in many things that life is very great. It is incomparably great in its material aspects, in its body of wealth, in the diversity and sweep of its energy, in the industries which have been conceived and built up by the genius of individual men and the limitless enterprise of groups of men. It is great, also, very great, in its moral force.

Nowhere else in the world have noble men and women exhibited in more striking forms the beauty and the energy of sympathy and helpfulness and counsel in their efforts to rectify wrong, alleviate suffering, and set the weak in the way of strength and hope. We have built up, moreover, a great system of government, which has stood through a long age as in many respects a model for those who seek to set liberty upon foundations that will endure against fortuitous change, against storm and accident. Our life contains every great thing, and contains it in rich abundance.

But the evil has come with the good, and much fine gold has been corroded. With riches has come inexcusable waste. We have squandered a great part of what we might have used, and have not stopped to conserve the exceeding bounty of nature, without which our genius for enterprise would have been worthless and impotent, scorning to be careful, shamefully prodigal as well as admirably efficient. We have been proud of our industrial achievements, but we have not hitherto stopped thoughtfully enough to count the human cost, the cost of lives snuffed out, of energies overtaxed and broken, the fearful physical and spiritual cost to the men and women and children upon whom the dead weight and burden of it all has fallen pitilessly the years through. The groans and agony of it all had not yet reached our ears, the solemn, moving undertone of our life, coming up out of the mines and factories and out of every home where the struggle had its intimate and familiar seat. With the great Government went many deep secret things which we too long delayed to look into and scrutinize with candid, fearless eyes. The great Government we loved has too often been made use of for private and selfish purposes, and those who used it had forgotten the people.

At last a vision has been vouchsafed us of our life as a whole. We see the bad with the good, the debased and decadent with the sound and vital. With this vision we approach new affairs. Our duty is to cleanse, to reconsider, to restore, to correct the evil without impairing the good, to purify and humanize every process of our common life without weakening or sentimentalizing it. There has been something crude and heartless and unfeeling in our haste to succeed and be great. Our thought has been "Let every man look out for himself, let every generation look out for itself," while we reared giant machinery which made it impossible that any but those who stood at the levers of control should have a chance to look out for themselves. We had not forgotten our morals. We remembered well enough that we had set up a policy which was meant to serve the humblest as well as the most powerful, with an eye single to the standards of justice and fair play, and remembered it with pride. But we were very heedless and in a great hurry to be great.

We have come now to the sober second thought. The scales of heedlessness have fallen from our eyes. We have made up our minds to square every process of our national life again with the standards we so proudly set up at the beginning and have always carried at our hearts. Our work is a work of restoration.

We have itemized with some degree of particularity the things that ought to be altered and here are some of the chief items: A tariff which cuts us off from our proper part in the commerce of the world, violates the just principles of taxation, and makes the Government a facile instrument in the hands of private interests; a banking and currency system based upon the necessity of the Government to sell its bonds fifty years ago and perfectly adapted to concentrating cash and restricting credits; an industrial system which, take it on all its sides, financial as well as administrative, holds capital in leading strings, restricts the liberties and limits the opportunities of labor, and exploits without renewing or conserving the natural resources of the country; a body of agricultural activities never yet given the efficiency of great business undertakings or served as it should be through the instrumentality of science taken directly to the farm, or afforded the facilities of credit best suited to its practical needs; water-courses undeveloped, waste places unreclaimed, forests untended, fast disappearing without plan or prospect of renewal, unregarded waste heaps at every mine. We have studied as perhaps no other nation has the most effective means of production, but we have not studied cost or economy as we should either as organizers of industry, as statesmen, or as individuals.

Nor have we studied and perfected the means by which government may be put at the service of humanity, in safeguarding the health of the Nation, the health of its men and its women and its children, as well as their rights in the struggle for existence. This is no sentimental duty. The firm basis of government is justice, not pity. These are matters of justice. There can be no equality or opportunity, the first essential of justice in the body politic, if men and women and children be not shielded in their lives, their very vitality, from the consequences of great industrial and social processes which they can not alter, control, or singly cope with. Society must see to it that it does not itself crush or weaken or damage its own constituent parts. The first duty of law is to keep sound the society it serves. Sanitary laws, pure food laws, and laws determining conditions of labor which individuals are powerless to determine for themselves are intimate parts of the very business of justice and legal efficiency.

These are some of the things we ought to do, and not leave the others undone, the old-fashioned, never-to-be-neglected, fundamental safeguarding of property and of individual right. This is the high enterprise of the new day: To lift everything that concerns our life as a Nation to the light that shines from the hearthfire of every man's conscience and vision of the right. It is inconceivable that we should do this as partisans; it is inconceivable we should do it in ignorance of the facts as they are or in blind haste. We shall restore, not destroy. We shall deal with our economic system as it is and as it may be modified, not as it might be if we had a clean sheet of paper to write upon; and step by step we shall make it what it should be, in the spirit of those who question their own wisdom and seek counsel and knowledge, not shallow self-satisfaction or the excitement of excursions whither they can not tell. Justice, and only justice, shall alway be our motto.

And yet it will be no cool process of mere science. The Nation has been deeply stirred, stirred by a solemn passion, stirred by the knowledge of wrong, of ideals lost, of government too often debauched and made an instrument of evil. The feelings with which we face this new age of right and opportunity sweep across our heartstrings like some air out of God's own presence, where justice and mercy are reconciled and the judge and the brother are one. We know our task to be no mere task of politics but a task which shall search us through and through, whether we be able to understand our time and the need of our people, whether we be indeed their spokesmen and interpreters, whether we have the pure heart to comprehend and the rectified will to choose our high course of action.

This is not a day of triumph; it is a day of dedication. Here muster, not the forces of party, but the forces of humanity. Men's hearts wait upon us; men's lives hang in the balance; men's hopes call upon us to say what we will do. Who shall live up to the great trust? Who dares fail to try? I summon all honest men, all patriotic, all forward-looking men, to my side. God helping me, I will not fail them, if they will but counsel and sustain me!

## PART EIGHT

# The Quest for an Old Order, 1912–1929

Americans entered World War I optimistically and confidently, carrying the Progressive spirit of domestic reform into the world arena; but they grew disillusioned very quickly, first about their ventures abroad, then about conditions at home. The 1920s, for all the popular notions of a roaring time, with flappers frenetically dancing the Charleston in gay speakeasies, was a decade marked by the most fundamental kinds of doubts and fears, an era when Americans were hard put to accept external responsibilities or to tolerate internal differences. Their responses ranged from private escapism to public repression. The 1920s, in other words, was an era not so much of song and dance as of isolationism, prohibition, immigration restriction, and the Ku Klux Klan.

Although Woodrow Wilson won re-election in 1916 on the slogan, "He kept us out of war," the President did not keep his promise very long. No doubt Wilson and his countrymen would have preferred to remain neutral in World War I; there were the many problems of industrialism, and no tradition was stronger than avoiding entanglement in European affairs. Yet they were drawn into the conflict, as Wilson, a proud and moralistic man, insisted on exercising and defending the right of neutral American ships to carry on trade. When the German command decided that all-out submarine warfare could bring victory and ignored the rights of neutrals to execute the strategy, American ships were sunk and Wilson had no choice except to ask Congress to declare war; but to compensate the nation, Wilson promised in the best Progressive tradition that this would be no ordinary war. It would accomplish nothing less than to end all wars, and to make the world safe for democracy. Rather than insist that our national self-interest was at stake or that an Allied victory was critical to America's immediate welfare, Wilson turned the war into a crusade, elevating participation to the highest possible plane. Indeed the rhetoric made it seem that the very millennium would accompany the peace.

However, peace brought conferences and further entanglements in the intricacies of European diplomacy, unavoidable compromises, and eventual disillusionments. Wilson went to meet the Allies at Paris and tried his best to keep the treaty negotiations as open and as democratic as possible; still, secret treaties often undermined his efforts. He argued vigorously and persuasively for self-determination for hitherto dependent nationalities, but all too often the ambitions of victorious powers determined the drawing of new boundary lines.

Yet Wilson achieved one critical victory: the creation of a League of Nations that would, he believed, be able to correct any errors or injustices. Linking it to the peace treaty as the best guarantee of future world security, Wilson returned home to defend his work.

Critics, especially in the Senate, immediately took him to task. They pointed to every instance in the peace treaty where the provisions had fallen short of Wilson's ideals, reiterating their distrust of European diplomatic maneuvers. They made the focus of their attacks the League, asserting that membership would imperil national sovereignty, that American troops would be at the beck and call of an international power. Wilson explained that the commitments would be moral, not legal, and that only Congress could declare war, but still the debate and stances hardened. A majority of the electorate would probably have preferred the country to join the League, but Wilson could not translate popular sentiments into a legislative victory. He suddenly fell ill in the midst of the battle, and his debility, his heavy-handed moralism, and his lack of political astuteness together with the determination of hard-core opponents combined to defeat the League. All the promises of war and peace evaporated.

These events cast a pall over the next decade, breeding a deep and widely shared cynicism. Wilson became the President who promised peace and delivered war; Americans were deceived by Allied propaganda or were the helpless victims of the munitions makers in search of greater profits. The promises of a war to end all wars rang hollow in the 1920s and robbed all ideological or high-sounding phrases of meaning. Having been taken in by one set of grandiose promises, Americans were not going to open themselves to similar disappointments again. Isolationism came to dominate public opinion. The country would have no part of the notion that power brought responsibility in world affairs. It turned its back on Europe—and as Franklin D. Roosevelt would discover in the 1930s, it would not easily be persuaded to change posture.

Americans also abandoned during this decade the Progressive faith that immigrants would easily and creditably integrate into the society. Progressives had confidently sponsored a variety of institutions to assimilate the newcomer: schools, settlement houses, and charitable organizations taught the immigrant to substitute American customs for eastern or southern European ones. These institutions, to be sure, showed little respect for Old World traditions and were impatient with non-American ways of doing things; but they operated on a voluntary basis, without threat or compulsion, hoping to set a persuasive example. In the 1920s, however, Americans grew far more distrustful of the immigrant and uneasy with the implications of a heterogeneous society. They were angry, on the one hand, that immigrants did not disappear or totally assimilate into the melting pot; they were jealous, on the other hand, when immigrants made advances in politics, business, or culture. Without the essential optimism of the Progressives, this generation turned from persuasion to coercion, from voluntary institutions to binding laws, moving at once to cut off the flow of newcomers and to harass those already here.

One of the first results of this shift was Prohibition as expressed in the Eighteenth Amendment, adopted in 1919, outlawing the sale of liquor. Convinced that it was no coincidence that bars and taverns flourished in lower-class immigrant neighborhoods, many Americans concluded that drinking made the immigrant poor, disorderly, and dangerous. Drunkedness was an unwelcome remnant of corrupt Old World customs, and by avoiding temptation, the immigrant could become a hard-working citizen and better American. No longer certain that persuasion would do, the country turned to compulsory legislation. Prohibition, still half-rooted in the Progressive era, was a mild step compared to later measures. Indeed one of the reasons that Prohibition was never vigorously enforced through the 1920s was because the groups that supported it most eagerly at first soon turned to still more coercive and compulsory measures: immigration restriction and Ku Klux Klan activities.

The movement for immigration restriction achieved its major goals in the 1920s. Congressional legislation not only limited the total number of immigrants but placed special restrictions on those from southern and eastern Europe. The law established yearly quotas for various national groups; and to insure that the newer immigrants—the Poles, the Slovaks, the Italians, the Jews—would no longer compose the bulk of entering foreigners, it based the quotas on the percentages of immigrants here in 1890. The date was carefully chosen, for very few of these groups were as yet present in any size. The popular rationale for this decision rested on the prevailing theories of race superiority and inferiority—arguments that enjoyed a great vogue during these years. The Anglo-Saxons stood at the highest end of the scale; Africans were at the bottom, and the Mediterranean types (Jews and Italians) near them. Popular prejudice armed with a specious but general theory combined effectively to cut off the flow of immigrants.

The Ku Klux Klan for its part tried to make life as terrifying as possible for immigrants already here, especially the Catholics. Although Southern in inspiration and origins, the bulk of the Klan's membership and activities in the 1920s centered in Midwestern and border states, often in cities with mixed populations like Chicago or Indianapolis. The Klan filled two critical functions for its members. First, through ceremonies, passwords, costumes, and marches, it gave the lower middle-class Americans a sense of comradeship and excitement, enlivening life in dull, drab, and isolated small towns, supplying a sense of identity and belonging in larger cities. Secondly, and most important, it permitted members to express frustrations and prejudices against anyone or anything that was different. Bewildered by change, threatened by the unfamiliar, frightened that others were making their mark in a changing America while they stood still, Klansmen donned masks, burned crosses, and somehow hoped to preserve their importance and their values.

They achieved some victories. They saw in Prohibition a national law that wrote their values into the Constitution; they saw in immigration restriction a confirmation of their mistrust of foreigners; but soon internal corruption and scandal struck the Klan, and condemnations of the secret organization increased. By the end of the decade the Klan was practically dead. Still its power and influence in the 1920s were testimony to the extraordinary fears that gripped many Americans.

The more serious problems confronting the nation in this decade received far too little attention. Caught up in worrying about immigrants and intemperance, Americans did not look closely at their economy to see whether the surface prosperity went very deep. Well before the Depression, farmers had fallen on hard times; having expanded their production during World War I, they now faced glutted markets at home and abroad. Labor-union victories in the first decade of the twentieth century were not maintained into the 1920s, and the bulk of workers had no protection against wage reductions or unemployment. Moreover, no one looked with any care at business practices, content to abdicate the task of regulation; but business did not fulfill its responsibility adequately. The manipulation of the stock market was the outstanding example of the unchecked dominance of private over public welfare. These failings became only too apparent when Black Friday 1929, crash day at Wall Street, signaled the start of a decade-long depression.

The nation's political leaders sat undisturbed, content to utter truisms rather than educate the public to necessary reforms. The Presidents set the tone. Warren Harding was a jovial, warm-hearted, and incompetent President, who also had the misfortune of being betrayed by his friends. Corruption during his administration was even more widespread than during the worst days of the Gilded Age. His successor Calvin Coolidge had risen to national prominence as the Governor who broke a Boston police strike; in the White House he was known as a man of few words rather than for the quality of anything he said or did. Perhaps the most qualified was Herbert Hoover. His reputation as a brilliant administrator was well earned. In charge of distributing American war relief to Europe, he fulfilled the task efficiently and humanely; but as President he was a prisoner of his unwavering hostility to any interference by government in the economy. He too was content to let matters take their own course, even in the first years of the Depression. With these men in the White House, it was not surprising that a good part of the nation never understood the irrationality of its fears or the issues that needed its attention. One of Franklin D. Roosevelt's many accomplishments would be the skillful education in realities that he gave his countrymen.

# 62

## Over There

With high-minded slogans, Americans entered World War I, on their way to make the world safe for democracy. But the crusade had to be organized—men were to be trained, shipped abroad, supplied, put into units, deployed on a European front, and coordinated in battle with the Allies. Yet Americans had little military experience on which to draw. The Spanish-American War had been too brief and against too weak an enemy to teach the nation much. Yet despite their inexperience, Americans made quick progress, and their effort in World War I was remarkable for its effectiveness and efficiency. The troops fought bravely. They were well trained and well supplied.

The letters between General of the Army John J. Pershing and Woodrow Wilson's Secretary of War, Newton D. Baker, reveal some of the dimensions and details of this accomplishment. Pershing was a critical figure, a general who could not only fight, but who could organize. Graduating from West Point in 1886 at the age of twenty-six, Pershing had no military experience until the Spanish-American War. He served first as a captain in the army, and subsequently was an officer in the Philippine Occupation Army. He also led an unsuccessful expedition in 1916 against the Mexican outlaw Pancho Villa. In 1917 Pershing took command of the American forces and helped to put together a modern, organized, and efficient army.

### EXPERIENCES IN THE WORLD WAR
#### *John J. Pershing*

**1   General John J. Pershing
to Newton D. Baker, June 18, 1918**

*My Dear Mr. Secretary:*

I wish to take up a subject of very great importance. That is the burning one of getting troops over here and forming an army as rapidly as possible. I think it is imperative that our whole program for the next ten or twelve months be reconstructed. The Department's estimate of 91,000 men per month after August is

From *My Experiences in the World War* (New York, 1931), II: 107–108, 110–113, 181–191, with permission of the Estate of General Pershing.

not nearly as much as we must do. Mr. Secretary, I cannot emphasize this point too forcibly. We should have at least three million men in France by next April ready for the spring and summer campaign. To achieve this will involve the shipment of 250,000 men per month for the eight months ending April 1st. This is the smallest program that we should contemplate. The situation among our Allies is such that unless we can end the war next year we are likely to be left practically alone in the fight. If further serious reverses come to us this year it is going to be very difficult even to hold France in the war.

The morale of both the French and British troops is not what it should be. The presence of our troops has braced them up very much but their staying powers are doubtful. Our 2d and 3d Divisions actually stopped the Germans. The French were not equal to it. I fear that I must put some of our regiments into the weaker French divisions, temporarily, to give them courage.

After checking the German offensive, we must be prepared to strike as soon as possible. The German divisions are growing weaker and their manpower is running low. The German people would be inclined to make peace if they felt a few very heavy blows. We should be ready to give them. On the other hand, if we do not hasten, and the war is allowed to drag along during next year and the year after, we shall run a very great risk that Germany will recuperate by conscripting manpower from the Western Provinces of Russia. The British and French Governments are alarmed about this, as you know, and I consider it a real danger.

Then, we must bear in mind the effect of a long war upon our own people. The idea seems prevalent at home that the war is going to be finished within a year and our people are wrought up and wish to see a big effort at once. But if we do not make ourselves strong enough on this front to assume the offensive and push the war to a finish, there is going to be criticism and dissatisfaction at home and a general letting down of our war spirit. Moreover, by using a large force and ending the war we shall avoid the large losses that have so dreadfully depleted our Allies. Let us take every advantage of the high tide of enthusiasm and win the war.

I think that with proper representations as to the necessity for shipping, the British would do all they could to assist us. In fact, Sir Graeme Thomson said he thought the British would be able to continue the recent shipping schedule indefinitely. On our side, we should demand a greater amount of American tonnage than has hitherto been allotted to the army from the sum total of our available shipping, which is constantly increasing. Our shipping advisers here say that several hundred thousand tons can be added to the army allotment by proper paring.

As to the preparation of this new army, may I not beg of you to consider a draft of 2,000,000 men by December 1st? My recent cable asking that 1,500,000 be called out should now be increased to 2,000,000. They should be called out, beginning now, at the rate of 400,000 per month for the next five months. We should not again be without trained men as we find ourselves now. Every possible means should be exhausted to train, clothe, and equip this force by the end of the year. These are strong words and the force looks large, but we are face to face with the most serious situation that has ever confronted a nation, and it must be met at any sacrifice and without any delay.

I think we must bring women into our factories, transforming the whole country into an organization to push the war. The British could help on clothing. As to munitions, it matters little whether we have a particular kind of artillery; if we cannot get the French, we should take the British. The same can be said of small arms and personal equipment. If our ordnance cannot furnish them, the French and British have them. So in equipment and armament, there should be no delay.

I am having a detailed study made of the supply and shipping questions involved, especially as to the amount of supplies that can be obtained in Europe. The pooling program will soon be in operation and I think we shall be able to obtain a greater amount of supplies here than we had anticipated. Spain is practically a virgin field for us which is as yet undeveloped and which, with diplomatic handling, should yield much more than she has hitherto yielded. I shall look into this further.

The question of accommodations for our troops may have to be considered. If that stands in the way, then I am in favor of asking Congress to permit the billeting of troops. The French people are standing for it even by the forces of two foreign nations, why should not we at home be willing to billet our own troops among our own people?

As to handling everything that must be sent over under this program, I stand ready now, without waiting for detailed study, to say that we can do it. The supply question will be less difficult as the pooling and the feeding of our troops by the Allies develop. The great port of Marseille is largely unused and will handle much additional tonnage. Our port construction and port facilities are progressing, the railroads are getting better and storage is becoming easier because the French are finding more and more room. The horse question will also probably be worked out here. So that there need be no hesitation in adopting the plan. We should do all that is humanly possible to carry it out.

There is nothing so dreadfully important as winning this war and every possible resource should be made immediately available. Mr. Secretary, the question is so vital to our country, and the necessity of winning the war is so great, that there is no limit to which we should not go to carry out the plan I have outlined for the next ten months, and we must be prepared to carry it on still further after that at the same rate or maybe faster.

I have outlined the plan as the least we should count upon to insure success, and I hope, with your strong support, that the President will approve it.


2    **General John J. Pershing**
     **to Newton D. Baker, June 21, 1918**

*My Dear Mr. Secretary:*

The present state of the war under the continued German offensive makes it necessary to consider at once the largest possible military program for the United States. The morale of the French Government and of the High Command is believed to be good but it is certain that the morale of the lower grades of the French Army is distinctly poor. Both the French and British people are extremely tired of the war and their troops are reflecting this attitude in their frequent inability to meet successfully the German attacks. It is the American soldiers now in France upon whom they rely. It is the moral as well as material aid given by the American soldier that is making the continuation of the war possible. Only the continual arrival of American troops and their judicious employment can restore the morale of our Allies and give them courage. The above represents the views of the Allied Military leaders as told me in person by General Foch himself, and I believe it is also the view of the civil leaders. We must start immediately on our plans for the future and be ready to strike this fall in order to tide us over till spring, when we should have a big army ready. The war can be brought to a successful conclusion next year if we only go at it now. From a purely military point of view it is essential that we make this effort, especially for the reasons above stated and on account of the grave possibility that the enemy will obtain supplies and men from Russia before next year.

To meet the demands imposed by the above plan our minimum effort should be based on sending to France prior to May, 1919, a total force, including that already here, of 66 divisions (or better, if possible) together with the necessary corps and army troops, service of supply troops, and replacements. This plan would give an available force of about 3,000,000 soldiers for the summer campaign of 1919, and if this force were maintained, would in conjunction with our Allies give us every hope of concluding the war in 1919.

### 3   Newton D. Baker
### to General John J. Pershing, July 6, 1918

*My Dear General Pershing:*

I have your letter of June 18, which reached me promptly. I have been studying with more than ordinary care and interest the dispatches of the past week or two with reference to the enlargement of our military effort and program. When your cablegram suggesting a 60-division program came I immediately set about the necessary inquiries to discover just how far it fell within the range of industrial possibility. When the 100-division program came it occurred to me that we ought to study the situation with the view of determining the maximum amount we can do. I have the feeling that this war has gone on long enough and if any exertion on our part or any sacrifice can speed its successful termination even by a single day, we should make it. We are therefore now having studies made to show the things necessary to be done for three possible programs, one involving 60, one 80, and the other 100 divisions by the first of July, 1919. As soon as these programs are worked out we will, in consultation with the War Industries Board, determine how far manufacturing facilities already in existence or possible to be created can supply the necessary material, and the assistance we shall have to have in the way of heavy artillery and transportation from the British and French. It will then be possible to take up with those Governments a frank exhibition of the possibilities and to arrange for concerted action among us which will lead to the increase in our effort which you and General Foch recommend. In the meantime, I have asked the British Government to continue the troop ships which they have had in our service during June through July and August, and have told them frankly that we are considering an enlargement of our program which may require for a time at least the uninterrupted service of all the ships which we have been using. If we are able in July and August to match the performance of June, it will mean another half-million men in France, as the June embarkation figures from this country show slightly more than 279,000 men. Our own ships carried during that month something more than 100,000, which is, of course, doing better than our part as we originally calculated it. I think it highly important that neither General Foch nor the British and French Governments should assume our ability to carry out an enlarged program until we ourselves have studied it. There is no disposition on the part of the United States to shrink from any sacrifice or any effort, and yet experience has taught us that great as our capacity is in industry it takes time to build new factories, get the necessary machine tools, and bring together the raw materials for any large increase in industrial output, and I am especially concerned that there should be no disappointment on the part of our Allies. I would very much rather they expect less and receive more, than to expect more and be disappointed in the result. One of the happy effects of the recent accelerated shipment of troops has been that we have out-stripped our promises and, if I judge correctly the effect of this in Europe, it has been most agreeable and heartening.

The Operations Committee of the General Staff is pressing forward the necessary studies. They involve, of course, questions of clothing, small arms, ammunition, transportation, and training. On the latter subject I am beginning to be fairly free from doubts; the troops which we have recently sent you have admittedly been of an uneven quality, chiefly because we have made up deficiencies in divisions about to sail by taking men from other divisions, with consequent dis-organization of those divisions from which men were repeatedly taken, and when we got to a place where we could no longer carry out this process, fairly raw men had to be used in order to keep divisions from sailing short. The plan inaugurated by General March of having replacement divisions in this country from which deficiencies could be supplied without robbing other divisions and disorganizing them, seems to me to solve the problem, and the divisions which come to you in August and September will, I am sure, show highly beneficial results from this policy. In the meantime, we have discovered two things about training in this country which apparently nobody knew or thought of before we went into the war; first, that while it may take nine months or a year to train raw recruits into soldiers in peace time, when there is no inspiration from an existing struggle, it takes no such length of time now when the great dramatic battles are being fought and men are eager to qualify themselves to participate in them. We are certainly able to get more training into a man now in three months than would be possible in nine months of peace-time training. And, second, we have learned that to keep men too long in training camps in this country makes them go stale and probably does as much harm by the spirit of impatience and restlessness aroused as it does good by the longer drilling. The men in our training camps are champing at the bit, and this applies not only to the officers, who naturally want their professional opportunity, but to the men as well. Indeed, one of the difficulties in America is to make people content with the lot which keeps them here for any length of time, so impatient are we all, military men and civilians alike, to get to France where the real work is being done. As a consequence of these discoveries, I feel that we will be perfectly safe if we have a million men in training in the United States at all times. That will enable us to feed them out to you at the rate of 250,000 a month and bring that number in by draft at the other end, which will always give us an adequate supply of men who have had as much training as they can profitably secure here in the United States. The finishing touches in any event will have to be given in France, and I think you will find that men who have had four months' training here are pretty nearly ready for use in association with your veteran and experienced troops, and that no prolonged period of European training, for infantry at least, will be found necessary. This makes the problem very simple from the point of view of the draft and the training camps. A number of the camps originally established by us have now been developed for specialized technical uses, but we still have a large number, and I think an adequate number, of camps which can be enlarged without great expense, and there seems little likelihood of our being obliged to resort to the billeting system, although of course we should not hesitate to do it if the need arose.

All accounts which we receive in this country of the conduct of our men are most stimulating and encouraging. Apparently the common opinion is that we have rendered valuable, if not indispensable, service already, in a purely military way, in the great battles. I saw a letter a day or two ago from Mr. Cravath to Mr. Leffingwell, in which he gave the opinion of British and French men of affairs on the subject of the American troops, and it was enthusiastic. I was a little afraid that too enthusiastic comment might create a feeling of resentment on the part of our allies. Their men, of course, have stood these attacks for a long time, and it would only be human if they resented the newcomers getting too much attention at the expense of organizations which are battle-scarred and have had their valor tested in great conflicts; and I have a little feared, too, that if our people here at home were fed too many stories of success they might get the notion that this great task is going to be easy for Americans and be ill-prepared for any reverse, no matter how slight, which might come. For that reason I have exercised a good deal of self-restraint in my own discussion with the newspapermen and in such public addresses as I have made, seeking always to couple up the British and the French with our American soldiers and to make the whole war a matter of common effort, rather than of our own national effort. This has been especially easy because the spirit of America is now very high. The country is thoroughly unified and is waiting only to be shown how it can make further effective sacrifices and efforts. It occurs to me in this connection that it might be wise for you in your communiqués, from time to time, to refer to slight repulses suffered by our men; but of course I do not want our men to be repulsed merely to balance the news.

On the 1st of July I wrote the President that 1,019,000 men had embarked from the United States for France. There had been so much speculation about numbers that it seemed necessary to be frank and tell the facts. The American people are accustomed to demanding the facts and there was some impatience manifested with the Department for its continued policy of silence on this subject. I realized when I made the statement that in all likelihood I should have to discontinue further reference to numbers, at least further specific references. The Germans, French, and British of course make no such announcements, and our allies will not like to have us adopting a different course. There are doubtless good military reasons for not being very generous with information of this kind, which finds its way to the enemy and enables them to make more certain calculations. Still, if the rate of shipments which we have maintained for the last two or three months can be kept up for another six months, I am not very sure that exact news carried to Germany of the arrival of Americans in France might not be helpful to us, rather than harmful. The German Government cannot fail to be impressed by this steady stream of fresh soldiers to the Western front.

The President and I have had several conferences about your situation in France, both of us desiring in every possible way to relieve you of unnecessary burdens, but of course to leave you with all the authority necessary to secure the best results from your forces and to supply all the support and assistance we possibly can. As the American troops in France become more and more numerous and the battle initiative on some parts of the front passes to you, the purely military part of your task will necessarily take more and more of your time, and both the President and I want to feel that the planning and executing of military undertakings has your personal consideration and that your mind is free for that as far as possible. The American people think of you as their "fighting General," and I want them to have that idea more and more brought home to them. For these reasons, it seems to me that if some plan could be devised by which you would be free from any necessity of giving attention to services of supply it would help, and one plan in that direction which suggested itself was to send General Goethals over to take charge of the services of supply, establishing a direct relationship between him and Washington and allowing you to rely upon him just as you would rely upon the supply departments of the War Department if our military operations were being conducted in America, instead of in France. Such a plan would place General Goethals rather in a coördinate than a subordinate relationship to you, but of course it would transfer all of the supply responsibilities from you to him and you could then forget about docks, railroads, storage houses, and all the other vast industrial undertakings to which up to now you have given a good deal of your time and, as you know, we all think with superb success. I would be very glad to know what you think about this suggestion. I realize that France is very far from the United States and that our reliance upon cables makes a very difficult means of communication, so that you may prefer to have the supply system as one of your responsibilities. I would be grateful if you would think the problem over and tell me quite frankly just what you think on the subject. The President and I will consider your reply together, and you may rely upon our being guided only by confidence in your judgment and the deep desire to aid you.

One other aspect of your burdens the President feels can be somewhat lightened

189

by a larger use of General Bliss as diplomatic intermediary. The President is adopting as a definite rule of action an insistence upon Inter-Allied military questions being referred to the Permanent Military Representatives. Our difficulty here has been that the British representative would present something for consideration without the knowledge of the French, or the French without the knowledge of the British, and when we took the matter up for decision we would sometimes find that the other nation felt aggrieved at not being consulted. As each of the Allied Nations is represented at Versailles, the President is now uniformly saying with regard to all Inter-Allied military questions, that their presentation to him should come through the Permanent Military Representatives who, in a way, are a kind of staff for General Foch and undoubtedly maintain such close relations with him as to make any proposition which they consider one upon which his views are ascertained. As the President deals in matters of military diplomacy with General Bliss, it would seem that he could with propriety relieve you of some part of the conferences and consultations which in the early days you were obliged to have with the British War Office and the French War Office, thus simplifying the presentation of Inter-Allied questions to the President.

Mr. Stettinius will leave very shortly for Europe; I enclose you copy of a letter which I have given him, outlining the inquiries which I desire to have him make. You will find him a very considerate man in the matter of demands upon your time, as he is accustomed to dealing with busy men and not prolonging conferences beyond their useful limit.

It seems not unlikely at present that I shall myself come over to Europe in connection with our enlarged military program. If we find that our ability to do the thing depends upon French and British coöperation it will be a good deal simpler to put the whole question up to the British and French Cabinets and get definite agreements of coöperation and concerted action. Cablegrams are of course inconclusive and uncertain, and I constantly find that even letters fail to carry just the spirit in which they are dictated. When I write you, of course I know that our personal relations and knowledge of each other are too cordial and entire to allow any sort of misunderstanding, but I haven't the same acquaintance with the British and French Cabinet officers, and with them the presumptions do not obtain which are always implied in our correspondence. I confess I am somewhat moved to this idea of the necessity for my going by my desire to go; it is a tremendous inspiration to see our forces and to look at the work which you and they have done.

*Cordially Yours.*


### 4    General John J. Pershing
to Newton D. Baker, July 28, 1918

*My Dear Mr. Secretary:*

I have your letter of July 6th and have gone over it very carefully.

I realize that a very large undertaking has been proposed in the 80 to 100 division program, and that to carry it out is going to require very great sacrifices on our part. But, as you say, the war has gone on long enough and should be brought to a close as early as it is possible for us to do it.

The main reason for an extreme effort on our part next year is the stimulating effect that our immediate entry into the war in a large way will have upon our allies. If we should not demonstrate our wish thus to bring the war to a speedy end our allies might not hold on over another year, and we shall need every ounce of fight they have left in them to win, not that we have not the men and the resources at home, but that if left to carry on the war alone, even on French soil, we would soon come to the limit of our ability to bring them over and supply them.

I realize that we shall be put to it to furnish all the equipment, the aviation, the artillery, the ammunition, the tanks, and especially the horses, but if we can win next year it will be worth the supreme effort necessary to provide all these things. I do not, of course, overlook the shipping, nor the very strenuous work necessary at this end to handle the immense quantity of freight that will be required. Our port facilities must be increased, our railroads must be improved, and we must have a large increase in cars and locomotives. These things must come along rapidly from now on. We are preparing estimates for what we shall need and will forward them by cable as soon as finished.

Just now we are passing through a very critical time. When the shipment of infantry and machine guns was increased during May, June and July, of course we had to reduce, or rather postpone, the corresponding troops for our service of the rear, with the result that we now find ourselves shorthanded and unable to handle as quickly as we should like the increase of supplies incident to the great expansion of our combatant forces.

To add to the difficulties there has been a shortage of replacements in men, as we have had to throw all available troops into the lines to stop the German advance. So that we have not even had any troops to spare for work to help out the rear, making it appear that we are unnecessarily falling behind in unloading ships. I have cabled a request for service of the rear troops to be sent at once and hope they will not be delayed. We have a lot to do to catch up and get our ports and lines of communication in shape to meet the heavy demands that are to be made upon them.

On June 23d, when Mr. Clemenceau was at my headquarters for the conference, I had an opportunity to speak about the use of our troops. I told him that they were being wasted and that instead of the Allies being always on the defensive, an American Army should be formed at once to strike an offensive blow and turn the tide of the war. He was very much impressed at such boldness, as he had heard only of our men going into French divisions as platoons or at most as regiments. Soon after that Pétain was called to Paris and I have heard was told my views. Anyway Pétain soon began to take another view.

Our troops have done well for new troops and the part they have taken has encouraged our allies, especially the French, to go in and help put over a counteroffensive. This offensive, between Soissons and Château-Thierry, was planned some time ago, to be undertaken especially in the event of the Germans attempting to push their line south of the Marne; or to the east between the Marne and Reims. I had conferred with General Pétain and had arranged to put the 1st, 2d, and 26th Divisions in the attack north of the Marne, supported by the 4th, while the 3d and 28th were to be used south of the Marne. As it turned out, all these troops were engaged with results you already know. The participation by our troops made this offensive possible and in fact the brunt of it fell to them. Our divisions in this advance completely outstepped the French and had to slow down their speed occasionally for them to catch up.

Two American corps are now organized and on the active front. These are to be organized into the Field Army which will take its place in line under my immediate command on August 10th. We shall occupy a sector north of the Marne and probably replace the 6th French Army. At the same time we shall take over a permanent sector north of Toul and Nancy, where I shall organize a second army at an early date. After that we shall soon have troops enough for a third army. So that before long I shall have to relinquish command of the Field Army and command the group.

I have had to insist very strongly, in the face of determined opposition, to get our troops out of leading strings. You know the French and British have always advanced the idea that we should not form divisions until our men had three or four months with them. We have found, however, that only a short time was necessary to learn all they know, as it is confined to trench warfare almost entirely, and I have insisted on open warfare training. To get this training, it has been necessary to unite our men under our own commanders, which is now being done rapidly.

The additional fact that training with these worn-out French and British troops, if continued, is detrimental, is another reason for haste in forming our own units and conducting our own training. The morale of the Allies is low and association with them has had a bad effect upon our men. To counteract the talk our men have heard, we have had to say to our troops, through their officers, that we had come over to brace up the Allies and help them win and that they must pay no attention to loose remarks along that line by their Allied comrades.

The fact is that our officers and men are far and away superior to the tired Europeans. High officers of the Allies have often dropped derogatory remarks about our poorly trained staff and high commanders, which our men have stood as long as they can. Even Mr. Tardieu said some of these things to me a few days ago. I replied, in rather forcible language, that we had now been patronized as long as we would stand for it, and I wished to hear no more of that sort of nonsense. Orders have now been given by the French that all of our troops in sectors with the French would be placed under our own officers and that American division commanders would be given command of their own sectors. This has come about since my insistence forced the French to agree to the formation of an American Field Army.

At a conference called by General Foch last Wednesday, the 24th instant, plans for assuming the offensive this year were discussed, as well as tentative plans for 1919. This is the first time the American Army has been recognized as a participant, as such, alongside the Allies. I shall give you from time to time an outline of what our plans are, but hope you will soon be here so that I may discuss them with you.

I entirely agree with what you say regarding General Bliss as a diplomatic intermediary. However, very little of my time has been taken up with that sort of thing, except as it concerned questions of troop shipments and their use with British and French. As you know, I have the highest regard for General Bliss and our relations have been the most pleasant. I think he is admirably fitted to represent the President in many of these perplexing diplomatic questions that come up. He has excellent judgment, and is very highly regarded by the Allied official world.

Mr. Stettinius has arrived and we have had several conferences. I am very much delighted to have him here. His presence is going to relieve me entirely of all those difficult questions pertaining to the allocation of materials, and the determination of manufacturing programs and the like. His action will be able to prevent the continuous flow of cablegrams from the Allies to our War Department on all these subjects.

On the subject of General Goethals, I thank you very much for referring this matter to me. Mr. Secretary, our organization here is working well. It is founded upon sound principles. May I not emphasize again the principle of unity of command and responsibility. It has always been my understanding that you believed that full power should be given to the man on the spot and responsible for results. I would say this regardless of the person in command. Our organization here is so bound up with operations, and training, and supply, and transportation of troops, that it would be impossible to make it function if the control of our service of the rear were placed in Washington. Please let us not make the mistake of handicapping our army here by attempting to control these things from Washington, or by introducing any coördinate authority. All matters pertaining to these forces, after their arrival in France, should be under the General Staff here where they are being and can be handled satisfactory.

May I say a word about our training. Our successes here should not be hastily accepted as the basis for conclusions on the possibilities of building up efficient units by intensive training for short periods. Four months should be the minimum for drafts that are to enter as replacements in among old soldiers in organized units. But, it requires a much longer time than that to build units from the ground up. Eight or nine months, or even a year, would be better, so that if we could get all of next year's army in the ranks by November we should be much better prepared in the Spring for the immense task we are preparing for.

May I again express my warm appreciation of your confidence, and say also how gratifying it is to me to enjoy the personal relations that exist between us.

Will you please convey to the President my best compliments and the Army's faith in his leadership.

With very warm regards and sincere good wishes, I am

*Very Faithfully.*

# 63

## The Diplomacy of Woodrow Wilson

Woodrow Wilson's efforts at the negotiating table in Paris were not as successful as his armies in the field. The Treaty of Versailles was far from perfect. At times secret covenants and imperialism played a larger role than open diplomacy and national self-determination. Still, there had been victories for democratic procedures at Versailles, and some of the new national boundaries were excellent. But most important to Wilson was the provision for a League of Nations. The peace treaty itself might not be perfect, but the League, Wilson believed, would correct deficiencies. Confidently he returned home to defend his work.

The history of his effort in the fall and winter of 1919–1920 is still a subject of controversy. Was Wilson stubborn, refusing to make limited concessions to gain more important ends? Did his moralism and his sudden illness blind him to political realities? And what of his opponents? Was the leading foe of the League, Henry Cabot Lodge, acting from a personal dislike of Wilson? Joseph Tumulty, Wilson's private secretary, close friend, and adviser, addressed himself to these questions in a volume written in 1921. As one would expect, he gave Wilson the benefit of every doubt; but his account is an inside story with sufficient detail to allow the reader an opportunity to reach his own conclusions.

### WOODROW WILSON AS I KNEW HIM
*Joseph Tumulty*

**The Treaty Fight**

Upon his return home from Paris, the President immediately invited, in most cordial fashion, the members of the Senate Foreign Relations Committee to confer with him at the White House. Some of those who received the invitation immediately announced that as a condition precedent to their acceptance they

From *Woodrow Wilson as I Knew Him* (New York: Doubleday, 1921), 422–425, 430–431, 434–435, 438–448, 452–455.

would insist that the conference should not be secret in character and that what would happen there should be disclosed to the public. The President quickly accepted the conditions proposed by the Republican senators and made a statement from the White House that the conditions which the conferees named were highly acceptable to him and that he was willing and anxious to give to the public a stenographic report of everything that transpired. Never before did the President show himself more tactful or more brilliant in repartee. Surrounded by twenty or thirty men, headed by Senator Lodge, who hated him with a bitterness that was intense, the President, with quiet courtesy, parried every blow aimed at him.

No question, no matter how pointed it was, seemed to disturb his serenity. He acted like a lawyer who knew his case from top to bottom, and who had confidence in the great cause he was representing. His cards were frankly laid upon the table and he appeared like a fighting champion, ready to meet all comers. Indeed, this very attitude of frankness, openness, sincerity, and courtesy, one could see from the side-lines, was a cause of discomfort to Senator Lodge and the Republicans grouped about him, and one could also see written upon the faces of the Democratic senators in that little room a look of pride that they had a leader who carried himself so gallantly and who so brilliantly met every onslaught of the enemy. The President anticipated an abrupt adjournment of the conference with a courteous invitation to luncheon. Senator Lodge had just turned to the President and said: "Mr. President, I do not wish to interfere in any way, but the conference has now lasted about three hours and a half, and it is half an hour after the lunch hour." Whereupon, the President said: "Will not you gentlemen take luncheon with me? It will be very delightful."

It was evident that this invitation, so cordially conveyed, broke the ice of formality which up to that time pervaded the meeting, and like boys out of school, forgetting the great affair in which they had all played prominent parts, they made their way to the dining room, the President walking by the side of Senator Lodge. Instead of fisticuffs, as some of the newspaper men had predicted, the lion and the lamb sat down together at the dining table, and for an hour or two the question of the ratification of the Treaty of Versailles was forgotten in the telling of pleasant stories and the play of repartee.

Although, at this conference of August 19, 1919, the President had frankly opened his mind and heart to the enemies of the Treaty, the opposition instead of moderating seemed to grow more intense and passionate. The President had done everything humanly possible to soften the opposition of the Republicans, but, alas, the information brought to him from the Hill by his Democratic friends only confirmed the opinion that the opposition to the Treaty was growing and could not be overcome by personal contact of any kind between the President and members of the Foreign Relations Committee.

It is plain now, and will become plainer as the years elapse, that the Republican opposition to the League was primarily partisan politics and a rooted personal dislike of the chief proponent of the League, Mr. Wilson. His reëlection in 1916, the first reëlection of an incumbent Democratic President since Andrew Jackson, had greatly disturbed the Republican leaders. The prestige of the Republican party was threatened by this Democratic leader. His reception in Europe added to their distress. For the sake of the sacred cause of Republicanism, this menace of Democratic leadership must be destroyed, even though in destroying it the leaders should swallow their own words and reverse their own former positions on world adjustment.

An attempt was made by enemies of the President to give the impression to the country that an association of nations was one of the "fool ideas" of Woodrow Wilson; that in making it part of his Fourteen Points, he was giving free rein to his idealism.

The storm centre of the whole fight against the League was the opposition personally conducted by Senator Lodge and others of the Republican party against the now famous Article X. The basis of the whole Republican opposition was their fear that America would have to bear some responsibility in the affairs of the world, while the strength of Woodrow Wilson's position was his faith that out of the war, with all its blood and tears, would come this great consummation.

It was the President's idea that we should go into the League and bear our responsibilities; that we should enter it as gentlemen, scorning privilege. He did not wish us to sneak in and enjoy its advantages and shirk its responsibilities, but he wanted America to enter boldly and not as a hypocrite.

With reference to the argument made by Senator Lodge against our going into the League, saying that it would be a surrender of American sovereignty and a loss of her freedom, the President often asked the question on his Western trip: How can a nation preserve its freedom except through concerted action? We surrender part of our freedom in order to save the rest of it. Discussing this matter one day, he said: "One cannot have an omelet without breaking eggs. By joining the League of Nations, a nation loses, not its individual freedom, but its selfish isolation. The only freedom it loses is the freedom to do wrong. Robinson Crusoe was free to shoot in any direction on his island until Friday came. Then there was one direction in which he could not shoot. His freedom ended where Friday's rights began."

There would have been no Federal Union to-day if the individual states that went to make up the Federal Union were not willing to surrender the powers they exercised, to surrender their freedom as it were.

Opponents of the League tried to convey the impression that under Article X we should be obliged to send our boys across the sea and that in that event America's voice would not be the determining voice.

Lloyd George answered this argument in a crushing way, when he said:

> We cannot, unless we abandon the whole basis of the League of Nations, disinterest ourselves in an attack upon the existence of a nation which is a member of that league and whose life is in jeopardy. That covenant, as I understand it, does not contemplate, necessarily, military action in support of the imperilled nation. It contemplates economic pressure; it contemplates support for the struggling people; and when it is said that if you give any support at all to Poland it involves a great war, with conscription and with all the mechanism of war with which we have been so familiar in the last few years, that is inconsistent with the whole theory of the covenant into which we have entered.

Tentative plans for a Western trip began to be formed in the White House because of the urgent insistence from Democratic friends on the Hill that nothing could win the fight for the League of Nations except a direct appeal to the country by the President in person.

Admiral Grayson, the President's physician and consistent friend, who knew his condition and the various physical crises through which he had passed here and on the other side, from some of which he had not yet recovered, stood firm in his resolve that the President should not go West, even intimating to me that the President's life might pay the forfeit if his advice were disregarded. Indeed, it needed not the trained eye of a physician to see that the man whom the senators were now advising to make a "swing around the circle" was on the verge of a nervous breakdown. More than once since his return from the Peace Conference I had urged him to take a needed rest; to get away from the turmoil of Washington and recuperate; but he spurned this advice and resolved to go through to the end.

No argument of ours could draw him away from his duties, which now involved not only the fight for the ratification of the Treaty, but the threatened railway strike, with its attendant evils to the country, and added administrative burdens growing out of the partisanship fight which was being waged in Congress for the ostensible purpose of reducing the high cost of living.

One day, after Democratic senators had been urging the Western trip, I took leave to say to the President that, in his condition, disastrous consequences might result if he should follow their advice. But he dismissed my solicitude, saying in a weary way: "I know that I am at the end of my tether, but my friends on the Hill say that the trip is necessary to save the Treaty, and I am willing to make whatever personal sacrifice is required, for if the Treaty should be defeated, God only knows what would happen to the world as a result of it. In the presence of the great tragedy which now faces the world, no decent man can count his own personal fortunes in the reckoning. Even though, in my condition, it might mean the giving up of my life, I will gladly make the sacrifice to save the Treaty."

He spoke like a soldier who was ready to make the supreme sacrifice to save the cause that lay closest to his heart.

As I looked at the President while he was talking, in my imagination I made a comparison between the man, Woodrow Wilson, who now stood before me and the man I had met many years before in New Jersey. In those days he was a vigorous, agile, slender man, active and alert, his hair but slightly streaked with gray. Now, as he stood before me discussing the necessity for the Western trip, he was an old man, grown grayer and grayer, but grimmer and grimmer in his determination, like an old warrior, to fight to the end.

When it became evident that the tide of public opinion was setting against the League, the President finally decided upon the Western trip as the only means of bringing home to the people the unparalleled world situation.

At the Executive offices we at once set in motion preparations for the Western trip. One itinerary after another was prepared, but upon examining it the President would find that it was not extensive enough and would suspect that it was made by those of us—like Grayson and myself—who were solicitious for his health, and he would cast them aside. All the itineraries provided for a week of rest in the Grand Canyon of the Colorado, but when a brief vacation was intimated to him, he was obdurate in his refusal to include even a day of relaxation, saying to me, that "the people would never forgive me if I took a rest on a trip such as the one I contemplate taking. This is a business trip, pure and simple, and the itinerary must not include rest of any kind." He insisted that there be no suggestion of a pleasure trip attaching to a journey which he regarded as a mission.

As I now look back upon this journey and its disastrous effects upon the President's health, I believe that if he had only consented to include a rest period in our arrangements, he might not have broken down at Pueblo.

Never have I seen the President look so weary as on the night we left Washington for our swing into the West. When we were about to board our special train, the President turned to me and said: "I am in a nice fix. I am scheduled between now and the 28th of September to make in the neighbourhood of a hundred speeches to various bodies, stretching all the way from Ohio to the coast, and yet the pressure of other affairs upon me at the White House has been so great that I have not had a single minute to prepare my speeches. I do not know how I shall get the time, for during the past few weeks I have been suffering from daily headaches; but perhaps to-night's rest will make me fit for the work of to-morrow."

No weariness or brain-fag, however, was apparent in the speech at Columbus, Ohio. To those of us who sat on the platform, including the newspaper group who accompanied the President, this speech with its beautiful phrasing and its effective delivery seemed to have been carefully prepared.

Day after day, for nearly a month, there were speeches of a similar kind, growing more intense in their emotion with each day. Shortly after we left Tacoma, Washington, the fatigue of the trip began to write itself in the President's face. He suffered from violent headaches each day, but his speeches never betrayed his illness.

In those troublous days and until the very end of our Western trip the President would not permit the slightest variation from our daily programme. Nor did he ever permit the constant headaches, which would have put an ordinary man out of sorts, to work unkindly upon the members of his immediate party, which included Mrs. Wilson, Doctor Grayson, and myself. He would appear regularly at each meal, partaking of it only slightly, always gracious, always good-natured and smiling, responding to every call from the outside for speeches—calls that came from early morning until late at night—from the plain people grouped about every station and watering place through which we passed. Even under the most adverse physical conditions he was always kind, gentle, and considerate to those about him.

I have often wished, as the criticisms of the Pullman smoking car, the cloak room, and the counting house were carried to me, picturing the President's coldness, his aloofness and exclusiveness, that the critics could for a moment have seen the heart and great good-nature of the man giving expression to themselves on this critical journey. If they could have peeped through the curtain of our dining room, at one of the evening meals, for instance, they would have been ashamed of their misrepresentations of this kind, patient, considerate, human-hearted man.

It was on the Western trip, about September 12th, while the President, with every ounce of his energy, was attempting to put across the League of Nations, that Mr. William C. Bullitt was disclosing to the Committee on Foreign Relations at a public hearing the facts of a conference between Secretary Lansing and himself, in which Mr. Bullitt declared that Mr. Lansing had severely criticized the League of Nations.

The press representatives aboard the train called Mr. Bullitt's testimony to the President's attention. He made no comment, but it was plain from his attitude that he was incensed and distressed beyond measure. Here he was in the heart of the West, advancing the cause so dear to his heart, steadily making gains against what appeared to be insurmountable odds, and now his intimate associate, Mr. Lansing, was engaged in sniping and attacking him from behind.

On September 16th, Mr. Lansing telegraphed the following message to the President:

> On May 17th, Bullitt resigned by letter giving his reasons with which you are familiar. I replied by letter on the 18th without any comment on his reasons. Bullitt on the 19th asked to see me to say good-bye and I saw him. He elaborated on the reasons for his resignation and said that he could not conscientiously give countenance to a treaty which was based on injustice. I told him that I would say nothing against his resigning since he put it on conscientious grounds, and that I recognized that certain features of the Treaty were bad, as I presumed most everyone did, but that was probably unavoidable in view of conflicting claims and that nothing ought to be done to prevent the speedy restoration of peace by signing the Treaty. Bullitt then discussed the numerous European commissions provided for by the Treaty on which the United States was to be represented. I told him that I was disturbed by this fact because I was afraid the Senate and possibly the people, if they understood this, would refuse ratification, and that anything which was an obstacle to ratification was unfortunate because we ought to have peace as soon as possible.

When the President received this explanation from Mr. Lansing, he sent for me to visit with him in his compartment. At the time I arrived he was seated in his little study, engaged in preparing his speech for the night's meeting. Turning to me, with a deep show of feeling, he said: "Read that, and tell me what you think of a man who was my associate on the other side and who confidentially expressed himself to an outsider in such a fashion? Were I in Washington I would at once demand his resignation! That kind of disloyalty must not be permitted to go unchallenged for a single minute. The testimony of Bullitt is a confirmation of the suspicions I have had with reference to this individual. I found the same attitude of mind on the part of Lansing on the other side. I could find his trail everywhere I went, but they were only suspicions and it would not be fair for me to act upon them. But here in his own statement is a verification at last of everything I have suspected. Think of it! This from a man who I raised from the level of a subordinate to the great office of Secretary of State of the United States. My God! I did not think it was possible for Lansing to act in this way. When we were in Paris I found that Lansing and others were constantly giving out statements that did not agree with my viewpoint. When I had arranged a settlement, there would appear from some source I could not locate unofficial statements telling the correspondents

199

not to take things too seriously; that a compromise would be made, and this news, or rather news of this kind, was harmful to the settlement I had already obtained and quite naturally gave the Conference the impression that Lansing and his kind were speaking for me, and then the French would say that I was bluffing."

I am convinced that only the President's illness a few days later prevented an immediate demand on his part for the resignation of Mr. Lansing.

Uncomplainingly the President applied himself to the difficult tasks of the Western trip. While the first meeting at Columbus was a disappointment as to attendance, as we approached the West the crowds grew in numbers and the enthusiasm became boundless. The idea of the League spread and spread as we neared the coast. Contrary to the impression in the East, the President's trip West was a veritable triumph for him and was so successful that we had planned, upon the completion of the Western trip, to invade the enemy's country, Senator Lodge's own territory, the New England States, and particularly Massachusetts. This was our plan, fully developed and arranged, when about four o'clock in the morning of September 26, 1919, Doctor Grayson knocked at the door of my sleeping compartment and told me to dress quickly, that the President was seriously ill. As we walked toward the President's car, the Doctor told me in a few words of the President's trouble and said that he greatly feared it might end fatally if we should attempt to continue the trip and that it was his duty to inform the President that by all means the trip must be cancelled; but that he did not feel free to suggest it to the President without having my coöperation and support. When we arrived at the President's drawing room I found him fully dressed and seated in his chair. With great difficulty he was able to articulate. His face was pale and wan. One side of it had fallen, and his condition was indeed pitiful to behold. Quickly I reached the same conclusion as that of Doctor Grayson, as to the necessity for the immediate cancellation of the trip, for to continue it, in my opinion, meant death to the President. Looking at me, with great tears running down his face, he said: "My dear boy, this has never happened to me before. I felt it coming on yesterday. I do not know what to do." He then pleaded with us not to cut short the trip. Turning to both of us, he said: "Don't you see that if you cancel this trip, Senator Lodge and his friends will say that I am a quitter and that the Western trip was a failure, and the Treaty will be lost." Reaching over to him, I took both of his hands and said: "What difference, my dear Governor, does it make what they say? Nobody in the world believes you are a quitter, but it is your life that we must now consider. We must cancel the trip, and I am sure that when the people learn of your condition there will be no misunderstanding." He then tried to move over nearer to me to continue his argument against the cancellation of the trip; but he found he was unable to do so. His left arm and leg refused to function. I then realized that the President's whole left side was paralyzed. Looking at me he said: "I want to show them that I can still fight and that I am not afraid. Just postpone the trip for twenty-four hours and I will be all right."

But Doctor Grayson and I resolved not to take any risk, and an immediate statement was made to the inquiring newspaper men that the Western trip was off.

Never was the President more gentle or tender than on that morning. Suffering the greatest pain, paralyzed on his left side, he was still fighting desperately for the thing that was so close to his heart—a vindication of the things for which he had so gallantly fought on the other side. Grim old warrior that he was, he was ready to fight to the death for the League of Nations.

During the illness of the President his political enemies sought to convey the impression that he was incapacitated for the duties of his office. As one who came in daily contact with him I knew how baseless were these insinuations. As a matter of fact, there was not a whole week during his entire illness that he was not in touch with every matter upon which he was called to act and upon which he was asked to render judgment.

That there was no real devotion on the part of Mr. Lansing for the President is shown by the following incident.

A few days after the President returned from the West and lay seriously ill at the White House, with physicians and nurses gathered about his bed, Mr. Lansing sought a private audience with me in the Cabinet Room. He informed me that he had called diplomatically to suggest that in view of the incapacity of the President we should arrange to call in the Vice-President to act in his stead as soon as possible, reading to me from a book which he had brought from the State Department, which I afterward learned was "Jefferson's Manual," the following clause of the United States Constitution:

> In case of the removal of the President from office, or his death, resignation, or inability to discharge the powers and duties of the said office, the same shall devolve upon the Vice-President.

Upon reading this, I coldly turned to Mr. Lansing and said: "Mr. Lansing, the Constitution is not a dead letter with the White House. I have read the Constitution and do not find myself in need of any tutoring at your hands of the provision you have just read." When I asked Mr. Lansing the question as to who should certify to the disability of the President, he intimated that that would be a job for either Doctor Grayson or myself. I immediately grasped the full significance of what he intimated and said: "You may rest assured that while Woodrow Wilson is lying in the White House on the broad of his back I will not be a party to ousting him. He has been too kind, too loyal, and too wonderful to me to receive such treatment at my hands." Just as I uttered this statement Doctor Grayson appeared in the Cabinet Room and I turned to him and said: "And I am sure that Doctor Grayson will never certify to his disability. Will you, Grayson?" Doctor Grayson left no doubt in Mr. Lansing's mind that he would not do as Mr. Lansing suggested. I then notified Mr. Lansing that if anybody outside of the White House circle attempted to certify to the President's disability, that Grayson and I would stand together and repudiate it. I added that if the President were in a condition to know of this episode he would, in my opinion, take decisive measures. That ended the interview.

It is unnecessary to say that no further attempt was made by Mr. Lansing to institute ouster proceedings against his chief.

I never attempted to ascertain what finally influenced the action of the President peremptorily to demand the resignation of Mr. Lansing. My own judgment is that the demand came as the culmination of repeated acts of what the President considered disloyalty on Mr. Lansing's part.

When I received from the President's stenographer the letter to Mr. Lansing, intimating that his resignation would not be a disagreeable thing to the President, I conferred with the President at once and argued with him that in the present state of public opinion it was the wrong time to do the right thing. At the time the President was seated in his invalid chair on the White House portico. Although physically weak, he was mentally active and alert. Quickly he took hold of my phrase and said, with a show of the old fire that I had seen on so many occasions: "Tumulty, it is never the wrong time to spike disloyalty. When Lansing sought to oust me, I was upon my back. I am on my feet now and I will not have disloyalty about me."

When the announcement of Lansing's resignation was made, the flood-gates of fury broke about the President; but he was serene throughout it all. When I called at the White House on the following Sunday, I found him calmly seated in his bathroom with his coloured valet engaged in the not arduous task of cutting his hair. Looking at me with a smile in his eye, he said: "Well, Tumulty, have I any friends left?" "Very few, Governor," I said. Whereupon he replied: "Of course, it will be another two days' wonder. But in a few days what the country considers an indiscretion on my part in getting rid of Lansing will be forgotten, but when the sober, second thought of the country begins to assert itself, what will stand out will be the disloyalty of Lansing to me."

### Reservations

On June 25, 1919, I received from President Wilson the following cabled message:

> My clear conviction is that the adoption of the treaty by the Senate with reservations will put the United States as clearly out of the concert of nations as a rejection. We ought either to go in or stay out. To stay out would be fatal to the influence and even to the commercial prospects of the United States, and to go in would give her a leading place in the affairs of the world. Reservations would either mean nothing or postpone the conclusion of peace, so far as America is concerned, until every other principal nation concerned in the treaty had found out by negotiation what the reservations practically meant and whether they could associate themselves with the United States on the terms of the reservations or not.
> *Woodrow Wilson*

The President consistently held to the principle involved in this statement. To his mind the reservations offered by Senator Lodge constituted a virtual nullification on the part of the United States of a treaty which was a contract, and which should be amended through free discussion among all the contracting parties. He did not argue or assume that the Covenant was a perfected document, but he believed that, like our American Constitution, it should be adopted and subsequently submitted to necessary amendment through the constitutional processes of debate. He was unalterably opposed to having the United States put in the position of seeking exemptions and special privileges under an agreement which he believed was in the interest of the entire world, including our own country. Furthermore, he believed that the advocacy for reservations in the Senate proceeded from partisan motives and that in so far as there was a strong popular opinion in the country in favour of reservations it proceeded from the same sources from which had come the pro-German propaganda. Before the war pro-German agitation had sought to keep us out of the conflict, and after the war it sought to separate us in interest and purpose from other governments with which we were associated.

By his opposition to reservations the President was seeking to prevent Germany from taking through diplomacy what she had been unable to get by her armies.

The President was so confident of the essential rightness of the League and the Covenant and of the inherent right-mindedness of the American people, that he could not believe that the people would sanction either rejection or emasculation of the Treaty if they could be made to see the issue in all the sincerity of its motives and purposes, if partisan attack could be met with plain truth-speaking. It was to present the case of the people in what he considered its true light that he undertook the Western tour, and it was while thus engaged that his health broke. Had he kept well and been able to lead in person the struggle for ratification, he might have won, as he had previously by his determination and conviction broken down stubborn opposition to the Federal Reserve system.

So strong was his faith in his cause and the people that even after he fell ill he could not believe that ratification would fail. What his enemies called stubbornness was his firm faith in the righteousness of the treaty and in the reasonableness of the proposition that the time to make amendments was not prior to the adoption of the Treaty and by one nation, but after all the nations had agreed and had met together for sober, unpartisan consideration of alterations in the interest of all the contracting parties and the peace and welfare of the world.

Even when he lay seriously ill, he insisted upon being taken in his invalid chair along the White House portico to the window of my outer office each day during the controversy in the Senate over the Treaty. There day after day in the coldest possible weather I conferred with him and discussed every phase of the fight on the Hill. He would sit in his chair, wrapped in blankets, and though hardly able, because of his physical condition, to discuss these matters with me, he evidenced in every way a tremendous interest in everything that was happening in the Capitol that had to do with the Treaty. Although I was warned by Doctor Grayson and Mrs. Wilson not to alarm him unduly by bringing pessimistic reports, I sought, in the most delicate and tactful way I could, to bring the atmosphere of the Hill to him. Whenever there was an indication of the slightest rise in the tide for the League of Nations a smile would pass over the President's face, and weak and broken though he was, he evidenced his great pleasure at the news. Time and time again during the critical days of the Treaty fight the President would appear outside my office, seated in the old wheel chair, and make inquiry regarding the progress of the Treaty fight on Capitol Hill.

One of the peculiar things about the illness from which the President suffered was the deep emotion which would stir him when word was brought to him that this senator or that senator on the Hill had said some kind thing about him or had gone to his defense when some political enemy was engaged in bitterly assailing his attitude in the Treaty fight. Never would there come from him any censure or bitter criticism of those who were opposing him in the fight. For Senator Borah, the leader of the opposition, he had high respect, and felt he was actuated only by sincere motives.

I recall how deeply depressed he was when word was carried to him that the defeat of the Treaty was inevitable. On this day he was looking more weary than at any time during his illness. After I had read to him a memorandum that I had prepared, containing a report on the situation in the Senate, I drew away from his wheel chair and said to him: "Governor, you are looking very well to-day." He shook his head in a pathetic way and said: "I am very well for a man who awaits disaster," and bowing his head he gave way to the deep emotion he felt.

A few days later I called to notify him of the defeat of the Treaty. His only comment was, "They have shamed us in the eyes of the world." Endeavouring to keep my good-nature steady in the midst of a trying situation, I smiled and said: "But, Governor, only the Senate has defeated you. The People will vindicate your course. You may rely upon that." "Ah, but our enemies have poisoned the wells of public opinion," he said. "They have made the people believe that the League of Nations is a great Juggernaut, the object of which is to bring war and not peace to the world. If I only could have remained well long enough to have convinced the people that the League of Nations was their real hope, their last chance, perhaps, to save civilization!"

# 64

## Selling the Ford

The 1920s was the decade of the automobile. During these years, the automobile spread through urban and rural counties, putting America on wheels. The Ford system of mass production became a model of organization. By virtue of the needs of the automobile, the production and use of steel and other commodities climbed, stimulating economic growth. The social effects of the automobile are harder to measure, but the feeble remains of a system of chaperons soon died, as the young came to enjoy new mobility and freedom. The auto also gave mobility and freedom to the farmers, bringing them closer to urban centers for their purchases and sales and for entertainment and companionship. At the same time, city people were able to live at even greater distances from their places of work, at the price, of course, of commuting daily in an automobile.

Yet for all their popularity, cars had to be sold day in and day out. An industry established and run on a mass-production system depended on its markets for survival; the economies of large-scale purchases and production needed a high and constant volume of sales in order to bring in profits. Thus, the agent selling the automobiles, located at a key point in the process, often felt the heavy hand of the company on him. In 1927, a reporter for *Harper's Magazine,* Jesse Rainsford Sprague, interviewed a Midwestern Ford dealer, and his "Confession" tells the story, somewhat one-sidedly to be sure, of how the industry went about insuring the continuing sale of its products.

### THE CONFESSIONS
### OF A FORD DEALER

The former Ford dealer said:

Things have changed a lot around here since 1912, when I bought out the man who had the Ford agency and paid him inventory price for his stock, plus a bonus of five hundred dollars for good-will. A dealer didn't have to hustle so hard then to

From "The Confessions of a Ford Dealer," by Jesse Rainsford Sprague, *Harper's Magazine,* June, 1927, 26–31, 34–35. Copyright © 1927, by Harper's Magazine, Inc. Reprinted from the June, 1927 issue of Harper's Magazine by Special Permission.

make both ends meet. You kept a few cars on your floor and when you needed more you bought them. You were your own boss. There weren't any iron-clad rules laid down for you saying how you had to run your business.

Sometimes I wonder if Mr. Ford knows how things have changed. I have just finished reading his book, and in one place he says: "Business grows big by public demand. But it never gets bigger than the demand. It cannot control or force the demand."

Understand me, I think Mr. Ford is a wonderful man. They say he is worth a billion dollars; and no one can make that much money unless he has plenty of brains. Still and all, when Mr. Ford says business cannot control or force the demand I can't quite think he means it. Or maybe it's his little joke. You *can* force demand if you ride people hard enough. And, believe me, you have only to get on the inside of a Ford agency to learn how.

Take my own case, for instance. Like I say, when I first took the agency I was my own boss like any other business man, selling as many cars as I could and buying more when I needed them. I didn't have to make many sales on installments, because people who wanted cars usually saved up in advance and had the cash in hand when they got ready to buy. Occasionally some man that I knew would want a little time, in which case I just charged it the same as if it was a bill of dry goods or groceries, and when the account fell due he paid me. There was no such thing then as putting a mortgage on the car and taking it away from him if he didn't pay up. If I didn't believe a man was honest I simply didn't give him credit.

I did a pretty good business this way and by 1916 was selling an average of about ten cars a month. Then one day a representative of the Company came to see me. I'll call him by the name of Benson, though that was not his real name. In fact wherever I mention a man's name in giving my experiences I shall call him something different because some of them probably would not like to be identified. Well, anyway, this man that I call Benson came into my place at the time I speak of and said ten cars a month was not enough for a dealer like me to sell. It seems the Company had made a survey of my territory and decided that the sales possibilities were much greater. Benson said my quota had been fixed at twenty cars a month, and from then on that number would be shipped me.

Naturally, I got a little hot under the collar at this kind of a proposition, and I told Benson where he could get off at. I said I was doing all the business that could be done and I intended to buy only the cars that I needed. The Company could ship me as many as they wanted to, but I would pay for what I could sell, and no more.

Benson was pretty hard boiled. He said there was no need of my getting mad at him because he was only doing what he had been ordered to do, and I could take my choice. Either I could buy twenty cars a month or the Company would find another agent. There were plenty of live wires who would jump at the chance.

Of course I knew this last was true. I had got to making a little money during the four years I was Ford agent, and there are always fellows who will go into a thing when someone else has done the hard sledding. My wife had got used to living pretty well and, beside that, my boy was fixing to go away to college. I knew there would be an awful roar at home if I gave up a sure thing and started over again at something else. Still, I couldn't see how I could possibly sell twenty cars a month in my territory. There were only about nine thousand people in the town, and possibly that many more on the farms. Most of them were poor folks. It wasn't, I told Benson, like an Eastern manufacturing community where there are a lot of moneyed people and a big bunch of well-paid mechanics who can afford to have their own cars.

Benson only laughed and said that didn't make any difference. There was a certain population in my territory that called for a certain number of sales, and the Company would show me how to do business. All I had to do was to follow instructions.

Well, I finally decided to take a chance on twenty cars a month rather than lose the agency. I had read a lot of nice things about Mr. Ford in the newspapers and I felt sure he wouldn't ask me to do anything he wouldn't be willing to do himself. Benson said he was glad I looked at things in a businesslike way and promised me plenty of assistance in moving my twenty cars a month. He called it "breaking down sales resistance."

I guess I should explain that out West here an ordinary Ford dealer doesn't do business direct from the factory in Detroit, but works under a general agency. The agency that I worked under was located in the city about a hundred and fifty miles from here, and I suppose the manager there took his orders from the factory. During the fourteen years I was in business there were eight different managers, and some of them rode us local agents pretty hard. I always thought I wouldn't have so many troubles if I could have done business direct with Mr. Ford, but I can realize how busy a big man like him must be, and I guess it is necessary for him to leave things pretty much in the hands of his managers that way. A few times when I thought they were riding me too hard I wrote in to the factory and complained about certain things, but I never got any answer. My letters were sent on to the branch manager, and of course that got me in bad with him. I found that if I wanted to hold my agency I had better do what I was told. Out of the eight managers six were transferred to other branches and two threw up their jobs to go into other lines of business. I met one of these fellows after he had quit and asked him why there were so many changes. He said he guessed it was because the Company believed a man had a tendency to get too friendly with the local agents if he stayed too long in one territory, and to see things too much from the agent's viewpoint. Personally, he said he quit the Company's service altogether because he couldn't stand the pace.

Maybe it was true that a branch manager would get to see things too much from the local agents' standpoint if he stayed too long, but it never seemed that way in my own case. Shortly after I agreed to take my twenty cars a month the War came on, and it was not a case of how many cars I could sell, but of how many I could get. Every day people came in wanting to buy new Fords and, as I never had any stock of cars on hand, all I could do was to take their deposit and set down their

207

names, promising each one that he should have his car according to his number on the waiting list. Then what should develop but a lot of bootleggers in Fords! These fellows would come in, or send someone else in, make a deposit, and get their names on the waiting list. Then when one of their cars came they would pay the balance due, drive it around the corner and sell it for fifty dollars' profit. Sometimes they could even sell their place on the waiting list for that much. Seeing what was going on, I thought I might as well make some of the easy money myself. I entered some fake names on my waiting list and sold myself two or three cars that I sent out on the street and sold over again for a bonus. It was like getting money from home, but it didn't last long. How the Company detectives found out about it I don't know, but one day I got word from the branch manager in the city saying he knew what I was doing and if I wanted to hold my agency I would have to quit it. I guess a lot of local agents were doing the same thing I was, because I understand the order came direct from Detroit. I guess Mr. Ford was right and we had no business to bootleg his product that way. Everything I read in the papers about him is one hundred per cent favorable. Just the same, I thought at the time he might as well let us agents who were making money for him get the extra profit instead of its going to the bootleggers.

Certainly I could have used some of that easy money later on. Of course business kept up fine during the War and for nearly two years afterward, and I made enough money to move out of my rented quarters and put up a nice brick building for my show room, garage, etc. But I sure got it in the neck when the slump of 1920 came on. If anyone wants to know what hard times are he ought to try to do business in a Western farming community during a panic. Almost overnight half of our sheep men went bankrupt when wool dropped from sixty cents a pound to twenty cents, and hardly any buyers at that price. The potato growers couldn't get enough for their stuff to pay freight to the Chicago market, and most of them let their crop rot in the ground. Of our four banks in town two went into the hands of receivers and the other two had to call in every possible loan in order to save their own necks. A lot of our Main Street retailers fell into the hands of their creditors that year, too.

I was in about as bad a fix as anyone else. By then I had agreed to take thirty Fords a month, which was a pretty heavy job to get away with in good times, to say nothing of the sort of a situation we were going through. These cars came in each month, regular as clock work, and I had stretched my credit at the bank about as far as it would go in paying for them as they arrived. The bank kept hounding me all the time to cut down my loan, which I couldn't do with my expenses running on all the time and hardly any business going on. From September to January that year I sold exactly four cars.

Pretty bad? I'll say it was. But the worst was yet to come. Altogether I had more than one hundred and forty new cars on hand, besides a lot of trade-ins, and no immediate prospect of selling any. Then all of a sudden came notice that a shipment of fifteen Fords was on the way to me, and that I would be expected to pay for them on arrival. I thought there must be some mistake, and got the branch manager in the city on the long distance. He was a pretty hard-boiled egg named Blassingham.

"What's the meaning of these fifteen cars that are being shipped me?" I asked. "I've already taken my quota for the month."

"It don't mean anything," Blassingham answered, "except that you're going to buy fifteen extra cars this month."

I tried to explain to him that I was in no position to get hold of the cash for such a purchase, and even if I was I wanted to know the whys and wherefores.

"You know as much about it as I do," he snapped. "Those are the orders, and my advice to you is to pay for those cars when they arrive."

Of course I sensed the reason later on, when it came out in the newspapers about Mr. Ford's little tilt with the money sharks down in New York, how they tried to get a hold on his business and how he fooled them by getting the cash without their help and then told them to go chase themselves.

If you ask me, I'd say Mr. Ford is an absolute humdinger when it comes to handling a lot of crooks who are bent on feathering their own nests off other people. At the moment, however, I was too busy with personal problems to think much about the battles of Big Business. Like I say, my credit at the bank was used up, and the bank had no money to loan, anyhow. I was taking in enough cash to pay my mechanics in the garage, but I had to stand off the office help Saturday nights with part of their wages and ask them to wait on me for the balance. I couldn't sleep much for worrying, and I guess my wife worried as much as I did because at three and four o'clock in the morning she would ask me if I had been to sleep yet and when I would say no, she would say she hadn't either.

I had fully made up my mind I was going on the rock pile when just a couple of days before the extra shipment of Fords was due to arrive I had an unexpected stroke of luck. There was a sheep man named Flanagan I knew who had made a trip out west to Salt Lake City just before the market broke and closed out his entire holdings for something like a hundred thousand dollars in cash, which he put into Liberty Bonds. He had a Ford that he ran around in sometimes, and one day when he drove up to the garage I happened to think about his money and asked him how he would like to come in with me as a silent partner. To make a long story short, he became interested in the proposition and bought a third interest. Of course I had to sell him his share for a lot less than it was worth, but it saved my scalp.

There was kind of a funny sequel to this deal, and I don't know yet whether my taking a moneyed partner had anything to do with it, or whether it would have happened anyway. We took the fifteen extra Fords all right when they arrived and thought everything was settled, but a few days later Blassingham came down from the city and told me fifteen more were about to be shipped to our town. It seems these were extra cars that were intended for some dealers in little nearby villages but they were absolutely flat broke and unable to pay for them. Blassingham didn't actually tell me I had to buy these cars, but from his conversation I knew it would be wise for me to do so if I expected to stay in the automobile business.

I went to my silent partner, Flanagan, and told him he would have to put up a few thousand dollars more. He made an awful roar and said he would see Mr. Ford in Hades before he would pay for any more new cars when we already had nearly a hundred and fifty on hand. I explained that Mr. Ford had nothing to do with it, that it was the branch manager, Blassingham, who was riding us; but Flanagan, mad as a hornet, asked me who in hell I supposed gave Blassingham *his* orders. He made me give him my agency contract and took it to a lawyer. Pretty soon he came back, a good deal milder than when he went away, and said he guessed we had better buy those fifteen extra cars, though if he had known what he was getting into he wouldn't have been so quick to invest his money in the Ford game.

Of course, the trouble with Flanagan was that he had been a sheep man all his life and didn't understand big business. Still, I couldn't blame him for getting still madder at what happened next. Counting our trade-ins, we had about a hundred and eighty cars in stock, which was a pretty heavy load to carry with business like it was; but I told him we would come out all right because Ford cars were just as staple as wheat or sugar and we would eventually get our profit on them. But shortly afterward the Company announced a reduction in price in order to stimulate sales. Altogether we ran behind about thirteen thousand dollars between January and July that year.

I am willing to confess that we rode the public a little ourselves while we were getting rid of our big surplus of cars. There are always some people that you can sell anything to if you hammer them hard enough. We had a salesman named Nichols who was a humdinger at running down prospects, and one day he told me he had a fellow on the string with a couple of hundred dollars who would buy a car if we would give him a little extra time on the balance. This prospect was a young fellow that had come out West on account of his health and was trying to make a living for his family as an expert accountant. Just at that time the referee in bankruptcy was doing most of the accounting business around town, and I knew the young fellow wasn't getting on at all. He had about as much use for a car as a jack rabbit. I told Nichols this, but you know how plausible these go-getter salesmen are; he told me it wasn't our business whether the young fellow had any use for a Ford or not; the main thing was he had two hundred dollars in cash.

Well, we went ahead and made the sale, but we never got any more payments. The young fellow took to his bed just after that, and the church people had to look out for him and his family until he died. In the final showdown it turned out that the two-hundred dollar equity in the car was everything they had on earth, and by the time we replevined it and sold it as a trade-in there wasn't anything at all. I gave twenty dollars toward his funeral expenses. I know this sounds pretty tough; but when it's a case of your own scalp or some other fellow's you can't afford to be too particular.

By 1922 things had picked up a little in my territory, though the farmers hadn't entirely recovered from the 1920 setback and our town population had shrunk considerably on account of scarcity of work. It was pretty hard under these conditions to sell my quota of thirty cars a month, but the branch manager in the city held me to it. By this time Blassingham had been transferred, but another man named Cosgrove took his place who rode me harder than Blassingham had done. Like I say, he held me to my quota of Fords though I had fewer people to sell to; and not only that, but he also told me I would have to buy fifteen tractors every year besides. That wasn't all, either. Eventually I was saddled with two Lincoln cars a year and also supposed to take a certain number of subscriptions for a magazine called the *Dearborn Independent* that is owned by Mr. Ford and has a page every week entitled "Mr. Ford's Page." I guess even the best of us like to see our names in print.

I say I was required to do all these things, but there was in reality a little leeway. I learned on the quiet that Cosgrove would not take away my agency if I fell down a little on the fifteen tractors and two Lincolns. But on the thirty Fords a month there was no alibi allowed, and the same thing applied to the *Dearborn Independent*. This last gave me a lot of trouble.

About the most nagging thing to me were the visits of the expert salesmen who came around every so often to show us how to sell cars. It seemed to me that so long as I was taking my quota every month I ought to be the best judge of how and who to sell. There was one expert I specially remember by the name of Burke. Among other things I had to do was to keep a card file of people in the territory who had not bought cars, and usually on these cards we wrote items like "says maybe will be in market this fall," or "not ready to buy yet." Burke was always raising Cain because we didn't make people give more explicit reasons for not buying. I remember once he laid me out because a card said only "Can't sell him." The man was a poor devil of a renter seven or eight miles out of town who never had enough cash ahead to buy a wheelbarrow, but Burke insisted that one of my salesmen go out there with him to try and land a sale. When they got there a couple of the children were down with whooping cough and a hailstorm had laid out his bean crop, but Burke came back and told me he would expect me to put over a Ford on the fellow before he came on his next trip.

The thing that made me quit the Ford game was the campaign they put on for farm machinery. Understand, I was in sympathy with it too, because I knew Mr. Ford was trying to make things easier for the farmers—like he says, help them do their whole year's work in twenty days. Still and all, I didn't feel I wanted to go broke even in a good cause.

The first thing I knew of Mr. Ford's plans was on a Saturday afternoon when I got a long-distance call from the city saying the branch manager was coming out next day and for me to be in my office at eleven o'clock. I usually go to church Sunday mornings, and besides I always understood Mr. Ford was against Sunday work; but an order is an order and I wasn't taking any chances on getting in bad with the branch manager. In our town there are laws on Sabbath observance, but if a business man wants to work a little no one bothers him just so he keeps the shades down.

211

The branch manager was a new man by the name of Biggs, and he told me that from then on I would be required to carry a line of farm machinery suitable to go with the Ford tractors. As I remember it, there were no ifs or ands; I understood it to be an order, and I knew what Biggs could do to me if I didn't obey orders. Anyhow I thought it might be a good thing to help move the tractors, which were always harder to sell than Ford cars. I asked Biggs if he wanted me to sign a contract and he said no, that wouldn't be necessary in this case, but when the salesman came along it would be indicated to me what I should buy.

Biggs left that afternoon to see the dealers in some small towns farther up the line, and some time later the machinery man called. I never did quite understand Mr. Ford's arrangements with the machinery manufacturers. The salesman who called on me represented a big jobbing house in the city, and apparently there was no connection between this jobbing house and the branch manager's office; but there must have been some kind of a working agreement because the salesman had my assortment of stuff all lined up for me and all I had to do was to sign the order. Altogether it amounted to about seven thousand dollars' worth. There were seeders, 12-inch plows, etc., all sorts of implements to be hauled by the Ford tractors.

Well, so far as our section of the country was concerned, the farm machinery campaign was a pretty bad flop. In the first place, it was hard to convince the farmers that they ought to buy their machines from the Ford dealers instead of from regular implement merchants. Naturally the implement merchants were down on us for trying to take away their trade, and knocked Ford cars every time they had a chance. Then it was found that 12-inch plows weren't suitable for our territory, and some of the other machines proved too heavy for the Ford tractor. Biggs sent out a lot of demonstrators and high-powered salesmen to help us move the stuff, but none of us could make a go of the line and after a while so many squawks came from the dealers that Biggs called a meeting to hear complaints. As I was the biggest agent in that part of the state the meeting was held in my office and the smaller dealers came there.

Biggs called the meeting to order and asked the different ones to air their complaints. Believe me, there were a plenty. One fellow would tell his troubles with the farm machinery line, and then another, and then half a dozen would be on their feet at once, blaming Biggs, and the Ford Motor Company, and the farm machinery company, and pretty near everyone else, for their griefs. In the midst of it Biggs hopped to his feet and pounded the table.

"If any man here can show a scratch of the pen," he yelled, "to prove he bought his farm machinery at the orders of the Ford Motor Company, I dare him to get up and say so!"

Of course no one could show a scratch of the pen because there wasn't any. Biggs hadn't made any of us sign a contract for our farm machinery. He had just *told* us to buy it, and we took it to be an order from headquarters.

I sold out my business as soon after that as I could find a buyer. I was afraid after Mr. Ford got through helping the farmers he might decide to help out the Hottentots or someone, and I didn't feel like I could afford to assist him. The

212

fellow I sold my business to wouldn't take the farm machinery stock at any price. Since then I have been peddling it wherever I could, but it's a hard game. I sold one machine that cost me $800 for $300, and took the farmer's notes for it, spread out over three years, without interest.

I am sure Mr. Ford can't know about all these things, because if he did he couldn't have written in his book this grand sentiment:

"The principle of the service of business to the people has gone far in the United States and it will spread through and remake the world."

# 65

# The Movies' Early Years

The period after World War I saw the beginnings of mass culture in America. Earlier, the high culture of the well-to-do had its counterpart in the low culture of the immigrant. There were separate magazines, separate theaters, separate newspapers, and no medium spoke to all groups. In the 1920s, this particularism broke down before the new modes of art and communication, especially the movies and radio. Not that the stylish literary magazine or the immigrant stage lost their following. Rather, radio and movies were national media and made some effort to appeal to all classes in their audiences.

The promise and potential of these new forms of communication were still unclear in the 1920s; but as the piece by critic Gilbert Seldes makes clear, many people took them seriously. No one, certainly not Seldes, had a fine sense of what standards ought to apply. Were radio and movies entertainment? What aesthetic values were appropriate? Was a radio show to be judged as theater, a movie as art? The answers were less important than the debate. Seldes, born in New Jersey in 1893, made his career by writing for magazines on the "lively arts," and for a time it seemed that culture might be to some degree reunited in these arts. Seldes' article in 1927, reviewing the accomplishments and failures of the first movies, points to a promise of a union—one, however, that was not to be fulfilled.

## THE SEVEN LIVELY ARTS
### Gilbert Seldes

**An Open Letter to the Movie Magnates**

*Ignorant and Unhappy People:*

The Lord has brought you into a narrow place—what you would call a tight corner—and you are beginning to feel the pressure. A voice is heard in the land saying that your day is over. The name of the voice is Radio, broadcasting nightly to announce that the unequal struggle between the tired washerwoman and the captions written by or for Mr Griffith is ended. It is easier to listen than to read. And it is long since you have given us anything significant to see.

Reprinted with permission of the author from *The Seven Lively Arts* (New York, 1924), 275–287.

You may say that radio will ruin the movies no more than the movies ruined the theatre. The difference is that your foundation is insecure: you are monstrously over-capitalized and monstrously undereducated; the one thing you cannot stand is a series of lean years. You have to keep on going because you have from the beginning considered the pictures as a business, not as an entertainment. Perhaps in your desperate straits you will for the first time try to think about the movie, to see it steadily and see it whole.

My suggestion to you is that you engage a number of men and women: an archæologist to unearth the history of the moving picture; a mechanical genius to explain the camera and the projector to you; a typical movie fan, if you can find one; and above all a man of no practical capacity whatever: a theorist. Let these people get to work for you; do what they tell you to do. You will hardly lose more money than in any other case.

If the historian tells you that the pictures you produced in 1910 were better than those you now lose money on, he is worthless to you. But if he fails to tell you that the pictures of 1910 pointed the way to the real right thing and that you have since departed from that way, discharge him as a fool. For that is exactly what has occurred. In your beginnings you were on the right track; I believe that in those days you still looked at the screen. Ten years later you were too busy looking at, or after, your bank account. Remember that ten years ago there wasn't a great name in the movies. And then, thinking of your present plight, recall that you deliberately introduced great names and chose Sir Gilbert Parker, Rupert Hughes, and Mrs Elinor Glyn. If I may quote an author you haven't filmed, it shall not be forgiven you.

Your historian ought to tell you that the moving picture came into being as the result of a series of mechanical developments; your technician will add the details about the camera and projector. From both you will learn that you are dealing with *movement governed by light*. It will be news to you. You seem not to realize the simplest thing about your business. Further, you will learn that everything you need to do *must* be by these two agencies: movement and light. (Counting in movement everything of pace and in light everything which light can make visible to the eye, even if it be an emotion: do not recall the unnatural splash of white in a street scene in *Caligari*?) It will occur to you that the cut-back, the alternating exposition of two concurrent actions, the vision, the dream, are all good; and that the close-up, dearest of all your finds, usually dissociates a face or an object from its moving background and is the most dangerous of expedients. You will learn much from the camera and from what was done with it in the early days.

I warn you again they were not great pictures except for *The Avenging Conscience* and—one you didn't make—*Cabiria*. To each of these a poet contributed. (Peace, Mr Griffith; the poet in your case was E. A. Poe; and the warrior poet of Fiume contributed the scenario for the second.) Mr Griffith contrived in his picture to project both beauty and terror by combining *Annabel Lee* with *The Telltale Heart*. A sure instinct led him to disengage the vast emotion of longing and of lost love through an *action* of mystery and terror. (I think he made a happy

215

ending somehow—by having the central portion of his story appear as a dream. How little it mattered since the *real* emotion came through the story.) The picture was projected in a palpable atmosphere; it was *felt*. After ten years I recall dark masses and ghostly rays of light. And if I may anticipate the end, let me compare it with a picture of 1922, a picturization as you call it, of Annabel Lee. It was all scenery and captions; it presented a detestable little boy and a pretty little girl doing æsthetic dancing along cliffs by the sea; one almost saw the Ocean View Hotel in the background. Mercilessly the stanzas appeared on the screen; but nothing was allowed to *happen* except a vulgar representation of calf love. I cannot bear to describe the disagreeable picture of grief at the end; I do not dare to think what you may now be preparing with a really great poem. The lesson is not merely one of taste; it is a question of knowing the camera, of realizing that you *must* project emotion by movement and by picture combined.

I am trying to trace for you the development of the serious moving picture as a *bogus* art, and I can't do better than assure you that it was best before it was an "art" at all. (Or I can indicate that slap-stick comedy, which you despise, is not bogus, is a real, and valuable, and delightful entertainment.) I believe that you went out West because the perpetual sun of southern California made taking easy; there you discovered the lost romance of America, its Wild West and its pioneer days, its gold rush and its Indians. You had it in your hands, then, to make that past of ours alive; a small written literature and a remnant of oral tradition remained for you to work on. On the whole you did make a good beginning. You missed fine things, but you caught the simple ones; you presented the material directly, with appropriate sentiment. You relied on melodrama, which was the rightest thing you ever did. Combat and pursuit, the last-minute rescue, were the three items of your best pictures; and your cutting department, carefully alternating the fight between white men and red with the slow-starting, distant, approaching, arriving, victorious troops from the garrison appealed properly to our soundest instincts. You went into the bad-man period; you began to make an individual soldier, Indian, bandit, pioneer, renegade, the focus of your interest: still good because you related him to an active, living background. Dear Heaven! before you had filmed Bret Harte you had created legendary heroes of your own.

Meanwhile Mr Griffith, apparently insatiable, was developing small *genre* scenes of slum life while he thought of filming the tragic history of the South after the war. Other directors sought other fields—notably that of the serial adventure film. Since they made money for all concerned, you will not be surprised to hear these serials praised: *The Exploits of Elaine,* the whole Pearl White adventure, the thirty minutes of action closing on an impossible and unresolved climax were, of course, infinitely better pictures that your version of Mr Joseph Conrad's *Victory,* your *Humoreske,* your *Should a Wife Forgive?* They were extremely silly; they worked too closely on a scheme: getting out of last week's predicament and into next week's can hardly be called a "form." But within their limitations they used the camera for all it was worth. It didn't matter a bit that the perils were preposterous, that the flights and pursuits were all fakes composed by the speed of the projector.

You were back in the days of Nick Carter and the Liberty Boys; you hadn't heard of psychology, and drama, and art; you were developing the camera. You bored us when your effects didn't come off and I'm afraid amused us a little even when they did. But you were on the right road.

There was very little *acting* in these films and in the Wild West exhibitions. There was a great deal of *action*. I can't recall Pearl White *registering* a single time; I recall only movement, which was excellent. It was later that your acting developed; up to this time you were working with people who hadn't succeeded in or were wholly ignorant of the technique of the stage; they moved before the camera gropingly at first, but gradually developing a technique suited to the camera and to nothing else. I am referring to days so far back that the old Biograph films used to be branded with the mark AB in a circle, and this mark occurred in the photographed sets to prevent stealing. In those days your actors and actresses were exceptionally naïve and creative. You were on the point of discovering mass and line in the handling of crowds, in the defile of a troop, in the movement of individuals. Mr Griffith had already discovered that four men running in opposite directions along the design of a figure 8 gave the effect of sixteen men—a discovery lightly comparable to that of Velasquez in the crossed spears of the Surrender of Breda. You should have done well to continue your experiments with nameless individuals and chaotic masses; but you couldn't. You developed what you called personalities—and after that, actresses.

Before *The Birth of a Nation* was begun Mary Pickford had already left Griffith. I have heard that he vowed to make Mae Marsh a greater actress—as if she weren't one from the start, as if acting mattered, as if Mary Pickford ever could or needed to act. Conceive your own stupidity in not knowing what Vachel Lindsay discovered: that "our Mary" was literally "the Queen of my People," a radiant, lovely, childlike girl, a beautiful figurehead, a symbol of all our sentimentality. Why did you allow her to become an actress? Why is everything associated with her later work so alien to beauty? You did not see her legend forming; you began to advertise her salary; you have, I believe unconsciously, tried to restore her now by giving her the palest rôle in all literature, that of Marguerite in *Faust*. You are ten years too late. In the same ten years Blanche Sweet has almost disappeared and Mae Marsh has not arrived; Gishes and Talmadges and Swansons and other fatalities have triumphed. You have taken over the stage and the opera; you have filmed Caruso and Al Jolson, too, for all I know. You now have acting and no playing.

This is a matter of capital importance and I am willing to come closer to a definition. Acting is the way of impersonating, of rendering character, of presenting action which is suitable to the stage; it has, in the first place, a specific relation to the size of the stage and to that of the auditorium; it has also a second important relation to the lines spoken. Good actors—they are few—will always suit the gesture to the utterance in the sense that their gesture will be on the beat of the words; failure to know this ruined several of John Barrymore's soliloquies in *Hamlet*. Neither of these two primary and determinant circumstances affect the moving

217

picture. It should be obvious that if good acting is adapted to the stage, nothing less than a miracle could make it also suitable to the cinema. The same thing is true of opera, which is in a desperate state because it failed to develop a type of representation adapted to musical instead of spoken expression. Opera and the pictures both needed "playing"—by which I cover *other forms* of representation, of impersonation, characterization, without identifying them. It is unlikely that opera and pictures require the same kind of playing; but neither of them can bear acting. Chaplin, by the way, is a player, not an actor—although we all think of him as an actor because the distinction is tardily made. I should say that Mae Marsh, too, was a player in *The Birth,* and there have been others.

The emergence of Mary Pickford and the production of *The Birth of a Nation* make the years 1911–14 the critical time of the movies. Nearly all your absurdities began about this time, including your protest against the word movies as no longer suited to the dignity of your art. From the success of *The Birth* sprang the spectacle film which was intrinsically all right and only corrupted Griffith and the pictures because it was unintelligently handled thereafter. From the success of Mary Pickford came the whole tradition of the movie as a genteel intellectual entertainment. The better side is the spectacle and the fact that in 1922 the whole mastery of the spectacular film has passed out of your hands ought to be sufficient proof that you bungled somewhere. Or, to drive it home, what can you make of the circumstance that one of the very greatest successes, in America and abroad, was *Nanook of the North,* a spectacle film to which the producer and the artistic director contributed nothing—for it was a picture of actualities, made, according to rumour, in the interests of a fur-trading company? You will reply that my assertions are pure theory. It is true that I have never filmed a scenario in my life. But as a spectator I am the one who is hard headed and you the theorists. What I and several million others know is that something wrong crept into the spectacle film.

In *The Birth* Mr Griffith had two stories with no perceptible internal relation, but with sufficient personal interest to carry; even here not one person in ten thousand saw the significance of the highfalutin title. But after the time of *Intolerance* Mr Griffith receded swiftly, and his latest pictures are merely lavish.

Everywhere Mr Griffith now gives us excesses— everything is big: the crowds, the effects, the rainstorms, the ice floes, and everything is informed with an overwhelming dignity. He has long ago ceased to create beauty—only beautiful effects, like set pieces in fireworks. And he was the man destined by his curiosity, his honesty, his intelligence, to reach the heights of the moving picture.

It is a hard thing to say, but it is literally true that something in Mr Griffith has been corrupted and died—his imagination. *Broken Blossoms* was a last expiring flicker. Since then he has constructed well; I understand that his success has been great; I am not denying that Mr Griffith is the man to do *Ben-Hur.* But he has imagined nothing on a grand scale, nor has he created anything delicate or fine. People talk of *The Birth* as if the battle scenes were important; they were very good and a credit to Griffith, who directed, and to George Bitzer, who photographed them; the direction of the ride of the Klansmen was better, it had some imagination. And far better still was a moment earlier in the piece, when Walthall returned to the shattered Confederate home and Mae Marsh met him at the door, wearing raw cotton smudged to resemble ermine—brother and sister both pretending that they had forgotten their dead, that they didn't care what happened. And then—for the honours of the scene went to Griffith, not even to the exquisite Mae Marsh—then there appeared from within the doorway the arm of their mother and with a gesture of unutterable loveliness it enlaced the boy's shoulders and drew him tenderly into the house. To have omitted the tears, to have shown nothing but the arm in that single curve of beauty, required, in those days, high imagination. It was the emotional climax of the film; one felt from that moment that the rape and death of the little girl was already understood in the vast suffering sympathy of the mother. So much Mr Griffith never again accomplished; it was the one moment when he stood beside Chaplin as a creative artist—and it was ten years ago.

Of course if Griffith hasn't come through there is hardly anything to hope for from the others. Mr Ince always beat him in advertized expenditure; Fox was always cheaper and easier and had Annette Kellerman and did *The Village Blacksmith*. The logical outcome of Griffithism is in the pictures he didn't make: in *When Knighthood Was in Flower* and in *Robin Hood,* neither of which I could sit through. The lavishness of these films is appalling; the camera runs mad in everything but action, which dies a hundred deaths in as many minutes. Of what use are sets by Urban if the action which occurs in them is invisible to the naked eye? The old trick of using a crowd as a background and holding the interest in the individual has been lost; the trick of using the crowd as an individual hasn't been found because we must have our love story. The spectacle film is slowly settling down to the level of the stereopticon slide.

Comparison with German films is inevitable. They are as much on the wrong track as we are; and the exception, *Caligari*, is defective because in a proper attempt to relieve the camera from the burden of recording actuality, the producers gave it the job of recording modern paintings for background. The acting was, however, playing; and the destruction of realism, even if it was accomplished by a questionable expedient, will have much to do with the future of the film. Yet even in the spectacle film the Germans managed to do something. *Passion* and *Deception* and the Pharaoh film and the film made out of *Sumurun* were not lavish. And in the manipulation of material (not of the instrument, where we know much more than they) there came occasionally flashes of the real thing. In *Deception* there was a scene where the courtyard had to be cleared of an angry mob. Every American producer has handled the parallel scene and every one in the same way, centring in the mêlée between civilians and police. What Lubitsch did was to form a single line of pike staffs and to show a solid mass of crowd—the feeling of hostility was projected in the opposition of line and mass. And slowly the *space behind* the pike staffs opened. The bright calm sunlight fell on a wider and widening strip of the courtyard. One was hardly aware of struggle; all one saw was that gradually broadening patch of open, uncontested *space in the light.* And suddenly one knew that the courtyard was cleared, one seemed to hear the faint murmur of the crowd outside, and then silence. I am lost in admiration of this simplicity which involves *every correct principle of the æsthetics of the moving picture.* The whole thing was done with movement and light—the movement massed and the light on the open space. That is the true, the imaginative camera technique, which we failed to develop.

The object of that technique is *the indirect communication of emotion*—indirect because that is the surest way, in all the arts, of multiplying the degree of intensity. The American spectacle film still communicates a thrill in the direct way of a highwayman with a blackjack. But the American serious film drama communicates not even this: it is at this moment entirely dead, or in other words, wholly bogus. I may be wrong in thinking that our present position develops out of the creation of Mary Pickford as a star. The result is the same.

For as soon as the movie became "the silent drama" it took upon itself responsibilities. It had to be dignified and artistic; it had to have literature and actors and ideals. The simple movie plots no longer sufficed, and stage and novel were called upon to contribute their small share to the success of an art which seriously believed itself to be the consummation of all the arts. The obligation remained to choose only those examples which were suitable to the screen. It was, however, not adaptability which guided the choice, but the great name. Eventually everything was filmed because what couldn't be adapted could be spoiled. The degree of vandalism passes words; and what completed the ruin was that good novels were spoiled not to make good films, but to make bad ones. *Victory* was a vile film in addition to being a vulgar betrayal of Conrad; even the good Molnar with his exciting second-rate play, *The Devil,* found himself so foully, so disgustingly changed on the screen that the whole idea, not a great one, was lost and nothing remained but a sentimental vulgarity which had no meaning of its own, quite apart from any meaning of his. In each of these the elements are the same: a psychological development through an action. By corrupting the action the producers changed the idea; bad enough in itself, they failed to understand what they were doing and supplied nothing to take the place of what they had destroyed. The actual movies so produced refused to project any consecutive significant action whatsoever.

It would be futile to multiply examples—as futile as to note that there have been well-filmed novels and plays. The essential thing is that nearly every picture made recently has borrowed something, usually in the interest of dignity, gentility, refinement—and the picture side, the part depending upon action before the camera, has gone steadily down. Long subtitles explain everything except the lack of action. Carefully built scenes are settings in which nothing takes place. The climax arrives in the masterpieces of the de Mille school. They are "art." They are genteel. They offend nothing—except the intelligence. High life in the de Mille manner is not recognizable as decent human society, but it is refined, and the picture with it is refined out of existence. Ten years earlier there was another type of drama: the vamp, in short, and Theda Bara was its divinity, I have little to say in its defense because it was unalterably stupid (I don't say I didn't like it). But it wasn't half so pretentious as the de Mille social drama, and not half so vulgar. What it had to say, false or banal or ridiculous, it said entirely with the camera. It appealed to low passions and it truckled to imitative morality; there was in it a sort of corruption. Yet one could resist that frank ugliness as one can't resist the polite falsehood of the new culture of the movies.

It would be easy to exaggerate your failures. Your greatest mistake was a natural one—in taking over the realistic theatre. You knew that a photograph can reproduce actuality without significantly transposing it, and you assumed that that was the duty of the film. But you forgot that the rhythm of the film was creating something, and that this creation adapted itself entirely to the projection of emotion by means *not realistic;* that in the end the camera was as legitimately an instrument of distortion as of reproduction. You gave us, in short, the pleasure of *verification* in every detail; the Germans who are largely in the same tradition—they should have known better because their theatre knew better—improved the method at times and counted on significant detail. But neither of you gave us the pleasure of *recognition.* Neither you nor they have taken the first step (except in *Caligari*) toward giving us the highest degree of pleasure: that of escaping actuality and entering into a created world, built on its own inherent logic, keeping time in its own rhythm—where we feel ourselves at once strangers and at home. That has been done elsewhere—not in the serious film.

I would be glad to temper all of this with praise. I have liked many more films than I have mentioned here. But you are familiar with praise and there remains to say what you have missed. The moving picture when it became pretentious, when it went upstage and said, "dear God, make me artistic" at the end of its prayers, killed its imagination and foreswore its popularity. At your present rate of progress you will in ten years—if you survive—be no more a popular art than grand opera is. You had in your hands an incalculable instrument to set free the imagination of mankind—and the atrophy of our imaginative lives has only been hastened by you. You had also an instrument of fantasy—and you gave us Marguerite Clark in films no better than the "whimsy-me" school of stage plays. Above all, you had something fresh and clean and new; it was a toy and should have remained a toy—something for our delight. You gave us problem plays. Beauty you neither understood nor cared for; and although you talked much about art you never for a moment tried to fathom the secret sources, nor to understand the secret obligations, of art.

Can you do anything now? I don't know and I am indifferent to your future—because there is a future for the moving picture with which you will have nothing to do. I do not know if the movie of the future will be popular—and to me it is the essence of the movie that it should be popular. Perhaps there will be a period of semi-popularity—it will be at this time that you will desert—and then the new picture will arrive without your assistance. For when you and your capitalizations and your publicity go down together, the field will be left free for others. The first cheap film will startle you; but the film will grow less and less expensive. Presently it will be within the reach of artists. With players instead of actors and actresses, with fresh ideas (among which the idea of making a lot of money may be absent) these artists will give back to the screen the thing you have debauched—imagination. They will create with the camera, and not record, and will follow its

221

pulsations instead of attempting to capture the rhythm of actuality. It isn't impossible to recreate exactly the atmosphere of Anderson's *I'm a Fool;* it isn't impossible (although it may not be desirable) to do studies in psychology; it is possible and desirable to create great epics of American industry and let the machine operate as a character in the play—just as the land of the West itself, as the corn must play its part. The grandiose conceptions of Frank Norris are not beyond the reach of the camera. There are painters willing to work in the medium of the camera and architects and photographers. And novelists, too, I fancy, would find much of interest in the scenario as a new way of expression. There is no end to what we can accomplish.

The vulgar prettiness, the absurdities, the ignorances of your films haven't saved you. And although the first steps after you take away your guiding hand may be feeble, although bogus artists and culture-hounds may capture the movie for a time—in the end all will be well. For the movie is the imagination of mankind in action—and you haven't destroyed it yet.

# 66

## The Idea of Greenwich Village

The legendary quality of the 1920s, the speak-easies, the flappers, the wild parties and dances, as well as the artists who lived their art, were all summed up in the notion of Greenwich Village. The Village was the symbol of new morals and fashions, located, as was to be expected, in the midst of the nation's largest city and representing all that was European, exotic, and different. For many, the lure of the freedom of the Village was either illusory or insufficient, and they went usually to Paris, living there as expatriates. But others hoped to find in the Village an atmosphere in which they could work creatively, or at least away from the Babbitts of Main Street.

Malcolm Cowley was one writer-critic who stopped off briefly in the Village and then moved to Europe before finally returning home in 1929. Born in 1898 in a small Pennsylvania town, Cowley was educated at Harvard and went on to a distinguished career as a literary critic and editor. In 1934 he looked back on the decade of the 1920s and the Greenwich Village experience, and his reminiscenses help to capture much of the ethos of the period.

### EXILE'S RETURN
#### *Malcolm Cowley*

In those days when division after division was landing in Hoboken and marching up Fifth Avenue in full battle equipment, when Americans were fighting the Bolshies in Siberia and guarding the Rhine—in those still belligerent days that followed the Armistice there was a private war between Greenwich Village and the *Saturday Evening Post*.

Other magazines fought in the same cause, but the *Post* was persistent and powerful enough to be regarded as chief of the aggressor nations. It published stories about the Villagers, editorials and articles against them, grave or flippant serials dealing with their customs in a mood of disparagement or alarm, humorous pieces done to order by its staff writers, cartoons in which the Villagers were depicted as long-haired men and short-haired women with ridiculous bone-rimmed spectacles—in all, a long campaign of invective beginning before the steel strike or the Palmer Raids and continuing through the jazz era, the boom and the depression. The burden of it was always the same: that the Village was the haunt of affectation; that it was inhabited by fools and fakers; that the fakers hid Moscow heresies under the disguise of cubism and free verse; that the fools would eventually be cured of their folly: they would forget this funny business about art and return to domesticity in South Bend, Indiana, and sell motorcars, and in the evenings sit with slippered feet while their children romped about them in paper caps made from the advertising pages of the *Saturday Evening Post*. The Village was dying, had died already, smelled to high heaven and Philadelphia. . . .

The Villagers did not answer this attack directly: instead they carried on a campaign of their own against the culture of which the *Post* seemed to be the final expression. They performed autopsies, they wrote obituaries of civilization in the United States, they shook the standardized dust of the country from their feet. Here, apparently, was a symbolic struggle: on the one side, the great megaphone of middle-class America; on the other, the American disciples of art and artistic living. Here, in its latest incarnation, was the eternal warfare of bohemian against bourgeois, poet against propriety—Villon and the Bishop of Orléans, Keats and the quarterly reviewers, Rodolphe, Mimi and the landlord. But perhaps, if we review the history of the struggle, we shall find that the issue was other than it seemed, and the enmity less ancient.

When the American magazines launched their counteroffensive, in 1919, a curious phenomenon was to be observed. The New York bohemians, the Greenwich Villagers, came from exactly the same social class as the readers of the *Saturday Evening Post*. Their political opinions were vague and by no means dangerous to Ford Motors or General Electric: the war had destroyed their belief in political action. They were trying to get ahead, and the proletariat be damned. Their economic standards were those of the small American businessman.

The art-shop era was just beginning. Having fled from Dubuque and Denver to escape the stultifying effects of a civilization ruled by business, many of the Villagers had already entered business for themselves, and many more were about to enter it. They would open tea shops, antique shops, book shops, yes, and bridge parlors, dance halls, night clubs and real-estate offices. By hiring shop assistants, they would become the exploiters of labor. If successful, they tried to expand their one restaurant into a chain of restaurants, all with a delightfully free and intimate atmosphere, but run on the best principles of business accounting. Some of them leased houses, remodeled them into studio apartments, and raised the rents three or four hundred per cent to their new tenants. Others clung faithfully to their profession of painting or writing, rose in it slowly, and at last had their stories or illustrations accepted by *Collier's* or the *Saturday Evening Post*. There were occasions, I believe, when Greenwich Village writers were editorially encouraged to write stories making fun of the Village, and some of them were glad to follow the suggestion. Of course they complained, when slightly tipsy, that they were killing themselves—but how else could they maintain their standard of living? What they meant was that they could not live like *Vanity Fair* readers without writing for the *Saturday Evening Post*.

And so it was that many of them lived during the prosperous decade that followed. If the book succeeded or if they got a fat advertising contract, they bought houses in Connecticut, preferably not too far from the Sound. They hired butlers; they sent their children to St. Somebody's; they collected highboys, lowboys, tester beds; they joined the local Hunt and rode in red coats across New England stone fences and through wine-red sumacs in pursuit of a bag of imported aniseed. In the midst of these new pleasures they continued to bewail the standardization of American life, while the magazines continued their polemic against Greenwich Village. You came to suspect that some of the Villagers themselves, even those who remained below Fourteenth Street, were not indignant at a publicity that brought tourists to the Pirates' Den and customers to Ye Olde Curiowe Shoppe and increased the value of the land in which a few of them had begun to speculate. The whole thing seemed like a sham battle. Yet beneath it was a real conflict of ideas and one that would soon be mirrored in the customs of a whole country.

Greenwich Village was not only a place, a mood, a way of life: like all bohemias, it was also a doctrine. By 1920, it had become a system of ideas that could roughly be summarized as follows:

1. The idea of salvation by the child.—Each of us at birth has special potentialities which are slowly crushed and destroyed by a standardized society and mechanical methods of teaching. If a new educational system can be introduced, one by which children are encouraged to develop their own personalities, to blossom freely like flowers, then the world will be saved by this new, free generation.

2. The idea of self-expression.—Each man's, each woman's, purpose in life is to express himself, to realize his full individuality through creative work and beautiful living in beautiful surroundings.

3. The idea of paganism.—The body is a temple in which there is nothing unclean, a shrine to be adorned for the ritual of love.

4. The idea of living for the moment.—It is stupid to pile up treasures that we can enjoy only in old age, when we have lost the capacity for enjoyment. Better to seize the moment as it comes, to dwell in it intensely, even at the cost of future suffering. Better to live extravagantly, gather June rosebuds, "burn my candle at both ends. . . . It gives a lovely light."

5. The idea of liberty.—Every law, convention or rule of art that prevents self-expression or the full enjoyment of the moment should be shattered and abolished. Puritanism is the great enemy. The crusade against puritanism is the only crusade with which free individuals are justified in allying themselves.

6. The idea of female equality.—Women should be the economic and moral equals of men. They should have the same pay, the same working conditions, the same opportunity for drinking, smoking, taking or dismissing lovers.

7. The idea of psychological adjustment.—We are unhappy because we are maladjusted, and maladjusted because we are repressed. If our individual repressions can be removed—by confessing them to a Freudian psychologist—then we can adjust ourselves to any situation, and be happy in it. (But Freudianism is only one

225

method of adjustment. What is wrong with us may be our glands, and by a slight operation, or merely by taking a daily dose of thyroid, we may alter our whole personalities. Again, we may adjust ourselves by some such psycho-physical discipline as was taught by Gurdjieff [a teacher of Yoga]. The implication of all these methods is the same—that the environment itself need not be altered. That explains why most radicals who became converted to psychoanalysis or glands or Gurdjieff gradually abondoned their political radicalism.)

8. The idea of changing place.—"They do things better in Europe." England and Germany have the wisdom of old cultures; the Latin peoples have admirably preserved their pagan heritage. By expatriating himself, by living in Paris, Capri or the South of France, the artist can break the puritan shackles, drink, live freely and be wholly creative.

All these, from the standpoint of the business-Christian ethic then represented by the *Saturday Evening Post*, were corrupt ideas. This older ethic is familiar to most people, but one feature of it has not been sufficiently emphasized: Substantially, it was a *production* ethic. The great virtues it taught were industry, foresight, thrift and personal initiative. The workman should be industrious in order to produce more for his employer; he should look ahead to the future; he should save money in order to become a capitalist himself; then he should exercise personal initiative and found new factories where other workmen would toil industriously, and save, and become capitalists in their turn.

During the process many people would suffer privations: most workers would live meagerly and wrack their bodies with labor; even the employers would deny themselves luxuries that they could easily purchase, choosing instead to put back the money into their business; but after all, our bodies were not to be pampered; they were temporary dwelling places, and we should be rewarded in Heaven for our self-denial. On earth, our duty was to accumulate more wealth and produce more goods, the ultimate use of which was no subject for worry. They would somehow be absorbed, by new markets opened in the West, or overseas in new countries, or by the increased purchasing power of workmen who had saved and bettered their position.

That was the ethic of a young capitalism, and it worked admirably, so long as the territory and population of the country were expanding faster than its industrial plant. But after the war the situation changed. Our industries had grown enormously to satisfy a demand that suddenly ceased. To keep the factory wheels turning, a new domestic market had to be created. Industry and thrift were no longer adequate. There must be a new ethic that encouraged people to buy, a *consumption* ethic.

It happened that many of the Greenwich Village ideas proved useful in the altered situation. Thus, *self-expression* and *paganism* encouraged a demand for all sorts of products—modern furniture, beach pajamas, cosmetics, colored bathrooms with toilet paper to match. *Living for the moment* meant buying an automobile, radio or house, using it now and paying for it tomorrow. *Female equality* was capable of doubling the consumption of products—cigarettes, for example—that had formerly been used by men alone. Even *changing place* would help to stimulate business in the country from which the artist was being expatriated. The exiles of art were also trade missionaries: involuntarily they increased the foreign demand for fountain pens, silk stockings, grapefruit and portable typewriters. They drew after them an invading army of tourists, thus swelling the profits of steamship lines and travel agencies. Everything fitted into the business picture.

I don't mean to say that Greenwich Village was the source of the revolution in morals that affected all our lives in the decade after the war, and neither do I mean that big business deliberately plotted to render the nation extravagant, pleasure worshiping and reckless of tomorrow.

The new moral standards arose from conditions that had nothing to do with the Village. They were, as a matter of fact, not really new. Always, even in the great age of the Puritans, there had been currents of licentiousness that were favored by the immoderate American climate and held in check only by hellfire preaching and the hardships of settling a new country. Old Boston, Providence, rural Connecticut, all had their underworlds. The reason puritanism became so strong in America was perhaps that it had to be strong in order to checkmate its enemies. But it was already weakening as the country grew richer in the twenty years before the war; and the war itself was the puritan crisis and defeat.

All standards were relaxed in the stormy-sultry wartime atmosphere. It wasn't only the boys of my age, those serving in the army, who were transformed by events: their sisters and younger brothers were affected in a different fashion. With their fathers away, perhaps, and their mothers making bandages or tea-dancing with lonely officers, it was possible for boys and girls to do what they pleased. For the first time they could go to dances unchaperoned, drive the family car and park it by the roadside while they made love, and come home after midnight, a little tipsy, with nobody to reproach them in the hallway. They took advantage of these stolen liberties—indeed, one might say that the revolution in morals began as a middle-class children's revolt.

But everything conspired to further it. Prohibition came and surrounded the new customs with illicit glamour; prosperity made it possible to practice them; Freudian psychology provided a philosophical justification and made it unfashionable to be repressed; still later the sex magazines and the movies, even the pulpit, would advertise a revolution that had taken place silently and triumphed without a struggle. In all this Greenwich Village had no part. The revolution would have occurred if the Village had never existed, but—the point is important—it would not have followed the same course. The Village, older in revolt, gave form to the movement, created its fashions, and supplied the writers and illustrators who would render them popular. As for American business, though it laid no plots in advance, it was quick enough to use the situation, to exploit the new markets for cigarettes and cosmetics, and to realize that, in advertising pages and movie palaces, sex appeal was now the surest appeal.

The Greenwich Village standards, with the help of business, had spread through the country. Young women east and west had bobbed their hair, let it grow and bobbed it again; they had passed through the period when corsets were checked in the cloakroom at dances and the period when corsets were not worn. They were not very self-conscious when they talked about taking a lover; and the conversations ran from mother fixations to birth control while they smoked cigarettes between the courses of luncheons eaten in black-and-orange tea shops just like those in the Village. People of forty had been affected by the younger generation: they spent too much money, drank too much gin, made love to one another's wives and talked about their neuroses. Houses were furnished to look like studios. Stenographers went on parties, following the example of the boss and his girl friend and her husband. The "party," conceived as a gathering together of men and women to drink gin cocktails, flirt, dance to the phonograph or radio and gossip about their absent friends, had in fact become one of the most popular American institutions; nobody stopped to think how short its history had been in this country. It developed out of the "orgies" celebrated by the French 1830 Romantics, but it was introduced into this country by Greenwich Villagers—before being adopted by salesmen from Kokomo and the younger country-club set in Kansas City.

Wherever one turned the Greenwich Village ideas were making their way: even the *Saturday Evening Post* was feeling their influence. Long before Repeal, it began to wobble on Prohibition. It allowed drinking, petting and unfaithfulness to be mentioned in the stories it published; its illustrations showed women smoking. Its advertising columns admitted one after another of the strictly pagan products— cosmetics, toilet tissues, cigarettes—yet still is continued to thunder against Greenwich Village and bohemian immorality. It even nourished the illusion that its long campaign had been successful. On more than one occasion it announced that the Village was dead and buried: "The sad truth is," it said in the autumn of 1931, "that the Village was a flop." Perhaps it was true that the Village was moribund—of that we can't be sure, for creeds and ways of life among artists are hard to kill. If, however, the Village was really dying, it was dying of success. It was dying because it became so popular that too many people insisted on living there. It was dying because women smoked cigarettes on the streets of the Bronx, drank gin cocktails in Omaha and had perfectly swell parties in Seattle and Middletown—in other words, because American business and the whole of middle-class America had been going Greenwich Village.

# 67

## The Klan in Mississippi

A darker side of American life in the 1920s revealed itself in immigration restriction, Prohibition, discrimination against ethnic and racial minorities, and, most dramatically, in the Ku Klux Klan. The optimism that led a nation to call for Europe's wretched masses seemed to be replaced with the fears of a hooded man who mumbled magical phrases, burned crosses, and denounced the immigrant at every opportunity.

The KKK had a slow beginning in the years before World War I; but in the 1920s, with leaders capable of effective promotion, it grew popular not only in the South but in the Midwest, not only in small towns but in cities like Chicago as well. The object of its hatred and fear was more often the Catholic than the Negro—the black, after all, was usually kept well in hand by Southern whites. The Catholic, entering business and politics, and often enjoying success, posed a graver threat to the Klan mentality. Its response, at times, was physical coercion, flogging, riding out of town, occasionally murder. More often the Klan used verbal intimidation and carried its program into politics. It enjoyed much success in the 1920s, but ultimately the public's good sense and decency, combined with the Klan's corruption and greed, ended its power.

The account below by William Percy describes the Klan's abortive efforts to take power in a small Southern town. But even where unsuccessful, the Klan, as Percy's reminiscenses make clear, was a serious danger and a threat to community life.

## LANTERNS ON THE LEVEE
### *William A. Percy*

The years following the war were a time of confusion not only to ex-soldiers but to all Americans. The tension of high endeavor and unselfish effort snapped, and Americans went "ornery." In the South the most vital matter became the price of cotton, in the North the price of commodities. Idealism was followed by the grossest materialism, which continues to be the order of the day.

From pp. 229–238 of *Lanterns on the Levee*, by William A. Percy. Copyright 1941 by Alfred A. Knopf, Inc. Reprinted by permission of the publisher.

Our town of about ten thousand population was no better or worse, I imagine, than other little Southern towns. My townsfolk had got along pretty well together—we knew each other so well and had suffered so much together. But we hadn't suffered a common disaster, one that was local and our very own, like a flood or a yellow-fever epidemic, since the flood of 1913, and that had failed as a binder because it didn't flood the town. Unbeknownst, strangers had drifted in since the war—from the hills, from the North, from all sorts of odd places where they hadn't succeeded or hadn't been wanted. We had changed our country attractively for them. Malaria had been about stamped out; electric fans and ice had lessened the terror of our intolerable summer heat; we had good roads and drainage and schools, and our lands were the most fertile in the world. We had made the Delta a good place in which to live by our determination and our ability to endure hardships, and now other folks were attracted by the result of our efforts. The town was changing, but so insidiously that the old-timers could feel but could not analyze the change. The newcomers weren't foreigners or Jews, they were an alien breed of Anglo-Saxon.

Although I was always traveling to strange places, I loved Greenville and never wanted any other place for home. Returning to it was the most exciting part of a trip. You could find friendly idlers round the post-office steps pretending they were waiting for the mail. You could take a coke any time of day with someone full of important news. There'd be amiable people running in and out of the house, without knocking, for tennis or golf or bridge or poker or to join you at a meal or just to talk. It was a lovable town.

I suppose the trait that distinguished it from neighboring towns was a certain laxity in church matters. We didn't regard drunkenness and lechery, Sabbath-breaking and gambling as more than poor judgment or poor taste. What we were slow to forgive was hardness of heart and all unkindness. Perhaps we were overstocked with sinners and pariahs and publicans, but they kept the churches in their places and preserved the tradition of sprightliness. Of course we had church folk, plenty of them—Episcopalians, not numerous but up-stage, whose forebears came from Virginia, Kentucky, or South Carolina; Catholics from Italy or Ireland or New Orleans; Methodists, indigenous and prolific; Baptists, who loved Methodists less but Catholics least, swarms of them; Presbyterians, not directly from Geneva or Edinburgh, but aged in the wood, fairly mellow considering they were predestined; and Jews too much like natives even to be overly prosperous. There were bickerings and fights during election time, but day in and day out we were pretty cozy and neighborly, and nobody cared what to hell was the other fellow's route to heaven. There was no embattled aristocracy, for the descendants of the old-timers were already a rather seedy remnant, and there was no wealth. White folks and colored folks—that's what we were—and some of us were nice and some weren't.

I never thought of Masons. Most of my friends wore aprons at funerals and fezzes (over vine leaves) at knightly convocations. Even Père had been a Mason, to the scandal of the Church and the curtailment of his last rites, but he took it easy. I thought Masonry a good thing for those who liked that sort of thing.

We had read in the newspapers that over in Atlanta some fraud was claiming to have revived the old Ku Klux Klan which during reconstruction days had played so desperate but on the whole so helpful a part in keeping the peace and preventing mob violence. This Atlanta monstrosity was not even a bastard of the old organization which General Forrest had headed and disbanded. This thing obviously was a money-making scheme without ideals or ideas. We were amused and uninterested. Even in Forrest's day the Klan had never been permitted to enter our county. It couldn't happen here. But reports of the Atlanta organization's misdeeds—masked night parades to terrorize the Negro, threatening letters, forcible closing of dance-halls and dives, whippings, kidnappings, violent brutalities—crowded the headlines. As citizens of the South we were ashamed; as citizens of Greenville we were not apprenhensive.

Then in the spring of 1922 a "Colonel" Camp was advertised to speak in our courthouse for the purpose of forming a branch of the Klan in Greenville. Thoroughly aroused, we debated whether to permit the speech in the courthouse or to answer it there. We couldn't learn who had invited him to speak or who had given him permission to use the courthouse, but evidently some of our own people were already Klansmen—fifth-column tactic before there was a Hitler. Our best citizens, those who thought for the common good, met in Father's office and agreed almost unanimously that the Colonel should be answered and by Father.

The Klan organizer made an artful speech to a tense crowd that packed every cranny of the room; and every man was armed. Who killed Garfield? A Catholic. Who asssinated President McKinley? A Catholic. Who had recently bought a huge tract of land opposite West Point and another overlooking Washington? The Pope. Convents were brothels, the confessional a place of seduction, the basement of every Catholic church an arsenal. The Pope was about to seize the government. To the rescue, Klansmen! These were statements which any trained mind recognized as lies, but which no man without weeks of ridiculous research could disprove. It was an example of Nazi propaganda before there were Nazis. The very enormity and insolence of the lie carried conviction to the simple and the credulous. The Colonel was listened to with courtesy.

To his surprise, Father answered him: he had never been answered before. I have never heard a speech that was so exciting and so much fun. The crowd rocked and cheered. Father's ridicule was amusing but bitter; and as he continued, it became more bitter, until it wasn't funny, it was terrifying. And the Colonel was terrified: he expected to be torn limb from limb by the mob. I don't blame him. At the close of Father's speech the crowd went quite mad, surging about, shouting and cheering, and thoroughly dangerous. A resolution was passed condemning the Klan. Colonel Camp scuttled out of a side door, appealing to a passing deputy for protection. The deputy, an Irish Catholic and the kindliest of men (out of *Henry IV*), escorted him ceremoniously to his hotel.

It was a triumphant meeting, but for the next two years our town was disintegrated by a bloodless, cruel warfare, more bitter and unforgiving than anything I encountered at the front. In the trenches soldiers felt sorry for one another, whether friend or enemy. In Father's senatorial fight, we were surrounded by ferocious stupidity rather than by hatred. But in the Klan fight the very spirit of hatred materialized before our eyes. It was the ugliest thing I have ever beheld. You didn't linger on the post-office steps or drink cokes with random companions: too many faces were hard and set, too many eyes were baleful and venomous. You couldn't go a block without learning by a glance that someone hated you.

The Klan did not stand for, but against. It stood against Catholics, Jews, Negroes, foreigners, and sin. In our town it chose Catholics as the object of its chief persecution. Catholic employees were fired, Catholic businessmen were boycotted, Catholic office-holders opposed. At first this seemed strange to me, because our Catholics were a small and obscure minority, but I came to learn with astonishment that of all the things hated in the South, more hated than the Jew or the Negro or sin itself, is Rome. The evangelical sects and Rome—as different and un-comprehending of each other as youth and old age! One seems never to have glimpsed the sorrowful pageant of the race and the other, profoundly disillusioned, profoundly compassionate, sees only the pageant. One has the enthusiasm and ignorance of the pioneer, the other the despair of the sage. One's a cheer-leader, the other an old sad-eyed family doctor from Samaria. We discovered that the Klan had its genesis, as far as our community was involved, in the Masonic Temple. The state head of that fraternal organization, a well-meaning old simpleton, had been preaching anti-Catholicism for years when conferring Masonic degrees. He joined the Klan early and induced other Masonic leaders to follow his example. These composed the Klan leadership in our county, though they were aided by a few politicians who knew better but who craved the Klan vote. It was a pretty leadership—fanatics and scalawag politicians. But not all Masons or all the godly were so misguided. The opposition to the Klan at home was led by a Protestant committee (and every denomination was represented in its ranks), who fought fearlessly, intelligently, and unceasingly this evil which they considered as unchristian as it was un-American. Father was not only head of the Protestant anti-Klan committee but of the anti-Klan forces in the South. He spoke as far north as Chicago and published probably the first article on the Klan in any distinguished magazine. It was reprinted from the *Atlantic Monthly* and distributed over the whole country. He felt the Klan was the sort of public evil good citizens could not ignore. Not to fight it was ineffectual and craven.

It's hard to conceive of the mumbo-jumbo ritual of the Klan and its half-wit principles—only less absurd than the Nazi principles of Aryan superiority and lebensraum—as worthy of an adult mind's attention. But when your living, your self-respect, and your life are threatened, you don't laugh at that which threatens. If you have either sense or courage you fight it. We fought, and it was high time someone did.

The Klan's increasing atrocities culminated in the brutal murders at Mer Rouge, where Skipwith was Cyclops. Mer Rouge is across the river from us, on the Louisiana side. It is very near and the murders were very ghastly. The Klan loathed and feared Father more than any other man in the South. For months I never let him out of my sight and of course we both went armed. Never before nor since have our doors been shut and locked at night.

One Sunday night of torrential rain when Father, Aunt Lady, and I sat in the library and Mother was ill upstairs I answered a knock at the door. It was early and I opened the door without apprehension. A dark, heavy-set man with two days' growth of beard and a soft-brimmed black hat stood there, drenched to the skin. He asked for Father and I, to his obvious surprise, invited him in. He wouldn't put down his hat, but held it in front of him. I didn't like his looks, so while Father talked to him I played the piano softly in the adjoining room and listened. The man's story was that he came from near our plantation, his car had run out of gas a few miles from town, he'd left his sister in the car and walked to town, he couldn't find a service station open, and would Father help him? Father, all sympathy, started phoning. The stranger seemed neither interested nor appreciative. I watched him with mounting suspicion. Father's efforts to find a service station open having failed, he said: "My car is here. We might run out and get your sister—I suppose you can drive my car?" The stranger brightened and observed he could drive any make of car. The two of them were still near the phone when Father's three bridge cronies came stamping in, laughing and shaking out the rain. As they came toward Father, the stranger brushed past them and had reached the door when I overtook him. "Say, what's the matter with you?" I asked. "Wait a minute and some of us will get you fixed up." He mumbled: "Got to take a leak," walked into the rain, and disappeared.

We waited for him, but we did not see him again for two years. Then he was in jail charged with a string of robberies. When he saw I recognized him, he grinned sourly and remarked: "Old Skip nearly put that one over." He refused to enlarge on this statement, which presumably referred to Skipwith, Cyclops of Mer Rouge. We found from the neighbors that the night of his visit to us he had arrived in a car with another man and parked across the street from our house.

It looked too much like an attempt at kidnapping and murder for me to feel easy. I went to the office of the local Cyclops. He was an inoffensive little man, a great Mason, and partial to anti-Catholic tirades. I said: "I want to let you know one thing: if anything happens to my Father or to any of our friends you will be killed. We won't hunt for the guilty party. So far as we are concerned the guilty party will be you."

There were no atrocities, no whippings, no threatening letters, no masked parades in our town. The local Klan bent all of its efforts toward electing one of its members sheriff. If they could have the law-enforcement machinery under their control, they could then flout the law and perpetrate such outrages as appealed to them. Our fight became a political fight to prevent the election of the Klan's choice for sheriff. The whole town was involved and the excitement was at fever heat. What appalled and terrified us most was the mendacity of Klan members. You never knew if the man you were talking to was a Klansman and a spy. Like German parachute jumpers, they appeared disguised as friends. For the Klan advised its members to lie about their affiliation with the order, about anything that concerned another Klansman's welfare, and about anything pertaining to the Klan—and its members took the advice. The most poisonous thing the Klan did to our town was to rob its citizens of their faith and trust in one another. Everyone

233

was under suspicion: from Klansmen you could expect neither frankness nor truth nor honor, and you couldn't tell who was a Klansman. If they were elected judges and law-enforcement officers, we would be cornered into servility or assassination.

Our candidate for sheriff was George B. Alexander, a powerful, square-bearded, Kentucky aristocrat drawn by Holbein. He was one of those people who are always right by no discernible mental process. His fearlessness, warm-heartedness, and sheer character made him a person you liked to be with and for. He was Father's favorite hunting companion and friend.

On election night the town was beside itself with excitement. Crowds filled the streets outside the voting booths to hear the counting of the ballots as it progressed. Everyone realized the race was close and whoever won would win by the narrowest of margins. The whole population was in the street, milling, apprehensive, silent. When the count began, Father went home and started a bridge game. I waited at the polls. About nine o'clock a sweating individual with his collar unbuttoned and his wide red face smeared with tears rushed out on the steps and bellowed: "We've won, we've won! Alexander's elected! God damn the Klan!" Pandemonium broke loose. Men yelled and screamed and hugged one another. Our town was saved, we had whipped the Klan and were safe. I ran home with the news and Father's bridge game broke up in a stillness of thanksgiving that was almost religious.

Mother was away. Being a Frenchwoman, she had been neither hysterical nor sentimental during the months and months of tension and danger. But none of us knew what she went through silently and it was then her health began to fail.

While we were talking about the victory, a tremendous uproar came to us from the street. We rushed out on the gallery. From curb to curb the street was filled with a mad marching crowd carrying torches and singing. They swarmed down the street and into our yard. It was a victory celebration. Father made a speech, everybody made a speech, nobody listened and everybody cheered. Klansmen had taken to cover, but the rest of the town was there, seething over the yard and onto the gallery. They cut Mr. Alexander's necktie to bits for souvenirs. And still they cheered and swarmed.

Father, nonplussed, turned to Adah and me and laughed: "They don't seem to have any idea of going home and I haven't a drop of whisky in the house—at least, I'm not going to waste my *good* liquor on them." Adah and Charlie dashed off in their car and returned with four kegs. Father called to the crowd: "Come on in, boys," and into the house they poured. That was a party never to be forgotten.

# 68

## The Intellectual as Cynic

No writer better personified the stance of the intellectual leaders of his generation than H. L. Mencken, the outstanding newspaper and magazine journalist of the 1920s. Mencken spoke a language that was congenial to many others in this decade. His tone was scoffing, skeptical, disbelieving, cynical, and hard-boiled. It was for these qualities that he won a large and devoted following. The villians in Mencken's pieces were often the sacred cows of the society. The "boobocracy" took its licks from him (the masses, after all, were boobs, and their government behaved accordingly) and so did virtues like chastity, to Mencken nothing more than a lack of courage and funds. To be sure, his mocking tone could get repetitious and stale, and finally, in the 1930s, often irrelevent, as the nation faced the depression; but at its best, it could puncture the pretentions and illuminate the foibles of society. If many Americans went about their business in the 1920s convinced that all was well with their country, Mencken's readers at least knew something of the other side of the story.

Mencken's essay, "The Anglo-Saxon," aptly illustrates his style and his contribution to his time. The 1920s witnessed an unprecedented enthusiasm for notions of race in America, inevitably to the glory of the Anglo-Saxon and the degradation of the Negro, the Jew, and southern Italian. In such a climate, it was helpful to have a critic like Mencken on the scene.

## THE ANGLO-SAXON
### H. L. Mencken

When I speak of Anglo-Saxons, of course, I speak inexactly and in the common phrase. Even within the bounds of that phrase the American of the dominant stock is Anglo-Saxon only partially, for there is probably just as much Celtic blood in his veins as Germanic, and his norm is to be found, not south of the Tyne and west of the Severn, but on the two sides of the northern border. Among the first English colonists there were many men of almost pure Teutonic stock from the east and south of England, and their influence is yet visible in many characteristic American

Reprinted with permission from *The Baltimore Evening Sun*, July, 1923; reprinted in *The Vintage Mencken*, Alistair Cooke, ed. (New York, 1959), 127–137.

folkways, in certain traditional American ideas—some of them now surviving only in national hypocrisies—and, above all, in the fundamental peculiarities of the American dialect of English. But their Teutonic blood was early diluted by Celtic strains from Scotland, from the north of Ireland, from Wales, and from the west of England, and today those Americans who are regarded as being most thoroughly Anglo-Saxons—for example, the mountaineers of the Appalachian slopes from Pennsylvania to Georgia—are obviously far more Celtic than Teutonic, not only physically but also mentally. They are leaner and taller than the true English, and far more given to moral obsessions and religious fanticism. A Methodist revival is not an English phenomenon; it is Welsh. So is the American tendency, marked by every foreign student of our history, to turn all political combats into moral crusades. The English themselves, of course, have been greatly polluted by Scotch, Irish and Welsh blood during the past three centuries, and for years past their government has been largely in the hands of Celts, but though this fact, by making them more like Americans, has tended to conceal the difference that I am discussing, it has certainly not sufficed to obliterate it altogether. The English notion of humor remains different from the American notion, and so does the English view of personal liberty, and on the same level of primary ideas there are many other obvious differences.

But though I am thus convinced that the American Anglo-Saxon wears a false label, and grossly libels both of the great races from which he claims descent, I can imagine no good in trying to change it. Let him call himself whatever he pleases. Whatever he calls himself, it must be plain that the term he uses designates a genuinely distinct and differentiated race—that he is separated definitely, in character and habits of thought, from the men of all other recognizable strains—that he represents, among the peoples of the earth, almost a special species, and that he runs true to type. The traits that he developed when the first mixture of races took place in colonial days are the traits that he still shows; despite the vast changes in his material environment, he is almost precisely the same, in the way he thinks and acts, as his forefathers were. Some of the other great races of men, during the past two centuries, have changed very noticeably, but the American Anglo-Saxon has stuck to his hereditary guns. Moreover, he tends to show much less variation than other races between man and man. No other race, save it be the Chinese, is so thoroughly regimented.

The good qualities of this so-called Anglo-Saxon are many, and I am certainly not disposed to question them, but I here pass them over without apology, for he devotes practically the whole of his literature and fully a half of his oral discourse to celebrating them himself, and so there is no danger that they will ever be disregarded. No other known man, indeed, is so violently the blowhard, save it be his English kinsman. In this fact lies the first cause of the ridiculous figure he commonly cuts in the eyes of other people: he brags and blusters so incessantly that, if he actually had the combined virtues of Socrates, the Cid and the Twelve Apostles, he would still go beyond the facts, and so appear a mere Bombastes Furioso. This habit, I believe, is fundamentally English, but it has been exaggerated in the Americano by his larger admixture of Celtic blood. In late years in America it has taken on an almost pathological character, and is to be explained, perhaps, only in terms of the Freudian necromancy. Braggadocio, in the 100% American—"we won the war," "it is our duty to lead the world," and so on—is probably no more than a protective mechanism erected to conceal an inescapable sense of inferiority.

That this inferiority is real must be obvious to any impartial observer. Whenever the Anglo-Saxon, whether of the English or of the American variety, comes into sharp conflict with men of other stocks, he tends to be worsted, or, at best, to be forced back upon extraneous and irrelevant aids to assist him in the struggle. Here in the United States his defeat is so palpable that it has filled him with vast alarms, and reduced him to seeking succor in grotesque and extravagant devices. In the fine arts, in the sciences and even in the more complex sorts of business the children of the later immigrants are running away from the descendants of the early settlers. To call the roll of Americans eminent in almost any field of human endeavor above the most elemental is to call a list of strange and often outlandish names; even the panel of Congress presents a startling example. Of the Americans who have come into notice during the past fifty years as poets, as novelists, as critics, as painters, as sculptors and in the minor arts, less than half bear Anglo-Saxon names, and in this minority there are few of pure Anglo-Saxon blood. So in the sciences. So in the higher reaches of engineering and technology. So in philosophy and its branches. So even in industry and agriculture. In those areas where the competition between the new and the old bloodstreams is most sharp and clear-cut, say in New York, in seaboard New England and in the farming States of the upper Middle West, the defeat of the so-called Anglo-Saxon is overwhelming and unmistakable. Once his predominance everywhere was actual and undisputed; today, even where he remains superior numerically, it is largely sentimental and illusory.

The descendants of the later immigrants tend generally to move upward; the descendants of the first settlers, I believe, tend plainly to move downward, mentally, spiritually and even physically. Civilization is at its lowest mark in the United States precisely in those areas where the Anglo-Saxon still presumes to rule. He runs the whole South—and in the whole South there are not as many first-rate men as in many a single city of the mongrel North. Wherever he is still firmly in the saddle, there we look for such pathological phenomena as Fundamentalism, Prohibition and Ku Kluxery, and there they flourish. It is not in the northern cities, with their mixed population, that the death-rate is highest, and politics most corrupt, and religion nearest to voodooism, and every decent human aspiration suspect; it is in the areas that the recent immigrations have not penetrated, where "the purest Anglo-Saxon blood in the world" still flows. I could pile up evidences, but they are not necessary. The fact is too plain to be challenged. One testimony will be sufficient: it comes from two inquirers who made an exhaustive survey of a region in southeastern Ohio, where "the people are more purely Americans than in the rest of the State":

Here gross superstition exercises strong control over the thought and action of a large proportion of the people. Syphilitic and other venereal diseases are common and increasing over whole counties, while in some communities nearly every family is afflicted with inherited or infectious disease. Many cases of incest are known; inbreeding is rife. Imbeciles, feeble-minded, and delinquents are numerous, politics is corrupt, and selling of votes is common, petty crimes abound, the schools have been badly managed and poorly attended. Cases of rape, assault, and robbery are of almost weekly occurrence within five minutes' walk of the corporation limits of one of the county seats, while in another county political control is held by a self-confessed criminal. Alcoholic intemperance is excessive. Gross immorality and its evil results are by no means confined to the hill districts, but are extreme also in the towns.

As I say, the American of the old stock is not unaware of this steady, and, of late, somewhat rapid deterioration—this gradual loss of his old mastery in the land his ancestors helped to wring from the Indian and the wildcat. He senses it, indeed, very painfully, and, as if in despair of arresting it in fact, makes desperate efforts to dispose of it by denial and concealment. These efforts often take grotesque and extravagant forms. Laws are passed to hobble and cage the citizen of newer stocks in a hundred fantastic ways. It is made difficult and socially dangerous for him to teach his children the speech of his fathers, or to maintain the cultural attitudes that he has inherited from them. Every divergence from the norm of the low-cast Anglo-Saxon is treated as an *attentat* against the commonwealth, and punished with eager ferocity.

It so happens that I am myself an Anglo-Saxon—one of far purer blood, indeed, than most of the half-bleached Celts who pass under the name in the United States and England. I am in part Angle and in part Saxon, and what else I am is safely white, Nordic, Protestant and blond. Thus I feel free, without risk of venturing into bad taste, to regard frankly the *soi-disant* Anglo-Saxon of this incomparable Republic and his rather less dubious cousin of the Motherland. How do the two appear to me, after years spent largely in accumulating their disfavor? What are the characters that I discern most clearly in the so-called Anglo-Saxon type of man? I may answer at once that two stick out above all others. One is his curious and apparently incurable incompetence—his congenital inability to do any difficult thing easily and well, whether it be isolating a bacillus or writing a sonata. The other is his astounding susceptibility to fears and alarms—in short, his hereditary cowardice.

To accuse so enterprising and successful a race of cowardice, of course, is to risk immediate derision; nevertheless, I believe that a fair-minded examination of its history will bear me out. Nine-tenths of the great feats of derring-do that its sucklings are taught to venerate in school—that is, its feats as a race, not the isolated exploits of its extraordinary individuals, most of them at least partly of other stocks—have been wholly lacking in even the most elementary gallantry. Consider, for example, the events attending the extension of the two great empires, English and American. Did either movement evoke any genuine courage and resolution? The answer is plainly no. Both empires were built up primarily by swindling and butchering unarmed savages, and after that by robbing weak and friendless nations. Neither produced a hero above the average run of those in the movies; neither exposed the folks at home to any serious danger of reprisal. Almost always, indeed, mercenaries have done the Anglo-Saxon's fighting for him—a high testimony to his common sense, but scarcely flattering, I fear, to the truculence he boasts of. The British empire was won mainly by Irishmen, Scotchmen and native allies, and the American empire, at least in large part, by Frenchmen and Spaniards. Moreover, neither great enterprise cost any appreciable amount of blood; neither presented grave and dreadful risks; neither exposed the conqueror to the slightest danger of being made the conquered. The British won most of their vast dominions without having to stand up in a single battle against a civilized and formidable foe, and the Americanos won their continent at the expense of a few dozen puerile skirmishes with savages. The total cost of conquering the whole area from Plymouth Rock to the Golden Gate and from Lake George to the Everglades, including even the cost of driving out the French, Dutch, English and Spaniards, was less than the cost of defending Verdun.

So far as I can make out there is no record in history of any Anglo-Saxon nation entering upon any great war without allies. The French have done it, the Dutch have done it, the Germans have done it, the Japs have done it, and even such inferior nations as the Danes, the Spaniards, the Boers and the Greeks have done it, but never the English or Americans. Can you imagine the United States resolutely facing a war in which the odds against it were as huge as they were against Spain in 1898? The facts of history are wholly against any such fancy. The Anglo-Saxon always tries to take a gang with him when he goes into battle, and even when he has it behind him he is very uneasy, and prone to fall into panic at the first threat of genuine danger. Here I put an unimpeachably Anglo-Saxon witness on the stand, to wit, the late Charles W. Eliot. I find him saying, in an article quoted with approbation by the *Congressional Record,* that during the Revolutionary War the colonists now hymned so eloquently in the school-books "fell into a condition of despondency from which nothing but the steadfastness of Washington and the Continental army *and the aid from France* saved them," and that "when the War of 1812 brought grave losses a considerable portion of the population experienced a moral collapse, from which they were rescued only by the exertions of a few thoroughly patriotic statesmen and the exploits of three or four American frigates on the seas"—to say nothing of an enterprising Corsican gentleman, Bonaparte by name.

In both these wars the Americans had enormous and obvious advantages, in terrain, in allies and in men; nevertheless, they fought, in the main, very badly, and from the first shot to the last a majority of them stood in favor of making peace on almost any terms. The Mexican and Spanish Wars I pass over as perhaps too obscenely ungallant to be discussed at all; of the former, U. S. Grant, who fought in it, said that it was "the most unjust war ever waged by a stronger against a weaker nation." Who remembers that, during the Spanish War, the whole Atlantic Coast trembled in fear of the Spaniards' feeble fleet—that all New England had hysterics every time a strange coal-barge was sighted on the sky-line, that the safe-deposit boxes of Boston were emptied and their contents transferred to Worcester, and that the Navy had to organize a patrol to save the coast towns from depopulation? Perhaps those Reds, atheists and pro-Germans remember it who also remember that during World War I the entire country went wild with fear of an enemy who, without the aid of divine intervention, obviously could not strike it a blow at all—and that the great moral victory was gained at last with the assistance of twenty-one allies and at odds of eight to one.

But the American Civil War remains? Does it, indeed? The almost unanimous opinion of the North, in 1861, was that it would be over after a few small battles; the first soldiers were actually enlisted for but three months. When, later on, it turned unexpectedly into a severe struggle, recruits had to be driven to the front by force, and the only Northerners remaining in favor of going on were Abraham Lincoln, a few ambitious generals and the profiteers. I turn to Dr. Eliot again. "In the closing year of the war," he says, "large portions of the Democratic party in the North *and of the Republican party,* advocated surrender to the Confederacy, *so downhearted were they.*" Downhearted at odds of three to one! The South was plainly more gallant, but even the gallantry of the South was largely illusory. The Confederate leaders, when the war began, adopted at once the traditional Anglo-Saxon device of seeking allies. They tried and expected to get the aid of England, and they actually came very near succeeding. When hopes in that direction began to fade (*i.e.,* when England concluded that tackling the North would be dangerous), the common people of the Confederacy threw up the sponge, and so the catastrophe, when it came at last, was mainly internal. The South failed to bring the quaking North to a standstill because, to borrow a phrase that Dr. Eliot uses in another connection, it "experienced a moral collapse of unprecedented depth and duration." The folks at home failed to support the troops in the field, and the troops in the field began to desert. Even so early as Shiloh, indeed, many Confederate regiments were already refusing to fight.

This reluctance for desperate chances and hard odds, so obvious in the military record of the English-speaking nations, is also conspicuous in times of peace. What a man of another and superior stock almost always notices, living among so-called Anglo-Saxons, is (*a*) their incapacity for prevailing in fair rivalry, either in trade, in the fine arts or in what is called learning—in brief, their general incompetence, and (*b*) their invariable effort to make up for this incapacity by putting some inequitable burden upon their rivals, usually by force. The Frenchman, I believe, is the worst of chauvinists, but once he admits a foreigner to his country he at least treats that foreigner fairly, and does not try to penalize him absurdly for his mere foreignness. The Anglo-Saxon American is always trying to do it; his history is a history of recurrent outbreaks of blind rage against peoples who have begun to worst him. Such movements would be inconceivable in an efficient and genuinely self-confident people, wholly assured of their superiority, and they would be equally inconceivable in a truly gallant and courageous people, disdaining unfair advantages and overwhelming odds. Theoretically launched against some imaginary inferiority in the non-Anglo-Saxon man, either as patriot, as democrat or as Christian, they are actually launched at his general superiority, his greater fitness to survive in the national environment. The effort is always to penalize him for winning in fair fight, to handicap him in such a manner that he will sink to the general level of the Anglo-Saxon population, and, if possible, even below it. Such devices, of course, never have the countenance of the Anglo-Saxon minority that is authentically superior, and hence self-confident and tolerant. But that minority is pathetically small, and it tends steadily to grow smaller and feebler. The communal laws and the communal *mores* are made by the folk, and they offer all the proof that is necessary, not only of its general inferiority, but also of its alarmed awareness of that inferiority. The normal American of the "pure-blooded" majority goes to rest every night with an uneasy feeling that there is a burglar under the bed, and he gets up every morning with a sickening fear that his underwear has been stolen.

This Anglo-Saxon of the great herd is, in many important respects, the least civilized of white men and the least capable of true civilization. His political ideas are crude and shallow. He is almost wholly devoid of esthetic feeling. The most elementary facts about the visible universe alarm him, and incite him to put them down. Educate him, make a professor of him, teach him how to express his soul, and he still remains palpably third-rate. He fears ideas almost more cravenly than he fears men. His blood, I believe, is running thin; perhaps it was not much to boast of at the start; in order that he may exercise any functions above those of a trader, a pedagogue or a mob orator, it needs the stimulus of other and less exhausted strains. The fact that they increase is the best hope of civilization in America. They shake the old race out of its spiritual lethargy, and introduce it to disquiet and experiment. They make for a free play of ideas. In opposing the process, whether in politics, in letters or in the ages-long struggle toward the truth, the prophets of Anglo-Saxon purity and tradition only make themselves ridiculous.

241

# 69

## Calvin Coolidge in the White House

National political life in the 1920s, to such Presidents as Warren Harding and Calvin Coolidge, was a straightforward and uncomplicated matter, only demanding an occasional adjustment of the rudder to keep the ship going smoothly on its course. In perspective, however, it is evident that inaction and complacency were hardly justified by existing economic and social conditions. In the economy, agriculture, for example, was in serious difficulty. Having overexpanded to satisfy the American and European demand generated by World War I, farmers were caught in a situation of rising costs and declining markets. Other sectors of the economy also needed assistance, and so did much of the unskilled part of the labor force. Moreover, as events would make all too clear, business was in dire need of regulation; when left to itself, it showed little restraint or a sense of the national welfare. Yet the nation's political leaders perceived little of this—and they talked even less about it.

What happened to the inquiring, critical spirit of the Progressive era? What replaced its outlook in the 1920s? The attitudes and actions of Calvin Coolidge as set down in his *Autobiography* may shed some light on these questions. For the President recorded here in simple language his guiding assumptions; and, to a surprising degree, they coincided with the sentiments of many of his fellow Americans.

## THE PRESIDENT'S AUTOBIOGRAPHY

It is a very old saying that you never can tell what you can do until you try. The more I see of life the more I am convinced of the wisdom of that observation.

Surprisingly few men are lacking in capacity, but they fail because they are lacking in application. Either they never learn how to work, or, having learned, they are too indolent to apply themselves with the seriousness and the attention that is necessary to solve important problems.

Reprinted with permission of John Coolidge from Calvin Coolidge, *Autobiography* (New York, 1931), 171–177, 182–185, 188–190, 200–204, 222–232, 234–235.

Any reward that is worth having only comes to the industrious. The success which is made in any walk of life is measured almost exactly by the amount of hard work that is put into it.

It has undoubtedly been the lot of every native boy of the United States to be told that he will some day be President. Nearly every young man who happens to be elected a member of his state legislature is pointed to by his friends and his local newspaper as on the way to the White House.

My own experience in this respect did not differ from that of others. But I never took such suggestions seriously, as I was convinced in my own mind that I was not qualified to fill the exalted office of President.

I had not changed this opinion after the November elections of 1919, when I was chosen Governor of Massachusetts for a second term by a majority which had only been exceeded in 1896.

When I began to be seriously mentioned by some of my friends at that time as the Republican candidate for President, it became apparent that there were many others who shared the same opinion as to my fitness which I had so long entertained.

But the coming national convention, acting in accordance with an unchangeable determination, took my destiny into its own hands and nominated me for Vice-President.

Had I been chosen for the first place, I could have accepted it only with a great deal of trepidation, but when the events of August, 1923, bestowed upon me the Presidential office, I felt at once that power had been given me to administer it. This was not any feeling of exclusiveness. While I felt qualified to serve, I was also well aware that there were many others who were better qualified. It would be my province to get the benefit of their opinions and advice. It is a great advantage to a President, and a major source of safety to the country, for him to know that he is not a great man. When a man begins to feel that he is the only one who can lead in this republic, he is guilty of treason to the spirit of our institutions.

On the night of August 2, 1923, I was awakened by my father coming up the stairs calling my name. I noticed that his voice trembled. As the only times I had ever observed that before were when death had visited our family, I knew that something of the gravest nature had occurred.

His emotion was partly due to the knowledge that a man whom he had met and liked was gone, partly to the feeling that must possess all of our citizens when the life of their President is taken from them.

But he must have been moved also by the thought of the many sacrifices he had made to place me where I was, the twenty-five-mile drives in storms and in zero weather over our mountain roads to carry me to the academy and all the tenderness and care he had lavished upon me in the thirty-eight years since the death of my mother in the hope that I might sometime rise to a position of importance, which he now saw realized.

He had been the first to address me as President of the United States. It was the culmination of the lifelong desire of a father for the success of his son.

243

He placed in my hands an official report and told me that President Harding had just passed away. My wife and I at once dressed.

Before leaving the room I knelt down and, with the same prayer with which I have since approached the altar of the church, asked God to bless the American people and give me power to serve them.

The oath was taken in what we always called the sitting room by the light of the kerosene lamp, which was the most modern form of lighting that had then reached the neighborhood. The Bible which had belonged to my mother lay on the table at my hand. It was not officially used, as it is not the practice in Vermont or Massachusetts to use a Bible in connection with the administration of an oath.

Where succession to the highest office in the land is by inheritance or appointment, no doubt there have been kings who have participated in the induction of their sons into their office, but in republics where the succession comes by an election I do not know of any other case in history where a father has administered to his son the qualifying oath of office which made him the chief magistrate of a nation. It seemed a simple and natural thing to do at the time, but I can now realize something of the dramatic force of the event.

My fundamental idea of both private and public business came first from my father. He had the strong New England trait of great repugnance at seeing anything wasted. He was a generous and charitable man, but he regarded waste as a moral wrong.

Wealth comes from industry and from the hard experience of human toil. To dissipate it in waste and extravagance is disloyalty to humanity. This is by no means a doctrine of parsimony. Both men and nations should live in accordance with their means and devote their substance not only to productive industry, but to the creation of the various forms of beauty and the pursuit of culture which give adornments to the art of life.

When I became President it was perfectly apparent that the key by which the way could be opened to national progress was constructive economy. Only by the use of that policy could the high rates of taxation, which were retarding our development and prosperity, be diminished, and the enormous burden of our public debt be reduced.

Without impairing the efficient operation of all the functions of the government, I have steadily and without ceasing pressed on in that direction. This policy has encouraged enterprise, made possible the highest rate of wages which has ever existed, returned large profits, brought to the homes of the people the greatest economic benefits they ever enjoyed, and given to the country as a whole an unexampled era of prosperity. This well-being of my country has given me the chief satisfaction of my administration.

While there have been newspapers which supported me, of course there have been others which opposed me, but they have usually been fair. I shall always consider it the highest tribute to my administration that the opposition have based so little of their criticism on what I have really said and done.

I have often said that there was no cause for feeling disturbed at being misrepresented in the press. It would be only when they began to say things detrimental to me which were true that I should feel alarm.

Perhaps one of the reasons I have been a target for so little abuse is because I have tried to refrain from abusing other people.

The words of the President have an enormous weight and ought not to be used indiscriminately.

It would be exceedingly easy to set the country all by the ears and foment hatreds and jealousies, which, by destroying faith and confidence, would help nobody and harm everybody. The end would be the destruction of all progress.

While every one knows that evils exist, there is yet sufficient good in the people to supply material for most of the comment that needs to be made.

The only way I know to drive out evil from the country is by the constructive method of filling it with good. The country is better off tranquilly considering its blessings and merits, and earnestly striving to secure more of them, than it would be in nursing hostile bitterness about its deficiencies and faults.

There is only one form of political strategy in which I have any confidence, and that is to try to do the right thing and sometimes be able to succeed.

Many people at once began to speak about nominating me to lead my party in the next campaign. I did not take any position in relation to their efforts. Unless the nomination came to me in a natural way, rather than as the result of an artificial campaign, I did not feel it would be of any value.

The people ought to make their choice on a great question of that kind without the influence that could be exerted by a President in office.

After the favorable reception which was given to my Message, I stated at the Gridiron Dinner that I should be willing to be a candidate. The convention nominated me the next June by a vote which was practically unanimous.

With the exception of the occasion of my notification, I did not attend any partisan meetings or make any purely political speeches during the campaign. I spoke several times at the dedication of a monument, the observance of the anniversary of an historic event, at a meeting of some commercial body, or before some religious gathering. The campaign was magnificently managed by William M. Butler and as it progressed the final result became more and more apparent.

My own participation was delayed by the death of my son Calvin, which occurred on the seventh of July. He was a boy of much promise, proficient in his studies, with a scholarly mind, who had just turned sixteen.

He had a remarkable insight into things.

The day I became President he had just started to work in a tobacco field When one of his fellow laborers said to him, "If my father was President I would not work in a tobacco field," Calvin replied, "If my father were your father, you would."

After he was gone some one sent us a letter he had written about the same time to a young man who had congratulated him on being the first boy in the land. To this he had replied that he had done nothing, and so did not merit the title, which should go to "some boy who had distinguished himself through his own actions."

We do not know what might have happened to him under other circumstances, but if I had not been President he would not have raised a blister on his toe, which resulted in blood poisoning, playing lawn tennis in the South Grounds.

In his suffering he was asking me to make him well. I could not.

When he went the power and the glory of the Presidency went with him.

The ways of Providence are often beyond our understanding. It seemed to me that the world had need of the work that it was probable he could do.

I do not know why such a price was exacted for occupying the White House.

Every day of the Presidential life is crowded with activities. When people not accustomed to Washington came to the office, or when I met them on some special occasion, they often remarked that it seemed to be my busy day, to which my stock reply came to be that all days were busy and there was little difference among them. It was my custom to be out of bed about six-thirty, except in the darkest mornings of winter. One of the doormen at the White House was an excellent barber, but I always preferred to shave myself with old-fashioned razors, which I knew how to keep in good condition. It was my intention to take a short walk before breakfast, which Mrs. Coolidge and I ate together in our rooms. For me there was fruit and about one-half cup of coffee, with a home-made cereal made from boiling together two parts of unground wheat with one part of rye. To this was added a roll and a strip of bacon, which went mostly to our dogs.

Soon after eight found me dictating in the White House library in preparation for some public utterance. This would go on for more than an hour, after which I began to receive callers at the office. Most of these came by appointment, but in addition to the average of six to eight who were listed there would be as many more from my Cabinet and the Congress, to whom I was always accessible. Each one came to me with a different problem requiring my decision, which was usually made at once. About twelve-fifteen those began to be brought in who were to be somewhat formally presented. At twelve-thirty the doors were opened, and a long line passed by who wished merely to shake hands with the President. One one occasion I shook hands with nineteen hundred in thirty-four minutes, which is probably my record. Instead of a burden, it was a pleasure and a relief to meet people in that way and listen to their greeting, which was often a bendiction. It was at this same hour that the numerous groups assembled in the South Grounds, where I joined them for the photographs used for news purposes and permanent mementoes of their White House visit.

Lunch came at one o'clock, at which we usually had guests. It made an opportunity for giving our friends a little more attention than could be extended through a mere handshake. About an hour was devoted to rest before returning to the office, where the afternoon was reserved for attention to the immense number of documents which pass over the desk of the President. These were all cleaned up each day. Before dinner another walk was in order, followed by exercises on some of the vibrating machines kept in my room. We gathered at the dinner table at seven o'clock and within three-quarters of an hour work would be resumed with my stenographer to continue until about ten o'clock.

At ten-thirty on Tuesdays and Fridays the Cabinet meetings were held. These were always very informal. Each member was asked if he had any problem he wished to lay before the President. When I first attended with President Harding at the beginning of a new administration these were rather numerous. Later, they decreased, as each member felt better able to solve his own problems. After entire freedom of discussion, but always without a vote of any kind, I was accustomed to announce what the decision should be. There never ought to be and never were marked differences of opinion in my Cabinet. As their duties were not to advise each other, but to advise the President, they could not disagree among themselves. I rarely failed to accept their recommendations. Sometimes they wished for larger appropriations than the state of the Treasury warranted, but they all cooperated most sincerely in the policy of economy and were content with such funds as I could assign to them.

The Congress has sometimes been a sore trial to Presidents. I did not find it so in my case. Among them were men of wonderful ability and veteran experience. I think they made their decisions with an honest purpose to serve their country. The membership of the Senate changed very much by reason of those who sacrificed themselves for public duty. Of all public officials with whom I have ever been acquainted, the work of a Senator of the United States is by far the most laborious. About twenty of them died during the eight years I was in Washington.

Sometimes it would seem for a day that either the House or the Senate had taken some unwise action, but if it was not corrected on the floor where it occurred it was usually remedied in the other chamber. I always found the members of both parties willing to confer with me and disposed to treat my recommendations fairly. Most of the differences could be adjusted by personal discussion. Sometimes I made an appeal direct to the country by stating my position at the newspaper conferences. I adopted that course in relation to the Mississippi Flood Control Bill. As it passed the Senate it appeared to be much too extravagant in its rule of damages and its proposed remedy. The press began a vigorous discussion of the subject, which caused the House greatly to modify the bill, and in conference a measure that was entirely fair and moderate was adopted. On other occasions I appealed to the country more privately, enlisting the influence of labor and trade organizations upon the Congress in behalf of some measures in which I was interested. That was done in the case of the tax bill of 1928. As it passed the House, the reductions were so large that the revenue necessary to meet the public expenses would not have been furnished. By quietly making this known to the Senate, and enlisting support for that position among their constituents, it was possible to secure such modification of the measure that it could be adopted without greatly endangering the revenue.

But a President cannot, with success, constantly appeal to the country. After a time he will get no response. The people have their own affairs to look after and can not give much attention to what the Congress is doing. If he takes a position, and stands by it, ultimately it will be adopted. Most of the policies set out in my first Annual Message have become law, but it took several years to get action on some of them.

One of the most perplexing and at the same time most important functions of the President is the making of appointments. In some few cases he acts alone, but usually they are made with the advice and consent of the Senate. It is the practice to consult Senators of his own party before making an appointment from their state. In choosing persons for service over the whole or any considerable portion of a single state, it is customary to rely almost entirely on the party Senators from that state for recommendations. It is not possible to find men who are perfect. Selection always has to be limited to human beings, whatever choice is made. It is therefore always possible to point out defects. The supposition that no one should be appointed who has had experience in the field which he is to supervise is extremely detrimental to the public service. An Interstate Commerce Commissioner is much better qualified, if he knows something about transportation. A Federal Trade Commissioner can render much better service if he has had a legal practice which extended into large business transactions. The assertion of those who contend that persons accepting a government appointment would betray their trust in favor of former associates can be understood only on the supposition that those who make it feel that their own tenure of public office is for the purpose of benefiting themselves and their friends.

Every one knows that where the treasure is, there will the heart be also. When a man has invested his personal interest and reputation in the conduct of a public office, if he goes wrong it will not be because of former relations, but because he is a bad man. The same interests that reached him would reach any bad man, irrespective of former life history. What we need in appointive positions is men of knowledge and experience who have sufficient character to resist temptations. If that standard is maintained, we need not be concerned about their former activities. If it is not maintained, all the restrictions of their past employment that can be conceived will be of no avail.

The more experience I have had in making appointments, the more I am convinced that attempts to put limitations on the appointing power are a mistake. It should be possible to choose a well qualified person wherever he can be found. When restrictions are placed on residence, occupation, or profession, it almost always happens that some one is found who is universally admitted to be the best qualified, but who is eliminated by the artificial specifications. So long as the Senate has the power to reject nominations, there is little danger that a President would abuse his authority if he were given the largest possible freedom in his choices. The public service would be improved if all vacancies were filled by simply appointing the best ability and character that can be found. That is what is done in private business. The adoption of any other course handicaps the government in all its operations.

In determining upon all his actions, however, the President has to remember that he is dealing with two different minds. One is the mind of the country, largely intent upon its own personal affairs, and, while not greatly interested in the government, yet desirous of seeing it conducted in an orderly and dignified manner for the advancement of the public welfare. Those who compose this mind wish to have the country prosperous and are opposed to unjust taxation and public extravagance. At the same time they have a patriotic pride which moves them with so great a desire to see things well done that they are willing to pay for it. They gladly contribute their money to place the United States in the lead. In general, they represent the public opinion of the land.

But they are unorganized, formless, and inarticulate. Against a compact and well drilled minority they do not appear to be very effective. They are nevertheless the great power in our government. I have constantly appealed to them and have seldom failed in enlisting their support. They are the court of last resort and their decisions are final.

They are, however, the indirect rather than the direct power. The immediate authority with which the President has to deal is vested in the political mind. In order to get things done he has to work through that agency. Some of our Presidents have appeared to lack comprehension of the political mind. Although I have been associated with it for many years, I always found difficulty in understanding it. It is a strange mixture of vanity and timidity, of an obsequious attitude at one time and a delusion of grandeur at another time, of the most selfish preferment combined with the most sacrificing patriotism. The political mind is the product of men in public life who have been twice spoiled. They have been spoiled with praise and they have been spoiled with abuse. With them nothing is natural, everything is artificial. A few rare souls escape these influences and maintain a vision and a judgment that are unimpaired. They are a great comfort to every President and a great service to their country. But they are not sufficient in number so that the public business can be transacted like a private business.

It is because in their hours of timidity the Congress becomes subservient to the importunities of organized minorities that the President comes more and more to stand as the champion of the rights of the whole country. Organizing such minorities has come to be a well-recognized industry at Washington. They are oftentimes led by persons of great ability, who display much skill in bringing their influences to bear on the Congress. They have ways of securing newspaper publicity, deluging Senators and Representatives with petitions and overwhelming them with imprecations that are oftentimes decisive in securing the passage of bills. While much of this legislation is not entirely bad, almost all of it is excessively expensive. If it were not for the rules of the House and the veto power of the President, within two years these activities would double the cost of the government.

Under our system the President is not only the head of the government, but is also the head of his party. The last twenty years have witnessed a decline in party spirit and a distinct weakening in party loyalty. While an independent attitude on the part of the citizen is not without a certain public advantage, yet it is necessary under our form of government to have political parties. Unless some one is a partisan, no one can be an independent. The Congress is organized entirely in accordance with party policy. The parties appeal to the voters in behalf of their platforms. The people make their choice on those issues. Unless those who are elected on the same party platform associate themselves together to carry out its provisions, the election becomes a mockery. The independent voter who has joined with others in placing a party nominee in office finds his efforts were all in vain, if the person he helps elect refuses or neglects to keep the platform pledges of his party.

Many occasions arise in the Congress when party lines are very properly disregarded, but if there is to be a reasonable government proceeding in accordance with the express mandate of the people, and not merely at the whim of those who happen to be victorious at the polls, on all the larger and important issues there must be party solidarity. It is the business of the President as party leader to do the best he can to see that the declared party platform purposes are translated into legislative and administrative action. Oftentimes I secured support from those without my party and had opposition from those within my party, in attempting to keep my platform pledges.

Such a condition is entirely anomalous. It leaves the President as the sole repository of party responsibility. But it is one of the reasons that the Presidential office has grown in popular estimation and favor, while the Congress has declined. The country feels that the President is willing to assume responsibility, while his party in the Congress is not. I have never felt it was my duty to attempt to coerce Senators or Representatives, or to take reprisals. The people sent them to Washington. I felt I had discharged my duty when I had done the best I could with them. In this way I avoided almost entirely a personal opposition, which I think was of more value to the country than to attempt to prevail through arousing personal fear.

Under our system it ought to be remembered that the power to initiate policies has to be centralized somewhere. Unless the party leaders exercising it can depend on loyalty and organization support, the party in which it is reposed will become entirely ineffective. A party which is ineffective will soon be discarded. If a party is to endure as a serviceable instrument of government for the country, it must possess and display a healthy spirit of party loyalty. Such a manifestation in the Congress would do more than anything else to rehabilitate it in the esteem and confidence of the country.

All of these trials and encouragements come to each President. It is impossible to explain them. Even after passing through the Presidential office, it still remains a great mystery. Why one person is selected for it and many others are rejected can not be told. Why people respond as they do to its influence seems to be beyond inquiry. Any man who has been placed in the White House can not feel that it is the result of his own exertions or his own merit. Some power outside and beyond him becomes manifest through him. As he contemplates the workings of his office, he comes to realize with an increasing sense of humility that he is but an instrument in the hands of God.

## PART NINE

# The End of the Old Order, 1929–1947

In 1929 the bubble burst. The stock market, which seemed to Americans of the golden era destined to spiral ever upward, suddenly collapsed. Respected leaders insisted that the economy was fundamentally sound and was only undergoing healthy readjustment, but stock prices continued to plunge downward and wiped out hundreds of thousands of investors. By January 1933 the typical stock sold for only one-fifth of its value on the eve of the October 1929 panic.

Only a modest fraction of the American population actually owned securities, but reverberations of the crisis were felt in every home. Decisions made on Wall Street determined the level of production and employment in the entire economy, and disaster there meant trouble everywhere. Wages plummeted, unemployment shot upward, production fell, prices dropped. In less than four years wages and farm income were halved and unemployment had tripled. One-quarter of the labor force was out of work, and only one-fourth of the jobless were covered by existing public or private relief programs. Municipal garbage dumps, accordingly, swarmed with hungry people; in Philadelphia a family was found subsisting on a diet of dandelions.

The Depression, and the failure of the Hoover administration to arrest its course, provoked a massive political upheaval. Franklin D. Roosevelt, swept into the Presidency in 1932, pledged to bring "a New Deal" to the American people. The extent to which he succeeded is still being debated by historians, but there can be no debate about the political achievement of the New Deal. It forged a new political coalition that brought an end to more than three decades of Republican ascendancy in national politics, and made the Democratic party the majority party in the United States for a generation to come. Prior to the New Deal, farmers outside the South and Negroes leaned strongly to the Republicans, and there was significant GOP strength in the ranks of organized labor and recent immigrant groups. John L. Lewis and many other AF of L leaders threw their support to the Republicans in the 1920s; Fiorello LaGuardia was a Republican. Bitter memories of the Depression and personal attachment to the charismatic FDR brought many of these elements into the Democratic camp and kept them there.

The shock of the economic collapse weakened traditional American assumptions about rugged individualism. "Success is not gained by leaning upon government to solve all the problems before us," declared Hoover in 1931. "That way leads to enervation of will and destruction of character." This belief was repudiated by a large majority of the electorate in 1932, and there followed a wave of new public programs to stimulate, regulate, and reform the sagging economy. The banking system was rearranged; the stock market was subjected to a variety of new restraints; industrial prices and wages were regulated; labor was assisted in the struggle to win recognition and the right of collective bargaining; farmers and homeowners burdened by debt were granted credit; federal relief, public works, and unemployment insurance programs eased the difficulties of the jobless. Some of the hastily planned New Deal efforts proved ineffective, and some were declared unconstitutional by the conservative Supreme Court. But the principle of federal responsibility for the economic welfare of every citizen was securely established.

A measure of recovery had been attained by 1935, and the administration was forced to make some difficult political choices. Until that year there had been a program to benefit virtually every interest, and the President had support throughout the society. By 1935 the honeymoon was over. There were complaints from the left, not so much from the tiny Socialist and Communist sects as from Senator Huey Long, Father Coughlin, and Dr. Francis Townsend, who insisted that the ordinary American was still prey to economic insecurity and that some sharing of wealth was required. A secret poll conducted by the Democratic National Committee in 1935 indicated that such discontent might draw enough votes to cost FDR the election in 1936. At the same time, the Republican opposition and business leaders began to argue that the New Deal had already gone too far. These pressures induced Roosevelt to launch a somewhat more radical "second New Deal." The Wealth Tax Act of 1935 provided a graduated income tax; though its schedules were only mildly progressive, some saw in it the beginnings of a "soak the rich" tax policy. The Wagner-Connery Labor Relations bill of the same year put the federal government more squarely behind the cause of organized labor than ever before, and enabled organizers of the newly formed CIO to exhort the unorganized "FDR wants you to join the union." A federally financed social-security system, providing old-age pensions, aid to dependent children, and unemployment insurance marked the beginnings of the modern American welfare state.

None of these reforms overcame the economic stagnation that plagued the United States in the Depression era, nor did the administration's cautious experiments with pump-priming and deficit financing. John Maynard Keynes had not fully outlined his theory of how fiscal policy could be used to combat business fluctuations until 1936, and even after that New Dealers left the federal budget unbalanced only when they were unable to do otherwise. A sharp cut in federal spending in 1937 provoked another downturn. Unemployment levels shot upward and remained high until rising military expenditures took up the slack toward the end of the decade.

Despite the efforts of New Deal reformers, there remained millions of desperately poor people in America. Few New Deal measures reached to the very bottom of the social order. Conservative political pressures led to the exclusion of many of the disadvantaged from much of the new social legislation. The share of the national income going to the bottom fifth of the population did not increase significantly during the New Deal years. The concentration of wealth in the hands of the very rich diminished modestly by some measures, but the gains went to groups in the middle brackets. It took the tight full employment of the booming World War II economy to lift up the very poor, and then the improvement was modest and short-lived.

American intellectuals of the Depression years were coming to think in increasingly collectivist terms and were more inclined to view society as a struggle between economic interests and classes. Some mechanically applied Marxist ideas to the analysis of American capitalism but more interesting and independent social criticism came from the pens of theologian Reinhold Niebuhr, sociologists Robert and Helen Lynd, and lawyer Thurman Arnold. Economist Paul Douglas, later a distinguished United States Senator from Illinois, spoke for many of these when he wrote in 1933: "Along with the Rooseveltian program must go . . . the organization of those who are at present weak, and who need to acquire that which the world respects, namely, power. Unless these things are done, we are likely to find the permanent benefits of Rooseveltian liberalism to be as illusory as were those of the Wilsonian Era."

By this criterion the New Deal was at best a moderate success. The most significant shift in power relations in American society that it produced, or helped to produce, was the spread of industrial unionism in the mass production industries, automobiles, steel, and rubber, in the latter half of the decade. The semiskilled operatives at Ford Motors, U.S. Steel, and Goodyear's had no place in the American Federation of Labor, which by this time had shed all pretension to any objectives more visionary than better wages for the elite of skilled craftsmen within it. Aided by the National Labor Relations Board, the investigations of the LaFollette Committee, the sympathy of liberal public officials like Governor Frank Murphy of Michigan, and the tactic of well-planned sit-down strikes, the CIO won a series of dramatic victories and gave millions of previously powerless men some control over their wages and working conditions. The new CIO unions became a

253

key source of Democratic strength, and a strong liberal influence on the national scene.

Observers who saw the thrust of labor organization as a challenge to American capitalism and the beginnings of class warfare, however, were mistaken. If manual laborers were more inclined to vote Democratic than their bosses, the class polarization of American parties was never as sharp as in many European countries, nor was the Democratic party comparable to European labor, Social-Democratic, or Communist organizations. The first efforts by social scientists like A. W. Jones to study the nature of the American class structure revealed a class-stratified society, but they also showed that few Americans on the lower rungs of the class ladder felt that the entire system was unfair and in need of radical alteration. This was not surprising, for even in the tight Depression years the social system retained considerable fluidity. Large numbers of Americans had experienced social mobility above the level of their father's occupations and their own first jobs. The closing of the "golden door" to European immigrants in the 1920s had cut off a classic source of fluidity, but the continued influx of rural people, especially from the South, had much the same effect. The Depression slowed the process of social circulation somewhat, and inspired class resentments, but during World War II it reached normal levels again. American workers were sufficiently class-conscious to join unions, to vote heavily Democratic, and to insist that the government intervene in the workings of the private enterprise system when it failed to function efficiently; they were not, however, disposed to think that the concentration of great wealth and economic power in private hands was fundamentally inequitable. However inadequate and incomplete the New Deal was, it did enough to prevent that.

Problems of foreign affairs did not intrude much into the American consciousness in the early Depression years. The isolationist mood was dominant, symbolized by neutrality legislation that forbade shipments to belligerents in time of war, outlawed travel by American nationals on belligerent vessels, and prevented the granting of commercial credits to warring parties. All this was intended to prevent the entanglements that had led us into what many citizens regarded as a tragically mistaken world war two decades earlier. The coming to power of Fascist regimes in Italy, Germany, and Spain, however, and of a military clique in Japan, disturbed Americans and eroded isolationist assumptions. Many felt moral outrage at the domestic brutalities of the totalitarian regimes, for instance, Hitler's persecution of the Jews. Some were concerned as well about the aggressively nationalist and expansionist foreign policies of Germany, Italy, and Japan, either out of the conviction that the Axis countries would ultimately seek to conquer America as well, or because such expansion challenged the influence and power of the United States and her allies in Europe and the underdeveloped world. Few Americans were sympathetic to the internal policies of the totalitarian powers, but there was deep and bitter division over the dangers of Fascist expansionism. Many believed that whatever happened across the seas, "fortress America," was safe. There was, in addition, serious questioning of the premise that the existing international status quo was a just one, and of the corollary that the demands of the dissatisfied "have-not" powers were so unjustified that we should risk war to deny them. The isolationist "America First" movement was consequently a potent force in national politics, and both FDR and his Republican opponent in 1940 were forced to pledge that no American troops would be sent overseas. These policy disagreements came to a sudden end in December 1941, when the Japanese attack at Pearl Harbor united the American public in opposition to the Axis powers, but the troubling questions that had been raised about America's role in the world would soon recur.

# 70

# From the Jazz Age
# to the Thirties

In his essay "The Literary Consequences of the Crash," Edmund Wilson sketches the intellectual climate of the 1920s and suggests some of the influences that drove American intellectuals to the left after the collapse in 1929. Wilson, perhaps America's most distinguished literary critic in this century, was on the staff of the *New Republic* throughout the period discussed in this essay. In 1932 he was one of several dozen prominent American writers to sign the manifesto "Culture and the Crisis," an endorsement of the Communist Party's candidates in the elections of that year. His generalizations about the alienation of the intellectuals apply more to writers and artists than to intellectuals of other types—historians and social scientists, for example. The latter felt less of a revulsion against the material achievements of American civilization, and were inclined to believe that the spread of science and technology would foster social progress. Both groups, however, were drawn together by the crash and stimulated to consider plans for the radical reconstruction of American society. The candidates running on the Socialist or Communist tickets never seriously threatened the political dominance of the two major parties, but pressure from disaffected intellectuals was an important influence upon the New Deal.

## THE LITERARY CONSEQUENCES
## OF THE CRASH
### *Edmund Wilson*

Even before the stock market crash of October, 1929, a kind of nervous dissatisfaction and apprehension had begun to manifest itself in American intellectual life. The liberating movement of the twenties had by that time accomplished its work of discrediting the gentility and Puritanism of the later nineteenth century; the orgy of spending of the Boom was becoming more and more grotesque, and the Jazz Age was ending in hysteria. The principal points of

Reprinted with permission of the author from *The Shores of Light* (New York: Farrar, Straus, and Company, Inc., 1952), 492–499.

view of this period I tried, after the crash, to sum up in an article of March 23, 1932:

The attitudes of the decade that followed the war, before the depression set in, already seem a long way off:

The attitude of the Menckenian gentleman, ironic, beer-loving and "civilized," living principally on the satisfaction of feeling superior to the broker and enjoying the debauchment of American life as a burlesque show or three-ring circus; the attitude of old-American-stock smugness, with its drawing aloof from the rabble in the name of old Uncle Gilead Pilcher who was Governor of Connecticut or Grandfather Timothy Merrymount who was killed in the Civil War—though the parvenus kept crashing the gate so fast, while the prosperity boom was on, that it was becoming harder and harder to get one's aloofness properly recognized; the liberal attitude that American capitalism was going to show a new wonder to the world by gradually and comfortably socializing itself and that we should just have to respect it in the meantime, taking a great interest in Dwight W. Morrow and Owen D. Young; the attitude of trying to get a kick out of the sheer size and energy of American enterprises, irrespective of what they were aiming at; the attitude of proudly withdrawing and cultivating a refined sensibility or of losing oneself completely in abstruse intellectual pursuits—scholastic philosophy, symbolic logic or metaphysical physics; the attitude of letting oneself be carried along by the mad hilarity and heartbreak of jazz, living only for the excitement of the evening; the attitude of keeping one's mind and morals impregnably disinfected with the feeble fascism-classicism of humanism.

I have in one mood or another myself felt some sympathy with all of these different attitudes—with the single exception of humanism; and they have all, no doubt, had their validity for certain people, for special situations. Yet today they all look rather queer: they are no use in our present predicament, and we can see how superficial they were. We can see now that they all represented attempts on the part of the more thoughtful Americans to reconcile themselves to a world dominated by salesmen and brokers—and that they all involved compromises with the salesman and the broker. Mencken and Nathan laughed at the broker, but they justified the system which produced him and they got along with him very well, provided he enjoyed George Moore and had pretensions to a taste in liquor; the jazz-age romantics spent the broker's money as speedily and wildly as possible and tried to laugh off the office and the factory with boyish and girlish jokes; the old-American-stockers sniffed at him, but though they salved their consciences thus, they were usually glad to get in on any of his good things that were going; the liberals, who had been vaguely unhappy, later became vaguely resigned and could never bring themselves to the point of serious quarrelling with him; the poets and philosophers hid from him—and the physicists grew more and more mystical in the laboratories subsidized mainly by the profits from industrial investments; the humanists, in volume after volume, endeavored by sheer hollow thunder to induce people to find in the stock exchange the harmony and dignity of the Parthenon.

I did not include in this catalogue a cult that was spreading in New York and that had converts in and around the *New Republic:* that of the Russo-Greek charlatan Gurdjieff, who undertook to renovate the personalities of discontented well-to-do persons. He combined making his clients uncomfortable in various gratuitous ways—such as waking them up in the middle of the night and training them to perform grotesque dances—with reducing them to a condition of complete docility, in which they would hold, at a signal, any position, however awkward, that they happened to be in at the moment, They were promised, if they proved themselves worthy of it, an ultimate initiation into the mysteries of an esoteric doctrine. Gurdjieff's apostle in the United States was the English ex-journalist A. R. Orage, a funereal and to me a distasteful person, who drilled his pupils, not in dancing, but in a kind of dialectic and who acquired at one time a considerable influence over the mind of Herbert Croly, whose inhibited personality and unsatisfied religious instincts laid him open to the lures of a cult that pretended to liberate the mind and to put one in touch with some higher power. But Croly was a fastidious man, and in the long run he found Orage grating. I was myself the object of several attempts to recruit me to the Orage group, but the only interchange of influence that took place between Orage and me consisted of my once persuading him to go to the National Winter Garden; when I next saw him, he told me with a severity that suggested a sense of outrage that he had not enjoyed it at all. Gurdjieff, however, whom I never met, had apparently a rogue's sense of humor. A young man in the office, a bishop's son who had lost his faith and was groping for something to take its place, told me of the banquets of roast sheep or goat, served in great pots in the Caucasian style and eaten with the fingers, to which Gurdjieff would invite his disciples and at which he would have read aloud to them a book he had written called *A Criticism of the Life of Man: Beëlzebub's Tale to His Grandson*. "It sounds as if it had been written," said this neophyte, "just on purpose to bore you to death. Everybody listens in silence, but every now and then Gurdjieff will suddenly burst out laughing—just roaring—nobody knows about what."

I did not read *Beëlzebub's Tale*, but I did read *Das Kapital*. Not that I want to compare the two works, but there *was* a certain similarity in the way in which people then approached them; and I was surprised to find that an apparently social evening that would turn out to be a conspiracy to involve one in some Communist organization resembled a dinner I had once attended at which I was chilled to discover that the springes of Orage had been laid for me—and these both recalled to me an earlier occasion on which a literary conversation, in the rooms of the proselytizing rector of the Episcopal Church at Princeton, had been prodded by amusing remarks in the direction of the Christian faith. People did want faiths and churches badly, and though I am good at resisting churches, I caught a wave from the impulsion of the Marxist faith.

The stock market crash was to count for us almost like a rending of the earth in preparation for the Day of Judgment. In my articles of the months just before it, I had often urged writers to acquaint themselves with "the realities of our contemporary life," to apply themselves to "the study of contemporary reality," etc. I myself had not exercised enough insight to realize that American "prosperity" was an inflation that was due to burst. I had, however, become aware that we liberals of the *New Republic* were not taking certain recent happenings so seriously as we should. The execution of Sacco and Vanzetti in August, 1927, had made liberals lose their bearings. During the months while the case was working up to its climax, Herbert Croly had been away in Honolulu attending a conference called by the Institute of Pacific Relations. When he returned, I was surprised to learn that he did not entirely approve of the way in which we had handled the case. Croly's method of commenting on current events was impersonal and very abstract; and, in his absence, we had given way to the impulse to print certain articles which were certainly, for the *New Republic*, unusually concrete and militant. I first became aware of a serious divergence between my own point of view and Croly's when I was talking with him one day about a leader called *A Nation of Foreigners* that I wrote for the paper in October. He did approve of this editorial, but for reasons that put me in a false position. My article had dealt with the futility of attempting to identify "Americanism" with the interests and ideas of the Anglo-Saxon element in the United States, pointing out that, in this case, the Irish, who had been snubbed by the Anglo-Saxon Bostonians, had combined with them in the most wolfish way to persecute the immigrant Italians; and I discovered that Croly was pleased at my treating the subject from this angle rather than from that of class animosities. This class aspect he wanted to deny; it was one of the assumptions of his political thinking—I had not then read *The Promise of American Life*—that the class struggle should not, and in its true form did not, occur in the United States.

I had been running the literary department, and this was my first excursion on the political side of the paper, which Croly had kept strictly in line with his own very definite ideas. Sometime in the later months of 1928, he had the first of several strokes, and was never able again to perform his full functions as editor-in-chief. When he died in May, 1930, the paper was carried on by the editors as a group, with no one in Croly's position, and we had—rather difficult with men of conflicting opinions and temperaments, with nobody to make final decisions—to work out a policy of our own. I had been troubled by another incident that took place in the autumn of 1929. The bitter and violent Gastonia strike of the textile workers in North Carolina had been going on ever since spring. It was the first major labor battle conducted by a Communist union. Sixteen union members, including three women, were being tried for the murder of a chief of police, who had invaded without a warrant the tent-colony in which the strikers had been living; and the death penalty was being asked for all of them except the women. Feeling on both sides had been roused to the point of ferocity—we were not then familiar with the Communists' habit of manufacturing martyrs—and, after the execution of Sacco and Vanzetti, one was apprehensive of another judicial lynching. John Dos Passos and Mary Heaton Vorse both asked the *New Republic* to send them to report on Gastonia, but both were thought to be too far to the Left to be reliable from our point of view. "The liberals," Dos Passos said to me, "are all so neurotic about Communists!" This was perfectly true; and the pressure on us to do something about Gastonia had at the time almost no effect. The young man who had been hooked by Orage—who had had no experience of labor disputes—was going down to a fashionable wedding at Asheville, not far from Gastonia, and he was asked to drop in at the seat of trouble. When he came back, this young man reported that there was nothing of interest going on. I do not know whom he could have talked to. He had been in Gastonia on the very day, September 14, when the hostilities were coming to a climax. In an attempt to prevent a union meeting, an armed mob had fired on unarmed strikers and had killed a woman named Ella May

259

Wiggins, a widow with five children, who had written songs for the strikers and was extremely popular among them. Her death gave the Communists a battle-cry and the strikers an unforgettable grievance. It was obvious that the *New Republic*, which was supposed to cover labor sympathetically, was falling down on this part of its program.

The next month the slump began, and, as conditions grew worse and worse and President Hoover, unable to grasp what had happened, made no effort to deal with the breakdown, a darkness seemed to descend. Yet, to the writers and artists of my generation who had grown up in the Big Business era and had always resented its barbarism, its crowding-out of everything they cared about, these years were not depressing but stimulating. One couldn't help being exhilarated at the sudden unexpected collapse of that stupid gigantic fraud. It gave us a new sense of freedom; and it gave us a new sense of power to find ourselves still carrying on while the bankers, for a change, were taking a beating. With a businessman's president in the White House, who kept telling us, when he told us anything, that the system was perfectly sound, who sent General Douglas MacArthur to burn the camp of the unemployed war veterans who had come to appeal to Washington, we wondered about the survival of republican American institutions; and we became more and more impressed by the achievements of the Soviet Union, which could boast that its industrial and financial problems were carefully studied by the government, and that it was able to avert such crises. We overdid both these tendencies; but the slump was like a flood or an earthquake, and it was long before many things righted themselves.

# 71

# A Christian Marxist Critique
# of Liberal Rationalism

The tradition of preaching the "social gospel," of relating religion to the burning social issues of the day, began in late nineteenth-century America. Reinhold Niebuhr, a brilliant young minister and theologian, gave it new relevance in the 1930s, when he blended Christian pessimism about human rationality and Marxist notions of class self-interest into a potent attack upon many of the assumptions of American culture. In books like *Moral Man and Immoral Society* (1932) and in numerous essays for religious and political journals like that reprinted here, Niebuhr called attention to glaring social injustice and argued that it was an integral, not an accidental, feature of capitalist civilization. His judgments that "capitalism is dying" and "liberalism in politics is a spent force" proved mistaken, but it is revealing of the depth of the crisis of American society in the early Depression years that they were widely shared by responsible thinkers.

## AFTER CAPITALISM—WHAT?
### *Reinhold Niebuhr*

The following analysis of American social and political conditions is written on the assumption that capitalism is dying and with the conviction that it ought to die. It is dying because it is a contracting economy which is unable to support the necessities of an industrial system that requires mass production for its maintenance, and because it disturbs the relations of an international economic system with the anarchy of nationalistic politics. It ought to die because it is unable to make the wealth created by modern technology available to all who participate in the productive process on terms of justice.

The conviction that capitalism is dying and that it ought to die gives us no clue to the method of its passing. Will it perish in another world war? Or in the collapse of the credit structure through which it manipulates its various functions? Will it, perhaps, give way to a new social order created by the political power of those who have been disinherited by it? Or will it be destroyed by a revolution? These questions are difficult to answer for any portion of Western civilization, and they

From "After Capitalism—What?", *The World Tomorrow*, March 1, 1933, 203–205. Reprinted by permission of Reinhold Niebuhr.

are particularly puzzling when directed to the American scene. We may believe that the basic forces moving in modern industrial society are roughly similar in all nations. Yet we cannot evade the fact that various nations reveal a wide variety of unique social and economic characteristics and that our own nation is particularly unique in some of the aspects of its political and economic life. Our wealth has been greater than that of any modern nation, the ideals of a pioneer democracy have retarded the formation of definite classes, the frontier spirit belongs to so recent a past that its individualism is not yet dissipated, and the complete preoccupation of the nation with its engineering task to the exclusion of political and social problems makes us singularly incompetent as a people in the field of politics. All these factors, and some others which might be mentioned, warn the prophet to be circumspect in applying generalizations derived from European conditions to our situation. It is therefore advisable to divide our problem of analysis by considering first those aspects of the situation about which generalizations equally applicable to Europe and America can be made; the uniquely American aspects may then be seen in clearer light.

The most generally applicable judgment which can be made is that capitalism will not reform itself from within. There is nothing in history to support the thesis that a dominant class ever yields its position or privileges in society because its rule has been convicted of ineptness or injustices. Those who still regard this as possible are rationalists and moralists who have only a slight understanding of the stubborn inertia and blindness of collective egoism.

Politically this judgment implies that liberalism in politics is a spent force. In so far as liberalism is based upon confidence in the ability and willingness of rational and moral individuals to change the basis of society, it has suffered disillusion in every modern nation. As the social struggle becomes more sharply defined, the confused liberals drift reluctantly into the camp of reaction and the minority of clear-sighted intellectuals and idealists are forced either to espouse the cause of radicalism or to escape to the bleachers and become disinterested observers. The liberal middle ground has been almost completely wiped out in Germany. It is held today only by the Catholic party, a unique phenomenon in Western politics. In England only the free-trade liberals who managed to extricate themselves from the Tory embrace and the quite lonely and slightly pathetic Mr. Lloyd George stand in the liberal position. The English liberals who interpreted their position as a championship of the community of consumers against warring camps of producers have had to learn that the stakes which men have in the productive process outweigh their interests as consumers. Mr. Roosevelt's effort at, or pretension to, liberalizing the Democratic Party may be regarded as a belated American effort to do what Europe has proved to be impossible. Equally futile will be the efforts of liberals who stand to the left of Mr. Roosevelt and who hope to organize a party which will give the feverish American patient pills of diluted socialism coated with liberalism, in the hope that his aversion to bitter pills will thus be circumvented.

All this does not mean that intellectual and moral idealism are futile. They are needed to bring decency and fairness into any system of society; for no basic reorganization of society will ever guarantee the preservation of humaneness if good men do not preserve it. Furthermore, the intelligence of a dominant group will determine in what measure it will yield in time under pressure or to what degree it will defend its entrenched positions so uncompromisingly that an orderly retreat becomes impossible and a disorderly rout envelops the whole of society in chaos. That ought to be high enough stake for those of us to play for who are engaged in the task of education and moral suasion among the privileged. If such conclusions seems unduly cynical they will seem so only because the moral idealists of the past century, both religious and rational, have been unduly sentimental in their estimates of human nature. Perhaps it will be permitted the writer to add, by way of parenthesis, that he has been greatly instructed by the number of letters which have come to him in late months complaining that a religious radical ought not to give up his faith in human nature so completely lest he betray thereby his lack of faith in the divine. Classical religion has always spoken rather unequivocally of the deprivity of human nature, a conclusion at which it arrived by looking at human nature from the perspective of the divine. It is one of the strange phenomena of our culture that an optimistic estimate of human nature has been made the basis of theistic theologies.

Next to the futility of liberalism we may set down the inevitability of fascism as a practical certainty in every Western nation. A disintegrating social system will try to save itself by closing ranks and eliminating the anarchy within itself. It will thus undoubtedly be able to perpetuate itself for several decades. It will not finally succeed because it will have no way of curing the two basic defects of capitalism, inequality of consumption and international anarchy. It will probably succeed longer in Italy and Germany than in America, because fascism in those countries derives its strength from a combination of the military and capitalistic castes. The military caste has a greater interest in avoiding revolution than in preserving the privileges of the capitalists. It may therefore be counted upon to circumscribe these privileges more rigorously than will be the case in America, where such a caste does not exist and where military men lack social prestige. A von Schleicher can always be counted on to build a more stable fascism than a "committee of public safety" consisting of Owen Youngs, et al., to whom the fascist task will undoubtedly be entrusted in America.

The certainty that dominant social groups which now control society will not easily yield and that their rule is nevertheless doomed raises interesting problems of strategy for those who desire a new social order. In America these problems are complicated by the fact that there is no real proletarian class in this country. All but the most disinherited workers still belong to the middle class, and they will not be united in a strong political party of their own for some years to come. Distressing social experience will finally produce radical convictions among them, but experience without education and an adequate political philosophy will merely result in sporadic violence. We are literally in the midst of a disintegrating economic empire with no receiver in bankruptcy in sight to assume responsibility for the defunct institution. All this probably means that capitalism has many a

263

decade to run in this country, particularly if it should find momentary relief from present difficulties through some inflationary movement. The sooner a strong political labor movement, expressing itself in socialist terms develops, the greater is the probability of achieving essential change without undue violence or social chaos.

One of the difficulties of the situation is that America may have to go through a period of purely parliamentary socialism even after Europe has proved that a socialism which makes a fetish of parliamentarism will not be able to press through to its goal. Though we will probably have to go through the experience of parliamentarism, we may be able to qualify our faith in it sufficiently to be pragmatic and experimental in the choice of our radical techniques. To disavow pure parliamentarism does not mean to espouse revolution. Any modern industrial civilization has a natural and justified instinctive avoidance of revolution. It rightly fears that revolution may result in suicide for the whole civilization. When European nations are unable to achieve a bare Socialist majority in their legislative bodies, it is hardly probable that in America we will ever have such a preponderance of Socialist conviction that Socialist amendments to the constitution could be enacted. But revolution is equally unthinkable. There is no possibility of a purely revolutionary movement establishing order on this continent without years of internecine strife. For this reason it is important that parliamentary socialism seek to enact as much of its program as possible within the present constitutional framework during the next decades, without hoping, however, that socialism itself can be established in this manner. The final struggle between socialism and fascism will probably be a long and drawn-out conflict in which it is possible that fascism will finally capitulate without a military or revolutionary venture being initiated against it. It will capitulate simply because the inexorable logic of history plus the determined opposition of the labor group will finally destroy it. The final transfer of power may come through the use of a general strike or some similar technique.

Prediction at long range may seem idle and useless. But it is important to recognize that neither the parliamentary nor the revolutionary course offers modern society an easy way to the mastery of a technological civilization. If this is the case, it becomes very important to develop such forms of resistance and mass coercion as will disturb the intricacies of an industrial civilization as little as possible, and as will perserve the temper of mutual respect within the area of social conflict. Political realists have become cynical about moral and religious idealism in politics chiefly because so frequently it is expressed in terms of confusion which hide the basic facts of the social struggle. Once the realities of this struggle are freely admitted, there is every possibility of introducing very important ethical elements into the struggle in the way, for instance, that Gandhi introduces them in India.

The inability of religious and intellectual idealists to gauge properly the course of historical events results from their constant over-estimate of idealistic and unselfish factors in political life. They think that an entire nation can be educated toward a new social ideal when all the testimony of history proves that new societies are born out of social struggle, in which the positions of the various social groups are determined by their economic interests.

Those who wish to participate in such a struggle creatively, to help history toward a goal of justice and to eliminate as much confusion, chaos and conflict in the attainment of the goal as possible, will accomplish this result only if they do not permit their own comparative emancipation from the determining and conditioning economic factors to obscure the fact that these factors are generally determining. No amount of education or religious idealism will ever persuade a social class to espouse a cause or seek a goal which is counter to its economic interest. Social intelligence can have a part in guiding social impulse only if it does not commit the error of assuming that intelligence has destroyed and sublimated impulse to such a degree that impulse is no longer potent. This is the real issue between liberalism and political realism. The liberal is an idealist who imagines that his particular type of education or his special kind of religious idealism will accomplish what history has never before revealed: the complete sublimation of the natural impulse of a social group.

Dominant groups will always have the impulse to hold on to their power as long as possible. In the interest of a progressive justice they must be dislodged, and this will be done least painfully and with least confusion if the social group which has the future in its hands becomes conscious of its destiny as soon as possible, is disciplined and self-confident in the knowledge of it destiny and gradually acquires all the heights of prestige and power in society which it is possible to acquire without a struggle. When the inevitable struggle comes (for all contests of power must finally issue in a crisis) there is always the possibility that the old will capitulate and the new assume social direction without internecine conflict. That is why an adequate political realism will ultimately make for more peace in society than a liberalism which does not read the facts of human nature and human history right, and which is betrayed by these errors into erroneous historical calculations which prolong the death agonies of the old order and postpone the coming of the new.

It may be important to say in conclusion that educational and religious idealists shrink from the conclusions to which a realistic analysis of history forces the careful student, partly because they live in the false hope that the impulses of nature in man can be sublimated by mind and conscience to a larger degree than is actually possible, and partly because their own personal idealism shrinks from the "brutalities" of the social struggle which a realistic theory envisages. But this idealism is full of confusion. It does not recognize that everyone but the ascetic is a participant in the brutalities of the social struggle now. The only question of importance is on what side of the struggle they are. Think of all the kind souls who stand in horror of a social conflict who are at this moment benefiting from, and living comfortable lives at the expense of, a social system which condemns 13 million men to misery and semi-starvation. Failure to recognize this covert brutality of the social struggle is probably the greatest weakness of middle-class liberals, and it lends a note of hypocrisy and self-deception to every moral pretension which seeks to eliminate violence in the social struggle.

The relation of the sensitive conscience to the brutal realities of man's collective behavior will always create its own problem—a problem in the solution of which orthodox religion has frequently been more shrewd than liberalism because it did not over-estimate the virtue of human society, but rather recognized the "sinful" character of man's collective life. This problem has its own difficulties, and they ought not to be confused with the problem of achieving an adequate social and political strategy for the attainment of a just society or for the attainment of a higher approximation of justice than a decadent capitalism grants.

# 72

## The Philosophy
## of the New Deal

To find a clear, coherent philosophy in the New Deal
or in the mind of the leader, Franklin D. Roosevelt,
who presided over the country in the New Deal years is
exceptionally difficult. The twistings and turnings, the
ambiguities and uncertainties, the pragmatic drifting
that characterized New Deal policy allow many diver-
gent interpretations; but there was something new about
the New Deal: there were assumptions about the
character of America's problems and the proper role of
government that FDR did not share with his predeces-
sor. The most important and vigorous statement of
these assumptions appeared in Roosevelt's 1932 campaign address before San Francisco's Commonwealth
Club.

### COMMONWEALTH CLUB ADDRESS
### *Franklin D. Roosevelt*

I count it a privilege to be invited to address the Commonwealth Club. It has stood
in the life of this city and state, and it is perhaps accurate to add, the nation, as a
group of citizen leaders interested in fundamental problems of government, and
chiefly concerned with achievement of progress in government through non-partisan
means. The privilege of addressing you, therefore, in the heat of a political
campaign, is great. I want to respond to your courtesy in terms consistent with your
policy.

I want to speak not of politics but of government. I want to speak not of
parties, but of universal principles. They are not political, except in that larger
sense in which a great American once expressed a definition of politics, that
nothing in all of human life is foreign to the science of politics.

The issue of government has always been whether individual men and women
will have to serve some system of government or economics, or whether a system of
government and economics exists to serve individual men and women. This
question has persistently dominated the discussion of government for many
generations. On questions relating to these things men have differed, and for time
immemorial it is probable that honest men will continue to differ.

The final word belongs to no man; yet we can still believe in chance and in progress. Democracy, as a dear old friend of mine in Indiana, Meredith Nicholson, has called it, is a quest, a never-ending seeking for better things, and in the seeking for these things and the striving for them, there are many roads to follow. But, if we map the course of these roads, we find that there are only two general directions.

When we look about us, we are likely to forget how hard people have worked to win the privilege of government. The growth of the national governments of Europe was a struggle for the development of a centralized force in the nation, strong enough to impose peace upon ruling barons. In many instances the victory of the central government, the creation of a strong central government, was a haven of refuge to the individual. The people preferred the master far away to the exploitation and cruelty of the smaller master near at hand.

But the creators of national government were perforce ruthless men. They were often cruel in their methods, but they did strive steadily toward something that society needed and very much wanted, a strong central state, able to keep the peace, to stamp out civil war, to put the unruly nobleman in his place, and to permit the bulk of individuals to live safely. The man of ruthless force had his place in developing a pioneer country, just as he did in fixing the power of the central government in the development of nations. Society paid him well for his services and its development. When the development among the nations of Europe, however, had been completed, ambition and ruthlessness, having served its term, tended to overstep its mark.

There came a growing feeling that government was conducted for the benefit of a few who thrived unduly at the expense of all. The people sought a balancing—a limiting force. There came gradually, through town council, trade guilds, national parliaments, by constitution and by popular participation and control, limitations on arbitrary power.

Another factor that tended to limit the power of those who ruled, was the rise of the ethical conception that a ruler bore a responsibility for the welfare of his subjects.

The American colonies were born in this struggle. The American Revolution was a turning point in it. After the revolution the struggle continued and shaped itself in the public life of the country. There were those who because they had seen the confusion which attended the years of war for American independence surrendered to the belief that popular government was essentially dangerous and essentially unworkable. They were honest people, my friends, and we cannot deny that their experience had warranted some measure of fear. The most brilliant, honest and able exponent of this point of view was Hamilton. He was too impatient of slow-moving methods. Fundamentally he believed that the safety of the republic lay in the autocratic strength of its government, that the destiny of individuals was to serve that government, and that fundamentally a great and strong group of central institutions, guided by a small group of able and public spirited citizens could best direct all government.

But Mr. Jefferson, in the summer of 1776, after drafting the Declaration of

Independence turned his mind to the same problem and took a different view. He did not deceive himself with outward forms. Government to him was a means to an end, not an end in itself; it might be either a refuge and a help or a threat and a danger, depending on the circumstances. We find him carefully analyzing the society for which he was to organize a government. "We have no paupers. The great mass of our population is of laborers, our rich who cannot live without labor, either manual or professional, being few and of moderate wealth. Most of the laboring class possess property, cultivate their own lands, have families and from the demand for their labor, are enabled to exact from the rich and the competent such prices as enable them to feed abundantly, clothe above mere decency, to labor moderately and raise their families."

These people, he considered, had two sets of rights, those of "personal competency" and those involved in acquiring and possessing property. By "personal competency" he meant the right of free thinking, freedom of forming and expressing opinions, and freedom of personal living each man according to his own lights. To insure the first set of rights, a government must so order its functions as not to interfere with the individual. But even Jefferson realized that the exercise of the property rights might so interfere with the rights of the individual that the government, without whose assistance the property rights could not exist, must intervene, not to destroy individualism but to protect it.

You are familiar with the great political duel which followed; and how Hamilton, and his friends, building towards a dominant centralized power were at length defeated in the great election of 1800, by Mr. Jefferson's party. Out of that duel came the two parties, Republican and Democratic, as we know them today.

So began, in American political life, the new day, the day of the individual against the system, the day in which individualism was made the great watchword of American life. The happiest of economic conditions made that day long and splendid. On the Western frontier, land was substantially free. No one, who did not shirk the task of earning a living, was entirely without opportunity to do so. Depressions could, and did, come and go; but they could not alter the fundamental fact that most of the people lived partly by selling their labor and partly by extracting their livelihood from the soil, so that starvation and dislocation were practically impossible. At the very worst there was always the possibility of climbing into a covered wagon and moving west where the untilled prairies afforded a haven for men to whom the East did not provide a place. So great were our natural resources that we could offer this relief not only to our own people, but to the distressed of all the world; we could invite immigration from Europe, and welcome it with open arms. Traditionally, when a depression came a new section of land was opened in the West; and even our temporary misfortune served our manifest destiny.

It was in the middle of the 19th century that a new force was released and a new dream created. The force was what is called the industrial revolution, the advance of steam and machinery and the rise of the forerunners of the modern industrial plant. The dream was the dream of an economic machine, able to raise

269

the standard of living for everyone; to bring luxury within the reach of the humblest; to annihilate distance by steam power and later by electricity, and to release everyone from the drudgery of the heaviest manual toil. It was to be expected that this would necessarily affect government. Heretofore, government had merely been called upon to produce conditions within which people could live happily, labor peacefully, and rest secure. Now it was called upon to aid in the consummation of this new dream. There was, however, a shadow over the dream. To be made real, it required use of the talents of men of tremendous will, and tremendous ambition, since by no other force could the problems of financing and engineering and new developments be brought to a consummation.

So manifest were the advantages of the machine age, however, that the United States fearlessly, cheerfully, and, I think, rightly, accepted the bitter with the sweet. It was thought that no price was too high to pay for the advantages which we could draw from a finished industrial system. The history of the last half century is accordingly in large measure a history of a group of financial Titans, whose methods were not scrutinized with too much care, and who were honored in proportion as they produced the results, irrespective of the means they used. The financiers who pushed the railroads to the Pacific were always ruthless, often wasteful, and frequently corrupt; but they did build railroads, and we have them today. It has been estimated that the American investor paid for the American railway system more than three times over in the process; but despite this fact the net advantage was to the United States. As long as we had free land; as long as population was growing by leaps and bounds; as long as our industrial plants were insufficient to supply our own needs, society chose to give the ambitious man free play and unlimited reward provided only that he produced the economic plant so much desired.

During this period of expansion, there was equal opportunity for all and the business of government was not to interfere but to assist in the development of industry. This was done at the request of business men themselves. The tariff was originally imposed for the purpose of "fostering our infant industry", a phrase I think the older among you will remember as a political issue not so long ago. The railroads were subsidized, sometimes by grants of money, oftener by grants of land; some of the most valuable oil lands in the United States were granted to assist the financing of the railroad which pushed through the Southwest. A nascent merchant marine was assisted by grants of money, or by mail subsidies, so that our steam shipping might ply the seven seas. Some of my friends tell me that they do not want the Government in business. With this I agree but I wonder whether they realize the implications of the past. For while it has been American doctrine that the government must not go into business in competition with private enterprises, still it has been traditional particularly in Republican administrations for business urgently to ask the government to put at private disposal all kinds of government assistance. The same man who tells you that he does not want to see the government interfere in business—and he means it, and has plenty of good reasons for saying so—is the first to go to Washington and ask the government for a prohibitory tariff on his product. When things get just bad enough—as they did two years ago—he will go with equal speed to the United States government and ask for a loan; and the Reconstruction Finance Corporation is the outcome of it. Each group has sought protection from the government for its own special interests, without realizing that the function of government must be to favor no small group at the expense of its duty to protect the rights of personal freedom and of private property of all its citizens.

In retrospect we can now see that the turn of the tide came with the turn of the century. We were reaching our last frontier; there was no more free land and our industrial combinations had become great uncontrolled and irresponsible units of power within the state. Clear-sighted men saw with fear the danger that opportunity would no longer be equal; that the growing corporation, like the feudal baron of old, might threaten the economic freedom of individuals to earn a living. In that hour, our antitrust laws were born. The cry was raised against the great corporations. Theodore Roosevelt, the first great Republican progressive, fought a Presidential campaign on the issue of "trust busting" and talked freely about malefactors of great wealth. If the government had a policy it was rather to turn the clock back, to destroy the large combinations and to return to the time when every man owned his individual small business.

This was impossible; Theodore Roosevelt, abandoning the idea of "trust busting", was forced to work out a difference between "good" trusts and "bad" trusts. The Supreme Court set forth the famous "rule of reason" by which it seems to have meant that a concentration of industrial power was permissible if the method by which it got its power, and the use it made of that power, was reasonable.

Woodrow Wilson, elected in 1912, saw the situation more clearly. Where Jefferson had feared the encroachment of political power on the lives of individuals, Wilson knew that the new power was financial. He saw, in the highly centralized economic system, the despot of the twentieth century, on whom great masses of individuals relied for their safety and their livelihood, and whose irresponsibility and greed (if it were not controlled) would reduce them to starvation and penury. The concentration of financial power had not proceeded so far in 1912 as it has today; but it had grown far enough for Mr. Wilson to realize fully its implications. It is interesting, now, to read his speeches. What is called "radical" today (and I have reason to know whereof I speak) is mild compared to the campaign of Mr. Wilson. "No man can deny", he said, "that the lines of endeavor have more and more narrowed and stiffened; no man who knows anything about the development of industry in this country can have failed to observe that the larger kinds of credit are more and more difficult to obtain unless you obtain them upon terms of uniting your efforts with those who already control the industry of the country, and nobody can fail to observe that every man who tries to set himself up in competition with any process of manufacture which has taken place under the control of large combinations of capital will presently find himself either squeezed out or obliged to sell and allow himself to be absorbed." Had there been no World War—had Mr.

271

Wilson been able to devote eight years to domestic instead of to international affairs—we might have had a wholly different situation at the present time. However, the then distant roar of European cannon, growing ever louder, forced him to abandon the study of this issue. The problem he saw so clearly is left with us as a legacy; and no one of us on either side of the political controversy can deny that it is a matter of grave concern to the government.

A glance at the situation today only too clearly indicates that equality of opportunity as we have known it no longer exists. Our industrial plant is built; the problem just now is whether under existing conditions it is not overbuilt. Our last frontier has long since been reached, and there is practically no more free land. More than half of our people do not live on the farms or on lands and cannot derive a living by cultivating their own property. There is no safety valve in the form of a Western prairie to which those thrown out of work by the Eastern economic machines can go for a new start. We are not able to invite the immigration from Europe to share our endless plenty. We are now providing a drab living for our own people.

Our system of constantly rising tariffs has at last reacted against us to the point of closing our Canadian frontier on the north, our European markets on the east, many of our Latin American markets to the south, and a goodly proportion of our Pacific markets on the west, through the retaliatory tariffs of those countries. It has forced many of our great industrial institutions who exported their surplus production to such countries, to establish plants in such countries, within the tariff walls. This has resulted in the reduction of the operation of their American plants, and opportunity for employment.

Just as freedom to farm has ceased, so also the opportunity in business has narrowed. It still is true that men can start small enterprises, trusting to native shrewdness and ability to keep abreast of competitors; but area after area has been preempted altogether by the great corporations, and even in the fields which still have no great concerns, the small man starts under a handicap. The unfeeling statistics of the past three decades show that the independent business man is running a losing race. Perhaps he is forced to the wall; perhaps he cannot command credit; perhaps he is "squeezed out," in Mr. Wilson's words, by highly organized corporate competitors, as your corner grocery man can tell you. Recently a careful study was made of the concentration of business in the United States. It showed that our economic life was dominated by some six hundred odd corporations who controlled two-thirds of American industry. Ten million small business men divided the other third. More striking still, it appeared that if the process of concentration goes on at the same rate, at the end of another century we shall have all American industry controlled by a dozen corporations, and run by perhaps a hundred men. Put plainly, we are steering a steady course toward economic oligarchy, If we are not there already.

Clearly, all this calls for a re-appraisal of values. A mere builder of more industrial plants, a creator of more railroad systems, an organizer of more corporations, is as likely to be a danger as a help. The day of the great promoter or the financial Titan, to whom we granted anything if only he would build, or develop, is over. Our task now is not discovery or exploitation of natural resources, or necessarily producing more goods. It is the soberer, less dramatic business of administering resources and plants already in hand, of seeking to reestablish foreign markets for our surplus production, of meeting the problem of underconsumption, of adjusting production to consumption, of distributing wealth and products more equitably, of adapting existing economic organizations to the service of the people. The day of enlightened administration has come.

Just as in older times the central government was first a haven of refuge, and then a threat, so now in a closer economic system the central and ambitious financial unit is no longer a servant of national desire, but a danger. I would draw the parallel one step farther. We did not think because national government had become a threat in the 18th century that therefore we should abandon the principle of national government. Nor today should we abandon the principle of strong economic units called corporations, merely because their power is susceptible of easy abuse. In other times we dealt with the problem of an unduly ambitious central government by modifying it gradually into a constitutional democratic government. So today we are modifying and controlling our economic units.

As I see it, the task of government in its relation to business is to assist the development of an economic declaration of rights, an economic constitutional order. This is the common task of statesman and business man. It is the minimum requirement of a more permanently safe order of things.

Every man has a right to life; and this means that he has also a right to make a comfortable living. He may by sloth or crime decline to exercise that right; but it may not be denied him. We have no actual famine or dearth; our industrial and agricultural mechanism can produce enough and to spare. Our government formal and informal, political and economic, owes to every one an avenue to possess himself of a portion of that plenty sufficient for his needs, through his own work.

Every man has a right to his own property; which means a right to be assured, to the fullest extent attainable, in the safety of his savings. By no other means can men carry the burdens of those parts of life which, in the nature of things, afford no chance of labor; childhood, sickness, old age. In all thought of property, this right is paramount; all other property rights must yield to it. If, in accord with this principle, we must restrict the operations of the speculator, the manipulator, even the financier, I believe we must accept the restriction as needful, not to hamper individualism but to protect it.

These two requirements must be satisfied, in the main, by the individuals who claim and hold control of the great industrial and financial combinations which dominate so large a part of our industrial life. They have undertaken to be, not business men, but princes—princes of property. I am not prepared to say that the system which produces them is wrong. I am very clear that they must fearlessly and competently assume the responsibility which goes with the power. So many enlightened business men know this that the statement would be little more than a platitude, were it not for an added implication.

273

This implication is, briefly, that the responsible heads of finance and industry instead of acting each for himself, must work together to achieve the common end. They must, where necessary, sacrifice this or that private advantage; and in reciprocal self-denial must seek a general advantage. It is here that formal government—political government, if you choose, comes in. Whenever in the pursuit of this objective the lone wolf, the unethical competitor, the reckless promoter, the Ishmael or Insull whose hand is against every man's, declines to join in achieving an end recognized as being for the public welfare, and threatens to drag the industry back to a state of anarchy, the government may properly be asked to apply restraint. Likewise, should the group ever use its collective power contrary to the public welfare, the government must be swift to enter and protect the public interest.

The government should assume the function of economic regulation only as a last resort, to be tried only when private initiative, inspired by high responsibility, with such assistance and balance as government can give, has finally failed. As yet there has been no final failure, because there has been no attempt; and I decline to assume that this nation is unable to meet the situation.

The final term of the high contract was for liberty and the pursuit of happiness. We have learnt a great deal of both in the past century. We know that individual liberty and individual happiness mean nothing unless both are ordered in the sense that one man's meat is not another man's poison. We know that the old "rights of personal competency"—the right to read, to think, to speak, to choose and live a mode of life, must be respected at all hazards. We know that liberty to do anything which deprives others of those elemental rights is outside the protection of any compact; and that government in this regard is the maintenance of a balance, within which every individual may have a place if he will take it; in which every individual may find safety if he wishes it; in which every individual may attain such power as his ability permits, consistent with his assuming the accompanying responsibility.

Faith in America, faith in our tradition of personal responsibility, faith in our institutions, faith in ourselves demands that we recognize the new terms of the old social contact. We shall fulfill them, as we fulfilled the obligation of the apparent Utopia which Jefferson imagined for us in 1776, and which Jefferson, Roosevelt and Wilson sought to bring to realization. We must do so, lest a rising tide of misery engendered by our common failure, engulf us all. But failure is not an American habit; and in the strength of great hope we must all shoulder our common load.

# 73

## The Persistence
## of the American Work Ethic

This autobiographical story, "Grass," was taken from *The Quest for Identity*, by psychoanalyst Allen Wheelis. Wheelis was mainly interested in defining what had changed about the American character as of 1958, but included this story, based on his childhood in Texas in the 1920s and early 1930s, as a point of comparison. As he himself notes, this episode "portrays a relationship of father to son which was more characteristic of the nineteenth century," and seems "alien to our time, exaggerated in its harshness." Yet this was what happened, not only in this case but in many others, especially in rural America. Americans of the 1930s were recognizably the offspring of Lucy Larcom, E. W. Howe, Russell Conwell, and Benjamin Franklin.

## THE QUEST FOR IDENTITY
### *Allen Wheelis*

**Grass**

It was the last day of school. The report cards had been distributed, and—to his great relief—Larry found that he had passed. Now at eleven o'clock in the morning he was on his way home with two of his friends. They felt exhilaration at the prospect of three months of freedom and manifested it by pushing each other, yelling, throwing rocks at a bottle, chasing a grass snake, and rolling a log into the creek. Being nine years old, it took them a long time to reach their homes. Before parting they made plans to meet that afternoon to play ball. Larry ran through the tall grass up to the back door and into the kitchen. His mother was stirring something on the stove.

"Mama, I passed!"

"Not so loud, hon." She leaned over and kissed him, then looked at the report card. "This is very good. Show it to Daddy if he's not asleep."

He took the card and went through the bedroom to the porch. The bed faced away from the door and he could not tell whether his father were asleep or not.

"Daddy?"

"Come in, son."

Reprinted from *The Quest for Identity* by Allen Wheelis (103–125). By permission of W. W. Norton & Company, Inc. and Victor Gollancz Ltd. Copyright © 1958 by W. W. Norton & Company, Inc.

"I passed," he said, offering the card.

Morris smiled and Larry averted his glance. He could never bring himself to face for long the level gaze of those gray eyes which seemed effortlessly to read his mind. His father looked over the report. "I see you got seventy-five in conduct."

"Yes, sir."

"Do you have an explanation?"

"No, sir."

"Do you think you deserved a better grade?"

"No . . . sir."

"Then you *do* have an explanation?"

Larry twisted one foot around the other. "Yes, sir. I guess so, sir."

"What is the explanation?"

This tireless interrogation could, Larry knew, be carried on for hours. Mumbling his words he began to recount his sins.

"I guess I . . . talked too much."

"Speak up, son."

"Yes, sir. I talked too much . . . and laughed . . . and cut up."

"Do you find silence so difficult?"

"Sir?"

"Was it so hard to be quiet?"

"Yes . . . sir. I guess so."

"You don't seem to find it difficult now."

He looked up and found his father smiling. It wasn't going to be so bad after all. "But the other grades are good," Morris said. Larry grinned and turned to look out the window. Heat waves shimmered above the tin roof of the barn, and away to the west was an unbroken field of sunflowers. Everything was bathed in, and seemed to be made drowsy by, the hot, bright sunlight. He thought of playing ball and wished dinner were over so that he could go now.

"Daddy, can I go over to Paul's house after dinner?"

Almost before the words were out he realized his mistake. He should have asked his mother first. She might have said yes without mentioning it to his father.

"No. You have to work, son."

"What've I got to do?"

Morris looked out over the several acres which were loosely referred to as the back yard. "You have to cut the grass."

Through a long wet spring the grass had sprung up until it was nearly a foot high. Now, in June, the rain was over and the heat was beginning to turn the grass brown. As the family had no lawn mower, any cutting of grass or weeds was done by hoe, scythe, or sickle. It was with one of these instruments that Larry assumed the grass would be cut, but he was mistaken. After dinner Morris gave him directions. The tool was to be an old, ivory-handled straight edge razor. The technique would be to grasp a handful of grass in the left hand and cut it level with the ground with the razor. The grass was to be put in a basket, along with any rocks or sticks that might be found on the ground. When the basket was full it was to be removed some hundred yards where the grass could be emptied and burned. When the razor was dull it was to be sharpened on a whetstone in the barn.

Larry changed his clothes, put on a straw hat, and went to work. Unable to realize the extent of the task or to gauge the time required, his only thought was to finish as soon as possible so as to be able to play before the afternoon were over. He began in the center of the yard and could see his father watching from the bed on the porch. After a few experimental slashes an idea occurred to him. He walked to the house and stood under the windows.

"Daddy."

"Yes, son."

"When I've finished can I play baseball?"

"Yes."

He resumed his work, thinking that he would cut fast and get it over in a couple of hours. For a few minutes the work went well, containing the satisfaction of watching the thin steel cut easily through dry grass. He grabbed big handfuls and hacked away with gusto. Soon his father called. Obediently he walked to the porch.

"Yes, sir?"

Morris was looking through a field glass at the small patch of ground that had been cleared.

"Son, I want you to cut the grass level with the ground. Therefore you will have to cut slower and more carefully. And it's better to hold a smaller handful because you can cut it more evenly. Also, you must pick up every stone." This referred to the few pebbles left in the cleared area. "Do you understand?"

"Yes, sir."

"Now go back and do that patch over again, and cut it even with the ground."

"Yes, sir."

Walking back he wondered why he had not started in some part of the yard out of his father's view. The work was now harder; for the stubble was only one or two inches high and was difficult to hold while being cut. It took an hour to do again the area originally cleared in a few minutes. By this time he was tired and disheartened. Sweat ran down his forehead and into his eyes, and his mouth was dry. The razor could not be held by the handle, for the blade would fold back. It had to be held by its narrow shank which already had raised a blister. Presently he heard his friends, and soon they came into view and approached the fence.

"Whatya doin'?"

"Cuttin' the grass."

"What's that you're cuttin' it with?"

"A razor."

They laughed. "That's a funny thing to be cuttin' grass with."

"Larry!" The boys stopped laughing and Larry went to the porch.

"Yes, sir?"

"If you want to talk to your friends, you may; but don't stop working while you talk."

"Yes, sir." He went back to the basket and resumed cutting.

277

"What'd he say?" Paul asked in a lowered voice.

"He said I had to work."

"You cain't play ball?"

"No."

"How long is he going to make you work?"

"I don't know."

"Well . . . I guess we might as well go on."

Larry looked up with longing. They were standing outside the fence, poking their toes idly through the palings. James was rhythmically pounding his fist into the socket of a first baseman's mitt.

"Yeah, let's get goin'."

"Can you get away later on?" Paul asked.

"Maybe I can. I'll try. I'll see if he'll let me." The two boys began to wander off. "I'll try to come later," he called urgently, hoping his father would not hear.

When they were gone he tried for a while to cut faster, but his hand hurt. Several times he had struck rocks with the razor, and the blade was getting dull. Gingerly he got up from his sore knees, went to the hydrant, allowed the water to run until cool, and drank from his cupped hands. Then he went to the barn and began whetting the blade on the stone. When it was sharp he sat down to rest. Being out of his father's sight he felt relatively secure for the moment. The chinaberry tree cast a liquid pattern of sun and shadow before the door. The berries were green and firm, just right for a slingshot.

"Larry!"

With a sense of guilt he hurried to his father's window. "Yes, sir."

"Get back to work. It's not time to rest yet."

At midafternoon he looked about and saw how little he had done. The heat waves shimmered before his eyes as he realized that he would not finish today and perhaps not tomorrow. Leavin the razor on the ground, he made the familiar trek to his father's window.

"Daddy."

"Yes."

"Can I quit now?"

"No, son."

"I cain't finish it this afternoon."

"I know."

"Then cain't I go play ball now and finish it tomorrow?"

"No."

"When can I play ball?"

"When you have finished cutting the grass."

"How long do you think it'll take me?"

"Two or three months."

"Well, can . . . ?"

"Now that's enough. Go back to work."

He resumed the work at a sullenly slow pace. To spare his knees he sat down, cutting around him as far as he could reach, then moving to a new place and sitting down again.

"Larry!"

He went back to the porch. "Yes, sir."

"Do you want to be a lazy, no-account scoundrel?" The voice was harsh and angry.

"No, sir."

"Then don't you ever let me see you sitting down to work again! Now you get back there as quick as you can and stand on your knees."

The afternoon wore on with excruciating slowness. The sun gradually declined. The thin shank of the razor cut into his hand and the blisters broke. He showed them to his father, hoping they would prove incapacitating, but Morris bandaged them and sent him back. Near sundown he heard the sounds of his friends returning home, but they did not come by to talk. Finally his mother came to the back door and said that supper was ready. The day's work was over.

When he awoke the next morning he thought it was another school day. Then he remembered the preceding afternoon and felt that school was not nearly as bad as cutting grass. He knew that his father intended for him to continue the work, but as no specific order had been given for this particular day there was possibility of escape. He decided to ask his mother for permission to play, and be gone before his father realized what had happened. His mother was cooking breakfast when he finished dressing. He made himself useful and waited until, for some reason, she went on the back porch. Now they were separated from his father by four rooms and clearly out of earshot.

"Mama, can I go over to Paul's house?"

"Why yes, hon, I guess so."

That was his mother. To the reasonable request she said yes immediately; the unreasonable required a varying amount of cajolery, but in the end that, too, would be granted. When breakfast was over, he quickly got his cap, whispered a soft good-bye, and started out. He had reached the back door when she called. "Be sure you come back before dinner."

"Larry!"

He stopped short. In another minute he would have been far enough away to pretend he had not heard. But though his conscience might be deaf to a small voice, it was not deaf to this sternly audible one. If he ran now he would never be able to look at his father and say, "No, I didn't hear you". He gave his mother a reproachful glance as he went back through the kitchen. "Now I won't get to go," he said darkly.

He entered the porch and stood by the bed, his eyes lowered. He was conscious of omitting the usual verbal obeisance of "Yes, sir," but did not care.

"Where were you off to?"

"To Paul's."

"Who told you you could go?"

"Mama."

"Did you ask her?"

"Yes."

"Yes *what?*"

"Yes, sir," he said sulkily.

"Didn't you know I wanted you to work today?"

"No, sir."

"Don't you remember my telling you that you could not play until you finished cutting the grass?"

"No, sir." One lie followed another now. "Anyway . . . that will take just about . . . all summer." His mouth was dry and he was swallowing heavily. "James and Paul . . . don't have to work and . . . I don't see why . . . I . . . have to work all the time."

He flushed, his eyes smarted, and tears were just one harsh word away. After a moment of silence he saw the covers of the bed move. His father's long, wasted legs appeared. The tears broke, flooding his face. Morris stood up, found his slippers, and put on a bathrobe. Larry's ear was grasped and twisted by a bony hand, and he was propelled into the bathroom. Morris sat on the edge of the tub and held Larry in front of him. The fingers were relentless, and it seemed that the ear would be torn from his head.

"Look at me, son."

Tears were dripping from his chin, and every other moment his chest was convulsed by a rattling inspiration. Trying to stop crying, he managed at last to raise his head and look in his father's face. The head and neck were thin. The skin had a grayish glint, and the lines that ran down from his nose were straight. His eyes were steady, and on their level, searching gaze Larry's conscience was impaled.

"Do you know why you are going to be punished?"

The pose of injured innocence was gone now. His guilt seemed everywhere, and there was no place to hide.

"Why?"

"Because . . . I . . . didn't tell the . . . truth." It was agony to look into those eyes.

"And?" The question was clipped and hard.

He tried to search his conscience and enumerate his sins, but his mind was a shambles and his past was mountainous with guilt. He could not speak. His eyes dropped.

"Look at me, son."

Painfully the wet eyes were again lifted to the steady gray ones above.

"You are being punished because you tried to get your mother's permission for an act you knew to be wrong. You were scoundrel enough to do that!" the knifelike voice said. "Do you understand?"

"Yes . . . sir."

"You are being punished, further, because you spoke in an ugly, sulky manner. Do you understand?"

"Yes . . . sir."

He saw the other hand move and felt the old, sick terror. The hand grasped the clothes of his back and lifted him onto his father's knees. His head hung down almost to the floor. The hand began to rise and fall.

"Do you understand why you're being punished?"

"Ye . . . es . . . sir."

The blows were heavy and he cried loudly.

"Will you ever do any of those things again?"

"No . . . sir."

The whipping lasted about a minute, after which he was placed on his feet. "Now, stop crying and wash your face. Then go out in the yard to work."

Still sobbing, he approached the lavatory and turned on a trickle of water. Behind him he heard his father stand and slowly leave the room. He held both hands under the faucet and with unseeing eyes stared at the drops of water tumbling over his fingers. Gradually the sobs diminished and presently ceased. He washed his face and left the room, closing the door softly. Passing through the kitchen he was aware that his mother was looking at him with compassion, but he avoided her eyes. To look at her now would be to cry again.

All that day he worked steadily and quietly. He asked no questions and made no requests. The work was an expiation and Morris found no occasion to criticize. Several times his mother brought out something cold for him to drink. She did not mention his punishment but knowledge of it was eloquent in her eyes. In the afternoon he began to feel better and thought of his friends and of playing ball. Knowing it to be out of the question for him, he merely dreamed about it.

That evening when supper was over and the dishes washed Morris called him.

"Tell him you're sorry," his mother whispered.

In their house after every punishment there must be a reconciliation. The integrity of the bonds that held them must be reaffirmed. Words of understanding must be spoken, tokens of love given and received. He walked out on the porch. The sky was filled with masses of purple and red.

"Do you feel better now, son?"

"Yes, sir." The gray eyes contained a reflection of the sunset. "I'm sorry I acted the way I did this morning."

A hand was laid on his head. "You said you didn't know why you had to work, didn't you?"

"Yes, sir but I . . ."

"That's all right son. I'll tell you. You ought to know. When you are grown you will have to work to make a living. All your life you'll have to work. Even if we were rich you would labor, because idleness is sinful. The Bible tells us that. I hope some day you will be able to work with your head, but first you've got to work with your hands." The color of the ponderous clouds was deepening to blue and black. "No one is born knowing how to work. It is something we have to learn. You've got to learn to set your mind to a job and keep at it, no matter how hard it is or how long it takes or how much you dislike it. If you don't learn that you'll never

281

amount to anything. And this is the time to learn it. Now do you know why you have to cut the grass?"

"Yes, sir."

"I don't like to make you work when you want to play, but it's for your own good. Can you understand that?"

"Yes, sir."

"Will you be a good boy and work hard this summer until the job is done?"

"Yes, sir."

He left the room feeling better. It was good to be forgiven, to be on good terms with one's father.

Day after day he worked in the yard, standing on his knees, cutting the grass close to the ground. There were few interruptions to break the monotony. Three or four times a day he went to the barn and sharpened the razor, but these trips were no escape. If he went too often or stayed too long his father took notice and put a stop to it. Many times each day he carried away the full basket of grass and stones, but the times of his departure and return were always observed. No evasions were possible because nothing escaped his father's eyes.

One day in July, at noon, he heard the rattle of dishes indicating that the table was being set. He was hot and tired and thirsty. He could almost smell the dinner cooking and thought of the tall glasses of iced tea. His mother came to the back door. At first he thought it was to call him, but she only threw out dishwater. Suddenly he dropped his razor and ran to the back steps.

"Mama," he called eagerly, but not loud enough for his father to hear. "Is dinner ready?"

"Yes, hon."

He came in, washed his hands, and sat in the kitchen to wait.

"Larry!"

It was his father's voice, the everlasting surveillance which he could not escape.

"Yes, sir."

"What did you come in for?"

"Mama said dinner was ready."

"Did you *ask* her?"

"Yes, sir."

"You trifling scoundrel! Get on back outside to work! And wait till she *calls* you to dinner! You understand?"

As weeks passed the heat increased and the grass withered. Had a match been touched to it the work of a summer would have been accomplished in a few minutes. No rain fell, even for a day, to interrupt the work. The grass did not grow, and the ground which was cleared on the first day remained bare. The earth was baked to a depth of four or five feet and began to crack. The only living thing he encountered was an occasional spider climbing desperately in or out of the crevices in search of a more habitable place to live. His friends knew he had to work and no longer came looking for him. Occasionally he would hear them playing in a nearby field, and sometimes in the mornings would see them pass with fishing poles over their shoulders. He knew that he was not missed, that they had stopped thinking of him and probably did not mention his name.

He became inured to the work but not reconciled to it, and throughout the summer continued to resist. Whippings—which had been rare before—were now common, and after each he would, in the evening, be required to apologize. He would go out on his father's porch, say he was sorry, and then listen guiltily to a restatement of the principles involved. Tirelessly Morris would explain what he had done wrong, the importance of learning to work, and the benefit to his character which this discipline would eventually bring about. After each of these sessions Larry would feel that he was innately shiftless, lazy, and impulsive. Each time he would resolve to try harder, but each time would relapse. After two or three days he would again become sullen or rebellious and again would be punished. Sometimes he saw his mother in tears and he knew that often she interceded in his behalf, but her efforts were ineffective.

Throughout June and July he worked every day except Sundays. As the job seemed endless he made no future plans. Anything that was apt to last all summer was too large an obstacle to plan beyond, any happiness that lay at its end too remote for practical anticipation. About the middle of August, however, his outlook changed. One evening at sundown he noticed that relatively little grass remained standing. For the first time since the beginning of summer he realized that his job would have an end and that he would soon be free. Surveying the area remaining to be cut, he attempted to divide it by the area which could be cleared in a single day and reached an estimate of five days. He felt a resurgence of hope and began visualizing what he would do when he was through. During the next several days he worked faster and more willingly, but found that he had been too sanguine in his estimate. He did not finish on the fifth day or the sixth. But on the evening of the seventh it was apparent to Morris as well as to him that the next day the job would be done. Only one or two hours of work remained.

The following morning—for the first time since May—he woke to the sound of rain. He wanted to work anyway, but was told that he could not. Then he asked if he could go to Paul's house to play until the rain stopped. Again the answer was no. About nine o'clock the rain let up and he hurriedly began to work. But the lull proved to be temporary and after a few minutes he had to stop. He stood under the awning which extended out over the windows of his father's porch and waited. After a while he sat on the ground and leaned against the house. A half hour passed. The rain was steady now, and seemingly would last all day. It dripped continuously from the canvas and formed a little trench in the earth in front of his feet. He stared out at the gray sky with a faraway, unseeing expression.

"I wish I could go to Paul's house."

He spoke in a low, sullen voice, hardly knowing whether he were talking to himself or to his father.

"It's not fair not to let me play . . . just because it's raining. It's not fair at all."

There was no comment from above. Minutes passed.

"You're a mean bastard!"

It seemed strange to be profane. He had never cursed before and was not at ease in the use of such words. Now, however, something violent was stirring in him, something that had been long stifled and was rankling for expression.

"If you think you can kick me around all the time you're wrong . . . you damned old bastard!"

At any moment he expected to be called. He would go inside and receive a whipping worse than he had thought possible. A long minute passed in silence.

Could it be that his father had not heard? That seemed unlikely, for often he had spoken from this place and been understood. The windows were open. There was nothing to prevent his hearing. Oh he had heard, all right. He was sure of that. Still, why wasn't he called? The waiting began to get on his nerves. Feeling that he could not make matters worse, he continued. This time he spoke louder and more viciously.

"You're the meanest man in the world. You lie up there in bed and are mean to everybody. I hate you!"

He began to feel astonished at himself. How incredible that he should be saying such things—he who had never dared a word of disrespect!

But why didn't his father call? What was he waiting for? Was he waiting for him to say his worst so as to be able to whip him all the harder? The rain drizzled down. The day was gray and quiet. The incident began to seem unreal. The absence of reaction was as incredible as the defamation. Both seemed impossible. It was like a bad dream.

But it's real! he thought furiously. He *had* said those things, and would keep on saying them till he made him answer. He became frantic and poured forth a tirade of abuse, a voluble, repetitious improvisation of profanity. He searched his memory for every dirty word he had heard, and when his store of obscene expletives was exhausted and he stopped, breathless, to listen . . . there was no response.

"You God damn dirty son of a bitch!" he screamed, "I wish you were dead! I wish you were dead, do you hear? Do you hear me?"

He had finished. Now something would happen. He cowered and waited for it, but there was no word from the porch. Not a sound. Not even the stir of bedclothes.

His rage passed and he became miserable. He sat with arms locked around his knees, staring blankly at the indifferent rain. As the minutes passed he became more appalled by what he had done. Its meaning broadened, expanded in endless ramifications, became boundless and unforgivable. He had broken the commandment to honor thy father and mother He had taken the name of the Lord in vain, and that was the same as cursing God. He though of his mother. What would she say when she learned? He pictured her face. She would cry.

For another half hour he sat there. He no longer expected to be called. For some reason the matter was to be left in abeyance. Finally, unable to endure further waiting, he got up and walked away. He went to the barn and wandered about morosely, expecting momentarily to see his mother enter to say that his father wanted him. But she did not come, and the morning passed without further incident.

On entering the house for lunch his first concern was to learn whether she knew. When she smiled he knew that she did not. Now that he was indoors he felt sure something would happen. He stayed as far from the porch as possible and spoke in low tones. Yet his father must know him to be present. He could not eat, and soon left the house and went back to the barn, where he felt somewhat less vulnerable.

He spent the afternoon there alone, sitting on a box, waiting. Occasionally he would get up and walk around aimlessly. Sometimes he would stand in the doorway looking out at the rain. Though unrestrained he felt himself a prisoner. He searched through his small understanding of his father but found no explanation of the delay. It was unlike him to postpone a whipping. Then it occurred to him that his act might have so far exceeded ordinary transgressions that it would require a special punishment. Perhaps he would not be whipped at all but would be sent away.

When supper time came he sneaked into the house and tried to be inconspicuous. His appearance was so haggard and agitated that his mother was concerned. She looked at him inquiringly and ran her hand affectiontely through his hair. "What's the matter son? Don't you feel well?"

"I feel all right," he said.

He escaped her and sat alone on the back porch until called to the table. When supper was safely over his situation was unimproved. It was too late to go outside again, and he could not long remain in the house without meeting his father. At the latest it could be put off only till family prayer. Perhaps that was the time when his crime would be related. Maybe they would pray for him and then expel him from home. He had just begun drying the dishes when the long awaited sound was heard.

"Larry."

It was not the wrathful voice he had expected. It was calm, just loud enough to be audible. Nevertheless it was enough to make him tremble and almost drop a plate. For a moment it seemed that he could not move.

"Your daddy wants you, dear."

He put down the dishtowel and went to the door of the porch.

"Yes, sir."

"Come out here where I can see you."

He approached the bed. His hands were clenched and he was biting his lip, trying not to cry.

"Your mother tells me you haven't been eating well today. You aren't sick, are you?"

"No, sir."

"You feel all right?"

"Yes, sir."

"Sit down, son. I just called you out here to talk for a while. I often think we don't talk to each other enough. I guess that's my fault. We'll have to do better in the future. I'd like to hear more about what you're interested in and what you think, because that's the only way I can get to know you." He paused a moment.

285

"Maybe you think because I'm grown up I understand everything, but that's not true. You'll find as you get older that no matter how much you learn there's always much you don't know. For example you're my own son and I ought to know you pretty well, but every now and then something'll happen that'll make me realize I don't understand you at all."

Larry choked back a sob and tried to brace himself for the coming blow.

"I don't think I ever understood my father," Morris went on presently, "until it was too late. We were very poor—much poorer, son, than you can imagine. From year in to year out we might see only a few dollars in our house, and what little there was had to be spent for essentials. When we sold our cotton we'd have to buy a plow or an ax. And there were staple foods we had to buy like flour and sugar. We bought cloth, too, but never any ready-made clothes. Until I was a grown man I never had any clothes except what my mother made. I got my first store-bought suit to go away to medical school in, and I don't believe my mother ever had a store-bought dress. My father worked hard and made his boys work hard. We resented it and sometimes even hated him for it, but in the end we knew he was right. One of my brothers never could get along with Daddy, and he ran away from home when he was about fifteen. He turned out to be a no-account scoundrel, and the last I heard of him he was a saloon keeper in New Orleans.

"In the summer we hoed corn and picked cotton, and in the winter we fixed rail fences and chopped wood and hauled it home. And we always had mules and pigs to take care of. It was a very different life from yours . . . and in some ways a better one." He looked at Larry affectionately. "At any rate, we learned how to work, and there's nothing more important for a boy to learn. It's something you haven't yet learned, son. Isn't that right?"

"Yes, sir."

"You will, though. If you ever amount to anything you'll learn. You're learning now. I wish you could understand that I wouldn't be trying to teach you so fast if I knew I would live long enough to teach you more slowly." He paused a moment. "Do you have anything to say?"

"No, sir."

"Then I guess you'd better see if your mother needs you."

Larry stood up, hardly able to believe that this was all.

"Son."

"Yes, sir."

"Come here a minute."

He went to the bed and his father put a hand on his shoulder. "Remember, son," he said in a husky voice, "whenever it seems I'm being hard on you . . . it's because I love you."

Late that night Larry woke frightened from a nightmare. For several minutes he lay in bed trembling, unable to convince himself that the vision was unreal. Presently he got up and tiptoed through the dark house to the porch.

"Daddy?" he whispered. "Daddy . . . are you all right?"

There was no reply, but soon he became aware of his father's regular breathing. He returned to bed but almost immediately got up and knelt on the floor.

"Dear God, please don't let anything happen to Daddy. Amen."

Still he could not sleep. He lay in bed and thought of many things, and after a while began worrying about the razor. What had he done with it? Was it still on the ground under the awning? Perhaps he had left it open. If so, someone might accidentally get cut. He got up again and went outside looking for it. In the dark he felt about on the ground under his father's windows but did not find it. Then he went to the barn and found it in its usual place and properly closed.

The following morning shortly before noon he completed his job. The last blade of grass was cut and carried away and the back yard was as bald as a razor could make it.

"Daddy," he said, standing under the porch window, "I've finished. Is it all right?"

Morris looked over the yard, then took his binoculars and scrutinized it in more detail, particularly the corners.

"That's well done, son."

Larry put away the basket and razor and came inside. After dinner he began to feel uncomfortable. It seemed strange not to be working. Restless and unable to sit still, he wandered about the house, looking out the windows and wondering what to do. Presently he sought and obtained permission to go to Paul's house, but he felt he was doing something wrong.

During the next two weeks he often played with his friends but never fully lost himself in play and was secretly glad when school started and life settled down to a routine again. He was more quiet than before and better behaved, and when next the report cards were distributed he had a nearly perfect score in conduct.

# 74

## Labor on the March

At the outset of the Depression the American labor movement was smaller and weaker than the labor movement of most other advanced societies. Organization was largely confined to the skilled crafts; the millions of semiskilled operatives in such mass production industries as steel, automobiles, and rubber were without effective voice. One of the most dramatic developments of the decade was the breaking away of the newly formed Congress of Industrial Organizations, the CIO, from the craft-dominated American Federation of Labor, and its phenomenal successes in winning the support of previously unorganized workers against the bitter and sometimes brutal resistance of great corporations. The journalist Edward Levinson provides a spirited and sympathetic narrative of a decisive battle between GM and the fledgling United Automobile Workers, a battle won by the workers via the new tactic of the sit-down strike, in which strikers refused to concede that the plants in which they worked were private property from which they could be expelled at the whim of the employer. This seemed to many Americans a violation of a sacred principle, but the strikes succeeded and helped to establish a new and competing principle: that workers are entitled to collective bargaining and that the power of a corporation over its property is not absolute. In many previous labor conflicts in the American past the government had interpreted the law narrowly and had employed force to break strikes. Its refusal to do so in this struggle marked a new stage in the definition of human rights and property rights.

## LABOR ON THE MARCH
### *Edward Levinson*

The strike of General Motors workers in January and February of 1937 was the most significant industrial battle since labor's defeat at Homestead. It held in its hands the future of the C.I.O. and the new labor movement which was soon to sweep millions of American breadwinners into its ranks. It aroused bitterness equal

Reprinted with permission from *Labor on the March* (New York: University Books, 1938), 149–168.

to that which accompanied the brief heyday of the Knights of Labor. It was more than a strike. It was a momentous struggle between the aroused forces of labor and the third largest corporation in the country, typifying years of unchallenged anti-unionism. It involved seizure of industrial plants worth more than $50,000,000 and the failure of the owners, vigilantes, courts, police, and military to recapture them.

Automobiles and steel-manufacturing form the backbone of American capitalism, and in the realm of autos General Motors was second to none in financial importance and in the 250,000 workers it employed. Its control lay in the hands of the Du Ponts and J. P. Morgan. The Corporation recovered strikingly from the depression years. Its net profit in 1934 was $167,000,000, while 1936 brought a profit of $227,940,000. Its average wage to its workers in 1935 was $1,150, which meant that many workers received far less. The auto workers were not comforted at all to know that the Corporation paid Alfred P. Sloan its president, $374,505 in 1935, vice-president William F. Knudsen $325,868, and a total of $3,779,730 to seventeen top officials. General Motors employees felt the speed-up more keenly than low wages. Belt-line production and the conveyor system were based on speed, and in the quest for ever-quicker, uninterrupted production the limbs and eyes and strength of the workers were geared to meet the pace of the machines. The workers had to meet competition between corporations, between plants and even sections of plants. Foremen, driven to bring up production, in turn drove the workers under them. The mere twist of a dial determined the speed of the line, and those workers who could not meet it faced the scrapheap. Automobile manufacturing yearly consigned men who had given their best years to the horror of being "old" at forty years or less. Over and over again, the strikers of 1937 summarized their chief complaints.

"We don't want to be driven," they said; and "We don't want to be spied on."

The espionage activities financed and promoted by General Motors sought several general objectives: to keep men from evading the demands of the speeded belt-line; to keep their unions, when they joined them, weak and ineffective; and eventually to destroy the unions. Without union grievance committees to speak up for them, many workers conspired in simple manner to keep down production. Word would pass through a section of a plant: "Only ten crank-shafts to be turned this hour; let's not burn ourselves up." To workers deprived of recognized spokesmen this was one way out of an intolerable situation. Here the work of the plant stool pigeon came in. General Motors accumulated weekly sheafs of reports on workers who had joined to keep down production. These "ears" also reported friendly references to unionism. It became so that no man could tell whether his neighbor was a friend or a company spy. In the ranks of the unionists, the General Motors espionage system had another function: to ferret out the leaders, to turn them in for discharge or discrimination and to watch the "outside agitators," i.e., the organizers. The La Follette committee which investigated violations of labor and civil rights discovered that General Motors spent $994,855 on private detective services from January 1, 1934, to July 31, 1936. As the probe got under way, most of the files of the company were stripped of spy reports. Knudsen sought to explain

289

the use of Pinkerton men and detectives of the Railway Audit and Inspection Company as the maintenance of a force to police and protect G.M.'s vast properties. But that did not explain how shadowing Adolph Germer, spies' attendance at picnics of Fisher Body employees, and spy reports on the reading habits of employees contributed to protection of its properties.

The strike which General Motors reaped from these practices had an inconspicuous start in the Fisher Body plant at Atlanta, Georgia. Four men who appeared in the plant with U.A.W. buttons on their workshirts were fired. A strike followed on November 18, 1936. The Atlanta unionists wanted the walkout extended to other plants, but the union and C.I.O. strategists felt such a move would be premature. A month later, the Kansas City Fisher Body plant discharged a unionist for an infraction of what was felt to be an unimportant, constantly violated rule. The response to the C.I.O. organizing campaign had meanwhile become so great, that Lewis and the auto union leaders on December 21st wired Knudsen, asking for a collective bargaining conference. They took as the text of their request, an address in which the corporation's executive head had said that "collective bargaining should take place before a shut-down, rather than after." General Motors replied that the respective plant managers should be approached with grievances that came within their jurisdictions. The U.A.W. locals thereupon handed in contract forms to the plant heads, and met with universal rebuffs. There appeared to be no alternative to spreading the walkout.

The efficiency of the specialized production units of the General Motors system proved its fatal weakness in the strike. Simple strategy indicated to the auto-union leaders that with the key plants tied up, production would inevitably be brought to a halt throughout the entire system. The principal organizing efforts had therefore been directed at the key plants, and these were now brought to a standstill. The Cleveland Fisher Body plant stamped turret tops for General Motors models. Organized under the leadership of Vice-president Mortimer, its workers had one of the strongest of the U.A.W. locals. On December 28th, all of the 7,000 Cleveland workers went on strike, more than a thousand remaining in the plant. The Cleveland and local promptly announced that any settlement of its grievances would have to be part of a settlement for the entire General Motors system.

Flint was next in the line of the union's attack. In Fisher Body No. 1 plant were important dies, which, if removed to a less strong union center, might become the instruments for breaking the strike. On the evening of December 30th the night-shift men at Fisher No. 1 saw the dies being loaded on to trucks, bound for Grand Rapids and Pontiac. The events of that memorable day in Flint's history are detailed in the "Song of the Fisher Body No. One Strikers," a homespun parody to the music of "The Martins and the Coys," which soon became the epic song of the great strike. As the song told the story:

> *Now this strike it started one bright Wednesday evening*
> *When they loaded up a box car full of dies.*
> *When the union boys they stopped them,*
> *And the railroad workers backed them,*
> *The officials in the office were surprised.*

*CHORUS*
*These 4,000 union boys*
*Oh, they sure made lots of noise.*
*They decided then and there to shut down tight.*
*In the office they got snooty,*
*So we started picket duty,*
*Now the Fisher Body shop is on a strike.*

*Now they really started out to strike in earnest.*
*They took possession of the gates and buildings too.*
*They placed a guard in either clock-house,*
*Just to keep the non-union men out,*
*And they took the keys and locked the gates up too.*

Closing of the Cleveland and Flint plants would have been enough to paralyze General Motors' sixty-five automotive plants, but the union in fifteen other units were too restive to await shut-downs by order of the Corporation. Sit-down strikers ensconsed themselves in the Fleetwood and Cadillac plants in Detroit, in Fisher Body No. 2. Flint, and in the Guide Lamp factory at Anderson, Indiana. The Cleveland local, strong enough to keep the plant closed without a sit-down, called its members out within a week after they had ceased working. In the last weeks of the strike the Chevrolet motor assembly plant at Flint also was occupied by the strikers. Strikes of the traditional type were called in Janesville, Wisconsin; Norwood, Atlanta, St. Louis, Kansas City, and Toledo, Ohio. A shortage of glass, brought about by a strategically timed strike of C.I.O. glass workers, closed several other plants. By January 11, 112,800 of the Corporation's 150,000 production workers were idle. Before the strike ended the total rose to 140,000.

A detailed statement of the union's grievances was forwarded to the Corporation on January 4th. It requested an immediate conference to discuss eight demands: signing of a national agreement; abolition of piece work and fixing of day rates of pay; a thirty-hour week, six-hour day, and time-and-a-half for overtime; minimum rates of pay; reinstatement of men discharged for union activities; a seniority system to govern employment and reemployment after slack periods; recognition of the U.A.W. as the sole bargaining agency of all G.M. employees; and regulation of the speed of the belt-line and other machinery by union plant committees and the management. This appeal, like the union's previous requests, was turned down, and the conflict became a belligerent endurance test. An effort by General Motors to create a united front of all automobile manufacturers broke down when the Ford Motor Company refused to coöperate. *Steel*, the trade journal of the iron-and-steel industry, reported on January 18th that the Automobile Chamber of Commerce had sponsored a meeting at which such a plan was broached. General Motors proposed that all companies cease operations. *Steel* reported the Ford management feared such a move would precipitate a national panic, responsibility for which would be placed at the doors of the auto industry.

During the second week in January, Governor Frank Murphy vigorously took over the task of peacemaker. Elected to office in the Roosevelt landslide of the previous November, he had received the endorsement of the auto union and the entire Michigan labor movement. The difficulties which Governor Murphy encountered were enlarged by the sit-down strikes. General Motors insisted that the sit-downs constituted illegal seizure of its property and refused to confer with the union until the sitters were withdrawn. The strike leaders and the C.I.O., on the other hand, declared they had no faith in the verbal promises of General Motors and would not order their men out of the plants until assurances of sincere collective bargaining efforts were given in writing and surrounded by conditions which would make resumption of operations impossible until collective bargaining conferences had been concluded. In this stand, the U.A.W. leaders had their backs stiffened by Lewis.

After days and nights of effort, Governor Murphy on January 15th announced that a truce had been arranged under which bargaining conferences might proceed. The union agreed to evacuate all the plants its members were holding; the corporation promised that negotiations would start at once on the union's eight-point memorandum of January 4th. This represented a substantial gain for the union, since the corporation had insisted that many of the eight points were not subjects for a general conference. The negotiations were to continue "until a satisfactory settlement of all issues shall be effected, if possible." In no event were the negotiations to be terminated in less than fifteen days. The corporation, meanwhile, was not to remove any dies, tools, machinery, material or equipment from any of the plants on strike, nor to endeavor to resume operations.

Hundreds of workers carrying blankets, radios, accordions paraded out of the Fleetwood and Cadillac plants on Saturday afternoon, January 17th. At the same time, the Guide Lamp sitters gave over the Anderson factory. The spirit of the strikers was high with the confidence that they had won important concessions. The Flint plants were to be surrendered the following day.

Flint held the key to peace as well as to the strength of the strike. The Cadillac, Fleetwood, and Guide Lamp plants had no great strategic importance, but the Flint Fisher Body No. 1 plant, which sprawled over half a mile, was an ace in the auto strikers' hands. Much of the bitterness of the battle was concentrated in Flint, where the C.I.O. and General Motors, respectively, despatched their specialists in striking and strike-breaking. The entire city of 163,000 men, women, and children was dependent on the local General Motors plants for its existence. More than 50,000 Flint workers toiled in Chevrolet and Buick plants, as well as in Fisher Body factories. Several times in the course of the six weeks' strike Flint was on the verge of serious violence. Early in the strike, the Flint Alliance came into existence. Chairmanned by George E. Boysen, a former General Motors' paymaster and owner of a spark-plug factory, the Alliance set itself up as the true voice of the Flint citizenry and its General Motors' employees. To translate this voice into propaganda and organization, Floyd E. Williamson, a New York promoter-publicity man, was imported. The Alliance attack varied from righteous appeals to civic pride, through Williamson's denunciation of outside agitators, to threats of violence against the strikers. Its financing has not been revealed to this date, but Boysen made no secret of its dependence on the business interests of the city. Before the strike had ended, the Alliance was publicly reprimanded by Governor Murphy as would-be instigators of violence.

The tense atmosphere of the city boiled over but once into bloodshed, in what has become known as "The Battle of the Running Bulls." "Fisher 2," two miles away and across the city from "Fisher 1," had been held by sit-down strikers since the day their fellow-unionists had "locked the gates" of their plant. During the afternoon of January 11th, while Governor Murphy was laboring for a basis on which the plants would be evacuated and negotiations set in motion, the heat in Fisher 2 was shut off. The need to protect plant equipment, including its water system, had hitherto led the corporation to maintain the heating supply without interruption. A few hours later, the Flint police surrounded the entrance and announced there would be no further shipments of food. A ladder placed to a window by strikers was immediately torn down. Dinner time on a cold day came with the police still at their stations. The strikers faced an effort to freeze and starve them out of the plant. The Fisher 2 sitters, captained by William (Red) Mundale, a union rank-and-filer, had been considered one of the weak links in the strike. The shutting off of heat and food for them, the union felt, would be followed by similar efforts at Fisher 1.

A union sound truck pulled up at Fisher 2 in the early evening. Scores of strikers soon surrounded it. Victor Reuther, U.A.W. organizer, was at the microphone. The police were asked to permit delivery of food. The voice inside the car, carried to the strikers in and out of the plant, as well as to the police, first made pleas of labor solidarity to the officers. These failing, more belligerent appeals were uttered. Shortly before seven P.M., pickets rushed the door, swept the police aside, and moved coffee and bread into the plant. Two hours later, fifty policemen, almost half of Flint's entire force, attacked the pickets at the doors with clubs, driving some inside the building and attempting to scatter the others. A policeman shattered the glass pane in the door, poked a tear gas gun through the crevice and fired it. The gassed strikers inside fell back, and the battle was on. The police poured buckshot into the pickets and through the windows of the plant. Tear gas discharges alternated with the crack of the guns. The strikers fought back with sticks, metal pipes, nuts and bolts, soda-pop bottles, coffee-mugs, and a continuous rain of two-pound steel automobile door hinges. Throughout the three hours of fighting which followed a group of stalwart strikers surrounded the automobile with the loud speaker and resisted efforts to dismantle it. First one strike leader, then another, took the microphone, directing the strategy of the battle, cheering on the strikers and shouting pleas and threats at the police. "We wanted peace. General Motors chose war. Give it to them," the voice would shout.

Sheriff Thomas Wolcott drove his sedan into the battle zone. Before many minutes, strikers turned it on its side, its headlights still glaring and lighting up a wide path strewn with broken glass, rocks, and door hinges. Before the battle had ended, three other police cars had been captured. The police reformed for a new attack at midnight, but at a shouted signal from the car the nozzle of a rubber hose appeared at the door of the plant, and the strikers turned a powerful stream of cold water on their attackers. The Flint police retreated under the barrage of water and door hinges. They ran fifty yards to a bridge that approached the plant gate; then they went fifty yards more to the far end of the bridge. The fighting was over.

The strikers' guard continued their vigil through the wintry night while the strident battle cries from the plant and the car gave way to labor songs and cheers of victory. Fourteen strikers were removed to the hospital with bullet wounds, but by dawn the strikers were unchallenged in their possession of the plant. "Solidarity Forever" and cheers for the C.I.O. from tired voices pierced the cold morning air as determined bands of men and women, huddled around two street fires, guarded against a possible new attack on their fellow strikers in the plant. "The Battle of the Running Bulls" proved to be the only effort forcibly to remove sit-down strikers from General Motors plants.

The battle brought 1,500 Michigan national guardsmen to Flint, but Governor Murphy refused to yield to demands of the Flint Alliance and local authorities that the troops be employed to dislodge the sit-down strikers. Instead, the Governor ordered the corporation to make no further efforts to halt the food supplies. While Boysen bitterly denounced him, Murphy summoned union and corporation heads to meet him in the state Capitol at Lansing. There he worked out the truce of January 15th which brought the sitters out of the Detroit and Anderson factories.

The Flint strikers were to evacuate their plants on Sunday, the 17th, and negotiations, under the terms of the Lansing truce, were to start the following day. Sunday morning, the auto union leaders learned of an exchange of telegrams between Boysen and Knudsen. The chairman of the Flint Alliance, assaying the rôle of unionist, wired the General Motors' executive asking for a conference in behalf of G.M. workers said to be members of the Alliance. The request was written to challenge the growing confidence of the auto union that it might win sole bargaining rights in the negotiations. Knudsen's reply sought to assure Boysen that no such rights would be granted. He agreed to meet with Boysen and asserted, "we stand ready always to discuss with your group or any group of our employees any questions without prejudice to anyone." The strike leaders now charged a "double-cross." The telegrams were not to have been made public until Sunday evening, after the Flint strikers had given up the plants. It was only by accident that a reporter learned of Boysen's wire on Sunday morning. He had then sought Robert Travis's comment and the entire auto union knew within a few hours that the Flint Alliance had been promised a collective bargaining conference.

The national and Flint strike leaders, after acquainting Lewis of the development, declared that General Motors had presumed to rule out the union's demand for sole recognition before negotiations had even started. Sole recognition was, in fact, one of the eight points which were to have been debated at the parleys. The truce had been violated, the strike leaders announced. To the Flint incident they added charges that in Anderson local police had dispersed a picket line and demolished picket shanties, and that in Detroit some employees of the Cadillac plant had received instructions to return to work. Knudsen denied all three charges, but the Flint strikers reinforced their makeshift "fortifications" of the plants. The negotiations of the following day consisted of Knudsen's handing Brophy, Martin, Mortimer, and other U.A.W. officials a refusal to meet until the plants were evacuated. A few days later, G.M. promised not to confer with the Flint Alliance until U.A.W. negotiations had ended, but the union responded that it no longer had the slightest faith in the corporation's words. It insisted on an agreement before evacuation.

With the breakdown of the Lansing truce, Governor Murphy turned to Washington for assistance. In the national capital General Motors was impatient for word from Secretary of Labor Frances Perkins that the sit-downs were illegal; and the C.I.O. was as vigorously seeking intercession of the federal government in behalf of recognition of the auto union. Miss Perkins persuaded Sloan and Knudsen to meet with her. She was making slight progress when the conference recessed. Meanwhile, Lewis had told a full complement of the Washington newspapermen that labor was expecting Presidential support for its crucial struggle.

"For six months during the Presidential campaign," said Lewis, "the economic royalists represented by General Motors and the Du Ponts contributed their money and used their energy to drive this Administration from power. The Administration asked labor for help to repel this attack and labor gave it. The same economic royalists now have their fangs in labor. The workers of this country expect the Administration to help the strikers in every reasonable way."

Scanning a newspaper as he left Miss Perkins' office, Sloan read Lewis' pointed remarks, which included also a reiteration of his refusal to urge evacuation of the plants pending a settlement of basic union demands. The General Motors' president seized upon the statement and announced that it made further peace efforts futile. Pressed by interviewers, Sloan said he particularly resented Lewis' references to the President. That evening Sloan left the capital for New York.

At a White House interview, the next day, President Roosevelt indirectly but deliberately rebuked the C.I.O. leader for his plea that the Administration aid the strikers. Unperturbed, Lewis said that Miss Perkins' only success with Sloan was to have him meet with her in the Department of Labor Building, instead of secretly in the recesses of the plutocratic Metropolitan Club, where a first conference betwen the Secretary of Labor and the G.M. president had been held. The press, largely unfriendly to Lewis and the auto strikers, made much of the Presidential rebuke. A few days later the President spanked Sloan, evening things up but bringing a settlement of the strike no nearer. Miss Perkins had invited both Lewis and Sloan to meet with her. Lewis agreed, but Sloan declined, and President Roosevelt declared that the automobile magnate had made a "very unfortunate decision." A few days later Sloan returned to the city for a second meeting with the Secretary of Labor. When the conference ended, Miss Perkins was under the impression that a basis for ending the strike had been found. "Sloan had promised to have the corporation attend another peace conference in Lansing," said Miss Perkins. Later he called to say it was "all off."

"He ran out on me," said the troubled Secretary of Labor, providing avid headline-writers with ready-made text.

The central stage of the strike had meanwhile shifted back to Flint, where General Motors for the second time turned to the courts for aid in recapturing its plants. The first court proceeding had reacted in the strikers' favor when it was

295

revealed that Judge Edward D. Black, Genesee County's most venerable jurist, was the owner of G.M. stock worth $150,000 at the time he ordered the strikers to vacate the factories. The embarrassing publicity attendant on the revelation made Black's order a dead letter. The sitters laughed and jeered when Sheriff Wolcott read them the text.

On January 29th the corporation went before Circuit Judge Paul V. Gadola. The corporation told the court that the occupation of the two Fisher Body plants was maintained by force and violence as part of a conspiracy by Martin, Mortimer, and all other international officers of the union, Bud Simons and Red Mundale, leaders of the sitters in the Fisher Body plants, and Travis and Roy Reuther, U.A.W. organizers, to cripple the business of the corporation. This had been accomplished by the "continuous trespass" of the sit-down strikers, by the refusal of the strikers to permit G.M. executives access to the plants, and by the "clubs, sticks, and other weapons" of the strikers, it was alleged. Almost coincidental with the application for an injunction came a brutal physical attack on several auto union and C.I.O. organizers. Six organizers were driven by a mob from Bay City, Michigan, to Saginaw, both of them G.M. centers. Some were slugged and all were piled into a taxi which was forced to drive to Flint, thirty miles away, with a caravan of vigilantes behind them. As the unionists' car reached the outskirts of Flint, one of the pursuing automobiles forced the taxi to crash into a telegraph pole. Anthony Federoff, organizer for the C.I.O. and a Pennsylvania miner, had his scalp torn away; three others also had to be taken to the hospital with bad injuries. Ring-leaders of the mob were identified as G.M. foremen, but none were apprehended in the investigation which Saginaw, Flint, and county authorities set in motion. The incident served to heighten the tenseness of an already jittery city.

Argument on the corporation's plea for an injunction took place before Judge Gadola on February 2nd. It dragged through the day as Pressman, Maurice Sugar, and Larry S. Davidow, U.A.W. lawyers, insisted that the corporation was violating the National Labor Relations Act, and thus came into the court with unclean hands. The guilt of trespass was denied, while the General Motors' lawyers insisted the sitters had violated every tenet of the law by seizing property which was not their own. Meanwhile, more potent affairs were transpiring outside the crowded courtroom.

The huge Chevrolet works in Flint had been operating a few days a week, stocking up a reserve of parts. Since no cars could be completed, the strikers had no objections to this work and urged their members to take advantage of the opportunity to earn a few dollars. Unionists employed at Chevrolet soon complained, however, that they had been unjustly fired. Strike-leader Travis requested a conference with the plant management. A meeting was promised, then postponed as more union men were sent home. Demands for a sit-down strike in Chevrolet began to be heard. The strike leaders weighed the possibilities of success of a sit-down, which in this case would mean capturing a plant. It would be a difficult task. The troops were still in the city and the strikers' ranks had scores of informers among them. Nevertheless, the strike strategists felt it would be a worthwhile effort. The strike was not more than a month old. Capture of another huge plant would enthuse all the strikers and set at rest reports that their spirit was weakening. It might have a salutary effect on negotiations for a settlement which finally appeared to be getting under way in Detroit. There was also the consideration that it would be a practical demonstration, in the midst of the court proceedings, of the strikers' contempt for judge-made law and injunctions.

With the increase of discharges at Chevrolet, U.A.W. members insisted that they be allowed to make a counter attack. Travis, Hapgood, and the other leaders agreed. The problem of how to plan and then take over a large plant worth millions of dollars without betraying the preparations to G.M. spies required consummate strategy. Travis, Hapgood, and Kermit Johnson, "Chevvy" union leader, were equal to it. Of the several buildings which made up the Flint Chevrolet works, Plant No. 4, the motor-assembly division, was the most important. Should the Fisher 1 strikers be ousted, possession of Chevvy 4 would still prevent a single shiny Chevrolet from rolling out of any G.M. factory in the world. The Chevrolet workers insisted Plant 4 was the ideal place to sit down. The strike leaders knew this to be true, but since the project had been discussed by a large committee, they felt it necessary to keep the details a secret until the plan was ready for execution. Travis and Hapgood proposed that Chevrolet 9, a ball-bearing plant, was the one to be taken. The strikers set up a derisive howl. Ball-bearings could be gotten here, there, and everywhere, they said. It would do no good to take Chevvy 9, they argued hotly, sometimes with contempt for the ignorance of the outside organizers who presumed to tell G.M. workers that a ball-bearing plant was more important than a motor-assembly plant. The strike leaders stood their ground and their authority prevailed. Then came the problem of selecting a spy-proof committee which could be trusted with the truth, since their services would be needed at Chevvy 4. Each prospective committeeman was interviewed separately so that no striker knew what others had been considered for the task. Those appointed to the committee were ordered not to talk; those suspected and rejected were secretly and impressively told to proceed to Fisher 1, more than a mile away from Chevvy 4, on the afternoon of the projected plant capture.

Monday afternoon, several thousand strikers were in and near Pengelly Hall, the old three-story brick-and-wood structure which housed the union headquarters. By a prearranged plan word came to the strikers that some of their number were being attacked outside of Chevvy 9. Led by Hapgood, Roy Reuther, and an inevitable sound-truck, the strikers proceeded to Plant 9, arriving at 3:30 P.M. at the change of the shifts. Inside the ball-bearing plant, a group of unionists set up a shout for a sit-down strike. Warned by the false reports of informers, the plant management was fully prepared. The strikers in Chevvy 9, not one of the strongest union plants, staged a valiant battle for half an hour, many of them sustaining severe beatings from G.M. plant police, Flint detectives and other burly men who had been installed in the factory. Tear gas was thrown by company guards and police. Outside, several score members of the union's Emergency Brigade, made up exclusively of women and daughters of the strikers, smashed all windows within reach to permit air into the plant. Surrounded by hundreds of strikers, Hapgood

297

was at the microphone of the sound-truck, keeping alive the impression that the striker's interest was concentrated at Chevvy 9.

Shortly after four o'clock, a union messenger brought Hapgood word that the occupation of Chevvy 4 had been accomplished peacefully and completely. The strike leader called upon the strikers to disperse, an order promptly obeyed. He then joined the sitters in Plant 4, located several hundred yards from Plant 9. The strategy had worked, completing one of the most audacious bits of strike strategy the country had ever seen. Some 400 Chevvy 4 strikers, joined by a few score from near-by Chevvy 6, had taken the motor-assembly plant with no more difficulty than a few harsh words to amazed foremen. Within a few minutes union guards had been placed at the doors and gates and patrol committees organized to guard against surprise attacks. The sitters blossomed into expert barricade-builders. Steel-plant trucks weighing several hundred pounds were piled on each other in front of entrances and windows until they reached from floor to ceiling. By morning of February 2nd, national guardsmen patrolled the plant, but Chevy 4 strikers, perched on the roof, were serenading Fisher 2 strikers, heroes of the "Battle of the Running Bulls," with "Solidarity Forever." And from the roof and windows of Fisher 2, across and fifty yards down the street, husky voices shouted the union song back. Below, in the street, khaki-clad troops with bayoneted rifles walked to and fro, while machine-guns were focused on the captive plants.

For an entire day, soldiers' bayonets barred delivery of food to the men in Chevvy 4 plant and Fisher 2, which had been included in the militarized zone. Pressure was again exerted on Governor Murphy to use the troops to clear the plants. Among some national guard officers plans to attack were being suggested. Some proposed simply to shoot the strikers out; another hoped to project vomiting gas through the ventilating systems. The intelligence division furnished the press with a lurid tale of 500 "loyal" Chevrolet employees being held as hostages by the strikers. The plans and military propaganda came to nothing, however, as Murphy's abhorrence and fear of violence continued to dominate his efforts. Again General Motors looked to the courts. On the day following the capture of Chevvy 4, Judge Gadola signed an order directing the men to leave the Fisher body plants under pain of imprisonment for conempt and of having a fine of $15,000,000—the estimated value of the plants—levied against them. Sheriff Wolcott proceeded to Plant 2 to read the order. A few strikers came to the door, dropped a steel barrier they had erected, and listened to the labored reading of the legal edict. At Fisher 1, the strikers permitted the sheriff to enter and stood about him in the cafeteria, gibing and assuming poses of mock seriousness while the recital was repeated. The order gave the strikers until three o'clock of the afternoon of February 3 to leave the factories.

The sit-down strikers called meetings in their plants on the evening before the ominous deadline. Seated on boxes, cans of paint, and kegs of nails, determined men in gray shirts, overalls, and work pants, all with loved ones at home, discussed a problem which they knew held life or death for some of them. The entire nation watched, fearing the bloodiest of industrial battles. It was obvious that only an army of sheriff's deputies and militiamen could enforce the court's ruling. In Fisher

2, surrounded by troops who barred all civilians from approaching, the sitters could not take counsel with their outside leaders. Nevertheless, the discussion in both plants was brief and arrived at unanimous conclusions. The decisions were conveyed to Governor Murphy in two telegrams.

"We the workers in the plant," said the message sent by the strikers in Fisher 1, "are completely unarmed, and to send in the military, armed thugs and armed deputies . . . will mean a bloody massacre of the workers.

"We have carried on a stay-in strike over a month in order to make General Motors Corporation obey the law and engage in collective bargaining. . . . Unarmed as we are, the introduction of the militia, sheriffs, or police with murderous weapons will mean a blood bath of unarmed workers. . . . We have decided to stay in the plant. We have no illusions about the sacrifices which this decision will entail. We fully expect that if a violent effort is made to oust us many of us will be killed, and we take this means of making it known to our wives, to our children, to the people of the state of Michigan and the country that if this result follows from the attempt to reject us, you are the one who must be held responsible for our deaths."

The temperature was again near zero in Flint the next day, but the vision of thousands of strikers battling armed deputies and possibly the militia was colder still. There was a spirit of a zero hour before an army's charge into enemy territory. Hysteria, mixed with eager anticipation, was evident in some quarters. Into the early hours of the morning plant executives, Flint Alliance leaders, and Flint police heads drank potent liquor in the exclusive Town Club at the Durant Hotel. Boisterously, they sang the songs of the strikers, giving them raucous, mocking accents. In the plants the strikers sat silently at their radios and card games. Wooden clubs and blackjacks produced with belt-line technique and speed hung at their waists.

Early morning of the ominous day, the roads to Flint were filled with strikers from near-by cities, some many miles away. Thousands of workers, many women among them, came with squared jaws to take their places on a picket line around Fisher 1. By noon delegations of workers had arrived in battered and new cars and trucks from Detroit, Lansing, Toledo, and Pontiac. Akron sent rubber workers, shock troops of the C.I.O. Walter Reuther came at the head of 500 strong from the West Side of Detroit. The Dodge workers from Detroit also arrived in disciplined phalanxes. Kelsey-Hayes Wheel unionists waved aloft a banner, "Kelsey-Hayes workers never forget their friends." As three o'clock approached, a long train of almost 5,000 workers, two abreast, circled the lawn that fronted the approach to Fisher 1. An American flag led the procession, then came members of the women's Emergency Brigades, their red and green berets the only color spots in a grim assembly. Men and women carried clubs and stout sticks; several had crowbars, stove pokers, and lengths of pipe. A few had knocked the base off clothes-trees, and carried the poles, with metal hangers, on their shoulders. Like the Minute Men of '76 and as fully determined that their cause was righteous, they had seized whatever weapon lay at hand and rushed off to do battle. The constantly arriving auto-loads of workers soon blocked the street, and strikers, aided by sound-trucks, took over direction of traffic. Not a policeman was in sight. At the windows of the plant were the sit-down strikers, their number augmented from the usual 400 to almost 2,000. Strips of cheesecloth hung round their necks, ready for use as some slight protection against tear gas. Windows were barricaded by steel plate, pierced with holes for the nozzles of hoses which lay on the floors nearby. A street valve that controlled the plant's water supply had been enclosed by a new wooden picket shanty. A special detail of strikers guarded the shanty. Inside were drums of gasoline, fuel for a protective wall of fire should an effort be made to capture the valve and cut off the plant's water system.

The zero hour at Fisher 2 and Chevvy 4 was far different. Here there were no crowds of cheering comrades, only a dreary, deserted broad street dotted with soldiers carrying muskets in a ceaseless patrol. The strikers at the windows of the plants displayed no outward reaction to the machine guns and 37-milimeter howitzers poised in the gutters. For hours as the afternoon fraught with tragedy wore on, the Chevvy and Fisher strikers chanted back and forth, "Solidarity Forever, For the Union Makes Us Strong."

Thus the deadline passed, Governor Murphy, in Detroit, where he had finally prevailed upon Knudsen to meet with Lewis, wired Sheriff Wolcott that he was to take no action. The sheriff, more than eager to comply, thereupon became a legal authority and asserted Judge Gadola's order was directed at the strikers alone and did not yet call upon him for enforcement. Boysen and local General Motors' attorneys raged at both the sheriff and the Governor. Meanwhile, the strikers' battle lines turned into celebrating. The sit-down strikers' band in Fisher 1 played hill-billy airs, and before many minutes the pickets, men and women, were square-dancing on the hard-frozen lawns. Flint's day of fear ended in hilarious, nervous joy for the strikers.

Two days later, Judge Gadola, refusing to postpone action any longer, ordered Sheriff Wolcott to arrest all officials and leaders of the auto union, and every striker in the Fisher Body plants. The sheriff, refusing to swear in new deputies, declared he did not have a sufficient force to make the arrests and asked Governor Murphy for the assistance of militiamen. Murphy noted the request, postponed a decision, and resumed his efforts to effect a settlement.

The end of the General Motors strike came on February 11th. A request from President Roosevelt that the corporation meet with spokesmen of the strikers brought about a conference on February 4th, Knudsen stating that the wish of the President left no alternative but compliance. The conference met in Detroit, with Governor Murphy in the rôle of peacemaker. For a week he shuttled back and forth between Lewis, Pressman, Martin and Mortimer, and Knudsen, John Thomas Smith, and G. Donaldson Brown, the corporation negotiators. Most of the time the two groups did not meet together; frequently they were on the verge of a complete break. At one point, Knudsen insisted that the talks would go no further until the plants were evacuated. "You have an injunction which disposes of that issue," Lewis replied. The chief issue was the insistence of Lewis that the auto union be given exclusive recognition. As the possibilities of forcible eviction of the Flint strikers dwindled, the resistance of G.M. weakened.

The settlement which Governor Murphy finally announced included a written pledge by the corporation that it would not, without the Governor's consent, for a period of six months recognize or deal with any other employee spokesman than the United Automobile Workers in the seventeen plants closed by strikes. In all other G.M. automotive plants, the union was to be recognized as the agent of its members. There was to be no discrimination against union members, and all strikers were to be rehired regardless of their union membership or strike activities. Union members were to be permitted to discuss the union with other workers during lunch and rest hours in the plant. Injunction and contempt proceedings against the Flint sit-down strikers were to be dropped. Negotiations were to start at once looking toward a signed contract on those of the eight original union demands which were not disposed of.

The agreement constituted a monumental advance for unionism in the automobile industry. The mere fact of General Motors signing a contract with a union would in itself have been an historic victory. The exclusive recognition accorded the U.A.W. in seventeen plants, however, was the outstanding union gain. The plants affected were those which held within their grasp the entire G.M. system. The prestige of the union was enhanced in all union plants, and as Lewis had foreseen, led to enrollment in the union of a great majority of all G.M.'s production workers. The pledge of no discrimination against union men might have been a mere pious declaration were it not for the lifting of restrictions on the right to talk about the union and the right to wear union buttons on plant property. The right to talk during one's lunch hour and to wear the insignia of one's organization seems an obvious enough privilege in a free country but the auto workers had never enjoyed it. These were more than academic gains. They effectively ended the spy system, for every man could now talk freely and proclaim openly his union affiliation without fear of reprisal. The agreement to reëmploy all strikers was a reversal of G.M.'s determination that all the sit-down strikers had been fired. Coincidental with the signing of the agreement, General Motors announced a general wage increase of five per cent. This was fixed in the auto workers' minds as a by-product of the strike.

There was good ground for the night-long celebrations which filled Flint and the auto workers' halls in Cleveland, Detroit, Toledo, and other G.M. centers. The auto workers had won a great victory for themselves, and for the Committee for Industrial Organization they had created the psychology of success and the enthusiasm which were needed to raise a great campaign to the dimensions of a crusade.

# 75

# Class Consciousness
# in an Industrial City

The preceding selection well conveys a sense of the social ferment of the 1930s, but Levinson and many other observers were inclined to exaggerate the extent to which American workingmen had become alienated from the capitalist system. Many were disrespectful of *particular* propertied interests when these seemed to conflict with their own welfare, but outside of intellectual circles there was little generalized antagonism toward an economy dominated by large corporations and wealthy individuals. A useful antidote to the view that class consciousness and class hatreds were acute in the New Deal era is Alfred Winslow Jones' pioneering study, *Life, Liberty and Property*. In 1938–1939 Jones went to Akron, Ohio, a city that had experienced violent labor conflicts in its rubber plants shortly before. If class antagonisms and the polarization of attitudes concerning public policy were sharp anywhere in the United States they were so in Akron; however, Jones' careful analysis of the relationship between class position and attitudes toward corporate property, based on interviews in which men were asked to respond to six stories involving conflicts between property rights and other values, revealed that even in Akron the trend toward cleavage was weak and the pull of what Jones calls "the central morality" strong. On the scale referred to in the selection, a score of 32 represented the choice of property rights over all other values in each of the stories: a score of 0 represented the complete subordination of property to other values.

## LIFE, LIBERTY AND PROPERTY
### Alfred W. Jones

The investigator is bound to approach with considerable trepidation the drawing of conclusions from a type of study that has never before been attempted. There are not many generalizations that can be fully supported by the data from a single study. It needs, therefore, to be pointed out that the following statements are in varying degrees borne out by the evidence gathered in Akron, and that they range from those that we regard as well-substantiated by the data to those that can be advanced only tentatively, as hypotheses, pending further investigation.

1. The attitude toward corporate property of industrial executives and business leaders, corresponds closely to their economic position.

The leaders of industry in Akron have prospered under the auspices of the corporate form of organization. They have advanced themselves to managerial positions of power and prestige and have acquired wealth in the form of corporate securities. It would have been a handicap to them, to say the least, if they had turned aside to show sympathy for the other side in any of the conflict situations in which they found themselves. This applies, of course, to the struggle they have had with each other as well as to the conflicts as in our stories—in which the general rights of corporate property were involved. The leaders of economic life in Akron are in the main line of American business with its tradition of self-reliance and ruthless, competitive acquisitiveness.

At first glance, there might be reason to expect a difference of interests and therefore of attitude between management and the absentee stockholders. In *The Modern Corporation and Private Property,* Berle and Means have demonstrated that a cleavage of interests exists between "control" and stockholders. The "pure" property rights of the stockholders do not correspond exactly to the rights of the managers of industry either in so far as the latter have their own interests, or in so far as they represent the "control," although the rights of both management and "control" derive traditionally from ownership. If managers were concerned wholly with the technical problems of production, we might expect from them a lower regard for corporate property rights than from the stockholders. In practice we could not, in Akron, isolate the three groups, stockholders, "control," and management. Even if we could have done so, it is doubtful whether our interview method would have uncovered any differences in attitudes between them.

Management is forced to be concerned with many considerations other than the problems of production. Managers are almost always wealthy men and stockholders themselves, and all three groups obviously derive benefits from the corporate form of wealth, whatever quarrels they may have with each other.

So it is not surprising that the scores of the eighteen Akron business leaders whom we interviewed tend to pile up at the 32 end of our scale.

2. Attitude toward corporate property corresponds to economic position fairly closely among the workers—especially those organized along industrial lines, *i.e.*, in the C.I.O., but less clearly than among the business leaders.

The worker derives no such special benefit from the existence of corporate property as does the manager of industry. On the contrary, "labor" is popularly supposed to, and does actually, confront "capital" on a variety of issues such as we have described in our stories, and it is conceivable that the working man would invariably set himself against the property rights of corporations wherever they come into conflict with the rights of interests of workers or poor people. We might expect that the economic position at least of manual workers would cause them to take a position exactly opposed to that of the leaders of industry.

There is a tendency for the scores of the 193 C.I.O. rubber workers in Akron to pile up at the lower end of our scale. But whereas ten out of eighteen, or 56.3 per cent, of the business leaders scored in the four highest places, no more than seventy-five out of 193 C.I.O. rubber workers, or 38.9 per cent, scored in the four lowest places.

Turning to other workers, the difference is even more marked. Random samples were taken of rubber workers who are not members of the C.I.O. (some of whom may be members of the Employee Associations); members of the A.F. of L. (mostly from the building trades); W.P.A. manual workers.

We can get a composite picture of the manual workers of Akron by taking the above groups along with the C.I.O. members.

No more than 28 per cent scored in the 0-3 class.

If we may say that the four highest scores represent at least the immediate economic interests of the business leaders, and the four lowest scores at least the immediate economic interests of the workers in Akron, then it is clear that the former show attitudes more in accordance with their interests. A majority (56 per cent) of our small sample of business executives scored in the 29-32 class. Only 28 per cent of the workers scored in the 0-3 class.

3. The middle groups, taken as a whole, show a greater tendency to divergence in their attitude toward corporate property than either the business leaders or the workers, with a predominant tendency to a moderate attitude, but with many individuals drawn toward the extremes. Other than immediately economic interests seem to play a considerable part in the divergence.

By middle groups we mean those whose position in industry is considered to be intermediate between that of the top management and the manual workers: or, if outside of big industry, those independent merchants and producers whose status and wealth is intermediate. Thus we should include both the new and old middle classes, along with the lower-salaried employees, some of whom may not be so well paid as many manual workers. Such a category would admit all such groups as technicians, white collar workers, salespeople, professionals (with certain exceptions), small storekeepers, independent producers, etc.

The best composite result that we can get is by throwing together the scores of the five middle groups that we studied in Akron—24 chemists, 97 female office workers, 40 teachers, 26 ministers, and 52 small merchants.

We saw above that these groups are not as bunched in the middle as our small sample of farmers. It is an easy conclusion that life in the city has exerted a pull upon them and has subjected some in each group to the influence of extreme ideas about corporate property. This is true both of those that are connected with big industry and of those independent of it.

5. Even in Akron, with almost everything in its background making for cleavage, the trend toward conformity with the compromising position seems to be stronger than the trend toward cleavage.

In a placid farm community, to which only echoes of industrial conflict penetrate, we might expect that the opinions of the middle people (who would be the bulk of the community) would pile up in the middle of the range—perhaps in a manner even more marked than was the case with our farmers to whose ears the shouts of the Akron battles come rather clearly. Or even in an industrial city where the issues between capital and labor have been peacefully worked out—either because unions have never appeared or because the employers have easily accommodated themselves to unionism—we might look for a marked middle-of-the-road tendency among the bulk of the middle people. We might then further expect that this would have an influence on the attitudes of the workers, drawing a great number of them in toward the central area. On the whole, then, the tendency toward conformity would be great and the tendency toward cleavage so slight that the end lines might even disappear entirely.

Akron, on the other hand, was the first city in this country (and, for that matter, in the world) in which large-scale sitdown strikes were deliberately used by the workers. Akron was the first city of any importance in which the C.I.O. succeeded in setting up a new industrial union. Nor was this done with the complacent non-interference of the big companies. Not only was the help of the Federal government called for, but also a series of militant strikes took place. In the fierceness of the industrial struggle of recent years, Akron is an extreme case among American cities, along with such others as Minneapolis, Toledo, and San Francisco. Akron is a one-industry town, and the theory can be advanced and defended that extreme points of view and attitudes build up more readily and quickly the more homogeneous the population. Not only is social interaction in Akron heightened because all have in common an interest in the rubber industry, but there is also, owing to the preponderance of "American" stock, an unusual absence of ethnic heterogeneity. Furthermore, if extreme attitudes develop out of suffering, we might expect to find them in the city that had been earlier keyed to such high expectations and had then been so hard hit by the depression. Finally, Akron is to an extraordinary degree an industrial city. According to the 1940 census it is the thirty-eighth city in the country in population, and according to Department of Commerce figures it is the twelfth in the country in value of manufactured goods. Akron is not a city of wealthy and middle class consumers—making for culture (in the narrow sense) and for the presence of a multitude of small service businesses. It is rather a city of producers with a minimum of the cushioning effect provided by administration, consumption, and leisure for education and the arts. Therefore, if anywhere, we might expect to find in Akron a city in which a great degree of polarization in economic attitudes had taken place, the middle groups having deserted their traditional middle position and therefore providing no point of attraction either for workers or capitalists.

Instead we find that the population of Akron yields a random sample of its citizens 76 per cent of whose scores fall within the central tendency rather than within the area piled up at the ends, and over half of whose scores are between 6 and 18.

6. No distinction is made between the property rights of corporations and of individuals, but rather between the rights of the wealthy, the "big interests," the banks etc., on the other hand, and the small property holders on the other.

For many decades the Supreme Court has interpreted the due process clause of

305

the Fourteenth Amendment (". . . nor shall any state deprive any person of life, liberty, or property, without due process of law") in such a way as to uphold firmly the legal fiction that corporations are persons. In a dissenting opinion that stands by itself, Justice Black said, "The words 'life' and 'liberty' do not apply to corporations. . . . However, the decisions of this court which the majority follows hold that corporations are included in this clause insofar as the word 'property' is concerned." In the same opinion he said, "I do not believe the word 'person' in the Fourteenth Amendment includes corporations. . . . I believe this court should overrule previous decisions which interpreted the Fourteenth Amendment to include corporations."

Clearly, a man is related in one way to the farm soil that he has worked and cherished, or to any product of toil, "with which he hath mixed his labour" and thereby made it part of himself (whether it is intended for further production or immediate consumption); and in another way to a gigantic factory that he may never have seen and whose ownership he shares with thousands of others. It is equally clear that the emotional impact on the common man of these two relationships must be vastly different. Simple private property—the right of a man to his farm, his tools, his dwelling place—is valued only lower than the even more basic personal rights—life and liberty. If a way in which these personal rights might be secured could be clearly and cogently shown, and if such a way should happen to infringe that vast complex of prerogatives and control that we call corporate property (without violating the basic personal security of the owners) there is every reason to believe that corporate property rights would crack up and fall apart, and those parts that demonstrably stand in the way of the general welfare would disappear.

But no such persuasive demonstration has been given, and, in the meantime, Justice Black's is a lone voice. At least as far as Akron is concerned, its common people show merely a tendency rather vaguely and blindly to project over to the companies and their owners the property rights that they readily accord to private persons in general. To be sure, this is one of the tentative conclusions from our work for which there is no statistical evidence, since we asked no direct questions allowing a differentiation between corporate property and private property in general. But it is based on negative evidence in the remarks made by the respondents, and on the general impression received by the investigators. Many of the persons interviewed were quick to see that each of our stories was concerned with a conflict between property rights and "human" rights, and even more mentioned "bank" and "companies" in such a way as to make clear that their opinions would be different if the property of humble individuals were involved. The blurring and confusion of the people of the central area derives plainly from the attribution to corporations of property rights, and then the two-way pull— toward the protection of property and toward human welfare. Our society has in the past protected both tolerably well, and the people of the central area somehow uneasily think it should continue to do so.

On the other hand, if the persuasive demonstration should ever be provided, it is more than possible that Justice Black, who would like to see the corporation lose its character as a person, would find an echo among the people, and then corporate property would lose its character as private property.

7.a. The persons whose scores fall in the central area make marked concessions to corporate property.

Something more than half (155) of the 303 scores in the random sample are clustered between the scores 6 and 18, inclusive. These 155 scores are the most closely grouped of any of the central area, and, if we leave out of account the zeros, they are the most closely grouped in the entire range. Of the 155, a majority (55 per cent) disapprove of the action of the farmer's neighbors in helping him to get rid of his obligation to the bank. An even larger majority (61 per cent) are in favor of having the stockholders of the given company get at least part of the net profits. (The card giving the stockholders everything was put in first place by 12 per cent and the compromise card—stockholders and employees—by 49 per cent.)

7.b. The persons whose scores fall in the central area accept violations of corporate property in the interest of human welfare and the alleviation of suffering, such as to suggest that they would accept changes curtailing—even sharply—the rights of corporate property.

8. The group with the highest regard for corporate property (most top business executives and some others) is not likely to gain (or regain) political and social leadership and a broad popular following if it bases its statements and actions on the sentiments and attitudes it manifested in our study.

"This is not a moral question, but a matter of sheer business. The company owes nothing to the workers or to the town. Its only obligation is to make money for the stockholders. If the management considers morals in this case, the stockholders ought to vote for a change in management." This was not an exceptional statement to hear from the industrial leaders in Akron. It corresponded to their scores, as did also, in a way, their hatred of the New Deal and almost all of its works. The difference between a score of 32 and one of 8 corresponds to the difference between such a statement and the following: "I used to think differently —I wouldn't be so willing now to let things take their course, and have people suffer. If a way can be found to prevent all this misery it ought to be put into effect—and I don't hardly see why big companies and rich people should be allowed to stand in the way."

A recent survey shows that Federal provision for all the needy having no other means of subsistence is now a desire of a considerable majority of the American people, and the assertion is made that this function of the Federal government was not accepted before the New Deal. In earlier times when things went relatively well there was little reason why the majority of people in the middle groups, and even a majority of workers, should not allow the big business man to speak for them. But our study shows that in Akron he is still speaking an old language that does not now meet the emotional needs of very many beside those of his own kind.

9. The central morality exerts a powerful pull upon the attitudes of the workers.

The leaders of industry sit secure and confident in the stronghold of their opinions—at least to all outward appearances. They feel that the law fortifies them

307

in their ideas, as do the traditions of the system that has elevated them. If they are in fact frightened, we may venture that it is because they are not really sure that they know what to do to bring back the confidence of others in them. They have learned, however, since the early days of the Roosevelt administration to work off their anxiety in the form of anger against the New Deal. In any case they enjoy a sort of ideological autonomy.

So do the middle groups, in spite of the conflicting pulls upon them and in spite of the fact they are troubled and confused. In fact the middle groups have perhaps an advantage over the capitalists in that they are not only willing to make concessions to the traditional claims of property, but also to the claims of humanitarianism which are likewise deeply rooted in our culture. Humanitarianism, of course, can lie dormant during good times. Even in times of general suffering, if there is no way to implement it, it will not add to the self-confidence of the groups that entertain it. That confidence has, in a measure, been provided by the New Deal, which made its appeal to the "people" and which provided a hope (a powerful hope for a time, and still a hope, though a weaker one) that its values could be realized. We have seen what an influence this hope had in Akron on most of the population and particularly on the workers.

It is significant that the staunchest supporters of the New Deal have been the workers, both organized and unorganized, in spite of the fact that it has shown no inclination to abolish the rights of corporate property. We have seen also that without the help of the Federal administration, and, probably, without the good will of the middle groups in Akron, the rubber workers would not have been able to organize. It is also important that workers in Akron (and elsewhere) have shown themselves willing to give up the sitdown strike as a weapon, in spite of its effectiveness, because it offended the middle groups. The evidence gathered in the present study indicates further how little ideological independence the workers possess, even on the subject and in a community where we might expect it to be the greatest.

Of course our study does not prove conclusively anything concerning the future. But the Akron data would seem to strengthen the further contention that the conforming, central morality or ideology of our society bears on the workers so heavily as to make it unlikely that they can shake it off as long as the conditions that have created and perpetuated it persist.

10. The group with the lowest regard for corporate property (some industrially organized workers, fewer other workers, and still fewer others) would find it possible to gain social and political leadership and a broad popular following only under extraordinary circumstances, if at all.

This statement, like (7) above and the two following, is in the nature of a speculation concerning the future and is, of course, merely hinted at by our data, rather than fully supported. Furthermore, the influences of the country as a whole upon any city are such that a statement of this sort is meaningless when applied to Akron alone. It ought, therefore, to be prefaced—"If the rest of the country were like Akron." As we have seen, the rest of the country is not like Akron, and this statement could be much more easily supported for the country as a whole than for Akron.

For the lowest scoring group to gain leadership there would almost certainly have to be (1) a united labor movement and (2) the fairly complete organization of the unorganized. (3) This would have to come about under a labor leadership with no regard for corporate property, and yet be achieved through statements and actions acceptable to the central tendency. (4) A competent leadership, political and economic, would have to be developed along with a workable and plausible program, ahead of what would probably also be called for, namely (5) such an economic breakdown as to demoralize the other groups.

We have seen in the scores of the workers (even many of the C.I.O.), in their remarks, and in the actual behavior of the labor unions in Akron, ample evidence of dependence on the ideas and values that are commonly associated with the middle groups. So much is this the case that it is hard to conceive of a unified labor movement and then the drawing in of those as yet unorganized unless this were to be brought about through statements and actions that would be approved of by the "central tendency." This would not be a barrier to organization, to be sure, since what we heard in Akron indicates amply that the central tendency is not opposed to unions nor even to their militant action where that seems to be called for by the intransigence of the employers. But even the first condition—the early settlement of labor's internal problems such as would permit the emergence of a strong and unified labor movement—has not yet taken place.

For it to come about under the necessary circumstances seems still more unlikely, and for the remaining conditions making for the leadership of the lowest scoring group to be fulfilled seems very improbable.

11. Economic and social action that satisfied the people whose scores fall in the central area could also satisfy the preponderant number of workers of all categories.

It is fairly safe speculation that the central mode in our distribution has been shifted toward the zero end of the scale by the events of the 1930's. It is likely that in earlier, more prosperous times the middle groups had a higher regard for corporate property and the complex of authority established around it. It is possible that this higher regard would have been represented by a sharper peak and one perhaps located above the middle of the range.

At present, however, the peak comes at 8, which is only one-third of the distance from zero that it is from 32. There can be little doubt but that it will be easier for the middle groups and workers (in so far as they are represented in the central tendency) to come together even with the lowest scoring group than with those that scored the highest.

The central morality is humanitarian and approves of acts in the interest of human welfare and alleviation of suffering even if they entail the infringement of corporate property. It approves of trade unions, and would like to see a well-led, unified, strong labor movement, but one that refrained from violence. The central morality is not pacifist, however, and would even approve of violence if there were wrongdoers that it thinks could be met in no other way. In all of these particulars it could completely satisfy the workers, with the exception of those few that have taken the point of view of the employers.

We believe that the considerations just mentioned are paramount with the workers. If they are met the workers would go along with the people of the central area in their desire to make some concessions to the rights of corporate property.

12. There exists widespread anxiety and doubt, which will persist and even grow, not merely if conditions become worse, but if they remain as they are. Further consequences are unpredictable, but it is not likely that the rights of corporate property will be strengthened.

Our stories reflect the times and put particular emphasis on the hardship and insecurity to which a considerable proportion of our population is subject. It is therefore only natural that they should have brought out in the respondents, as their remarks showed, feelings of pessimism and apprehension. It was equally clear that very few think they know what ought to be done, or have faith that anyone else is in possession of a program capable of meeting the country's present needs.

# 76

# A Definition of America's Role in the Far East

In the early 1930s Japan began to flex its muscles and to extend its influence throughout eastern Asia by military and other means. Its invasion of Manchuria in 1931 resulted in the creation of a satellite government there; soon after, Japan announced that she would no longer be bound by the provisions of the Washington Naval Treaty of 1922, and that she would strive to attain parity of strength with the United States and Great Britain. In this letter of December 1934 the U.S. Ambassador to Japan, Joseph C. Grew, comments on Japanese ambitions. Grew feared that Japan sought the establishment of "a Pax Japonica, with eventual complete commercial control, and, in the minds of some, eventual complete political control of East Asia." From the Japanese point of view, however, the status quo Grew was defending amounted to a "Pax Americana," in which through somewhat more subtle economic and political pressures America assured a dominant power position for itself in an area of the world several thousand miles removed from its natural sphere of interest. Grew's assumptions about the importance and legitimacy of protecting America's "varied interests in the Far East," even at the cost of war, continued to influence United States foreign policy down to the present day.

## LETTER TO THE SECRETARY OF STATE
### Joseph C. Grew

Sir:

Now that the London Naval Conversations have terminated, I should like to convey to the Department various thoughts in this general connection to which the Department may desire to give consideration if and when the conversations are renewed or a naval conference convoked. I shall be contributing little that is new, for most of the facts and opinions set forth herein have already been brought to the Department's attention in previous reports. Furthermore the attitude, policy and

From *Peace and War: United States Foreign Policy, 1931–1941* (Washington, D.C., 1943), 236–244.

action of our delegation in London, as directed by the Government and as revealed in the various summaries of developments telegraphed to this Embassy on October 25 and 31, November 22 and December 10, and in certain press reports, have indicated a sound comprehension of the situation in the Far East as it exists today. The firm stand of our Government and delegation to maintain the present naval ratios intact in the face of Japanese intransigence, as well as their decision that the action of the Japanese Government in denouncing the Washington Naval Treaty automatically created a new situation in which the conversations must be suspended *sine die,* leaving the Japanese to return home empty handed, were especially gratifying to those of us who have watched the developments in London from this angle. The purpose of this despatch is therefore mainly to summarize and to place my views in concise form on record for the future.

The thought which is uppermost in my mind is that the United States is faced, and will be faced in future, with two main alternatives. One is to be prepared to withdraw from the Far East, gracefully and gradually perhaps, but not the less effectively in the long run, permitting our treaty rights to be nullified, the Open door to be closed, our vested economic interests to be dissolved and our commerce to operate unprotected. There are those who advocate this course, and who have advocated it to me personally, on the ground that any other policy will entail the risk of eventual war with Japan. In their opinion, "the game is not worth the candle" because the United States can continue to subsist comfortably even after relinquishing its varied interests in the Far East, thereby eliminating the risk of future war.

The other main alternative is to insist, and to continue to insist, not aggressively yet not the less firmly, on the maintenance of our legitimate rights and interests in this part of the world and, so far as practicable, to support the normal development of those interests constructively and progressively.

There has already been abundant indication that the present Administration in Washington proposes to follow the second of these alternatives. For purposes of discussion we may therefore, I assume, discard the hypothesis of withdrawal and examine the future outlook with the assurance that our Government has not the slightest intention of relinquishing the legitimate rights, vested interests, non-discriminatory privileges for equal opportunity and healthful commercial development of the United States in the Far East.

In following this second and logical course, there should be and need be nothing inconsistent, so far as our own attitude is concerned, with the policy of the good neighbor. The determination to support and protect our legitimate interests in the Far East can and should be carried out in a way which, while sacrificing no point of principle, will aim to restrict to a minimum the friction between the United States and Japan inevitably arising from time to time as a result of that determination.

The administration of that policy from day to day becomes a matter of diplomacy, sometimes delicate, always important, for much depends on the method and manner of approach to the various problems with which we have been, are, and will continue to be faced. With the ultrasensitiveness of the Japanese, arising out of a marked inferiority complex which manifests itself in the garb of an equally marked superiority complex, with all its attendant bluster, chauvinism, xenophobia and organized national propaganda, the method and manner of dealing with current controversies assumes a significance and importance often out of all proportion to the nature of the controversy. That the Department fully appreciates this fact has been amply demonstrated by the instructions issued to this Embassy since the present Administration took office, and it has been our endeavor to carry out those instructions, or to act on our own initiative when such action was called for, with the foregoing considerations constantly in view.

But behind our day to day diplomacy lies a factor of prime importance, namely national support, demonstrated and reinforced by national preparedness. I believe that a fundamental element of that preparedness should be the maintenance of the present naval ratios in principle and the eventual achievement and maintenance of those ratios, so far as they apply to Japan, in fact. With such a background, and only with such a background, can we pursue our diplomacy with any confidence that our representations will be listened to or that they will lead to favorable results. General Douglas MacArthur, Chief of Staff of the United States Army, was recently reported in the press as saying: "Armies and navies, in being efficient, give weight to the peaceful words of statesmen, but a feverish effort to create them when once a crisis is imminent simply provokes attack." We need thorough preparedness not in the interests of war but of peace.

It is difficult for those who do not live in Japan to appraise the present temper of the country. An American Senator, according to reports, has recently recommended that we should accord parity to Japan in order to avoid future war. Whatever the Senator's views may be concerning the general policy that we should follow in the Far East, he probably does not realize what harm that sort of public statement does in strengthening the Japanese stand and in reinforcing the aggressive ambitions of the expansionists. The Japanese press of course picks out such statements by prominent Americans and publishes them far and wide, thus confirming the general belief in Japan that the pacifist element in the United States is preponderantly strong and in the last analysis will control the policy and action of our Government. Under such circumstances there is a general tendency to characterize our diplomatic representations as bluff and to believe that they can safely be disregarded without fear of implementation. It would be helpful if those who share the Senator's views could hear and read some of the things that are constantly being said and written in Japan, to the effect that Japan's destiny is to subjugate and rule the world (*sic*), and could realize the expansionist ambitions which lie not far from the surface in the minds of certain elements in the Army and Navy, the patriotic societies and the intense nationalists throughout the country. Their aim is to obtain trade control and eventually predominant political influence in China, the Philippines, the Straits Settlements, Siam and the Dutch East Indies, the Maritime Provinces and Vladivostok, one step at a time, as in Korea and Manchuria, pausing intermittently to consolidate and then continuing as soon as the intervening obstacles can be overcome by diplomacy or force. With such dreams of empire cherished by many, and with an army and navy capable of taking the bit in

313

their own teeth and running away with it regardless of the restraining influence of the saner heads of the Government in Tokyo (a risk which unquestionably exists and of which we have already had ample evidence in the Manchurian affair), we would be reprehensibly somnolent if we were to trust to the security of treaty restraints or international comity to safeguard our own interests or, indeed, our own property.

I may refer here to my despatch No. 608 of December 12, 1933, a re-reading of which is respectfully invited because it applies directly to the present situation. That despatch reported a confidential conversation with the Netherlands Minister, General Pabst, a shrewd and rational colleague with long experience in Japan, in which the Minister said that in his opinion the Japanese Navy, imbued as it is with patriotic and chauvinistic fervor and with a desire to emulate the deeds of the Army in order not to lose caste with the public, would be perfectly capable of descending upon and occupying Guam at a moment of crisis or, indeed, at any other moment, regardless of the ulterior consequences. I do not think that such an insane step is likely, yet the action of the Army in Manchuria, judged from the point of view of treaty rights and international comity, might also have been judged as insensate. The important fact is that under present circumstances, and indeed under circumstances which may continue in future (although the pendulum of chauvinism throughout Japanese history has swung to and fro in periodic cycles of intensity and temporary relaxation) the armed forces of the country are perfectly capable of over-riding the restraining control of the Government and of committing what might well amount to national "hara-kiri" in a mistaken conception of patriotism.

When Japanese speak of Japan's being the "stabilizing factor" and the "guardian of peace" of East Asia, what they have in mind is a Pax Japonica with eventual complete commercial control, and, in the minds of some, eventual complete political control of East Asia. While Ambassador Saito may have been misquoted in a recent issue of the Philadelphia Bulletin as saying that Japan will be prepared to fight to maintain that conception of peace, nevertheless that is precisely what is in the minds of many Japanese today. There is a swashbuckling temper in the country, largely developed by military propaganda, which can lead Japan during the next few years, or in the next few generations, to any extremes unless the saner minds in the Government prove able to cope with it and to restrain the country from national suicide.

The efficacy of such restraint is always problematical. Plots against the Government are constantly being hatched. We hear, for instance, that a number of young officers of the 3rd Infantry Regiment and students from the Military Academy in Tokyo were found on November 22 to have planned to assassinate various high members of the Government, including Count Makino, and that students of the Military Academy were confined to the school area for a few days after the discovery of that plot, which had for its object the placing in effect at once of the provisions of the now celebrated "Army pamphlet" (see despatch No. 1031 of November 1, 1934). A similar alleged plot to attack the politicians at the opening of the extraordinary session of the Diet—another May 15th incident—is also said to have been discovered and nipped in the bud. Such plots aim to form a military dictatorship. It is of course impossible to substantiate these rumors, but they are much talked about and it is unlikely that so much smoke would materialize without some fire. I wish that more Americans could come out here and live here and gradually come to sense the real potential risks and dangers of the situation instead of speaking and writing academically on a subject which they know nothing whatever about, thereby contributing ammunition to the Japanese military and extremists who are stronger than they have been for many a day. The idea that a great body of liberal thought lying just beneath the surface since 1931 would be sufficiently strong to emerge and assume control with a little foreign encouragement is thoroughly mistaken. The liberal thought is there, but it is inarticulate and largely impotent, and in all probability will remain so for some time to come.

At this point I should like to make the following observation. From reading this despatch, and perhaps from other reports periodically submitted by the Embassy, one might readily get the impression that we are developing something of an "anti-Japanese" complex. This is not the case. One can dislike and disagree with certain members of a family without necessarily feeling hostility to the family itself. For me there are no finer people in the world than the type of Japanese exemplified by such men as . . . and a host of others. I am rather inclined to place . . . in the same general category; if he could have his way unhampered by the military I believe that he would steer the country into safer and saner channels. One of these friends once sadly remarked to us: "We Japanese are always putting out worst foot foremost, and we are too proud to explain ourselves." This is profoundly true. Theirs has been and is a "bungling diplomacy." They habitually play their cards badly. Amau's statements of April 17 was a case in point. The declaration of the oil monopoly in Manchuria at this particular juncture, thereby tending to drive Great Britain into the other camp at a moment when closer Anglo-Japanese cooperation was very much in view, was another. While it is true that the military and the extremists are primarily responsible for the "bungling diplomacy" of Japan, the Japanese as a race tend to be inarticulate, more at home in action than with words. The recent negotiations in Batavia amply illustrated the fact that Japanese diplomats, well removed from home influences and at liberty to choose their own method and manner of approach, are peculiarly insensitive to the unhappy effects of arbitrary pronouncements. They have learned little from the sad experience of Hanihara. But the military and the extremists know little and care little about Japan's relations with other countries, and it is the desire of people like Shiratori, Amau and other Government officials to enhance their own prestige at home and to safeguard their future careers by standing in well with the military that brings about much of the trouble. Perhaps we should be grateful that they so often give their hand away in advance.

But all this does not make us less sympathetic to the better elements in Japanese life or in any sense "anti-Japanese." Japan is a country of paradoxes and extremes, of great wisdom and of great stupidity, an apt illustration of which may be found in connection with the naval conversations; while the naval authorities and the press have been stoutly maintaining that Japan cannot adequately defend her shores with

315

less than parity, the press and the public, in articles, speeches and interviews, have at the same time been valiantly boasting that the Japanese Navy is today stronger than the American Navy and could easily defeat us in case of war. In such an atmosphere it is difficult, very difficult, for a foreigner to keep a detached and balanced point of view. We in the Embassy are making that effort, I hope with success, and in the meantime about all we can do is to keep the boat from rocking dangerously. Constructive work is at present impossible. Our efforts are concentrated on the thwarting of destructive influences.

Having placed the foregoing considerations on record, I have less hesitation in reiterating and emphasizing with all conviction the potential dangers of the situation and the prime importance of American national preparedness to meet it. As a nation we have taken the lead in international efforts towards the restriction and reduction of armaments. We have had hopes that the movement would be progressive, but the condition of world affairs as they have developed during the past twelve years since the Washington Conference has not afforded fruitful ground for such progress. Unless we are prepared to subscribe to a "Pax Japonica" in the Far East, with all that this movement, as conceived and interpreted by Japan, is bound to entail, we should rapidly build up our navy to treaty strength, and if and when the Washington Naval Treaty expires we should continue to maintain the present ratio with Japan regardless of cost, a peace-time insurance both to cover and to reduce the risk of war. In the meantime every proper step should be taken to avoid or to offset the belligerent utterances of jingoes no less than the defeatist statements of pacifists in the United States, many of which find their way into the Japanese press, because the utterances of the former tend to enflame public sentiment against our country, while the statements of the latter convey an impression of American weakness, irresolution and bluff.

My own opinion, although it can be but guesswork, is that Japan will under no circumstances invite a race in naval armaments, and that having found our position on the ratios to be adamant, further propositions will be forthcoming within the next two years before the Washington Treaty expires, or before our present building program is fully completed. When the United States has actually completed its naval building program to treaty limits, then, it is believed, and probably not before then, Japan will realize that we are in earnest and will seek a compromise. We believe that Japan's naval policy has been formulated on the premise that the United States would never build up to treaty strength, a premise which has been strengthened in the past by the naval policy of the past two Administrations, by the apparent strength of the pacifist element in the United States, and more recently by the effects of the depression.

While it is true that Japan, by sedulously forming and stimulating public opinion to demand parity with the United States in principle if not in fact, has burned her bridges behind her, nevertheless the Japanese leaders are past-masters at remoulding public opinion in the country by skillful propaganda to suit new conditions. Once convinced that parity is impossible, it is difficult to believe that she will allow matters to come to a point where competitive building becomes unavoidable. With a national budget for 1935–1936 totaling 2,193,414,289 yen, of which about 47% is for the Army and Navy, and with an estimated national debt in 1936 of 9,880,000,000 yen, nearly equal to the Cabinet Bureau of Statistics estimate of the national income for 1930, namely 10,635,000,000 yen; with her vast outlay in Manchuria, her already heavily taxed population and the crying need of large sections of her people for relief funds, it is difficult to see how Japan could afford to embark upon a program of maintaining naval parity with the United States and Great Britain.

Having registered our position firmly and unequivocally, we can now afford to await the next move on the part of Japan. I believe that it will come.

So far as we can evaluate here the proceedings of the recent preliminary naval conversations in London, I am of the opinion that the most important and the most valuable result issuing therefrom has been the apparent tendency towards closer Anglo-American cooperation in the Far East. If we can count in future—again as a direct result of Japan's "bungling diplomacy"—on a solid and united front between the United States and Great Britain in meeting Japan's flaunting of treaty rights and her unrestrained ambitions to control East Asia, the future may well assume a brighter aspect for all of us.

Theodore Roosevelt enunciated the policy "Speak softly but carry a big stick." If our diplomacy in the Far East is to achieve favorable results, and if we are to reduce the risk of an eventual war with Japan to a minimum, that is the only way to proceed. Such a war may be unthinkable, and so it is, but the spectre of it is always present and will be present for some time to come. It would be criminally short-sighted to discard it from our calculations, and the best possible way to avoid it is to be adequately prepared, for preparedness is a cold fact which even the chauvinists, the military, the patriots and the ultra-nationalists in Japan, for all their bluster concerning "provocative measures" in the United States, can grasp and understand. The Soviet Ambassador recently told me that a prominent Japanese had said to him that the most important factor in avoiding a Japanese attack on the Maritime Provinces was the intensive Soviet military preparations in Siberia and Vladivostok. I believe this to be true, and again, and yet again, I urge that our own country be adequately prepared to meet all eventualities in the Far East.

The Counselor, the Navail Attaché and the Military Attaché of this Embassy, having separately read this despatch, have expressed to me their full concurrence with its contents both in essence and detail.

*Respectfully yours,*
*Joseph C. Grew*

# PART TEN

# Peace in a World of Conflict, 1945–1968

The deadly mushroom clouds that rose over Hiroshima and Nagasaki in August 1945 brought World War II to a close and opened an era in which every inhabitant of the planet lived under the threat of nuclear destruction. A World War III was by no means impossible, but it was evident that World War IV would have to be fought with clubs, if indeed there were humans alive to fight it at all.

In 1945 two giant powers stood over the ruins of a war-torn world. The United States was the richest country in the world; it had suffered fewer casualties than any other of the leading belligerents, and it was sole possessor of the most deadly weapon mankind had ever devised. Its wartime ally, the Soviet Union, had suffered far more from the war, and as yet it had no nuclear arsenal, but Russian troops had pushed the Nazi invaders out of eastern Europe and were in de facto control of virtually all of eastern Europe and half of Germany. Stalin, Roosevelt, and Churchill had made tentative agreement about the shape of the postwar world in wartime conferences at Teheran and Yalta, but the apparent consensus was superficial and ambiguous. The Russians sought firm guarantees of friendly regimes in the territories they had conquered, and heavy reparations from Germany, both to bolster the damaged Soviet economy and to prevent still another German attack upon Russia in the future. The United States was hesitant about conceding eastern

Europe as a Soviet sphere of influence, and extracted from Stalin a vague promise that free elections be held in the captured areas.

The peace soon revealed that the Soviet conception of a "free" election was far removed from that of the United States and Roosevelt's successor, Harry Truman, emboldened by America's nuclear monopoly, initiated a "get tough" policy. From the American point of view, this was intended to liberate eastern Europe; from the Russian perspective it was an effort to deprive the USSR of the security she had won through bloody battles against the Germans and to draw eastern Europe into the American sphere of influence that already extended over western Europe. The Cold War had begun.

The United States soon committed itself to the containment policy, the rationale for which was outlined by foreign service officer George F. Kennan in a famous article in 1947. Kennan's assumption that Russian fears of the West were based solely on the internal stresses of its totalitarian regime rather than on the long record of anti-Communist behavior by the Western powers since 1917, and his conclusion that toughness accordingly was invariably more successful than accommodation may have been doubtful. Kennan himself was later to see greater possibilities for compromise and conciliation with the Soviet Union, and to argue that American reliance upon military threats was excessive; but amidst the pervasive fear of the Red menace that swept through the United States in the early postwar years and sparked by the career of Senator Joseph McCarthy, such questions were swept aside. A bipartisan consensus on the main elements of cold-war foreign policy emerged; disagreement and debate stopped at the water's edge. The dismal failure of Henry Wallace's campaign for the Presidency in 1948 was in part due to Wallace's innocence about the Communist Party's dominating influence in his Progressive Party, but in any event the public mood at the time was entirely unreceptive to pleas for a less militantly anti-Communist foreign policy.

In Europe containment was carried out via the Marshall Plan, providing economic assistance to restore war-devastated economies, the North Atlantic Treaty Organization, and the ultimate threat of nuclear retaliation should NATO forces prove unable to repel Soviet attack. There were no further Russian gains in Europe, evidence either that the policy had been successful, or that it had been based on a misreading of Soviet intentions. The Russians, however, remained in control over the satellite regimes behind the Iron Curtain. President Dwight Eisenhower and his Secretary of State John Foster Dulles spoke of liberating the captive people of eastern Europe and rolling back the Iron Curtain, but by then the USSR possessed a nuclear striking force. The test of American willingness to risk total war came in 1956, when a popular uprising temporarily established an independent government in Hungary. Russian troops quickly moved in to crush the revolution, and America dared not intervene. The threat of total nuclear war loomed ominously on later occasions, notably in the Cuban missile crisis of 1962, but in each instance the uneasy balance of terror was preserved in the end. A nuclear test ban treaty with the Russians later slackened the pace of the arms race slightly, but there was no progress toward actual disarmament. The peace of the world still depended on the caution and restraint of men in the Kremlin and the

White House, and recurrent crises continued to put dangerous strains on this delicate equilibrium.

The locus of American-Soviet conflict shifted increasingly from Europe toward the less developed and less stable "third world." Here the task of containing Communism and preserving the integrity of "the free world" was far more difficult. Revolutionary ferment was rising in many parts of the globe. In many cases it was being directed against oppressive landlord or military regimes. At times it seemed that the United States government equated "free" with "pro-American," and that it was determined to preserve in power, through military and economic aid and even American troops, governments that would follow its lead, however undemocratic their character. Though the Soviet Union, and after its establishment in 1949 Communist China, generally looked with favor upon the attempts to overturn these regimes, actual Communists were rarely dominant in the rebel groups. Instead there was a medley of disaffected men of a wide variety of political leanings. Some Americans were incapable of making these distinctions, but more sophisticated defenders of American policy argued that whatever the composition of the revolutionary movement, a situation of revolutionary turmoil was one in which actual Communists were likely to triumph in the long run, and this justified propping up weak pro-American governments as lesser evils.

The difficulties of serving as self-appointed policeman imposing order in the underdeveloped world were not immediately apparent in the first venture of this kind—President Truman's 1947 decision to assist the Greek government to suppress a guerrilla uprising there. The revolutionary forces had considerable popular support, but the government had sufficient strength to put them down with few American troops. Twenty years later, reflecting on the military dictatorship reigning in Greece and the modest easing of totalitarian controls in Communist but neutral Yugoslavia, some observers were wondering how much Greece had been benefited by being saved for the free world, but in 1947 the answer seemed easy to most Americans. The Korean War, too, appeared self-evidently necessary, for it involved a blatant military invasion of one state by another. The public divided only over the question of whether the war was to be fought as a limited war within Korea or whether the United States should run the risk of attacking China.

In subsequent years there were other instances of overt or covert American intervention to prevent or undo political changes regarded as dangerous—in Guatemala in 1954, Lebanon in 1958, Cuba in 1961, and the Dominican Republic in 1965; but not until the Vietnam War was there deep popular revulsion against the fundamentals of cold-war foreign policy, and the beginnings of a searching national debate over America's role in the world. Many Americans viewed the attempt of the National Liberation Front to topple the pro-United States regime as essentially an indigenous popular uprising, albeit one aided and encouraged by Communist North Vietnam; they also believed that America was inflicting fearful casualties on helpless peasants in both sections of the country in a tragically mistaken effort to preserve American prestige and power in Southeast Asia, regardless of the cost in lives. Many others, however, took the administration's position that this was a classic, if somewhat more subtle, instance of aggression

321

against a duly constituted state, and that a peaceful world could be preserved only through resolute action to demonstrate that aggression does not pay. By 1968 there were faint signs that a settlement might be reached in Vietnam, but whether there would be other Vietnams in the future seemed destined to be a central issue in American politics for years to come.

In the years of uneasy peace and intermittent limited war that made up the cold-war years, the American economy performed at a generally high level. There were modest recessions in the late 1940s and the late 1950s, but the major depression many feared following the close of the world war did not materialize then or later. The built-in economic stabilizers developed during the New Deal, and a new sophistication about the functioning of a modern economy, symbolized by the creation of the President's Council of Economic Advisors in 1946, were part of the explanation. The extent of sustained prosperity could not be determined so long as the arms race with the Soviet Union and our extensive military commitments around the world kept the economy on a partial wartime basis. In any event, the gross national product moved steadily upward, and it seemed as though America had become an "affluent society," in which poverty had virtually disappeared and every group had been able to develop "countervailing power" to obtain its fair share.

In the 1960s, however, such optimism about the workings of the economy was weakened, and there was a new wave of public concern about poverty. The Kennedy administration had begun planning a new attack on the problem shortly before the President's assassination, and his successor launched a national War on Poverty in 1964. It had become evident that low-income groups were receiving roughly the same small portion of the national wealth they had been receiving thirty years before. Few Americans were poor by the standards of other societies, or of the American past, but a substantial minority of citizens were living in conditions that had begun to seem intolerable.

This was particularly true of Negroes, who remained impoverished far out of proportion to their representation in the population. The postwar years saw dramatic progress in the Negro's struggle to win a place in American society—the integration of the armed forces, the Supreme Court's striking down of racially segregated schools in 1954, the elimination of segregated public facilities, the beginnings toward protection of voting rights in areas where blacks had been deprived of them. Federal legislation, passed during the Presidency of Lyndon Johnson, climaxed the drive to assure American Negroes of the elementary civil rights long denied them. These gains brought not contentment, but new awareness of problems beyond the purview of traditional civil-rights measures. Negroes living in liberal Northern states like New York had been free of formal segregation for many years without winning economic and social advances as impressive as those of earlier migrants to the urban world. As increasing numbers of blacks concentrated in Northern cities, and the South itself began to evolve toward the Northern pattern of race relations, it began to appear that genuine integration in housing, education, and jobs would continue to elude the mass of Negroes for decades to come, and that other strategies for group advance were required. The riots that

322

erupted in the cities reflected the frustration induced by this disturbing discovery. The slogan "black power" was becoming ever more fashionable, at least among articulate Negroes, but this loose concept embraced everything from internal guerrilla warfare in pursuit of a separate black state to efforts to create a class of responsible Negro businessmen along the lines suggested by Booker T. Washington at the turn of the century. What black power might mean in practice, and what the response of white society would be remained to be seen. A Presidential commission of moderate leaders warned that "white racism" was a dominant fact of American life, and that the United States was rapidly becoming two societies. Some thought this overly pessimistic, but it was difficult to deny that the crisis in black and white was the most painful and challenging domestic problem on the horizon.

# 77

# The Doctrine of Containment

George F. Kennan wrote this essay on "The Sources of Soviet Conduct" and published it in the magazine *Foreign Affairs* under the pen name "Mr. X" in 1947, while serving in the United States Department of State. It quickly became the classic statement of the rationale for the policy of containment adopted by the Truman administration and followed by subsequent administrations as well. Kennan did not recommend an aggressive military assault upon the Soviet Union, but rather "the adroit and vigilant application of counter-force at a series of constantly shifting geographical and political points, corresponding to the shifts and maneuvers of Soviet policy"; and he was later to complain that America had relied too heavily upon military threats as a technique of containment. The fundamental premise of his essay, however, was that expansion was integral to the Soviet system, the inevitable consequence of the inner dynamics of totalitarian rule, and that nothing but the threat of superior force could prevent it. The USSR was like "a persistent toy automobile wound up and headed in a given direction, stopping only when it meets some unanswerable force." If that premise was correct, it was difficult to dissent from the main outlines of postwar American foreign policy.

## THE SOURCES
## OF SOVIET CONDUCT
*George F. Kennan*

### I

The political personality of Soviet power as we know it today is the product of ideology and circumstances: ideology inherited by the present Soviet leaders from the movement in which they had their political origin, and circumstances of the power which they now have exercised for nearly three decades in Russia. There can be few tasks of psychological analysis more difficult than to try to trace the interaction of those two forces and the relative role of each in the determination of official Soviet conduct. Yet the attempt must be made if that conduct is to be understood and effectively countered.

Reprinted by special permission from *Foreign Affairs*, July 1947 issue (4:566–582). Copyright by the Council on Foreign Relations, Inc., New York.

It is difficult to summarize the set of ideological concepts with which the Soviet leaders came into power. Marxian ideology, in its Russian-Communist projection, has always been in process of subtle evolution. The materials on which it bases itself are extensive and complex. But the outstanding features of Communist thought as it existed in 1916 may perhaps be summarized as follows: (*a*) that the central factor in the life of man, the fact which determines the character of public life and the "physiognomy of society," is the system by which material goods are produced and exchanged; (*b*) that the capitalist system of production is a nefarious one which inevitably leads to the exploitation of the working class by the capital-owning class and is incapable of developing adequately the economic resources of society or of distributing fairly the material goods produced by human labor; (*c*) that capitalism contains the seeds of its own destruction and must, in view of the inability of the capital-owning class to adjust itself to economic change, result eventually and inescapably in a revolutionary transfer of power to the working class; and (*d*) that imperialism, the final phase of capitalism, leads directly to war and revolution.

The rest may be outlined in Lenin's own words: "Unevenness of economic and political development is the inflexible law of capitalism. It follows from this that the victory of Socialism may come originally in a few capitalist countries or even in a single capitalist country. The victorious proletariat of that country, having expropriated the capitalists and having organized Socialist production at home, would rise against the remaining capitalist world, drawing to itself in the process the oppressed classes of other countries." It must be noted that there was no assumption that capitalism would perish without proletarian revolution. A final push was needed from a revolutionary proletariat movement in order to tip over the tottering structure. But it was regarded as inevitable that sooner or later that push be given.

For fifty years prior to the outbreak of the Revolution, this pattern of thought had exercised great fascination for the members of the Russian revolutionary movement. Frustrated, discontented, hopeless of finding self-expression—or too impatient to seek it—in the confining limits of the Tsarist political system, yet lacking wide popular support for their choice of bloody revolution as a means of social betterment, these revolutionists found in Marxist theory a highly convenient rationalization for their own instinctive desires. It afforded pseudo-scientific justification for their impatience, for their categoric denial of all value in the Tsarist system, for their yearning for power and revenge and for their inclination to cut corners in the pursuit of it. It is therefore no wonder that they had come to believe implicitly in the truth and soundness of the Marxian-Leninist teachings, so congenial to their own impulses and emotions. Their sincerity need not be impugned. This is a phenomenon as old as human nature itself. It has never been more aptly described than by Edward Gibbon, who wrote in *The Decline and Fall of the Roman Empire:* "From enthusiasm to imposture the step is perilous and slippery; the demon of Socrates affords a memorable instance how a wise man may deceive himself; how a good man may deceive others, how the conscience may slumber in a mixed and middle state between self-illusion and voluntary fraud."

325

And it was with this set of conceptions that the members of the Bolshevik Party entered into power.

Now it must be noted that through all the years of preparation for revolution, the attention of these men, as indeed of Marx himself, had been centered less on the future form which Socialism would take than on the necessary overthrow of rival power which, in their view, had to precede the introduction of Socialism. Their views, therefore, on the positive program to be put into effect, once power was attained, were for the most part nebulous, visionary and impractical. Beyond the nationalization of industry and the expropriation of large private capital holdings, there was no agreed program. The treatment of the peasantry, which according to the Marxist formulation was not of the proletariat, had always been a vague sport in the pattern of Communist thought; and it remained an object of controversy and vacillation for the first ten years of Communist power.

The circumstances of the immediate post-Revolution period—the existence in Russia of civil war and foreign intervention, together with the obvious fact that the Communists represented only a tiny minority of the Russian people—made the establishment of dictatorial power a necessity. The experiment with "war Communism" and the abrupt attempt to eliminate private production and trade had unfortunate economic consequences and caused further bitterness against the new revolutionary regime. While the temporary relaxation of the effort to communize Russia, represented by the New Economic Policy, alleviated some of this economic distress and thereby served its purpose, it also made it evident that the "capitalistic sector of society" was still prepared to profit at once from any relaxation of governmental pressure, and would, if permitted to continue to exist, always constitute a powerful opposing element to the Soviet regime and a serious rival for influence in the country. Somewhat the same situation prevailed with respect to the individual peasant who, in his own small way, was also a private producer.

Lenin, had he lived, might have proved a great enough man to reconcile these conflicting forces to the ultimate benefit of Russian society, though this is questionable. But be that as it may, Stalin, and those whom he led in the struggle for succession to Lenin's position of leadership, were not the men to tolerate rival political forces in the sphere of power which they coveted. Their sense of insecurity was too great. Their particular brand of fanaticism, unmodified by any of the Anglo-Saxon traditions of compromise, was too fierce and too jealous to envisage any permanent sharing of power. From the Russian-Asiatic world out of which they had emerged they carried with them a skepticism as to the possibilities of permanent and peaceful coexistence of rival forces. Easily persuaded of their own doctrinaire "rightness," they insisted on the submission or destruction of all competing power. Outside of the Communist Party, Russian society was to have no rigidity. There were to be no forms of collective human activity or association which would not be dominated by the Party. No other force in Russian society was to be permitted to achieve vitality or integrity. Only the Party was to have structure. All else was to be an amorphous mass.

And within the Party the same principle was to apply. The mass of Party members might go through the motions of election, deliberation, decision and action; but in these motions they were to be animated not by their own individual wills but by the awesome breath of the Party leadership and the overbrooding presence of "the world."

Let it be stressed again that subjectively these men probably did not seek absolutism for its own sake. They doubtless believed—and found it easy to believe—that they alone knew what was good for society and that they would accomplish that good once their power was secure and unchallengeable. But in seeking that security of their own rule they were prepared to recognize no restrictions, either of God or man, on the character of their methods. And until such time as that security might be achieved, they placed far down on their scale of operational priorities the comforts and happiness of the peoples entrusted to their care.

Now the outstanding circumstance concerning the Soviet regime is that down to the present day this process of political consolidation has never been completed and the men in the Kremlin have continued to be predominantly absorbed with the struggle to secure and make absolute the power which they seized in November 1917. They have endeavored to secure it primarily against forces at home, within Soviet society itself. But they have also endeavored to secure it against the outside world. For ideology, as we have seen, taught them that the outside world was hostile and that it was their duty eventually to overthrow the political forces beyond their borders. The powerful hands of Russian history and tradition reached up to sustain them in this feeling. Finally, their own aggressive intransigence with respect to the outside world began to find its own reaction; and they were soon forced, to use another Gibbonesque phrase, "to chastise the contumacy" which they themselves had provoked. It is an undeniable privilege of every man to prove himself right in the thesis that the world is his enemy; for if he reiterates it frequently enough and makes it the background of his conduct he is bound eventually to be right.

Now it lies in the nature of the mental world of the Soviet leaders, as well as in the character of their ideology, that no opposition to them can be officially recognized as having any merit or justification whatsoever. Such opposition can flow, in theory, only from the hostile and incorrigible forces of dying capitalism. As long as remnants of capitalism were officially recognized as existing in Russia, it was possible to place on them, as an internal element, part of the blame for the maintenance of a dictatorial form of society. But as these remnants were liquidated, little by little, this justification fell away; and when it was indicated officially that they had been finally destroyed, it disappeared altogether. And this fact created one of the most basic of the compulsions which came to act upon the Soviet regime: since capitalism no longer existed in Russia and since it could not be admitted that there could be serious or widespread opposition to the Kremlin springing spontaneously from the liberated masses under its authority, it became necessary to justify the retention of the dictatorship by stressing the menace of capitalism abroad.

This began at an early date. In 1924, Stalin specifically defended the retention of the "organs of suppression," meaning, among others, the army and the secret police, on the ground that "as long as there is a capitalist encirclement there will be danger of intervention with all the consequences that flow from that danger." In accordance with that theory, and from that time on, all internal opposition forces in Russia have consistently been portrayed as the agents of foreign forces of reaction antagonistic to Soviet power.

By the same token, tremendous emphasis has been placed on the original Communist thesis of a basic antagonism between the capitalist and Socialist worlds. It is clear, from many indications, that this emphasis is not founded in reality. The real facts concerning it have been confused by the existence abroad of genuine resentment provoked by Soviet philosophy and tactics and occasionally by the existence of great centers of military power, notably the Nazi regime in Germany and the Japanese government of the late 1930's, which did indeed have aggressive designs against the Soviet Union. But there is ample evidence that the stress laid in Moscow on the menace confronting Soviet society from the world outside its borders is founded not in the realities of foreign antagonism but in the necessity of explaining away the maintenance of dictatorial authority at home.

Now the maintenance of this pattern of Soviet power, namely, the pursuit of unlimited authority domestically, accompanied by the cultivation of the semi-myth of implacable foreign hostility, has gone far to shape the actual machinery of Soviet power as we know it today. Internal organs of administration which did not serve this purpose withered on the vine. Organs which did serve this purpose became vastly swollen. The security of Soviet power came to rest on the iron discipline of the Party, on the severity and ubiquity of the secret police, and on the uncompromising economic monopolism of the state. The "organs of suppression," in which the Soviet leaders had sought security from rival forces, became in large measure the masters of those whom they were designed to serve. Today the major part of the structure of Soviet power is comfitted to the perfection of the dictatorship and to the maintenance of the concept of Russia as in a state of siege, with the enemy lowering beyond the walls. And the millions of human beings who form that part of the structure of power must defend at all costs this concept of Russia's position, for without it they are themselves superfluous.

As things stand today, the rulers can no longer dream of parting with these organs of suppression. The quest for absolute power, pursued now for nearly three decades with a ruthlessness unparalleled (in scope at least) in modern times, has again produced internally, as it did externally, its own reaction. The excesses of the police apparatus have fanned the potential opposition to the regime into something far greater and more dangerous than it could have been before those excesses began.

But least of all can the rulers dispense with the fiction by which the maintenance of dictatorial power has been defended. For this fiction has been canonized in Soviet philosophy by the excesses already committed in its name; and it is now anchored in the Soviet structure of thought by bonds far greater than those of mere ideology.

## II

So much for the historical background. What does it spell in terms of the political personality of Soviet power as we know it today?

Of the original ideology, nothing has been officially junked. Belief is maintained in the basic badness of capitalism, in the inevitability of its destruction, in the obligation of the proletariat to assist in that destruction and to take power into its own hands. But stress has come to be laid primarily on those concepts which relate most specifically to the Soviet regime itself: to its position as the sole truly Socialist regime in a dark and misguided world, and to the relationships of power within it.

The first of these concepts is that of the innate antagonism between capitalism and Socialism. We have seen how deeply that concept has become imbedded in foundations of Soviet power. It has profound implications for Russia's conduct as a member of international society. It means that there can never be on Moscow's side any sincere assumption of a community of aims between the Soviet Union and powers which are regarded as capitalism. It must invariably be assumed in Moscow that the aims of the capitalist world are antagonistic to the Soviet regime and, therefore, to the interests of the peoples it controls. If the Soviet government occasionally sets its signature to documents which would indicate the contrary, this is to be regarded as a tactical maneuver permissible in dealing with the enemy (who is without honor) and should be taken in the spirit of *caveat emptor*. Basically, the antagonism remains. It is postulated. And from it flow many of the phenomena which we find disturbing in the Kremlin's conduct of foreign policy: the secretiveness, the lack of frankness, the duplicity, the war suspiciousness, and the basic unfriendliness of purpose. These phenomena are there to stay, for the foreseeable future. There can be variations of degree and of emphasis. When there is something the Russians want from us, one or the other of these features of their policy may be thrust temporarily into the background; and when that happens there will always be Americans who will leap forward with gleeful announcements that "the Russians have changed," and some who will even try to take credit for having brought about such "changes." But we should not be misled by tactical maneuvers. These characteristics of Soviet policy, like the postulate from which they flow, are basic to the internal nature of Soviet power, and will be with us, whether in the foreground or the background, until the internal nature of Soviet power is changed.

This means that we are going to continue for a long time to find the Russians difficult to deal with. It does not mean that they should be considered as embarked upon a do-or-die program to overthrow our society by a given date. The theory of the inevitability of the eventual fall of capitalism has the fortunate connotation that there is no hurry about it. The forces of progress can take their time in preparing the final *coup de grâce*. Meanwhile, what is vital is that the "Socialist father-land"—that oasis of power which has been already won for Socialism in the person of the Soviet Union—should be cherished and defended by all good Communists at home and abroad, its fortunes promoted, its enemies badgered and confounded. The promotion of premature, "adventuristic" revolutionary projects abroad which might embarrass Soviet power in any way would be an inexcusable, even a counter-revolutionary act. The cause of Socialism is the support and promotion of Soviet power, as defined in Moscow.

This brings us to the second of the concepts important to contemporary Soviet outlook. That is the infallibility of the Kremlin. The Soviet concept of power, which permits no focal points of organization outside the Party itself, requires that the Party leadership remain in theory the sole repository of truth. For if truth were to be found elsewhere, there would be justification for its expression in organized activity. But it is precisely that which the Kremlin cannot and will not permit.

The leadership of the Communist Party is therefore always right and has been always right ever since in 1929 Stalin formalized his personal power by announcing that decisions of the Politburo were being taken unanimously.

On the principle of infallibility there rests the iron discipline of the Communist Party. In fact, the two concepts are mutually self-supporting. Perfect discipline requires recognition of infallibility. Infallibility requires the observance of discipline. And the two together go far to determine the behaviorism of the entire Soviet apparatus of power. But their effect cannot be understood unless a third factor be taken into account: namely, the fact that the leadership is at liberty to put forward for tactical purposes any particular thesis which it finds useful to the cause at any particular moment and to require the faithful and unquestioning acceptance of that thesis by the members of the movement as a whole. This means that truth is not a constant but is actually created, for all intents and purposes, by the Soviet leaders themselves. It may vary from week to week, from month to month. It is nothing absolute and immutable—nothing which flows from objective reality. It is only the most recent manifestation of the wisdom of those in whom the ultimate wisdom is supposed to reside, because they represent the logic of history. The accumulative effect of these factors is to give to the whole subordinate apparatus of Soviet power an unshakeable stubbornness and steadfastness in its orientation. This orientation can be changed at will by the Kremlin but by no other power. Once a given party line has been laid down on a given issue of current policy, the whole Soviet governmental machine, including the mechanism of diplomacy, moves inexorably along the prescribed path, like a persistent toy automobile wound up and headed in a given direction, stopping only when it meets with some unanswerable force. The individuals who are the components of this machine are unamenable to argument or reason which comes to them from outside sources. Their whole training has taught them to mistrust and discount the glib persuasiveness of the outside world. Like the white dog before the phonograph, they hear only the "master's voice." And if they are to be called off from the purposes last dictated to them, it is the master who must call them off. Thus the foreign representative cannot hope that his words will make any impression on them. The most that he can hope is that they will be transmitted to those at the top, who are capable of changing the party line. But even those are not likely to be swayed by any normal logic in the words of the bourgeois representative. Since there can be no appeal to common purposes, there can be no appeal to common mental approaches. For this reason, facts speak louder than words to the ears of the Kremlin; and words carry the greatest weight when they have the ring of reflecting, or being backed up by, facts of unchallengeable validity.

But we have seen that the Kremlin is under no ideological compulsion to accomplish its purposes in a hurry. Like the Church, it is dealing in ideological concepts which are of long-term validity, and it can afford to be patient. It has no right to risk the existing achievements of the revolution for the sake of vain baubles of the future. The very teachings of Lenin himself require great caution and flexibility in the pursuit of Communist purposes. Again, these precepts are fortified by the lessons of Russian history: of centuries of obscure battles between nomadic forces over the stretches of a vast unfortified plain. Here caution, circumspection, flexibility and deception are the valuable qualities; and their value finds natural appreciation in the Russian or the oriental mind. Thus the Kremlin has no compunction about retreating in the face of superior force. And being under the compulsion of no timetable, it does not get panicky under the necessity for such retreat. Its political action is a fluid stream which moves constantly, wherever it is permitted to move, toward a given goal. Its main concern is to make sure that it has filled every nook and cranny available to it in the basin of world power. But if it finds unassailable barriers in its path, it accepts these philosophically and accommodates itself to them. The main thing is that there should always be pressure, increasing constant pressure, toward the desired goal. There is no trace of any feeling in Soviet psychology that that goal must be reached at any given time.

These considerations make Soviet diplomacy at once easier and more difficult to deal with than the diplomacy of individual aggressive leaders like Napoleon and Hitler. On the one hand it is more sensitive to contrary force, more ready to yield on individual sectors of the diplomatic front when that force is felt to be too strong, and thus more rational in the logic and rhetoric of power. On the other hand it cannot be easily defeated or discouraged by a single victory on the part of its opponents. And the patient persistence by which it is animated means that it can be effectively countered not by sporadic acts which represent the momentary whims of democratic opinion but only by intelligent long-range policies on the part of Russia's adversaries—policies no less steady in their purpose, and no less variegated and resourceful in their application, than those of the Soviet Union itself.

In these circumstances it is clear that the main element of any United States policy toward the Soviet Union must be that of a long-term, patient but firm and vigilant containment of Russian expansive tendencies. It is important to note, however, that such a policy has nothing to do with outward histrionics: with threats or blustering or superfluous gestures of outward "toughness." While the Kremlin is basically flexible in its reaction to political realities, it is by no means unamenable to considerations of prestige. Like almost any other government, it can be placed by tactless and threatening gestures in a position where it cannot afford to yield even though this might be dictated by its sense of realism. The Russian leaders are keen judges of human psychology, and as such they are highly conscious that loss of temper and of self-control is never a source of strength in political affairs. They are quick to exploit such evidences of weakness. For these reasons, it is a *sine qua non* of successful dealing with Russia that the foreign government in question should

331

remain at all times cool and collected and that its demands on Russian policy should be put forward in such a manner as to leave the way open for compliance not too detrimental to Russian prestige.

## III

In the light of the above, it will be clearly seen that the Soviet pressure against the free institutions of the Western world is something that can be contained by the adroit and vigilant application of counter-force at a series of constantly shifting geographical and political points, corresponding to the shifts and maneuvers of Soviet policy, but which cannot be charmed or talked out of existence. The Russians look forward to a duel of infinite duration, and they see that already they have scored great successes. It must be borne in mind that there was a time when the Communist Party represented far more of a minority in the sphere of Russian national life than Soviet power today represents in the world community.

But if ideology convinces the rulers of Russia that truth is on their side and that they can therefore afford to wait, those of us on whom that ideology has no claim are free to examine objectively the validity of that premise. The Soviet thesis not only implies complete lack of control by the West over its own economic destiny, it likewise assumes Russian unity, discipline and patience over an infinite period. Let us bring this apocalyptic vision down to earth, and suppose that the Western world finds the strength and resourcefulness to contain Soviet power over a period of ten to fifteen years. What does that spell for Russia itself?

The Soviet leaders, taking advantage of the contributions of modern technique to the arts of despotism, have solved the question of obedience within the confines of their power. Few challenge their authority; and even those who do are unable to make that challenge valid as against the organs of suppression of the state.

The Kremlin has also proved able to accomplish its purpose of building up in Russia, regardless of the interests of the inhabitants, an industrial foundation of heavy metallurgy, which is, to be sure, not yet complete but which is nevertheless continuing to grow and is approaching those of the other major industrial countries. All of this, however, both the maintenance of internal political security and the building of heavy industry, has been carried out at a terrible cost in human life and in human hopes and energies. It has necessitated the use of forced labor on a scale unprecedented in modern times under conditions of peace. It has involved the neglect or abuse of other phases of Soviet economic life, particularly agriculture, consumers' goods production, housing and transportation.

To all that, the war has added its tremendous toll of destruction, death and human exhaustion. In consequence of this, we have in Russia today a population which is physically and spiritually tired. The mass of the people are disillusioned, skeptical and no longer as accessible as they once were to the magical attraction which Soviet power still radiates to its followers abroad. The avidity with which people seized upon the slightest respite accorded to the Church for tactical reasons during the war was eloquent testimony to the fact that their capacity for faith and devotion found little expression in the purposes of the regime.

In these circumstances, there are limits to the physical and nervous strength of people themselves. These limits are absolute ones, and are binding even for the cruelest dictatorship, because beyond them people cannot be driven. The forced labor camps and the other agencies of constraint provide temporary means of compelling people to work longer hours than their own volition or mere economic pressure would dictate; but if people survive them at all they become old before their time and must be considered as human casualties to the demands of dictatorship. In either case their best powers are no longer available to society and can no longer be enlisted in the service of the state.

Here only the younger generation can help. The younger generation, despite all vicissitudes and sufferings, is numerous and vigorous; and the Russians are a talented people. But it still remains to be seen what will be the effects on mature performance of the abnormal emotional strains of childhood which Soviet dictator-ship created and which were enormously increased by the war. Such things as normal security and placidity of home environment have practically ceased to exist in the Soviet Union outside of the most remote farms and villages. And observers are not yet sure whether that is not going to leave its mark on the over-all capacity of the generation now coming into maturity.

In addition to this, we have the fact that Soviet economic development, while it can list certain formidable achievements, has been precariously spotty and uneven. Russian Communists who speak of the "uneven development of capitalism" should blush at the contemplation of their own national economy. Here certain branches of economic life, such as the metallurgical and machine industries, have been pushed out of all proportion to other sectors of economy. Here is a nation striving to become in a short period one of the great industrial nations of the world while it still has no highway network worthy of the name and only a relatively primitive network of railways. Much has been done to increase efficiency of labor and to teach primitive peasants something about the operation of machines. But mainte-nance is still a crying deficiency of all Soviet economy. Construction is hasty and poor in quality. Depreciation must be enormous. And in vast sectors of economic life it has not yet been possible to instill into labor anything like that general culture of production and technical self-respect which characterizes the skilled worker of the West.

It is difficult to see how these deficiencies can be corrected at an early date by a tired and dispirited population working largely under the shadow of fear and compulsion. And as long as they are not overcome, Russia will remain economi-cally a vulnerable, and in a certain sense an impotent, nation, capable of exporting its enthusiasms and of radiating the strange charm of its primitive political vitality but unable to back up those articles of export by the real evidences of material power and prosperity.

Meanwhile, a great uncertainty hangs over the political life of the Soviet Union. That is the uncertainty involved in the transfer of power from one individual or group of individuals to others.

This is, of course, outstandingly the problem of the personal position of Stalin. We must remember that his succession to Lenin's pinnacle of preeminence in the

Communist movement was the only such transfer of individual authority which the Soviet Union has experienced. That transfer took twelve years to consolidate. It cost the lives of millions of people and shook the state to its foundations, the attendant tremors were felt all through the international revolutionary movement, to the disadvantage of the Kremlin itself.

It is always possible that another transfer of preeminent power may take place quietly and inconspicuously, with no repercussions anywhere. But again, it is possible that the questions involved may unleash, to use some of Lenin's words, one of those "incredibly swift transitions" from "delicate deceit" to "wild violence" which characterize Russian history, and may shake Soviet power to its foundations.

But this is not only a question of Stalin himself. There has been, since 1938, a dangerous congealment of political life in the higher circles of Soviet power. The All-Union Party Congress, in theory the supreme body of the Party, is supposed to meet not less often than once in three years. It will soon be eight full years since its last meeting. During this period membership in the Party has numerically doubled. Party mortality during the war was enormous, and today well over half of the Party members are persons who have entered since the last Party congress was held. Meanwhile, the same small group of men has carried on at the top through an amazing series of national vicissitudes. Surely there is some reason why the experiences of the war brought basic political changes to every one of the great governments of the West. Surely the causes of that phenomenon are basic enough to be present somewhere in the obscurity of Soviet political life, as well. And yet no recognition has been given to these causes in Russia.

It must be surmised from this that even within so highly disciplined an organization as the Communist Party there must be a growing divergence in age, outlook and interest between the great mass of Party members, only so recently recruited into the movement, and the little self-perpetuating clique of men at the top, whom most of these Party members have never met, with whom they have never conversed, and with whom they can have no political intimacy.

Who can say whether, in these circumstances, the eventual rejuvenation of the higher spheres of authority (which can only be a matter of time) can take place smoothly and peacefully, or whether rivals in the quest for higher power will not eventually reach down into these politically immature and inexperienced masses in order to find support for their respective claims. If this were ever to happen, strange consequences could flow for the Communist Party: for the membership at large has been exercised only in the practices of iron discipline and obedience and not in the arts of compromise and accommodation. And if disunity were ever to seize and paralyze the Party, the chaos and weakness of Russian society would be revealed in forms beyond description. For we have seen that Soviet power is only a crust concealing an amorphous mass of human beings among whom no independent organizational structure is tolerated. In Russia there is not even such a thing as local government. The present generation of Russians have never known spontaneity of collective action. If, consequently, anything were ever to occur to disrupt the unity and efficacy of the Party as a political instrument, Soviet Russia might be changed overnight from one of the strongest to one of the weakest and most pitiable of national societies.

Thus the future of Soviet power may not be by any means as secure as Russian capacity for self-delusion would make it appear to the men in the Kremlin. That they can keep power themselves, they have demonstrated. That they can quietly and easily turn it over to others remains to be proved. Meanwhile, the hardships of their rule and the vicissitudes of international life have taken a heavy toll of the strength and hopes of the great people on whom their power rests. It is curious to note that the ideological power of Soviet authority is strongest today in areas beyond the frontiers of Russia, beyond the reach of its police power. This phenomenon brings to mind a comparison used by Thomas Mann in his great novel *Buddenbrooks*. Observing that human institutions often show the greatest outward brilliance at a moment when inner decay is in reality farthest advanced, he compared the Buddenbrook family, in the days of its greatest glamour to one of these stars whose light shines most brightly on this world when in reality it has long since ceased to exist. And who can say with assurance that the strong light still cast by the Kremlin on the dissatisfied peoples of the Western world is not the powerful afterglow of a constellation which is in actuality on the wane? This cannot be proved. And it cannot be disproved. But the possibility remains (and in the opinion of this writer it is a strong one) that Soviet power, like the capitalist world of its conception, bears within it the seeds of its own decay, and that the sprouting of these seeds is well advanced.

## IV

It is clear that the United States cannot expect in the foreseeable future to enjoy political intimacy with the Soviet regime. It must continue to regard the Soviet Union as a rival, not a partner, in the political arena. It must continue to expect that Soviet policies will reflect no abstract love of peace and stability, no real faith in the possibility of a permanent happy coexistence of the Socialist and capitalist worlds, but rather a cautious, persistent pressure toward the disruption and weakening of all rival influence and rival power.

Balanced against this are the facts that Russia, as opposed to the Western world in general, is still by far the weaker party, that Soviet policy is highly flexible, and that Soviet society may well contain deficiencies which will eventually weaken its own total potential. This would of itself warrant the United States entering with reasonable confidence upon a policy of firm containment, designed to confront the Russians with unalterable counter-force at every point where they show signs of encroaching upon the interests of a peaceful and stable world.

But in actuality the possibilities for American policy are by no means limited to holding the line and hoping for the best. It is entirely possible for the United States to influence by its actions the internal developments, both within Russia and throughout the international Communist movement, by which Russian policy is largely determined. This is not only a question of the modest measure of informational activity which this government can conduct in the Soviet Union and elsewhere, although that, too, is important. It is rather a question of the degree to which the United States can create among the peoples of the world generally the impression of a country which knows what it wants, which is coping successfully with the problems of its internal life and with the responsibilities of a World Power, and which has a spiritual vitality capable of holding its own among the major ideological currents of the time. To the extent that such an impression can be created and maintained, the aims of Russian Communism must appear sterile and quixotic, the hopes and enthusiasm of Moscow's supporters must wane, and added strain must be imposed on the Kremlin's foreign policies. For the palsied decrepitude of the capitalist world is the keystone of Communist philosophy. Even the failure of the United States to experience the early economic depression which the ravens of the Red Square have been predicting with such complacent confidence since hostilities ceased would have deep and important repercussions throughout the Communist world.

By the same token, exhibitions of indecision, disunity and internal disintegration within this country have an exhilarating effect on the whole Communist movement. At each evidence of these tendencies, a thrill of hope and excitement goes through the Communist world; a new jauntiness can be noted in the Moscow trade; new groups of foreign supporters climb on to what they can only view as the band wagon of international politics; and Russian pressure increases all along the line in international affairs.

It would be an exaggeration to say that American behavior unassisted and alone could exercise a power of life and death over the Communist movement and bring about the early fall of Soviet power in Russia. But the United States has it in its power to increase enormously the strains under which Soviet policy must operate, to force upon the Kremlin a far greater degree of moderation and circumspection than it has had to observe in recent years, and in this way to promote tendencies which must eventually find their outlet in either the break-up or the gradual mellowing of Soviet power. For no mystical, Messianic movement—and particularly not that of the Kremlin—can face frustration indefinitely without eventually adjusting itself in one way or another to the logic of that state of affairs.

Thus the decision will really fall in large measure in this country itself. The issue of Soviet-American relations is in essence a test of the over-all worth of the United States as a nation among nations. To avoid destruction the United States need only measure up to its own best traditions and prove itself worthy of preservation as a great nation.

Surely, there was never a fairer test of national quality than this. In the light of these circumstances, the thoughtful observer of Russian-American relations will find no cause for complaint in the Kremlin's challenge to American society. He will rather experience a certain gratitude to a Providence which, by providing the American people with this implacable challenge, has made their entire security as a nation dependent on their pulling themselves together and accepting the responsibilities of moral and political leadership that history plainly intended them to bear.

# 78

## The Distribution
## of Economic Power

In *American Capitalism: The Concept of Countervailing Power,* economist John Kenneth Galbraith argued that while the old-fashioned competition between large numbers of small producers had been eliminated from much of the American economy, there still were mechanisms that automatically checked the exercise of monopoly power. The general proposition that private economic power stimulated the demand for countervailing power by those subject to it was well suited to the complacent national mood that prevailed in the Age of Eisenhower, when Galbraith's influential book was published. Today's readers, however, may be struck by the brief qualification included in section VI of this excerpt, concerning the varying capacities of different groups to organize effectively, a very important fact of life that such efforts as the community action phase of the federal War on Poverty and the black power movement currently seek to alter.

## AMERICAN CAPITALISM
### *John Kenneth Galbraith*

On the night of November 2, 1907, the elder Morgan played solitaire in his library while the panic gripped Wall Street. Then, when the other bankers had divided up the cost of saving the tottering Trust Company of America, he presided at the signing of the agreement, authorized the purchase of the Tennessee Coal & Iron Company by the Steel Corporation to encourage the market, cleared the transaction with President Roosevelt and the panic was over. There, as legend has preserved and doubtless improved the story, was a man with power a self-respecting man could fear.

A mere two decades later, in the crash of 1929, it was evident that the Wall Street bankers were as helpless as everyone else. Their effort in the autumn of that year to check the collapse in the market is now recalled as an amusing anecdote; the heads of the New York Stock Exchange and the National City Bank fell into the toils of the law and the first went to prison; the son of the Great Morgan went

From *American Capitalism* (108–128). Copyright © 1952, 1956 by John Kenneth Galbraith. Reprinted by permission of the publishers Houghton Mifflin Company and Hamish Hamilton (London).

to a Congressional hearing in Washington and acquired fame, not for his authority, but for his embarrassment when a circus midget was placed on his knee.

As the banker, as a symbol of economic power, passed into the shadows his place was taken by the giant industrial corporation. The substitute was much more plausible. The association of power with the banker had always depended on the somewhat tenuous belief in a "money trust"—on the notion that the means for financing the initiation and expansion of business enterprises was concentrated in the hands of a few men. The ancestry of this idea was in Marx's doctrine of finance capital; it was not susceptible to statistical or other empirical verification at least in the United States.

By contrast, the fact that a substantial proportion of all production was concentrated in the hands of a relatively small number of huge firms was readily verified. That three or four giant firms in an industry might exercise power analogous to that of a monopoly, and not different in consequences, was an idea that had come to have the most respectable of ancestry in classical economics. So as the J. P. Morgan Company left the stage, it was replaced by the two hundred largest corporations—giant devils in company strength. Here was economic power identified by the greatest and most conservative tradition in economic theory. Here was power to control the prices the citizen paid, the wages he received, and which interposed the most formidable of obstacles of size and experience to the aspiring new firm. What more might it accomplish were it to turn its vast resources to corrupting politics and controlling access to public opinion?

Yet, as was so dramatically revealed to be the case with the omnipotence of the banker in 1929, there are considerable gaps between the myth and the fact. The comparative importance of a small number of great corporations in the American economy cannot be denied except by those who have a singular immunity to statistical evidence or striking capacity to manipulate it. In principle the American is controlled, livelihood and soul, by the large corporation; in practice he seems not to be completely enslaved. Once again the danger is in the future; the present seems still tolerable. Once again there may be lessons from the present which, if learned, will save us in the future.

## II

The paradox of the unexercised power of the large corporation begins with an important oversight in the underlying economic theory. In the competitive model—the economy of many sellers each with a small share of the total market—the restraint on the private exercise of economic power was provided by other firms on the same side of the market. It was the eagerness of competitors to sell, not the complaints of buyers, that saved the latter from spoliation. It was assumed, no doubt accurately, that the nineteenth-century textile manufacturer who overcharged for his product would promptly lose his market to another manufacturer who did not. If all manufacturers found themselves in a position where they could exploit a strong demand, and mark up their prices accordingly, there would soon be an inflow of new competitors. The resulting increase in supply would bring prices and profits back to normal.

As with the seller who was tempted to use his economic power against the customer, so with the buyer who was tempted to use it against his labor or suppliers. The man who paid less than prevailing wage would lose his labor force to those who paid the worker his full (marginal) contribution to the earnings of the firm. In all cases the incentive to socially desirable behavior was provided by the competitor. It was to the same side of the market—the restraint of sellers by other sellers and of buyers by other buyers, in other words to competition—that economists came to look for the self-regulatory mechanism of the economy.

They also came to look to competition exclusively and in formal theory still do. The notion that there might be another regulatory mechanism in the economy has been almost completely excluded from economic thought. Thus, with the widespread disappearance of competition in its classical form and its replacement by the small group of firms if not in overt, at least in conventional or tacit collusion, it was easy to suppose that since competition had disappeared, all effective restraint on private power had disappeared. Indeed this conclusion was all but inevitable if no search was made for other restraints and so complete was the preoccupation with competition that none was made.

In fact, new restraints on private power did appear to replace competition. They were nurtured by the same process of concentration which impaired or destroyed competition. But they appeared not on the same side of the market but on the opposite side, not with competitors but with customers or suppliers. It will be convenient to have a name for this counterpart of competition and I shall call it *countervailing power*.

To begin with a broad and somewhat too dogmatically stated proposition, private economic power is held in check by the countervailing power of those who are subject to it. The first begets the second. The long trend toward concentration of industrial enterprise in the hands of a relatively few firms has brought into existence not only strong sellers, as economists have supposed, but also strong buyers as they have failed to see. The two develop together, not in precise step but in such manner that there can be no doubt that the one is in response to the other.

The fact that a seller enjoys a measure of monopoly power, and is reaping a measure of monopoly return as a result, means that there is an inducement to those firms from whom he buys or those to whom he sells to develop the power with which they can defend themselves against exploitation. It means also that there is a reward to them, in the form of a share of the gains of their opponents' market power, if they are able to do so. In this way the existence of market power creates an incentive to the organization of another position of power that neutralizes it.

The contention I am here making is a formidable one. It comes to this: Competition which, at least since the time of Adam Smith, has been viewed as the autonomous regulator of economic activity and as the only available regulatory mechanism apart from the state, has, in fact, been superseded. Not entirely, to be sure. I should like to be explicit on this point. Competition still plays a role. There are still important markets where the power of the firm as (say) a seller is checked or circumscribed by those who provide a similar or a substitute product or service. This, in the broadest sense that can be meaningful, is the meaning of competition. The role of the buyer on the other side of such markets is essentially a passive one. It consists in looking for, perhaps asking for, and responding to the best bargain. The active restraint is provided by the competitor who offers, or threatens to offer, a better bargain. However, this is not the only or even the typical restraint on the exercise of economic power. In the typical modern market of few sellers, the active restraint is provided not by competitors but from the other side of the market by strong buyers. Given the convention against price competition, it is the role of the competitor that becomes passive in these markets.

It was always one of the basic presuppositions of competition that market power exercised in its absence would invite the competitors who would eliminate such exercise of power. The profits of a monopoly position inspired competitors to try for a share. In other words competition was regarded as a *self-generating* regulatory force. The doubt whether this was in fact so after a market had been pre-empted by a few large sellers, after entry of new firms had become difficult and after existing firms had accepted a convention against price competition, was what destroyed the faith in competition as a regulatory mechanism. Countervailing power is also a self-generating force and this is a matter of great importance. Something, although not very much, could be claimed for the regulatory role of the strong buyer in relation to the market power of sellers, did it happen that as an accident of economic development, such strong buyers were frequently juxtaposed to strong sellers. However the tendency of power to be organized in response to a given position of power is the vital characteristic of the phenomenon I am here identifying. As noted, power on one side of a market creates both the need for, and the prospect of reward to, the exercise of countervailing power from the other side. This means that, as a common rule, we can rely on countervailing power to appear as a curb on economic power. There are also, it should be added, circumstances in which it does not appear or is effectively prevented from appearing. To these I shall return. For some reason, critics of the theory have seized with particular avidity on these exceptions to deny the existence of the phenomenon itself. It is plain that by a similar line of argument one could deny the existence of competition by finding one monopoly.

In the market of small numbers or oligopoly, the practical barriers to entry and the convention against price competition have eliminated the self-generating capacity of competition. The self-generating tendency of countervailing power, by contrast, is readily assimilated to the common sense of the situation and its existence, once we have learned to look for it, is readily subject to empirical observation.

Market power can be exercised by strong buyers against weak sellers as well as by strong sellers against weak buyers. In the competitive model, competition acted as a restraint on both kinds of exercise of power. This is also the case with countervailing power. In turning to its practical manifestations, it will be convenient, in fact, to begin with a case where it is exercised by weak sellers against strong buyers.

## III

The operation of countervailing power is to be seen with the greatest clarity in the labor market where it is also most fully developed. Because of his comparative immobility, the individual worker has long been highly vulnerable to private economic power. The customer of any particular steel mill, at the turn of the century, could always take himself elsewhere if he felt he was being overcharged. Or he could exercise his sovereign privilege of not buying steel at all. The worker had no comparable freedom if he felt he was being underpaid. Normally he could not move and he had to have work. Not often has the power of one man over another been used more callously than in the American labor market after the rise of the large corporation. As late as the early twenties, the steel industry worked a twelve-hour day and seventy-two-hour week with an incredible twenty-four-hour stint every fortnight when the shift changed.

No such power is exercised today and for the reason that its earlier exercise stimulated the counteraction that brought it to an end. In the ultimate sense it was the power of the steel industry, not the organizing abilities of John L. Lewis and Philip Murray, that brought the United Steel Workers into being. The economic power that the worker faced in the sale of his labor—the competition of many sellers dealing with few buyers—made it necessary that he organize for his own protection. There were rewards to the power of the steel companies in which, when he had successfully developed countervailing power, he could share.

As a general thought not invariable rule one finds the strongest unions in the United States where markets are served by strong corporations. And it is not an accident that the large automobile, steel, electrical, rubber, farm-machinery and non-ferrous metal-mining and smelting companies all bargain with powerful unions. Not only has the strength of the corporations in these industries made it necessary for workers to develop the protection of countervailing power: it has provided unions with the opportunity for getting something more as well. If successful they could share in the fruits of the corporation's market power. By contrast there is not a single union of any consequence in American agriculture, the country's closest approach to the competitive model. The reason lies not in the difficulties in organization; these are considerable, but greater difficulties in organization have been overcome. The reason is that the farmer has not possessed any power over his labor force, and at least until recent times has not had any rewards from market power which it was worth the while of a union to seek. As an interesting verification of the point, in the Great Valley of California, the large farmers of that area have had considerable power vis-à-vis their labor force. Almost uniquely in the United States, that region has been marked by persistent attempts at organization by farm workers.

Elsewhere in industries which approach the competition of the model one typically finds weaker or less comprehensive unions. The textile industry, boot and shoe manufacture, lumbering and other forest industries in most parts of the country, and smaller wholesale and retail enterprises, are all cases in point. I do not, of course, advance the theory of countervailing power as a monolithic

341

explanation of tradeunion organization. No such complex social phenomenon is likely to have any single, simple explanation. American trade unions developed in the face of the implacable hostility, not alone of employers, but often of the community as well. In this environment organization of the skilled crafts was much easier than the average, which undoubtedly explains the earlier appearance of durable unions here. In the modern bituminous coal-mining and more clearly in the clothing industry, unions have another explanation. They have emerged as a supplement to the weak market position of the operators and manufacturers. They have assumed price- and market-regulating functions that are the normal functions of managements, and on which the latter, because of the competitive character of the industry, have been forced to default. Nevertheless, as an explanation of the incidence of trade-union strength in the American economy, the theory of countervailing power clearly fits the broad contours of experience. There is, I venture, no other so satisfactory explanation of the great dynamic of labor organization in the modern capitalist community and none which so sensibly integrates the union into the theory of that society.

## IV

The labor market serves admirably to illustrate the incentives to the development of countervailing power and it is of great importance in this market. However, its development, in response to positions of market power, is pervasive in the economy. As a regulatory device one of its most important manifestations is in the relation of the large retailer to the firms from which it buys. The way in which countervailing power operates in these markets is worth examining in some detail.

One of the seemingly harmless simplifications of formal economic theory has been the assumption that producers of consumers' goods sell their products directly to consumers. All business units are held, for this reason, to have broadly parallel interests. Each buys labor and materials, combines them and passes them along to the public at prices that, over some period of time, maximize returns. It is recognized that this is, indeed, a simplification; courses in marketing in the universities deal with what is excluded by this assumption. Yet it has long been supposed that the assumption does no appreciable violence to reality.

Did the real world correspond to the assumed one, the lot of the consumer would be an unhappy one. In fact goods pass to consumers by way of retailers and other intermediaries and this is a circumstance of first importance. Retailers are required by their situation to develop countervailing power on the consumer's behalf.

As I have previously observed, retailing remains one of the industries to which entry is characteristically free. It takes small capital and no very rare talent to set up as a seller of goods. Through history there have always been an ample supply of men with both and with access to something to sell. The small man can provide convenience and intimacy of service and can give an attention to detail, all of which allow him to co-exist with larger competitors.

The advantage of the larger competitor ordinarily lies in its lower prices. It lives constantly under the threat of an erosion of its business by the more rapid growth of rivals and by the appearance of new firms. This loss of volume, in turn, destroys the chance for the lower prices on which the firm depends. This means that the larger retailer is extraordinarily sensitive to higher prices by its suppliers. It means also that it is strongly rewarded if it can develop the market power which permits it to force lower prices.

The opportunity to exercise such power exists only when the suppliers are enjoying something that can be taken away; i.e., when they are enjoying the fruits of market power from which they can be separated. Thus, as in the labor market, we find the mass retailer, from a position across the market, with both a protective and a profit incentive to develop countervailing power when the firm with which it is doing business is in possession of market power. Critics have suggested that these are possibly important but certainly disparate phenomena. This may be so, but only if all similarity between social phenomena be denied. In the present instance the market context is the same. The motivating incentives are identical. The fact that it has characteristics in common has been what has caused people to call competition competition when they encountered it, say, in agriculture and then again in the laundry business.

Countervailing power in the retail business is identified with the large and powerful retail enterprises. Its practical manifestation, over the last half-century, has been the rise of the food chains, the variety chains, the mail-order houses (now graduated into chain stores), the department-store chains, and the co-operative buying organizations of the surviving independent department and food stores.

This development was the countervailing response to previously established positions of power. The gains from invading these positions have been considerable and in some instances even spectacular. The rubber tire industry is a fairly commonplace example of oligopoly. Four large firms are dominant in the market. In the thirties, Sears, Roebuck & Co. was able, by exploiting its role as a large and indispensable customer, to procure tires from Goodyear Tire & Rubber Company at a price from twenty-nine to forty per cent lower than the going market. These it resold to thrifty motorists for from a fifth to a quarter less than the same tires carrying the regular Goodyear brand.

As a partial consequence of the failure of the government to recognize the role of countervailing power many hundreds of pages of court records have detailed the exercise of this power by the Great Atlantic & Pacific Tea Company. There is little doubt that this firm, at least in its uninhibited days, used the countervailing power it had developed with considerable artistry. In 1937, a survey by the company indicated that, for an investment of $175,000, it could supply itself with corn flakes. Assuming that it charged itself the price it was then paying to one of the three companies manufacturing this delicacy, it could earn a modest sixty-eight per cent on the outlay. Armed with this information, and the threat to go into the business which its power could readily make effective, it had no difficulty in bringing down the price by approximately ten per cent. Such gains from the exercise of countervailing power, it will be clear, could only occur where there is an exercise of original market power with which to contend. The A & P could have reaped no comparable gains in buying staple products from the farmer. Committed as he is to the competition of the competitive model, the farmer has no gains to surrender. Provided, as he is, with the opportunity of selling all he produces at the impersonally determined market price, he has not the slightest incentive to make a special price to A & P at least beyond that which might in some circumstances be associated with the simple economies of bulk sale.

The examples of the exercise of countervailing power by Sears, Roebuck and A & P just cited show how this power is deployed in its most dramatic form. The day-to-day exercise of the buyer's power is a good deal less spectacular but also a good deal more significant. At the end of virtually every channel by which consumers' goods reach the public there is, in practice, a layer of powerful buyers. In the food market there are the great food chains; in clothing there are the department stores, the chain department stores and the department store buying organizations; in appliances there are Sears, Roebuck and Montgomery Ward and the department stores; these latter firms are also important outlets for furniture and other house furnishings; the drug and cosmetic manufacturer has to seek part of his market through the large drug chains and the department stores; a vast miscellany of consumers' goods pass to the public through Woolworth's, Kresge's, and other variety chains.

The buyers of all these firms deal directly with the manufacturer and there are few of the latter who, in setting prices, do not have to reckon with the attitude and reaction of their powerful customers. The retail buyers have a variety of weapons at their disposal to use against the market power of their suppliers. Their ultimate sanction is to develop their own source of supply as the food chains, Sears, Roebuck and Montgomery Ward have extensively done. They can also concentrate their entire patronage on a single supplier and, in return for a lower price, give him security in his volume and relieve him of selling and advertising costs. This policy has been widely followed and there have also been numerous complaints of the leverage it gives the retailer on his source of supply.

The more commonplace but more important tactic in the exercise of counter-vailing power consists, merely, in keeping the seller in a state of uncertainty as to the intentions of a buyer who is indispensable to him. The larger of the retail buying organizations place orders around which the production schedules and occasionally the investment of even the largest manufacturers become organized. A shift in this custom imposes prompt and heavy loss. The threat or even the fear of this sanction is enough to cause the supplier to surrender some or all of the rewards of his market power. He must frequently, in addition, make a partial surrender to less potent buyers if he is not to be more than ever in the power of his large customers. It will be clear that in this operation there are rare opportunities for playing one supplier off against another.

A measure of the importance which large retailing organizations attach to the deployment of their countervailing power is the prestige they accord to their buyers. These men (and women) are the key employees of the modern large retail organization; they are highly paid and they are among the most intelligent and resourceful people to be found anywhere in business. In the everyday course of business, they may be considerably better known and command rather more respect than the salesmen from whom they buy. This is a not unimportant index of the power they wield.

There are producers of consumers' goods who have protected themselves from exercise of countervailing power. Some, like the automobile and the oil industry, have done so by integrating their distribution through to the consumer—a strategy which attests the importance of the use of countervailing power by retailers. Others have found it possible to maintain dominance over an organization of small and dependent and therefore fairly powerless dealers. It seems probable that in a few industries, tobacco manufacture for example, the members are ordinarily strong enough and have sufficient solidarity to withstand any pressure applied to them by the most powerful buyer. However, even the tobacco manufacturers, under conditions that were especially favorable to the exercise of countervailing power in the thirties, were forced to make liberal price concessions, in the form of advertising allowances, to the A & P and possibly also to other large customers. When the comprehensive representation of large retailers in the various fields of consumers' goods distribution is considered, it is reasonable to conclude—the reader is warned that this is an important generalization—that most positions of market power in the production of consumers' goods are covered by positions of countervailing power. As noted, there are exceptions and, as between markets, countervailing power is exercised with varying strength and effectiveness. The existence of exceptions does not impair the significance of the regulatory phenomenon here described. To its devotees the virtues of competition were great but few if any ever held its reign to be universal.

Countervailing power also manifests itself, although less visibly, in producers' goods markets. For many years the power of the automobile companies, as purchasers of steel, has sharply curbed the power of the steel mills as sellers. Detroit is the only city where the historic basing-point system was not used to price steel. Under the basing-point system, all producers regardless of location quoted the same price at any particular point of delivery. This obviously minimized the opportunity of a strong buyer to play one seller off against the other. The large firms in the automobile industry had developed the countervailing power which enabled them to do precisely this. They were not disposed to tolerate any limitations on their exercise of such power. In explaining the quotation of "arbitrary prices" on Detroit steel, a leading student of the basing-point system some years ago recognized, implicitly but accurately, the role of countervailing power by observing that "it is difficult to apply high cartel prices to particularly large and strong customers such as the automobile manufacturers in Detroit."

The more normal operation of countervailing power in producers' goods markets has, as its point of departure, the relatively small number of customers which firms in these industries typically have. Where the cigarette or soap manufacturer numbers his retail outlets by the hundreds of thousands and his final consumers by the millions, the machinery or equipment manufacturer counts his customers by the hundreds or thousands and, very often, his important ones by the dozen. But here, as elsewhere, the market pays a premium to those who develop power as buyers that is equivalent to the market power of those from whom they buy. The reverse is true where weak sellers do business with strong buyers.

## V

There is an old saying, or should be, that it is a wise economist who recognizes the scope of his own generalizations. It is now time to consider the limits in place and time on the operations of countervailing power. A study of the instances where countervailing power fails to function is not without advantage in showing its achievements in the decisively important areas where it does operate. As noted, some industries, because they are integrated through to the consumer or because their product passes through a dependent dealer organization have not been faced with countervailing power. There are a few cases where a very strong market position has proven impregnable even against the attacks of strong buyers. And there are cases where the dangers from countervailing power have, apparently, been recognized and where it has been successfully resisted.

An example of successful resistance to countervailing power is the residential-building industry. No segment of American capitalism evokes less pride. Yet anyone approaching the industry with the preconceptions of competition in mind is unlikely to see, very accurately, the reasons for its shortcomings. There are many thousands of individual firms in the business of building houses. Nearly all are small; the capital of the typical housebuilder runs from a few hundred to a few thousand dollars. The members of the industry oppose little market power to the would-be house owner. Except in times of extremely high building activity there is aggressive competition for business.

The industry does show many detailed manifestations of guild restraint. Builders are frequently in alliance with each other, unions, and local politicians to protect prices and wages and to maintain established building techniques. These derelictions have been seized upon avidly by the critics of the industry. Since they represent its major departure from the competitive model, they have been assumed to be the cause of the poor performance of the housing industry. It has long been an article of faith with liberals that if competition could be brought to the housing business all would be well.

In fact were all restraint and collusion swept away—were there full and free competition in bidding, no restrictive building codes, no collusion with union leaders or local politicians to enhance prices—it seems improbable that the price of new houses would be much changed and the satisfaction of customers with what they get for what they pay much enhanced. The reason is that the typical builder would still be a small and powerless figure buying his building materials in small quantities at high cost from suppliers with effective market power and facing in this case essentially the same problem vis-à-vis the unions as sellers of labor. It is these factors which, very largely, determine the cost of the house.

The builder is more or less deliberately kept without power. With few exceptions, the manufacturers of building supplies decline to sell to him direct. This prevents any builder from bringing pressure to bear on his source of supply; at the same time it helps keep all builders relatively small and powerless by uniformly denying them the economies of direct purchase. All must pay jobbers' and retailers' margins. A few builders—a spectacular case is Levitt & Sons of Long Island—have managed to circumvent this ban. As the result of more effective buying, a much stronger position in dealing with labor, and the savings from large-scale production of houses, they have notably increased the satisfaction of customers with what they receive for their money. Few can doubt that the future of the industry, if its future is to improve on its past, lies with such firms.

Thus it is the notion of countervailing power, not of competition, which points the way to progress in the housing industry. What is needed is fewer firms of far greater scale with resulting capacity to bring power to bear upon unions and suppliers. It is the absence of such firms, and of the resulting economies, which helps explain why one sector of this industry—low-cost housing where cost is especially important in relation to ability-to-pay—has passed under government management. In the absence of an effective regulating mechanism within the industry in the form of countervailing power, private entrepreneurship has been superseded. In accordance with classical expectations the state has had to intervene. Only the failure was not of competition but of countervailing power.

## VI

The development of countervailing power requires a certain minimum opportunity and capacity for organization, corporate or otherwise. If the large retail buying organizations had not developed the countervailing power which they have used, by proxy, on behalf of the individual consumer, consumers would have been faced with the need to organize the equivalent of the retailer's power. This would have been a formidable task but it has been accomplished in Scandinavia where the consumer's co-operative, instead of the chain store, is the dominant instrument of countervailing power in consumers' goods markets. There has been a similar though less comprehensive development in England and Scotland. In the Scandinavian countries the co-operatives have long been regarded explicitly as instruments for bringing power to bear on the cartels; i.e., for exercise of countervailing power. This is readily conceded by many who have the greatest difficulty in seeing private mass buyers in the same role. But the fact that consumer co-operatives are not of any great importance in the United States is to be explained, not by any inherent incapacity of the American for such organization, but because the chain stores pre-empted the gains of countervailing power first. The counterpart of the Swedish Kooperative Forbundet or the British Co-operative Wholesale Societies has not appeared in the United States simply because it could not compete with the A & P and other large food chains. The meaning of this, which incidentally has been lost on devotees of the theology of co-operation, is that the chain stores are approximately as efficient in the exercise of countervailing power as a co-operative would be. In parts of the American economy where proprietary mass buyers have not made their appearance, notably in the purchase of farm supplies, individuals (who are also individualists) have shown as much capacity to organize as the Scandinavians and the British and have similarly obtained the protection and rewards of countervailing power. The Grange League Federation, the Eastern States Farmers' Exchange and the Illinois Farm Supply Company, co-operatives with annual sales running to multi-million-dollar figures, are among the illustrations of the point.

However, it must not be assumed that it is easy for great numbers of individuals to coalesce and organize countervailing power. In less developed communities, Puerto Rico for example, one finds people fully exposed to the exactions of strategically situated importers, merchants and wholesalers and without the apparent capacity to develop countervailing power in their own behalf. Anyone, incidentally, who doubts the force of the countervailing power exercised by large retailer-buying organizations would do well to consider the revolution which the entry of the large chain stores would work in an economy like that of Puerto Rico and also how such an intrusion would be resented and perhaps resisted by importers and merchants now able to exercise their market power with impunity against the thousands of small, independent and inefficient retailers who are their present outlets.

In the light of the difficulty in organizing countervailing power, it is not surprising that the assistance of government has repeatedly been sought in this task. Without the phenomenon itself being fully recognized, the provision of state assistance to the development of countervailing power has become a major function of government—perhaps *the* major domestic function of government. Much of the domestic legislation of the last twenty years, that of the New Deal episode in particular, only because fully comprehensible when it is viewed in this light.

# 79

## Farewell to Progressivism

Lionel Trilling was one of America's most distinguished literary critics in an era in which, as this essay
from his book *The Liberal Imagination* (1950) illustrates, literary criticism had become an important
vehicle of political and social criticism as well. Distressed about what he considered the simplistic and
crude assumptions of the American liberal and progressive tradition, Trilling argued that "the job of criticism"
was to "recall liberalism to its first essential imagination of variousness and possibility, which implies the
awareness of complexity and difficulty," and that the
study of literature had a unique relevance to that task
because "literature is the human activity that takes the
fullest and most precise account of variousness, possibility, complexity, and difficulty." In the following
attack upon literary historian Vernon L. Parrington and
novelist Theodore Dreiser, two men who took a
different view of the relationship between literature and
life, Trilling raised penetrating questions about the
American liberal imagination.

## THE LIBERAL IMAGINATION
### *Lionel Trilling*

**I**

It is possible to say of V. L. Parrington that with his *Main Currents in American
Thought* he has had an influence on our conception of American culture which is
not equaled by that of any other writer of the last two decades. His ideas are now
the accepted ones wherever the college course in American literature is given by a
teacher who conceives himself to be opposed to the genteel and the academic and
in alliance with the vigorous and the actual. And whenever the liberal historian of
America finds occasion to take account of the national literature, as nowadays he
feels it proper to do, it is Parrington who is his standard and guide. Parrington's
ideas are the more firmly established because they do not have to be imposed—the
teacher or the critic who presents them is likely to find that his task is merely to
make articulate for his audience what it has always believed, for Parrington
formulated in a classic way the suppositions about our culture which are held by

the American middle class so far as that class is at all liberal in its social thought and so far as it begins to understand that literature has anything to do with society.

Parrington was not a great mind; he was not a precise thinker or, except when measured by the low eminences that were about him, an impressive one. Separate Parrington from his informing idea of the economic and social determination of thought and what is left is a simple intelligence, notable for its generosity and enthusiasm but certainly not for its accuracy or originality. Take him even with his idea and he is, once its direction is established, rather too predictable to be continuously interesting; and, indeed, what we dignify with the name of economic and social determinism amounts in his use of it to not much more than the demonstration that most writers incline to stick to their own social class. But his best virtue was real and important—he had what we like to think of as the saving salt of the American mind, the lively sense of the practical, workaday world, of the welter of ordinary undistinguished things and people, of the tangible, quirky, unrefined elements of life. He knew what so many literary historians do not know, that emotions and ideas are the sparks that fly when the mind meets difficulties.

Yet he had after all but a limited sense of what constitutes a difficulty. Whenever he was confronted with a work of art that was complex, personal and not literal, that was not, as it were, a public document. Parrington was at a loss. Difficulties that were complicated by personality or that were expressed in the language of successful art did not seem quite real to him and he was inclined to treat them as aberrations, which is one way of saying what everybody admits, that the weakest part of Parrington's talent was his aesthetic judgment. His admirers and disciples like to imply that his errors of aesthetic judgment are merely lapses of taste, but this is not so. Despite such mistakes as his notorious praise of Cabell, to whom in a remarkable passage he compares Melville, Parrington's taste was by no means bad. His errors are the errors of understanding which arise from his assumptions about the nature of reality.

Parrington does not often deal with abstract philosophical ideas, but whenever he approaches a work of art we are made aware of the metaphysics on which his aesthetics is based. There exists, he believes, a thing called *reality*; it is one and immutable, it is wholly external, it is irreducible. Men's minds may waver, but reality is always reliable, always the same, always easily to be known. And the artist's relation to reality he conceives as a simple one. Reality being fixed and given, the artist has but to let it pass through him, he is the lens in the first diagram of an elementary book on optics: Fig. 1, Reality; Fig. 2, Artist; Fig. 1', Work of Art. Figs. 1 and 1' are normally in virtual correspondence with each other. Sometimes the artist spoils this ideal relation by "turning away from" reality. This results in certain fantastic works, unreal and ultimately useless. It does not occur to Parrington that there is any other relation possible between the artist and reality than this passage of reality through the transparent artist; he meets evidence of imagination and creativeness with a settled hostility the expression of which suggests that he regards them as the natural enemies of democracy.

In this view of things, reality, although it is always reliable, is always rather sober-sided, even grim. Parrington, a genial and enthusiastic man, can understand how the generosity of man's hopes and desires may leap beyond reality; he admires will in the degree that he suspects mind. To an excess of desire and energy which blinds a man to the limitations of reality he can indeed be very tender. This is one of the many meanings he gives to *romance* or *romanticism,* and in spite of himself it appeals to something in his own nature. The praise of Cabell is Parrington's response not only to Cabell's elegance—for Parrington loved elegance—but also to Cabell's insistence on the part which a beneficent self-deception may and even should play in the disappointing fact-bound life of man, particularly in the private and erotic part of his life.

The second volume of *Main Currents* is called *The Romantic Revolution in America* and it is natural to expect that the word romantic should appear in it frequently. So it does more frequently than one can count, and seldom with the same meaning, seldom with the sense that the word, although scandalously vague as it has been used by the literary historians, is still full of complicated but not wholly pointless ideas, that it involves many contrary but definable things; all too often Parrington uses the word romantic with the word romance close at hand, meaning *a* romance, in the sense that *Graustark* or *Treasure Island* is a romance, as though it signified chiefly a gay disregard of the limitations of everyday fact. Romance is refusing to heed the counsels of experience p. iii); it is ebullience (p. iv); it is utopianism (p. iv); it is individualism (p. vi); it is self-deception (p. 59)— "romantic faith . . . in the beneficent processes of trade and industry" (as held, we inevitably ask, by the romantic Adam Smith?); it is the love of the picturesque (p. 49); it is the dislike of innovation (p. 50) but also the love of change (p. iv); it is the sentimental (p. 192); it is patriotism, and then it is cheap (p. 235). It may be used to denote what is not classical, but chiefly it means that which ignores reality (pp. ix, 136, 143, 147, and *passim*); it is not critical (pp. 225, 235), although in speaking of Cooper and Melville, Parrington admits that criticism can sometimes spring from romanticism.

Whenever a man with whose ideas he disagrees wins from Parrington a reluctant measure of respect, the word romantic is likely to appear. He does not admire Henry Clay, yet something in Clay is not to be despised—his romanticism, although Clay's romanticism is made equivalent with his inability to "come to grips with reality." Romanticism is thus, in most of its significations, the venial sin of *Main Currents;* like carnal passion in the *Inferno*, it evokes not blame but tender sorrow. But it can also be the great and saving virtue which Parrington recognizes. It is ascribed to the transcendental reformers he so much admires; it is said to mark two of his most cherished heroes, Jefferson and Emerson: "they were both romantics and their idealism was only a different expression of a common spirit." Parrington held, we may say, at least two different views of romanticism which suggest two different views of reality. Sometimes he speaks of reality in an honorific way, meaning the substantial stuff of life, the ineluctable facts with which the mind must cope, but sometimes he speaks of it pejoratively and means the world of established social forms; and he speaks of realism in two ways: sometimes as the power of dealing intelligently with fact, sometimes as a cold and conservative resistance to idealism.

351

Just as for Parrington there is a saving grace and a venial sin, there is also a deadly sin, and this is turning away from reality, not in the excess of generous feeling, but in what he believes to be a deficiency of feeling, as with Hawthorne, or out of what amounts to sinful pride, as with Henry James. He tells us that there was too much realism in Hawthorne to allow him to give his faith to the transcendental reformers: "he was too much of a realist to change fashions in creeds"; "he remained cold to the revolutionary criticism that was eager to pull down the old temples to make room for nobler." It is this cold realism, keeping Hawthorne was critically examining the question of evil as it appeared in the light sympathy—"Eager souls, mystics and revolutionaries, may propose to refashion the world in accordance with their dreams; but evil remains, and so long as it lurks in the secret places of the heart, utopia is only the shadow of a dream. And so while the Concord thinkers were proclaiming man to be the indubitable child of God, Hawthorne was critically examining the question of evil as it appeared in the light of his own experience. It was the central fascinating problem of his intellectual life, and in pursuit of a solution he probed curiously into the hidden, furtive recesses of the soul." Parrington's disapproval of the enterprise is unmistakable.

Now we might wonder whether Hawthorne's questioning of the naïve and often eccentric faiths of the transcendental reformers was not, on the face of it, a public service. But Parrington implies that it contributes nothing to democracy, and even that it stands in the way of the realization of democracy. If democracy depends wholly on a fighting faith, I suppose he is right. Yet society is after all something that exists at the moment as well as in the future, and if one man wants to probe curiously into the hidden furtive recesses of the contemporary soul, a broad democracy and especially one devoted to reality should allow him to do so without despising him. If what Hawthorne did was certainly nothing to build a party on, we ought perhaps to forgive him when we remember that he was only one man and that the future of mankind did not depend upon him alone. But this very fact serves only to irritate Parrington; he is put out by Hawthorne's loneliness and believes that part of Hawthorne's insufficiency as a writer comes from his failure to get around and meet people. Hawthorne could not, he tells us, establish contact with the "Yankee reality," and was scarcely aware of the "substantial world of Puritan reality that Samuel Sewall knew."

To turn from reality might mean to turn to romance, but Parrington tells us that Hawthorne was romantic "only in a narrow and very special sense." He was not interested in the world of, as it were, practical romance, in the Salem of the clipper ships; from this he turned away to create "a romance of ethics." This is not an illuminating phrase but it is a catching one, and it might be taken to mean that Hawthorne was in the tradition of, say, Shakespeare; but we quickly learn that, no, Hawthorne had entered a barren field, for although he himself lived in the present and had all the future to mold, he preferred to find many of the subjects in the past. We learn too that his romance of ethics is not admirable because it requires the hard, fine pressing of ideas, and we are told that "a romantic uninterested in adventure and afraid of sex is likely to become somewhat graveled for matter." In short, Hawthorne's mind was a thin one, and Parrington puts in evidence his use of allegory and symbol and the very severity and precision of his art to prove that he suffered from a sadly limited intellect, for so much fancy and so much art could scarcely be needed unless the writer were trying to exploit to the utmost the few poor ideas that he had.

Hawthorne, then, was "forever dealing with shadows, and he knew that he was dealing with shadows." Perhaps so, but shadows are also part of reality and one would not want a world without shadows, it would not even be a "real" world. But we must get beyond Parrington's metaphor. The fact is that Hawthorne was dealing beautifully with realities, with substantial things. The man who could raise those brilliant and serious doubts about the nature and possibility of moral perfection, the man who could keep himself aloof from the "Yankee reality" and who could dissent from the orthodoxies of dissent and tell us so much about the nature of moral zeal, is of course dealing exactly with reality.

Parrington's characteristic weakness as a historian is suggested by his title, for the culture of a nation is not truly figured in the image of the current. A culture is not a flow, nor even a confluence; the form of its existence is struggle, or at least debate—it is nothing if not a dialectic. And in any culture there are likely to be certain artists who contain a large part of the dialectic within themselves, their meaning and power lying in their contradictions; they contain within themselves, it may be said, the very essence of the culture, and the sign of this is that they do not submit to serve the ends of any one ideological group or tendency. It is a significant circumstance of American culture, and one which is susceptible of explanation, that an unusually large proportion of its notable writers of the nineteenth century were such repositories of the dialectic of their times—they contained both the yes and the no of their culture, and by that token they were prophetic of the future. Parrington said that he had not set up shop as a literary critic; but if a literary critic is simply a reader who has the ability to understand literature and to convey to others who he understands, it is not exactly a matter of free choice whether or not a cultural historian shall be a literary critic, nor is it open to him to let his virtuous political and social opinions do duty for percipience. To throw out Poe because he cannot be conveniently fitted into a theory of American culture, to speak of him as a biological sport and as a mind apart from the main current, to find his gloom to be merely personal and eccentric, "only the atrabilious wretchedness of a dipsomaniac," as Hawthorne's was "no more than the skeptical questioning of life by a nature that knew no fierce storms," to judge Melville's response to American life to be less noble than that of Bryant or of Greeley, to speak of Henry James as an escapist, as an artist similar to Whistler, a man characteristically afraid of stress—this is not merely to be mistaken in aesthetic judgment; rather it is to examine without attention and from the point of view of a limited and essentially arrogant conception of reality the documents which are in some respects the most suggestive testimony to what America was and is, and of course to get no answer from them.

Parrington lies twenty years behind us, and in the intervening time there has developed a body of opinion which is aware of his inadequacies and of the inadequacies of his coadjutors and disciples, who make up what might be called the literary academicism of liberalism. Yet Parrington still stands at the center of American thought about American culture because, as I say, he expresses the chronic American belief that there exists an opposition between reality and mind and that one must enlist oneself in the party of reality.

## II

This belief in the incompatibility of mind and reality is exemplified by the doctrinaire indulgence which liberal intellectuals have always displayed toward Theodore Dreiser, an indulgence which becomes the worthier of remark when it is contrasted with the liberal severity toward Henry James. Dreiser and James: with that juxtaposition we are immediately at the dark and bloody crossroads where literature and politics meet. One does not go there gladly, but nowadays it is not exactly a matter of free choice whether one does or does not go. As for the particular juxtaposition itself, it is inevitable and it has at the present moment far more significance than the juxtaposition which once used to be made between James and Whitman. It is not hard to contrive factitious oppositions between James and Whitman, but the real difference between them is the difference between the moral mind, with its awareness of tragedy, irony, and multitudinous distinctions, and the transcendental mind, with its passionate sense of the oneness of multiplicity. James and Whitman are unlike not in quality but in kind, and in their very opposition they serve to complement each other. But the difference between James and Dreiser is not of kind, for both men addressed themselves to virtually the same social and moral fact. The difference here is one of quality, and perhaps nothing is more typical of American liberalism than the way it has responded to the respective qualities of the two men.

Few critics, I suppose, no matter what their political disposition, have ever been wholly blind to James's great gifts, or even to the grandiose moral intention of these gifts. And few critics have ever been wholly blind to Dreiser's great faults. But by liberal critics James is traditionally put to the ultimate question: of what use, of what actual political use, are his gifts and their intention? Granted that James was devoted to an extraordinary moral perceptiveness, granted too that moral perceptiveness has something to do with politics and the social life, of what possible practical value in our world of impending disaster can James's work be? And James's style, his characters, his subjects, and even his own social origin and the manner of his personal life are adduced to show that his work cannot endure the question. To James no quarter is given by American criticism in its political and liberal aspect. But in the same degree that liberal criticism is moved by political considerations to treat James with severity, it treats Dreiser with the most sympathetic indulgence. Dreiser's literary faults, it gives us to understand, are essentially social and political virtues. It was Parrington who established the formula for the liberal criticism of Dreiser by calling him a "peasant": when Dreiser thinks stupidly, it is because he has the slow stubbornness of a peasant; when he writes badly, it is because he is impatient of the sterile literary gentility of the bourgeoisie. It is as if wit, and flexibility of mind, and perception, and knowledge were to be equated with aristocracy and political reaction, while dullness and stupidity must naturally suggest a virtuous democracy, as in the old plays.

The liberal judgment of Dreiser and James goes back of politics, goes back to the cultural assumptions that make politics. We are still haunted by a kind of political fear of the intellect which Tocqueville observed in us more than a century ago. American intellectuals, when they are being consciously American or political, are remarkably quick to suggest that an art which is marked by perception and knowledge, although all very well in its way, can never get us through gross dangers and difficulties. And their misgivings become the more intense when intellect works in art as it ideally should, when its processes are vivacious and interesting and brilliant. It is then that we like to confront it with the gross dangers and difficulties and to challenge it to save us at once from disaster. When intellect in art is awkward or dull we do not put it to the test of ultimate or immediate practicality. No liberal critic asks the question of Dreiser whether *his* moral preoccupations are going to be useful in confronting the disasters that threaten us. And it is a judgment on the proper nature of mind, rather than any actual political meaning that might be drawn from the works of the two men, which accounts for the unequal justice they have received from the progressive critics. If it could be conclusively demonstrated—by, say, documents in James's handwriting—that James explicitly intended his books to be understood as pleas for co-operatives, labor unions, better housing, and more equitable taxation, the American critic in his liberal and progressive character would still be worried by James because his work shows so many of the electric qualities of mind. And if something like the opposite were proved of Dreiser, it would be brushed aside—as his doctrinaire anti-Semitism has in fact brushed aside—because his books have the awkwardness, the chaos, the heaviness which we associate with "reality." In the American metaphysic, reality is always material reality, hard, resistant, uninformed, impenetrable, and unpleasant. And that mind is alone felt to be trustworthy which most resembles this reality by most nearly reproducing the sensations it affords.

In *The Rise of American Civilization,* Professor Beard uses a significant phrase when, in the course of an ironic account of James's career, he implies that we have the clue to the irrelevance of that career when we know that James was "a whole generation removed from the odors of the shop." Of a piece with this, and in itself even more significant, is the comment which Granville Hicks makes in *The Great Tradition* when he deals with James's stories about artists and remarks that such artists as James portrays, so concerned for their art and their integrity in art, do not really exist: "After all, who has ever known such artists? Where are the Hugh Verekers, the Mark Ambients, the Neil Paradays, the Overts, Limberts, Dencombes, Delavoys?" This question, as Mr. Hicks admits, had occurred to James himself, but what answer had James given to it? "If the life about us for the last thirty years refused warrant for these examples," he said in the preface to volume xii of the New York Edition, "then so much the worse for that life. . . . There are decencies that in the name of the general self-respect we must take for granted, there's a rudimentary intellectual honor to which we must, in the interest of civilization, at least pretend." And to this Mr. Hicks, shocked beyond argument, makes this reply, which would be astonishing had we not heard it before: "But this is the purest romanticism, this writing about what ought to be rather than what is!"

The "odors of the shop" are real, and to those who breathe them they guarantee a sense of vitality from which James is debarred. The idea of intellectual honor is not real, and to that chimera James was devoted. He betrayed the reality of what is in the interests of what ought to be. Dare we trust him? The question, we remember, is asked by men who themselves have elaborate transactions with what ought to be. Professor Beard spoke in the name of a growing, developing, and improving America. Mr. Hicks, when he wrote *The Great Tradition,* was in general sympathy with a nominally radical movement. But James's own transaction with what ought to be is suspect because it is carried on through what I have called the electrical qualities of mind, through a complex and rapid imagination and with a kind of authoritative immediacy. Mr. Hicks knows that Dreiser is "clumsy" and "stupid" and "bewildered" and "crude in his statement of materialistic monism"; he knows that Dreiser in his personal life—which is in point because James's personal life is always supposed to be so much in point—was not quite emancipated from "his boyhood longing for crass material success," showing "again and again a desire for the ostentatious luxury of the successful business man." But Dreiser is to be accepted and forgiven because his faults are the sad, lovable, honorable faults of reality itself, or of America itself—huge, inchoate, struggling toward expression, caught between the dream of raw power and the dream of morality.

"The liability in what Santayana called the genteel tradition was due to its being the product of mind apart from experience. Dreiser gave us the stuff of our common experience, not as it was hoped to be by any idealizing theorist, but as it actually was in its crudity." The author of this statement certainly cannot be accused of any lack of feeling for mind as Henry James represents it; nor can Mr. Matthiessen be thought of as a follower of Parrington—indeed, in the preface to American Renaissance he has framed one of the sharpest and most cogent criticisms of Parrington's method. Yet Mr. Matthiessen, writing in the *New York Times Book Review* about Dreiser's posthumous novel, *The Bulwark,* accepts the liberal cliché which opposes crude experience to mind and establishes Dreiser's value by implying that the mind which Dreiser's crude experience is presumed to confront and refute is the mind of gentility.

This implied amalgamation of mind with gentility is the rationale of the long indulgence of Dreiser, which is extended even to the style of his prose. Everyone is aware that Dreiser's prose style is full of roughness and ungainliness, and the critics who admire Dreiser tell us it does not matter. Of course it does not matter. No reader with a right sense of style would suppose that it does matter, and he might even find it a virtue. But it has been taken for granted that the ungainliness of Dreiser's style is the only possible objection to be made to it, and that whoever finds in it any fault at all wants a prettified genteel style (and is objecting to the ungainliness of reality itself). For instance, Edwin Berry Burgum, in a leaflet on Dreiser put out by the Book Find Club, tells us that Dreiser was one of those who used—or, as Mr. Burgum says, utilized—"the diction of the Middle West, pretty much as it was spoken, rich in colloquialism and frank in the simplicity and directness of the pioneer tradition," and that this diction took the place of "the literary English, formal and bookish, of New England provincialism that was closer to the aristocratic spirit of the mother country than to the tang of everyday life in the new West." This is mere fantasy. Hawthorne, Thoreau, and Emerson were for the most part remarkably colloquial—they wrote, that is, much as they spoke; their prose was specifically American in quality, and, except for occasional lapses, quite direct and simple. It is Dreiser who lacks the sense of colloquial diction—that of the Middle West or any other. If we are to talk of bookishness, it is Dreiser who is bookish; he is precisely literary in the bad sense; he is full of flowers of rhetoric and shines with paste gems; at hundreds of points his diction is not only genteel but fancy. It is he who speaks of "a scene more distingué than this," or of a woman "artistic in form and feature," or of a man who, although "strong, reserved, aggressive, with an air of wealth and experience, was *soi-disant* and not particularly eager to stay at home." Colloquialism held no real charm for him and his natural tendency is always toward the "fine:"

> . . . . Moralists come and go; religionists fulminate and declare the pronounce-ments of God as to this; but Aphrodite still reigns. Embowered in the festal depths of the spring, set above her altars of prophyry, chalcedony, ivory and gold, see her smile the smile that is at once the texture and essence of delight, the glory and despair of the world! Dream on, oh Buddha, asleep on your lotus leaf, of an undisturbed Nirvana! Sweat, oh Jesus, your last agonizing drops over an unregenerate world! In the forests of Pan still ring the cries of the worshippers of Aphrodite! From her altars the incense of adoration ever rises! And see, the new red grapes dripping where votive hands new-press them!

Charles Jackson, the novelist, telling us in the same leaflet that Dreiser's style does not matter, remarks on how much still comes to us when we have lost by translation the stylistic brilliance of Thomas Mann or the Russians or Balzac. He is in part right. And he is right too when he says that a certain kind of conscious, supervised artistry is not appropriate to the novel of large dimensions. Yet the fact is that the great novelists have usually written very good prose, and what comes through even a bad translation is exactly the power of mind that made the well-hung sentence of the original text. In literature style is so little the mere clothing of thought— need it be insisted on at this late date?—that we may say that from the earth of the novelist's prose spring his characters, his ideas, and even his story itself.

To the extent that Dreiser's style is defensible, his thought is also defensible. That is, when he thinks like a novelist, he is worth following—when by means of his rough and ungainly but no doubt cumulatively effective style he creates rough, ungainly, but effective characters and events. But when he thinks like, as we say, a philosopher, he is likely to be not only foolish but vulgar. He thinks as the modern crowd thinks when it decides to think: religion and morality are nonsense, "religionists" and moralists are fakes, tradition is a fraud, what is man but matter and impulses, mysterious "chemisms," what value has life anyway? "What, cooking, eating, coition, job holding, growing, aging, losing, winning, in so changeful and

357

passing a scene as this, important? Bunk! It is some form of titillating illusion with about as much import to the superior forces that bring it all about as the functions and gyrations of a fly. No more. And maybe less." Thus Dreiser at sixty. And yet there is for him always the vulgarly saving suspicion that maybe, when all is said and done, there is Something Behind It All. It is much to the point of his intellectual vulgarity that Dreiser's anti-Semitism was not merely a social prejudice but an idea, a way of dealing with difficulties.

No one, I suppose, has ever represented Dreiser as a masterly intellect. It is even commonplace to say that his ideas are inconsistent or inadequate. But once that admission has been made, his ideas are hustled out of sight while his "reality" and great brooding pity are spoken of. (His pity is to be questioned: pity is to be judged by kind, not amount, and Dreiser's pity—*Jennie Gerhardt* provides the only exception—is either destructive of its object or it is self-pity.) Why has no liberal critic ever brought Dreiser's ideas to the bar of political practicality, asking what use is to be made of Dreiser's dim, awkward speculation, of his self-justification, of his lust for "beauty" and "sex" and "living" and "life itself," and of the showy nihilism which always seems to him so grand a gesture in the direction of profundity? We live, understandably enough, with the sense of urgency; our clock, like Baudelaire's, has had the hands removed and bears the legend, "It is later than you think." But with us it is always a little too late for mind, yet never too late for honest stupidity; always a little too late for understanding, never too late for righteous, bewildered wrath; always too late for thought, never too late for naïve moralizing. We seem to like to condemn our finest but not our worst qualities by pitting them against the exigency of time.

But sometimes time is not quite so exigent as to justify all our own exigency, and in the case of Dreiser time has allowed his deficiencies to reach their logical, and fatal, conclusion. In *The Bulwark* Dreiser's characteristic ideas come full circle, and the simple, didactic life history of Solon Barnes, a Quaker business man, affirms a simple Christian faith, and a kind of practical mysticism, and the virtues of self-abnegation and self-restraint, and the belief in and submission to the hidden purposes of higher powers, those "superior forces that bring it all about"—once, in Dreiser's opinion, so brutally indifferent, now somehow benign. This is not the first occasion on which Dreiser has shown a tenderness toward religion and a responsiveness to mysticism. *Jennie Gerhardt* and the figure of the Reverend Duncan McMillan in *An American Tragedy* are forecasts of the avowals of *The Bulwark,* and Dreiser's lively interest in power of any sort led him to take account of the power implicit in the cruder forms of mystical performance. Yet these rifts in his nearly monolithic materialism cannot quite prepare us for the blank pietism of *The Bulwark,* not after we have remembered how salient in Dreiser's work has been the long surly rage against the "religionists" and the "moralists," the men who have presumed to believe that life can be given any law at all and who have dared to suppose that will or mind or faith can shape the savage and beautiful entity that Dreiser liked to call "life itself." Now for Dreiser the law may indeed be given, and it is wholly simple—the safe conduct of the personal life requires only that we follow the Inner Light according to the regimen of the Society of Friends, or according to some other godly rule. And now the smiling Aphrodite set above her altars of porphyry, chalcedony, ivory, and gold is quite forgotten, and we are told that the sad joy of cosmic acceptance goes hand in hand with sexual abstinence.

Dreiser's mood of "acceptance" in the last years of his life is not, as a personal experience, to be submitted to the tests of intellectual validity. It consists of a sensation of cosmic understanding, of an overarching sense of unity with the world in its apparent evil as well as in its obvious good. It is no more to be quarreled with, or reasoned with, than love itself—indeed, it is a kind of love, not so much of the world as of oneself in the world. Perhaps it is either the cessation of desire or the perfect balance of desires. It is what used often to be meant by "peace," and up through the nineteenth century a good many people understood its meaning. If it was Dreiser's own emotion at the end of his life, who would not be happy that he had achieved it? I am not even sure that our civilization would not be the better for more of us knowing and desiring this emotion of grave felicity. Yet granting the personal validity of the emotion, Dreiser's exposition of it fails, and is, moreover, offensive. Mr. Matthiessen has warned us of the attack that will be made on the doctrine of *The Bulwark* by "those who believe that any renewal of Christianity marks a new 'failure of nerve.' " But Dreiser's religious avowal is not a failure of nerve—it is a failure of mind and heart. We have only to set his book beside any work in which mind and heart are made to serve religion to know this at once. Ivan Karamazov's giving back his ticket of admission to the "harmony" of the universe suggests that *The Bulwark* is not morally adequate, for we dare not, as its hero does, blandly "accept" the suffering of others; and the Book of Job tells us that it does not include enough in its exploration of the problem of evil, and is not stern enough. I have said that Dreiser's religious affirmation was offensive; the offense lies in the vulgar ease of its formulation, as well as in the comfortable untroubled way in which Dreiser moved from nihilism to pietism.

*The Bulwark* is the fruit of Dreiser's old age, but if we speak of it as a failure of thought and feeling, we cannot suppose that with age Dreiser weakened in mind and heart. The weakness was always there. And in a sense it is not Dreiser who failed but a whole way of dealing with ideas, a way in which we have all been in some degree involved. Our liberal, progressive culture tolerated Dreiser's vulgar materialism with its huge negation, its simple cry of "Bunk!," feeling that perhaps it was not quite intellectually adequate but certainly very *strong*, certainly very *real*. And now, almost as a natural consequence, it has been given, and is not unwilling to take, Dreiser's pietistic religion in all its inadequacy.

Dreiser, of course, was firmer than the intellectual culture that accepted him. He *meant* his ideas, at least so far as a man can mean ideas who is incapable of following them to their consequences. But we, when it came to his ideas, talked about his great brooding pity and shrugged the ideas off. We are still doing it. Robert Elias, the biographer of Dreiser, tells us that "it is part of the logic of [Dreiser's] life that he should have completed *The Bulwark* at the same time that he joined the Communists." Just what kind of logic this is we learn from Mr. Elias's further statement. "When he supported left-wing movements and finally, last year, joined the Communist Party, he did so not because he had examined the details of the party line and found them satisfactory, but because he agreed with a general program that represented a means for establishing his cherished goal of greater equality among men." Whether or not Dreiser was following the logic of his own life, he was certainly following the logic of the liberal criticism that accepted him so undiscriminatingly as one of the great, significant expressions of its spirit. This is the liberal criticism, in the direct line of Parrington, which establishes the social responsibility of the writer and then goes on to say that, apart from his duty of resembling reality as much as possible, he is not really responsible for anything, not even for his ideas. The scope of reality being what it is, ideas are held to be mere "details," and, what is more, to be details which, if attended to, have the effect of diminishing reality. But ideals are different from ideas; in the liberal criticism which descends from Parrington ideals consort happily with reality and they urge us to deal impatiently with ideas—a "cherished goal" forbids that we stop to consider how we reach it, or if we may not destroy it in trying to reach it the wrong way.

# 80

# McCarthyism
# and the Intellectuals

Shock at the post-World War II expansion of the Soviet Union and frustration at the inability of even the most powerful country in the world to control the course of events led many Americans to search within their own society for subversives whose misdeeds could explain our impotence. In 1950 the obscure junior Senator from Wisconsin, Joseph R. McCarthy, claimed that he had a list of fifty-seven Communists employed by the United States Department of State, declared that the Roosevelt and Truman years had been "twenty years of treason," and began a brilliantly successful career as a demagogue and character assassin. Though uncomfortable about McCarthy's inability to distinguish between dissent and disloyalty, many liberal intellectuals did not condemn him flatly, partly because they believed the country had been blind to a serious internal subversive threat, partly for the reasons critic Harold Rosenberg pungently analyzes here.

## COUCH LIBERALISM
## AND THE GUILTY PAST
### *Harold Rosenberg*

**1**

What is remarkable about the manufacture of myths in the twentieth century is that it takes place under the noses of living witnesses of the actual events and, in fact, cannot dispense with their collaboration.

Everyone is familiar with the Communist method of transforming the past; the formula for the production of historical fictions is no longer any more secret than for the atom bomb. Through a series of public confessions a new collective Character is created, retrospectively responsible for the way things happened. The Trotskyite Assassin or the Titoist Agent of Imperialism who emerges from the judicial vaudeville changes events after they have taken place. But to accomplish this, former builders of the future must agree to destroy their personal pasts in order to substitute the one offered them by the political police. At their trials, the condemned Communists are still making history—only this time backwards.

Reprinted with permission of the author from *The Tradition of the New* (New York, 1959), 221–240.

In the United States, too, recent history is being re-made. If Russia has purloined our nuclear know-how, we have evened the score by mastering her technique of psychological fission and fusion. To be able to dissolve segments of time is at least as important in modern politico-military struggle as the capacity to devastate areas of space. It is now definitely in our power to alter at will the contents of the past twenty years.

Since under our free system the government undertakes enterprises only when private initiatives fail, our official investment in mythology has so far been a limited one. Save for occasional contributions by Congress and the Attorney General's office, most of the work of changing American history has been carried on by volunteers; although various Republican Party leaders have indicated their bafflement at their Administration's refusal to use to the hilt a weapon which has been proved so effective. A single full-scale blast and the years 1932–1952 could have been turned into the desert of "twenty years of treason."

Modern history-changing needs the help of persons prepared to make a gift of their own pasts to the new one under construction. Confession is a species of autobiography; but in the political confession the "I" of the confessor is not the genuine interest of either the accused or his prosecutor. The photo of the final verdict is not of a collection of individuals but of a single "we." The Enemy is *one*—the effect of a composite of self-accusations, each of which, through fitting into the rest, exceeds the specific guilt assumed by the accused.

The reason for this overlapping was made clear by Radek in his last plea, after indicating in his testimony that he was the Fermi of psyche splitting. "There are in the country," he explained, "semi-Trotskyites, one-eighth Trotskyites and . . . people who from liberalism . . . gave us help." The guilty "we" being fashioned at his trial had to cover all of these. Vishinsky's counter-revolutionary Mad Dog had to resemble equally the desperado with the bomb, the ideologically skeptical professor, the gossipy and all-but-innocent clerk. A problem of intersecting planes and contrasting hues and light values. In the end, the Adversary had to have the face of almost anybody.

Precisely in these wider radiations of his guilt lies the reward of the confessor. An act at once individual and collective, his confession, besides giving effective vent to his resentment against those both less and more guilty than he, becomes the means by which he rejoins society. His opposition to the regime, no matter if it consisted only of an occasional doubt, isolated him through having the tonality of his individual conscience; especially if he was *not* part of an organized conspiracy his hidden criticism burdened him with the full weight of subversion. To whom could he communicate its exact nuance? Did not his friends, his wife, his children, exist in the façade of common agreement? His arrest had been but the physical confirmation of his removal from society.

In being forced to accuse himself the distracted dissident is given a chance for uniformity. Models of guilt are placed before him; he is invited to make full use of them in portraying himself. His confession will not only bestow upon him solidarity with other confessing culprits, it will supply him with a community definition. Out of the solitude of his dungeon he marches in an ensemble of comrades into the full tableau of pre-fabricated history. That the scene is a hoax matters less than that he is no longer alone and has a role to play.

In America the part of the repentant history maker has been played by the ex-radical intellectuals, some, former Communists, others, liberals and rebels who could no longer find any substance but anti-Communism in their earlier dissent. Which category they had belonged to made little difference once the confessions began. In accordance with the recipe for recasting history, all threw themselves into the same melting pot, were changed into the same Person and assumed the identical guilt. Looking backwards, paying dues to the Party or following its line were only deeper shadings of criticizing capitalism, questioning the motives of certain of America's foreign policies or making distinctions between Red and White totalitarianism.

## II

Though confessing in America lacked the fatal finale of Iron Curtain confessions, it was not without its difficulties. The very absence of the bludgeon created special problems. It is possible that without the inspiration of the Russian originals, as an earlier generation was inspired by the Moscow Art Theatre, the entire effort would have failed. Far from being goaded to their parts by police agents hidden in the wings, the American guilty had to all but force their way on to the stage. Chambers himself, that witness of witnesses (one almost slips into calling him The Supreme Witness), came close to breaking under the ordeal of gaining the notice of people whose vital interests he was determined to defend. In time, we know, the barriers went down and whoever had a story to tell found a campfire waiting.

Still, the fact that one had possessed a radical bent did not of itself make him the star of a Congressional hearing nor supply him with a list of interesting names. Some leading confessors have probably never even been interviewed by the FBI. When the appetite of the ex-radicals for at least a spear-carrying assignment exceeded their stock of misdeeds, they were compelled to draw upon a psychological reserve of guilt, the confession of dangerous frames of mind to which "we the intellectuals" are prone—what had been called in totalitarian courts *moral responsibility* for sabotage or assassination performed by strangers. Obviously, the exposure of such data was as urgently needed as of dates and places when packages of film were passed. How else than through "our" instruction could a cop or a congressman understand and guard against the obscure mental processes of an Oppenheimer? Yet the sales resistance of the dumb outsiders to these more refined services could never be quite overcome.

Since there was no one effectively to extract confessions—even the threats of McCarthy fell far short of propelling the ultimate self-doubt that was the specialty of Russian interrogation—the potential confessor had to supply his own heckling. In the United States psychoanalysis assumed the function of the secret police. If Americans spoke in order to escape from a dungeon, it was from the dungeons of their own selves. Yet hasn't the Russian prosecutor since *Crime and Punishment* been rather easily recognizable as the personification of an inner voice? Despite the handicap of the Bill of Rights, our fugitive radicals succeeded admirably in making themselves victims; their example of Do-It-Yourself initiative ought to convince Khrushchev that prisons and torture are obsolete and that the cellars of the Lubianka may as well be refitted as a game room.

The final result was that a neo-liberal became available to admit the justice of any accusation, no matter how ridiculous. Since Oppenheimer gave money to aid the Spanish Loyalists, it mattered not that at the height of Russian-American cooperation he unequivocally rejected the approaches of Communist agents; "we," including Oppenheimer, may as well own up that we are unreliable types and deserve to be fired, regardless of actual service to the country. When McCarthy attempted to bully James Wechsler and spread his invented history into the headlines, the confessing liberal showed his objectivity by conceding that "we" never tendered names to the FBI unless we were forced to and are, consequently, "McCarthyites of the Left," in fighting distortion with distortion. Guilty ex-radicalism has even evolved of its Freudian researches a a new GUILT BY RHETORIC, consisting of a contaminating passion for certain words and phrases. "How desperately," exclaims a characteristic document, "they [the guilty liberals] wish in each case that the Hiss, the Lattimore *who speaks their language* might be telling the truth." The important step here beyond mere Guilt By Association is that to be incriminated it is no longer necessary to know Hiss or Lattimore personally.

The quotation above regarding complicity through language with persons with whom we may violently disagree is from Leslie Fiedler's *An End to Innocence,* a collection of "essays on culture and politics," recently published by Beacon Press. This book is as representative of what I hereby christen Couch Liberalism as anything one may hope to find. Most of the pieces in it have appeared during the past five years in the leading organs of this sect: *Commentary, Encounter, Partisan Review*; and its meditations on the evils "we" have wrought are headed by a passage from that St. John of the Couch, Whittaker Chambers, to the effect that History will get you if you don't get it first.

Half of Fiedler's book is devoted to an essay apiece on the Hiss Case, the Rosenberg Case and McCarthy, in each of which it turns out that whoever suffered deserved what he got for not confessing and that we intellectuals with our "shorthand" that the people cannot understand are deeply implicated; the rest of the book consists of literary essays with a strong discovery-of-the-true-America motif.

When I first read some of these political articles, together with pieces like them by other writers, I must confess (it's contagious) that I did not grasp what was happening. These slippery arguments that directed themselves against persons who had already been punished by law, that complained about "our" over-fussiness on the subject of civil rights, that while believing McCarthy was a crook placed under suspicion those who called him one, seemed to me simply odd. I could not grasp especially why these messages appeared under the name of liberalism. I, too, believed that Hiss was guilty, but so had the jury, he was in jail—so why these profound evocations of his perfidy and of Chambers's ordeal and triumph by a "liberal?" Or why a "liberal" indictment of Lattimore to supplement that of the

364

Attorney General's office? Or an assault on people who, conceding the guilt of the Rosenbergs, opposed their electrocution? It was only after I had noticed that these ideas were appearing in concert that I recognized that a collective person was in the process of formation which named itself "liberal" out of the same default of historical truth that caused the Communist sympathizers to cling to this title.

Fiedler's essays blend the new fake-liberal anti-Communist with that of the old fake-liberal fellow traveler to produce a "liberal" who shares the guilt for Stalin's crimes through the fact alone of having held liberal or radical opinions, *even anti-Communist ones!* For Fiedler *all* liberals are contaminated by the past, if by nothing else than through having spoken the code language of intellectuals.

Fertilized by left-wing sophistication and by Freud, Fiedler's essays are confessions on another plane than autobiography. He has no facts to relate—one does not learn that he ever did anything in politics. The guilt he assumes is that of an essence; he confesses for the guilty "we" without an "I." His theorizing about American politics derives from a vision of wrestling stereotypes, Right and Left wing, in which the collective Left sinks under a bad conscience. As one of our new volunteer cultural ambassadors "explaining us" to the Europeans, Fiedler must have done as much as anyone to confirm the belief that everybody in America lives on a billboard.

## III

*An End to Innocence* adds perhaps the final dimension to penitence. Fiedler's line is: We have been guilty of being innocent. Only by confessing will we terminate our culpability. In a rhetoric in which the kettles predominate, Fiedler laments Alger Hiss's refusal to confess as a defeat for all of "us." Hiss "failed all liberals, all who had, in some sense and at some time shared his illusions (and who that calls himself a liberal is exempt?), all who demanded of him that he speak aloud a common recognition of complicity. And yet . . . at the bottom of their hearts, they did not finally want him to admit anything, but preferred the chance he gave them to say: He is, we are, innocent." Hiss's drama of Hush Or Tell could have cleansed us all had but its protagonist acknowledged his "mistake."

Whom Fiedler is here describing, except possibly repentant Communists who haven't confessed yet, I defy anyone to specify. His "all liberals" is a made-up character with an attributed past. To his question "Who is exempt?" I raise my right hand and reply that I never shared anything with Mr. Hiss, including automobiles or apartments; certainly not illusions, if my impression is correct that he was a typical government Communist or top-echelon fellow traveler. I shall have a few words to say about these "innocents" later. Here I insist that it was Chambers who shared with Hiss, not "all liberals"; Chambers who was never a liberal, who in his book gives no hint of having ever criticized the Communist Party in his radical days from a libertarian position and who after he broke with Communism became something quite different from a liberal. Fiedler's "common recognition of complicity" is simply slander, ex-Communist style. Had Hiss testified according to his suggestion he would have deserved another five years.

Perhaps from the point of view of the Department of Justice or of Couch Liberalism Hiss made a "mistake" by not confessing as Chambers did. But from the point of view of liberals and independent radicals the activities of the Chambers-Hisses when they were Communists were never "mistakes." Communists on this level belonged to the Party's apparatus of intimidation and bribery. Their respectability did not conflict with their support of Communist treachery and violence against non-Party Leftists or radical democrats throughout the world. On the contrary, boycotting, informing against or condemning to the executioner socialists, anarchists, Trotskyites, POUMists, strengthened their patriotic disguise. Nor did confession ever purge these agents of power of their passion to browbeat critics of their historical mission. The same people who as Communists persecuted free opinion continued to do so with the same vehemence after they had turned themselves inside out and become organizers of anti-radical penance. Conversion alters the world in which a man acts; it does not change his character. Before he confessed the GPU chief Yagoda executed countless dissenters; by his confession he dragged down unnumbered others. The first law of the spurious "we" is its malice.

How could we intellectuals, asks Fiedler, have been so wrong about Communism, as against its lowbrow enemies? And if so wrong about the issue of the age might we not be equally wrong about everything else? Ought we not therefore abandon our intellectuals' ghetto and take our place in the citizens' non-intellectual America? In a word, the end of innocence is a guilty return, as with the Moscow defendants, to the defined community—the address of "responsibility" is not the library, the study or the café but Main Street.

"The unpalatable truth we have been discovering is that the buffoons and bullies, those who *knew* really nothing about the Soviet Union at all, were right—stupidly right, if you will, accidentally right, right for the wrong reasons, but damnably right. This most continuing liberals, as well as ex-Communists and former fellow travelers, are prepared to grant in the face of the slave labor and oppression and police terror in the Soviet Union; but yet they, who have erred out of generosity and open-mindedness (!), cannot feel even yet on the same side as Velde or McCarthy or Nixon or Mundt."

It takes devotion to compile so gross a statement. Under the radiations of the fused "we," facts have grown bulbous, lost their outlines, finally dissolved. Nothing is left but a conflict of opinions. I will leave to Fiedler the explanation of how a man can be "right" without knowing anything about his subject. One recalls Lenin's incognito discussions with peasants who *knew* as against the damnably wrong intellectuals; their knowledge remains one of the mysteries of Bolshevik dialectic. Fiedler, however, cannot avail himself of Lenin's epistemology. His demand for self-surrender and intellectual abdication has nothing behind it but the will to move to the right side.

In this project Fiedler is aided by his approach, which consists of a literary critcism of events; actually, of their journalistic caricatures. Instead of political ideas, Fiedler relies upon "a sensibility trained by the newer critical methods." Through symbolist elaboration Kenneth Burke used to find endless sociological and psychological clues in a cigarette ad. Fiedler's method is to place facing each other the popular and fellow-traveler stereotypes of Hiss, Chambers, McCarthy; getting in between he lets his "sensibility" quiver with their possible meanings. For him the contrasting "myths" of Left-wing and public opinion have a wonderfully complex existence. But reality, the Soviet Union, for example, as the most baffling social, political and historical fact of our civilization, is so bare of literary suggestion, so obvious, that it may be left to the judgment of those who know nothing.

The effect of Fiedler's application of his sensibility to the public showcases of criminals, liars and corpses is that the history of the past two decades appears ultimately as a two-character melodrama. One character speaks in refined tones and idealistic abstractions in favor of the CIO, the New Deal, Socialism, defense of the Soviet Union, the dangers of Fascism—the other mutters "Dirty Reds!" Number Two wins the argument by throwing Number One in the clink. Let me reemphasize that the loser is not the *Communist* "liberal"—besides being "innocent" he has become also "generous and open-minded." But in return for these compliments to the fakers, fools and position-seekers of yesterday, all intellectuals are urged to crawl under the cloak of a spiritualized Hiss who would capitulate to the club wielder who was "right."

## IV

Fiedler's "Afterthoughts on the Rosenbergs" appeared originally in *Encounter,* the international magazine published in London by the Congress for Cultural Freedom. His thesis is "that there were two Rosenberg cases," the actual case and the legendary one concocted by the Communists. Naturally, Fiedler is not interested in the "first," or actual, case. His meat is the legendary one that placed before the world the fiction of a pair of persecuted innocents. The Rosenbergs themselves, Fiedler contends, believed in their fictional counterpart so completely that they neither had any conscious guilt for having stolen the atom secrets nor any cause which they could openly champion. Thus they died as neither heroes nor martyrs—more important, they were not even human. A couple of Red cardboard cutouts were burned; there was nobody to feel sorry for, and the liberals who protested the electrocution were dupes. Just the same, Fiedler argues, it was an error to kill them, since America could have won a moral victory over Communism by sparing them. By acting as if there were a core of personal reality inside these self-made nothings we could have appeared before the world as champions of humanity.

In this scholasticist apologia, shuffling between psychological speculation and the author's insulting pose of moral conscience—for what but apology could induce the exile from humanity of a pair of corpses—Fiedler supplies a model of how to becloud historical events and the issues arising therefrom. After reading his article, I wrote a letter to *Encounter* pointing out its distortions. Although I was a contributor, my letter was not published. In its sense of Cold War "responsibility." Couch Liberalism had learned to mimic the toughness of Red Front liberalism with its why-rock-the-boat cynicism. I suggest that in doing so they have been laying the ground for future confessions.

I reproduce below excerpts from my letter to *Encounter*. If my remarks are somewhat milder than they would be today, it is because in 1953 I still naively believed I was criticising the idiosyncrasies of an individual mind rather than of the spokesman of a trend.

Fiedler . . . was shrewd to deal with Stalinism (is this still the right word?) in terms of its bad poetry. The characteristic of our time is that corn can be killing.

The Rosenberg case was the absolutely deadly mixture of American corn and Moscow mash. That in this incredibly shallow farce the Rosenbergs were playing for their lives was, of course, pathetic. This pathos Fiedler brought out very well.

I cannot, however, accept the explanation that the execution represented merely a negative failing on the part of the United States, the absence of a higher humanity, resulting from "political innocence," a "lack of moral imagination" and a "certain incapacity to really believe in Communists as people."

Fiedler is gumming up the issue with misplaced profoundity . . . He is talking about psychology, morality and "myth," when we are confronted primarily with a question of injustice, the injustice of applying the death penalty in this case. What shocked liberal opinion was the objective factor of the disproportion between the crime as charged, and for which the defendants were convicted, and the death penalty. There was, and is, something hideous and unbelievable about transporting the act from the loose atmosphere of the time in which it was committed, when RESTRICTED DOCUMENTS used to lie around like leaves, to the tense one of the 1950s. When the act was committed no one was that serious . . . Granted that the Rosenbergs were justly convicted, and I don't question that any more than any other liberal, they did not seem to deserve the electric chair. (This question of timing was implicit in Justice Douglas' desire to review which law applied.)

Sure, it was easier to perpetrate this injustice because Communists de-humanize themselves . . . But Sacco and Vanzetti, with whom Fiedler contrasts the Rosenbergs, weren't saved by their innocence or their human reality. Massachusetts did not experience them as "people" either. The fact is that no defendant is a "person"— *nor ought to be.* The law defines a man by his act. Justice requires only that he shall not be made to personify an act that he did not perform; and that the punishment shall not be cruel and inhuman and shall fit the crime.

The psychological question regarding the inability of many people (including myself) to feel sympathy for the Rosenbergs as individuals . . . would never have arisen had it not been for the disproportion I have mentioned between the crime, in its specific quality as an act, and the penalty. Because of this disproportion the government itself, the press, the whole "official" U.S., had to be the first to resort to psychology and the "moral imagination," that is, to unreality . . . This monster-making, which took place before the Communists countered with their own milksop Frankenstein, is something quite different from "political innocence" or an "incapacity to accept Communists as human beings."

In denying the appeal for clemency, President Eisenhower devoted his statement entirely, as I recall, to overcoming the disproportion between the crime and the legal penalty and to justifying the death sentence . . . by holding these two feeble tools responsible for starting the Korean War and for the potential death of millions of Americans, in opposition to the statements of atomic scientists that the Rosenbergs could not possibly have transmitted, by the means alleged, information worth a good goddamn . . .

The scandal of the Rosenberg Case would not exist if, as Fiedler contends, the United States had simply failed in the opportunity to save the defendants from their own masquerade as patriotic Americans. The scandals exists, not because of lack of humanity, but because of human-all-too-human passions not properly restrained by law but on the contrary making use of law. Instead of preserving the objectivity and *abstractness* of law, the government took up the slack in the law by creating its own fictional person, that of the fiendishly efficient underground incendiary capable of setting whole continents on fire. This caricature, which caused every act of the defendants to take on a enormous magnitude, was needed to enable the court to render a brutal decision and the officialdom and the press to justify it. The dramatic imagination, *with its power of creating the person it judges,* supplemented the law and replaced the creature with the creation. This is demonism, not just an absence of Christian charity.

Fiedler is exactly wrong. It seemed to him there was too little humanity in the Case, instead of too much, because he looked at this affair as if it were a stage performance and compared the Rosenbergs as bad actors to Sacco and Vanzetti as genuine personalities . . . I think it is gruesome and a bit cowardly to drag out the corpses of Communists in order to show that there are no dead bodies here but self-constructed dummies incapable of bleeding. If the Communist executes not men but devils and animals that is his basic crime. If we in turn take over this process and forget about justice because we are dealing with "made" people, we are making our own contribution to the nightmare of the twentieth century.


## V

To impede the process of turning American intellectual history of our own lifetime into a comic-strip encounter between a cock-eyed egghead and a right-thinking goon, I beg leave to cite a few data.

1. Whatever its weakness in understanding Communist power and techniques, liberalism was in no sense responsible for Communist vileness. It is false to say that a belief too naive in freedom, equality, individuality, induced adherence to the band, with its underband of party bosses, spies and masterminds. The liberal sentiment for radical equality and freedom was, in fact, the single intellectual mooring that held against the powerful drag of the totalitarian "we," supported by the offer of a heroic part, social scheming and material reward. Moreover, the sentiment of freedom alone *presented Marxism itself in its living intellectual form, that is, as a problem.* One of the few serious discussions concerning the Bolshevik conception of ends and means was begun by John Dewey around the time he went to Mexico to sit on the commission of inquiry before which Trotsky crushed the Moscow Trials and permanently damaged the revolutionary pretensions of international Communism (no, it was not Fiedler's buffoons who did that). The totalitarian liberals were too "responsible" to let the fate of an individual get in the way of the prestige of the USSR "just when we are fighting fascism." Like the Couch Liberals they were also too "responsible" to take thinking seriously.

2. The intellectuals and fellow travelers who remained with Communism through the execution of the old Bolsheviks, the extermination of POUMists and anarchists in Spain, the Stalin-Hitler Pact, the fight of the Communist International against French and British resistance to the Nazis, the partition of Poland, all of which took place in public and behind no curtain of any kind, were not innocent, to

369

say nothing of "generous and open-minded." They were, as a type, middle-class careerists, closed both to argument and evidence, impatient with thought, psychopaths of their "radical" conformity. The "idealism" of this sodden group of Philistines, distinguished from the rest of their species by their more up-to-date smugness and systematic malice, can be emphasized only by one who ignores its function in hiding from themselves the cynicism which hardened their minds against any human plea or valid idea embarrassing to the Party. Feeling themselves on The Stage of History, they were prepared to execute the particular atrocities assigned to them, while keeping one eye on a post in the future International Power, the other on the present Good Spot in the government, the university, Hollywood, publishing. Most of their assignments were *intellectual* crimes, the concoction of arguments and boycotts to cover up acts of the Party anywhere. One recalls, for instance, the international libel let loose against André Gide when he published his account of his trip to the USSR.

All criticism by any one but the "buffoons" was met with the stare of the social climber or busy man of affairs. During the Spanish Civil War, Left professors and party-givers identified themselves with Malraux and Hemingway as ruthless franc-tireurs of the International. Without an appreciation of slapstick in both its absurdity and cruelty, it is impossible to recall these "innocents" accurately. A leadership mania centering on a dream of the power that would fall into their hands after a new Ten Days That Shook The World staged under their direction transformed these sorry bourgeois into sleep-walking social highwaymen. Undoubtedly, there were individual sympathizers whom this image does not fit, professionals too busy to look beyond the Communist explanation of events. But these innocents, if it be innocent to be made a tool through phrases and flattery, were in a minority. The Communist intellectual, *as a distinct figure* produced by the movement, was innocent in one sense only: the *non sui juris* of pathology. He had been taken over completely by a false or assumed "we"—which is the basis of mystification in our century. But the spurious "we" is also the basis of modern terrorism. If the Communist intellectuals were merely "mistaken" so were the *gauleiters*. And the Couch Liberals, with their repentant "we," are bringing more innocents of this stamp into the world.

3. The most significant falsification of the ex-Communist confessional is the suppression of the account of the struggle that raged on the Left during the epoch of Communist influence in America. This omission in itself would be almost enough to prove that Couch Liberalism is a Communist Party spirit that has changed its spots.

Like their master in Moscow, the Communist intellectuals in America detested above all, not capitalism nor even fascism, to both of which the switching Party line taught them to accommodate themselves—their one hatred which knew no amelioration was that toward the independent radical intellectual. New ideas, modern art and literature, non-conformity in taste, behavior, morals, inevitably produced in them a venomous recoil; to the antipathy officially demanded by the Party toward its foes on the Left, the sordid leftish mass willingly added its own spite toward the outsiders who undermined their revolutionary conceit, especially in the days when the Party had traded in revolution for Defense Of The USSR. Soft to the point of servility to its foes on the Right, the Stalinist front never varied in its violence against those who struck in any form against its vanguard hijacking.

Instead of Communists, fellow travelers, liberals and radicals in one lump, the reality of the period lay in its battles. Nor were the attacks all from one side. I have before me a manifesto of the "League for Cultural Freedom and Socialism," published in the *Partisan Review* in Summer, 1939. Signed by 34 writers, it denounces the "so-called cultural organizations under control of the CP" as "the most active forces of reaction among advanced intellectual circles in the United States. Pretending to represent progressive opinion, these bodies are in effect but apologists for the Kremlin dictatorship. They outlaw all dissenting opinion from the Left, they poison the intellectual atmosphere with slander." At the time this statement was issued Fiedler's bullies were more concerned with what they could sweat out of a Federal road-building contract than with the truth about the USSR. That some who signed it have, shrinking from the word "socialism" in the title, today adapted their past to the Couch Liberal distortion, does not alter the fact that such demands of the Left upon the intellectual conscience cost the Communist Party dear each time it swung at the end of the tail of the Moscow bureaucracy. Granted that no permanent victory could have been won by intellectual means alone, the FBI, the courts and Committees have not assured that victory either. Let the Cold War give way to an era of East-West trade and collaboration, and Russian caviar and contracts, citations and free trips, will begin to count their ideological votes. Yet as a major intellectual current in the United States Communism had been rather decisively defeated long before a single ex-Communist had voided his memory from the witness stand.

The Communist who "passed" from Red to Ex is himself, very often, the product of this criticism. Is Fiedler, in his idolization of Chambers, simple-minded enough to believe the Witness' yarn that it was the light of God glowing through his offspring's ear and not an argument drummed in his own by his anti-Communist radical friends that first revealed to him what was wrong with Communism? The new Good Citizen cannot change his ancestry by forgetting his disreputable father.

The Confession Era in the United States is about over. It is hard to imagine anyone adding facts likely to prove useful to the government's prophylaxis. Beyond the facts, each repentant Communist or radical has contributed his bit of himself to the collective protagonist of subversion and vanished into the common life.

The attempt to change past history has probably failed, largely because of the two-party system and the common sense and boredom of the public. Mystification has been quarantined in the quarters where it originated: the colony of the ex-radical intelligentsia.

*An End to Innocence* is already out of date. Its political and social morale belong to the days of McCarthy's putsch, when yesterday's vanguard saw itself blinking in the footlights with a pistol at its head. The moment this physical threat vanished the posture was bound to appear ludicrous.

# 81

# Voices from the City

One of the most important developments altering the character of American life in the second third of the twentieth century was the rise of scientific public-opinion polling. Public opinion, as measured by a questionnaire administered to a sample of respondents, was used to determine the dimensions of a new cake of soap, the style of a political candidate, and even of the course of public policy in some instances. The historian of this era, therefore, had to consider the poll an important source of evidence. The standard questionnaire, however, was ill-equipped to measure the full depth, complexity, and intensity of popular feeling. An alternative complementary method of feeling the public pulse is represented in the following selections from Studs Terkel's *Division Street: America*. Armed with a tape recorder. Terkel walked the streets of Chicago, and talked with seventy residents about their lives, their hopes, and their feelings about what was happening to their society. We cannot be sure of the representativeness of the four voices that speak here, or even of the full group of seventy. Terkel "played hunches" in selecting his cast of characters, instead of following systematic procedures that would permit scientific generalizations about the population of Chicago as a whole. But these interviews deepen our understanding of American life in the mid-1960s.

## DIVISION STREET: AMERICA
### *Studs Terkel*

**Tom Kearney, 53**

*An apartment in a high-rise complex on the Near Side of the city, adjacent to Michael Reese Hospital. A well-thumbed copy of Gunnar Myrdal's* An American Dilemma *was on the coffee table.*

I've been a policeman for twenty-three hard years. . . .

I worked as a patrolman and a detective. Then I was promoted to a detective sergeant and from there I went to the traffic division. So I've covered all bases so far.

From pp. 79–88, 135–139, 159–165, 285–289 of *Division Street: America*, by Studs Terkel. © Copyright 1967 by Studs Terkel. Reprinted by permission of Pantheon Books, a division of Random House, Inc.

Sometimes you're disenchanted, you're disillusioned, you're cynical. When people attempt to offer a bribe. I know I've been negligent in my duty because I should have arrested the person. At the same time, that's universal, everywhere. I turn it down. I told him, you know, "No harm trying. But I just don't go that way." (Laughs sadly.) It's a corrupt society. . . .

I was born in Chicago, my father was born in Chicago, and my grandfather was born here. His father came to America to dig the Sag Canal. They were promised they could have farmland where they could grow anything. In the winter, they'd dig the canal. Unfortunately, it was all rocks. So they wound up with a rock farm.

There's something you gotta understand about the Irish Catholics in Chicago. Until recently, being a policeman was a wonderful thing. 'Cause he had a steady job and he knew he was gonna get a pension and they seemed to think it was better than being a truck driver, although a truck driver earns far more than a policeman today.

Someone had to be police, you know? They sacrified anything. They just knew that so-and-so in the family would be. It was another step out of the mud. You figured at least you'd have some security. They felt they no longer worked with their hands. They weren't laborers any more.

If the Depression hadn't come along, my father would have been able to do more educational-wise for us. He couldn't provide. There was no money for two years. At that time, the firemen and policemen weren't paid. My father was a fireman for forty years. They were the only ones who didn't get their back pay. Whoever could work and earn anything at all . . . that's what kept us going.

I recall the hunger marches. I remember the police at that time, they had mounted police. I had a job at Madison and Canal, and they were marching, trying to get into the Downtown area, from the west to the east. The police charged them. Whether they were right or wrong, I didn't know then. I was too much concerned with my own self. 'Cause things were rather brutal and you expected that, you know.

I remember at Blue Island and Ashland—there's a lumber company there now—that was a big transient camp. I remember the food lines. I also remember getting off the Elevated and men waiting in line for the newspaper. If you were through reading it, they'd take it. They had a little code among themselves. What they used them for was probably to sleep on. . . .

There's no colored there [Bridgeport]. A mixture of white—different ethnic groups: Polish, Slavic, Irish, Italian, anything and everything. A few Jewish families. In the old days, it was all Irish. The streets, the names were Irish. The street my grandmother lived on was named after one of my father's sisters who died very young.

We moved farther south, to Roseland. My father was assigned there. It was a community begun by people who had left Pullman. They had rebelled against the company by moving out. If you worked for him you had to live in one of his Company houses. You bought from the Company store. If profits fell below a certain level, wages were cut. The rents weren't lowered, the rents remained the same. Now, of course, there's nothing much over there.

373

My father was one of the radicals. Even though he had status, you know, being a fireman and the fact he got a pension, he used to say, "Why should I get a pension when the fellow next door doesn't get one?" He was a good Irish Catholic, so he wasn't a Commie, but at the same time he used to say, "You know, maybe they got something over there that we should know about, because they keep on talking about how bad it is over there."

My family wasn't devout. Certain things my mother, of course, insisted upon. On Good Fridays, you had to sit in a chair in the kitchen. In those days they didn't have any foam rubber seats. It was hard wood. And you had to sit there till about five minutes to twelve. Don't laugh and don't talk. You sat for three hours. She had some of an idea that it helped you spiritually. But I don't think we were deeply religious.

I find myself at odds with the Church at various times. I knew the nuns taught me some things that weren't true. At the same time, I realized they themselves didn't know whether they were true or not. They were simple women, you know. You say you'd rather have your son go to a public school because he's gonna have to get along with those people and he might as well start young. The same as going to school with the colored. You're going to have to get along with them. They're here, so you might as well go to school with them and get along with them.

### HOW DO YOU FEEL ABOUT YOUNG NUNS AND PRIESTS TAKING PART IN STREET DEMONSTRATIONS?

They have every right to do so, although not to violate the law. I'm not saying that because I'm a policeman, but simply because having been in parochial school all my life, all I ever heard was: "Don't do anything wrong." Respect for authority.

Today things are changing. If one married outside the religion I remember this: "Oooh, tear out all my hair. I can't face my friends, we gotta move." Oooh, terrible, terrible. And what happened? I have five brothers and one sister. Of the brothers, one is a bachelor. The rest of us married Protestants. My sister married a Protestant. My older brother had two daughters. They raised one a Catholic and one a Protestant. The girl raised a Catholic married a Protestant and the one raised a Protestant married a Catholic. Today, for convenience's sake, my brother and his wife go to the Catholic Church. She hasn't been converted, but just goes for convenience's sake. It isn't any big deal any more.

It's changing rapidly. Look at the city. Of course, everyone resists change, good or bad. Even if it's good for them, they resist it. Take the color situation today. The whites, they're only fighting a rear-guard action. The walls are coming down, that's all. The tragedy is that the program of the colored is still negative. There's no reason to lead a march or sit in the streets any more, as I see it. Because they've won, there's no question about it. They've got to find a way to have the whites accept them.

Unfortunately, the colored man came to the industrial North just too late. He came after there were so few jobs to begin with. The Caucasian immigrants came with nothing but their hands and they worked in steel mills and maybe they were snapping cinders, which is one of the most difficult jobs and the lowest paid. They watched another fellow do a job and they learned his job and climbed up. Well, the colored man didn't have that opportunity after the wave of migration from the South. There were so few labor jobs that he could start out from and learn how to get up. The machine took care of that. They didn't need him any more. One man can do the work of ten today.

WHAT DO YOU THINK THE OBJECTIVE
OF THE COLORED IS?

The same as mine, the same as mine. Everything best for him and his family that he can possibly have. I can see where they'd want to move away from a completely colored neighborhood and integrate. I can understand that. He also understands that his family is gonna have to live with whites and if he doesn't live with the whites he can't understand them either. The colored man says: "Well, you don't know us." Naturally we don't. They don't know the white either.

I think people are intelligent enough to accept integration. We've done one thing, it's a bad thing, but I can't think of anything better. The quota. It's bad because you have to exclude someone sometimes, but the whites wouldn't have any fear of being overwhelmed. And the colored wouldn't have any fear that the white would run. This high-rise complex I live in now works on a quota. It's highly controlled.

Most of urban renewal is bad in a sense. People were displaced. Yet it had to be done. Where we're sitting now was one of the foulest slums in America. It was worse than Calcutta, believe me. I've been in here as a police officer on many occasions. Right across the street, they had a fence to protect the institution there. It must have been eighteen feet in the air, with barbed wire.

Actually it's not really integrated now because there's no community life here at all. You don't know the fella next door usually. Your wife may meet them or something like that, but you yourself come and go, that's all. There's no way for people to know one another. You at least vote together, you know, at election time. Well, each building is its own precinct. So people just go in and out. There isn't any standing outside like you do normally at an election. There's no church in the immediate vicinity. Most people, they have to go several blocks to an known place. And these complexes have very few children. An adult population, more or less concerned with their own problems. When we first moved in here, I thought I'd go insane, being cooped in and actually nowhere to go, because the neighborhood is sterile. It's not a neighborhood at all.

People don't want to become involved. Most people have had some dealings with court, like traffic courts. People have sat for long periods of time, waiting for their case to be called. In criminal court, they've found themselves returning there and then continuances being granted after continuances. This man, he loses his day's pay from work. If it's a woman, she becomes frightened, that they might retaliate in some way. The fear. Like many cabdrivers that don't report a robbery, 'cause normally they might not have eight or ten dollars when he's held up. He won't report it because he'd lose a day's work if they finally apprehended the offender and the loss is a loss.

This fear of involvement. I wondered why there were so few colored in the crowd greeting the astronauts yesterday. Most of the fellows said, "They don't care if anybody went to the moon. They don't have any feeling about it." I said, I don't think that's true. We were briefed to search for colored people who might be a threat, you know. It was the week of demonstrations. The average colored person is just like you and I. If there was a great crowd some place and there was a threat to all people wearing blue shirts, you certainly wouldn't go down there in a blue shirt.

DO YOU HAVE ANY COLORED FRIENDS?

Oh yes. Yes. (Pause.) I *say* colored friends and I *think* colored friends . . . but actually I really don't know.

YOU DON'T KNOW WHAT THEY THINK OF YOU?

Not really. I can understand that. Because if I were colored, I'd be bitter, too. I *think* I'd try to control myself, try to be rational about it. I remember one night, a colored schoolteacher I know, we're at a party, an interracial party, very nice. She forgot the potency of martinis and I sitting talking to her and suddenly she looked at me very hard and said, "You're my Caucasian enemy." Very indignantly. Of course, I realized, you know . . . I mean, she just didn't realize how potent a martini was. So you really don't know.

Some guys that I know, colored, we talk and discuss the family and how things are going, and how their wives are and things like that, but I don't think I know. (Pause.) I don't think I know.

My son, a twenty-two-year-old boy, who's been going to college, I really don't think I know *him*. I think he knows me better than I know him. That's one thing he really doesn't like. I think he'd like it the other way around. The younger generation doesn't think too highly of us. They think we made a mess of things, which we did. We seem to lead disorganized lives. Most of us dislike the work we're doing. Most of us are anxious to go someplace else, thinking we could leave our troubles behind. They love us, our sons and daughters. But at the same time, they don't think we did things correctly. They're critical of us. They discuss things far more intelligently than we do. They think for themselves.

One day he brought up a charming little blond girl, not overly dressed, but not ragged or beatnik type. She was going down South to teach in one of the Freedom schools. Very much enthused about it. And she seemed to have a good idea why she was doing it. I mean she wasn't looking for publicity or anything like that. She really thought she should be doing this. And then again, he met a colored girl, a beautiful creature, who also had a brilliant mind, you know, straight-A student, one of those types. And she had absolutely no interest in civil rights. None. couldn't mean less to her, although she identifies with the colored people. She makes no attempt to pass, 'cause she could very easily. And then he has a friend whose sister and mother are both active in the civil-rights movement. The sister was arrested twice in the last week.

DID YOU HAVE TO ARREST HER?

No, I . . . (Laughs.) It woulda really been funny, you know. I asked her, "Now what is this about police brutality?" And she said, the way some policeman talk, you know, and then I suppose holler at them at some degree or another, I mean to keep them in control and get them in the wagon or something. But I said, "What happened to you?" I mean, the voice means nothing, I mean, I holler at people, too, you know—stand back, or something. Well, she said, "When the policeman arrested me, he said, 'Now come along, honey, step up in the wagon.'" (Laughs.) That was police brutality.

. . . So the difference in them, more freedom. You never say, "Go to your room, I want to talk to your mother." When I was a boy, when they had company, I was always excluded. Today, even when our son was young, he sat in on conversation and he learned to judge and evaluate things. In my home, when my father was there, he got the paper. When he was through with it, you got it. That's all. Sometimes he didn't get through with it until you were in bed. About the only thing that was discarded was the comics on Sunday. They didn't think you were interested in other things.

I was surprised to see what these young people were thinking. Civil rights. Some couldn't care less. Others were militant. Then others like himself approved of what was going on but didn't participate. They had some very good ideas about it. Some of the most controversial things, Vietnam, Cuba.

They began wondering. Of course they have more time. You and I have to make a living. But their level of conversation is much higher than the adults' level today. I think we tend to be more humorous, even if we force it, probably because of age and years of work. I find myself in a group, visiting, where there's very little conversation of any depth. Did you hear the latest Polish joke? or things like that. Or talk about some play or movie. You know, there's no . . .

But these young people really have a feeling. They trade views. I find they seldom argue in a—in disagreement. They give and take, back and forth, but they don't stand on their points. They want to know the other person. They seem to accept other people more easily than we did.

The only thing is there's a great many pressures on them. The fear of the draft is always there. It's stupid, they feel. It doesn't accomplish a thing, and why do it. They don't seem—outside of this one girl who was arrested twice in one week for sitting in the streets—they don't seem to have any great drive. I mean, it's a problem. Everything is so complex.

They see all our values changing. Just as we see the city changing, with the expressways and with the high-rise living, which I never thought I'd live or could possibly afford.

YOU'RE TWO YEARS AWAY FROM RETIREMENT.
DO YOU LOOK FORWARD TO IT?

Not particularly. I do in one way. I'd like to take up something else if I can. Be able to enter—this sounds sort of corny—more of a community life, in a smaller community where you participated more, you know. *In doing something.*

I myself haven't done everything a man should do. Some guy once said the four things a man had to do: he had to be in love, he had to get married, he had to have children, and he had to fight a war. So you accomplish these things, and I did. Now there's the Bomb. As far as I'm concerned, I'd hold on as long as I could. I don't think this is as serious with the older generation, this fear, as it is with the young. They believe here's a possibility of working your way out of this intelligently and we don't seem to work toward that end. We're constantly in turmoil. That's the older generation. After you're fifty, it's all the way down, no speed limits. That's it, you've had it. I mean you have nothing left.

A policeman starts out young and very impressionable, and you see people at their worst, naturally. You don't go into the better homes, because they have fewer problems, or they keep them under control. Sure, a man and wife argue, but usually it's on a quiet level. In the poorer classes of homes, frustrations are great, pressures are tremendous. They turn on the TV set and they have these give-away programs and someone's winning thousands of dollars. Or if they're watching a play of some kind, everything's beautiful and lovely. They watch this and they don't have any of it and they can't get any of it. Then when an argument breaks out, the closest one to 'em, he's gonna get it. We were taught, you know, if my mother and father argued, my mother went around shutting down the windows and the doors because they didn't want the neighbors to hear 'em. But they deliberately open the doors and open the windows, screaming and hollering, and it's a release from their emotions. So when they have an argument, it's a good argument and it necessitates the police coming to quiet it down. Naturally, the impression of a young police officer is that they aren't really people, you know, get rid of them.

I've often worked with policemen who became very angry when we'd arrest a narcotic addict, a burglar. And then have to notify the parents. This one police officer, he used to get insane, he'd be so mad. Why couldn't you do something with your son? One day I finally said to him, "What would you do if your son came home and said he was a junkie?" He wouldn't know what to do. He wouldn't know why his son did it. The son would know, but he wouldn't. You understand?

### Mike Kostelnik, 36

*His home is on the Far Northwest Side of the city, bordering the suburb Norridge. An area primarily of one-family dwellings of a new middle class.*

*He is a window washer, earning $160 a week. He has worked eighteen years for the same contractor. He has a wife and two children, a boy and a girl.*

I'm losing a very good neighbor. He's a fireman, captain, and he's retiring. As a matter of fact, he's leaving today. So before I went to work this morning, I even had to say goodbye to him and his wife. They had one boy, but he's gone now. He's married, you know. So he decided to retire, a man fifty-some years old. He's doing very well. Shelby, Michigan. When you're owning individual property you have a community feeling. Everyone's more interested because they have more at stake. And when you come outside, I mean, there's Joe Blow or whatever his name is, he's doing a concrete job. Well, the thing to do is go over and give him a hand. I've got a neighbor across the way, well, he can't do heights, so I cut his trees. So the next time the guy comes over my house, he's gonna do my plumbing.

We had our street paved where we were living. Now everybody had to do this, because you wanted the block to look right, you know. And if you didn't—'cause a couple were real slow at it—all the rest of the people looked at them: "Hey, when are you going to get yours?" A month or two and you see the guy's not doing it, so you, well, you sort of look it over every time you go by. You give the guy a subtle hint that this should be done. You know. "Lookit, uh, why should you leave it this way? You like the area? That's why you moved here. You like the area? Keep it up." I mean, why should you go into an area that you pick and then right away let the weeds grow, you know? Why should I be a nonconformist? You have to conform to society.

What makes people scared of the colored race is they're scared of deteriorating property. Now if these people just go ahead and show that they're intelligent enough . . . And there are a lot of wonderful people. I've done work for colored lawyers, educated people, and you couldn't find a better group of people. These people don't like their own type, they don't like their own people in their own race. Now there must be a reason for it. I have quite a few Negro friends. I've discussed this basic thing with them. I know a parking-lot fella here. I've met a lot of wonderful Negro people, don't get me wrong. It's never a question of color, it's the way a lot of them live.

So why should anybody tell me, the property I'm sweating for right now and I'm working every day and sweating for . . . why should I be told who to sell it? Where are *my* civil rights? There's the twister. Why should I be told what I sweated for and earned—this is against the constitution actually—how I should dispose of it? Don't you think that's wrong? I don't want to infringe on any man's freedom. But I also don't want mine infringed on.

SUPPOSE A NEIGHBOR LEFT
AND SOLD HIS HOUSE TO A NEGRO?

I would not run. But I tell you one thing, he better keep up his property, because then I'd get disturbed. I'd be one of the first guys on the phone and keep on calling City Hall and telling them: "Here's your man now, let's see how he keeps up his property." 'Cause I bought my property and I want my property value to be up. I'm taking care of mine and so are all my neighbors. Now if this gentleman conforms to this type of situation, there's no restriction. Of course, his moral code I would watch out for, too. . . .

Maybe I've gotten in contact with some poor ones, but the few of them have left me with a very poor idea. It seems the biggest thing to do is to live with two, three women. Well, maybe I'm a little old-fashioned, but I've been married to the same woman for sixteen years and I'm pretty happy with her.

Now, I'm just a window washer, okay, I'm just a bum window washer, some people would say. But I'll tell you one thing, when I walk away from a building, I like it to look like it's been done. Follow me? It might be a simple thing to other people, but when it's done, it's done. I mean I can go up and take a look at this

379

glass and say, great. And then I don't have to take back seat from my boss. I do my work. No brown-nosing, no nothing: "If I'm not doing it for you, I'll do it for another man. I stayed here for eighteen years because you wanted me and I enjoyed being here. But I don't have to kowtow to you." And this is the point of pleasure. If you're willing to do your job, everybody wants you.

Window cleaners, like I told you, they're independent people. And they love challenges. They'll match against each other to see how much speed they have. Now I'm getting a little out of the stage, but when I was a little younger man, I used to enjoy it. When I was eighteen or nineteen, My God, the worst thing that could be told about you was he could beat you. You were the Johnny-on-the-spot, man, you went and moved. To show him that you were as good as him, if not better. Personal pride in work. This we're losing in window cleaning. And when we used to race like this, against each other, any streak on the window, that window was discounted. These were the challenges, this is what made your job interesting. A different group of men, they were big, burly men, rough, big drinkers, and all this . . . but they had a feeling about it, they took pride in their work. Today, a lot of it's gone.

It's a new age. Automation's the big thing. People who're really getting hurt are the office people, as of now. Factory workers was hurt before, now it's got to the office field. You know I heard this—they said something Henry Ford said to Martin Luther . . . no, it wasn't Martin Luther . . .

THOMAS EDISON?

No, no, the big union man. Walter Reuther, that's it. He took him through the plant. I heard this story somehow, it hit me pretty good. He said, "I like that machine there," he says. "It does the work of six men." "And yet," as an added remark, he tells him, he says, "it doesn't have to pay union dues." And Martin Luther told him, he says, "Yeah, it's a good part. But you tell me how many cars that machine will buy. You can produce all you want, but you have to have a market for it. And if you don't have a market for it, you're not gonna sell your products." So . . .

They can work a man, heat, cold, snow. You want a job, you want to earn a living, you go in, go do it. You know these machines have to have a 72 temperature. So they talk about a working man fighting for better working conditions. Here's a machine, just don't work, has nobody to support. It doesn't have to work. It just sits there, unless you give it the proper working conditions, it just don't work. . . .

My kids are gonna have a better education than me. When my boy hits a certain age, when he's qualified to be a window washer, which I hope is another two years, he'll be working with me in the summer months, picking up about a thousand dollars for the summer months. He's hoping to get a scholarship through football.

He told the boys he didn't want to have any part of smoking, because it kills his wind, and he intended to play football. These are things that make a man feel good. He doesn't have to impress anybody. His size impresses, you know what I mean?

He doesn't have to make like a bully. Nobody picks on him, because anybody in his age bracket doesn't want no part of him.

Today he's got a beautiful arm on him. I like strength myself. I'm one of these individuals that enjoys a good Indian rassle or a handshake, or stuff like that. If it's a nice bout or challenge. I enjoy it. My son, I guess he gets it from me. We've been doing this—God, since he's about ten years old. Now he's got an arm on him, he could take a grown man, at fourteen, you know. And this is the fun of it.

I've got an insurance policy, this will guarantee his education, the one I couldn't get. This will make him a better man. And this isn't done overnight. My dad was a laborer all his life. He came from Poland. We used to speak it in the home. I read and write it. My dad never owned a home. My dad never owned a car. I own all this. And this is true, generation after generation.

Yet, these kids today . . . I've got four nephews in the teaching profession. One, he's six feet two, but at times he's a little scared. He says a fifteen-, sixteen-year-old with a switchblade sort of scares you.

A regular school, not only colored. Maybe a Puerto Rican kid might do this or another white kid. We're talking about people. What did it do to these kids? When I was a kid, I came from an awful rough neighborhood. You don't like someone, man, you matched up against him with your fists. If he whipped you, you knew him better next time. But this idea of switchblades and knives and what have you, it scares a man.

And these kids come from good homes. What is a good home? If you don't spend your time with those kids . . . no, I'm trying my best. For all I know, maybe next year, or two years from now, my son might change and become one of these big bullies. Right now, he's a wonderful kid. Who knows what happens to a kid? Who knows what happens to anything?

### Helen Peters, "slightly past forty"

*A middle-class area in the city. Two-flats and three-flats are being suddenly surrounded by high-rises. It is near the lake.*

*She came to Chicago in the early Forties from a farm near Pontiac, about a hundred miles southwest of Chicago. "Most people leave. The town isn't progressive."*

*She does market research a couple of days a week, thus a second car has become necessary for the family. One of her discoveries on the job: "The more successful a man is—and you can tell by going into his office how successful he is—the more anxious he is to help you."*

*She is active in the PTA, a neighborhood bowling league, and numerous fundraising activities. She keeps house for her husband and two children. Her eldest daughter is married and has "two babies."*

We have right on this street almost every class. I shouldn't say class because we don't live in a nation of classes. But we have janitors living on the street, we have doctors, we have businessmen, CPA's.

Take janitors, for instance. The ones we have contact with and happen to know are very class-conscious. And it's not because people make them feel that way. It's something . . . they have come from a family of janitors, they feel they have to

381

prove themselves, that they are as good as the next person. One of our mutual friends calls this the janitor syndrome. (Laughs.) They are constantly trying to prove that they are as good as someone else. Well, that isn't necessary. Just because he cleans boilers or carries garbage, he's making an honest dollar.

My husband, as he says, is a Jack-of-all-trades. He's assistant to the president of a corporation right now. He's primarily interested in over-all management. He's very machine-conscious. He's a sort of systems-and-procedures man. It expedites things. I mean, he's a firm believer, do it the best way possible, the fastest. And he—blowing my own horn—is a very smart man.

I think when your children are small, a woman's place is definitely in the home. But once they're partially grown a woman is foolish if she sits around and stagnates. I think you become unhappy.

I know many women who have become bridge bums, they've become alcoholics, or they are doing clubwork which they do not enjoy. Because it's the thing to do. There are women who play bridge every afternoon. They also play bridge every night. Their whole life, their whole outlet, is bridge. And I feel that if these women don't have bridge, they would be hitting the bottle quite hard. In fact, there are a lot of so called bridge players that are very heavy drinkers. And some of them take dope, too.

Also in PTA, there are women there are in their sixties that are still in the PTA. Their grandchildren must be out of PTA. I feel sorry for them. Their life must be so empty that their only outlet is PTA, and they are to be pitied.

. . . The kids . . . I wonder if they're getting the proper education. I went to a country school, out in the country where a teacher taught all eight grades. I learned the eight parts of speech when I was in grammar school. I could still give them if I had to. Most kids in school now don't know there are eight parts. They do not teach grammar as such.

You know, nouns, verbs, prepositions, and so forth. But the kids are not taught to diagram sentences, that is no longer considered necessary. I don't know, they just aren't taught. If they write a composition, if it's correct, it's strictly an accident. Not by thought, word, or deed, shall we say? It's a subject I think should be brought back. We hear all children say, "I don't got any"—and, mine included, until I could strangle them.

My boy is sixteen, he likes to go out. I trust him. I know he won't go out and steal or break into a car, what do you call it? Mug somebody? But maybe he's going to be the one who gets mugged. I don't know all his friends. You can't possibly know. Most of them have been to the house. But you can't keep them in the house all the time. So I'm one of those worrying mothers who stands in the window and watches (laughs) for them to come home, and if they're five minutes after curfew, yell, "If you're picked up by the police, you can stay there all night."

And especially with an eleven-year-old girl, you worry about some mentally deranged people. I'm not neurotic about it. But if they come home later than they should, then I'm always, shall we say, a little upset.

I love Chicago, contacting people, talking to people. Despite the violence. If I go out late in the car, and I can't park right out here on the street, I jump out and run in the house and get Cliff and say, "Come on." (Laughs.)

. . . I would think it was all right if a Negro family moved next door to me. If he moved on this street to begin with, he's going to have to have a job that supports himself and his family in order to pay the rent around here. Rents on this particular street are not excessively high, but they are not low. On the next street, there is a colored woman living, did you know? She is married to a white man, she came to the PTA the other day, and I'm very sorry to say there were only three of us who talked to her. We invited her to join our bowling league, and as you know, asked her to please come again. She is very nice. She is a very pretty Negro woman.

In Pontiac, we knew one Negro man down there. He was a junkman and came out and I imagine he made as good a living as anyone else. Buying and selling junk. Probably better than most people, during the Depression. (Laughs.) But somehow or other, well, there was an incident when I was a child. A colored man shot a white man, and they put a curfew on the colored people. They had to be off the streets at six o'clock. Whenever this man came, we weren't exactly afraid of him, because we knew he was Les Summerville, he was the junkman. But he was different. If he was at our house collecting junk over the noon hour, call it dinner hour on all farms, Les was asked to come in and eat with us, and he ate with us at the table. And I can remember as a child that the insides of his hands were white, which amazed us when we were small. That the insides of his hands should be so white and the backs of his hands so dark.

We have a neighborhood school policy. I believe in the neighborhood school policy. I also believe in open housing. I think a man should be able to live in the neighborhood of his choosing, where he can afford to pay the rent. Like they say, water will seek its own level.

But I think these demonstrations are horrible. I don't think they prove a thing. I don't know how much patience I could have if I were a policeman, with these people laying down in the streets. When they are asked to move, they will not move. The demonstration in what was that place, the so-called ghetto in the West Coast? Watts. I think that was the most disgraceful thing that ever happened in any country. I think the National Guard were within their rights, if they just mowed them down wholesale with machine guns.

I think somebody has come in and stirred these people up. I know they are not brilliant people, they are easily led, they're poorly educated. A lot of them are from the South where they really have been forced down. They really don't have rights in the South, but I think here, I mean, everyone has the opportunity to go to school, he has the opportunity to go to college if he chooses. I'm sure if they want to work and earn a living that they can.

I think it's highly possible that there's a communist influence here, that if you don't have it, go out and take it. It is your right, which these people did by looting and taking things out of stores, that that man was walking away with a couch on his back. (Laughs.) It's horrible even to think, but I really couldn't have blamed those troopers if they had . . . because they were being shot at by snipers.

383

About that march in the South . . . this woman that was killed from Michigan. I think that's awful that the Ku Klux Klan, we know they're a violent group, but to shoot people in the dark, it's not . . . it sounds trite to say, it's not nice. She felt, from what I read in the paper, that she was helping those poor people. Each one has his own compulsions and drives, and maybe she felt it was her moral obligation, maybe she had a feeling of religion about it. I don't know. But she did have a home and five children, and I don't feel she had a place down there.

DO YOU AND YOUR HUSBAND TALK POLITICS MUCH?

We have mixed politics in our family, and the name of Roosevelt can almost turn my husband purple. I think he's the greatest president, or what have you, that ever lived. Of course, I think Truman is too. And I like Johnson. We are not solid Democrats or Republicans. We both vote a split ticket. But primarily he's a Republican and I'm a Democrat, and we have friendly arguments. We also have, shall I call them discussions?—like what year did Baumholtz play for the Cubs, and I'm up in the middle of the night looking up references to find out. (Laughs.)

At parties, Vietnam always makes a good topic of conversation. I think it has to be cleaned up. It just cannot continue and continue. And even though my son-in-law is going to have to go—by the first of the year I know he will have to go—he's in the Strategic Air Command, and SAC is stationed on Guam, where they take off, these big planes, B-52's. They're going to have to get more men in there and just clean it up. War can't go on forever and ever and ever, and you get sick when you think, gee, Cliffy is only sixteen, in two years he's going to have to register. And he's going to be seventeen pretty soon. And you think: Holy smoke, I would hate to have to see him . . . I lived through that Second World War, it was horrible; the Korean War was horrible. But now your own kids are coming up into it again.

I don't think they will come to a truce. They're going to have to clean out all the guerillas, and something has to be done. It's too much a drain on our young men, too much of a dollar drain. We have to get enough boys in there to bring things to a sudden halt somewhere along the line.

WE'RE TOLD THAT H-BOMBS TODAY CAN DESTROY THE WORLD.
DOES IT EVER BOTHER YOU?

Yes, because in August of this year we went to South Dakota. We were lucky enough to tour Ellsworth Air Force Base. We saw these terrific bombers, these tremendous B-52's. We went through the bomber. It amazed us, all the equipment that is in this plane. The plane is so loaded down, if I'm not mistaken it can carry only two bombs. This multimillion-dollar thing. Then we drove up the country of South Dakota. We saw these, they're called silos. They're the missiles, I think they're called. They're out in the middle of wheat fields. Evidently at a moment's notice a button can be pushed and these things will be shot off.

It makes you feel, oh, aren't we lucky to have such an organization as SAC And then you see these young kids, these eighteen-year-olds, and they're responsible for your safety. But they are put through rigid training. So you feel, gee, aren't we lucky? That we have this.

You feel so insignificant when you see this tremendous B-52 plane, with eight engines, four on each wing. And the wingspan of the plane we were under. We went out and saw the launching, and they take off on their practices within fifteen seconds of each other, and if you think that isn't a sight! To see these tremendous big planes come at you. The first plane you can see, the second one, in the fifteen-second time that it takes, is completely blacked out because of this jet take-off from those eight engines. You see it come up out of this black mess, and when the third plane comes up, it is wavering because of the air current. But they all get off and they're gone, but you're so glad that they're for our side.

YOU FEEL SO INSIGNIFICANT, YOU SAID?

Yes, I wonder if we'll ever come to a time that will be like the Dark Ages again . . . it's highly possible. And I don't think I can do one lousy, miserable thing. Look how crazy Hitler was. We could get another man like that. We don't know the Russians. Red China, probably. Or one of those little grubby hungry countries that are playing both sides against the middle: "If you don't do this, we'll go over here."

SO THE INDIVIDUAL FEELS HELPLESS?

I think there are a lot of people in very prominent, important places that can cause an awful lot of trouble for the whole world. I think these Vietnam protesters ought to be taken home and whipped with a strap. (Laughs.) Really I do. I honestly do. These boys are over there for something they believe in, and these smart-aleck upstarts, because we have freedom of speech, are allowed to go and more or less demoralize people that are over there. They're doing our country an awful lot of harm. This gives us a black eye in the eyes of the world.

I think that some people are professional dissenters. They take the opposite point of view whether they believe it or not, just for the sake of argument. There are those who dissent because they are looking for the overthrow of our government. (Almost whispers.) They infiltrate all our organizations, even the PTA.

YOU FEEL THAT?   .

It's a known fact.

COMMUNISTS, YOU'RE TALKING ABOUT NOW?

Yes, and Birchers. I think Birchers are an obnoxious lot. I came in contact with one on our trip to the West. He cannot come out openly against or for anything, so he's a fence rider, he's not a member. But I tell you he's the biggest John Birch leaner I have ever seen. I think that the John Birch Society flourishes in small communities where people have no outlet. This is a town of only nine hundred people. If someone comes in with any highfalutin ideas and all these people that don't get anywhere . . . every day they're out working in town in the little post offices or courthouses, you know, that probably has four rooms . . . they think this is marvelous. Why, he's right. I think they are easily led because they have not come in contact with the world.

Yes, I'd like to see a peaceful world. I mean, a world without war, the terrors of war and the abject poverty that comes from war. There'd have to be a meeting of the minds. It brings Kennedy to mind: his meeting with Khrushchev, where these two men of two great nations grew to respect each other. They knew they couldn't walk on each other. Do unto others as you would have others do unto you.

Maybe I've grown to appreciate more things. I think we all grow as we grow into more understanding people. You learn to be more tolerant of your fellow man.

### Gene Willis, Revisited

*Now he is one of the owners of another tavern on the Near North Side; his clientele, the same sort of "swingers" who patronized the place where he had worked as a bartender.*

You make your own break the best way you can. If I had to shovel streets for some guy for ten years and finally I can move up and own the sidewalk, I mean that's the break you take. I have many more things I want to do. I hope to get in real estate and buy some more things. But this takes time and I'm just a young guy anyways. Buy a couple of apartment buildings and let 'em pay . . . just like anything else. As soon as I can. It costs me a lot to live. I'm not a millionaire but I'd rather go first class and go out once a week than go out and spend forty cents a night and sit around and worry about having a good time. Find a good-lookin' chick, a few bucks in your pocket, and you can go many ways. I'm a high roller.

A high roller is after I've had a couple of drinks. If I walk into a bar and I see three guys and they're with ten people, I buy everybody a drink. I always leave a deuce or three bucks tip because I been in the business. Always paid my way. That's a high roller. I can't see a guy that worries about a nickle or a dime, because then he's in trouble.

I have a nice apartment that runs into a lotta dough. Very high-rise, seventeenth floor, overlooking the whole thing. My average day? After I kick my girl out . . . I get up at ten o'clock, breakfast, shower, the whole bit. Then we get a golf game going and we play in the afternoon. Then I cry for an hour while I have a drink, while I count all the money I lost. Grab a date about five o'clock for a drink or so. Dinner. Then I go to work. About nine now. I'm through at four. Whatever's happening, of course, you never know what's happening around Near North. You always try to grab something, so you never know what you're doing.

My philosophy is that I have only one life to live, and it's enough the way I'm doing. I don't have room for anything else.

*A ginger man, he recounts his early life and some picaresque experiences. Father, a burlesque comic, alcoholic. Mother, several bad-luck marriages. All-state basketball player out East. "We used to get CARE packages from Europe, sort of that kind of family, that's how poor we were." Coast to coast, after the army. Bellhop, fired for 'pushing booze, pushing broads." Bartender at posh joints and those less so; pocket-*

*ing about $125 a week on the side; shilled at a Las Vegas casino; swung all the way on a Diner's card left by some drunk at a bar; running up $600 hotel bill, friend stuck with it, but getting away with "towels, peppermills, dishes, glasses, the whole bit." Arrived in Chicago a year ago.*

DO YOU EVER FEEL GUILTY ABOUT THIS STUFF?

About what stuff?

YOU KNOW, WHEN YOU . . .

No, shit, no. I believe the world is based on gettin' a little bit of the pie, everything's hunky-dory. But as soon as you're not gettin' it, the first thing you say is, "Why aren't I in that?" And of course it's not right. But show me a person that's not makin' a few bucks on the side, goddam it. I believe that everybody, if they make a little bit more, get a little greedier, and they want a little bit more. There are a certain amount of straight arrows, they don't know any better. But they got a lotta dough or they don't care. But give like a guy that come up and he's up there by cutting a few fences, he's not gonna stop cuttin' fences. It's too late for him to stop cuttin' fences. When you cut a fence, you have to involve somebody else usually. So everybody's always helping somebody, one way or the other. Most guys I know would do anything for a buck. (Laughs.)

Like Vietnam. People think the reason whoever are gettin' their ass shot off, we love the other guy. I don't know anybody who want to get his ass shot off because he loves somebody else. It's not that way. The pressure is on us from the guy with the big buck. We have a lot of money invested. You have to go that way. With more power, you make more money. The Russians want the same thing. How does it change? Take the guy that sells peanuts. He's trying to make more peanuts, that's all. Or take the guy with more dough that's selling gold bars, it's the same.

Chicago is the only area of a big city that I've ever been, like in the Near North where I know everybody. They're all good people. A lotta bullshit goes on there, but you have to pass on it. I have a brother I brought back with me. He's bartending. He's a nice kid, but he's got so much shit that it's unbelievable. He's just a dreamer. He never had anything, you know. He bought a T-Bird, so he can impress the girls. He tells 'em he owns planes, yachts, and all this sort of stuff. Fantasy. A terrible dreamer. I don't mind it, but when I'm talkin' to a broad, I don't want him to lie.

SUPPOSE ONE OF YOUR BARTENDERS
DID WHAT YOU DID?

Impossible. You don't swing in the area, because you don't work in this area again if you do. The difference is in L.A., you can go anywhere and get a job with no reference. There are thousands of bars in L.A. and it's so spread out. Here a guy who swings wouldn't go anywhere. You can't get away with anything here.

But I don't bother anybody and I don't like anybody to bother me. If I were walkin' down the street and they were robbin' a bank, the guy would walk out and say, "Hi, Gene, how are you?" And if I knew him or didn't know him, I'd say, "Hi,

387

how are you?" And as long as he didn't step on my foot while I was walkin' by the bank, let him do what he wants to do. It's none of my goddam business. I could care less. (Indignantly.) Nothin' bothers me more than people that are tryin' all the time to say, "Oh, did you see what he did over there?" It's none of your business, he's not bothering you. If nobody hurt me, let them do what they want to do. I'm glad they're gettin' away with it. If they can get away with it, all the more power to 'em, that's their business. If I were a police officer, then of course that's my problem. I'm pleasant, get along, courteous.

I'll tell you what I want in life. I'd like to have a nice home in Evanston, on the lake. I'd like to have a ranch in Mexico, where I could retire a couple of months. I'd like to have a girl with a lot of qualities: intelligence, good-looking, which is tough to find, a little common sense, which could be very important. With high ideals, which you don't find around here. Morals. Broads around here, Christ, they screw you one night and they wanna screw someone else the next night, and they could care less. And they lie to you. I got all the broads I can handle now.

I'd like to find somebody that could be a companion. Some girl that you have to bend and sway. The way I am now, I could care less with the girls I meet. I'd like a girl you can discuss things, you can do things together, the important things. Respect and faith. Respect is the most important. You can't do anything in this life without respect for the other person. Once you lose respect for anybody, you can't go anywhere. If I find the right girl, I'll marry her tomorrow.

### WHAT KIND OF PEOPLE WOULD YOU LIKE YOUR KIDS TO BE?

Just like me. I want' em to work like I have. I want 'em to be open-minded like I am. I want them to be respectful and respect myself because I demand respect. If you don't respect me, I don't want you because I don't need you. I want the kids to have a good education which I never got. And I want a very close-knit family, because the close-knit family is the whole thing.

I like people. If you know somebody, you can give him an even break, and if you don't know him, you screw him. When I wake up in the morning, there's only one person thinking about me and that's me. If I were God, I couldn't say anything else that's different, because where else could you go? Everybody's human. You have to change the human being to change the world. The world is beautiful in itself, terrain-wise and etcetera. Everybody has greed, lust, and wants power, so you can't do it differently. As long as there's man, then that's it.

# 82

## Crisis in Black and White

In August 1966, a year after the Watts Riot, a subcommittee of the United States Senate, chaired by Senator Abraham Ribicoff, held hearings on "The Federal Role in Urban Problems." By this time the racial crisis shaking American society was becoming widely recognized. "Urban problems" and "the urban crisis" had become synonyms for the racial crisis. The Ribicoff Committee asked three Negroes to testify about conditions in the ghettoes of New York City. Claude Brown, a young law student, had recently published his sensational autobiography, *Manchild in the Promised Land*. Arthur Dunmeyer was his boyhood friend, who had never escaped the life both had lived as youths; at this time, aged 30, Dunmeyer had spent roughly half of his life in jail. Ralph Ellison, who offered a somewhat different perspective in his testimony, is the author of *The Invisible Man*, one of the finest American novels published since World War II.

### RIBICOFF HEARINGS: FEDERAL ROLE IN URBAN PROBLEMS

*Ribicoff:*   How old were you when you had your first child?

*Dunmeyer:*   Fifteen.

*Ribicoff:*   You were 15. And how old was your daughter when she had her first child?

*Dunmeyer:*   Twelve.

*Ribicoff:*   So your first child was born at 15 and your daughter's child was born when she was 12.

*Dunmeyer:*   That is right.

*Ribicoff:*   Is this a common situation where you live?

*Dunmeyer:*   Very much so. As I said before, it is our way of life. We have but so many ways to express ourselves, and when you are a kid you have the expressions that want to come out, and this is the closest thing that you can get as a solvent. You know you have a girl, you have a mother, you have a friend, or you have somebody away from the crowd, and you can express yourself sexually because you do know all of the facts about sex long before society thinks you know or says you know. This is a normal thing.

*Brown:*   I would like to say something here. Our society is always condemning

From the Ribicoff Committee hearings, as reprinted in *The New Leader*, September 26, 1966.

the high rate of illegitimacy in Negro ghettos, and it always seems so ridiculous to me to give any group of people so little means with which to cope with the dictates, the moral dictates of the society and expect them to live up to them. The Negroes' views on sex and the whites' views on sex are so completely diverse that the two will almost never get together. As has been said, never shall the twain meet, because Negroes don't have the money, they don't have the education.

The parents didn't have the education to send children to private schools, to give them the proper supervision. Both parents had to work. When I was say about nine years old, both of my parents had to work to make $50 a week—you know, eight hours a day. This is why at the age of six I was left out on the street to be brought up by the criminal elements, prostitutes, the hustlers, the pimps, the stick-up artists, the dope dealers, the fences and this sort of thing. I had to learn about sex because like—and this was at the age of six—everybody else was doing it, you know. It was the biggest. This was the most we had. We had no money to—well, TVs weren't even out at that time, but many of us couldn't afford radios. We had no money to go to any camps. Our parents weren't interested. They were from the South.

I am telling you, we were the progeny of the Southern generation that had migrated to the North during the 30s, the late 30s, early 40s, during the decade following the Depression. Anyway, it is like these people, they hadn't the slightest awareness of what the urban ghetto was all about, and they were ill-equipped to cope with it. They knew nothing about taking kids to Ys, to day nurseries and camps and this sort of thing, and so we were out on the streets learning about sex at five and six. We knew at five and six that, well, it was a nice thing. It was good. By the time we were 13 we knew it was a great anodyne, you know, before you got to heroin.

*Ribicoff:* What is the impact on the Negores who come from the South, the rural South, to the slums of New York? What do you find happens to them physically, emotionally, mentally, morally? What do you find happens when they have to make the change? Your parents came and you were born here, or you [Dunmeyer] were just a child in arms, and now you are older than you observe this. What happens?

*Brown:* Once they get there and become disillusioned, once they can see the streets aren't paved with gold and no great economic opportunities exist for them, they become pressured, you know. Many of the fathers who brought the families, they can't take the pressure any more, the economic pressure. How can you support a family of five kids on $65 a week. So they just leave. A father just ups one day and leaves, maybe becoming an alcoholic. Maybe he just goes out one night because he is so depressed about having missed a day's pay. During the week he was sick. He couldn't help it. And he wasn't in the union. And this depression leads to a sort of touchiness I will say, to become more mundane, so that in a bar a person can step on his foot and he or the person gets his throat cut. Somebody is dead. The other is in jail. He is going to the electric chair. It won't happen in New York today since they have abolished capital punishment. But this was one of the reactions.

Many take out their frustrations on their kids. They beat the hell out of them. My father used to beat me to death nearly everyday. But, still they take it out on their wives. They beat their wives. It is just frustration that they feel.

The wives will say—well, they lose respect for their husbands. The husbands can't really support their families. There are many affairs, you know. Like Mama—I am using the word generally—is screwing the butcher for an extra piece of meat. Pardon the term. Mama is having sexual relationships with the butcher for an extra piece of pork chop for the kids. She wants to see them well fed—this sort of thing.

Or maybe the numbers runner on the corner digs Mama or something. She has got a couple of kids. He can give her $25 a week. The most her husband can make is say $60 a week, and it isn't enough, and the $25 helps because she wants her kids to have the things that TV says they should have.

You know, these are many of the reactions. And then there is the shooting. The guy comes home. He is trying. He is trying. He comes home. He hears about his wife and he goes out one day and picks up a gun. He says, "Oh, Lord, I have tried so hard. It is just not for me. It is my lot to always be a day late and a dollar short. But this guy has been making it with my woman and he has got to die. This is an affront to my masculinity." So he goes out and kills him. Then he is in jail. His family is on welfare or he is in the electric chair. These are emotional and physical reactions.

*Dunmeyer:* I would like to bring this up also. In some cases this is the way you get your drug dealers and prostitutes and numbers runners. You get people that come here and it is not that they are disillusioned. They see that these things are the only way they can compete in the society, the only way to get some sort of status. The realize that there aren't any real doors open to them, and they can't go back south. There is nothing to go back to. This is understood; this is why they came.

The only thing to do is to get something going to benefit themselves, and in their minds this is not a criminal thing. It is a way to live, a way to have enough to keep your wife from going to bed with the butcher. It is a way to keep from killing the butcher. You kill him in small ways, by taking him off, by holding him up, by seeing that he don't hang out in the neighborhood after the store is closed. It is cheating. It is stealing. These things are just a way of life.

*Brown:* I would like to make an interjection at this point, just to avoid any misconstruing of what has been said. You know, there are many solid citizens in Harlem, the nice old people who get up and go to church every Sunday and pray for their sons. They hope he won't go out and get caught on none of that old dope. They work hard every day for $50 a week, you know, like for Mrs. Goldberg in the book.

These people believe in the game that has been run down, the con game of American society, equal opportunity and all that, and that everybody is supposed to be a solid citizen, like my friend here. You know, work hard every day. To most of the younger generation all this is a myth. But even to these people, the good solid citizens, the Christians, the church-going people who want to live righteously,

391

something like numbers is an economic institution in Harlem. It is not a crime to them, and they will go to war for it.

You would have a riot if everybody hit the numbers or something and the police came and wanted to make a bust—to arrest the guy who pays off for the numbers. These women who go to church every Sunday, and scrub floors every day during the week, would jump on top of the police. They would have to call out the entire precinct, you know, to calm this thing down. Even with the solid citizens, it is like they know they must have some kind of a dream. The only way they can possibly make it is one day maybe they will hit a number. So, if you take the numbers away from them you take away their dream. They know they are not going to be able to make it off their $50 a week.

*Dunmeyer:* Our people happen to be the minority, they are in the ghettos, so this is where all the limelight is focused and because of this we are considered people with problems, people who have something wrong with them. But, believe it or not, I would never think of going on the roof and jumping off. I would never think of going on the roof and taking a rifle and shooting five or six people for no reason at all. But I might think of having some children, not thinking of if the woman is married to me or not, because I want to have children, not thinking it is right or wrong. This is because I want to have children, you see. But I would never do a lot of things that I see the accepted standards allow and make excuses for it.

These things never come across my mind. I wouldn't steal just to be stealing. I'd steal for a purpose, if I stole. It means something to me, but perhaps not to you or any other person who is always asking why do we steal, who do we steal. They are not even thinking of what I stole. They are not thinking that I stole an orange because I was hungry, see, whereas another person may steal $10,000 and not be hungry. I might steal just an orange, but I am considered a criminal for two reasons—because I was caught, and because society says to steal is wrong, you see.

As I said before, it is not a matter of race. It is a matter of the upper class and the lower class, those who have and those who haven't got.

*Kennedy:* If you were in charge of the Establishment, whether it is the economic or the political or whatever it might be, whether it is state, city or Federal, if you had control over that, what would you do in the situation—whether it is Harlem, Bedford Stuyvesant, Watts, or whatever it might be?

*Dunmeyer:* First of all, I would find the numbers runners in the neighborhood, and all the dope pushers in the neighborhood who are doing this because, like I said, this is a way of life, but who have something more to offer in the way of intelligence. They know how to get around the police. These people I could use to my advantage. They might know how to get around another problem by using the same ideas, and I would use these people. And I wouldn't come out of this neighborhood until these people themselves felt that they were human again, not until I felt it, because unless I was living there, unless I was a part of this thing—you see, I couldn't sit behind a desk and do it. I would have to know what was going on inside and out.

And I would employ each person that I take on in any capacity and use him to the extent of what he can offer himself, not what the books say is right. I couldn't sit down and write any laws, any mandates for anyone to follow. I would have to feel out the block itself. I would have to feel out the people themselves.

You can walk three blocks in any direction in Harlem, or in the Bedford Stuyvesant section, and you will find a whole different world, class of people. For instance, I live in a block where the people are together and they don't even know it themselves. They have this gregarious thing going for them and they don't realize it. In the next block the people all have big fine cars, and they have their own homes, and there is no noise. The police are always walking up and down the streets protecting them. These people don't even know each other. These people don't even know each other and they are the ones who are played up to by the politicians when it is time to vote.

These are the people that are considered people. But the people that really are people are the ones who are suffering together, and they have something already together. Just to suffer makes them together, and this is what you have to look at. You have to go into a neighborhood or a block and look at it for that block, that neighborhood, those people. You can't say, well, all the black people all over the world, all the black people all over the country, all the ghettos are the same. All the ghettos are different. This is a name you put on it.

*Ellison:* I would like to suggest here that there is a basic difference between what has happened in the South, to the Southern Negro, and what has happened to people living in such slums as Harlem. At Tuskegee, for instance, in Macon County, Alabama, where I attended school, I knew exactly where I could go and where I could not go. The contempt which was held for me by whites was obvious in the most casual interracial contacts.

I got to know Alabama and North Georgia fairly well, because I was playing trumpet in a jazz orchestra. We played in the various country clubs, and for dances for both whites and Negroes, and we got to know the country people, the white people most antagonistic to my race, and there was a certain sense of security about knowing their ways. They were very interested—some of them—in provoking me to violence so that they could destroy me. And my struggle was to keep from being provoked, to keep my eye on my own goals. I was not there to hold a contest of violence with white people. I was there to get an education and go on to the North and become a composer of symphonies.

Now, I think that my experience, the discipline which I acquired, sums up a certain aspect of Southern Negro character. We have been disciplined for over 300 years not to be provoked. We have been disciplined for over 300 years to define the nature of the reality of society and the human predicament for ourselves. We have been disciplined to accept our *own* sense of life regardless of what those antagonistic to us thought about us.

Now, this makes for the most complex personalities among those so disciplined and it makes for a certain split, a certain ambivalence within the Negro American's conception of the United States. But of one thing I am certain: We were hopeful. We made the sacrifices necessary for survival. We tried to educate our children—as we still do—and we lived as we could live and had to live, because we had great hopes and great confidence in the promises of American democracy.

We Negroes have long memories. We know what went on before 1865 and after 1876. And if you think about it, there is hardly a Negro of my generation who can't touch a grandparent or two and be right back in slavery—it has been that recent. So, we have within our very lives and our memories a sense of the reality of slavery and what had been promised by Emancipation. So that by 1954, when the civil rights bills began to be passed, when the law of the land began to change, we were able to transform our old discipline, our fortitude before physical provocation and casual brutalization, into an agency to help ourselves achieve the freedom which was now guaranteed by the law. To walk through hostile groups of people now became a *political* instrumentality, and it has worked. And even little children, little Negro children, have been disciplined to confront the new possibilities unflinchingly. And this courage is not something found overnight, but is part of a heritage of over 300 years.

In the North, Southern tradition breaks down. You get to Harlem. You have expected a great deal of freedom that does not exist. Or when it does exist you haven't been taught how to achieve it. Too often, you don't have the education or experience necessary to go into many of the jobs and places which attract you and which others take for granted, and you find yourself frustrated. Thus when the civil rights laws began to be passed, they did not have the same impact within the Northern slums because we had certain of the rights which were symbols at least of what Southern Negroes had not had.

I think that the shock is apt to be sustained by the second generation of Southern Negroes. At least during the 30s and 40s and 50s this was true. The adult who came usually found some way of bettering himself. Even though he didn't get the good job that he expected, there was a greater freedom of movement about the cities.

With the children of such people, you had a different situation, because they could see what is possible within the big city. They could see the wonderful possibilities offered by the city to define one's own individuality, to amplify one's talent, to find a place for one's self.

But for many, many Negroes, this proved impossible. They came to the North with poor schooling. Very often their parents had no schooling, and thus two strikes were against them. This makes for a great deal of frustration.

Now, on the other hand, these are American children, and Americans are taught to be restless, to be mobile, to be daring. Our myths teach this, our cartoons teach us this, our athletic sports teach us this. The whole society is geared to making the individual restless, to making him test himself against the possibilities around him. He gets this from the motion pictures. He gets it from the television cameras, He gets it from every avenue of life, and Negroes are as much subjected to it as anybody else.

So you see little Negro Batmen flying around Harlem just as you see little white Batmen flying around Sutton Place. It is in the blood. But while the white child who is taken with these fantasies has many opportunities for working them into real life situations, too often the Negro child is unable to so do. This leads the Negro child who identifies with the heroes and outlaws of fantasy to feel frustrated and to feel that society has designated him the outlaw, for he is treated as one. Thus his sense of being outside the law is not simply a matter of fantasy, it is a reality based on the incontrovertible fact of race. This makes for frustration and resentment. And it makes for something else, it makes for a very cynical and sometimes sharp perspective on the difference between our stated ideals and the way in which we actually live. The Negro slum child knows the difference between a dishonest policeman and an honest one because he can go around and see the numbers men paying off the police. He observes what is in the policeman's eyes when he is being ordered around.

# 83

# Vietnam and the American Will to Power

The long and indecisive war in Vietnam provoked larger doubts about the general outlines of American foreign policy of the cold war era. Perhaps the most eloquent and influential critical statement on this issue was the essay "The Responsibility of Intellectuals" written by Noam Chomsky, an outstanding linguist from the Massachusetts Institute of Technology. The advent of the nuclear age had brought many members of the intellectual community into close relationships with political and military decision-makers; the expertise of social as well as physical scientists played an increasing role in the operations of government. This seemed entirely appropriate to those who accepted the premises upon which American foreign policy was based and believed in the essential righteousness of American actions in the world arena. The events of the Kennedy and especially the Johnson years, however, were deeply disillusioning to some who came to share Chomsky's revulsion against American policies in the underdeveloped areas of the world and his distrust of the academic "experts" who devised or at least rationalized those policies.

## THE RESPONSIBILITY
## OF INTELLECTUALS
### Noam Chomsky

Twenty years ago, Dwight Macdonald published a series of articles in *Politics* on the responsibilities of peoples, and specifically, the responsibility of intellectuals. I read them as an undergraduate, in the years just after the war, and had occasion to read them again a few months ago. They seem to me to have lost none of their power or persuasiveness. Macdonald is concerned with the question of war guilt. He asks the question: To what extent were the German or Japanese people responsible for the atrocities committed by their governments? And, quite properly, he turns the question back to us: To what extent are the British or American people responsible for the vicious terror bombings of civilians, perfected as a technique of warfare by the Western democracies and reaching their culmination in

Reprinted in abridged form from the *New York Review of Books*, February 23, 1967, with the permission of the author. Copyright © 1967 by Noam Chomsky.

Hiroshima and Nagasaki, surely among the most unspeakable crimes in history? To an undergraduate in 1945–1946—to anyone whose political and moral conscious- ness had been formed by the horrors of the 1930s, by the war in Ethiopia, the Russian purge, the "China Incident," the Spanish Civil War, the Nazi atrocities, the Western reaction to these events and, in part, complicity in them—these questions had particular significance and poignancy.

With respect to the responsibility of intellectuals, there are still other, equally disturbing questions. Intellectuals are in a position to expose the lies of govern- ments, to analyze actions according to their causes and motives and often hidden intentions. In the Western world, at least, they have the power that comes from political liberty, from access to information and freedom of expression. For a privileged minority. Western democracy provides the leisure, the facilities, and the training to seek the truth lying hidden behind the veil of distortion and misrepresentation, ideology and class interest, through which the events of current history are presented to us. The responsibilities of intellectuals, then, are much deeper than what Macdonald calls the "responsibility of peoples," given the unique privileges that intellectuals enjoy.

The issues that Macdonald raised are as pertinent today as they were twenty years ago. We can hardly avoid asking ourselves to what extent the American people bear responsibility for the savage American assault on a largely helpless rural population in Vietnam, still another atrocity in what Asians see as the "Vasco da Gama era" of world history. As for those of us who stood by in silence and apathy as this catastrophe slowly took shape over the past dozen years, on what page of history do we find our proper place? Only the most insensible can escape these questions. I want to return to them, later on, after a few scattered remarks about the responsibility of intellectuals and how, in practice, they go about meeting this responsibility in the mid-1960s.

It is the responsibility of intellectuals to speak the truth and to expose lies. This, at least, may seem enough of a truism to pass without comment. Not so, however. For the modern intellectual, it is not at all obvious. Thus we have Martin Heidegger writing, in a pro-Hitler declaration of 1933, that "truth is the revelation of that which makes a people certain, clear, and strong in its action and knowledge"; it is only this kind of "truth" that one has a responsibility to speak. Americans tend to be more forthright. When Arthur Schlesinger was asked by the *New York Times*, in November 1965, to explain the contradiction between his published account of the Bay of Pigs incident and the story he had given the press at the time of the attack, he simply remarked that he had lied; and a few days later, he went on to compliment the *Times* for also having suppressed information on the planned invasion, in "the national interest," as this was defined by the group of arrogant and deluded men of whom Schlesinger gives such a flattering portrait in his recent account of the Kennedy administration. It is of no particular interest that one man is quite happy to lie in behalf of a cause which he knows to be unjust; but it is significant that such events provoke so little response in the intellectual community—no feeling, for example, that there is something strange in the offer of a major chair in humanities to a historian who feels it to be his duty to persuade the world that an American-sponsored invasion of a nearby country is nothing of the sort. And what of the incredible sequence of lies on the part of our government and its spokesmen concerning such matters as negotiations in Vietnam? The facts are known to all who care to know. The press, foreign and domestic, has presented documentation to refute each falsehood as it appears. But the power of the government propaganda apparatus is such that the citizen who does not undertake a research project on the subject can hardly hope to confront government pronouncements with fact.

The deceit and distortion surrounding the American invasion of Vietnam is by now so familiar that it has lost its power to shock. It is therefore well to recall that although new levels of cynicism are constantly being reached, their clear antecedents were accepted at home with quiet toleration. It is a useful exercise to compare government statements at the time of the invasion of Guatemala in 1954 with Eisenhower's admission—to be more accurate, his boast—a decade later that American planes were sent "to help the invaders." Nor is it only in moments of crisis that duplicity is considered perfectly in order. "New Frontiersmen," for example, have scarcely distinguished themselves by a passionate concern for historical accuracy, even when they are not being called upon to provide a "propaganda cover" for ongoing actions. For example, Arthur Schlesinger describes the bombing of North Vietnam and the massive escalation of military commitment in early 1965 as based on a "perfectly rational argument": "so long as the Vietcong thought they were going to win the war, they obviously would not be interested in any kind of negotiated settlement." The date is important. Had the statement been made six months earlier, one could attribute it to ignorance. But this statement appeared after months of front-page news reports detailing the UN, North Vietnamese, and Soviet initiatives that preceded the February 1965 escalation and that, in fact, continued for several weeks after the bombing began, after months of soul-searching by Washington correspondents who were trying desperately to find some mitigating circumstances for the startling deception that had been revealed (Chalmers Roberts, for example, wrote with unconscious irony that late February 1965 "hardly seemed to Washington to be a propitious moment for negotiations [since] Mr. Johnson . . . had just ordered the first bombing of North Vietnam in an effort to bring Hanoi to a conference table where bargaining chips on both sides would be more closely matched"). Coming at this moment, Schlesinger's statement is less an example of deceit than of contempt—contempt for an audience that can be expected to tolerate such behavior with silence, if not approval.

To turn to someone closer to the actual formation and implementation of policy, consider some of the reflections of Walt Rostow, a man who, according to Schlesinger, brought a "spacious historical view" to the conduct of foreign affairs in the Kennedy administration. According to his analysis, the guerrilla warfare in Indochina in 1946 was launched by Stalin, and Hanoi initiated the guerrilla war against South Vietnam in 1958. Similarly, the Communist planners probed the "free world spectrum of defense" in Northern Azerbaijan and Greece (where Stalin "supported substantial guerilla warfare") operating from plans carefully laid in 1945. And in Central Europe, the Soviet Union was not "prepared to accept a solution which would remove the dangerous tensions from Central Europe at the risk of even slowly staged corrosion of communism in East Germany."

It is interesting to compare these observations with studies by scholars actually concerned with historical events. The remark about Stalin's initiating the first Vietnamese war in 1946 does not even merit refutation. As to Hanoi's purported initiative of 1958, the situation is more clouded. But even government sources concede that in 1959 Hanoi received the first direct reports of what Diem referred to as his own Algerian war and that only after this did they lay their plans to involve themselves in this struggle. In fact, in December 1958 Hanoi made another of its many attempts—rebuffed once again by Saigon and the United States—to establish diplomatic and commercial relations with the Saigon government on the basis of the status quo. Rostow offers no evidence of Stalin's support for the Greek guerrillas; in fact, though the historical record is far from clear, it seems that Stalin was by no means pleased with the adventurism of the Greek guerrillas, who, from his point of view, were upsetting the satisfactory postwar imperialist settlement.

Rostow's remarks about Germany are more interesting still. He does not see fit to mention, for example, the Russian notes of March—April 1952, which proposed unification of Germany under internationally supervised elections, with withdrawal of all troops within a year, *if* there was a guarantee that a reunified Germany would not be permitted to join a Western military alliance. And he has also momentarily forgotten his own characterization of the strategy of the Truman and Eisenhower administrations: "to avoid any serious negotiation with the Soviet Union until the West could confront Moscow with German rearmament within an organized European framework, as a *fait accompli*"—to be sure, in defiance of the Potsdam agreements.

But most interesting of all is Rostow's reference to Iran. The facts are that there was a Russian attempt to impose by force a pro-Soviet government in Northern Azerbaijan that would grant the Soviet Union access to Iranian oil. This was rebuffed by superior Anglo-American force in 1946, at which point the more powerful imperialism obtained full rights to Iranian oil for itself, with the installation of a pro-Western government. We recall what happened when, for a brief period in the early 1950s, the only Iranian government with something of a popular base experimented with the curious idea that Iranian oil should belong to the Iranians. What is interesting, however, is the description of Northern Azerbaijan as part of "the free world spectrum of defense." It is pointless, by now, to comment on the debasement of the phrase "free world." But by what law of nature does Iran, with its resources, fall within Western dominion? The bland assumption that it does is most revealing of deep-seated attitudes toward the conduct of foreign affairs.

In addition to this growing lack of concern for truth, we find, in recent statements, a real or feigned naiveté with regard to American actions that reaches startling proportions. For example, Arthur Schlesinger has recently characterized our Vietnamese policies of 1954 as "part of our general program of international goodwill." Unless intended as irony, this remark shows either a colossal cynicism or an inability, on a scale that defies comment, to comprehend elementary phenomena

399

of contemporary history. Similarly, what is one to make of the testimony of Thomas Schelling before the House Foreign Affairs Committee, January 27, 1966, in which he discusses the two great dangers if all Asia "goes Communist"? First, this would exclude "the United States and what we call Western civilization from a large part of the world that is poor and colored and potentially hostile." Second, "a country like the United States probably cannot maintain self-confidence if just about the greatest thing it ever attempted, namely to create the basis for decency and prosperity and democratic government in the underdeveloped world, had to be acknowledged as a failure or as an attempt that we wouldn't try again." It surpasses belief that a person with even minimal acquaintance with the record of American foreign policy could produce such statements.

It surpasses belief, that is, unless we look at the matter from a more historical point of view, and place such statements in the context of the hypocritical moralism of the past; for example, of Woodrow Wilson, who was going to teach the Latin Americans the art of good government, and who wrote (1902) that it is "our peculiar duty" to teach colonial peoples "order and self-control . . . [and] . . . the drill and habit of law and obedience." Or of the missionaries of the 1840's who described the hideous and degrading opium wars as "the result of a great design of Providence to make the wickedness of men subserve his purposes of mercy toward China, in breaking through her wall of exclusion, and bringing the empire into more immediate contact with western and Christian nations." Or, to approach the present, of A. A. Berle, who, in commenting on the Dominican intervention, has the impertinence to attribute the problems of the Caribbean countries to imperialism—*Russian* imperialism.

As a final example of this failure of skepticism, consider the remarks of Henry Kissinger in concluding his presentation in a Harvard-Oxford television debate on American Vietnam policies. He observed, rather sadly, that what disturbs him most is that others question not our judgment but our motives—a remarkable comment on the part of one whose professional concern is political analysis, that is, analysis of the actions of governments in terms of motives that are unexpressed in official propaganda and perhaps only dimly perceived by those whose acts they govern. No one would be disturbed by an analysis of the political behavior of Russians, French, or Tanzanians, questioning their motives and interpreting their actions in terms of long-range interests, perhaps well concealed behind official rhetoric. But it is an article of faith that American motives are pure and not subject to analysis. Although it is nothing new in American intellectual history—or, for that matter, in the general history of imperialist apologia—this innocence becomes increasingly distasteful as the power it serves grows more dominant in world affairs and more capable, therefore, of the unconstrained viciousness that the mass media present to us each day. We are hardly the first power in history to combine material interests, great technological capacity, and an utter disregard for the suffering and misery of the lower orders. The long tradition of naiveté and self-righteousness that disfigures our intellectual history, however, must serve as a warning to the Third World, if such a warning is needed, as to how our protestations of sincerity and benign intent are to be interpreted.

The basic assumptions of the "New Frontiersmen" should be pondered carefully by those who look forward to the involvement of academic intellectuals in politics. For example, I have referred to Arthur Schlesinger's objections to the Bay of Pigs invasion, but the reference was imprecise. True, he felt that it was a "terrible idea," but "not because the notion of sponsoring an exile attempt to overthrow Castro seemed intolerable in itself." Such a reaction would be the merest sentimentality, unthinkable to a tough-minded realist. The difficulty, rather, was that it seemed unlikely that the deception could succeed. The operation, in his view, was ill-conceived but not otherwise objectionable. In a similar vein, Schlesinger quotes with approval Kennedy's "realistic" assessment of the situation resulting from Trujillo's assassination: "There are three possibilities in descending order of preference: a decent democratic regime, a continuation of the Trujillo regime or a Castro regime. We ought to aim at the first, but we really can't renounce the second until we are sure that we can avoid the third." The reason why the third possibility is so intolerable is explained a few pages later: "Communist success in Latin America would deal a much harder blow to the power and influence of the United States." Of course, we can never really be sure of avoiding the third possibility; therefore, in practice, we will always settle for the second, as we are now doing in Brazil and Argentina, for example.

Or consider Walt Rostow's views on American policy in Asia. The basis on which we must build this policy is that "we are openly threatened and we feel menaced by Communist China." To prove that we are menaced is of course unnecessary, and the matter receives no attention; it is enough that we feel menaced. Our policy must be based on our national heritage and our national interests. Our national heritage is briefly outlined in the following terms: "Throughout the nineteenth century, in good conscience Americans could devote themselves to the extension of both their principles and their power on this continent," making use of "the somewhat elastic concept of the Monroe doctrine" and, of course, extending "the American interest to Alaska and the mid-Pacific island. . . . Both our insistence on unconditional surrender and the idea of post-war occupation . . . represented the formulation of American security interests in Europe and Asia." So much for our heritage. As to our interests, the matter is equally simple. Fundamental is our "profound interest that societies abroad develop and strengthen those elements in their respective cultures that elevate and protect the dignity of the individual against the state." At the same time, we must counter the "ideological threat," namely "the possibility that the Chinese Communists can prove to Asians by progress in China that Communist methods are better and faster than democratic methods." Nothing is said about those people in Asian cultures to whom our "conception of the proper relation of the individual to the state" may not be the uniquely important value, people who might, for example, be concerned with preserving the "dignity of the individual" against concentrations of foreign or domestic capital, or against semifeudal structures (such as Trujillo-type dictatorships) introduced or kept in power by American arms. All of this is flavored with allusions to "our religious and ethical value systems" and to our "diffuse and complex concepts" which are to the Asian mind "so much more difficult to grasp"

401

than Marxist dogma, and are so "disturbing to some Asians" because of "their very lack of dogmatism."

Such intellectual contributions as these suggest the need for a correction to De Gaulle's remark, in his *Memoirs*, about the American "will to power, cloaking itself in idealism." By now, this will to power is not so much cloaked in idealism as it is drowned in fatuity. And academic intellectuals have made their unique contribution to this sorry picture.

Let us, however, return to the war in Vietnam and the response that it has aroused among American intellectuals. A striking feature of the recent debate on Southeast Asian policy has been the distinction that is commonly drawn between "responsible criticism," on the one hand, and "sentimental," or "emotional," or "hysterical" criticism, on the other. There is much to be learned from a careful study of the terms in which this distinction is drawn. The "hysterical critics" are to be identified, apparently, by their irrational refusal to accept one fundamental political axiom, namely, that the United States has the right to extend its power and control without limit, insofar as is feasible. Responsible criticism does not challenge this assumption, but argues, rather, that we probably can't "get away with it" at this particular time and place.

A distinction of this sort seems to be what Irving Kristol has in mind, for example, in his analysis of the protest over Vietnam policy, in *Encounter,* August 1965. He contrasts the responsible critics, such as Walter Lippmann, the *New York Times*, and Senator Fulbright, with the "teach-in movement." "Unlike the university protesters," he maintains, "Mr. Lippmann engages in no presumptuous suppositions as to 'what the Vietnamese people really want'—he obviously doesn't much care—or in legalistic exegesis as to whether, or to what extent, there is 'aggression' or 'revolution' in South Vietnam. His is a *realpolitik* point of view; and he will apparently even contemplate the possibility of a *nuclear* war against China in extreme circumstances." This is commendable, and contrasts favorably, for Kristol, with the talk of the "unreasonable, ideological types" in the teach-in movement, who often seem to be motivated by such absurdities as "simple, virtuous 'anti-imperialism,'" who deliver "harangues on 'the power structure,'" and who even sometimes stoop so low as to read "articles and reports from the foreign press on the American presence in Vietnam." Furthermore, these nasty types are often psychologists, mathematicians, chemists, or philosophers (just as, incidentally, those most vocal in protest in the Soviet Union are generally physicists, literary intellectuals, and others remote from the exercise of power), rather than people with Washington contacts, who, of course, realize that "had they a new, good idea about Vietnam, they would get a prompt and respectful hearing" in Washington.

I am not interested here in whether Kristol's characterization of protest and dissent is accurate, but rather in the assumptions that it expresses with respect to such questions as these: Is the purity of American motives a matter that is beyond discussion, or that is irrelevant to discussion? Should decisions be left to "experts" with Washington contacts—that is, even if we assume that they command the necessary knowledge and principles to make the "best" decision, will they invariably do so? And, a logically prior question, is "expertise" applicable—that is, is there a body of theory and of relevant information, not in the public domain, that can be applied to the analysis of foreign policy or that demonstrates the correctness of present actions in some way that the psychologists, mathematicians, chemists, and philosophers are incapable of comprehending? Although Kristol does not examine these questions directly, his attitudes presuppose answers, answers which are wrong in all cases. American aggressiveness, however it may be masked in pious rhetoric, is a dominant force in world affairs and must be analyzed in terms of its causes and motives. There is no body of theory or significant body of relevant information, beyond the comprehension of the layman, which makes policy immune from criticism. To the extent that "expert knowledge" is applied to world affairs, it is surely appropriate—for a person of any integrity, quite necessary—to question its quality and the goals that it serves. These facts seem too obvious to require extended discussion.

A corrective to Kristol's curious belief in the administration's openness to new thinking about Vietnam is provided by McGeorge Bundy in a recent article. As Bundy correctly observes, "on the main stage . . . the argument on Viet Nam turns on tactics, not fundamentals," although, he adds, "there are wild men in the wings." On stage center are, of course, the President (who in his recent trip to Asia had just "magisterially reaffirmed" our interest "in the progress of the people across the Pacific") and his advisers, who deserve "the understanding support of those who want restraint." It is these men who deserve the credit for the fact that "the bombing of the North has been the most accurate and the most restrained in modern warfare"—a solicitude which will be appreciated by the inhabitants, or former inhabitants, of Nam Dinh and Phu Ly and Vinh. It is these men, too, who deserve the credit for what was reported by Malcolm Browne as long ago as May 1965: "In the South, huge sectors of the nation have been declared 'free bombing zones,' in which anything that moves is a legitimate target. Tens of thousands of tons of bombs, rockets, napalm and cannon fire are poured into these vast areas each week. If only by the laws of chance, bloodshed is believed to be heavy in these raids."

Fortunately for the developing countries, Bundy assures us, "American democracy has no enduring taste for imperialism," and "taken as a whole, the stock of American experience, understanding, sympathy and simple knowledge is now much the most impressive in the world." It is true that "four-fifths of all the foreign investing in the world is now done by Americans" and that "the most admired plans and policies . . . are no better than their demonstrable relation to the American interest"—just as it is true, so we read in the same issue of *Foreign Affairs*, that the plans for armed action against Cuba were put into motion a few weeks after Mikoyan visited Havana, "invading what had so long been an almost exclusively American sphere of influence." Unfortunately, such facts as these are often taken by unsophisticated Asian intellectuals as indicating a "taste for imperialism." For example, a number of Indians have expressed their "near exasperation" at the fact that "we have done everything we can to attract foreign capital for fertilizer plants, but the American and the other Western private companies know we are over a barrel, so they demand stringent terms which we just cannot meet," while "Washington . . . doggedly insists that deals be made in the private sector with private enterprise." But this reaction, no doubt, simply reveals once again how the Asian mind fails to comprehend the "diffuse and complex concepts" of Western thought.

It may be useful to study carefully the "new, good ideas about Vietnam" that are receiving a "prompt and respectful hearing" in Washington these days. The United States Government Printing Office is an endless source of insight into the moral and intellectual level of this expert advice. In its publications one can read, for example, the testimony of Professor David N. Rowe, Director of Graduate on Foreign Affairs. Professor Rowe proposes that the United States buy all surplus Studies in International Relations at Yale University, before the House Committee Canadian and Australian wheat, so that there will be mass starvation in China. These are his words: "Mind you, I am not talking about this as a weapon against the Chinese people. It will be. But that is only incidental. The weapon will be a weapon against the Government because the internal stability of that country cannot be sustained by an unfriendly Government in the face of general starvation." Professor Rowe will have none of the sentimental moralism that might lead one to compare this suggestion with, say, the *Ostpolitik* of Hitler's Germany. Nor does he fear the impact of such policies on other Asian nations, for example Japan. He assures us, from his "very long acquaintance with Japanese questions," that "the Japanese above all are people who respect power and determination." Hence "they will not be so much alarmed by American policy in Vietnam that takes off from a position of power and intends to seek a solution based upon the imposition of our power upon local people that we are in opposition to." What would disturb the Japanese is "a policy of indecision, a policy of refusal to face up to the problems [in China and Vietnam] and to meet our responsibilities there in a positive way," such as the way just cited. A conviction that we were "unwilling to use the power that they know we have" might "alarm the Japanese people very intensely and shake the degree of their friendly relations with us." In fact, a full use of American power would be particularly reassuring to the Japanese, because they have had a demonstration "of the tremendous power in action of the United States . . . because they have felt our power directly." This is surely a prime example of the healthy "*realpolitik* point of view" that Irving Kristol so much admires.

Having settled the issue of the political irrelevance of the protest movement, Kristol turns to the question of what motivates it—more generally, what has made students and junior faculty "go left," as he sees it, amid general prosperity and under liberal, Welfare State administrations. This, he notes, "is a riddle to which no sociologist has as yet come up with an answer." Since these young people are well-off, have good futures, etc., their protest must be irrational. It must be the result of boredom, of too much security, or something of this sort.

Other possibilities come to mind. It might be, for example, that as honest men the students and junior faculty are attempting to find out the truth for themselves rather than ceding the responsibility to "experts" or to government; and it might be that they react with indignation to what they discover. These possibilities Kristol does not reject. They are simply unthinkable, unworthy of consideration. More accurately, these possibilities are inexpressible; the categories in which they are formulated (honesty, indignation) simply do not exist for the tough-minded social scientist.

In this implicit disparagement of traditional intellectual values, Kristol reflects attitudes that are fairly widespread in academic circles. I do not doubt that these attitudes are in part a consequence of the desperate attempt of the social and behavioral sciences to imitate the surface features of sciences that really have significant intellectual content. But they have other sources as well. Anyone can be a moral individual, concerned with human rights and problems; but only a college professor, a trained expert, can solve technical problems by "sophisticated" methods. Ergo, it is only problems of the latter sort that are important or real. Responsible, nonideological experts will give advice on tactical questions; irresponsible "ideological types" will "harangue" about principle and trouble themselves over moral issues and human rights, or over the traditional problems of man and society, concerning which "social and behavioral science" have nothing to offer beyond trivialities. Obviously, these emotional, ideological types are irrational, since, being well-off and having power in their grasp, they shouldn't worry about such matters.

When we consider the responsibility of intellectuals, our basic concern must be their role in the creation and analysis of ideology. And, in fact, Kristol's contrast between the unreasonable ideological types and the responsible experts is formulated in terms that immediately bring to mind Daniel Bell's interesting and influential essay on the "end of ideology," an essay which is as important for what it leaves unsaid as for its actual content. Bell presents and discusses the Marxist analysis of ideology as a mask for class interest, in particular, quoting Marx's well-known description of the belief of the bourgeoisie "that the *special* conditions of its emancipation are the *general* conditions through which alone modern society can be saved and the class struggle avoided." He then argues that the age of ideology is ended, supplanted, at least in the West, by a general agreement that each issue must be settled on its own individual terms, within the framework of a welfare state in which, presumably, experts in the conduct of public affairs will have a prominent role. Bell is quite careful, however, to characterize the precise sense of "ideology" in which "ideologies are exhausted." He is referring only to ideology as "the conversion of ideas into social levers," to ideology as "a set of beliefs, infused with passion, . . . [which] . . . seeks to transform the whole of a way of life." The crucial words are "transform" and "convert into social levers." Intellectuals in the West, he argues, have lost interest in converting ideas into social levers for the radical transformation of society. Now that we have achieved the pluralistic society of the Welfare State, they see no further need for a radical transformation of society; we may tinker with our way of life here and there, but it would be wrong to try to modify it in any significant way. With this consensus of intellectuals, ideology is dead.

There are several striking facts about Bell's essay. First, he does not point out the extent to which this consensus of the intellectuals is self-serving. He does not relate his observation that, by and large, intellectuals have lost interest in "transforming the whole of a way of life" to the fact that they play an increasingly prominent role in running the Welfare State; he does not relate their general satisfaction with the Welfare State to the fact that, as he observes elsewhere, "America has become an affluent society, offering place . . . and prestige . . . to the onetime radicals." Secondly, he offers no serious argument to show that intellectuals are somehow "right" or "objectively justified" in reaching the consensus to which he alludes, with its rejection of the notion that society should be transformed. Indeed, although Bell is fairly sharp about the empty rhetoric of the "New Left," he seems to have a quite utopian faith that technical experts will be able to come to grips with the few problems that still remain; for example, the fact that labor is treated as a commodity, and the problems of "alienation."

It seems fairly obvious that the classical problems are very much with us; one might plausibly argue that they have even been enhanced in severity and scale. For example, the classical paradox of poverty in the midst of plenty is now an ever increasing problem on an international scale. Whereas one might conceive, at least in principle, of a solution within national boundaries, a sensible idea as to how to transform international society in such a way as to cope with the vast and perhaps increasing human misery is hardly likely to develop within the framework of the intellectual consensus that Bell describes.

A good case can be made for the conclusion that there is indeed something of a consensus among intellectuals who have already achieved power and affluence, or who sense that they can achieve them by "accepting society" as it is and promoting the values that are "being honored" in this society. And it is also true that this consensus is most noticeable among the scholar-experts who are replacing the free-floating intellectuals of the past. In the university, these scholar-experts construct a "value-free technology" for the solution of technical problems that arise in contemporary society, taking a "responsible stance" towards these problems, in the sense noted earlier. This consensus among the responsible scholar-experts is the domestic analogue to that proposed, in the international arena, by those who justify the application of American power in Asia, whatever the human cost, on the grounds that it is necessary to contain the "expansion of China" (an "expansion" which is, to be sure, hypothetical for the time being)—to translate from State Department Newspeak, on the grounds that it is essential to reverse the Asian nationalist revolutions, or at least to prevent them from spreading. The analogy becomes clear when we look carefully at the ways in which this proposal is formulated. With his usual lucidity, Churchill outlined the general position in a remark to his colleague of the moment, Joseph Stalin, at Teheran in 1943: ". . . the government of the world must be entrusted to satisfied nations, who wished nothing more for themselves than what they had. If the world-government were in the hand of hungry nations, there would always be danger. But none of us had any reason to seek for anything more. The peace would be kept by peoples who lived in their own way and were not ambitious. Our power placed us above the rest. We were like rich men dwelling at peace within their habitations."

For a translation of Churchill's biblical rhetoric into the jargon of contemporary social science, one may turn to the testimony of Charles Wolf, Senior Economist of the RAND Corporation, at the congressional committee hearings cited earlier:

> I am dubious that China's fears of encirclement are going to be abated, eased, relaxed in the long-term future. But I would hope that what we do in Southeast Asia would help to develop within the Chinese body politic more of a realism and willingness to live with this fear than to indulge it by support for liberation movements, which admittedly depend on a great deal more than external support . . . the operational question for American foreign-policy is not whether that fear can be eliminated or substantially alleviated, but whether China can be faced with a structure of incentives, of penalties and rewards, of inducements that will make it willing to live with this fear.

In short, we are prepared to live peaceably within our—to be sure, rather extensive—habitations. And quite naturally, we are offended by the undignified noises from the servants' quarters. If, let us say, a peasant-based revolutionary movement tries to achieve independence from foreign domination or to overthrow semifeudal structures supported by foreign powers, or if the Chinese irrationally refuse to respond properly to the schedule of reinforcement that we have prepared for them, if they object to being encircled by the benign and peace-loving "rich men" who control the territories on their borders as a natural right, then, evidently, we must respond to this belligerence with appropriate force.

It is this mentality that explains the frankness with which the United States government and its academic apologists defend the American refusal to permit a political settlement in Vietnam at a local level, a settlement based on the actual distribution of political forces. Even government experts freely admit that the NLF is the only "truly mass-based political party in South Vietnam"; that the NLF had "made a conscious and massive effort to extend political participation, even if it was manipulated, on the local level so as to involve the people in a self-contained, self-supporting revolution"; and that this effort had been so successful that no political groups, "with the possible exception of the Buddhists, thought themselves equal in size and power to risk entering into a coalition, fearing that if they did the whale would swallow the minnow." Moreover, they concede that until the introduction of overwhelming American force, the NLF had insisted that the struggle "should be fought out at the political level and that the use of massed military might was in itself illegitimate. . . . The battleground was to be the minds and loyalties of the rural Vietnamese, the weapons were to be ideas"; and correspondingly, that until mid-1964, aid from Hanoi "was largely confined to two areas—doctrinal know-how and leadership personnel." Captured NLF documents contrast the enemy's "military superiority" with their own "political superiority," thus fully confirming the analysis of American military spokesmen who define our problem as how, "with considerable armed force but little political power, [to] contain an adversary who has enormous political force but only modest military power."

Similarly, the most striking outcome of both the Honolulu conference in February and the Manila conference in October was the frank admission by high officials of the Saigon government that "they could not survive a 'peaceful settlement' that left the Vietcong *political* structure in place even if the Vietcong guerilla units were disbanded," that "they are not able to compete *politically* with the Vietnamese Communists." Officials in Washington understand the situation very well. Thus Secretary Rusk has pointed out that "if the Vietcong come to the conference table as full partners they will, in a sense, have been victorious in the very aims that South Vietnam and the United States are pledged to prevent" (January 28, 1966). Similarly, Max Frankel reported from Washington: "Compromise has had no appeal here because the Administration concluded long ago that the non-Communist forces of South Vietnam could not long survive in a Saigon coalition with Communists. It is for that reason—and not because of an excessively rigid sense of protocol—that Washington has steadfastly refused to deal with the Vietcong or recognize them as an independent political force."

In short, we will—magnanimously—permit Vietcong representatives to attend negotiations only if they will agree to identify themselves as agents of a foreign power and thus forfeit the right to participate in a coalition government, a right which they have now been demanding for a half-dozen years. We know well that in any representative coalition, our chosen delegates could not last a day without the support of American arms. Therefore, we must increase American force and resist meaningful negotiations, until the day when a client government can exert both military and political control over its own population—a day which may never dawn, for as William Bundy has pointed out, we could never be sure of the security of a Southeast Asia "from which the Western presence was effectively withdrawn." Thus if we were to "negotiate in the direction of solutions that are put under the label of neutralization," this would amount to capitulation to the Communists. According to this reasoning, then, South Vietnam must remain, permanently, an American military base.

All of this is of course reasonable, so long as we accept the fundamental political axiom that the United States, with its traditional concern for the rights of the weak and downtrodden, and with its unique insight into the proper mode of development for backward countries, must have the courage and the persistence to impose its will by force until such time as other nations are prepared to accept these truths—or simply to abandon hope.

If it is the responsibility of the intellectual to insist upon the truth, it is also his duty to see events in their historical perspective. Thus one must applaud the insistence of the Secretary of State on the importance of historical analogies, the Munich analogy, for example. As Munich showed, a powerful and aggressive nation with a fanatic belief in its manifest destiny will regard each victory, each extension of its power and authority, as a prelude to the next step. The matter was very well put by Adlai Stevenson, when he spoke of "the old, old route whereby expansive powers push at more and more doors, believing they will open, until, at the ultimate door, resistance is unavoidable and major war breaks out." Herein lies the danger of appeasement, as the Chinese tirelessly point out to the Soviet Union, which they claim is playing Chamberlain to our Hitler in Vietnam. Of course, the aggressiveness of liberal imperialism is not that of Nazi Germany, though the distinction may seem rather academic to a Vietnamese peasant who is being gassed or incinerated. We do not want to occupy Asia; we merely wish, to return to Mr. Wolf, "to help the Asian countries progress toward economic modernization, as relatively 'open' and stable societies, to which our access, as a country and as individual citizens, is free and comfortable." The formulation is appropriate. Recent history shows that it makes little difference to us what form of government a country has as long as it remains an "open society," in our peculiar sense of this term—a society, that is, that remains open to American economic penetration or political control. If it is necessary to approach genocide in Vietnam to achieve this objective, then this is the price we must pay in defense of freedom and the rights of man.

Quite often, the statements of sincere and devoted technical experts give surprising insight into the intellectual attitudes that lie in the background of the latest savagery. Consider, for example, the following comment by economist Richard Lindholm, in 1959, expressing his frustration over the failure of economic development in "free Vietnam": "the use of American aid is determined by how the Vietnamese use their incomes and their savings. The fact that a large portion of the Vietnamese imports financed with American aid are either consumer goods or raw materials used rather directly to meet consumer demands is an indication that the Vietnamese people desire these goods, for they have shown their desire by their willingness to use their piasters to purchase them."

In short, the Vietnamese *people* desire Buicks and air conditioners, rather than sugar-refining equipment or road-building machinery, as they have shown by their behavior in a free market. And however much we may deplore their free choice, we must allow the people to have their way. Of course, there are also those two-legged beasts of burden that one stumbles on in the countryside, but as any graduate student of political science can explain, they are not part of a responsible modernizing elite, and therefore have only a superficial biological resemblance to the human race.

In no small measure, it is attitudes like this that lie behind the butchery in Vietnam, and we had better face up to them with candor, or we will find our government leading us towards a "final solution" in Vietnam, and in the many Vietnams that inevitably lie ahead.

Let me finally return to Macdonald and the responsibility of intellectuals. Macdonald quotes an interview with a death-camp paymaster who bursts into tears when told that the Russians would hang him. "Why should they? What have I done?" he asked. Macdonald concludes: "Only those who are willing to resist authority themselves when it conflicts too intolerably with their personal moral code, only they have the right to condemn the death-camp paymaster." The question "What have I done?" is one that we may well ask ourselves, as we read, each day, of fresh atrocities in Vietnam—as we create, or mouth, or tolerate the deceptions that will be used to justify the next defense of freedom.

# Index of Documents

416